# Media Space 20+ Years of Mediated Life

# Computer Supported Cooperative Work



For other titles published in this series, go to
http://www.springer.com/2861

Steve Harrison
Editor

# Media Space 20 + Years of Mediated Life

*Editor*
Steve Harrison
Virginia Tech
USA

Computer Supported Cooperative Work ISSN 1431-1496
ISBN: 978-1-84996-842-3 e-ISBN: 978-1-84882-483-6
DOI: 10.1007/978-1-84882-483-6

British Library Cataloguing in Publication Data
A catalogue record for this book is available from the British Library



Printed on acid-free paper

Springer is part of Springer Science+Business Media (www.springer.com)

# Contents

# Chapter 1
# An Introduction to Media Space

**Steve Harrison**

In the mid-1980s, Bob Stults and I created the first media space at Xerox Palo Alto Research Center (PARC). From our initial office-to-office always-on real-time audio and video connections grew a switched network of continuous connections for a small laboratory split between Palo Alto, California and Portland, Oregon. Offices and public spaces had cameras, microphones, video monitors, and computers. Users were in charge; they could turn their cameras or audio off, or focus cameras out of the window; they could choose to connect to one person or another; however, the underlying connection was always there, with no setup, changeable with a click of a mouse button.

The images on the screens and the sound coming out of the speakers created shared offices, put offices onto hallways that were, in fact, 500 miles away, and "virtually" doubled the size of the common area for both the Portland and Palo Alto groups. Colleagues shared informal interactions, formal lab meetings, quick conversations, in-depth discussions, cross-site projects, and cross-site reporting relationships. There were difficulties in maintaining the technology-mediated communication, but the participants interacted regularly and continued to learn about each other (Stults, 1986; Bly et al., 1993; Harrison et al., 1997).[1]

Other research labs followed, with both internal-only and multiple-site configurations. EuroPARC in Cambridge (Gaver et al., 1992; Bellotti and Dourish, 1997), BellCore (Fish et al., 1990), US West in Denver (Bulick et al., 1989), Sun Labs in Palo Alto, (Tang et al., 1994), and the University of Toronto (Mantei, et al., 1991) all began experimenting with forms of real-time audio, video, and computer connection that put people into extended working situations with one another. These lab-based projects were quite different from one another in both (often important) subtle and (sometimes unimportant) obvious ways. These media spaces supported a sense of community, extended one-on-one close collaboration, and teleconferencing. "Media space" brought the topics of awareness, gaze

S. Harrison
Virginia Polytechnic Institute and State University
e-mail: srh@cs.vt.edu

[1] Before the PARC Media Space, the artists' collective, Mobile Image, created the *Hole in Space* that suggested many of the social and para-social relations that were observed at PARC and the follow-ons (Galloway and Rabinowitz, 1980).

S. Harrison (ed.), *Media Space 20+ Years of Mediated Life*,
Computer Supported Cooperative Work,

and attention, visual reciprocity, para-social relationships, control, notification, echo-canceling, spatialized real-time audio, collaborative sketching, and, of course, privacy to the research table (Gaver et al., 1993). Through these, media spaces engendered Computer-Supported Collaborative Work (CSCW) research in desktop video conferencing, shared drawing, e.g., VideoDraw (Tang and Minneman, 1990), TeamWorsktation (Ishii, 1990) and Clearboard (Ishii and Kobayashi, 1992), awareness servers, e.g., Portholes (Dourish and Bly, 1992), time-shifting technologies – WhereWereWe (Minneman and Harrison, 1993), and even some aspects of MUDs and MOOs – Jupiter (Curtis et al., 1995).

Since that time, technology has changed. Affordable real-time desktop conferencing is an everyday reality. However, these technological advances do not render the experiments of the past irrelevant. While there is a large array of devices – ubiquitous cell-phone cameras, web cams, iChat, architectural scale displays, the Internet, and globalized work – there is still little understanding of how and when to use them. By and large, our images of use are confined to procedures of calls between people. We have yet to fully understand and exploit the power of context, to design for space, task, and working relationships instead of short-term connections between (at most) talking heads. Space is explored in some connected system, such as through virtual environments like Second Life, but these environments do something different than media spaces. They literalize the shared spaces rather than drawing on the power of the real. Early research lauded the unfettering effects of virtual connectivity on feelings of freedom, for example, in MOOs or MUDs (Curtis et al., 1995). More recent work explores the detailed relationship between anonymity and experience (as in Bargh, 2002; Bargh et al., 2002). But the very power of fantasy and projection that this research explores may be too much for ordinary workplace interaction. Like Second Life, media spaces create spaces. Like the phone, it can be used to convey targeted messages using targeted informational tactics, both conscious and unconscious. But a media space is different. It cannot as easily be tailored to exclude all non-intentional elements of interaction. The real can be revealing, and, in that way, reassuring, and, furthermore, freeing. Connectivity and trust are deeply aligned concepts. I believe that over the next 10 years, as we have come to understand that connected space even better in the context of everyday life, the implicit balance between the nature of the media space, connectivity, trust, and the desired degree of risk taking in the environment will come to be more explicitly modeled.

But these elements are all here implicitly – even if not always emphasized and drawn out. Reflecting on past systems and experiences can help us understand what the roles are in the systems of what is displayed, what is known about the other, and the kinds of work done. They can help us think clearly about when and to what extent systems should employ socially negotiated control instead of enforcing an established policy. What is the meaning of "awareness," "presence," and "notification" apart from the systems that we happen to have on hand today? How do the current devices change our experience, and also, has our experience truly changed? What should the devices of tomorrow look like?

The basic media space idea is that continuously available media becomes part of the fabric of everyday experience. We see that many researchers today are unaware of the real motivations behind and the fundamental understandings that resulted from the first media spaces; we encourage those who rediscover some of these ideas in current research to learn about the work anew. Some topics include:

- Privacy
- Large-scale display
- Awareness
- Telepresence
- Mobile awareness (IM)
- Video chat
- Social triangulation
- Coordination
- Distributed work
- Multiplayer games
- Camera-projector integration research
- IRVEs
- Media and related critical theory
- Space and place issues
- And, of course, media space

We are part of an on-going engagement in research with space and technology. Everyone who considers ways to make the cell phone more socially aware, who is considering the next chat technology, or who finds they are changing the layout of their physical desk to better accommodate desk top video conferencing is working towards next generations of media spaces. This book takes perspectives evolved by a relatively small group of researchers over the last 20 plus years and position them in relation to this changing field.

## Structure of the Book

We invite the readers to use this book as reference, light reading, or as a textbook in a specialized CSCW course. In that regard, the organization is worth noting. The chapters are grouped into three different but interconnected approaches to media space research. Each implies a different exploration of the connectivity that constitutes a media space.

**Social**: Media technology (audio, video, text, etc.) that is used to link separated individuals and groups can support social relations that build upon, distort, or even cartoon those in physical space. In this approach, we focus on how media spaces can use elements of understood social practice in mediated ways to promote or suppress understanding. This might involve placing a monitor for negotiating whether one wants to engage in a casual conversation next to an office door in order to mimic the physical-space practice or creating connection control systems that expose who is talking to whom to all who might connect. Salient issues in this approach are sociality, community, and appropriate behavioral framing.

**Spatial**: Though a little less familiar to most people than social connectivity, spatial connectivity is the heart of my own concept of media space. Continuously available, always-on audio, video, and networked computing links separated places and times to create collections of visual, acoustic, and metaphoric connections. In this approach, the primary issues are framed in terms of space and place and the unfolding of experience. For example, places in media space are created using extensions of place-making as understood in the physical world. Of course, the illusions of cinema and broadcast television may also become part of the experiential fabric of physical space, yet these are themselves molded by their very different use in situ.

**(Embodied) Communications**: A third approach emphasizes the mechanisms of communication in support of content, task, and activity. In this approach, the resolution of deictic (i.e., indicating or pointing) reference through the showing of hands (aka "shared drawing"), the "efficiency" of teleconferencing, and the forms of meaning-making are drivers of using audio, video, and networked computing in novel combination. As a category, it encompasses considerable contention, engendered by competing analytic approaches including information theory, conversation analysis, task support, and conventional teleconferencing metrics. This, then, represents a microcosm of the contentions within HCI and CSCW over paradigms and "science" (see Harrison et al., 2007).

Each kind of characterization is strikingly different in values and concerns. It also differs in the kinds of media space systems considered within the domain. For example, the (embodied) communication's approach admits telephony-like interactions and information-theoretic frames of analysis, which the spatial definition excludes.

What ties the three together are (a) the use of real-time media in a physical context to connect people together, who are physically separated from one another; and (b) some elements of human experience that are used to describe the phenomena. The tight binding of experiential phenomena to utility highlights the difficulty of understanding what is and was powerful about this line of research and why it leads to such a diverse collection of investigations.

As with many truly radical research paradigms, a number of conditions hampered a broad understanding of the significance of the research in the moment in which it was conducted. These include the following:

- Many of the first media spaces were used as part of the infrastructure by researchers in and out of the media space research in ad hoc ways. Thus, the configurations would change from day to day, and week to week without much useful record of the changes.
- It was difficult to get "scientific" reports accepted for these first projects since the users were often the researchers themselves.
- Some media spaces were at odds with the "official" research agendas of the supporting institution.

- Reports actually published were focused on aspects specific to the dominant paradigms of the venues in which they were published. Thus, interfaces were reported at the CHI conference (the ACM sigCHI Conference on Human-Factors in Computing) and aspects of presence and membership reported at CSCW (the ACM Conference on Computer-Supported Collaborative Work). There was no comprehensive venue that pulled all the aspects together to understand subtle couplings.
- Excitement and realization of media space projects spread mostly through direct contact by researchers with other existing media spaces.[2]

In particular, one continuing, foundational issue for media space research is that it implicitly contravenes the dominant organizational idea in human–computer interaction and, indeed, in computation. Media space is a form of communication through a technology, but it is not centered on information. That is, the content is not easily organized into quanta and therefore "signal" and "noise" are not readily apparent; thus, "usage" is also not easily compared to other media like e-mail or phone calls.

Some of these issues were resolved as the various research disciplines matured; the rise of phenomenologically based investigations in CSCW may be seen as a "work around" for this problem inherent in several CSCW paradigms. Additionally, they have changed as computing companies have come to realize that networking brings them into the communications business. However, a paradigm shift, almost by definition, takes a long time to be fully understood and developed. By bringing together many perspectives over time in the context of this volume, the authors and I hope to make the trajectory clearer.

## *A Field Guide to the Phenomenology of Media Space*

Some chapters are reports of direct experience, while others present investigations of use in more traditional fashion. Scattered among the chapters are sidebars containing personal anecdotes that give some sense of the lived experience of the projects and also document aspects that were either not initially thought reportable or were too remote from reviewer's disciplines to be accepted for peer-reviewed publication. Thus, this book is both a report of research and of the working life using that research every day.

It may seem a bit disconcerting to mix first-hand reports of everyday use and research investigation. In fact, though, these accounts are a legitimate and important part of conducting science, similar to naturalists' field guides to spotting wildlife. The accounts of years of direct observation of wolves in Alaska are no less science than Newton's description of the mathematical relations of bodies at rest compared to those in motion.

---

[2] A brief description of media space projects can be found in Chapter 2. Among the first ones, only BellCore's Cruiser was not the result of first-hand experience with other media spaces.

In most books collecting together research, the introductory chapter of each part is an explanation of why these varied chapters are placed together. Our introductory chapters go beyond this. Since each part can be read as a "field guide" to that approach, each part is a "mini-field guide" appropriate to the approach. Each field guide then has a different kind of "naturalist" and a different form. So each part's introductory chapter establishes the ground rules of the guide's genre.

I. **Introduction**. Besides laying out how readers might approach the book, we also provide a basic guide to theory and research literature that has informed this work and a timeline of research, technology development, and other notable events in mediated life to help contextualize the book.
II. The **social** approach uses the rhetoric and methods that are more familiar to a CSCW audience to consider social spaces. However, the social approach asks more of the reader taking them into actual situations that include close working bonds, broken trust, shared joy, community building, interpersonal tension, and anxiety, among other things.
III. The **spatial** approach looks at "looking" to guide the reader through both the intellectual landscape of spatiality and the ways in which one can directly encounter the phenomena that is so present to the authors.
IV. **Communication** is a field guide to sense-making in the as-lived mediated condition. The "communications naturalist" goes meta to make sense of the sense that is made: media space sense-making is both the understanding in the moment and the sense made of the long unfolding of being in the world and reflection upon it. These jumps in levels of abstraction, timescale, and need both reflect vastly different paradigms and theories, and vastly different relationships to media in physical space.
V. **Lessons and Conclusions** reflect on the research agenda and its consequences for media space in particular and wider programs of interacting with and through information and communications technologies.

Underlying the three separate field guides is a basic question of the nature of science that has been present from the start of explorations of media space, the relationship between different kinds of media spaces from the points of view not necessarily held by their creators. This book tries to fill that gap by close juxtaposition of ideas. Nonetheless, we must confront the nature of very different world views in these scientific endeavors. Each part confronts the nature of the ontologies that are used in the section and discusses the conflicts that arise. In Part IV, for example, we will look at how the paradigms of CHI (such as information theory) alter and filter the results that are allowable.

We are asking you, dear reader, to be patient and clever. As with the consumption of any good postmodern text, you will be both in the position of an author steeped in information-theoretic thinking, for example, and able to stand apart from that approach. You will also be in the role of the adventurer going down the rapids with the authors as they live in the temporal stream of their mediated spaces.

## Previous Reporting

This book builds upon previous reports, journal articles, and book chapters. While we have an extensive cumulative bibliography at the conclusion, there are a few works that are referenced by many of our authors and would be good companion material, worth the reader's time to preemptively review. Foremost among them are Robert Stults' *Media Space Report* (1986) and *Video-Mediated Communication* (1997) edited by Kathleen Finn, Abigail Sellen, and Sylvia Wilbur. *The Media Space Report* provides a first-person account of the nature of being in a physical space that is "warped" by continuously available audio and video. In contrast, *Video-Mediated Communication* collects research about video mediation rather than media spaces, per se. Therefore, only six or seven chapters of this book could be said to be based on media space research, but of those, all are considered foundational to various directions of media space work.

**Acknowledgements** I want to thank the many people of Xerox PARC, who in the mid 1980's, began to recognize that distributed and virtual organizations were the next big thing and that it would be enabled by something that at the time they called "interpersonal computing". (We now call that enabler "CSCW".) In particular, that would be the members of the System Concepts Laboratory, its Laboratory Manager Adele Goldberg, and Area Manager, Bob Stults. It was Bob who first saw the interaction of media and space as key. And I also want to thank media space's first evangelist, Bill Buxton, who made the research world aware of the idea. I wish to thank all of the authors who contributed to this book for their efforts and insights. Most of all, I want to thank my wife, Deborah Tatar, who has encouraged me to stick with my ideas and this book; her persistent intellectual curiosity and unflagging support has made this work possible.

## References

Bargh, J. A. (2002). "Beyond simple truths: The human-Internet interaction." *Journal of Social Issues* **58**(1): 1–8.

Bargh, J. A., McKenna, K. Y. A., & Fitzsimmons, G. M. (2002). Can you see the real me? Activation and expression of the "true self" on the Internet. *Journal of Social Issues* 58: 33–48.

Bellotti, V. and Dourish, P. (1997). "Rant and RAVE: Experimental and experiential accounts of a media space." In K. Finn, A. Sellen, and S. Wilbur (eds.), *Video-Mediated Communication*. Lawrence Erlbaum, Mahwah, NJ, pp. 245–272.

Bly, S., Harrison, S., and Irwin, S. (1993). "Media spaces: Bringing people together in a video, audio, and computing environment." *Communications of the Association of Computing Machinery*, New York, vol. 36, no. 1, January 1993, pp. 28–45.

Bulick, S., Abel, M., Corey, D., Schmidt, J., and Coffin, S. (1989). "The US WEST Advanced Technologies Prototype Multi-media Communications System." *GLOBECOM '89: In Proceedings of the IEEE Global Telecommunications Conference*. Dallas, Texas.

Curtis, P., Dixon, M., Frederick, R., and Nichols, D., (1995). "The Jupiter audio/video architecture: secure multimedia in network places," *Proceedings of the Third ACM International Conference on Multimedia*, pp. 79–90, November 05–09, 1995.

Dourish, P. and Bly, S. (1992). "Portholes: supporting awareness in a distributed work group," *Proceedings of the SIGCHI Conference on Human Factors in Computing Systems*, pp. 541–547, May 03–07, 1992, Monterey, California, USA.

Finn, K., Sellen, A., and Wilbur, S (eds.) (1997). *Video-Mediated Communication*. Lawrence Erlbaum, Mahwah, NJ.

Fish, R., Kraut, R., and Chalfonte, B. (1990). "The VideoWindow system in informal communication," *Proceedings of the 1990 ACM Conference on Computer-Supported Cooperative Work*, pp. 1–11, October 07–10, 1990, Los Angeles, California, USA.

Galloway, K. and Rabinowitz, S. (1980). *Hole in Space* http://www.ecafe.com/getty/HIS/ project displayed at Lincoln Center, NYC and Century City, Los Angeles, November, 1980.

Gaver, W., Moran, T., MacLean, A., Lövstrand, L., Dourish, P., Carter, K., and Buxton, W. (1992). "Realizing a video environment: EuroPARC's RAVE system," *Proceedings of the SIGCHI Conference on Human Factors in Computing Systems*, pp. 27–35, May 03–07, 1992, Monterey, California, USA.

Gaver, W., Sellen, S., Heath, C., and Luff, P. (1993). "One is not enough: Multiple views in a media space," *Proceedings of the SIGCHI Conference on Human Factors in Computing Systems*, pp. 335–341, April 24–29, 1993, Amsterdam, The Netherlands.

Harrison, S., Bly, S., Anderson, S., and Minneman, S. (1997). "The media space." In K. Finn, A. Sellen, and S. Wilbur (eds.) *Video-Mediated Communication*, 1997. Lawrence Erlbaum, Mahwah, NJ, pp. 273–300.

Harrison, S., Tatar, D., and Sengers, P. (2007) "The Three Paradigms of HCI", *Proceedings of CHI 2007*, alt.chi, San Jose, CA, May 2007.

Ishii, H. (1990) "TeamWorkStation: towards a seamless shared workspace", *In Proceedings of the 1990 ACM Conference on Computer-Supported Cooperative Work* (Los Angeles, California, United States, October 07–10, 1990). CSCW '90. ACM, New York, NY, 13–26.

Ishii, H. and Kobayashi, M. (1992). "ClearBoard: a seamless medium for shared drawing and conversation with eye contact," *Proceedings of the SIGCHI Conference on Human Factors in Computing Systems*, pp. 525–532, May 03–07, 1992, Monterey, California, USA.

Mantei, M., Baecker, R., Sellen, A., Buxton, W., and Wellman, B. (1991). "Experiences in the use of a media space," *Proceedings of the SIGCHI Conference on Human Factors in Computing Systems: Reaching Through Technology*, pp. 203–208, April 27–May 02, 1991, New Orleans, Louisiana, USA.

Minneman, S. and Harrison, S. (1993). "Where were we: making and using near-synchronous, pre-narrative video," *Proceedings of the First ACM International Conference on Multimedia*, pp. 207–214, August 02–06, 1993, Anaheim, California, USA.

Stults, R. (1986). *Media Space*. Xerox PARC Technical Report, Palo Alto, California.

Tang, J. and Minneman, S. (1990). "VideoDraw: a video interface for collaborative drawing," *Proceedings of the SIGCHI Conference on Human Factors in Computing Systems: Empowering People*, pp. 313–320, April 01–05, 1990, Seattle, Washington, DC, USA.

Tang, J., Isaacs, E., and Rua, M. (1994). "Supporting distributed groups with a Montage of lightweight interactions," *Proceedings of the 1994 ACM Conference on Computer-Supported Cooperative Work*, pp. 23–34, October 22–26, 1994, Chapel Hill, North Carolina, USA.

# Chapter 2
# A Brief History of Media Space Research and Mediated Life

**Steve Harrison**

*To contextualize the events, research projects, and commercial deployment of media space, we have created the following timeline. Fundamentally, this timeline should remind the reader that there was a time when audio and video were distinctly separate from computing and their inclusion in computing research was considered unusual. In addition, there has been some confusion about the development of ideas, as the sequence of publication did not correspond to the sequence of investigation and innovation; as a rule of thumb, the earlier the work, the longer the time to publication. This confusion has even led to occasional mis-attribution.*

## Precursors

*These are a few of the noteworthy first instances of casual mediated connection and events that figured in the development of ideas in media space. Many of the items listed are quite remarkable and sometimes little known. Curiosity-seekers who follow the references will be rewarded with some images and ideas that should alter and deepen their appreciation for ICT research before the term was invented.*

**1930 – Bell Labs demonstrates two-way television** between offices at 195 Broadway and 463 West Street in Manhattan. (tvhistory.tv ND).

**1930**s – The comic strip, **Dick Tracy, features two-way wrist-mounted TV**. It only shows the faces of users. This becomes a classic "envisionment" used by the popular press to describe media space and related technologies.

**1962 – AT&T markets** Bell Lab's **Picturephone** in various desktop designs. The video unit integrates camera, monitor, and speakerphone. The video is black and white and is configured for showing faces. Most actual users are AT&T executives

S. Harrison
Virginia Polytechnic Institute and State University
e-mail: srh@cs.vt.edu

S. Harrison (ed.), *Media Space 20+ Years of Mediated Life*,
Computer Supported Cooperative Work,

because specialized networking is required. Public gets demonstrations at various fairs across the world and Disney theme parks (proticus.org ND).

**1960s** – The cartoon show, **The Jetsons**, features large-screen picturephones. Gags often involve irate callers reaching through the screen to yell or strangle one another. Screen location is used to represent the hierarchy of the caller (e.g., Jetson's boss would appear on a monitor above subservient employee Jetson). Some early media space researchers would informally cite the Jetsons for inspiration.

**1968** – **Doug Englebart** gives **NLS demo** to Fall Joint Computer Conference in San Francisco, using media space-like connection to SRI located in Menlo Park. Links between locations are for the duration of the demo and consist of one-way monochromatic video, two-way audio, and shared computing display. Englebart wears an audio headset and his colleague at SRI is visible on an inset window (sloan.stanford.edu ND).

**1970s** – As apparatus for the study of "intersubjectivity" in the relations between a mother and a newborn, developmental psychologist Colwyn Trevarthen creates probably the **first video tunnel**. Camera and monitor pairs are arranged to make eye contact reciprocal fields of view. This idea gets reinvented numerous times for many different purposes. (The tunnel was quite effective, recorded interaction would be switched for real interaction so that parent–child response cycle would be broken. It took 1-week-old babies about 1 s to get restive and about 5 s to be in tears.) (attachment.edu.ar ND).

**1980** – Video artists Kit Galloway and Sherrie Rabinowitz' **Hole in Space** project links Century City in Los Angeles to Lincoln Center in New York City. This is a real-time video and audio link. Images are monochromatic full-size rear-projected images of passersby. Audio is more or less full duplex with echo canceling handled by technicians manually adjusting levels. It is on display for three evenings (Galloway and Rabinowitz, 1980; Harrison, 2008).

**1981** – Ithia de Sola Pool gives presentation "Who Needs All This Bandwidth" to Optical Society of America. Presentation notes that digital transmission will make ubiquitous video connection nearly free. His vision of massive shared memory for networked computing foreshadows the Internet as ubiquitously accessible repository of knowledge. Together, these two ideas suggest a universal digital vehicle for ubiquitous-mediated connection.

## First Instances

*The first research experiments in media space carry analog audio and video in separate networks from the data network. Connection between locations is through costly teleconferencing codecs. This physical and logical separation of computing and media reflects separation of audio and video from office systems research;*

*these technical and organizational issues do not prevent investigations that presume ubiquitous media and computing.*

**1985 – Xerox PARC office-to-office media space**. The first instance links three offices with hardwired connections using consumer VCRs, cameras, and televisions for termination, and coaxial cables for audio and video signals (Stults, 1986).

– **PARC Palo Alto to Portland media space** hardwired link between Palo Alto and Portland provided by 56 Kbit teleconferencing codecs started on October 8 at 3:30 P.M.

– PARC Palo Alto to Portland **media space with switched connection**. Building on original hardwired media space, consumer video equipment used for termination and coaxial cabling used for video and audio distribution; link between Palo Alto and Portland provided by 56 Kbit teleconferencing codecs; professional studio switch provides one-to-one and one-to-many switching (Bly et al., 1993; Harrison et al., 1997).

**1986** – PARC **Office Design Project**. Demonstration of uses of video in design. Three architects meet asynchronously using video recordings organized as threaded conversations; they work together in three separate locations using hardwired video and audio links; recording is used to document and report process. Researchers use Wizard-of-Oz techniques to simulate media services (Weber and Minneman, 1987).

**1986 – EuroPARC** (Cambridge, UK) creates **media space** linking offices on three floors. The initial infrastructure (16 nodes) was based on coax cabling and a set of around eight Akai switches controlled by MIDI interface; later, a large BTS crossbar switch was introduced to relieve a trunking problem and serving 24 nodes and PictureTel codec enabled on-demand off-site linkage. Control infrastructure called "iiif" was written by Tom Milligan without any switches to test it on. When the switches arrived, he plugged them in, and it worked first time. The first reaction by staff and researchers was that it was "creepy," but they eventually became its staunchest supporters. Audio was balanced low impedance stereo and video was broadcast quality composite (Buxton and Moran, 1990; Gaver et al., 1992; Bellotti and Dourish, 1997; Henderson et al., 1996).

– Randy Smith and William Newman at **EuroPARC** develop a "**video tunnel**" using half-silvered mirrors that provides eye contact and visual reciprocity. Given the intrinsic dyadic nature of the terminal, it is used for extended office-sharing connections. This is a reinvention of the apparatus used by Colwyn Trevarthen in the 1970s and a telecommunication terminal patented in1987. Others also reinvent this idea such as the Gazecam (Acker and Levitt, 1987).

– System Concepts Lab at PARC is merged into the System Sciences Lab. To share culture of new organization, break areas of both Labs are linked with disastrous results.

– PARC Palo Alto to Portland link was decommissioned when Portland laboratory was shut down.

– **BellCore** (the joint research lab of the "Baby Bells" that resulted from the break up of the original AT&T) creates a media space and deploys **Video Window** and **Cruiser**. Cruiser allows researchers to "virtually walk the halls" to encounter colleagues for informal conversation (Fish et al., 1990; Kraut et al., 1994).

**1989 – US West** Research creates a media space (Bulick et al., 1989).

– EuroPARC and PARC create **video mail** service demo using computer-controlled VHS VCRs with time-code indexed messages – much like the audio-cassette based telephone answering machines. Tapes are sent by overnight delivery services.

## Digital Transition

*The early 1990s sees audio and images going digital with faster processors, improved compression and the rapid growth of high-speed networking.*

**1990 – University of Toronto Telepresence Project** begun by building on and extending design from EuroPARC. (Mantei et al., 1991; Buxton et al., 1997).

– **First video capture cards** become available for office workstation–class computers.

– PARC explores video-based shared drawing work ("**VideoDraw**," "VideoCom," "VideoWhiteBoard") (Tang and Minneman, 1990).

– Hiroshi Ishii and colleagues at NTT in Japan develop **TeamWorkstation** and other seamless computing + video interaction workstations (Ishii, 1990; Ishii and Kobayashi, 1992).

– **H.261** video conferencing compression standard established. Codecs are expensive as is the connection using T1 or other conditioned connections, but codecs from different vendors can now interconnect.

**1991** – EuroPARC- begins exploring "**awareness**." This leads to Portholes – low-resolution still images taken from media space cameras. It was inspired by Polyscope and Vrooms, systems built by Alan Borning in 1990. "Awareness" emerged from a survey and study of the infrastructure that was conducted in 1990 and overseen by Gary and Judy Olson, who were visiting that year (Dourish and Bly, 1992).

– **Dan's Apartment**. Artist Dan O'Sullivan creates a fake media space: a public-access channel cable television show allows users to "look around" in Dan's apartment by navigating images on a laserdisc. Users call a number that recognizes simple voice commands. This is the precursor to any number of voyeuristic webcams that come online a few years later (itp.nyu.edu ND).

– Quentin Stafford-Fraser at the Computer Laboratory at Cambridge University sets up a camera to observe a coffee pot in a shared break area. This is the **first known webcam**. The camera and the coffee pot stay online until 2001 (parkerinfo.com ND).

**1992** – At the University of Toronto, Bill Buxton and colleagues begin work on embodied displays such as **Hydra** and spatially organized displays such as a door-mouse that controls accessibility icon in Portholes and "**Brady Bunch**" display. The idea is that one should use the same mechanisms for social control in media space as in physical space, whenever possible (Buxton et al., 1997).

– **CuSeeMe** provides a method to connect personal computers using low-resolution video over standard networking. Originally for Macintoshs and video-only, it soon migrates to PCs and adds audio.

– University of Toronto extends Portholes to have sensing. By differencing two successive portholes images, motion was detected. Motion sensing let users know when spaces were occupied and was mapped to availability information (Buxton, 1995).

**1993** – **University of Calgary** establishes media space that shares computational artifacts. **TeamRooms** is MOO-based; it is followed by the **Notification Collage** and **Community Bar**. A multimedia notification server distributed multimedia information, including snapshot video frames, shared artifacts, and shared groupware workspaces to all group members. These systems are also toolkits, allowing programmers to craft new content and systems within them (Roseman and Greenberg, 1996).

– **SUN Labs** create a media space using the **DIME** (Digital Integrated Multimedia Environment) prototype platform for digitizing video and sending it around over IP networks. There were approximately 25 users, including a systematic study of 10 people. Conventional consumer analog video cameras were used as input, and displayed the video as a window on users' computer screens (Tang et al., 1994).

**1995** – **H.263** video conferencing compression standard set replacing H.261; eventually boards in PCs allow desktop conferencing through workstations using this standard.

– **Interval Research** creates an audio-only media space (Ackerman et al., 1997).

– The **Telegarden** goes on line. Created by Ken Goldberg and colleagues at the University of Southern California, remote users on the Internet can control a robotic arm to tend a garden. It is probably the first publicly accessible tele-operator (usc.edu ND).

## The Rise of Mediated Life

*In the second half of the 1990s and into the 2000s, the Internet and the cell phone become ubiquitous. Called a "convergence," digital media make audio and video an integral part of everyday computing. Users become produces of content. Sharing (legally and otherwise) of content becomes a* fait accompli. *Producing video like that of commercial cinema and manipulating images become standard educational fare setting expectations that anything can appear to be anywhere. New social conventions address appropriate behavior with cell phones and cameras. All of these phenomena reassert issues of privacy, control, the meaning of one's appearance, notions of space and place, and ownership.*

**1996** – NYNEX creates a media space.

**1997** – Phillipe Kahn introduces "**J-Phone**," the first cell phone with a built-in camera. A big hit from the start, cell phone cameras in a few years go from gimmick to a standard feature (wikipedia.org ND).

**1999** – PARC develops **DrawStreamStation**. DSS couples digital video recording and playback to real-time media space. The station supports a variety of media that includes marking and gesturing of hands coordinated with talk and display. Distributed nature of timestream architecture allows for local storage and coordinated playback across network (Harrison et al. 1999).

**2001 – Google image search** makes sharing (and appropriating) still images commonplace.
– **USB-connected cameras** such as the Logitech enter the market enabling ubiquitous webcams and desktop video conferencing.

**2002** – Apple markets iSight **firewire camera** enabling high resolution desktop video conferencing.

**2005 – Telemural** deployed in MIT dormitory.

**2007** – Apple introduces the **iPhone**. Digital convergence, long talked about by pundits, seems more at hand than ever, but the cost seems to be that connections fall into short attentional events rather than seamless whole.

## References

—(ND) http://attachment.edu.ar/intersubjectivity.html
—(ND) http://itp.nyu.edu/~dbo3/proj/apartment.htm
—(ND) http://www.parkerinfo.com/coffee.htm
—(ND) http://www.porticus.org/bell/telephones-picturephone.html
—(ND) http://sloan.stanford.edu/mousesite/1968 Demo.html
—(ND) http://www.tvhistory.tv/1930-ATT-BELL.htm
—(ND) http://www.usc.edu/dept/garden/
—(ND) http://en.wikipedia.org/wiki/Camera_phone

Acker, S. and Levitt, S. (1987). Designing videoconference facilities for improved eye contact. *Journal of Broadcasting & Electronic Media*, 31(2), 181–191.

Ackerman, M., Starr, B., Hindus, D., and Mainwaring, S. (1997). Hanging on the wire: A field study of an audio-only media space. *ACM Transactions on Computer-Human Interaction (TOCHI)*, 4(1), 39–66.

Adler, A. and Henderson, A. (1994). A Room of Our Own: Experiences from a Direct Office Share in *Proceedings of CHI'94, Human Factors in Computing Systems* (pp. 138–144), doi: 10.1145/191666.191727.

Bellotti, V. and Dourish, P. (1997). Rant and RAVE: Experimental and experiential accounts of a media space. In K. Finn, A. Sellen, and S. Wilbur (Eds.) *Video-Mediated Communication* (pp. 245–272). Mahwah, NJ: Lawrence Erlbaum.

Bly, S., Harrison, S., and Irwin, S. (1993). Media Spaces: Bringing people together in a video, audio, and computing environment. *Communications of the Association of Computing Machinery*, NY 36(1) January 1993. 28–45, doi: 10.1145/151233.151235.

Bulick, S., Abel, M., Corey, D., Schmidt, J., and Coffin, S. (1989). The US WEST Advanced Technologies Prototype Multi-media communications System. *GLOBECOM'89: Proceedings of the IEEE Global Telecommunications Conference*, Dallas, Texas.

Buxton, W. (1995). Integrating the periphery and context: A new model of telematics. *Proceedings of Graphics Interface'95* (pp. 239–246) http://www.billbuxton.com/BG_FG.html

Buxton, W. and Moran, T. (1990). EuroPARC's integrated interactive intermedia facility (iiif): Early experience. In S. Gibbs and A.A. Verrijn-Stuart (Eds.) *Multiuser Interfaces and Applications, Proceedings of the IFIP WG 8.4 Conference on Multi-user Interfaces and Applications* (pp. 11–34). Amsterdam: Elsevier Science Publishers B.V. (North-Holland) http://www.billbuxton.com/iiif.html

Buxton, W., Sellen, A.J., and Sheasby, M. (1997). Interfaces for multiparty videoconferences. In K. Finn, A. Sellen, and S. Wilbur (Eds.) *Video-Mediated Communication*. Mahwah, NJ: Lawrence Erlbaum.

Curtis, P., Dixon, M., Frederick, R., and Nichols, D. (1995). The Jupiter audio/video architecture: Secure multimedia in network places, *Proceedings of the third ACM international conference on Multimedia* (pp. 79–90), doi: 10.1145/217279.215128.

Dourish, P. and Bly, S. (1992). Portholes: Supporting awareness in a distributed work group, *Proceedings of the SIGCHI Conference on Human Factors in Computing Systems* (pp. 541–547), doi: 10.1145/142750.142982.

Fish, R., Kraut, R., and Chalfonte, B. (1990) The VideoWindow system in informal communication, *Proceedings of the 1990 ACM Conference on Computer-Supported Cooperative Work* (pp. 1–11), doi: 10.1145/99332.99335.

Galloway, K. and Rabinowitz, S. (1980) "Hole in Space" project displayed at Lincoln Center, NYC and Century City, http://www.ecafe.com/getty/HIS/ Los Angeles, November, 1980.

Gaver, W., Moran, T., MacLean, A., Lövstrand, L., Dourish, P., Carter, K., and Buxton, W. (1992) Realizing a video environment: EuroPARC's RAVE system, *Proceedings of the SIGCHI Conference on Human Factors in Computing Systems* (pp. 27–35), doi: 10.1145/142750.142754.

Greenberg S. and Roseman, M. (2003). Using a room metaphor to ease transitions in groupware. In M. Ackerman, V. Pipek, V. Wulf (Eds.) *Sharing Expertise: Beyond Knowledge Management* (pp. 203–256). Cambridge, MA: MIT Press.

Greenberg, S. and Rounding, M. (2001). The notification collage: Posting information to public and personal displays. *Proceedings of the ACM Conference on Human Factors in Computing Systems* (pp 514–521), doi: 10.1145/365024.365339.

Harrison, S. (2008) Seeing the hole in space *HCI Remixed* (pp 155–160). Cambridge: MIT Press.

Harrison, S., Bly, S., Anderson, S., and Minneman, S. (1997) The Media Space. In Finn, K., Sellen, A., and Wilbur, S. (Eds.) *Video-Mediated Communication* (pp. 273–300) Mahwah, NJ: Lawerence Erlbaum.

Harrison, S., Minneman, S., and Marinacci, J. (1999). The DrawStream Station or the AVC's of video cocktail napkins. *The Proceedings of the International Conference on Multimedia Systems'99*, doi: 10.1109/MMCS.1999.779259.

Henderson, A., Dourish, P., Adler, and A. Bellottii, V. (1996). Your place or mine? Learning from long-term use of audio-video communication. *Journal of Computer Supported Cooperative Work*, 5(1).

Ishii, H. (1990) TeamWorkStation: Towards a seamless shared workspace, *Proceedings of the 1990 ACM Conference on Computer-Supported Cooperative Work* (pp. 13–26), doi: 10.1145/99332.99337.

Ishii, H. and Kobayashi, M. (1992). ClearBoard: A seamless medium for shared drawing and conversation with eye contact, *Proceedings of the SIGCHI Conference on Human Factors in Computing Systems* (pp. 525–532), doi: 10.1145/142750.142977.

Kraut, R., Rice, R., Cool, C., and Fish, R. (1994). Life and death of new technology: task, utility and social influences on the use of a communication medium, *Proceedings of the 1994 ACM Conference on Computer Supported Cooperative Work* (pp. 13–21), doi: 10.1145/192844.192858.

Mantei, M., Baecker, R., Sellen, A., Buxton, W., and Wellman, B. (1991). Experiences in the use of a media space, *Proceedings of the SIGCHI Conference on Human Factors in Computing Systems: Reaching Through Technology* (pp. 203–208), doi: 10.1145/108844.108888.

McEwan, G., and Greenberg, S. (2005). Supporting social worlds with the community bar, *Proceedings of the ACM Group 2005 Conference*, doi: 10.1145/1099203.1099207.

Moran, T., Palen, L., Harrison, S., Chiu, P., Kimber, D., Minneman, S., van Melle, W., and Zellweger, P. (1997) "I'll get that off the audio": A case study of salvaging multimedia meeting records, *Proceedings of the SIGCHI Conference on Human Factors in Computing Systems* (pp. 202–209), doi: 10.1145/258549.258704.

Roseman, M. and Greenberg, S. (1996). TeamRooms: Network places for collaboration, *Proceedings of the SIGCHI Conference on Human Factors in Computing Systems* (pp. 325–333), doi: 10.1145/240080.240319.

Stults, R. (1986). *Media Space*. Xerox PARC Technical Report.

Tang, J., Isaacs, E., and Rua, M. (1994). Supporting distributed groups with a Montage of lightweight interactions, *Proceedings of the 1994 ACM Conference on Computer Supported Cooperative Work* (pp. 23–34), doi: 10.1145/192844.192861.

Tang, J. and Minneman, S. (1990). VideoDraw: A video interface for collaborative drawing, *Proceedings of the SIGCHI Conference on Human Factors in Computing Systems: Empowering People* (pp. 313–320), doi: 10.1145/97243.97302.

Weber, K. and Minneman, S. (1987). "Office Design Project." (videotape) Xerox Corporation, Palo Alto, CA.

# Chapter 3
# Section 1: The Social Space

**Paul M. Aoki and John C. Tang**

The development of the media space implementations drew on art installations and architectural conceptions of spatiality for initial inspiration. However, discussions of the impact of media spaces have always included social responses and implications as well. As Bly, Harrison, and Irwin (1993) noted:

> *The people participating in the media space have the greatest influence on the ways in which it will be used. The ways of working that people bring to a media space and create in that space can vary greatly. However, characteristics of the setting and the technology are also important in how a media space is used and what it becomes. We consider the setting to include the individuals using the technology, the relationships among these individuals, and their activities.*

The notion that a media space must be understood as embedded in a setting, or a technosocial situation (Ito and Okabe, 2005) that is largely socially defined is now often rendered in shorthand: "media spaces connect people." The above passage highlights this point, and also reminds us to keep in mind each of the individual elements – individuals, relationships, and activities – that relate a media space to the people who use it.

Over time, much of the research on media spaces has examined the dynamics of this embedding. That is, rather than focusing on theoretically derived design arguments or on technical novelty, these inquiries have focused on the social processes by which a media space "comes to be" a media space instead of a computer system. Such studies are not only about what people "do" with a media space, but also about how it is adopted and appropriated, how the practices of its users stabilize into communities, or how its availability shapes users' behaviors and perceptions.

---

P.M. Aoki
Intel Research Berkeley
e-mail: aoki@acm.org

J.C. Tang
Microsoft Research
e-mail: johntang@microsoft.com

S. Harrison (ed.), *Media Space 20+ Years of Mediated Life*,
Computer Supported Cooperative Work,

While this research shares a common emphasis on the social construction of media spaces, it can be useful to divide these inquiries into two general arcs.

## Stable Environment

The first arc is what might be described as the *stable environment* arc. In this arc, a communication technology is used to connect a collection of people who have existing relationships and relatively clear reasons to interact. The most common social unit studied is that of an office workgroup or a collection of such workgroups. This includes many of the classic empirical reports of media space use, such as that of Bly, Harrison, and Irwin (1993).

The goal here is typically what is glossed in the Introduction as "[understanding how] elements of understood social practice are used in mediated ways." While any environment can be expected to change over time, the relative stability of the goals and constitution of these kinds of groups often lead to a convergence of practices within a group. Indeed, we are often able to tie together results across studies of different groups and different technologies.

For example, we can see that just as the spatial definition of media spaces has its landmark features (always-on, high fidelity audio–video connections, real-time awareness), its social construction also has some core elements. Groups used media spaces to *share awareness and context* surrounding each others' activities. This affordance in turn enables people to *socially negotiate starting interactions* with each other at appropriate times and situations. Overall, media spaces were often used to *coordinate activities* among the participants. These general activities are often seen in informal workplace interaction (Whittaker et al., 1994), but they play out with different specifics in media spaces. As the chapter by Luff, Kuzuoka, Heath, Yamazaki and Yamashita shows, this is especially true when the activities involve access and reference to social and physical resources outside the scope of the media space.

As a second example, stable environments lend themselves to nuanced investigations of difficult issues such as privacy. Because participants generally have ongoing relationships as well as the time to negotiate with each other and reflect upon outcomes, the privacy questions that arise are different from issues raised by strangers in a similar situation. The complexity of these issues can be seen in the fact that these explorations continue today and indeed will likely never be completed in any meaningful sense. The chapter by Boyle, Neustaedter and Greenberg provides a systematic and insightful theoretical guide to privacy issues that have arisen thus far.

As a final example, there have been many fruitful investigations of what happens within organizations as media-based interaction becomes widely available. These range from highly informative case studies of use within workgroups to larger examinations of adoption within organizations (Bly et al., 1993).

The stable environment arc has been and continues to be extremely productive. The designers of the early media space systems at PARC, Bellcore, University of Toronto, etc. were able to refine their concepts by deploying systems in the context of their own workplaces. Indeed, the best-known uses and applications – linked common areas, office share, video window, and so on – came out of these highly productive explorations. However, if we posit that media spaces can be socially constructed from a design space broader than the well-defined technological configurations used at that time, it is clear that only a fraction of this design space could be explored in the laboratory.

## Design Elasticity

This leads to the second of our two arcs, which might be termed the *design elasticity* arc. Since the deployment of the initial media spaces, researchers have pushed on the design space by varying more widely the kinds of settings that can be established. This again poses the definitional question – how much can we change the setting and still know that it constitutes a media space?

In cases where designers are varying one or two specific dimensions (such as the physical context, the activities supported, or the technological medium used) in a straightforward way, this problem might be best addressed through the hoary adage that we know it when we see it. That is, one can draw on the reports from the early media spaces to identify particular orientations on the part of the users and then identify these same orientations in new settings. To use a simple technological example: can we think of the Interval audio spaces (Ackerman et al., 1997) as media spaces even though video was "left out"? From the reports we have of their use, the answer seems to be "yes." As we suggest elsewhere in this volume, drawing connections of this kind between old systems and new systems can still be very informative.

The definitional question becomes more acute – and interesting – as the setting is changed more radically. In particular, recent designs often aim to enable situations in which the activities are less focused or instrumental – on facilitating forms of interaction that are better characterized in terms of pure sociability (Simmel, 1911/1950) or play (Caillois, 1958/1961) as opposed to "work" or "tasks" in their commonly understood meanings. These design explorations can be seen as testing the boundaries of the design space in the following ways, among others:

**Elasticity of relationships ("audience").** From studies of use within groups of social familiars (colleagues and friends), we have seen an expansion into studies of what a media space means for ad hoc configurations of strangers, for collections of what are essentially familiar strangers (Milgram, 1977), and for communities defined more by weak ties than by strong ties. In this section, these are exemplified (respectively) in the chapters by Churchill and Nelson; by Friedman, Kahn,

Hagman, Severson and Gill; and by Karahalios. In the other direction, we have seen preliminary examinations of media space use in relationships that are more intimate than those usually found in the workplace. The chapter by Burge and Tatar provides initial insights into the specifics of interpersonal conflict in mediated communication.

**Elasticity of experience.** From systems that mainly use media to provide a high degree of fidelity with face-to-face interaction, we have seen an evolution toward providing reduced-fidelity representations that are not simply designed to enable obfuscatory "privacy" but are instead designed to require active engagement to explore and interpret. The chapter by Karahalios explores this design space and summarizes her experiences with several different systems of this type.

**Elasticity of temporality.** From the early emphasis on synchronous media and direct interaction between users, we have seen an emphasis on use of asynchronous media and of very different ways of using content to "draw in" users into initial states of engagement and "draw back" users as time goes on. In their chapter, Churchill and Nelson reflect on user engagement by drawing on their years of experience with emplaced media installations.

**Elasticity of setting persistence.** From environments in which the participants and sites were relatively stable, we have seen more exploration of settings that change over time. Mobility is one of the most important drivers for accommodating changes of environment. The increasing prevalence of public and semi-public displays also illustrates new environments to explore, as Churchill and Nelson demonstrate.

As might be expected, the goal in this arc tends to be more explicitly design-oriented. That is, even though an understanding of the social processes is still primary, the motivation is generally to tie this understanding back into concrete design points. The most common approach is to look at deployments of several media space variations and consider them in a comparative way. In some cases, the variations are chosen from reports on separate lines of research system and product use and the comparisons are knit together retrospectively (Our own chapters in Section 3 are examples of this). In other cases, researchers ambitiously produce these variations through systematic exploration of a design subspace. For example, one line of research (represented here by the chapter by Churchill and Nelson) takes the same basic asynchronous communication system (i.e., touchscreen-based Web applications designed for semi-public use) and deploys customized variations for a range of different audiences. By contrast, another line of research (of which the chapter by karahalios is representative) focuses on synchronous interaction within a particular type of audience (i.e., strangers) but then varies the experience through the use of very different systems.

While the two general arcs differ in the way in which the research is framed and explored, they clearly share an emphasis on the dynamics of how groups come together and how this is shaped by the design of a system. While each of the spatial, social, and embodied communication perspectives cannot help but include large aspects of "the social," work of the kind described here falls somewhere in between the metaphoric nature in the spatial perspective and the detailed particulars of interaction in the embodied communication perspective.

## Social Appropriation

An overlay on both arcs is a dynamic sense of *social appropriation.* As Ito and Okabe (2005) illustrate, the use of technology in a social setting leads to discovering new ways for its application. Media spaces started with the relatively simple proposition of outfitting workspaces with cameras and displays that could be connected under computer control. The socially agreed-upon uses that emerged over the past 20 years fill this book and more with a diverse range of applications. Sharing presentations over distance, encouraging impromptu interactions through remote common spaces, maintaining awareness of team members in different time zones, and sharing news and other timely status updates around the globe have all evolved from the initial media space experiences. While the media space research prototypes have helped the users discover the value of awareness and lightweight communication to support collaboration and coordination, these socially constructed functionalities may be accomplished without any video connections in the future. In this sense, the socially defined notions of media space may transcend technical implementations of the early research prototypes.

Along with socially invented ways of using the technology come socially agreed-upon conventions and mores around appropriate uses. The nature of media spaces has provoked thinking about how to address privacy concerns in such a connected environment. As observed in the conclusion of the chapter by Friedman et al., socially agreed-upon conventions of privacy continue to evolve as the pervasiveness of video has been extended and people gain more familiarity with its liabilities and limitations.

Reflecting on what we have learned from a social perspective on media spaces provides a nice complement to the spatial and embodied communication perspectives. While media spaces may have been one of the first systems to demonstrate the benefits of issues such as contextual awareness for social negotiation and coordination, we can apply the observations from this research to guide the ongoing evolution of technology. Indeed, as we note in Chapter 26, our understanding of the social response and appropriation of media spaces can explain the popularity of many systems that have emerged since then, such as IM, photo sharing, and video sharing. Furthermore, that understanding can be used to guide the design of new technologies that bring the social affordances of media spaces closer to widespread deployment, even though it may come in a very different form than the early research prototypes. These chapters explore a variety of approaches that help guide the design of future of socially constructed media spaces.

## References

Ackerman, M.S., Starr, B., Hindus, D., and Mainwaring, S.D. (1997). "Hanging on the wire: a field study of an audio-only media space." *TOCHI* 4 (1), 39–66.

Bly, S., Harrison, S., and Irwin, S. (1993). "Media spaces: bringing people together in a video, audio, and computing environment." *Communications of the Association of Computing Machinery*, NY, vol. 36, no. 1, January 1993, pp 28–45.

Caillois, R. (1958/1961). Man, play and games (M. Barash, trans.). New York: Free Press.
Ito, M. and Okabe, D. (2005). Technosocial situations: emergent structuring of mobile e-mail use. In M. Ito, D. Okabe, and M. Matsuda (eds.), Personal, portable, pedestrian: mobile phones in Japanese life. Cambridge, MA: MIT Press, pp 257–273.
Milgram, S. (1977). The familiar stranger: an aspect of urban anonymity. In S. Milgram (ed.), The individual in a social world: essays and experiments. Reading, MA: Addison-Wesley, pp 51–53.
Simmel, G. (1911/1950). Sociability. In K.H. Wolff (trans.), The sociology of Georg Simmel. New York: Free Press, pp 40–57.
Whittaker, S., Frohlich, D., and Daly-Jones, O. (1994). Informal workplace communication: what is it like and how might we support it? Proc. CHI 1994. New York: ACM, pp 131–137.

# *Anecdotes on the Social Space of Media Space*

***The following are short anecdotes about coming upon a media space for the first time and the social consequences of that***

## My First Reaction

**Victoria Bellotti**
Palo Alto Research Center

The media space (at EuroPARC) was going online when I started working there in October 1989. I remember that it was rather creepy at first as I was just a newcomer and did not have any say in what was put in my office. Several of the administrative staff were very upset about it too. Later on, we became some of its strongest advocates.

## Close Encounters of the Media Space Kind

**D. Scott McCrickard**
Virginia Polytechnic Institute and State University

*The author does not use video chat although he has used teleconferencing for distance learning and faculty meetings. This is his first experience of encountering a shared media space office. It happened in 2008, but bears remarkable similarity to experiences reported since the first media spaces.*

I went by "P"'s [a post-doc] office with my kids to raid his lollipop stash. I entered the room and saw that his girlfriend "C" [who attends a university 500 miles away] was in a video window on one of "P"'s two monitors (the smaller, secondary one). "P" announced our presence: "Hey, the

McCrickards are here!" and "C" put forth a greeting. I was a bit worried that I was interrupting something, but "P" immediately started engaging with the kids. I was left at a loss as to how to include "C" in the conversation; she seemed to be sitting there staring at us. I could not read her face – expectant? patient? anxious? I made occasional attempts to include her in the conversation, and she would politely respond and go back to the same look. I even invented my own media space interactions, holding a lollipop up to her camera so she could "lick" it. When we were getting ready to leave, I mentioned to "P" that he could get back to his conversation – but he said they both just leave the video chat up all the time so that they could stay connected. In reflecting on that, it seems odd to me (having some but not lots of video window usage experience), but perhaps it is something that works for "P" and "C".

## My Introduction to Media Space

**Deborah Tatar**
Virginia Polytechnic Institute and State University

In 1988, I was part of the CoLab group at Xerox PARC. It was located in a part of the building next to where the System Concepts Lab was housed. The SCL folks had this remarkable collaboration system, which they called the Media Space – but they did not talk about it as such. It seemed rather exotic and strangely useful.

They were rather generous in inviting researchers outside SCL to have it installed in their offices, but this was not open-ended. Only those who signed up to be part of the Media Space community and live in the visually open universe could get it. Many of the socially aware researchers (and "socially aware" was not the norm at PARC) had expressed well-founded concerns about being observed, "panopticons," power issues, representation issues, and – well, all this will be subverted by a malevolent Big Brother. I had opted-in knowing that the media space folks generally kept audio off. The visual appearance of office activity is not particularly revealing beyond presence and absence – and modulo the occasional digit that might end up in a nose, not particularly embarrassing.

So one day, after much crawling around under my desk by one of the SCLers, I had a camera, monitor, and microphone in my office. There was a simple interface that allowed me to switch what I was watching and who watched me. (I later came to realize that I could also see who was watching whom and even switch anyone's connection.)

I turned on the TV and what did I see: nothing but some empty office that I could not place. This seemed rather anti-climactic. Some time passed and I went back to writing. Minutes went by. Out of the corner of my eye, I saw a figure appear, turned toward the camera, unbuckled his belt, tucked in his shirt, tightened his belt and sat back down with his back to the camera. What a surprise, the Media Space turned out to be a lot like MTV: many minutes of nothing happening, punctuated by people taking their clothes off.

What really happened was that the person I happened to be connected to had returned from lunch and had turned away from his door in order to modestly tuck in his shirt. Even though he was one of the originators of the media space, he forgot that his camera was on.

I kept my Media Space connection for the remainder of my time at PARC. While my first impression set my expectations very high, the visual content never rivaled that first day.

## Windows

**Bill Buxton**
Microsoft Research

From about 1990-1994 I directed something called the Ontario Tele-presence Project at the University of Toronto and University of Ottawa. I was the project's scientific director, and perhaps for that reason, my second floor office had the best view. Hence, I had a "window cam" pointing out onto the main quad on the campus – a pretty beautiful sight. I knew that this was valued because of any piece of the entire system that ever failed (and in the early stages, things were – shall we say – not overly stable), the thing that caused my phone to ring the fastest was my window cam.

Lots of people (especially lowly graduate students) had landlocked offices, i.e., no windows. This was their only link to what it was like outside. Was it snowing? Raining? Or even daylight still? They had no other way of knowing from the bowels of the building.

But the day that the guy cleaned the outside of my windows was a special day, with various parts of his anatomy gyrating in front of the lens. This was only outdone by the time there was a car crash right in view of the camera. On such days people were not discussing video compression algo-rithms or the finer points of SMPTE time code over lunch.

The fact is, the power of the window became an effective tool for social engineering. Ron Riensenbach, my managing director, and I shared and administrative assistant. She sat in a landlocked area in the inner part of our office suite. When she started, following the "good form" established at PARC, I asked if she would like a media space node installed on her desk. Of course, I was just following form, so I was really taken aback when she said, "No. I am just an admin, and I don't want my bosses able to watch my every move and keep their eyes on my like that." Hmmm. Welcome to the real world Bill, where groups are not made up of trusting peers and you can't take things like trust and respect for granted.

Thanks to my deep experience with birds, window washers, car crashes and the weather, I at least had the wit to ask a different question: "Would you like a windowed office instead?" The answer was and immediate and definitive "Yes." So, we installed a monitor on her desk, and the software to let her hook up to the window cam, but no microphone or camera.

This was great. She was happy (as were a number of other admins in the general area, who while not related to our project, also requested – and got – similar "windowed offices"). Our new admin got a window, and some consequent brownie points with her peers.

We all settled in and work progressed. Working relationships were established, along with the inevitable dependencies on each other. One of these was that between Garry Beirne, one of our programmers, and Ron and my admin. I can't remember what the project was, but they needed to have constant interactions for a while. Consequently, one day she asked "Can someone hook my monitor up so that I can see Garry sometimes, instead the window? I need to know when I can call him." (Garry was on the 4th floor at the far side of the building. We were on the 2nd.)

The answer was "No – it would not be fair letting you see him if he can't see you." Which led to an immediate request, "So can I have a camera, microphone and speakers too?" To which the answer was an immediate "Yes."

The point is that the window, besides simply improving the working environment, also was an important tool in building trust and understanding - of the technology and the social mores associated with it. It provided a path to a pull for the technology and associated services, rather than a push. It was a valuable tool for social and cultural change.

And I wish that I could tell you that I was such a brilliant and insightful manager that I planned the whole thing. But that would be a lie.

However, like the birds, the lesson was not lost on me. Living the experience rather than just thinking about it, brings a whole different level of learning and depth of understanding. And I needed it. I still do.

# Chapter 4
# Creating Assemblies in Media Space: Recent Developments in Enhancing Access to Workspaces

**Paul Luff, Hideaki Kuzuoka, Christian Heath, Keiichi Yamazaki, and Jun Yamashita**

## Introduction

Media spaces offer an unprecedented opportunity to enhance communication and collaboration, and to transform the ways in which people are able to work together. The emergence of media spaces in the 1980s happened at a time of significant change in the workplace. With enhanced communications a new form of global economy was seen to emerge and the organisation of both private and public sector institutions was being rethought. While the distinctiveness of these new organisational arrangements are probably exaggerated, the growing commitment to devolved expertise, temporary collations, and highly flexible and contingent assemblies of dispersed activities seemed dependent on the ability of new technologies to enhance, if not replace, the conventional workplace and work space. With their promise of rich and real-time access to geographically dispersed colleagues, it seemed that media spaces provide the technological support necessary for the new workplace and these would be the jewel in the crown of the emerging field of Computer-Supported Collaborative Work (CSCW). And yet, despite the commitment and contributions of researchers from a number of academic disciplines, building successful, pliable and useable media spaces has proved highly intractable. Indeed, media spaces, not unlike their precursors, video telephony and conferencing, have had little impact on the ways in which people work together. Research in media spaces is often treated by many of our colleagues in CSCW, HCI and Ubiquitous Computing with some disdain.

P. Luff and C. Heath
Work Interaction and Technology Research Centre, Department of Management, King's College of London
e-mails: Paul.Luff@kcl.ac.uk; Christian.Heath@kcl.ac.uk

H. Kuzuoka and J. Yamashita
Department of Intelligent Interaction Technologies, University of Tsukuba, Graduate School of Systems and Information Engineering
e-mails: kuzuoka@iit.tsukuba.ac.jp; jun@iit.tsukuba.ac.jp

K. Yamazaki
Faculty of Liberal Arts, Saitama University
e-mail: By106561@nifty.com

S. Harrison (ed.), *Media Space 20+ Years of Mediated Life*,
Computer Supported Cooperative Work,

In this chapter, we discuss a programme of social and technical research that we have undertaken over the last few years concerned with the design, assessment and development of systems to support real-time, distributed work; work that relies upon a participants' ability to access a range of tangible and digital resources. The programme of work has been informed by findings from a range of studies of work and collaboration in environments that include architectural practices, control centres, surgeries, hospitals, news rooms, and the like. These studies have a framework of considerations, criteria, and insights into the organization of everyday work and interaction that have enabled us to identify some of the limitations of conventional media spaces, including systems which we have helped develop, and to pose a set of requirements and challenges, which we believe are fundamental to the creation of a media space that could support the flexible and contingent demands of seemingly simple forms of collaborative work. These studies, coupled with the development and assessment of a series of experimental systems, have enabled us to identify three key issues that we believe have to be addressed and resolved (in one way or another) if media space research is going to achieve its early potential.

The key issues that have underpinned our own programme of research are threefold:

- A satisfactory media space, like any other working environment, must provide participants with real-time access to a range of material and digital resources, including paper and digital documents, and the ability to produce, transform and annotate these resources.
- Media spaces consist of systems that interconnect participants in distinct physical environments and 'inevitably' create an ecology that provides participants with asymmetrical access to each other, to each others' environment, to the material and digital resources within those environments, and perhaps most fundamentally to each other in relation to the environment in which they are located. Media spaces must enable participants to manage or ameliorate the fragmentation that arises by virtue of these asymmetries; to enable the concerted and contingent production of collaborative work.
- Reference is a critical feature for the activities that people undertake when working together. Whereas in conventional face-to-face settings, participants largely accomplish reference to features of the local physical and material environment unproblematically, media spaces render reference, including pointing to features of particular objects, problematic. Media spaces must enable participants to flexibly invoke and achieve mutual reference: a problem that becomes increasingly complex as one enhances the range of materials and digital resources that one provides participants in the spaces.

In the next section, we briefly discuss extensions to the original media spaces that aim to address one or more of these issues. All media spaces fragment or fracture, in some way, the critical resources on which we rely to establish even a simple reference to a feature in the local environment. These difficulties suggest a reconsideration of the objectives of media spaces aimed at supporting distributed collaborative work activities. Rather than extending the scope of the technology to provide additional features to large numbers of participants or in locations away from the workplace, we should first pay close attention to how these systems could support people interacting and engaging in everyday activities. We briefly reflect on the critical problem of reference through distributed space, particularly to details of physical artefacts. In this regard we describe how we have configured an experimental system, Agora, to try and support detailed collaborative activities in the workspace, where we aimed to provide access to a range of documents in different ways. Agora uses a variety of techniques including multiple views of others and their workspaces, projections of spaces and conduct and ways of displaying the real-time conduct of a colleague related to the documents they have around them. We discuss, through a number of examples, the problems participants face when using the system and also how they appear to make sense of what appears to be a complex array of images of another's conduct. We conclude by suggesting further implications that might be of concern to those developing media spaces to support work activities and discuss how the problems raised by the very earliest media spaces – the curiously disembodied nature of visual conduct they present – are not necessarily avoided by shifting to alternative applications or shifting to other kinds of technology.

## Background: Neglecting the Artefact

By offering rich environments for communication and collaboration, the original media spaces suggested the great potential of technologies to support collaborative work. The visual, audio and computer-based communication services they offered would seem to be just the kind of resources necessary to support 'real-time', distributed collaborative work. Once deployed they would reduce the need for costly and wasteful travel, would bring isolated parts of an organisation together and allow people within an organisation to meet and work on tasks with others who may be in another country or continent at little or no notice. They seemed to provide the solution to the 'disaggregated' organisation.

Such hopes made over 20 years ago have curious similarities with those made for a diverse range of recent and emerging technologies including video-based desktop conferencing, powerful infrastructures to support distributed 'eResearch' like the ACCESSGRID and advanced collaboration rooms like HP's Halo system. No doubt that these systems are more sophisticated, more powerful and, in some cases, more accessible than the original media spaces, but this may not mean that they will be able to meet the expectations of their proponents. Moreover, it is unclear whether, and in what way, the motivations and development of these 'new generation' of media spaces draw from the research on the original media spaces. It may be worth revisiting some of these to consider whether the problems encountered when media spaces were originally used might also suggest how these and other new technologies might be shaped to support collaborative work.

One of the implications that could be drawn from the early research on media spaces and video connectivity was that the conventional 'face-to-face' view found in most of the systems did not provide the expected support required for many forms of collaboration. Despite the oft-reported importance of visual communication in interaction and collaborative work, these media spaces seemed to introduce a number of difficulties when configured to support face-to-face communication. Indeed, a number of studies suggested that critical resources for interaction were undermined by media spaces. They introduced interactional asymmetries that the participants had to manage, creating fragmented environments in which participants had to work to make the activities of their colleagues coherent (e.g. Heath and Luff, 1992; Gaver et al., 1993, 1995). It was noted that there were frequent perturbations in the talk between participants; that speakers had to engage in explicit activities to try and engender a change in the orientation of a co-participant; and that gestures frequently had to be upgraded and exaggerated in order to elicit an appropriate response from a colleague. Coupled with these difficulties, participants had little access to the domain of their remote colleagues. They had little access to the material objects or artefacts such as paper documents that are critical for the accomplishment of workplace activities. Perhaps most importantly they could not engage with, refer to or talk about the details of the written texts, drawings, sketches, images or notes, which pervade interaction and collaboration in most organisational activities (Luff et al., 1992; Sellen and Harper, 2002). In consequence, media spaces failed to provide systematic support for object-focused collaboration. Efforts were made to allow participants to see common objects on a desk, but these did not offer much access to the objects, providing restricted views and limited mobility of and manoeuvrability around physical objects. It is critical when supporting real-time distributed work to allow access to the artefacts that are used in that work; participants need to be able to point, reference and gesture to objects, and details of these objects, in both the local and the remote domains.

A number of attempts were made to circumvent these problems, for example, by providing a viewer with multiple views of the remote domain or allowing the view to change depending on what the viewer did. However, rather than alleviating the asymmetries between viewer and viewed they tended to exacerbate them (Gaver et al., 1993; Heath et al., 2001). An alternative was not to use video images but to try and provide all participants with more symmetrical resources through a Collaborative Virtual Environment (CVE) where avatars on the screen could orient to, talk about and refer to representations of objects in a screen-based interaction. However, producing conduct through an avatar, particularly detailed references to object in the space, was problematic. Even a simple activity like pointing to an object in the virtual space required work from both participants. In order to make sense of the 'visual' conduct the participants had to assemble the resources that made it possible to refer to objects – the avatar, the pointing devices (like visual representations of arms) and the object being referred to. This could prove difficult in a shifting and fractured environment (Hindmarsh et al., 1998).

Developing from media spaces a number of innovations have sought to provide better access to physical objects in the environment. Paying less attention to symmetrical environments and on offering generic support for communication and collaborations these initiatives have focused on activities such as remote instruction

(Kuzuoka, 1992; Fussell et al., 2003; Kuzuoka et al., 1994). Despite providing access to features of the remote environment and supporting participants to refer to remote objects, and features of those objects, these initiatives have paid little attention to supporting interactions in and around perhaps the most pervasive object in everyday work settings – the paper document (Luff and Heath, 1998; Sellen and Harper, 2002). This is despite the familiarity of the activities that occur on and around paper – reading and writing being perhaps the most obvious; the wide variety of collaborative activities that paper supports, and the detailed ways in which paper facilitates the shift between different and multiple forms of collaboration and participation (e.g. Luff and Heath, 1998). Previously, offering such support through technology might have been difficult due to the poor resolution of cameras and display devices, but recently there have been great improvements to the capabilities of video. It is now feasible to consider how media spaces might be enhanced to allow quite delicate ways of referring to and manipulating paper documents across remote domains.

## The Problem of Reference: Requirements for Enhanced Media Spaces

It is an obvious and important property of paper documents that they are transportable both between and within domains (e.g. Bellotti and Bly, 1996; Luff, et al., 1992), but there is another, quite distinct way that paper can be considered mobile; it can also be manoeuvrable at a much finer level of detail – what could be termed micro-mobility (Luff and Heath, 1998). It can be moved around a desk, for example, so that the workspace can be re-configured for new activities or so that co-participation in ongoing activities around the desk can be co-ordinated. Paper documents can be rotated, tilted or slid into position to achieve more comfortable access for reading or writing. The manouvrability of paper can also support transitions between different kinds of collaborative activity; its flexibility and manipulatability providing numerous ways for participants to shape their activities with regard to the shifting demands and changing concerns of colleagues.

Moreover, paper documents can be used alongside other materials and artefacts. When tasks involve multiple objects or materials participants will often carefully position them in particular places in relation to each other to enable easy access at the appropriate time. For example, participants can configure their local environment, their environment of documents, for their potentially upcoming activities. This is afforded by the ease with which paper documents can be overlaid and positioned (Fig. 4.1). In a range workplaces as diverse as school rooms, control centres, doctors surgeries, news rooms, architectural practices and trading rooms (e.g. Heath and Luff, 2000), we have observed how critical the micro-mobility of the paper document is for the accomplishment of everyday interactions and work.

Drawing from such observations concerning micro-mobility and our earlier research on media spaces (e.g. Heath and Luff, 1992; Kuzuoka, 1992; Yamazaki et al., 1999), we identified a number of demanding, yet critical, requirements that a

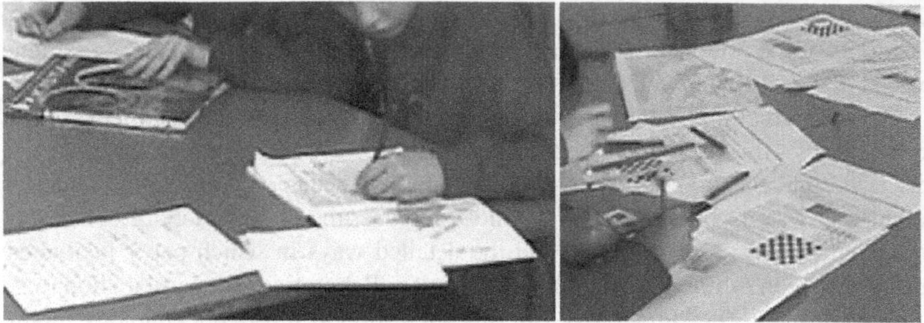

**Fig. 4.1** Paper positioned in ways to support different forms of collaboration so that particular activities are visible and accessible to others

media space designed to support distributed, synchronous collaborative work needs to address (Heath et al., 1995). These include:

- Providing participants with the ability to determine the location, orientation and frame of reference of others;
- Providing resources for participants to determine their standpoint with regard to other participants and the space(s) in which they and others are located;
- Providing resources through which participants can discriminate the actions of others, which involve shifts in orientation and references to the space and a range of objects, artefacts and features;
- Considering ways in which participants can refer to, invoke, grasp, manipulate, address and in various ways animate properties of the space, and coordinate such actions with the real-time conduct of others;
- Considering how participants can be provided with, and themselves preserve a stable constellation of relevant objects, artefacts and scenes within the space(s), so that they can produce and interpret activities with respect to a presupposed coherent and stable environment.

In the light of these requirements, we identified a number of capabilities that a motivating technology would need to support a pair of individuals collaboratively working, writing on and reading a set of documents. Such a system would have to provide:

- Access to details of materials in the remote environment;
- The ability to view a number of paper documents and types of documents in the remote domain;
- Multiple forms of access to another's documents, including focused collaborative activities such as shared writing, private work with documents and 'semi-public' activities where items may be referred to, but their details are not necessarily made public to the other;
- Easy ways of moving between different forms of access;
- Access to the ongoing conduct and orientation of the co-participant and ways of preserving common orientations to documents and others in collaborative activities (e.g. movements in and out of a side-by-side configuration)

These are a demanding set of requirements, particularly given the difficulties participants face in straightforward collaborative environments and media spaces. Moreover, as each person should be free to bring their own materials to the workspace, to read, write on and refer to these, the resources would need to be similar for each participant. Earlier innovations in video-supported systems suggested some ways in which these capabilities could be provided, for example, by using different qualities of projected images to support different forms of co-participation. With a little consideration it might be possible to configure a system with a number of areas that could facilitate transitions between different kinds of collaborative activity.

## The Agora Systems

To develop such a technology we brought together a team of social scientists and engineers from the UK and Japan. Together, we would undertake an iterative series of studies developing technological prototypes, analysing and assessing those prototypes in use which would in turn inform the redesign of the systems. We were particularly concerned to exploit the high resolution of images available through digital video systems and projectors. With such capabilities, rather than just have access to models, renderings of artefacts or some indications of the locations of documents, actual details of these objects could be read by the individuals using the technology (and the analysts considering its use). For these investigations we built upon experience with an existing system called Agora developed at the University of Tsukuba (Kuzuoka et al., 1999). The design of Agora was informed by a number of related initiatives to augment media spaces, such as VideoDraw (Tang and Minneman, 1991), ClearFace (Ishii and Kobayashi, 1992), TeamWorkstation (Ishii, 1990) and DigitalDesk (Wellner, 1991). The developments we made to Agora called AgoraPro and AgoraG aimed to support two participants interacting with a range of paper documents.

The Agora systems, as well as providing audio connections, offer a series of interrelated views that enable remote participants both to see and hear each other, access and share paper and digital documents and point to and gesture over documents both in their own domain and their co-participants', see Fig. 4.2.

More specifically the system consists of:

- A 120 cm screen situated along one side of the desk that projects a life-size image of the remote participant as they sit (or stand) at their desk. This provides a view of the other as well as a small portion of their desk. The camera associated with this view is attached to the middle of the screen; it is small enough not to be obtrusive.
- A large 'working area' (66 × 49 cm) on the desk in front of the participant. Here documents and hand gestures on and over the desktop are captured by a video camera above the desk, transmitted to a remote site and projected onto the remote desktop from beneath. In order to eliminate infinite video feedback, polarised films are placed both on the desk surface and in front of the camera lens. The resolution in this area is relatively low and with the polarised films rather dark. Also, since the image is projected from beneath, documents on the local desktop can cover the image of documents on the remote one.

**Fig. 4.2** A view of Agora showing the different spaces and the remote participant using a similar 'desk'

- A private space where documents are only available to the local participant.
- A smaller document space (the same size as an A3 piece of paper, 42 × 30 cm) where documents can be placed and worked upon. These were displayed on a shared touch-sensitive screen.
- Associated with this space we experimented with different ways of pointing into a remote domain. These configurations were called AgoroG and AgoraPro.

## *AgoraG*

The AgoraG variation is the slightly simpler configuration. In it a remotely controlled laser pointer is used to 'point' to objects in the remote domain. When a participant points at the shared screen the laser spot is directed to the appropriate place on the 'real' documents down on the remote participant's desk.

As the video image of the projected laser pointer is captured by the document camera it can also be seen on the shared document monitors at both sites (Fig. 4.3). Thus, the local participant can see that the laser pointer is pointing at the appropriate location in the remote domain, while the remote participant can see the laser spot both on the actual document on the desk in front of them and on the shared screen.

## *AgoraPro*

Rather than a laser pointer, in AgoraPro we use a hand-gesture camera and a hand-gesture projector which captures and shows hand gestures. A participant's gestures towards objects in the remote domain displayed on the shared screen are captured

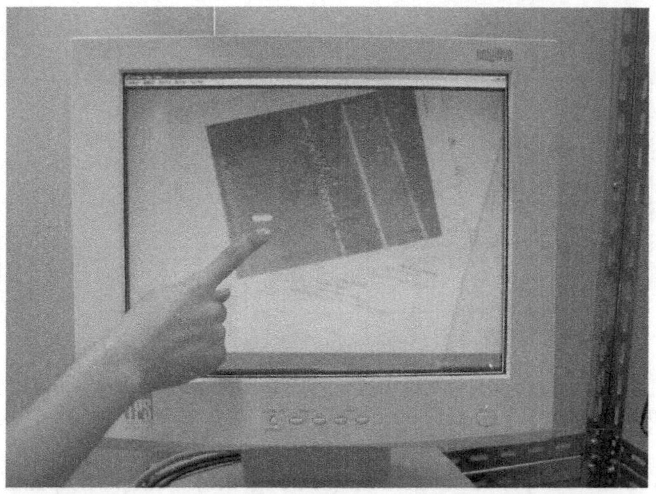

**Fig. 4.3** The laser spot pointing to a photograph on the remote desk positioned by the local participant touching the shared screen

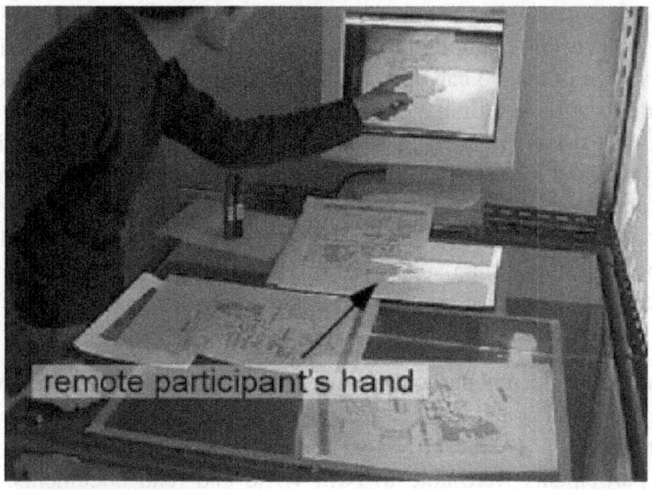


**Fig. 4.4** The remote participant's hand is projected onto the local document and onto the screen. As the local participant is also pointing to the screen the remote person would see something similar to this at their site

and projected down onto the document space at the remote site (see Fig. 4.4). They are also shown on the shared screen. This configuration aims to give the impression of reaching over and pointing to documents in the other workspace.

In order to eliminate infinite video feedback a polarised film is placed in front of the hand-gesture camera so that the camera captures only a hand image. This also means that the projected image of the hand, although still in colour, appears lighter and whiter than the images of other hands captured through the camera.

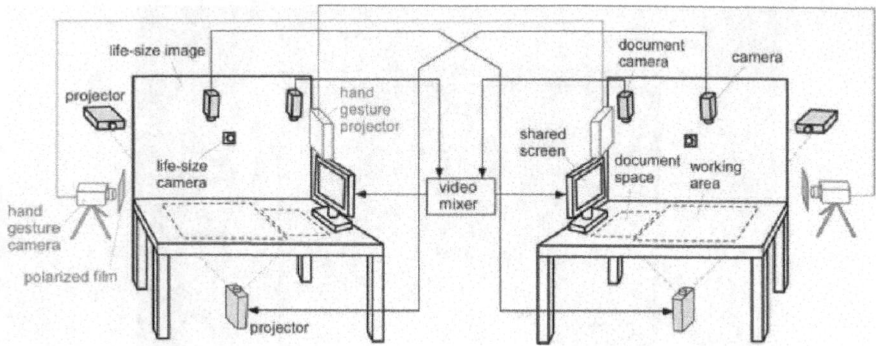


**Fig. 4.5** The additional cameras and projectors in AgoraPro required to display gestures to 'digital' documents

With this rather complex arrangement (see Fig. 4.5). both participants can point at real documents (in their own space) and at the same documents displayed on the shared screen. Whether they look at the document on the desk or the one on the screen they have the possibility of seeing any of their colleague's gestures above or around the documents. But, Agora also can present multiple images of the same features of conduct. For example, in the course of a simple pointing action across the desk the image of a hand can appear in four different places, and potentially in more than one location at a time.

Although they draw upon previous attempts at providing enhanced distributed workspaces (Ishii and Kobayashi, 1992; Freeman, 1994), the distinctive motivation for AgoraG and AgoraPro is to see not only the details of documents and objects in a remote space, but also the gestures made to, over and around them. To explore the extent to which the system supported mixed media, multiple document work, we organised a series of quasi-naturalistic experiments involving pairs of Japanese and English subjects. The experiments were designed to examine:

- How a number of documents of different kinds and sizes were used. We wanted to investigate whether and how the participants could manage the materials typically found on a 'messy' desk.
- Whether participants were able to both write and read documents. We were interested in seeing how participants coordinate their activities through the technology and the difficulties they faced.
- Whether participants could engage in activities on and around the documents together or individually. We were interested in the problems individuals face when shifting between different kinds of co-participation.
- Whether participants could move documents around and shift between different activities with different documents. We wanted to investigate whether and how the participants configure documents in the workspace.
- Whether participants could discuss details of the documents with their colleagues. We wanted to see whether and how, through the various areas and spaces on system, they talked about, referenced and in other ways pointed to documents and details of those objects.

We developed a number of tasks for subjects to undertake in the experiment that would encourage the use of a wide variety of documents including maps, photographs and textual documents, and demand changing alignment and shifting reference. The tasks principally involved planning and design, more specifically urban planning and solving transportation problems. To encourage discussion we gave the participants slightly different instructions and collections of materials. They were given a 5–10 min introduction to the technology and the task lasted around 30 min. After each experiment there followed a short debriefing where we asked the participants about the task and the technology. The two desks were located in different buildings that were 200 m apart and connected via a high-band-width network (155 Mbps ATM). This could result in a slight delay (0.3 s at the most). None of the participants remarked on this in the debriefing or when asked about it.

In all we carried out the tasks with 26 pairs of participants (16 Japanese- and 10 English- speaking pairs). We collected materials from five cameras (the two face-to-face views, the shared screen and two wide-angle views of the participants in relation to the Agora system). In this chapter, for ease of exposition we focus on those materials gathered when pairs of English speakers used the system.

Rather than providing an overview of the results of the assessment, in this chapter we will focus on the ways in which the participants established, or attempted to establish mutual alignment and reference to particular objects or aspects of those objects. We are interested in how participants respond to each other's attempts to establish a particular focal alignment, and the ways in which they are able to design reference with regard to actions, orientation and relevant ecologies of the remote participant. Our analysis draws on conversation analysis and recent studies of multi-modal interaction in everyday settings (Heath and Luff, 2000; Goodwin, 2003; Mondada, 2003). In this respect our concern is with the emergent and sequential character of practical action and the practices in and through which participants collaboratively accomplish particular activities, in this case pointing and reference. It is important to note that the very production of an action, such as an attempt to have another look at a specific aspect of a document, is, in the course of its accomplishment, sensitive and shaped with regard to the concurrent conduct of the co-participants. The fragments presented here are selected in order to provide a sense of some of the issues and complexities that arise in these brief moments of concerted action.

## Assembling and Handling Paperwork

Given the tasks involved the use of a range of different kinds of documents of different sizes and qualities, one initial observation is that participants have to manage a collection of documents on their desks and their workspaces. Just as in meetings or general office work, which involve the use of many paper documents, the participants had to arrange their workspaces, select documents to work on and refer to features of those they wished to talk about. Many of these adjustments require quite small movements of documents around the space. For example, in the following instance Elise asks Joan to go through the proposals 'what did you write?'. Joan has written down a series of titles and bulleted points on a piece of paper in front of her, which is also visible to Elise projected in the working area in front of her. As Elise asks her question she moves slightly forward, tilting her head towards the sheet. Joan whose pen has been over the title then moves the document slightly forward towards and angled towards Elise.

Just as Joan says ‘mark’ in ‘mark spaces’ her finger falls on the word ‘mark’. As she does this, Elise maintaining her orientation towards the document, confirms the proposal. Joan can then go on to the next point. The slight movement of document helping Joan to make visible a particular detail of the written text and secure an alignment to the proposal from Elise.

In the next fragment Linda and Bob are starting to look for places to locate a bus terminal on a map. As Linda begins to talk about possible locations she moves her page slightly forward a couple of centimetres.

As Linda does this Bob also moves his copy of the same map about a centimetre towards Linda. The documents displayed in the working areas of each desk are then used to discuss various proposals. The participants go on to talk and point out about the various locations where they have planned to place certain amenities on these two paper and projected maps.

In these experiments we see many of these micro-adjustments of documents. Most of these are to alter the assembly of documents in some way, to fit another document on the working area, to compare proposals, to make possible a juxtaposition of two features from different documents or to facilitate reading or writing. However, these small adjustments are also sensitive to the conduct of a colleague, to make some feature more visible or accompanying an issue that is being discussed, to elicit a reorientation to a feature, for example.

In its design Agora makes documents accessible by various means and requires users to orient the documents in different ways to be visible for their colleagues. On the working area the orientation of the documents is consistent across the desk, that is you need to spin the document around (180°) for another to read details the 'right way up'. In the document space they have to be moved perpendicular (90°) so that they can be best seen on the shared screen. The participants did manage to do this on occasions when they found it useful to see particular details. However, there were many examples of features being pointed at to emphasise an issue or invoke some form of participation or engagement from a colleague. Here, it was not necessary for the other to see the precise feature or read a particular word, and the movement of the material document coordinated with the talk and visual conduct supported the collaboration by not being too intrusive in the ongoing conduct. Agora, by quite simple means, often by the very fact that material documents are available and visible and displayed in relation to the conduct of both participants, provides for the micro-mobility of objects and hence for fine-grained collaboration over and around a distributed workspace, across a fragmented desk.

## (Re) Embedding Actions in Space

On the whole the tasks did seem to encourage reasonable collaboration and engagement from the participants. Indeed, it is rather surprising, given the number of spaces and the different qualities of the images available, that the participants could carry out all tasks. They manage to display documents of different kinds to each other, point to particular items and together produce the reports and summaries asked of them. Consider the following fragment, where Joan (J) and Elise (E) are using the AgoraG configuration to review their proposals for new traffic regulations for cyclists.

**Fragment 1**

J: and (0.3) its safe for bicycles because you can't steal them (0.7)
→ and ↑ its not you know you don't get this situation anymore (0.3)
E: yeah because you park er:: here

Joan has started to talk through the proposals they discussed earlier and she has made notes about it. As she does this Elise is writing a more formal report giving their justifications for the proposals. Joan gestures over her document in the projected working area with both her right hand and the pen she is holding.

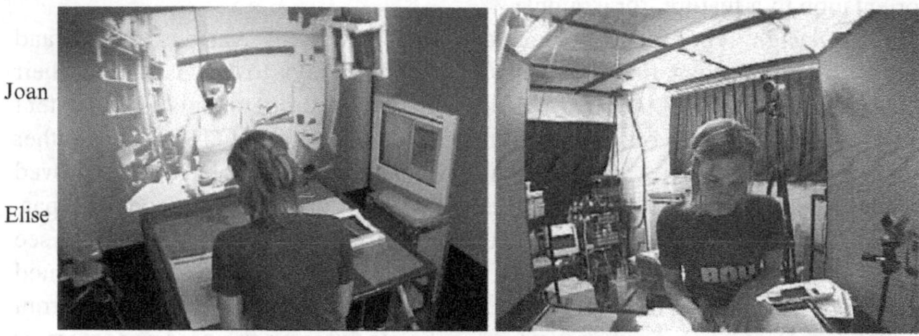


Although the text is barely legible in this area, Joan's gestures serve to 'annotate' the points she is making. When Joan completes the justification 'and (0.3) its safe for bicycles because ...' Elise moves her pen closer to the page holding it steady in preparation to write, and when Joan pauses, she begins to write. Elise is sensitive to the different activities of her colleague displayed through the projected surface, and coordinates her own activities with them.

As Joan begins 'and↑ its not you know' she shifts towards the shared screen and then points with her left hand to the photograph that is actually on Elise's desk. Once the gist of Joan's utterance emerges 'you don't get ...', Elise first looks up towards Joan and then, finding Joan pointing to her own 'shared' screen, Elise turns to her shared screen where (as it is in the AgoraG configuration) the laser dot appears over an area where some bicycles can be seen in poorly parked positions. Joan accompanies her utterance with pointing gestures to a number of other similar locations. Elise then moves her own right hand up to the screen, pointing, with the laser dot, to a location where (presumably) their regulations would require cycles to be parked, and says 'yeah because you park er:: here'.

Elise follows these gestures while Joan is speaking, moving gradually to an orientation of hand and body where she can begin to write on her own document. The projected surface, though providing an image of the hands and the text that is not very distinct, does seem to provide a resource for coordinating, quite delicately, the different activities of the two participants.

J: you don't get this situation anymore
(0.3)
E: 'yeah because you park er:: here'.

(Elise's laser dot appears above Joan's on the shared screen on the right)

In this brief fragment, the two participants use all the surfaces available to them, the back-projected working area and the shared screen (and the document space – where the photograph is positioned), as well as the projected pointing device (the laser dot). They also use the large screen in front of them, this being a resource to assess each other's orientation and participation in the activity at hand. The use of these resources is accomplished as part of a simple activity – recalling what has been written on a page and providing a visual example through the documents, the paper photographs, they have available to them. The participants therefore utilise the technology to refer to the details of materials that they have differential access to. Joan manages to tie what she is talking about with what she has written on her page and also to relate this to a document that is actually 200 m away on Elise's desk. Elise can, through the technology, make sense of Joan's conduct, and through a contribution of her own, display that understanding. In order to do this she draws on various resources, for example, the hand and pen's movement across the page on the working area, the orientation of her co-participant in the large display and the appearance of the laser dot. But these resources are not used in isolation from one another. They are used in relation to each other to make sense of the ongoing contributions of a co-participant. Perhaps surprisingly, the multitude of images and views, rather than exacerbating the fragmentation of an activity, seems to provide resources for participants to configure coherence to their actions in a distributed environment.

In the following instance Phoebe and Andrew are using the other configuration of Agora (AgoraPro). They are discussing the problems that occur when a path becomes blocked by parked bicycles. Phoebe has been talking about particular difficulties, pointing to areas on a photograph on her own workspace and projected in front of Andrew in the general working area. As Phoebe leans over and points to a place on the path on her photo with her left hand, she notices that the place is clearer on another photo in Andrew's workspace, which is also displayed on the monitor over to her right. She then begins to point to Andrew's photo with her right hand as she says 'but it comes up here right?'. Her pointing appears as a projected hand to Andrew which secures his orientation to the new document (as Phoebe says the word 'here').

P: this side I don't know, can't tell from the photo,

but it comes up here right?

(1,5)

P: er where?

(0.2)

P: errrrr I can't see on mine so:
A: err
P: up (.) right here
A: ah yeah yep

(0.2)

This reorientation is not entirely unproblematic. Although it is often sufficient to secure an alignment just to an object in the local environment, in many cases, particularly with documents, it is necessary to orient to a particular aspect of that document. When Andrew turns he sees a projected hand moving over a particularly complex photograph – it not being entirely clear the precise location Phoebe is talking about. After a couple of small readjustments of her fingers, Phoebe has to reproduce the whole gesture, dropping her hand down to the desk and re-raising it. This does seem to secure an appropriate alignment from Andrew ('ah yeah yep'). Once this has been accomplished Phoebe goes on to discuss the problem of 'weaving' through the bikes, which Andrew agrees it to be 'like an obstacle course'.

It is as if, although the participants can draw on the resources to locate a common document and even a general location on that document, there are some difficulties in securing an alignment to a specific location. In this case such a detail is important. Although Phoebe's hand is held over an area to the far left of the photograph the location of the tip of the finger is obscure. Even minor shifts of the fingers do not seem to help. When Phoebe puts her hand down and then brings it back up to the same location Andrew does seem to make sense of her conduct. It may be that these difficulties are a consequence of the way in which the production of a seemingly simple point is transformed by the technology.

When projecting images of three-dimensional hands on a work surface a number of technical decisions have to be made, each with consequences for what will remain visible and what obscure. The projections transform the conduct in some way, flattening out the image, and also making movements away from the surface or towards them less apparent than movements across them. In this case, Phoebe's point is almost perpendicular to the screen, so the tip of her finger can hardly be seen. Interestingly, her second pointing while she says 'up (.) right here' is slightly at an angle, so its image is slightly more distinct. This seems to secure an appropriate alignment from Andrew and allows Phoebe to proceed with her description of the problem at hand.

AgoraPro makes some minor transformations to the ways conduct is displayed and it is interesting to note that participants can be sensitive to these transformations. Nevertheless, after a little more effort, the participants do manage to move on. AgoraPro seems to provide ways of also repairing these anomalies and helping a participant reassemble the sense of another's conduct. AgoraPro provides participants with views that are related to each other and thereby resources for recovering sense from apparently disembodied action. The additional images, particularly the large life-size image of a colleague help secure alignment to an object, even a fine detail; the reference to an object being seen in the light of the emergence of the gesture and the orientation of a colleague. Even the general field of view offered by an image might provide some support for following the trajectory of another's conduct. In Agora, a small area of the desk is visible at the bottom of the large life-sized display. This provides a resource to see hands moving just above a desk and from the projected surface, and hence for tying the display of conduct in one space with that in another.

## Creative Combinations

Securing an alignment to an object or a detail of an object usually foreshadows some talk or activity about that object. In the experiments with Agora participants discuss the details of what they are looking at, confirm the problems they associate with them and make various proposals to solve these problems. In doing this the participants frequently produce gestures, for example, to contrast features on different photographs, to mark out where something could be drawn or annotated or to confirm the details of what they are proposing. So, once a common orientation to an object has been secured some work is required to sustain it, particularly as there may be a number of objects of concern, and some objects are remote and could be moved by a colleague.

Some time after the action in the previous fragment, Phoebe and Andrew discuss several proposals, including one involving the building of a new cycle path to avoid congestion on one of the main roads. They mark up on a plan of the area a suggested route, and then begin to write up why this new path should be constructed. In the following fragment Phoebe and Andrew are writing out the reasons for this path. Andrew has the plan in front of him on which he has marked the path as a line in red joining the main road. He has a black pen in his right hand with which he has been writing notes. Phoebe looks at the image of the map on the screen to her right and locates the proposed path.

P: so your (0.8) right here you have drawn this line right?=
A: =ye:p

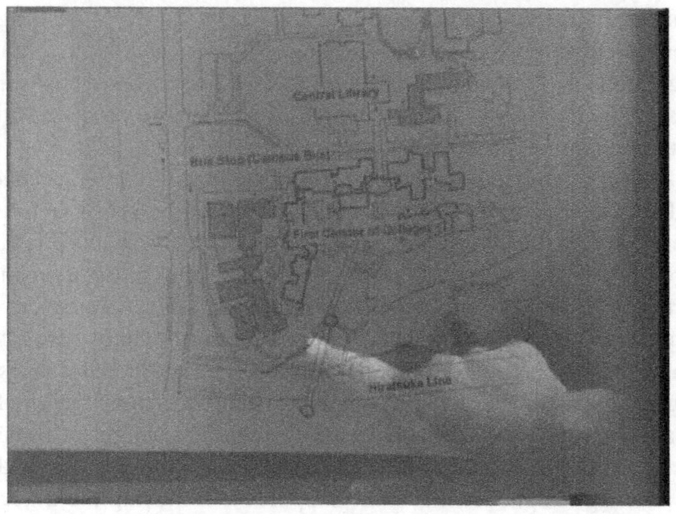

While Phoebe says her utterance she points to the path. Her conduct appears on both the screen to Andrews' left and projected over the real document in front of him. Phoebe's conduct is accomplished through a number of components. As she says 'so your' the forefinger of her right hand moves towards the screen over the road they are concerned about. She then readjusts her gesture first downwards to one of the circles Andrew has drawn on the map, then upwards towards the left of the new path and then across the whole distance of the line. As she continues her utterance she moves her finger up and down the line, then loops around another path that joins the road. Andrew, who has been looking down at the map on the desk in front of him looks up to the screen (on 'drawn') and then back to the desk (on 'right?'). He seems to juxtapose the two views of the same object with Phoebe's gestures, and then confirms the location of the path; his confirmation allowing Phoebe to go on with her suggestion.

P: So we have to say like
(1.5)
P: to build the: (1.3) the footpath or the:: bicycle path (or)
A: (yep)
P: whatever you want to call it↑
(0.1)

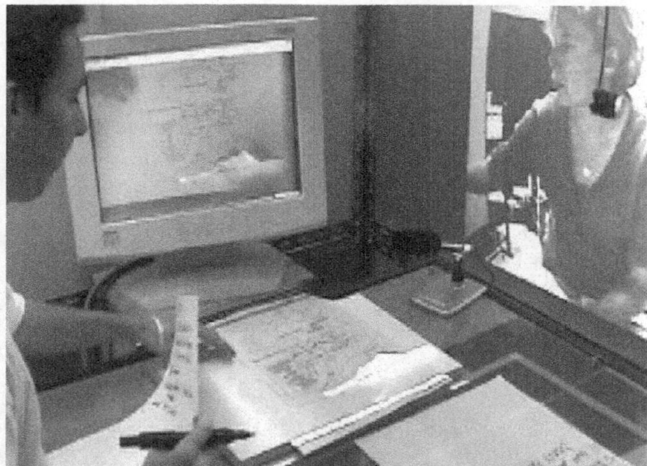

While Phoebe is saying 'so we have to' she continues to gesture over the map and Andrew moves his right hand to grab the bottom right corner of a large sheet of paper on which he has been writing. As Phoebe starts to say what to write, Andrew readjusts his left hand, so he can lift the paper up with both hands, turn it and place it in a location where he can write on it, and where his writing will be visible to Phoebe. In order to do this Andrew has to move the map to the right; a map to which Phoebe is still oriented and pointing with her left forefinger. These readjustments may account for the pauses and perturbations in Phoebe's speech. While she continues talking, Phoebe follows the object she is pointing to as it slides to her right. She then goes on to re-mark out the line several times more with her forefinger, coordinating several up and down movements along the line while she says 'footpath or the bicycle path (or) whatever you want to call it'.

It is not clear that all these efforts at pointing to the line are produced merely to identify a reference to an object which (for Phoebe) is in a remote space. Phoebe is dictating something for Andrew to write, a bulleted point of the kind 'to build a footpath'. However, when Andrew has placed the page on the desk, as Phoebe completes the word 'footpath' he does not begin to write. Indeed his right hand moves away from the point where he could start writing and his left comes off the sheet. Phoebe continues her utterance, but as she does this she turns to Andrew, who is picking up the red pen with his right hand and transferring it to his left hand. When she completes her suggestion, he moves forward and points to the sheet with the black pen saying: 'do you think it should join up here though?' (See Fragment 3.3).

Andrew quite delicately raises a problem with the drawing and the proposal at it currently stands that the route of the path, which Phoebe has taken a lot of trouble to point out, means that three paths will all join at the same place. They go on to discuss an alternative route.

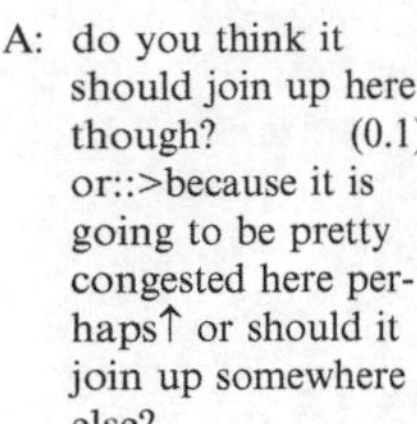
A: do you think it should join up here though? (0.1) or::>because it is going to be pretty congested here perhaps↑ or should it join up somewhere else?

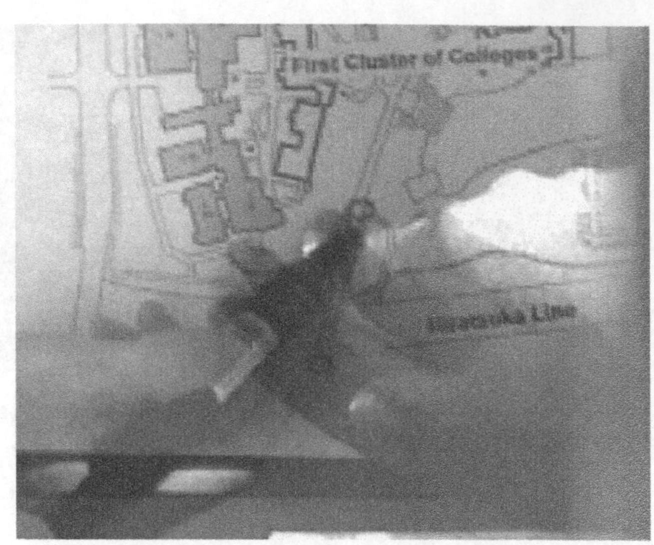


The participants are engaged through the Agora system in very detailed discussions about precise elements of the proposals they have made. By having various documents visible in both domains there are many different resources for discussion. Detailed locations, objects and features can be pointed out and the documents can be marked up and annotated. Moreover, it is possible to shift attention between documents, juxtapose different documents and kinds of documents, or read and write on one alongside another. Agora makes this possible, and in some ways straightforward to achieve, by providing a simulacrum of a desk space with real physical documents, maps, photographs and pieces of notepaper that can be read, written on and pointed to directly. But the space is transformed, by having to interleave projected images in two remote locations. The choices involved in making a 'common space' means that in most circumstances there are multiple views of the same object and at least one participant can choose where to look. It need not be the case that a participants' orientation 'reflects' that of their colleague. As in the above case, when Andrew can look down at the physical document that Phoebe sees only on the display to her right. And yet, it may be surprising that through Agora participants can point out, discuss and argue about quite fine details of the objects around them. They seem to do this with subtle sensitivity to the ongoing conduct of the other. This seems particularly apparent when they are pointing something out.

For pointing the visual appearance of the conduct is critical. By using video and projection techniques, AgoraPro provides details of the finger(s), hands and arms, and also allows participants to design their conduct so that this can be shaped with regard to what is being pointed at and why. Participants can point with different fingers, pens or pencils to identify a detail, contrast one place with another or discriminate a particular detail. They can also point along a line, around a circle or swerve along a loop. But the appearance and location of the pointings are not all that is critical. In the few examples discussed so far it is noticeable how often the pointing hand (or pen) arrives just as the relevant object is being referred to in the talk, whether this accompanies a direct referent (a path) or an indirect or deictic one ('here' or 'right here'). As in this case with Phoebe and Andrew participants take great care in coordinating their talk and visual conduct. This allows a co-participant to recover what is being referred to.

This relies upon the co-participant being able to see the gesture in relation to the ongoing talk. Participants have to co-ordinate their talk and gestures with the ongoing conduct of their colleague. Phoebe designs her conduct so that it can be seen at the right place and right time by Andrew, and Andrew, vice versa. This is despite of the small delay between when participants produce their conduct and when it is seen. Moreover, the participants have to accomplish this in a setting where their colleagues may be shifting alignment or, where, because of the arrangement of the images, a colleague is oriented to another domain.

Participants can draw on other resources to make sense of the ongoing conduct. As in the foregoing instance, participants can foreshadow their upcoming conduct through their actions. So, Phoebe's initial 'here' is made sense of not only in the light of her 'so your (0.8) ...', but also her turn towards the screen. Similarly, the gist of her suggestion 'to build the footpath' is foreshadowed by 'so we have to say like' and Andrew's contribution is produced in the light of his drawing first away from the page, picking up a pen he has previously used for drawing and then moving his hand (and pen) towards a detail on the document. Such actions project forthcoming activities, they help participants to co-ordinate their own conduct with another's actions and also to provide a local interactional context in which others can make sense of their conduct. What, therefore, might seem like a simple point, produced to identify a particular object, is designed and transformed from moment to moment in the light of the conduct of colleagues.

In the course of their work participants have to sustain an alignment and maintain involvement in an activity in particular ways. Even though Agora transforms the spatial and temporal nature of the participants' actions, the participants do seem to collaboratively produce coherent actions. This seems to be possible because of the ways Agora makes trajectories of conduct available. It provides ways for participants to assess the sequential development of a colleague's activities and draw on this to co-ordinate their own moment-to-moment contributions.

## Gestural Annotation

Previous studies have revealed quite long-standing problems in media space and CVEs, particularly with regard to the difficulties participants face in orienting to the conduct and gestures of others. As described elsewhere, simple pointing, gestures and other ways to achieve reference in these collaborative environments can be upgraded to such an extent that they can be commented on by another, be accompanied by talk about the gesture and in other ways actually enter the foreground as the topic of the conversation (Hindmarsh et al., 1998; Heath and Luff, 1992). Both in AgoraPro and AgoraG we find participants using gestures to annotate quite delicate features of the materials and environment around them and participants seem to be able to make sense of this conduct when working with documents.

In the next fragment Mary and Elizabeth are trying to identify some places where it might be possible to make it easier for pedestrians and cyclists to use the same road. Mary has been writing notes on a document to her left, on top of which she has placed a photograph of one of the roads. The participants are oriented to this photograph as they discuss ways of widening the road. Elizabeth asks whether 'they couldn't make this wider right?'. She accompanies this with a series of gestures over her shared screen with her left hand. First, as she begins this utterance she marks out the area with her first and fore fingers. Then, as she is uttering 'wider' she rotates her hand and marks approximately the same width with her first finger and thumb.

E: 'they couldn't make this wider right?'.

The new orientation of Elizabeth's hand marks out the possible direction of widening – across a pedestrian footpath on the right of the photo. However, as her thumb arrives over the path, and there is no response from Mary, Elizabeth continues her utterance with 'there is no more space so:' and she pulls her hand away. Mary then goes onto suggest some problems for the path if the road was widened.

M: No because then again the problem of the pedestrian walk here? but that if they make> they could make an extension this much right?

As Mary says 'they could do an extension this much, right' she produces a gesture with her right hand, mirroring in some ways Elizabeth's earlier gesture, Mary marks out the area with her first finger and thumb. This gesture is over the actual photograph on the desk and appears to Elizabeth on the screen to her left.

As Mary's utterance comes to completion, Elizabeth begins to point again with her finger to the screen (at an area to the right of the path), saying 'but could the pedestrian walk be extended here?'. Elizabeth's finger appears on the screen as a 'shadow hand' on a trajectory heading towards the path just below Mary's hand. As it reaches its destination Mary withdraws her hand upward.

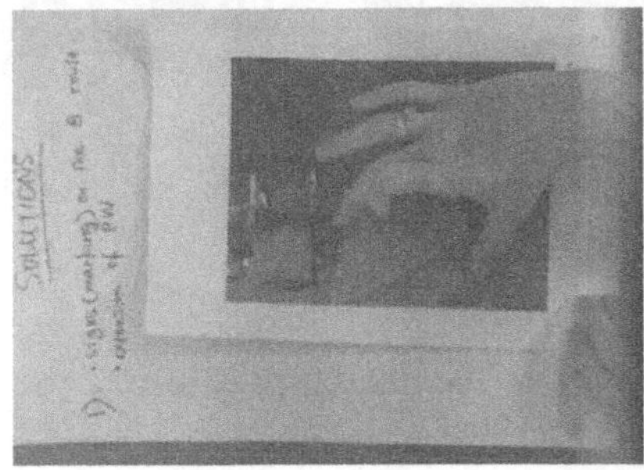


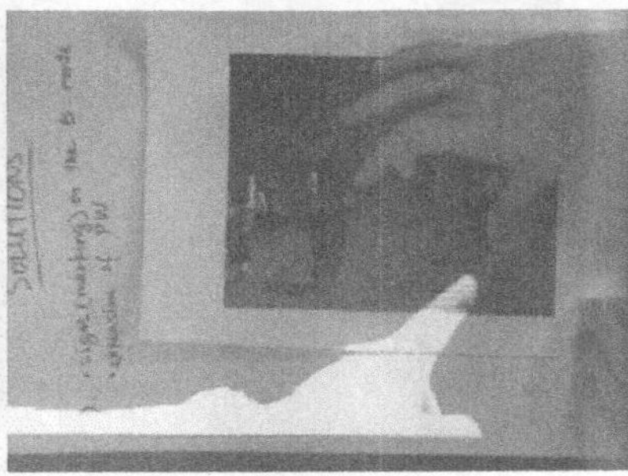


Mary

Elizabeth

E: 'but could the pedestrian walkway be extended here?'.
M: [ ]but then the pedestrians no

Mary does not withdraw her hand entirely from the scene. Indeed even as it is held towards the top right of the photo it maintains its configuration marking out the now smaller width of the path. As the gist of Elizabeth's suggestion emerges Mary overlaps her talk with 'but then the pedestrians' as well as move her hand further to the right and down over the green space where presumably the new path would go.

Both participants are now talking and gesturing over the same area of the document. Elizabeth once again transforms her hand gesture; her first two fingers marking out (from the bottom) a region approximately co-extensive with that marked out by Mary.

At this moment when both are talking in overlap, their hands are nearly touching in the virtual space, and as Elizabeth says 'here' they glance at each other on the large projected screen and Mary shakes her head and says 'no'. Mary then goes on to explain in more detail some of the difficulties with Elizabeth's proposal.

When viewed in detail the activities of the two participants using AgoraPro are complex and interleaved in quite intricate ways. This being while they are engaged in a discussion concerning the finer points of widening a road. The positioning of the cameras means that not only the projected hands appear on the screens and surfaces, but also at times additional hands can be seen fleeting across the image or on the periphery. However, despite this complexity the participants manage to interact through the system. From their visible conduct (and from the discussions afterwards) it is not apparent that the technology undermines in any significant way their attempts to point to objects in the remote domain, annotate their suggestions with gestures or generally work with documents in the distributed environment.

Indeed, the AgoraPro configuration appears to support the participants not only pointing and referring to the details of documents in the remote domain, but also animating their discussions with a range of fine-grained gestures. It may be that the quality of the images supports this. But it is also obvious that the projection of an image of a hand provides not only for a variety of ways of annotating the environment with the hands, but also allows for these animations to be transformed in their course in the light of the ongoing conduct of a co-participant. The system therefore supports the fluid transition between different kinds of collaborative activities over documents. The hands providing a resource for displaying trajectories of action and a means for co-participants to monitor moment by moment the prospective activities of a colleague and then to shape their next actions accordingly.

## Discussion

In the mid-1980s several research laboratories around the world took the innovative and bold step of deploying media spaces around their working environment. At the time these were expensive systems requiring special switches, the design of bespoke software and high-quality audio and video equipments, but this investment seemed to be set aside by the promise of revealing how we could better support collaborative work with new technologies. Media spaces were at the heart of the agenda to support collaborative work. However, except for a few unsustained experiments in organisations (e.g. Pagani and Mackay 1993; Harper and Carter, 1994) these deployments did not move far away from the research laboratory, and as their proponents left and research objectives of the laboratories changed the use of media spaces diminished and the infrastructures were gradually removed. The hope that this technology would become an undemanding yet invaluable resource for office work and workplace communications and the benefits so afforded would justify that its expense was not borne out. Perhaps this is not so surprising. The early developers of media spaces remained preoccupied with a face-to-face model of interaction. Recently, with infrastructures that have larger bandwidths and offer higher resolution many of the original promises of media spaces have been rehearsed, but few of these have sought to expand the space to provide greater access to the local material environment. In this chapter we have reported some investigations into enhancing media spaces in this way. Drawing on failures to do this in the past, many of them our own, we set out a number of general requirements that emerged from studies of workplaces. The Agora systems were developed and refined in the light of these requirements, focusing on the details of how activities are accomplished moment to moment in interaction, particularly those apparently insignificant movements and shifts of and between paper documents.

The systems were designed to allow participants a stable environment to determine the location, orientation and frame of reference of their co-participants and thereby provide resources through which they could discriminate the actions of others with regard to a range of objects, particularly paper documents. This required a configuration using many cameras, projectors and displays. Our earlier attempts at providing multiple views of another to support activities like pointing and reference, even replacing connected physical spaces with a CVE, revealed the difficulties for participants to reconcile incongruities and establish a reciprocity of perspective when undertaking even the simplest of tasks (Gaver et al., 1993; Heath et al., 2001; Heath and Luff, 1992; Hindmarsh et al., 1998).

In the light of these difficulties, AgoraPro and AgoraG proved surprisingly successful, at least within the framework of the small-scale experiments we have undertaken so far. With respect to our original requirements the participants cannot grasp and manipulate objects in the remote space. And yet through their actions with objects they do seem to be able to determine their own standpoint with regard to other participants and the space(s) in which they are located, and to coordinate their actions with the real-time conduct of others. For example, the bodily comportment, visual orientation and gestural activity of participants remain a pervasive and critical feature of work and collaboration, and in these experiments, we tried to enable participants to draw upon their ordinary bodily resources for acting and interacting in and through the material environment. Our preliminary observations suggest that participants are able to produce, recognise and coordinate quite complex, material-focused actions, with others in these media spaces. They create interesting and innovate solutions given the problems posed by the way in which the technologies position and display the objects. They are also able to design their actions so that they are sensible to a co-participant. Of particular significance is the large projected display and the resources it provides. This enables an individual to see, at a glance, how the other is participating, from their standpoint, within the developing and highly contingent course of an activity.

The AgoraG and AgoraPro configurations provide two different ways for a media space to support the ability to refer to material objects in a remote environment. With AgoraG, we have noticed that participants are able to make unproblematic and simple references to objects within the remote environment, in particular, when they are attempting to differentiate one document from another. For certain tasks this may be critical. Indeed, the laser dot can make it easier to point and recognise pointings to small objects. AgoraPro, on the other hand, enables participants to overlay remote objects with a complex array of gestures and accomplish actions, which involve much more than simple reference. For example, gestures can be used to demarcate different elements of an object, to exaggerate features and characteristics and to animate and embed action in materials, so that they gain a significance, then and there, that they might not otherwise have. Indeed, as in more conventional environments, AgoraPro provides participants with the resources to animate and annotate material objects through bodily action and thereby accomplish a range of actions, which are ordinarily precluded when the participant's body is either unavailable or disassociated from the material objects with which it is 'engaged'.

The significance of visible gestures to the organisation of collaboration goes far beyond the ability to animate objects. It has some bearing on the ways participants coordinate their actions with each other. The single dot or cursor simply appears in the relevant location on the document, whereas the hands emerge progressively, within the developing course of the activity. So for example, we find that participants are able to form and reform the shape and movement of the hands with regard to emerging demands of the activity and in particular the co-participation of the other. The hands are sensitive to the shifting character of the activity, and their sensitivity is visible and oriented by the co-participant. More fundamentally, rather than simply appearing in a location, the hands prospectively inform the co-participant; they provide sense of where they are going, what they are doing and what it will take for their action to be complete. The prospective orientation of the hands' work enables the co-participant to envisage and anticipate the actions of the other, and to align towards those actions within the developing course of their articulation. The single dot or cursor is denuded of its temporal and spatial development, whereas the hands enable the co-participant to envisage their character and completion and thereby produce sequentially appropriate conduct right at the point and moment at which it becomes relevant. The hands therefore do not simply provide resources for the elaboration of material objects, but, through their prospective orientation, enrich the ways in which participants are able to produce, recognise and coordinate their actions with one another.

One of the interesting features of Agora, in contrast to our earlier attempts to support collaboration, is the way in which the participants are able to interweave a range of resources and spaces within the developing course of a particular activity. For example, relatively subtle shifts in orientation, the delicate onset of particular actions and shifting glances between particular objects and domains are not only available to the co-participant, but also are oriented in sequentially relevant ways. In other words, participants are able to retrieve the sense and significance of particular actions from the standpoint of the co-participants and thereby produce a sequentially appropriate action. This sense and sensibility is achieved through the ways in which co-participants interweave the visibility of co-participants' actions on different displays and in different locales, so that, for example, a shift in orientation on the large projected display and the beginnings of an arm movement towards the co-participant's screen can be seen to prefigure some activity on a document – either on one's own shared screen or on a document on the desk.

The organisation of the 'work spaces' appears to support the participants' ability to interconnect the various scenes and their action displayed therein. For example, a movement of an arm to the right on the projected screen can be tied to a subsequent movement of a hand from the right of the shared screen. Similarly, fleeting movements of the hands appearing on the screen can be juxtaposed with the bodily conduct of a colleague displayed on the projected screen (either as a dot or a projected hand). The size, location and orientation of the screens therefore are critical to the participants' abilities to retrieve the course of activities as they arise on and through various displays; the arrangement of the scene providing a resource to establish the coherence of action.

The system and its arrangement however, have certain drawbacks. This media space consists of a complex configuration of cameras, projectors, filters, monitors and screens. Although the system is only intended to be experimental it is somewhat cumbersome, and it would need significant reconsideration before a system that could be developed to be deployed in an organisational setting (cf. Kuzuoka et al. 2006). By using more recent digital cameras and projectors even finer details can be oriented to, particularly in spaces other than the document space. At present, the organisation of the configuration is shaped by the qualities of the images each provides, ensuring also that there are obvious boundaries between the spaces. It would be interesting to experiment with more fluid boundaries between the spaces, or have larger areas to support focused collaborative work. Perhaps more problematic, especially when earlier media spaces are considered, the system appears particularly suitable for relatively intense forms of document-focused collaboration, where it is critical that participants require subtle and fine-grained access to each others' actions. AgoraG and AgoraPro are configured to support a different order of activity than addressed in earlier work on media spaces and CVEs. As a consequence of their design they are able to support materially mediated collaboration rather than broader access to other features of a participants' local environment. This suggests that in the future one direction we may need to explore is how we can integrate fine-grained details of work within the everyday environments of workspaces, interweaving the work on the desktop with activities on and around other spaces and with other objects and individuals. However, it would be unfortunate if such developments, by shifting attention towards the capabilities of mobile devices or the requirements of larger groups, neglected how to develop what is necessary for supporting the fine-grained accomplishment of everyday work and interaction.

One final observation should be mentioned. The quality of the images available in the experiments also has some bearing on more general social scientific concerns with the empirical analysis of material-focused collaboration. We are increasingly finding that digital video recordings of conduct and collaboration, whether in experimental or naturalistic settings, provide access to the organisation of action and interaction, which until recently was unavailable. So, for example, even our preliminary analysis of the data, which were collected as part of these experiments, reveal characteristics of social action and collaboration with and around documents that have not been addressed, as far as we are aware, in the social and cognitive sciences, and disregarded in much work in CSCW. This of course is not the first time that a technology, even in the behavioural sciences, might have a significant impact on the ability of researchers to see new phenomena. However, it is interesting to note in the case of CSCW that these developments could inform not only technological support for conduct and collaboration, but also our understanding of everyday behaviour. Ironically, studies of advanced media spaces crucially reveal not only the inadequacies of the technological solutions so far developed, but how little we still understand about the moment-to-moment accomplishment of everyday work and interaction.

**Acknowledgements** The research was supported in the UK by the EU Projects Paperworks (IST-2-516895) and Palcom (IST-002057) and in Japan by Oki Electric Industry Co. Ltd., the International Communications Foundation (ICF) Grant for Scientific Research (B) 2004-16300261, Strategic Information and Communications R&D Promotion Programme (SCOPE) of Ministry of Internal Affairs and Communications Grant for Scientific Research (B), 2005-16330095. Some of the experiments were supported by Tsukuba JGNII RC of NICT. We would like to thank colleagues who participated in many discussions about the technology and the analysis.

## References

Bellotti, V. and Bly, S. (1996). 'Walking Away from the Desktop Computer: Distributed Collaboration and Mobility in a Product Design Team', in Proceedings of CSCW '96, Cambridge, MA, 209–18.

Fussell, S., Setlock, L., and Kraut, R. (2003) Effects of Head-Mounted and Scene-Oriented Video Systems on Remote Collaboration on Physical Tasks, in Proceedings of CHI '93, ACM Press, pp. 513–20.

Gaver, W. W., Sellen, A., Heath, C. C. and Luff, P. (1993). 'One Is Not Enough: Multiple Views in a Media Space', in Proceedings of INTERCHI '93, Amsterdam, April 24–29, pp. 335–41.

Gaver, W. W., Smets, G. and Overbeeke, K. (1995). 'A Virtual Window on Media Space', in Proceedings of CHI '95, pp. 257–64.

Goodwin, C. (2003). Pointing as a Situated Practice. In S. Kita (Ed.), Pointing: Where Language, Culture and Cognition Meet (pp. 217–241). Mahwah, NJ: Lawrence Erlbaum.

Harper, R. and Carter, K. (1994). Keeping people apart: A research note. CSCW J., 2, 199–207.

Heath, C., Luff, P., Kuzuoka, H., Yamazaki, K. and Oyama, S. (2001). 'Creating Coherent Environments for Collaboration', in Proceedings of ECSCW 2001, Bonn, pp. 119–38.

Heath, C. C. and Luff, P. (1992). Media space and communicative asymmetries: Preliminary observations of video mediated interaction, Human-Computer Interaction. 7, 315–46.

Heath, C. C., Luff, P. and Sellen, A. (1995). 'Reconsidering the Virtual Workplace: Flexible Support for Collaborative Activity', in Proceedings of ECSCW'95, Stockholm, pp. 83–100.

Heath, C. C. and Luff, P. K. (2000). Technology in Action. Cambridge University Press, Cambridge.

Hindmarsh, J., Fraser, M., Heath, C. C., Benford, S. and Greenhalgh, C. (1998). 'Fragmented Interaction: Establishing Mutual Orientation in Virtual Environments. Proceedings of CSCW'98, ACM Press, New York, pp. 217–26.

Heath, C., Luff, P., Kuzuoka, H., Yamazaki, K. and Oyama, S. (2001). Creating coherent environments for collaboration. In Proceedings of the Seventh Conference on European Conference on Computer Supported Cooperative Work (Bonn, Germany, September 16–20, 2001). W. Prinz, M. Jarke, Y. Rogers, K. Schmidt, and V. Wulf, Eds. ECSCW. Kluwer, Norwell, MA, 119–138. Interaction: Establishing mutual orientation in virtual environments', in Proceedings of CSCW'98, Seattle, WA, pp. 217–26.

Ishii, H. (1990). 'TeamWorkStation: Towards a Seamless Shared Workspace', in Proceedings of CSCW '90, Los Angeles, CA, pp. 13–26.

Ishii, H. and Kobayashi, M. (1992). 'Clearface: A seamless medium for sharing drawing and conversation with eye contact', in Proceedings of CHI 92, Monterey, pp. 525–32.

Kuzuoka, H. (1992) Spatial Workspace Collaboration: A Shared-View Video Support System for Remote Collaboration Capability, in Proceedings of CHI '92, ACM Press, pp. 533–40.

Kuzuoka, H., Kosuge, T. and Tanaka, M. (1994) GestureCam: A Video Communication System for Sympathetic Remote Collaboration, in Proceedings of CSCW '94, ACM Press, pp. 35–43.

Kuzuoka, H., Yamashita, J., Yamazaki, K. and Yamazaki, A. A. (1999). 'Agora: A Remote Collaboration System that Enables Mutual Monitoring', in Proceedings of CHI'99 Extended Abstracts, Philadelphia, PA, pp. 190–1.

Kuzuoka, H., Kurihara, T. and Luff, P. (2006) 'Introduction to the AgoraDesk Project', in Conference Supplement of CSCW 2006, pp. 197–8.

Luff, P. and Heath, C. C. (1998). 'Mobility in Collaboration', in Proceedings of CSCW'98, Seattle, WA, pp. 105–14.

Luff, P., Heath, C. C. and Greatbatch, D. (1992). 'Tasks-in-Interaction: Paper and Screen Based Documentation in Collaborative Activity', in Proceedings of CSCW '92, Toronto, pp. 163–70.

Mondada, L. (2003). Working with video: how surgeons produce video records of their actions. Visual Studies, 18, 58–73.

Pagani, D.S. and Mackay, D. E. (1993). Bring Media Spaces into the Real World, in Proceedings of Third Conference on ECSCW Milan, Italy, pp. 341–56.

Sellen, A. and Harper, R. H. R. (2002). The Myth of the Paperless Office. MIT Press, Cambridge.

Tang, J. C. and Minneman, S. L. (1991). VideoDraw: A Video Interface for Collaborative Drawing, ACM Transactions on Information Systems. 9 (2), 170–84.

Wellner, P. (1991). The DigitalDesk Calculator: Tactile Manipulation on a Desk Top Display. Proceedings of the Symposium on User Interface Software and Technology (UIST '91), Hilton Head, NY.

Yamazaki, K, Yamazaki, A., Kuzuoka, H., Oyama, S., Kato, H., Suzuki, H. and Miki, H. (1999) GestureLaser and Gesturelaser Car: Development of an Embodied Space to Support Remote Instruction, in Proceedings of ECSCW'99, pp. 239–58.

# Chapter 5
# From Media Spaces to Emplaced Media: Digital Poster Boards and Community Connectedness

**Elizabeth F. Churchill and Les Nelson**

**Abstract** The influence of research in media spaces and desktop-based video communication portals extends to other forms of media experience. In this chapter we describe our work on interactive digital community bulletin boards. We give a brief overview of five installations of interactive poster boards, focusing on the similarities and differences in the details of the installation design, the setting and the adoption, and appropriation of the technology. Public space communication gives us another way to reflect on past models and elaborating future models of "informated" environments designed to promote social connection.

## Introduction

Media spaces are about connecting people. Inspired in part by art installations like Kit Galloway and Sherrie Rabinowitz's Hole-in-Space art installation, experiments beginning in the 1980s demonstrated how an A/V connection between rooms with large displays and between desktops with video windows could enrich social connection, allow close collaboration, and create a sense of being-in-place-together (for early descriptions and discussions see [Bly et al., 1993; Dourish and Bly, 1992; Harrison and Minneman, 1990; Mantei et al., 1991; Stults, 1986; Tang et al., 1994]).

As Gaver articulates in his 1992 paper on the affordances of media spaces, much of the design work in this arena drew clear analogies to everyday spaces. It was suggested that media spaces offer "virtual co-presence," and allow ' "tailorable office-spaces," "meeting rooms," and "hallways" ' (Bly, Harrison and Irwin 1993; Gaver, 1992; Gaver et al., 1992). These authors pinpointed the power of media spaces through the fact that they are "always on"; it is in this regard that they can

---

E.F. Churchill
Yahoo! Research
e-mail: Elizabeth@elizabethchurchill.com

L. Nelson
PARC – Palo Alto Research Center
e-mail: lesnelson@acm.org

S. Harrison (ed.), *Media Space 20+ Years of Mediated Life*,
Computer Supported Cooperative Work,

be compared to physical spaces. In this context, the authors state that "connections are a means of changing the arrangement of that space and access controls determine which connections are possible."

In the extensive literature on media spaces that was published through the late 1980s and early 1990s, researchers and developers explored aspects of connection, communication, and collaboration offering discussions of:

- *Awareness* of others through peripherally sensed movement and activity (e.g., Dourish et al., 1996; Dourish and Bly, 1992).
- *Access control* to preserve privacy and prevent snooping, "peeping Toms," and surveillance behaviors. Tested models for access control were based on social protocols familiar in the physical and embodied world – "glancing" to simulate a look in someone's direction (Tang et al., 1994), cruising hallways (Fish et al., 1992), and knocking on doors (e.g., Dourish et al., 1996; Dourish and Bly, 1992; Tang et al., 1994).
- *Close collaboration over content*, exploring the assertion that design documents are more important for collaboration in their making than in their exchange (Harrison and Minneman, 1990). These explorations led to a body of work on embodied conversation, considering how bodies orient to each other and to content when collaborating or simply working in parallel, and the importance of things like gaze direction and deictic reference for conversational flow and the creation of shared understanding (e.g., Heath and Luff, 1992). Notably, research into video conferencing (e.g., Sellen, 1997), multimedia and distributed virtual environments (Curtis et al., 1995), and the design of embodiments in collaborative virtual environments drew on, and in later years, fed into this body of work (Hindmarsh et al., 2000).

These explorations involved largely synchronous video feeds, but other forms of media space were also designed and evaluated (e.g., work on audio only spaces also explored how togetherness can be achieved by only sharing sound, Hindus et al., 1996).

## *Theorizing Media Spaces*

Media spaces proved an excellent grounding for exploring the ramifications of different philosophical and psychological approaches to social being and social interaction – from Gaver's reworking of Gibson's ecological psychological notions of "affordance" (Gaver, 1992), to Goffman's ideas on face-work (Goffman, 1963), to conversation analytic and ethnomethodological analyses of embodied interaction (Garfinkel, 1967; Sacks et al., 1974), to Goodwin's broader notion of environmental and social "semiotic resources" (Goodwin, 2003), to issues of eye gaze and body orientation in embodied social discourse (Kendon, 1990), and to cognitive models of conversation and "common ground" (Clark, 1996). Fascinating debates on the nature of privacy, attention, awareness, social presence (e.g., Lombard and Ditton,

1997), and so on continued in papers, panels, and discussion groups. Sparked perhaps by the notion of a "hole in space," much has also been written about the very nature of "place" and of "space" as concepts for ordering and understanding human experience (Harrison and Dourish, 1996).

Questions in this ongoing research that were posed included: What does it take for people to feel co-present (Lombard and Ditton, 1997) and connected in collaborative working situations (see also Daft and Lengel, 1986)? How is connection maintained on a moment-to-moment basis through conversation and body orientation (Heath and Luff, 1992)? How do people cognize in concert when not face to face but given rich cues of each other's behavior, and how can we evaluate the effect of different levels in the "richness" of cues (Daft and Lengel, 1986; Suh, 1999)? How do people establish shared or "common" understandings through language and paralinguistic cues in mediated communication contexts (Durnell Cramton, 2001; Clark, 1996; Kraut et al., 2003)? These questions and studies intersected with considerations of connectedness in other media. Can we combine video with other data streams to create greater possibilities for sharing (Curtis et al., 1995)? How do different kinds and amounts of perceptual stimulation relate to the degree of social presence people experience (Lombard and Ditton, 1997)? Do we need rich visual or graphical cues to feel connected and/or when will textual cues suffice (Churchill and Bly, 1999)?

Most recently, in 2008, a panel retrospective of media space research addressed the future of media space research, with some discussion of technological and market developments in media production and consumption from personal devices like cell phones and in large-screen display technologies (Baecker et al., 2008). The panel presenters foregrounded the value of being cognizant of previous research, but also pointed to new opportunities for detailed study of the use of media spaces in forging and maintaining relationships between individuals and groups in work and in recreational contexts. Indeed, many of the chapters in this volume address exactly this point.

## Our Work: Rich Media Content as a Proxy for Co-presence

In our own work we have focused on a particular aspect of communication through technologies, including media spaces: rather than seeing rich media content as secondary to creating connection, we have made content, rather than a synchronous link between people in conversation, as primary. There are several reasons for this: first we have been designing for cross time zone connections where the synchrony that is entailed with video-based media spaces was practically not possible. Secondly, our research agenda has largely been about how objects result from and themselves mediate relationships between people, in particular, social settings (see Nardi, 1996), what objects tell about a culture and how people orient to that culture (Miller, 1997), and how our relationships are built around and upon the exchange and sharing of objects (Komter, 2005). We have also drawn on notions of objects as social actors (Latour, 2005), and on anthropological work on biographical objects (Hoskins, 1998). This approach – the primacy of content, in this case of digital "things" – was also explored in our work on collaboration where we chose to subjugate people to content. Instead of pursuing detailed representation of people via avatars and rich spatial backdrops for collaboration as graphical landscapes, we chose to insert lightweight text conversations into preexisting collaborative documents and supported rich, fluid annotation and transformation of that content (Churchill et al., 2000). The social connection was seen to derive through work on the collaborative texts, rather than through rich representation of the conversants themselves. Other influences draw from studies and investigations into the nature of everyday encountering of people and things as people go about the daily business (de Certeau, 2002; Savolainen, 1995); this kind of encountering stands in contrast to purposive, goal-directed, and iterative information seeking behaviors that typify much of the research into information retrieval and information recommendation.

The research thread of communication through content has been instantiated in the design, development, and deployment of over 15 installations of digital community bulletin boards that act as windows between online social networking sites and the world of physical social spaces (see Fig. 5.1). Our work was conducted at Fuji Xerox's Palo Alto-based research center, FXPAL, between 2001 and 2004. The research center is well-known for research into audio/video innovation, and although we were inspired by video-oriented, synchronous connection, media space, and while we utilized video in one of our installations, it was not central to the designs we created. There were several reasons for this:

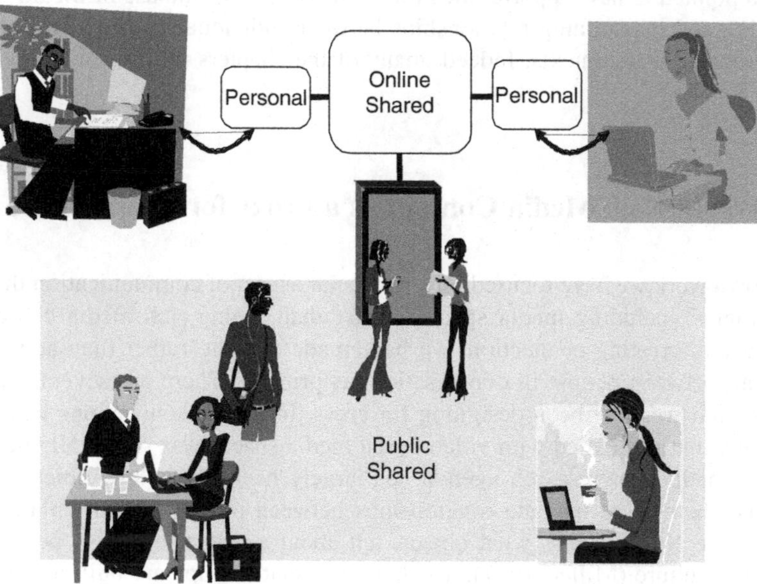


**Fig. 5.1** Information flows in online and physical public spaces

- Firstly, at the incept of the interactive community board design, we were working to connect places in different countries and across time zones: Japan and the US, specifically California. The time zone differences made video impractical in terms of creating an always-on persistent presence between the two locations. Indeed, in one experiment we conducted, we found ourselves staring at a darkened room for most of the time the connection was live; there was only minimal overlap in terms of time between the two spaces when they were inhabited, so this did not achieve our goal of increasing a sense of connection between the two social groups who inhabited the spaces.
- Secondly, language differences, and especially low competence in speaking Japanese on the US side, meant a video plus audio space would perhaps prove more frustrating than enabling.
- Thirdly, there seemed to be a natural fit between several ongoing research efforts and interests, including those above: what we called "polite technologies," collaborative filtering (Churchill et al., 1999), content-oriented collaboration in online social spaces (Churchill et al., 2000), social and collaborative annotation and sharing of media content (Marshall et al., 1999), and ambient, environmental information displays (Pedersen and Sokoler, 1997). As part of our initial design work, we conducted explorations along an elaborated design continuum in shared physical space technologies – a continuum between ambient and abstract social sharing resources (Ishii and Ullmer, 1997, Pedersen and Sokoler, 1997), "realist" co-presence tools like rooms augmented with media spaces, and technologies for co-presence focused on collaborations like shared whiteboards (Pedersen et al., 1993). We placed socially annotated/recommended content within this continuum, by (1) elaborating the potential for public space technologies rather than desktop or personal device technologies, by (2) elaborating the potential for community-generated/recommended content to provide peripheral awareness of other's presence and engagement in a community, and by (3) creating a roll-out strategy that focused on inviting, but not insisting, upon active engagement on the part team members in producing, reading, and annotating the content.

In the next section, we briefly describe five installations that were created and installed, each of which had slightly different characteristics. The last installation, YeTi, combined posted multimedia content with ad hoc video annotations to that content (Yamada et al., 2004). Although still exploring asynchronous sharing, this installation brings us almost full circle to media spaces in their original incarnation, but preserves our notion of the content itself as being central, with the interaction over that content as secondary.

Given our focus on information encountering of community media content in physical social places, rather than on synchronous human–human communication across geographical distance, we refer to our installations as "emplaced social media technologies," rather than "media space technologies." Therefore, a key aspect of understanding how these emplaced social media technologies operate is to comprehend the settings into which they are introduced. Our descriptions below are brief, but we refer readers to related papers for more details.

## *Blurring the Boundaries Between Online and Offline Interaction*

We have created a number of installations of interactive community bulletin boards. These bulletin boards are an exploration in both informating the physical world with social content, and represent a form of social recommendation and digital content book-marking, such as is offered by services like deli.ci.ous.com, but in public rather than in online space. The community bulletin boards are designed to provide a window onto online community activities and interests, offering a leakage between the world of single user at the screen contributing to a community and the encountering of information serendipitously in shared physical space (Fig. 5.1). These boards are not intended to be anonymous, broadcast message bearers as is more usual with commercial boards and advertising content; they are intended to host content generated or selected by community members, for the community itself. Therefore, content may be highly specialized and diverse, unlike general announcements and/or advertising content. The content represents a snapshot into the interests of community members – or rather a snapshot into what *they* think will be of interest to the community – offering a view onto what we informally called the "information zeitgeist" of the group.

Content can be posted to the network via desktop and personal devices (i.e., smart phones) using email or a webpage. Content types can be text, html, images, or video. Content is stored in a database, and is made available for the person posting the content via a personal site, and can be selected for posting publicly in three modes: to the online shared space, to a particular interactive bulletin board at a particular location, or to all the bulletin boards in the network. Content appears in the templated form designed for a given poster installation, as shown in the Fig. 5.2.

For each of our display layouts we have had variations on the component elements given in Fig. 5.2 (this figure shows the eyeCanvas design described below). The top area reflects the branding elements that identify the poster, giving clues to the audience about the context of the information being presented to them. Each posting is accompanied by a Title, allowing a degree of personalization of the content by the posting author. The main part of the display is for the content itself, shown in a foreground manner commanding the most attention and real estate. Various expressions of overview of other content are also shown, usually expressed as thumbnails. Touching the main content and thumbnails is the primary mode of poster interaction, scrolling, and navigating these display elements. And finally, at the bottom and reachable by all audience members is the control buttons for various forms of interaction with the content over and above the main touch interactions (e.g., invoking feedback displays, printing).

Underlying the bulletin boards is a social network site, essentially an information production and dissemination infrastructure; this infrastructure is the Plasma Poster Network (Fig. 5.3). Server components provide an infrastructure for managing and sharing content and meta-data. Client components support the posting of content (email, Web), maintenance and administration of the system, and content

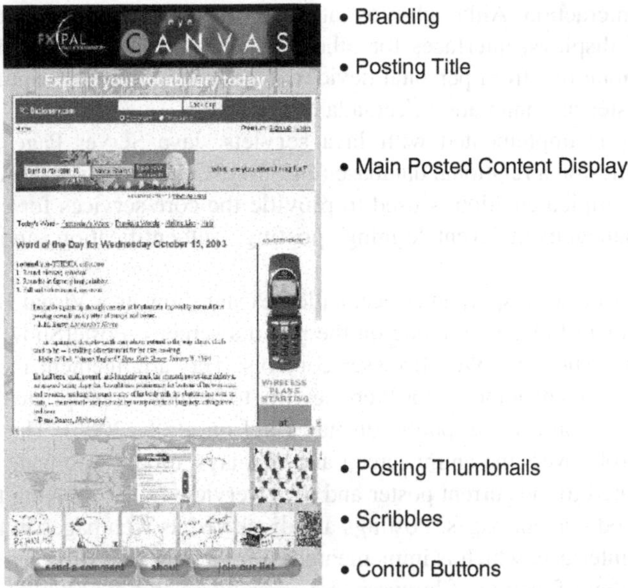


**Fig. 5.2** The public display is based on an adaptable design, allowing a layout and set of features appropriate for each installation setting

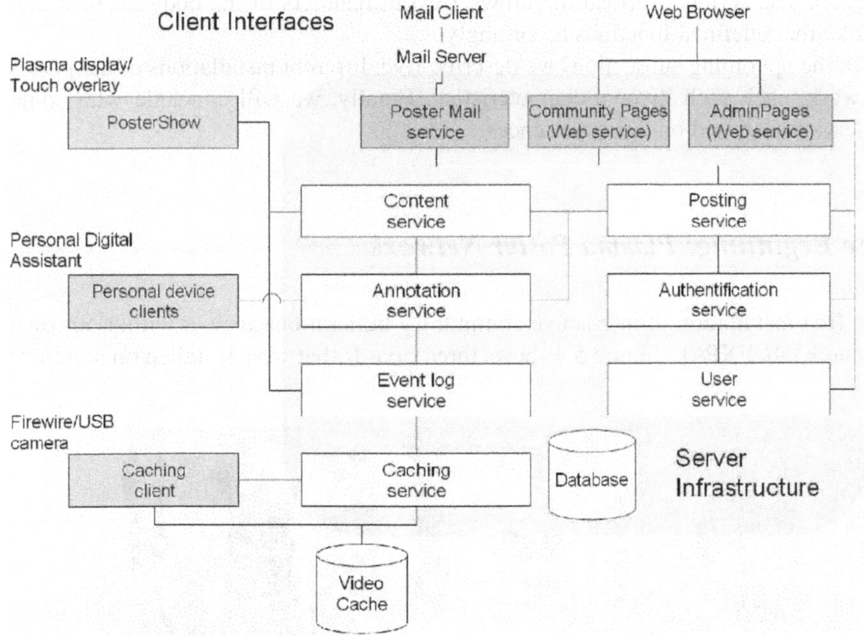


**Fig. 5.3** The Plasma Posters are based on a general client-server information publishing and distribution infrastructure, allowing different adaptation for the different needs of different settings

display and interaction. Although most attention has been focused on the Plasma Poster public displays, interfaces for other purposes are included in the system: capturing annotations from personal devices (Carter et al., 2004), capturing video activity as poster-use annotation (Yamada et al., 2004).

The server is implemented with Java servlets, Java Server Pages, and Java Beans, and relies on a relational database (e.g., MySQL from MySQL AB) to store all data. This implementation is used to provide the core services for content and annotation management, event logging, posting, authentification, and user data management.

The Plasma Poster display interface, called PosterShow, is a Visual Basic application that runs in full-screen mode on the plasma screens. PosterShow's interface consists of two Microsoft Web Browser controls. This arrangement facilitates the repurposing of content authored for Web viewing to be more appropriate for walk-up style interactions on a large, public display (Nelson et al., 2006). The main Web Browser control covers the entire screen and displays a local web page containing meta-data related to the current poster and the overview frame showing thumbnails of all the posted content pages. Postings are displayed as web pages in the content region of the interface, which is implemented as a second Web Browser control. To replace the default function of browser (e.g., scrollbars and hyperlinks), we access the Document Object Model (DOM) of the posted web pages and inject Javascript functions that implement the new interaction mechanism that help provide a "poster" user experience (e.g., finger gesture scrolling and redirecting the navigation window targets). The scripts overload the browser event handlers of the body element and invoke the redefined functions accordingly.

In the upcoming subsections we describe five different installations of the poster network, each with its own characteristics. Finally, we will conclude with some observations based on our experiences.

## *The Beginning: Plasma Poster Network*

The first installation of interactive community bulletin boards was within our own research lab, FXPAL. Figure 5.4 shows three boards that were installed on one floor

**Fig. 5.4** Three Plasma Posters installed at FXPAL; hallway, foyer, kitchen

of the building. As described above, the Plasma Poster Network is a distributed information-sharing architecture with a number of interfaces, designed for a number of platforms – cell phone, PDA (Carter et al., 2004), and most importantly for the current chapter, large-screen interactive public displays. Content types supported for display on the interactive poster boards are text, html, images, and videos. On personal devices where media format is not supported, readers see summarized meta-data about format, as well as poster-network-generated meta-data (e.g., date of posting) and meta-data that the author creates (title, comment, etc.).

The Plasma Poster network was originally envisioned to be a way of sharing content between FXPAL in California and a sister research lab outside Tokyo in Japan. However, its primary use was within the FXPAL research lab (see Churchill et al., 2003) for more details of posting activities including measures of use and analysis of posted content).

Our naivete about the power of content to transcend social boundaries and create a bridge between labs was revealed in the failure of our transnational experiment. Despite the fact that many of our colleagues in Japan read English well, and our encouragement to them to post content in Japanese, they did not use the Plasma Poster – they neither posted content nor read our posted content. On a visit to Japan to investigate what had "gone wrong," we discovered that the interactive poster was first placed in a non-conducive location. It was located between two (somewhat estranged) departments in a space that was only nominally a "lounge" – the lounge was in fact a corridor between the departments that led to the restricted area for smoking. The nature of this social place acted to exclude the interactive poster as a useful social sharing tool; it simply raised issues and concerns about maintaining "face." However, on moving the poster to a more sympathetic location (firmly in one department, and near a printer where people idled awaiting printouts), we discovered yet again that it was *apparently* not used. That is, not used by our indications from a distance monitoring of the shared database we had set up between FXPAL and the sister lab. Another visit to Japan and more data gathered revealed that in fact the Plasma Poster **was** in use, but that a separate database had been created, creating a local poster board. People posted only locally relevant content. This was not the transnational social technology we had envisaged but in hindsight, we were able to understand that the design encouraged local sharing more than cross-group sharing.

## *A Moving Show: CHIplace and CSCWplace Extended*

Having successfully installed three poster boards at FXPAL and one at our Japanese location, we investigated the possibility of creating moving installations that built on and connected an online community space. The questions we posed in this experiment were technology, business, and socially related. Technologically speaking we were interested in how swiftly we could repurpose an interface and redesign it for a new context (Nelson and Churchill, 2006). We also wanted to integrate the Plasma Poster infrastructure with that which already existed for the

**Fig. 5.5** CHIplace poster installation at CHI 2002 in Minneapolis and CSCW place installation at CSCW 2002 in New Orleans

CHIplace (www.chiplace.fxpal.com) online community (which was appropriated and re-implemented for CSCW to create CSCWplace). Finally we were interested in creating a connection between online community participants who were interested in CHI 2002, but could not attend, and people who were physically attending the conference (Churchill et al., 2004). Figure 5.5 shows the installation of the poster boards at CHI 2002 in Minneapolis and at CSCW 2002 in New Orleans.

By far the most popular use of these installations were the shared photos; attendees uploaded images taken at events during the conference for others, online and offline, to see. Announcements of upcoming events and impromptu gatherings (e.g., journal editorial board meetings, special interest group, and "birds of a feather" sessions) were also popular. Notably some but not all of these were documented in the materials all attendees received at registration so the boards and the online community space acted as an additional information dissemination mechanism. With CHIplace and CSCWplace, our layout and feature designs needed to be refined to accommodate a lower attention, higher distraction setting, allowing quick focus to selected community content (e.g., CHIplace) and event happenings (e.g., photos in CSCWplace).

## *Governmental Communications: Mitaka City*

An installation of the Plasma Poster Network was created for and deployed in a government building in Mitaka City in Japan (Fig. 5.6). Here the basic technological infrastructure and the interface remained as it had been for the FXPAL installation, but the social use changed. Instead of supporting a community of content creators who posted directly to the board, government officials and associates from the local community were encouraged to send potential content to a person, an official "poster," who exercised some editorial control and posted the content to the board itself. Communications from the government officials to the visitors of the municipal building were clearly scripted, a singular and consistent "face" from the group

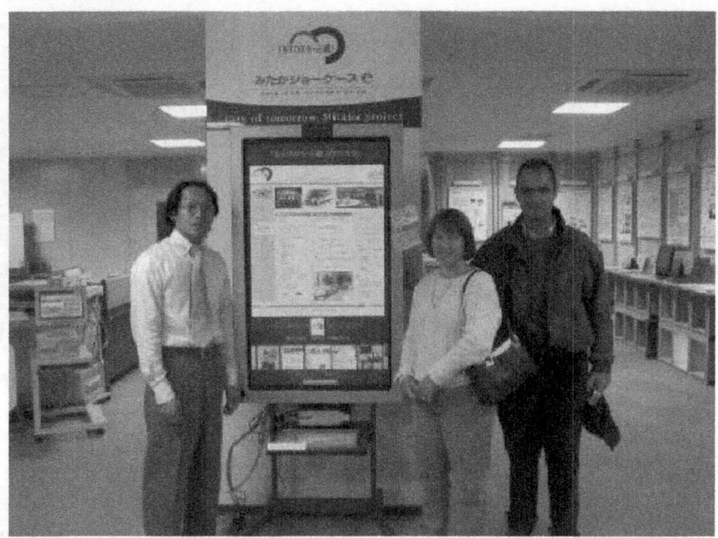

**Fig. 5.6** Mitaka City Plasma Poster

to the community. This was not community members informing each other directly. The poster was physically located at the entrance of the public offices; amongst general posting for the local area were postings about how the building itself functioned – what events were coming up and what meetings (albeit closed to the general public) were taking place. This was an interesting form of awareness – "we are working hard on your behalf" was the message, but the details of those actions were not of import. With the Mitaka City installation, the publishing interface we designed with informal community sharing in mind was well adopted for a single person to curate the more official and polished content.

## *Café Conversations: EyeCanvas*

Another major installation was the eyeCanvas display, designed for and deployed in a local café/art gallery. Details of the installation can be seen elsewhere (Churchill et al., 2006; Churchill and Nelson, forthcoming), but here again there were social setting issues that made this installation very different from the others we had created. In this instance the café/gallery owners controlled the content that was posted, community members (artists, musicians, café visitors) were never invited to the online community space we created. However, we deployed an interactive finger-scribble application that allowed patrons to create messages that were then posted to the board itself, thus enabling some form of participation. Figure 5.7 shows one of the local artists creating a drawing with an onlooker. These "scribbles" proved very popular, creating a flow of information into the public space from patrons (for more details see Churchill and Nelson, 2007). We have also described

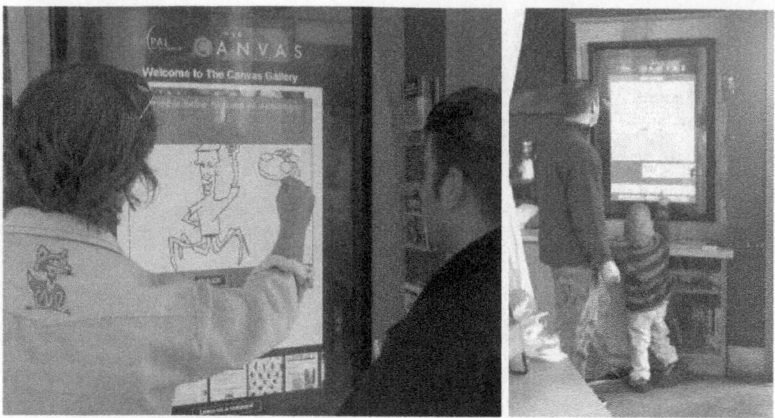


**Fig. 5.7** eyeCanvas public board at the Canvas Gallery in San Francisco

in detail elsewhere the design process of locating the interactive poster, and the design issues involved in the creation of the online social networking site (Churchill and Nelson, forthcoming). With the eyeCanvas, we did not foresee the sheer volume of use the poster received, ultimately bringing about difficult hardware and maintenance issues to address.

## *Who's Reading: Video Annotations on Content*

Lastly, we created a version of the interactive poster to encourage the sharing we intended with the first Plasma Poster installation – sharing content with colleagues in Japan as a means of fostering trust and connection between the distributed groups.

Called the YeTi interactive board (for Yesterday Today Interface, an allusion to the time zone differences between the locations, see Fig. 5.8), the interface was designed explicitly as a shared digital space between two departments – space on the board itself was visually dedicated to each department. In addition we added a video annotation capability – when people touched content, a short (soundless) video of their interaction with the content was captured and associated with the viewed content (see Yamada et al., 2004 for more details). A bit of a surprise for us with YeTI was that largely people did not object to a video camera presence. People appropriated the video snippets, using these asynchronous clips to accentuate both their expression (e.g., waving to the camera and the future readers of a posting) and their audience curiosity (e.g., seeing who was reading their own postings overnight).

## *Summary Points*

In this chapter we have described briefly several installations of a public space interactive community bulletin board and online community sharing space. In all

**Fig. 5.8** YeTi poster interface, with text and video annotations illustrated to the side

instances the basic infrastructure was the same, but the interface and placement differed. Our poster technology is now a product in Japan from Fuji Xerox, the "Collaboposter." This product is intended to be sold as part of a consultancy package, part of improving information flow in customer sites. Our work is continuing in this area; an installation of loosely coupled poster boards inspired by the Plasma Poster technology is planned for deployment in a sister research lab of FXPAL, where the original Plasma Posters are still in operation, 7 years after initial installation.

From a product or technology perspective the exploration has been successful. However, we are only just beginning to return to our original research questions, the questions that underpinned the original design. The basic design we have presented here was envisioned to be just one design instance in a broader design space focused on exploring human–human interaction in physical and digital social locales, on exploring sociopetal "polite" technologies, and on exploring interactions in media enriched physical, embodied place and space. So: What have we learned? And what questions remain firmly on the table?

## Looking Back and Forward

We now briefly reflect on what we have learned and how it builds on and contributes to previous work. We also speculate on what media spaces are becoming, and the future of emplaced media. First, we want to explicitly point out that each setting described above involved a subtle (sometimes unspoken) interchange between the "hosts" and "users" of the technology – this manifested through access control to the distribution network (who gets to post), access control to the posted content (placement of the poster and online login controlling who can most readily read/interact), editorial (what content is approved), and modification/extension (willingness to adapt the technology after first deployment to user responses). As with observations of media space use, emplaced social media technologies involve a coevolution of people's practices with technologies. In addition to the user–host issues, we have elaborated a number of dimensions for characterizing some of the differences between the installations described above:

- *Place matters* – there has been much written about space and place (e.g., see Low and Lawrence-Zuninga, 2003) and frequent restating of the fact that places are socially constructed, with space in some debates presented as the superset container from which places derive (see Harrison and Dourish [1996] and Casey [1997] for criticism and elaboration of this argument). Our installations have shown clearly the co-construction of technology and place – people adopt and adapt the technology by posting content, which is in turn saved, annotated, forwarded, and printed, moving on to play a role in conversations that are woven away from the boards themselves.
- *Media matters* – the form of media that are shared is determined by the setting. In a café-art gallery we found most of the posted content was imagery and were sketches. In our research lab, most of the posting were technology related, and many more videos were posted. In the government building, most documents were governmental information postings.
- *People matter(s)*: The adoption and adaptation of the boards and the media they host affect and are affected by the evolving practices of public media sharing. Sanctions, tests, creations all play a role in what is put on the boards, and over time a norming of what is acceptable occurs. The effect of setting on content type and the norming over time of content style is evident in the very different forms of adoption and adaptation in each of the deployment.

We can take media spaces with us in our mobile devices. We can have foci of media spaces we construct and control in our homes and office environments. With emplaced media, the exercise of design around place, media, and people gives special attention to the experience of "encountered" technology, where there is a different set of controls and ownership in play.

In writing this chapter, we have reflected on what we found to be "surprises" in the design, development, and deployment of these technologies. Perhaps the surprise is that we could have predicted, from the 10,000 ft view, that the technologies would create a stir, provoke interest, be adopted, and adapted in different ways by different social groups in different settings. However, for us the "devil was in the details" along the dimensions of place, media, and people we have outlined; and we *were* surprised where "surprising" means entrancing rather than shocking. The difference in content that was posted to the boards in the different settings, the editorial controls that were exerted on content, the ways people envisioned using the devices in other settings – these were all entrancing and exciting and a wonderful indicator of how "disruptive" technology interventions reveal hithertofore unseen aspects of a social setting. Perhaps this reflects a science and design project located in celebrating the details of what makes a social setting a place to share, and the ways in which content posted to social places can be read in multiple ways, and the ways in which people *want to* reach out and share content with others.

So what is next for media spaces and emplaced media? Certainly video conferencing on mobile devices is going to increase the sense of mobile co-presence people can enjoy (or not). We are already sharing content on urban displays, and texting to public and private devices. Further, video annotation over content on personalized devices is set to move forward. Finally, the domestication of media spaces is another rich area of research (e.g., see Hindus et al., 2001). We have outlined proposals for poster-like interfaces as part of home installations on refrigerators, for example. Homes are settings with particularly close ties between people, so these are perhaps where the sharing of rich content can have deepest impact.

In our ongoing work, we hope to elaborate and populate further the design dimensions of (em)placed media technologies elaborated above. We are also actively engaged in assessing the role of emplaced media in underpinning, reflecting, and transforming social settings and social connection.

## References

Baecker, R., Harrison, S., Buxton, B. Poltrock, S. and Churchill, E.F. Media spaces: past visions, current realities, future promise. In *Proceedings of CHI 2008*. New York, ACM Press, pp. 2245–2248, 2008.

Bly, S., Harrison, S., and Irwin, S. Media spaces: bringing people together in a video, audio, and computing environment. *Communications of the ACM*, 36(1), 28–47, 1993.

de Certeau, Michel. *The Practice of Everyday Life*. Berkeley, CA, University of California Press, 1984, 2002.

Carter, S., Churchill, E.F., Denoue, L., Helfman, J., and Nelson, L., Digital graffiti: public annotation of multimedia content, *CHI 2004*, 2004.

Casey, Edward S.: *The Fate of Place – A Philosophical History*, California, University of California Press, 1997.

Churchill, E. F. and Bly, S. Virtual environments at work: ongoing use of MUDs in the workplace. *Proceedings of the International Joint Conference on Work Activities Coordination and Collaboration*, 99–108, 1999.

Churchill, E.F. and Nelson, L., Interactive community bulletin boards as conversational hubs and sites for playful visual repartee, to appear in persistent conversations track at HICSS 2007.

Churchill, E.F. and Nelson, L., Information flows in a gallery-work-entertainment space: The effect of a digital bulletin board on social encounters. To appear in *Human Organization*.

Churchill, E.F., Nelson, L. Denoue, L., Murphy, P., Helfman, J., The plasma poster network social hypermedia on public display, in public and situated displays. In: K. O'Hara, M. Perry, E. Churchill and D. Russell (Eds.) *Social and Interactional Aspects of Shared Display Technologies*. London, Kluwer, 2003.

Churchill, E.F., Girgensohn, A., Nelson, L., and Lee, A., Blending digital and physical spaces for ubiquitous community, *Communications of the ACM*, 47(2), 38–44, 2004.

Churchill, E., Nelson, L., and Hsieh, G. Café life in the digital age: augmenting information flow in a café-work-entertainment space. In *Proceedings of CHI 2006*, Extended Abstracts, pp. 123–128. New York, ACM Press, 2006.

Churchill, E., Sullivan, J., Golovchinsky, G., and Snowdon, D. Collaborative and co-operative information seeking: CSCW'98 Workshop Report, SIGGROUP Bulletin, 20(1), 56–59, 1999.

Churchill, E.F., Trevor, J., Bly, S., Nelson, L., and Cubranic, D. Anchored conversations: chatting in the context of a document. *CHI 2000*. New York, ACM Press, pp. 454–461, 2000.

Clark, H. H. Using language. Cambridge, Cambridge University Press, 1996.

Curtis, P., Dixon, M., Frederick, R., and Nichols, D. A. The jupiter sudio/video architecture: secure multimedia in network Places. *ACM Multimedia 1995*: 79–90, 1995.

Daft, R.L. and Lengel, R.H. Organizational information requirements, media richness and structural design. *Management Science*, 32(5), 554–571, 1986.

Dourish, P., Adler, A., Bellotti, V., and Henderson, A. Your place or mine? Learning from long-term use of audio-video communication, *Computer Supported Cooperative Work*, 5(1), 33–62, 1996.

Dourish, P. and Bly, S. Portholes: supporting awareness in a distributed work group. *Proceedings of ACM CHI'92 Conference on Human Factors in Computing Systems*, pp. 541–547, May 3–7, 1992.

Durnell Cramton, C. The mutual knowledge problem and its consequences for dispersed collaboration. *Organization Science*, 12(3):346–371, 2001.

Fish, R., Kraut, R., Root, R., and Rice, R. Evaluating video as a technology for informal communication. *Proceedings of CHI'92*. ACM, New York, pp. 37–48, 1992.

Gaver, W. The affordances of media spaces for collaboration. *Proceedings of CSCW'92*, 1992.

Gaver, W., Moran, T., MacLean, A., Lovstrand, L., Dourish, P., Carter, K., and Buxton, W. Realizing a Video Environment: EuroPARC's RAVE System. *Proceedings of ACM CHI'92 Conference on Human Factors in Computing Systems*, pp. 27–35, May 3–7, 1992.

Garfinkel, H. Studies in ethnomethodology. Englewood Cliffs, NJ, Prentice Hall, 1967.

Goffman, E. On face-work. *Interaction Ritual*. New York, Anchor Books, 1963.

Goodwin, C. Pointing as situated practice. In Sotaro Kita. Mahwah (eds.). *Pointing: Where Language, Culture and Cognition Meet*. NJ, Lawrence Erlbaum, pp. 217–41, 2003.

Harrison, S. and S. Minneman. *The Media Space: A Research Project into the Use of Video as a Design Medium*. PaloAlto, CA, Xerox Corporation, 1990.

Harrison, S. and Dourish, P. Re-place-ing space: The roles of place and space in collaborative systems, *Proceedings of the ACM Conf. Computer-Supported Cooperative Work CSCW'96* (Boston, MA), pp. 67–76. New York, ACM, 1996.

Heath, C. and Luff, P. Media space and communicative asymmetries: preliminary observations of video mediated interaction. *Human-Computer Interaction*, 7, 315–346, 1992.

Hindmarsh, J., Fraser, M., Heath, C. and Benford, S. Virtually missing the point: configuring CVEs for object-focused interaction. In: Churchill, E. F., Snowdon, D. N. et al. (Ed.) *Collaborative Virtual Environments*. Springer, London, pp. 115–42, 2000.

Hindus, D., Ackerman, M., Mainwaring, S. D., Starr, B. Thunderwire: A field study of an audio-only media space. *Proceedings of CSCW 1996*, pp. 238–247, 1996.

Hindus, D., Mainwaring, S.D., Leduc, N., Hagstrom, A.E., and Bayley, O Casablanca: designing social communication devices for the Home. *Proceedings of CHI 2001* pp. 325–332, 2001.

Hoskins, J. *Biographical Objects: How Things Tell the Stories of People's Lives*. London, Routledge, 1998.

Ishii, H. and Ullmer, B. Tangible Bits: Towards Seamless Interfaces between People, Bits and Atoms, *Proceedings of CHI '97*, New York, ACM, pp. 234–241, 1997.

Kendon, A. *Conducting Interaction: Patterns of Behavior in Focused Encounters*. Cambridge, Cambridge University Press, 1990.

Komter, A.E. *Social Solidarity and the Gift*. New York, Cambridge University Press, 2005.

Kraut, R.E., Fussell, S.R., and Siegel, J. Visual information as a conversational resource in collaborative physical tasks. *Human–Computer Interaction*, 18: 13–49, 2003.

Latour, B. *Reassembling the Social: An Introduction to Actor-Network-Theory*. Oxford, Oxford University Press, 2005.

Lombard, M. and Ditton, T. At the heart of it all: the concept of presence. *Journal of Computer-Mediated Communication*, 3(2). http://www.ascusc.org/jcmc/vol3/issue2/lombard.html, 1997.

Low, S. and Lawrence-Zuniga, D. *The Anthropology of Space and Place*, Blackwell, Oxford, 2003.

Mantei, M., Baecker, R., Sellen, A., Buxton, W., Milligan, T., and Wellman, B. Experiences in the use of a media space. *Proceedings of CHI'91*. New York, ACM, pp. 203–208, 1991.

Marshall, C., Price, M.N., Golovchinsky, G., and Schilit, B.N. Introducing a digital library reading appliance into a reading group." In *Proceedings of ACM Digital Libraries 99*. New York, ACM, pp. 77–84, 1999.

Miller, D. Why some things matter. In: Miller, D. (Ed.) *Material Cultures*. London/Chicago: UCL Press/University of Chicago Press, pp. 3–21, 1997.

Nardi, B. A. *Context and Consciousness: Activity Theory and Human-computer Interaction*. Cambridge, MA, MIT Press, pp. 1–20, 1996.

Nelson, L. and Churchill, E.F. Repurposing: techniques for reuse and integration of interactive systems, *Proceedings of the 2006 IEEE International Conference on Information Reuse and Integration*, September 2006.

Pedersen, E., McCall, K., Moran, T. and Halasz, F. Tivoli. An electronic whiteboard for informal workgroup meetings. *Proceedings of InterCHI*, Amsterdam, April 1993, 1993.

Pedersen, E. and Sokoler, T. AROMA – Abstract representation of mediated presence supporting mutual awareness. *Proceedings of CHI 97 Conference*, Atlanta, ACM, 1997.

Sacks, H., Schegloff, E. A., and Jefferson, G. A simplest systematics for the organization of turn-taking for conversation. *Language*, 50, 696–735, 1974.

Savolainen, R. Everyday life information seeking: approaching information seeking in the context of 'Way of Life.' *Library and Information Science Research* 17, 259–294, 1995.

Sellen, A.J. Assessing video-mediated conduct: a comparison of different analytic approaches. In: K. Finn, A. Sellen, and S. Wilbur (Eds.), *Video-mediated Communication*, New Jersey, Lawrence Erlbaum, pp. 95–106, 1997.

Stults, R. *Media space*. Xerox PARC technical report, 1986.

Suh, K.S. Impact of communication medium on task performance and satisfaction: an examination of media-richness theory. *Information & Management*, 35, 295–312, 1999.

Tang, John C., Ellen A. Isaacs, and Monica Rua. Supporting distributed groups with a montage of lightweight interactions, *Proc. CSCW '94*, pp. 23–34, 1994.

Yamada, T., Shingu, J., Churchill, E.F., Nelson, L., Helfman, J., and Murphy, P. Who cares? Reflecting who is reading what on distributed community bulletin boards. *Proceedings of UIST 2004*, pp. 109–118.

# Chapter 6
# Social Catalysts for Creating Sociable Media Spaces

**Karrie G. Karahalios**

**Abstract** Mediated communication between public spaces is a relatively new concept. One current example of this interaction is video conferencing among people within the same organization. Large-scale video conferencing walls have begun to appear in public or semipublic areas, such as workplace lobbies and kitchens. These connections provide a link via audio and/or video to another public space within the organization.

When placed in public or semipublic work spaces, they are often designed for casual encounters among people within that community. Thus far, communicating via these systems has not met expectations. Some drawbacks of such systems have been lack of privacy, gaze ambiguity, spatial incongruity, and fear of appearing too social in a work environment.

In this chapter we explore a different aim and approach to linking public spaces. We are not creating a substitute for face-to-face interaction, but rather new modes of conversational and physical interaction within this blended space. This is accomplished through the introduction of what we define as a social catalyst.

We address the need for designs best suited for linking public spaces and present a series of design criteria for incorporating mediated communication between public and semipublic spaces.

This chapter focuses on design principles for intelligent social interfaces that serve as catalysts to encourage new interactions between people within and between two spaces. We call them *social catalysts*.

The main idea of the social catalyst is to initiate and create mutual involvement for people to engage in conversation. For example, in a public space, it is not customary to initiate conversation with random strangers. However, there are events that act as catalysts, which connect people who would not otherwise be communicating with each other. Such a catalyst may be an experience, a common object like a sculpture or map, or a dramatic event such as a street performer. The chess tables in Harvard Square's outdoor cafe are an interesting example. People flock to this

K.G. Karahalios
University of Illinois, Urbana-Champaign
e-mail: kkarahal@cs.uiuc.edu

S. Harrison (ed.), *Media Space 20+ Years of Mediated Life*,
Computer Supported Cooperative Work,

public space for coffee, walks, etc. The chess players usually draw a small crowd from the masses. The act of the game then provides an icebreaker and lowers the barriers to conversation.

## Social Catalysts

> *A sign of a great place is triangulation. This is the process by which some external stimulus provides a linkage between people and prompts strangers to talk to each other as if they were not.* (William H. Whyte)

Our hypothesis is that the creation of a social catalyst as an integral part of the environment will aid mediated communication between spaces by providing a spark to initiate conversation and the interest to sustain it.

The social catalysts of our installations extend Whyte's triangulation principle into the display and interface of the connected space. The form of our social catalyst is abstract, may defy physics, and allows one to interact in ways that are not possible in unmediated communication. It alters the space and communicative cues between the two spaces through the influence of the people in the space and their actions. One such social catalyst might be a connection where the current conversation of the users appears as graffiti in the environment. This would allow the occupants to see that they are affecting the space and might encourage them to alter it. While the possibilities are infinite, the challenge is to determine which agents on the interface are effective as social catalysts and why.

In our linking of two spaces, we are augmenting the appearance of the familiar audio–video wall interface with stimuli that are initiated at either end of the connection. The wall is extended to be not only a display but an event in itself; the system becomes both medium and catalyst. This work further emphasizes the design of the interface as a complement to the space. We want the communication link and display to blend into the physicality and aesthetics of the space and to make the interactions sociable and intuitive.

We will continue by examining a brief history of communication between remote spaces. We then discuss features of communication such as social cues and feedback that are the fundamental elements necessary in communication channels between connected sociable spaces for people.

This chapter explores social catalysts along four different axes:

- Transformation of Space through Interaction
- Abstraction for Visualizing Conversation
- Physical Manifestation of Virtual Presence
- Time and Motion for Blended Spaces

We describe these four features through an implemented installation called *Telemurals* and describe how the social catalysts influenced this interaction.

Throughout this chapter, we see that the four features mentioned above are not mutually exclusive and there is much overlap. We revisit the concepts of transformation, abstraction, physicality and scale, and time and motion over and over. We conclude with a brief overview of two other sociable media spaces that similarly adopt social catalysts.

## Background

There have been a number of "media space" projects that connect geographically distinct locales with some combination of audio and video (Agamanolis et al., 1997; Bly and Irwin, 1993; Buxton, 1992; Hindus et al., 1996; Ishii et al., 1992; Singer et al., 1999) as well as studies of the relative affordances of audio, video, and other media (Isaacs and Tang, 1993; Jancke et al., 2001; Tang and Minneman, 1991).

One of the main goals behind the creation of the original media space project at Xerox Parc was to find means to support cross-site work and to maintain the necessary social connection between remote research labs (Bly and Irwin, 1993). Following media space systems incorporated privacy controls so that one could refuse a connection, block a connection for several seconds, or filter the transmitted video (Boyle et al., 2002; Dourish and Bly, 1992; Jancke et al., 2001). Telecommunication art pieces such as Hole-in-Space (Galloway and Rabinowitz, 1980) have shown glimpses that people will use audio–video connections for social interaction.

There has also been relevant work focusing in the audio-only or audio-dominant media spaces. Smith and Hudson's work on low-disturbance audio found that audio, even when filtered to be incomprehensible (for privacy, in their application) provided a good sense of awareness of the presence and activity of others (Smith and Hudson, 1995).

One audio-only media space, Thunderwire, suggested that users originally had difficulty with the interface and modified their behavior in response (Hindus et al., 1996). The Somewire project is one of the most relevant, since it was designed to foster casual interactions among colleagues (Singer et al., 1999). Here, Singer et. al experimented with a number of visual interfaces in conjunction with an audio-only media space. They found that control over such features as localization or other attributes was not needed, but that information that supplemented users' knowledge of the social aspects of the space, such as awareness of the presence of others, was quite useful.

Few audio–video media spaces have ventured into the physical realm. One early example is Buxton's Hydra project, where small distinct physical modules containing cameras, microphones, and speakers were used to model a four-person meeting around a table (Buxton, 1992).

This work described in this chapter moves further into the physical realm. The social catalysts of these projects are designed to blend into the interface and space of the interaction. They incorporate the design concepts we cited earlier for creating sociable media spaces: transformation of space, abstraction of information, interaction in physical space, and motion in space. We start by describing how these relate to the *Telemurals* installation.

## *Telemurals*

*Telemurals* is an audio–video connection that abstractly blends two remote spaces. The initial setup is straightforward. Two disjoint spaces are connected through an audio–video wall. Video and audio from each space is captured. The two images are then rendered, blended together, and projected onto the wall of their respective space. The difference between *Telemurals* and traditional media space connections is that the image and audio transformations that evolve as people communicate through the system and the blending of the participating spaces (Karahalios and Donath, 2004).

Duplex audio is transmitted between the two locations. To provide feedback and comic relief, the audio is passed to a speech recognition algorithm. The algorithm returns text of the closest matching words in its dictionary. This text is then rendered on the shared wall of the two spaces. The goal here is to make it clear that the users' words are affecting the space without necessarily requiring 100% accuracy of the speech recognition system.

The first installation of *Telemurals* is shown in Fig. 6.1. Silhouettes of the participants in the local space are rendered in orange. The participants at the remote end are rendered in red. When they overlap, that region becomes yellow. The aim of this cartoon-like rendering is to transmit certain cues such as number of participants and activity level without initially revealing the identity of the participants.

Participation is required for this communication space to work. To reinforce a sense of involvement, we provide the system with some intelligence to modify its space according to certain movements and speech patterns. That is, the more

**Fig. 6.1** *Telemurals* installation inside MIT dormitory. Local participants are represented in yellow. The remote participant is represented as a red silhouette

conversation and movement between the two spaces, the more image detail will be revealed to the participants at each end. The silhouettes slightly fade to become more photo-realistic. This prompts the participants to move closer into the space to see. If conversation stops, the images fade back to their silhouette rendering. We want the participants to choose their own level of commitment in this shared space. The more effort they exert, the more they see of both spaces.

Much thought has been given to the design of the renderings in *Telemurals*. We wanted to maintain the benefits of video in their simplest form. Adding video to a communication channel improves the capacity for showing understanding, attention, forecasting responses, and expressing attitudes (Isaacs and Tang, 1993). A simple nodding of the head can express agreement or disagreement in a conversation. Gestures can convey concepts that are not easily expressed in words; they can express nonrational emotions and nonverbal experiences.

Yet these cues are not always properly transmitted. There may be dropped frames and audio glitches. Lack of synchronicity between image and audio can influence perceptions and trust of the speaker at the other end. Other challenges include equipment placement. For example, camera placement has long been a reason of ambiguous eye gaze in audio–video links. A large camera offset gives the impression that the person you are speaking to is constantly looking elsewhere.

With *Telemurals*, we are creating an environment where rendered video maintains subtle cues of expression such as posture and hand motion, yet also enhances other cues. For example, changes in volume alter the style of the rendered video. By adding another layer of abstraction into the video stream, we can enhance cues in a manner that is not possible in straight video streams.

In this project, the abstraction of person, the blending of participants, the graffiti conversation, and the fading from abstract to photo-realistic are the social catalysts for the experience. This new wall created by filtering creates an icebreaker, a common ground for interaction, and an object for experimentation. How will one communicate in this abstracted space? How will their behavior affect their appearance and the appearance of the setting? How different is communication using photorealistic versus non-photorealistic video? The goal here is to create new styles of movement and speech interaction by providing a common language across the two spaces.

The first *Telemurals* installation connected two common area halls of MIT graduate dormitories, Ashdown and Sidney-Pacific. The Telemural in Ashdown is located to the right of the main lobby. In Sidney-Pacific, it is placed in a high-traffic cross-way connecting the gym, the laundry room, and the elevators (see Fig. 6.1). This connection came about as the under-construction Sidney-Pacific Dormitory committee was looking to put public art in its public areas and create spaces to encourage students to gather. Ashdown, the oldest graduate dormitory on campus, was similarly undergoing renovations to create public spaces for social gatherings, and the two dormitories were open to the idea of creating a shared communication link. The sites within the dorms were chosen because they have traffic, are public to the community, and because a large video wall aesthetically blends into the space.

## Evaluation

This work combines the disciplines of technology, design, and communication. Evaluation of this work is therefore threefold.

### *Engineering*

We evaluate if the system functions. Does it work? That is, does it transmit audio and video? Is the sound quality acceptable? Is the video quality and speed acceptable? Are the interface and networks reliable?

### *Design*

This is in the form of a studio critique. Professors from various architecture and design departments and research scientists have been invited and have volunteered to participate in a series of critiques.

### *Ethnography*

The field for this observation study is the semipublic space within the two chosen dormitories. The participants are graduate students who live in the respective dormitory and their friends. We are primarily interested in seeing (1) how people use *Telemurals*, (2) whether the catalysts attract them, and (3) how we can improve the system.

The *Telemurals* observation took place in May and June 2003. Initially, *Telemurals* ran for 2 h each on Wednesday and Sunday nights in conjunction with a coffee hour/study break. Signage was placed in the entry ways of both spaces to describe what is being transmitted and the privacy concerns of the project.

We had requests from both spaces to increase the hours of the connection. *Telemurals* then ran every night for 2 h and then ran continuously for 24 h a day.

We performed three different types of observations.

- Observation while immersed in the environment
- Observation from mounted camera video
- Observation from abstract blended video

The footage from these tapes was used to annotate patterns of use for this study and were then discarded. Initially, we were interested in observing:

- How long people speak using *Telemurals*
- The number of people using the system at any one time
- The number of people present but not interacting
- The number of unique users (if possible)

- The number of repeat users (if possible)
- The number of times and the duration that people use *Telemurals* in one space only
- Repeated patterns of interaction: gestures, kicks, jumps, screams

These are factors that we believe are indicative of levels of interaction. However, one must always be open to the unexpected and attempt to find other underlying patterns as well in studying the social catalysts.

# Discussion

## *Engineering*

*Telemurals* works as an engineering project. It runs on the school network and typically uses less than 1 MB of bandwidth with audio latency varying from 500 ms to 1 s depending on network usage. The networking audio and image libraries are all written in C over UDP, and we use the Intel OpenCV library for image segmentation.

The video was reliable, the audio had acceptable lag, and the system ran continuously for over 2 months. The one technical challenge that could use improvement is the audio. Using just one microphone does not cover the intended space and the acoustics of each space play a huge role. We are experimenting with microphone arrays and with physical objects that one interacts with that contain the microphone.

*Telemurals* was evolving throughout its construction and connected installation period. We experimented with several different renderings of people at each end, we changed the fading algorithm, the hours of operation, and the *Telemural* wall site at Sidney-Pacific. These changes were made according to suggestions and critiques throughout a 5-month period.

### Social: Comparisons and Contrasts

Time-schedule, social events, signage, interface, trust, site selection, and a changing environment proved to influence population mass at the *Telemurals* sites. The motion of people, ambient noise, and the speech-to-text graffiti created from the users' own words kept people at the site.

#### Hours of Operation

The *Telemurals* observation took place in May and June 2003. Originally, *Telemurals* ran for 2 h each on Wednesday and Sunday nights in conjunction with a coffee hour/study break. We had requests from both spaces to increase the hours of the connection to the point where it ran 24 h, 7 days a week. We had a larger population of use per hour and longer linked interaction times when *Telemurals* was up for shorter intervals of time (2 h, 2 days a week, and 2 h every night versus 24 h a day). We believe that it became more of an event – something that should not be missed. Nevertheless, we continued getting requests to run it continuously.

### Events

Dormitory events such as meetings and social hours attracted large crowds to the *Telemurals*. One person at the *Telemural*, whether at the local or remote end, tended to attract more people. A wedding party proved to be the most interactive period, with children repeatedly running back and forth across the wall. Food associated with these events also attracted people.

### Signage

We were required to place signage in the entry ways of both spaces to describe what was being transmitted, where it was being sent, and to inform people of the presence of the camera, microphone, and the ubiquitous link. Of over 1,200 people living in both dorms, we had one complaint asking that we shut off the microphones between both spaces. This person felt the system was eavesdropping on them as they waited for the elevator. The abstracted images were not a concern in this case.

We suspect that the signage further emphasizing the cameras perhaps discouraged some use of the system. The signs were large and placed in such a manner that they would not be missed.

### Interface

The creation of the interface was an iterative process. It was modified every 2 weeks. At the end of each 2-week period, feedback was requested from the residents of the dormitories and the student council. Along the way, several key issues emerged:

1. Residents found the straight audio–video feed too surveillance-like. They avoided the camera.
2. The abstracted video was preferred. In this case, they wanted to see how they appeared at the other end as well. It was not enough to see the people at the remote end. It was important to see how they were represented in this new space. Furthermore, it appeared to be more of a shared space when all parties shared the screen real estate.
3. Prior to the described fading transformation, participants would slowly emerge as photorealistic black and white silhouettes. This was disturbing the participants as sometimes people would appear as disembodied heads.

4. Prior to adding the graffiti from speech, participants did not use the audio channel as much. When the text from the speech recognition was presented as graffiti on the screen, participation in *Telemurals* increased fivefold. Gestures decreased, perhaps because people could convey information through this other channel as well.

**Design**

*Telemurals* was critiqued by three professors while in use at each installation site. It was noted that the abstraction not only enhances certain social cues such as gesture, but also mitigates the confusion associated with gaze and audio–video synchronicity in teleconferencing systems. The interface was described as "evocative and fascinating" by one design professor. This evaluation is not enough. More observation and critique is necessary in a variety of venues and space to see the constraints and benefits of this interaction interface.

**Privacy**

Privacy control was one of the major forces behind the design of *Telemurals*. The privacy gained through abstracting people in the setting allowed for participation with less risk and without a covert feeling of surveillance.

However, in observing such an interface, we did record some video of the interactions and of the people. If straight video directly from the camera was captured, there was a large sign saying this might be happening. Abstracted video was captured at random times every day. All of the audio and video captured in the Telemurals interface was annotated, analyzed, and then destroyed.

## *Social Catalysts: Transformation, Abstraction, Physicality, and Time and Motion*

The previous sections described the *Telemurals* installation and the iterative process involved in its creation. In this section, we will look at the social catalysts that evolved in the installation that encouraged participation.

**Transformation**

Transformation manifests itself in several ways. First of all, people do not appear as they are, but rather as cartoon-like renderings of themselves. Second, this process is a transformation as a person first appears as a brief outline of a silhouette and slowly fills in based on movement and speech (see Fig. 6.2).

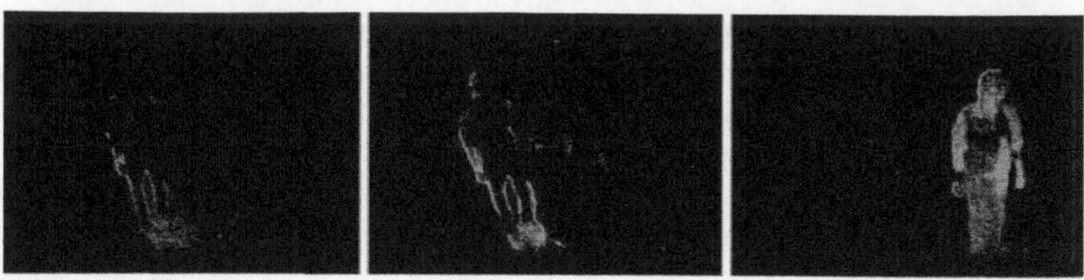

**Fig. 6.2** Fading in (from left to right) as participant exhibits more movement and speech

The displayed graffiti is another form of transformation. It starts as speech input is converted to text and then the text is rendered on the screen. Sometimes, the speech to text is not perfect; in this case, the transformation is not always what is expected.

Both places participating in the installation are further transformed to become blended spaces. They are not merely windows into a remote existing space, but a new space altogether.

### Abstraction

As mentioned earlier, the techniques for social catalysts are not mutually exclusive in the interface. In this case, the abstraction is the rendering of people as silhouettes and later cartoon-like renderings as opposed to rendering in a photorealistic style. This is also qualified as part of the transformation process.

Furthermore, a new abstract space is created whereby renderings of both spaces exist as well as the letters from their speech floating above their heads in the form of graffiti.

### Physicality

Physicality in *Telemurals* is evident in the life-size interactions of the participants and the displays. This interaction on a desktop computer or laptop using a webcam would be very different. The user would not use their entire body; they would probably not kick, or do a cartwheel. By interacting in a space that is the same scale as the body, movement is more familiar and intuitive. This is further helped by the interface in that no special commands need to be known by the users. They simply move as they normally would.

### Time/Motion

The effects of time and motion can be seen primarily in two ways. First, as someone moves or speaks, they appear to fill in over time. Second, it is movement that causes this change over a period of time.

The following sections will briefly describe two different installations and highlight their social catalysts.

## Other Examples of Sociable Media Spaces

In the latter half of this chapter, we discuss two projects: *Visiphone* and *Chit Chat Club*. We briefly describe their goal, design motivations, and the social catalysts that encouraged their use in their respective spaces.

### Visiphone

*Visiphone* is a communication object that bridges the distance between two physically separate spaces. We began with the notion of building a virtual portal between two spaces, one that would allow the inhabitants of the two separate spaces to communicate easily and to be intuitively aware of each other's presence (See Fig. 6.3).

It consists of two stations connected via the Internet. Each station has a dome on which the visualization is projected. When a live connection exists, the dome displays a continuing moving spiral of circles. The central dot represents the present moment. If it is a small gray dot, there is no sound going between the two spaces. When sound is originating locally, the current circle is orange; when sound originates at the outside location, the circles is blue. If sound is coming from both locations, the colors are shown as concentric blended circles. The dots spiral outward from the center, so the display shows the history of the last half minute or so of conversational rhythm.

The *Visiphone* display is a translucent dome sitting on a pedestal. The graphics are projected onto the dome from below. The dome shape makes it an interface in the round: one can view it from any side. This is essential for an object meant to create a connection between two inhabited, real-world spaces in which people move about. The design of the dome itself is a key element in this multimodal interface and its size, location, and appearance influence its use and ability to portray the sense of awareness and continuous connection in the space.

One can think of Visiphone as a speakerphone system with a graphical interface. Let us imagine for a moment that this is a speakerphone interface without the graphics similar to existing speakerphones and teleconferencing systems. Audio alone has several drawbacks, especially in terms of awareness. It is difficult, especially in a noisy environment to know if one's voice has carried or if others are speaking at the other end. Furthermore, lone periods of silence make it easy to forget the device, which then takes on a quality of covert surveillance.

Our approach is to connect the spaces aurally and then to visibly render the sound flowing between them. *Visiphone*'s graphics express the dynamics of the conversations originating at both locations, thus providing visual feedback that one's voice has carried sufficiently and indicating the presence of those on the other end.

It portrays the existence of the connection even in moments of silence, thus removing the surveillance-like aura of the audio-only system.

For a piece such as *Visiphone*, form is function: it must be attractive and intriguing enough to claim a central place in a space. The dome shape makes it readable from any location; its placement on the pedestal puts it into the category of sculptural object (as well as concealing the projector). The abstract graphics themselves are designed to convey a sense of rhythm and activity – to visibly represent the connection between the two spaces (Donath et al., 2000).

## Transformation

*Visiphone* transforms voice and creates a "picture" of a conversation. Because of this picture, one can "see" things in a conversation that were previously ephemeral. For example, one can see conversational dominance if all the dots are orange or blue. One can see arguments if the dots are shades of violet and concentric. Or one can see silence if the dots are small and gray. Motion of any kind implies a connection. An interaction that is usually audio-only now has been transformed to have

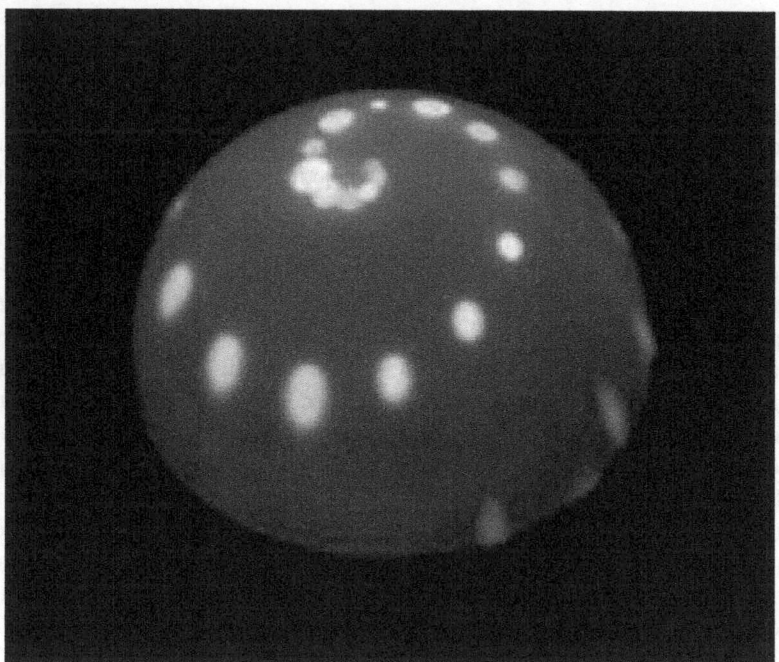

**Fig. 6.3** The *Visiphone* interface. Dots emanate from the top center and spiral down the dome. Orange dots represent the local space. Blue dots represent the remote space. The radius of the dot corresponds to the average volume at that interval of time. Concentric dots with blended color represent moments of concurrent speech

a physical component that provides cues into a conversation that were previously thoughts or suggestions rather than conversational metrics.

### Abstraction

Abstracting the traditional audio wave patterns into the simple graphical element of the circle allows one to think of audio from a different perspective. The circle representation divorces the technical connotations from audio channel and provides a new frame of reference to the conversations.

We are familiar with other forms of volume representation whether they be bar chart visualizations such as in Quicktime™ or waveforms as in many sound recorders and players. Although these representations are readable, they have a technical connotation and their representations are fleeting. The string of beads visualization in *Visiphone* separates itself from these traditional technical representations. Its simple graphical elements are easy to comprehend and, therefore, append to each other to add a historical context to the audio stream. The color and the discrete units display salient features such as turn-taking and interruptions far more clearly than would a continuous waveform representation of two audio streams.

### Physicality

Another function of the visible interface is to serve as a focus of attention. Anyone who has attended a meeting at which some participants are present via speakerphone knows the phenomenon by which the little black object on the table becomes a stand-in for the person: one addresses one's remarks to it, one looks at it when it is "speaking." We focus on the object because it is difficult to converse with a disembodied voice – if an object is associated with that disembodied voice, it becomes the representation for the connection and person. With the traditional speakerphone, the physical object neither provides information, nor is it designed to evoke a person, conversation, connection, etc. With *Visiphone* we sought to make an object that is abstract enough to be suitable to all users, contexts, and topics, yet that also reflects the rhythm of the ongoing conversation.

### Time/Motion

Revelation is key in *Visiphone*; this is made possible by the depiction of time and motion in the interface. Conversational dominance is made more apparent by the historical aspect of the dome – rendering audio graphically over time. Motion shows the progress of conversation as well as the existence of a link.

*Visiphone* allows you to see things you know but may not realize that you know. Abstraction makes this possible. This ability to perceive a wide spectrum of conversational patterns from the one cue of volume shows the power of this mediated connection. As previously mentioned, we are not adding information to the audio stream. Using what is already there, we are highlighting patterns that are not obvious in an audio-only mode or using more traditional representations of audio.

Although we have not conducted formal user studies of *Visiphone*, it has been on display in public environments and used by hundreds of people.[1] People have been enthusiastic about it. The form of the display has proved to be quite important – the spiraling dots are often described as mesmerizing and this aesthetic appeal is an intrinsic part of its value. One of the more surprising comments, but one we heard repeatedly, was that people thought it would be a good "therapy" tool; they were interested in the way the dots could show patterns of interruptions and of individual conversational dominance.

## Chit Chat Club

*Chit Chat Club* is an experiment in bringing people together in a mixed physical and virtual environment (Karahalios and Dobson, 2005). Online chat rooms and real-world cafes are both venues for social interaction, but with significant differences, e.g., the participants' knowledge of each other's expressions and identity and the more governing introductions, turn-taking, etc. Our goal was to create, through careful design of the physical environment and computer interface, a place that gracefully combines these two cultures; the analysis of how well this space actually functions will further our understanding of social interaction, both online and in person.

Figure 6.4 is a rendering of the two spaces that connect in the *Chit Chat Club*. It should be noted that the interaction is asymmetrical. For the discussion in this chapter, we will primarily be focusing on the café side of the installation.

There was a series of *Chit Chat Club* installations. We will begin by describing the spaces involved and then proceed to describe the interaction. Figure 6.5 shows three different *Chit Chat Club* tele-sculptures. They can be thought of as the physical counterpart of an avatar in an online space. When someone goes to a *Chit Chat Club* café, they can go with a friend to sit as they would in a typical café, or they can also talk to someone from a remote location that embodies one of the *Chit Chat Club* tele-sculptures (see Fig. 6.6).

Entering the *Chit Chat Club* from the remote setting was similar for the three tele-sculptures shown above. First, one went to the web site. The visitor was presented with an abstract view of the café where they could see which person chairs and tele-sculpture chairs were occupied and vacant. Then, they could create a look for their "face" in the first two tele-sculpture options shown in Fig. 6.5, from a mix-and-match pallet. The user could choose different eyes, lips, glasses, face color from hand-drawn faces, claymation faces, and cartoon faces. For a more detailed description of this process, please see the description in Karahalios and

[1] It was shown in the Emerging Technologies exhibit at Siggraph 1999 and has been a featured demonstration at the MIT Media Lab.

**Fig. 6.4** Rendering of the two *Chit Chat Club* spaces. The left represents the café where physical statues embody remote visitors to the café. On the right, remote visitors enter the physical statues via the *Chit Chat Club* website

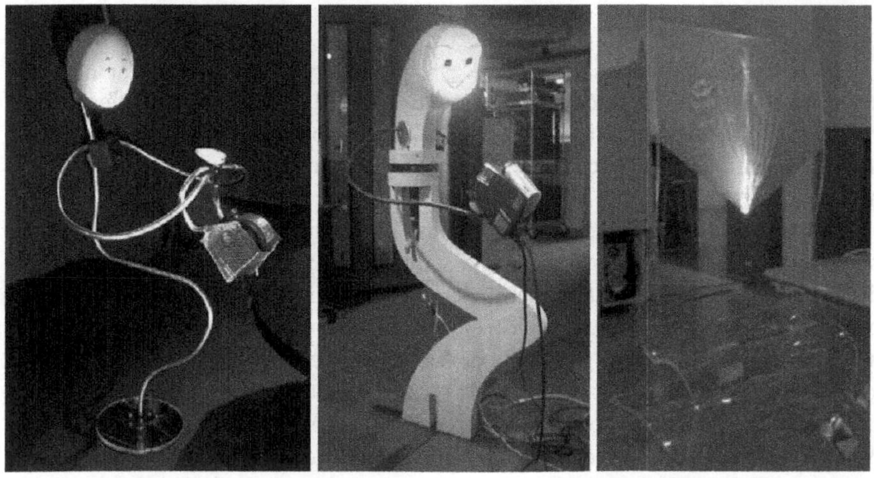

**Fig. 6.5** Three *Chit Chat Club* tele-sculptures. The image on the left is 'Slim'. This was the first tele-sculpture. The middle image is 'Orlando'. Orlando has a motor in the midsection to allow the remote visitor to control gaze during conversation. The tele-sculpture on the right is 'Ginger'. This is one of the most recent designs in abstraction of voice and body

Dobson (2005). With the Ginger tele-sculpture, there was no face. Once the visitors "dressed" for their encounter, they were brought into the communication interface (see Fig. 6.7). Each of the tele-sculptures have a camera so that the remote user sees live video of the café space as seen in all the communication interfaces.

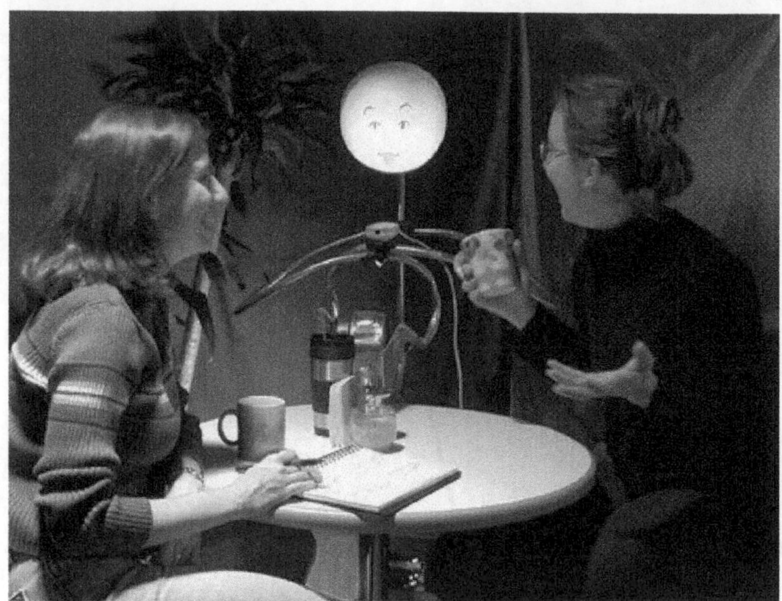

**Fig. 6.6** Two café goers and a *Chit Chat Club* tele-sculpture

The remote communication interfaces evolved over time. The first interface described in Fig. 6.7 allowed remote user to transmit their audio and to choose from five animated facial expressions. The chosen expression was projected onto the face of the telecommunication sculpture. The mouth on the face was morphed to match the audio communication.

This remote interface had some problems. When the remote user was not clicking on an expression, the face on the tele-sculpture was static. When this happened, visitors at the café end thought that the connection had dropped. They felt that no movement implied no connection. This led to the remote user clicking constantly to the extent that it distracted from the conversation. We remedied this in the second communication interface in two ways. First, the remote user no longer had to click for an expression. The expressions were determined by vocal parameters (Scherer, 1986). If the remote user did not like that expression, they could override that expression by mousing over a landscape of expressions on the expression wheel on the bottom left of the interface. In this manner, the remote user did not have to constantly click on the interface. Furthermore, they were able to see how they appeared at the other end as their face was also shown on their interface.

The final communication interface is more abstract. It does not have an anthropomorphic face, but rather an evocative rendering of voice. The lines emanating from the point resemble abstract vocal chords. The remote user can drag images from their computer and have them incorporated into the abstract visualization. Again, the remote user can see at their end how they appear at the café space.

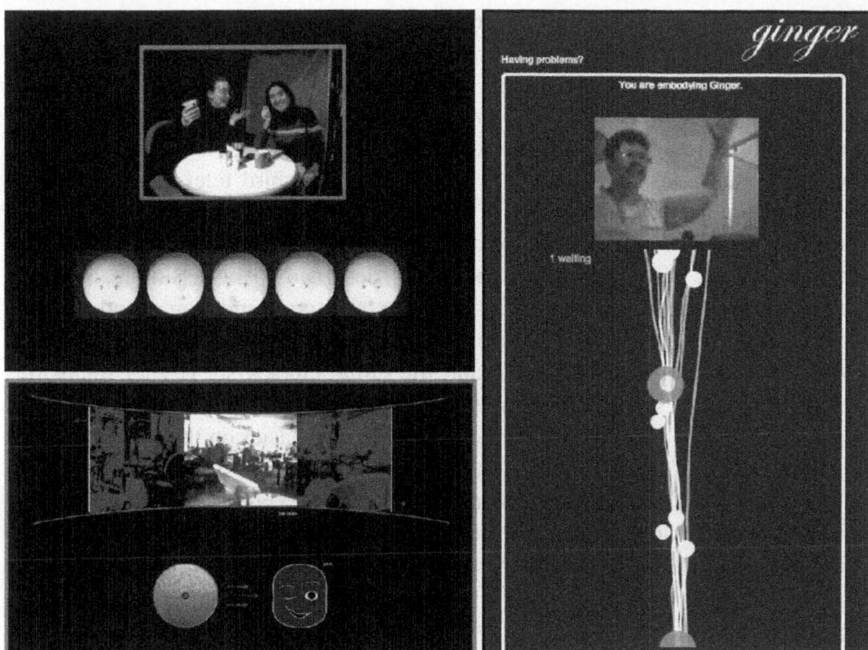


**Fig. 6.7** The three remote *Chit Chat Club* communication interfaces. (Top *left*) The Slim communication interface. The remote user would speak into a microphone. They could choose their facial expression by selecting one of the five available expressions: happy, sad, angry, 'duh', and bored. (Bottom *left*) The Orlando communication interface. The users voice controlled the facial expression, however, the user could override this expression by choosing one of their own from the expression wheel. The user could also control the gaze of the tele-sculpture by moving the frame left and right. (*Right*) The Ginger communication interface. The interface is abstract and is identical for all users at the onset. The lines emanating from the chair vibrate based on vocal parameters. The dots represent spoken words; the color of the dots are the pitch spoken at that time. Remote users can further convey intent by dragging images they want onto the display to be projected onto the chair so that they can be viewed by the café goers

## Transformation

Transformation in *Chit Chat Club* can be seen in several forms. In all cases, voice is transformed and expressed into graphical form. The remote visitors to the café are transformed to embody a sculpture in a different space.

## Abstraction

Abstraction can be seen at both the café end of *Chit Chat Club* and the remote interface. At the café end, the tele-sculpture form is an abstracted form. We designed the tele-sculptures to be anthropomorphic to a degree, but not so anthropomorphic that one would expect exact human movement and human expression (see Fig. 6.5). We also wanted it to be accepted as an interesting seated visitor. There was a head, a seated body, and arms. The faces were abstracted human faces rather than photo-realistic faces so that the participants would not focus on lag discrepancies in the interaction; we also wanted to explore the nature of the interaction with abstracted faces. The second tele-sculpture was motorized so that the remote user could direct the gaze. This offered more control to the remote user and a focus for attention to the local users at the physical *Chit Chat Club*. The third tele-sculpture moved further from the notion of a humanoid face.

At the remote end, the second communication interface contained an abstract expression wheel. The expression wheel was designed to be a simple, intuitive interface for performing facial expressions. Facial expressions composed of componential elements such as the lowering of eyebrows and the raising of lip corners are mapped in smooth transitions around the circle clockwise. Higher intensities of these expressions are at the perimeter of the circle and blend to more neutral expressions towards the center of the circle. To make it easier on the user, there was no clicking involved. One simply had to mouse over the area of the expression. To focus attention on communication while maintaining expression cues during the conversation, we decided to abstract the representation of the expression wheel and make the expression selection somewhat autonomous (see color expression wheel in Fig. 6.7). We do this by tracking the pitch of the remote user in real time and using simple heuristics to alter facial expression. One example of this is the correlation of rise in pitch to rise in eyebrows. Although, the expression selection is semi-autonomous, the user always has the ability to override the system and select their expression independently. We intentionally did not label expressions. Instead, the user could explore the expression landscape by speaking or moving the mouse.

The abstracted expression wheel allowed the remote user to focus more of their attention on the conversation and less on moving the mouse. There was, however, a trade-off in the expressiveness of the faces. With the automated expression selection, we were cautious not to deduce a false expression. Hence, the arc of the expressions did not always reach the extremes. In retrospect, it was the extreme, cartoon-like animations that provided more of a catalyst for interaction than the subdued ones.

The abstracted visualization in the third tele-sculpture and communication interface depicted excitement, anxiety, and anger in the form of animated lines and curves. The bezier curves were influenced by volume, pitch, and formants from the voice of the remote user. Slow-moving lines depicted calm speech; rapid-moving lines depicted high pitch audio. The radius of the dots along the lines represents the volume of speech. As the remote user drags an image into the remote interface, these images appeared in circles flowing in the stream of lines.

## Physicality

The physical "avatar" seat was designed to be of human scale. The idea was to communicate with an interface that was at the same head level as opposed to a monitor with similar proxemic codes as sitting face to face. If the seat is bigger and looks down on the person, it is intimidating; if it is much smaller, it is often ignored. This way, the remote participant occupied a similar space as the physical participants.

Physicality and human scale were the central social catalysts of *Chit Chat Club*. The physicality makes interaction far different from what happens while staring at a computer screen. In contrast to the *Hydra* system (Buxton, 1992), the human scale in *Chit Chat Club* provides gestural behaviors at eye-level and not to several chess-piece-like screens. The similarity in scale blends the physical and virtual world together to emphasize togetherness versus remoteness.

### Time/Motion

In Chit Chat Club motion proved more important than expected. In the interface with faces, users in early interaction were disconcerted when staring at faces with eyes that did not blink. Visitors to the café spent more time interacting with the remote visitors through the tele-sculptures when the eyes on the faces blinked than when they did not.

As mentioned earlier, motion was also an indicator of connection. Because the audio was rendered graphically, when the graphics stopped, visitors assumed that the connection had also "stopped."

The motion of the second tele-sculpture also reinforced the notion of gaze and indicated who was being spoken to by the remote visitor.

Time played more of a role in the third interface than in the other two. All the tele-sculptures became "bored" when no audio had passed through them for some time. They "spoke" to the café visitors saying "what happened?" or "why so silent?" The third chair was more affected by time, however, because its visualization had some persistent history. It was more obvious to see if no one said anything – the lines were perfectly straight and there were no dots.

No formal study was conducted using the *Chit Chat Club*. It was presented to hundreds of users and video was collected of the interactions. The first two tele-sculptures were installed in a laboratory setting. The third tele-sculpture, Ginger, was an exhibit at the San Jose Museum of Art during ISEA 2006.

A final note on *Chit Chat Club*: Although the installation emphasizes togetherness, there is an asymmetry in the public and the private. The local physical *Chit Chat Club* occupants perceive more of the social catalysts and the physicality, although they only see an abstracted representation of the remote cafe-goer. In contrast, the remote user sees a fuller view of the participants albeit at a smaller scale and in a physically remote setting.

## Summary

> *I am not, heaven forefend going on to argue for places of maximum gregariousness, social directors for plazas. Anomie would be preferable. What I am suggesting, simply, is that we make places friendlier. We know how. In both the design and management of spaces, there are many ways to make it much easier for people to mingle and meet.*
>
> (William Whyte)

The object of the social catalysts in these projects was not to attract the largest number of people, or was it to create the longest possible conversations. Rather, they were social interrogations to see if people could and would socialize in a mediated environment, and in what situations were best suited for such interaction. The biggest revelation for us was the impact of transformation, abstraction, physicality, and time (motion). We so often replicate face-to-face interaction with technology that we forget to incorporate the magical interactions that make storytelling, expression, and imagination so evocative.

## References

Agamanolis, S. Westner, A., and Bove, V.M. (1997). Reflection of Presence: Toward More Natural and Responsive Telecollaboration. *Proc. SPIE Multimedia Networks*, 3228A.

Bly, S. and Irwin, S. (1993). Media spaces: Bringing people together in a video, audio and computing environment. *Comm. ACM* 36, 1, 28–47.

Boyle, M., Edwards, C., and Greenberg, S. (2002). The Effects of Filtered Video on Awareness and Privacy. *Proceedings of CSCW 2002.*

Buxton, W. (1992). Telepresence: Integrating Shared Task and Person Spaces. *Proceedings of Graphics Interface 1992.*

Donath, J., Karahalios, K., and Viegas Fernanda (2000). Visiphone. *Proceedings of ICAD 2000.*

Dourish, P. and Bly, S. (1992). Portholes: Supporting Awareness in a Distributed Work Group. *Proceedings of CHI'92.*

Galloway, K. and Rabinowitz, S. (1980). Hole in Space. Available at http://www.ecafe.com/getty/HIS/ Accessed June 2008.

Goffman, E. (1963). *Behavior in Public Spaces: Notes on the Social Organization of Gathering.* New York: The Free Press.

Grudin, J. (1988) Why CSCW Applications Fail: Problems in the Design and Evaluation of Organizational Interfaces. *Proceedings of CSCW 1988.*

Hindus, D., Ackerman, M., Mainwaring, S., and Starr, B. (1996). Thunderwire: A Field Study of an Audio-Only Media Space. *CSCW 1996.*

Isaacs E. and Tang J. (1993). What Video Can and Can't Do for Collaboration: A Case Study. *Multimedia'93.*

Ishii, H., Kobayashi, M., and Grudin, J. (1992). Integration of Inter-personal Space and Shared Workspace: ClearBoard Design and Experiments. *Proceedings of CSCW 1992.*

Jacobs, J. (1961). *The Death and Life of Great American Cities.* New York: The Modern Library.

Jancke, G., Venolia, G., Grudin, J., Cadia, J., and Gupta, A. (2001). Linking Public Spaces: Technical and Social Issues. *Proceedings of CHI2001.*

Karahalios, K. and Dobson, K. (2005). Chit Chat Club: Bridging Virtual and Physical Space for Social Interaction. *Extended abstracts of CHI'05.*

Karahalios, K. and Donath, J. (2004). Telemurals: Linking Remote Spaces with Social Catalysts. *Proceedings of CHI'04.*

Krueger, M. (1991). *Artificial Reality II.* Reading, MA: Addison-Wesley.

McCloud, S. (1993). *Understanding Comics.* New York: Kitchen Sink Press.

Pederson, E.R. and Sokoler, T. (1997). AROMA: Abstract Representation of Presence Supporting Mutual Awareness. *Proceedings of CHI'97.*

Scherer, K.R. (1986). Vocal affect expression: A review and a model for future research. *Psychological Bulletin, 99, 143–165.*

Singer, A., Hindus, D., Stifelman, L., and White, S. (1999). Tangible Progress: Less is More in Somewire Audio Space. *Proceedings of CHI'99.*

Smith, I. and Hudson, S. (1995). Low disturbance Audio for Awareness and Privacy in Media Space Applications. *Proceedings of Multimedia'95.*

Tang, J. and Minneman, S. (1991). VideoWhiteboard: Video Shadows to Support Remote Collaboration. *Proceedings of CHI 1991.*

Whyte, W.H. (1988). *City: Rediscovering the Center*. New York: Doubleday.

# Chapter 7
# Privacy Factors in Video-Based Media Spaces

**Michael Boyle, Carman Neustaedter, and Saul Greenberg**

**Abstract** Media space research is accompanied by a long-standing debate on the value of awareness leading to casual interaction versus its potential for intended or unintended privacy invasion. This is not just a matter of technology: the trade-off between the two depends very much on the social makeup of the people using the space, how cameras are actually situated, the kinds of activities that typically happen in the space, and so on. This chapter offers a framework – a descriptive theory – that defines how one can think of privacy while analyzing media spaces and their expected or actual use. The framework outlines existing perspectives on privacy and then decomposes privacy into three normative controls for regulating interpersonal boundaries in an embodied dialectic: solitude, confidentiality, and autonomy. By considering the nuances of these controls, this theory yields a powerful vocabulary of terms that disambiguate the many interrelated and subtle meanings of "privacy."

## Introduction

Video media spaces (VMS) connect small groups of distance-separated collaborators with always-on or always-available video channels. Via these video channels, people gain informal awareness of others' presence and their activities. This awareness permits fine-grained coordination of frequent, light-weight casual interactions. While video media spaces are a promising way to increase group interaction, they are perceived by users and non-users alike to be privacy invasive and privacy insensitive, e.g., Gaver (1992), Bellotti and Sellen (1993), Lee et al. (1997). They permit privacy violations that range from subtle to obvious and from inconsequential to intolerable.

M. Boyle
SMART Technologies ULC

C. Neustaedter
Kodak Research Labs

S. Greenberg
University of Calgary
e-mail: saul.greenberg@ucalgary.ca

S. Harrison (ed.), *Media Space 20+ Years of Mediated Life*,
Computer Supported Cooperative Work,

Even early media spaces proponents, while enthusiastic about the technology, raised concerns about privacy and its potential for sociological and psychological impact. This is evident in the various anecdotes presented in this book from early media space researchers (and users) such as Victoria Bellotti, Bill Buxton, and Deborah Tatar.

Yet, what do we mean when we say "privacy"? If media space persons are concerned about their privacy, do they mean they are worried about others spying on them (surveillance), or being caught by their companions in an embarrassing act, or theft of their video image, or that they would be continually interrupted, or that others would masquerade as them? In reality, privacy is multifaceted, connected with much of daily life and highly dependant on context. Perhaps because of this, privacy has been given considerable diverse treatment by hundreds of authors in scientific, engineering, and humanities literature (Brierley-Newell, 1995). While many have articulated core concepts in privacy, its very diversity gives rise to confusion in the vocabulary crafted to discuss privacy nuances. Different authors may use the same word to describe different concepts or phenomena, or the same author may use different words to describe the same concept/phenomenon without relating the words to one another. Disciplines have their own language, and thus interdisciplinary discussion of privacy is complicated by obvious differences among the stereotypical conceptions of privacy in different domains. Lawyers stereotypically equate privacy with autonomy (being let alone). Psychologists stereotypically equate privacy with solitude (being away from others). Technologists, economists, architects, and others stereotypically equate privacy with confidentiality (keeping secrets).

The goal of this chapter is to unravel this confusion by describing a vocabulary of terms that permit unambiguous and holistic description of privacy in the context of video media space design and use. Collectively, this vocabulary creates a descriptive "theory" about factors affecting privacy and its perception. This vocabulary is built on a broad base formed by others' theoretical descriptions of privacy, e.g., Altman (1975), Bellotti (1998), Palen and Dourish (2003), and Schwartz (1968). The vocabulary explanations given below distil concepts explained in detail in our own prior work (Boyle et al., 2000; Neustaedter and Greenberg, 2003; Neustaedter, 2003; Boyle, 2005; Boyle and Greenberg, 2005; Neustaedter et al., 2006), which in turn should be used as a source for further explication.

Tables 7.1–7.5 outline the vocabulary of terms that will be discussed throughout the chapter. In the text below, terms are bolded and a reference to their location in the tables is included. For example, if the text reads normative (3.b.ii) then the vocabulary term, normative, can be found in Table 7.3 under item (b) and sub-item (ii). In some cases, slight derivations of the bolded words will appear in the table (in order to match the writing's structure). Our discussion of the vocabulary terms synthesizes the existing literature, presents new insights and organization, and directly relates the discussion to VMS design itself (at least as much as space allows).

We begin with an overview. Section 2 outlines the varying perspectives and approaches to understanding privacy in media space design. Section 3 builds on this work by outlining three control modalities for privacy in VMS – solitude, confidentiality, and autonomy – that form the core of our descriptive theory. The tables are central to our discussions, and should be read in their own right before starting. The tables by themselves should be considered a chart categorizing and classifying

**Table 7.1** Vocabulary terms for SOLITUDE

| 1. SOLITUDE | | |
|---|---|---|
| (a) Physical Dimensions | (b) Psychological Dimensions | (c) Presentation Dimensions |
| (i) Interpersonal Distance | (i) Interaction to withdrawal | (i) High-level Aawareness |
| 1. Isolation to crowding | 1. Anonymity and reserve to intimacy | 1. Availability |
| | | 2. Accessibility |
| (ii) Attention | (ii) Escape | (ii) Distraction |
| 1. Focus to periphery | 1. Refuge | 1. Relevance |
| | 2. Fantasy | 2. Salience |

**Table 7.2** Vocabulary terms for CONFIDENTIALITY

| 2. CONFIDENTIALITY | | |
|---|---|---|
| (a) Information Channels | (b) Information Characteristics | (c) Information Operations |
| (i) Medium | (i) Basic Characteristics | (i) Basic Operations |
| 1. Aural | 1. Sensitivity | 1. Capture |
| 2. Visual | 2. Persistence | 2. Archival |
| 3. Numeric | 3. Transitivity | 3. Edit |
| 4. Textual | | |
| (ii) Processing | (ii) Fidelity | (ii) Intention/Use |
| 1. Sampling | 1. Precision | 1. Accountability |
| 2. Interpolation | 2. Accuracy | 2. Misappropriation |
| 3. Aggregation | 3. Misinformation | 3. Misuse |
| 4. Inference | 4. Disinformation | |
| (iii) Topic | (iii) Certainty | (iii) Scrutiny |
| 1. Information about the self | 1. Plausible deniability | 1. Surreptitious surveillance |
| 2. Personally identifying information | 2. Ambiguity | 2. Analysis |
| 3. Activities | | |
| 4. Whereabouts | | |
| 5. Encounters | | |
| 6. Utterances | | |
| 7. Actions | | |
| 8. Relationships | | |

the various terms for privacy, while the text explicates the meanings of the words within it. Though the tables are presented as a hierarchy, it is really a semantic web; thus our descriptions of terms often cut across the categories and classification boundaries in Tables 7.1–7.5.

## Perspectives on Privacy

"Private" is often defined as the opposite of "public": public is to "being together" as private is to "being apart." Brierley-Newell (1998) found this to be the most fundamental and broad cross-cultural conceptualization of privacy. Being apart, though, is different from being alone. For example, one can be with one's lover and

**Table 7.3** Vocabulary terms for AUTONOMY

| 3. AUTONOMY | |
|---|---|
| (a) Social Constructions of the Self | (b) Social Environment |
| (i) Front | (i) Social relationships |
| 1. Identity | 1. Roles |
| 2. Digital persona | 2. Power |
| 3. Appearance | 3. Obligations |
| 4. Impression | 4. Status divisions |
| 5. Personal space | 5. Trust |
| (ii) Back | (ii) Norms |
| 1. Flaws | 1. Expectations |
| 2. Deviance | 2. Preferences |
| 3. Idealizations | 3. Social acceptability |
| (iii) Signifiers | 4. Conformance |
| 1. Territory | 5. Deviance |
| 2. Props | 6. Place |
| 3. Costumes | |
| (iv) Harms | |
| 1. Aesthetic | |
| 2. Strategic | |

**Table 7.4** Vocabulary terms for MECHANICS OF PRIVACY

| 4. MECHANICS OF PRIVACY | | |
|---|---|---|
| (a) Boundaries | (b) Process Characteristics | (c) Violations |
| (i) Disclosure | (i) Dialectic | (i) Risk |
| (ii) Temporal | (ii) Dynamic | (ii) Possibility |
| (iii) Spatial | (iii) Regulation | (iii) Probability |
| (iv) Identity | (iv) Cooperation | (iv) Severity |
| | | (v) Threat |
| (d) Behavioral and Cognitive Phenomena | (e) Environmental Support | |
| (i) Self-appropriation | (i) Situated action | |
| (ii) Genres of disclosure | (ii) Reflexive interpretability of action | |
| (iii) Policing | (iii) Constraints | |
| (iv) Reprimand | (iv) Transitions | |
| (v) Reward | (v) Choice | |
| (vi) Risk/reward trade-off | (vi) Reciprocity | |
| (vii) Disclosure boundary tension | (vii) Liberty | |
| (viii) Disinformation | (viii) Refuge | |
| (ix) Reserve | (ix) Embodiments | |
| (x) Signifiers | 1. Rich to impoverished | |
| 1. Implicit | (x) Cues | |
| 2. Explicit | 1. Feedback | |
| | 2. Feed-through | |

**Table 7.5** Vocabulary terms for COMPUTERS AND PRIVACY

| 5. COMPUTERS AND PRIVACY | | |
|---|---|---|
| (a) Support Methods | (b) Problems | (c) User Interface Issues |
| (i) Computer security | (i) Inadvertent privacy infractions | (i) Degrees of temporal/ spatial freedom for information access |
| (ii) Cryptography | (ii) Apprehension | (ii) Risk/reward disparity |
| (iii) Pseudonymity | (iii) Resentment | (iii) Feedback and Control |
| (iv) Access control | (iv) The four 'D's: decontextualization, disembodiment, dissociation, desituated action | 1. Believability |
| 1. Authentication | | 2. Socially natural qualities |
| 2. Authorization | | 3. Utility of privacy countermeasures |
| (v) Content Control | (v) Role conflict | (iv) Effort |
| 1. Distortion filtration | (vi) Deliberate abuse | 1. Cognitive |
| 2. Publication filtration | 1. Misappropriation | 2. Physical |
| (vi) Reliability | 2. Misuse | 3. Lightweight control |
| 1. Data integrity | 3. Identity theft | (v) Control Granularity |
| 2. Process integrity | 4. Impersonation | 1. Fine- to coarse-grained |
| 3. Stability | | |

the two together are apart from a larger group. The part of one's life lived apart from society was not highly valued in some ancient societies (Hixon, 1987) and strong emphasis was placed on social involvement. Palen and Dourish (2003) call this the **disclosure boundary tension** (4.d.vii): a tension between one wanting/needing/choosing/being private versus public. This tension carries over to VMS design. From an organizational perspective, the video media space is seen positively as it strives to increase the amount of "togetherness" experienced by group members, even though the heightened collaboration and cooperative work may not be something desired by all individuals at all times.

## *Privacy as an Interpersonal Process*

One perspective of privacy identified by Brierley–Newell is that human behaviors are part of a **privacy process** (4.b). Altman (1975) in particular sees it as a **boundary-regulation** (4.b.iii) process which facilitates the negotiation of access to the self. The **self** (3.a) broadly refers to the totality of a person: his/her body, thoughts and personality, and information about him/her. The negotiation occurs between the self and the **environment** (4.e): the physical environment and also the social environment, i.e., the people immediately nearby and society at large.

Altman's privacy process is a **dialectic** (4.b.i). The actual level of privacy attained is decided through a process of negotiation between the self and the environment. This dialectic is **normative** (3.b.ii). Altman draws a sharp distinction between desired privacy and attained privacy. People's desired privacy is constrained by the environment to socially accepted (normal) levels. What constitutes a privacy **violation** (4.c) is defined against the same set of norms, some of which may be codified as laws while others are part of the culture's tacit knowledge. Individual factors are also important. Each person possesses his/her own set of privacy **preferences** (3.b.ii.2) or "personal norms" that determine his/her initial desired privacy level and subsequently influence the privacy dialect. Also, group norms change in response to changes in group membership and so are influenced by individual preferences. This means that privacy regulation is **dynamic** (4.b.ii) and requires the **cooperation** (4.b.iv) of others. Making things even more complicated, there may be a number of norms that can apply in a given situation because one is typically involved in many groups simultaneously, or because of cross-cultural contact.

Altman's privacy process does not deny interactions between the self and the environment, rather it regulates them. When one has too many interactions or, in other words, too little privacy, these interactions can be throttled. For example, a person turns off the media space to get away from others. When the connections with others have been cut so deeply that one has "too much privacy" the privacy process can open access to the self so that a person gets the interactions he craves. For example, a person turns on the media space when he wants to chat with others. This process demands skill or, more likely, **power** (3.b.i.2) that not all persons share equally (Brierley-Newell, 1998) and power relationships become significant when addressing privacy problems in VMS design (Dourish, 1993).

## *Privacy as a Need, Right, and Freedom*

People place great value upon privacy in our society. Privacy is often defined as a legal and moral right and as an inalienable freedom that no other person or institution may lawfully or morally unduly curtail. A privacy that is a right or freedom can be **violated** (4.c). Others' actions may deny one this right or impair one's exercise of it. Thus, it is a privacy violation when others' actions prevent one from obtaining the privacy he needs, he normally enjoys, and society deems that he ought to enjoy. Outcomes vary in **severity** (4.c.iv), which is a subjective measure of how "bad" the harm due to the outcome is.

Privacy can be threatened without necessarily being violated. Privacy **threat** (4.c.v) and privacy **risk** (4.c.i) are used almost synonymously and seem to include the **possibility** (4.c.ii) of a violation, the **probability** (4.c.iii) that it will occur, and the severity of the harm it causes. Risk is quite inescapable: abstractly, if there is insufficient control to outrightly deny the possibility that a violation can occur, then there is some risk. Practically, however, opportunities for violation are held in check by **policing** (4.d.iii): providing punishments, taboos, social consequences such as **resentment** (5.b.iii), etc., to discourage others from doing things that violate one's privacy.

## *Privacy as a Balancing Act*

Aside from hermits and the like, people balance the benefits accrued from social interactions against the risks to privacy, engaging and withdrawing from others to satisfy both the need to be "apart" and the need to be "together." Even though there is risk, there may also be **reward** (4.d.v): benefits to having less privacy than may be possible. Thus, a **trade-off** between **risk and reward** (4.d.vi) exists.

People balance risk and reward in unmediated interactions but come up against problems when attempting to do so in mediated interactions. The technology itself, the ways it can be subverted, and the awkwardness of its interface may hinder their ability to port unmediated interaction skills to the virtual environment. For example, many video media space designs permit some form of **surreptitious surveillance** (2.c.iii.1), i.e., close monitoring or **analysis** (2.c.iii.2) of the environment – usually the presence and activities of others – without revealing much about oneself. This kind of surveillance can come about from seemingly innocent actions. Thus, video media space designs themselves foster **disparity** (5.c.ii) between risk and reward such that reward does not accrue accordingly with risk or, conversely, risk does rise with reward. This concept is illustrated in the subsequent chapter by Friedman et al. where they investigate privacy in public places. Surveillance is also brought up in Chapter 3.4 by Bill Buxton when the admin is concerned about her superiors watching her.

**Reciprocity** (4.e.vi) is a simple rule that states that if *A* can access *B* via channel *C*, then *B* can also access *A* via channel *C*. Reciprocity is often enforced over video media space channels as a technological means for rebalancing this risk/reward disparity (Root, 1988). Yet, reciprocity does not always hold for the physical environment, and sometimes breaking the reciprocity rule is beneficial. For example, it is possible to observe a person to deduce her/his **availability** (1.c.i.1) – willingness to engage in interaction – without disturbing her/him, such as by moving quietly and peeking around the corner of an open office doorway. Some VMS designs, such as the RAVE media, have explored privacy regulation in the absence of reciprocity but these design experiences underscore the need for multiple modalities of support for privacy in any one given system and across systems (Gaver, 1992).

## *Privacy Violations*

A fundamental premise of much privacy research is that privacy is a thing that can be intentionally controlled (to a limited extent) by groups and individuals. This control is afforded by environmental constraints to interactivity. Technology confounds privacy control by lifting or changing these constraints (Palen and Dourish, 2003; Grudin, 2001) and affords new **degrees of temporal and spatial freedom for information access** (5.c.i) (Palen and Dourish, 2003). There is an implicit assumption that there are times when some people – who may or may not be part of the VMS community – go out of their way to violate others' privacy. Thus, even though video media space users might never willingly violate their peers' privacy the system affords the potential for such **deliberate abuses** (5.b.vi). Worse, media spaces are not adequately designed to safeguard against malicious use arising from unauthorized access. Thus, they afford the potential for undiagnosed abuse by outsiders. One example is surreptitious surveillance, which comes up in Chapter 9 within Friedman et al.'s discussion of privacy in public.

Undoubtedly, not all privacy violations are deliberate nor are all opportunities for deliberate privacy abuses capitalized upon. Accidental violations are known to happen from time to time. **Inadvertent privacy infractions** (5.b.i) are believed to occur because media space designs fit poorly with individual human and social factors thereby causing breakdowns in normal social practice (Bellotti, 1998). Specifically, privacy regulation is **situated action** (4.e.i) (Suchman, 1987). Environmental constraints for interactivity keep interactions situated in a temporally and spatially localized context. Technology changes these constraints, causing actions and interactions to be **desituated** and **decontextualized** (5.b.iv) (Grudin, 2001). That is, actions are seen out of their context, or the context is not communicated along with the action.

Related to this is the concept of **self-appropriation** (4.d.i): a regulatory process where people modify their behavior and appearance according to social norms and expectations (Bellotti, 1998). Self-appropriation depends on cues for behavior sense from the environment, such as **place** (3.b.ii.6) and the people in it. For example when a person is at work, she acts, dresses, and speaks to match others' expectations of professionalism. This will differ markedly from how she appropriates herself on the basketball court. As people move between contexts – the office, the bathroom, the hallway, the basketball court, the home – they modify their expectations for social behavior (norms) and adapt their behavior accordingly. The impoverished nature of a video media space means that people often do not appropriate themselves correctly for viewing by distant colleagues. **Disembodiment** (5.b.iv) – where a user becomes cut off from the (multiple) contexts of those people viewing him – confounds self-appropriation and leads to inadvertent privacy violations (Bellotti, 1998).

Privacy violations can be **aesthetic** (3.a.iv.1) – affecting appearances and impressions – or **strategic** (3.a.iv.2) – affecting the execution of plans (Samarajiva, 1997). In social environments, aesthetic privacy violations can have consequences of a strategic nature. Humans, as social creatures, fear and resent both kinds of violations. Nonusers are often so suspicious of the media space that they go out of their way to sabotage the system (Jancke et al., 2001). Even users themselves are often wary about the system's handling of their privacy (Tang et al., 1994). Thus, in addition to specific deliberate or inadvertent privacy threats, prior analysis of video media space privacy indicates that **apprehension** (5.b.ii) itself is a significant problem. Specifically, participants are apprehensive about making bad **impressions** (3.a.i.4) in the media space and the aesthetic or strategic consequences of them.

### *Privacy Control in Media Spaces*

One way to solve deliberate privacy abuses is with **access control** (5.a.iv), which puts into place computer security and cryptographic measures to deny unauthorized individuals access to sensitive information (Smith et al., 1995). While access control is common on virtually all computers, those wishing to restrict access have faced a constant and unrelenting battle with those wishing to crack systems. Another way to solve deliberate privacy abuses is to simply remove sensitive information from the media space so that there is nothing of worth for others to access and to reduce the harm that may result if access control measures are defeated. We call this technique **content control** (5.a.v). It is hard to put this technique into practice in a VMS because the purpose of a media space is to reveal (Gaver, 1992). There is a fundamental trade-off between privacy and the **utility** (5.c.iii.3) of VMS for awareness: for one person in the media space to have richer awareness, others must have necessarily less privacy (Hudson and Smith, 1996).

Figure 7.1 shows several techniques for preserving privacy in video media spaces based on content control. **Distortion filters** (5.a.v.1) such as the blur filter in Fig. 7.1 mask sensitive details in video while still providing a low-fidelity overview useful for awareness (Zhao and Stasko, 1998; Boyle et al., 2000). The technique itself is a kind of **edit** (2.c.i.3) operation that occurs after **capture** (2.c.i.1).

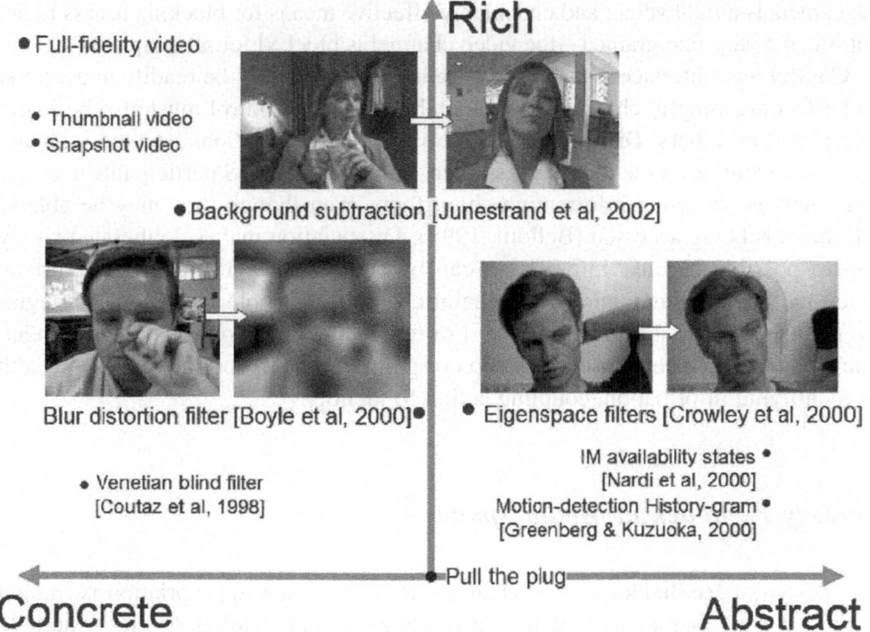


**Fig. 7.1** A design space showing some previously explored techniques for preserving privacy in video media spaces

Distortion filtration operates solely on the **visual information channel** (2.a.i.2). The information is obtained directly from **sampling** (2.a.ii.1) the visual field, rather than being **interpolated** (2.a.ii.2), **aggregated** (2.a.ii.3), or **inferred** (2.a.ii.4) from multiple other context sources. The distorted video image contains some **personally identifying information** (2.a.iii.2), namely people's faces, but mostly contains information that we call **information about the self** (2.a.iii.1): the **actions** (2.a.iii.7) and **activities** (2.a.iii.3), **whereabouts** (2.a.iii.4), and **encounters** (2.a.iii.5) of a person that may or may not be known to or identified by an observer. **Publication filters** (5.a.v.2) such as the background subtraction filter in Fig. 7.1 are similar to distortion filters. They work by removing details from the visual channel that are considered unimportant for awareness information (Coutaz et al., 1998; Junestrand et al., 2001). Finally, potentially privacy-threatening details can be also abstracted away from the video altogether such as in instant messenger status icons and in the eigenspace filter in the figure (Crowley et al., 2000).

The above approaches involve control over what information is in the media space and who gets to see it. It is hard to design a video media space that provides fine-grained control in a lightweight manner, yet both are vital to preserving privacy (Bellotti, 1998). **Fine-grained control** (5.c.v.1) can be adjusted on a person-by-person, instance-by-instance basis. **Lightweight control** (5.c.iv.3) needs little **cognitive** (5.c.iv.1) or **physical** (5.c.iv.2) effort. In the physical environment, strategies for controlling information access are both lightweight and fine-grained. Yet there are few fine-grained yet lightweight strategies for controlling a video media space. Unplugging the camera is a lightweight and undeniably effective means for blocking access to all, but it is not very fine-grained—the video channel is blocked for all recipients.

Control user interfaces must also be **believable** (5.c.iii.1): be readily understood and effect meaningful change in a predictable manner. Control must also be easily interpreted by others. **Dissociation** (5.b.iv), where one's actions become logically separated from one's identity, makes it very difficult for VMS participants to determine who is accessing information about them even though they may be able to tell that it is being accessed (Bellotti, 1998). Dissociation makes deliberate privacy abuses possible because information can be accessed in an unchecked, untraceable, and anonymous manner (Langheinrich, 2001). People have poor strategies for dealing with dissociation because it rarely occurs in the physical environment: one's body, as it is performing an action or gaining access, communicates a wealth of identifying information, coupling action to identity.

## *Privacy Feedback in Media Spaces*

The design of **feedback** (4.e.x.1) channels to support self-appropriation is fraught with technical factors that permit inadvertent privacy violations. It is hard to balance VMS feedback **salience** (1.c.ii.2) and **distraction** (1.c.ii) (Gaver, 1992; Hudson & Smith, 1996; Bellotti, 1998). If feedback cues are not saliently presented they will go unnoticed, fostering disembodiment and poor self-appropriation.

If feedback cues are too distracting, such as lacking **relevance** (1.c.ii.1), there is the risk that the VMS user will either disable the feedback channel or disable the VMS altogether. **Feed-through** (4.e.x.2)—the transmission of cues signaling an action as it is in progress—is related to feedback and is similarly problematic.

It is hard to design VMS feedback cues for self-appropriation that integrate well with social protocol for conversation initiation. In the physical environment, feedback cues are given **socially natural** (5.c.iii.2) forms, placements, and meanings. For example, a person in his office can hear, emanating from the corridor, the footsteps of a colleague approaching him to strike up a conversation. This audible cue signals the onset of interactivity (who, when, and where) and there is a rich, socially-based (and often unconscious) protocol for initiating conversations built around this doorway approach. Providing a media space user interface to support this protocol is full of subtle problems.

Bellotti presents a framework for analyzing deliberate and inadvertent privacy problems in systems and evaluating solutions (Bellotti, 1998). Her framework consists of topic areas for formulating questions about the feedback and control a system affords over information in it and topic areas for evaluating the feedback and control user interface. Bellotti's framework includes **intention** (2.c.ii) for access and minimal needed disclosure as feedback cues that are important to evaluating privacy options. In unmediated settings, intention may be revealed implicitly as a consequence of an attempt to access (prior to access is made) or through explicit (e.g., verbal) communication of it. In either case, the communication process is kept extremely lightweight. It is not lightweight in media spaces. Disembodiment and disassociation confound the implicit signaling of intentionality before access is made. Even if there are audio or text channels, getting everyone into a state where they can use them is not lightweight. Beyond cumbersome user interfaces, networking delays during the initiation of conversation denies quick and graceful transition into it (Tang et al., 1994).

## Privacy as Control Modalities

Many discussions of media spaces attribute privacy problems to inadequacies in control and its exercise (Bellotti, 1998; Grudin, 2001; Palen & Dourish, 2003). For this reason, our descriptive theory of privacy identifies three control modalities by which people control the self-environment boundary (Altman, 1975). These modalities are based on the elements of privacy outlined by Gavison (1980). The control modalities we identify are:

- **Solitude**: control over one's interpersonal interactions, specifically one's attention for interaction (1).
- **Confidentiality**: control over other's access to information about oneself, specifically the fidelity of such accesses (2).
- **Autonomy**: control over the observable manifestations of the self, such as action, appearance, impression and identity (3).

All three modalities of control are negotiated concurrently. Behaviors used to exert one modality of control also have strengthening and weakening implications for the other two. Moreover, the privacy-related actions of one individual operate concurrently with those of all other individuals. Altman's notion of attained privacy is thus the net effect of all these mutually, complementary and competitively interacting privacy-affecting actions.

A similar approach has been taken up by Palen & Dourish (2003). In their framework they identify three boundaries which are congruent to but not direct parallels of the three modalities of privacy control we describe here. The **disclosure boundary** (4.a.i) is regulated mostly by confidentiality, but also by solitude. The **identity boundary** (4.a.iv) is regulated by autonomy. The **temporal boundary** (4.a.ii) spans both identity and disclosure and is regulated by the norms and preferences that are part of solitude, confidentiality and autonomy.

In the next three sections we delve deeply into each of the three modalities of control—solitude, confidentiality and autonomy—to complete the construction of an integrated vocabulary for privacy.

## Solitude

Solitude controls help a person 'be apart' from others and are involved in many behaviors that are vital to human development, e.g., self-evaluation and ego development (Altman, 1975). Being apart is different from being alone: for example, two lovers can find solitude in each other's company, even in a crowded restaurant. 'Togetherness' is thus a continuum of states, and the extremes present failure conditions that yield negative behavioral, psychological, and physiological responses. For example, **crowding** (1.a.i.1) results when others are granted too much access to the self. **Isolation** (1.a.i.1) results when one cannot interact with others to the degree they wish. Both conditions indicate failures in solitude control. Westin (1967) introduces four states along a spectrum of social interactions arising from typical exercise of solitude. These include:

- Total isolation (Westin calls this 'solitude');
- **Intimacy** (1.b.i.1)—the state in which a small group (e.g., lovers) isolate themselves from others;
- **Anonymity** (1.b.i.1)—the state in which one is physically copresent with others and yet not expected to be recognized by them; thus, being free from interactions with them (e.g., 'lost in a crowd'); and,
- **Reserve** (1.b.i.1 and 4.d.ix)—the state in which we can ignore the presence of others who are nearby.

We also generalize solitude to include control over where one directs one's **attention** (1.a.ii)—ranging from one's **focus** to being in the **periphery** (1.a.ii.1)—and how one controls **distraction** (1.c.ii). Most video media spaces require that users expend extra effort to attend to awareness information by presenting it in ways that potentially distract or disrupt people. Thus, media spaces confound solitude, and presence and **availability** (1.c.i) are regulated by solitude. This also relates to problems of 'camera shyness' (Lee et al., 1997) where the heightened self-awareness that people are monitoring one's availability can lead to discomfort (Duval and Wicklund, 1972).

## *Verbal and Para-Verbal Solitude Controls*

A variety of individual and social behaviors are used to regulate solitude. Verbal and para-verbal mechanisms for controlling solitude usually involve signaling availability, e.g., verbally telling another you wish to be left alone or hanging a 'do not disturb' sign outside a hotel door. Desires can be signaled in both the content (the meaning of the words spoken) and the structure (pitch, duration, volume etc. of voice) of speech (Altman and Chemers, 1980). Para-verbal means for signaling one's desired solitude include a posture or facial expressions and explicit gestures to beckon or dismiss others. While these mechanisms are very lightweight in face to face settings, they are easily impaired by limitations of VMS technology. For example, low-quality video (i.e., low resolution, low frame rate, many visible artefacts of compression) mask subtle para-verbal cues for communicating availability. Because such desires must instead be communicated with speech, video media spaces can make the process of signaling solitude desires more explicit and heavyweight. These changes alter social interpretation of the expressed desires.

## *Affordances of Space for Solitude*

To regulate solitude, one can also go someplace to be alone. These places of **refuge** (1.b.ii.1 and 4.e.viii) permit one to 'get away' from the stresses incurred through interactions with others by utilizing **spatial boundaries** (4.a.iii). Yet VMS design complicates refuge-seeking. Although places of refuge from the media space are typically nearby—it is prohibitively expensive to put cameras in every room and so the media space is usually present in only a few locations (e.g., a person's personal office). Awkwardly, the office is where most will retreat to find refuge. A place of refuge can also be created by 'pulling the plug' on the video media space (Neustaedter and Greenberg, 2003). Unfortunately, this disconnected mode of operation is often misinterpreted in many media space implementations as an exceptional error case to which little developer attention is given. Consequently, most hardware and software infrastructures make reconnection so complicated that users are disinclined to 'pull the plug.'

Conversely, when one craves social stimulation, one can go to places where others are. Place partially determines **accessibility** (1.c.i.2), i.e., the effort people must expend to engage others for interaction (Harrison & Dourish, 1996). Architectural spaces can often be reconfigured to raise or lower their permeability to light, matter, and sound. In changing these attributes, people control the affordance of space for interactivity. For example, an office door can be closed to reduce visual and auditory distractions from the corridor and serve as a physical barrier to others' entry. Doors permit fine-grained control because they can be fully closed, slightly ajar, or wide open. Indeed, this becomes a social cue indicating one's solitude desires. In contrast, video media spaces generally provide only one modality for interactivity (an audio/video channel) and offer few ways to configure this channel to signal the desired level of engagement.

People can also capitalize upon the ambiguity inherent in some architectural changes to regulate solitude. For example, a closed door ambiguously symbolizes both absence as well as a wish to be left undisturbed (Root, 1988). People also capitalize on **ambiguity** (2.b.iii.2) when it is possible in computer-mediated environments. For example, Nardi et al. (2000) report that people use the inaccuracies of IM presence indicators as a form of **plausible deniability** (2.b.iii.1) where they ignore requests for conversation from people because they know that the other person will be uncertain if they are really there.

## *Personal Space*

Space and social behavior interoperate with respect to solitude. **Personal space** (3.a.i.5) refers to an invisible boundary in space around a person, separating him from others. The boundary's shape and size varies from moment to moment as part of the privacy dialectic. Although the boundary's characteristics are never made explicit, people show definite behavioral and physiological responses when others physically enter their personal space. **Territory** (3.a.iii.1) is similar, but usually implies a recognizably fixed spatial or psychological location, even if it is defined relative to its owner. Territories are important for the regulation of workspace artefacts and confidentiality and will be discussed later.

Personal space regulates solitude by reducing sensory stimulation due to the presence of or interactions with others. This, in turn, affects attention. At each distance, different sensory capabilities afford different modes for interaction. Hall describes four interpersonal zones, each with differing modalities for social interaction; these are given in Table 7.6 (Hall, 1966). Because of this relationship between distance and interaction, distance itself becomes imbued with social meaning (Altman, 1975). For example, consider when one person sits down at the same table as another. If the newcomer sits diagonally across the table and out of direct eye contact, he sends a solitude-related message that differs markedly from when he chooses to sit directly across the person and in easy eye contact.

Personal space, as a tool for solitude regulation, depends on having a range of **interpersonal distances** (1.a.i) at which people may space themselves. These distances define modalities for interaction that differ in both affordances for interaction and the attention or engagement needed to sustain such interactions. These distances are thus imbued with social meanings. Typically, in a video media

**Table 7.6** Interpersonal distances and the interactions supported at each (Hall, 1966)

| Distance | Modality | Interaction capabilities |
|---|---|---|
| Public distance (> 5 m) | Gross Vision | Gross assessments of posture and large gestures; facial expressions and gaze not visible |
| Social distance (< 4 m) | Hearing | Speech content and structure |
| Personal distance (< 2 m) | Detailed Vision | Posture, gestures, gaze, facial expressions involving eyes and mouth (e.g., wink, smile) |
| Interpersonal zone (< 0.5 m) | Touch and Smell | Exchange, inspect, and manipulate artifacts; physical contact (e.g., handshake, hug); perfume |

space the camera position and display size dictates the visual distance between people; these are sometimes arbitrary and do not represent the desired social distance. For example, seeing a tightly cropped face shot on a large video monitor places someone visually close, but the mannerisms exhibited by that person may reflect actions of someone who is in fact quite far away.

The concept of interpersonal distance in a VMS can be even further generalized to include engagement and connectivity. In a typical VMS, only two or three such distances are offered: full interconnectivity; connected to just one other person; and, disconnected from everyone. The limited choices for connectivity make the media space a crude tool for the selective expression of social interest for interactivity. Moreover, in physically colocated settings, adjusting distances is very lightweight and can be continuously adapted by just moving around. In contrast, media spaces offer highly discrete choices selected using heavyweight GUIs and limit degrees of freedom, e.g., it is awkward to reposition the VMS camera because of limited cable lengths, lighting, shelf space, and similar factors.

## Confidentiality

Confidentiality is the control of access to information about oneself, e.g., informal awareness cues, intentions, vital statistics, thoughts and feelings, medical history, criminal record. Thus, confidentiality is about controlling **aural** (2.a.i.1), **visual** (2.a.i.2), **numeric** (2.a.i.3), and even **textual** (2.a.i.4) information. Controlling access is as much granting access as it is restricting it. Secrecy is similar to confidentiality but narrower because secrecy emphasizes that the information is concealed from certain people. Secrecy modulates the communication of information to others, but this is only one aspect of confidentiality. Palen & Dourish (2003) use the term disclosure to describe deliberate control over what information is communicated, to whom, when, and how.

Confidentiality and solitude are of course related. Confidentiality directly regulates the outward flow of information and thereby indirectly others' attention, whereas solitude directly regulates one's own attention by indirectly regulating the inward flow of information from others. As noted earlier, there is a fundamental tension between confidentiality and the goal of the video media space to reveal informal awareness cues (the disclosure boundary tension described by Palen & Dourish). Hence, there is tension regarding confidentiality in the design of a video media space. Confidentiality and autonomy are related as information yields power to affect livelihood (e.g., coercion, competitive advantage), personal safety or autonomy (e.g., interference or intervention).

**Sensitivity** (2.b.i.1) is a property of a piece of information that can be defined as a perception of how important it is to maintain control over access to it (Adams, 2000). Others' impressions of a person are predicated upon their knowledge of her, and so confidentiality is part of impression management (Goffman, 1959). The harms that could arise from breeches of confidentiality include embarrassment, damage to ego and identity, loss of others' esteem, and possibly impairment of livelihood. Video media spaces can, of course, easily reveal sensitive information when they unintentionally capture and transmit a person's image that, for example, shows that person in a socially unacceptable act.

## *Computers and Confidentiality*

Increasingly, computers are being used to store or transmit confidential information and **computer security** (5.a.i) holistically addresses many aspects of confidentiality. **Authorization** (5.a.iv.2) is control not only over access, but also use, i.e., a person's intention for using the system or the information it provides, or outcomes of access. **Data integrity** (5.a.vi.1) concerns ensuring that persisted information about oneself is not modified or transmitted information is not modified en-route. Both of these are obviously part of confidentiality. **Process integrity** (5.a.vi.2), availability, responsiveness, and reliability concern ensuring that computers perform their intended function when requested correctly and completely in an expected amount of time with no undesired side-effects. Process integrity is an important component of confidentiality because, as stated in the introduction to this section, confidentiality includes ensuring a person has all the access he/she has been granted. **Cryptographic methods** (5.a.ii) are used to provide access control and verify the identity of the receiver or sender of information and check the integrity of the message (e.g., with digital signatures).

## *Fidelity*

**Fidelity** (2.b.ii) is one aspect of confidentiality that has been studied in detail as it relates to VMS design. Fidelity is a perception of how faithfully a piece of information represents some truth. It includes both **precision** (2.b.ii.1)—how detailed the information is perceived— and **accuracy** (2.b.ii.2)—the confidence or certainty one places in the information, or the error in its perception. The same essential truth or description of circumstance may be perceived at a variety of fidelities. Information about oneself—the object of confidentiality—may be known by different individuals at different fidelities. The perceived fidelity of information is also not static. It is influenced by the **trust** (3.b.i.5) one places in the sender and the number of recipients. We also consider that information has properties such as **persistency** (2.b.i.2) and **transitivity** (2.b.i.3) that are relevant to confidentiality. Information may change when it is transmitted between people, such as through oral or written statements or when it is permanently recorded. Hence, confidentiality also involves the regulation of the fidelity of information that third parties transmit about us.

Within VMS design, confidentiality includes control over fidelity. Confidentiality is breeched when a person is unable to control the fidelity at which others are able to access her/his information. Video media spaces have several dimensions for video fidelity, e.g., field of view, resolution, frame rate, codec quality, latency, jitter, etc. Technology places an upper bound on most of these parameters, and these bounds are usually much lower than in face to face situations. For example, although a person can move his head or body to very easily change his field of view to encompass virtually any area around that person, the field of view in a video media space is typically fixed because the cameras lack pan/tilt/zoom capabilities.

Despite these upper bounds, video is nonetheless a high-fidelity medium for informal awareness and casual interactions. This is both part of the appeal of video and a source of confidentiality problems. Undoubtedly, video offers more fidelity than is genuinely needed in many scenarios, even between intimate collaborators. Consequently, many video media space designs try to preserve confidentiality by discarding fidelity. This typically involves using techniques that mask the video with distortion filters such as a blur filter (Boyle et al., 2000). The premise is that appropriate masking can find a balance by providing just enough awareness information to be useful, while not too much to violate confidentiality. These techniques presume that sensitive information lies mostly in image details and so low-fidelity overviews of the video pose less risk (Hudson and Smith, 1996). Studies have shown, however, that the effectiveness of such techniques is limited when risky situations are captured by the VMS (Neustaedter, 2003; Neustaedter and Greenberg, 2003; Neustaedter et al., 2006).

## *Direct Controls*

Mechanisms for regulating confidentiality overlap greatly with those for solitude, emphasizing their synergistic relationship. The principle means for confidentiality control involve keeping our bodies, possessions, and thoughts accessible to some but inaccessible to others. We consider possessions because things like diaries, driver's licenses, and even automobiles reveal a great deal of sensitive information about a person and are used to mark status and individuality (Schwartz, 1968).

Territoriality and personal space use distance to afford fine-grained control over others' access to our bodies and our things. Similar control is available over speech: a person directs his voice and modulates its volume so as to whisper into the ear of someone nearby without allowing others to hear what is said. Private vocabularies can be used to talk openly among others yet obscure what is being said: e.g., pig latin among children and hand signals in baseball.

Architecture also plays a vital role in the preservation of confidentiality (minimizing leak outs) as well as the preservation of solitude (minimizing leak ins). Walls reduce access via visual and auditory channels. Walls may also be fortified with sound-proofing materials to preserve aural confidentiality as well as solitude. Window blinds may be raised or lowered and doors closed or open to modulate visual confidentiality. Video media spaces afford similar opportunities for regulating confidentiality, for example, turning down microphone volume so as not to be overheard, encoding information with cryptographic methods so others cannot eavesdrop, or using a filtration technique (Boyle et al., 2001).

## *Indirect Controls*

People explicitly state (verbally or para-verbally) their confidentiality desires and perceptions on information sensitivity. For example, one person can tell another to "Keep this secret, okay?" Telling a person that it is important to keep a piece of information secret does not prevent that person from revealing it to others. Yet, people can choose to – and sometimes do – keep others' secrets. People can intuit others' sensitivity perceptions and from these infer self-imposed limits to behavior. While people can keep secrets or assess sensitivity, a particular individual may not keep a secret well, or may ultimately choose not to respect the apparent sensitivity.

Information about others, including confidentiality preferences, are usually revealed over time as one builds and maintains **relationships** (2.a.iii.8) with others. Palen and Dourish (2003) introduce the notion of **genres of disclosure** (4.d.ii) to capture not only institutional (socially constructed) expectations regarding confidentiality but also situational ones that change with the temporal boundary. That is, genres of disclosure are loosely defined patterns of interactions that evolve over time. Because genres of disclosure are loosely defined between people, it is possible to feel that one's privacy has been violated through others' **misappropriation** (2.c.ii.2 and 5.b.vi.1) or **misuse** (2.c.ii.3 and 5.b.vi.2) of confidential information and not just inappropriate disclosure.

However, VMS may change the rules of engagement. For example, a VMS might permanently **archive** (2.c.i.2) video/audio exchanges for later replay, rendering requests to keep information confidential meaningless. Verbally telling those people present to keep matters confidential does not preclude others from listening in later. By the same token, people willingly and unwittingly spread **misinformation** (2.b.ii.3) – unintentionally inaccurate information – and **disinformation**

(2.b.ii.4 and 4.d.viii) – intentionally inaccurate information designed to obscure the truth, i.e., lies. Given this, it is important to incorporate into the VMS design various awareness and interaction channels that can be used to diagnose, police, and **reprimand** (4.d.iv) willful and damaging violations. Similarly, VMS designs should be **accountable** (2.c.ii.1) by letting users know how their sensitive information is being handled within the system.

## Autonomy

Collectively, the freedom to choose how one acts and interacts in the world (freedom of will, also liberty) and the power to act in such a way are taken as the third modality of privacy control: autonomy. In law, **personal liberty** (4.e.vii) is often used synonymously with autonomy. Self-appropriation, described earlier, and autonomy point to the same basic control – control over one's own behavior – yet, autonomy incorporates behaviors that facilitate self-definition and identity. Privacy problems in video media spaces can often be blamed on systems' poor support for managing behavior, identity and impressions. Thus, an understanding of autonomy – which regulates these things – is needed to design a privacy-preserving VMS.

### *Preserving and Constraining Autonomy*

Autonomy is like the "muscle" of privacy in that it must be routinely exercised or it will atrophy. The simplest mechanism for preserving autonomy is to try to do as one wishes. One can communicate to others how important it is that he/she be allowed to do precisely as he/she wishes. Such signaling may be **explicit** (4.d.x.2) in the content of speech or **implicit** (4.d.x.1) in the structure of spoken language, facial expressions, and posture. Informal awareness cues for availability and simultaneously reveals one's autonomy desires.

Autonomy can be impaired when technology robs media space users of the opportunity to choose when and how they participate in the media space community. While there are cases in which media space participation is effectively mandated by an organization's culture, in such cases the social fabric of the organization has evolved through an extended period of use (Harper, 1996). Introducing video into home offices also engenders several different kinds of privacy fears, one of which is related to loss of autonomy. One of the advantages of working from home is the ability to set one's own schedule. Home workers often work at irregular times outside the typical "9 to 5" hours to better accommodate the demands of family life they hope to balance by working at home in the first place. A video media space that connects home and corporate offices blurs the clear separation between one's presence at home and one's presence at work. This could introduce social pressure to schedule one's activities at home to fit the work context, effectively robbing them of the opportunity to decide when they work.

Exercising autonomy does not imply that one "always gets one's way." Although the sanctity of autonomy is enshrined in law – people are granted the rights and freedom needed to enjoy life, each according to her/his own will – both autonomy and our legal entitlement to it take part in a dialectic based on group norms. Each may do as he/she wishes, so long as her/his actions conform to group **expectations** (3.b.ii.1). Indeed, as part of the normal regulation of autonomy, one routinely adjusts one's behavior so that one may live cordially among others. This involves acting in a manner that is **socially acceptable** (3.b.ii.3), which may entail **conforming** (3.b.ii.4) to group norms. This is essentially self-appropriation. Thus, autonomy is generally constrained rather than compromised by group norms. Yet, if group norms change faster than people can adapt, or insufficient feedback about the presence and activities of others is offered to support self-appropriation, autonomy can be compromised.

Beyond self-imposed limits to autonomy, others may directly constrain it. For example, institutionalized people often incur great losses in autonomy (Altman, 1975). Parents often restrict the autonomy of their young children to keep them safe and to socialize them (teach them how to behave properly in society). Constraints to autonomy are the primary means for punishing bad behavior: adults who commit crimes are incarcerated and children who disobey their parents are grounded. These observations have implications for VMS design. Fundamentally, the single-user interface to a social technology like video media spaces eliminates social governance of its use.

## *Autonomy–Confidentiality–Solitude Symbiosis*

The second way in which autonomy is like the muscle of privacy regulation is that it provides people with the power to enact their privacy **choices** (4.e.v), i.e., to control information access and direct attention for interactions. Solitude and confidentiality intrinsically depend on autonomy in a readily understood way. Yet, the converse is also true: one cannot have autonomy without solitude and confidentiality. Solitude is needed for self-reflection and the formulation of future plans (Altman, 1975). Solitude also affords a person with confidentiality needed to perform socially unacceptable acts. Confidentiality is also needed to preserve autonomy when others can use privileged information to thwart one's short- and long-term plans. Because of the symbiotic relationship between solitude, confidentiality, and autonomy, when a VMS design impairs the regulation of one kind of control, the other two may also be negatively affected. For example, when cameras are ubiquitously embedded into every corner of our physical space, their pervasiveness makes it difficult for people to find opportunities to be apart from others (i.e., regulate solitude) and thus limits choices for autonomy where they cannot behave as desired because they are being watched.

Some important autonomy-related terms can be borrowed from Goffman's (1965) framework for self-presentation. People are actors who have **fronts** (3.a.i) which serve as conduits for the social expression of self and team identities. A front is manifested in actions: **utterances** (2.a.iii.6) and interactions, as well as various verbal and nonverbal **signifiers** (3.a.iii): social setting such as location, scenery, **props** (3.a.iii.2); **appearance** (3.a.i.3) such as **costumes** (3.a.iii.3) and props, posture, expressions, gestures; and, manners. These signifiers have social meanings which contribute to the front. As such, fronts can become institutionalized and the audiences' expectations of a front become part of the front itself. Fronts are carefully constructed and maintained (e.g., by confidentiality) to ensure homogeneity between performances. The **back** (3.a.ii) is a secondary presentation of the self to only the team (for team fronts) or the individual herself/himself. Here, **deviance** (3.a.ii.2 and 3.b.ii.5) occurs and the self is maintained. If left unchecked, there is the possibility that unconscious backstage performances such as **fantasy** (1.b.ii.2) can be made into lapses in a desired self-appropriation in the front.

## *Identity*

Autonomy also includes control over **identity** (3.a.i.1) and its expression, e.g., a person's likeness (visual physical appearance and mannerisms, and the sound of one's voice) and names (e.g., signature or seal). National identity cards, passports, driver's license, credit cards, and so forth are tangible artifacts revealing identity. These exist separately from a person's body and may be held in possession or reproduced by others. Electronic equivalents include email addresses, personal web pages, and network IDs. These make up part of one's **digital persona** (3.a.i.2) (Clarke, 1994). While there are legal safeguards to discourage others from mishandling one's conventional identity, such as civil penalties for libel or unauthorized use of one's identity to promote a product or service, these are still sadly lacking in the electronic medium. With no recourse to reprimand violators, computer system users must turn to privacy-enhancing technologies to protect their online identities, usually by preserving the confidentiality of one's digital persona (Burkert, 1998).

Identity is highly relevant to VMS design. Dissociation relates to identity because the virtual **embodiments** (4.e.ix) of people – which signal presence and afford means to interact with others and access information about them – do not, unlike our corporeal bodies, reveal identity. This is despite a range of possible embodiments offering varying degrees of information from **rich to impoverished** (4.e.ix.1). Computer security also relates. **Impersonation** (5.b.vi.4) is the act of assuming the identity of another, usually without authority. **Identity theft** (5.b.vi.3) is a form of impersonation that usually involves theft of documents used to **authenticate** (5.a.iv.1) (confirm the identity of) an individual. Confidentiality guards against this type of crime, but vigilance is required to keep identifying information and authenticating documents out of the hands of malicious individuals. Just as reserve promotes confidentiality, minimizing the amount of identifying material that exists physically separate from an individual preserves her/his control over her/his own identity. Oddly enough, certain privacy-preserving techniques used in video media spaces can create situations that confuse identity. For example, distortion filters that greatly blur an image, or substitute actors in the video with stock images can make one person unintentionally appear as another (Crowley et al., 2000).

## *Pseudonymity*

A person is typically involved in a number of intersecting and disjoint social worlds. **Pseudnyms** (5.a.iii) are alternate identities which one creates and uses for interactions within each environment. Often, each identity is used in a distinct social world and little is revealed that relates one's identity to the others. Transportation and telecommunication technologies facilitate pseudonymity by allowing social circles to extend across large geographic ranges and population bases, decreasing the likelihood that a person who is part of one social world is also part of or communicates with members of another. Also, some telecommunication technologies permit anonymity by allowing one's interactions with the environment to proceed in a way that limits the revealing of identifying information. Video media spaces are at odds with pseudonymity because much identifying information is communicated in the video image of one's face and body. While video manipulation techniques could conceivably replace a person's real visage with an artificial one, such algorithms are tricky to implement in practice, require considerable setup for creating replacement images for multiple identities, and likely reduce the value of the video channel for expressive communication.

## *Role Conflict*

People often assume different **roles** (3.b.i.1) as they move between social worlds. A single person may have the role of a stern leader when working with underlings, a supplicant when working with her boss, a parent when with her children, a lover when with her mate, and a slob when alone at home. This implies possible **status divisions** (3.b.i.4) and can also create certain role **obligations** (3.b.i.3). **Role conflict** (5.b.v) (Adler and Adler, 1991) can result when previously nonoverlapping social worlds collide and one is forced to assume two previously distinct roles simultaneously, exposing each to people whom one would rather not. The classical example of role conflict in the non-mediated environment is when parents go to visit their children at their college dormitory: the children must simultaneously play the role of "children" in the eyes of their parents and "adults" in the eyes of their peers.

Role conflict can be a major problem in video media spaces. The purpose of the media space is to connect physically distributed people, but its users will likely inhabit quite different physical contexts. By virtue of connecting two physically disjoint spaces – each embodying their own, possibly different sets of privacy norms – the media space creates opportunities for role conflict akin to problems with self-appropriation. Moreover, there is an analogue of role conflict for privacy norms: decontextualization confuses which norms apply in a given circumstance (Palen and Dourish, 2003). These problems are particularly evident when the VMS connects both home and corporate offices. The home worker must simultaneously play the role of an office worker (because he is connected to the remote office site), a disciplinarian parent and intimate partner (when children or mates enter the home office), and a relaxed home inhabitant (when he is alone at home and forgets he is connected). Role conflict fosters opportunities for inadvertent privacy violations and contributes to the apprehension participants feel towards the media space.

## Conclusion

This chapter has described a comprehensive vocabulary of privacy – a descriptive theory – that permits unambiguous description of privacy-related phenomena and issues connected with the design of video media spaces. This includes the discussion of various perspectives on privacy as it relates to video media space design, as well as three control modalities – solitude, confidentiality, and autonomy – used by people to regulate privacy in their environment.

The chapter does not explain how to apply this vocabulary. One approach is to systematically analyze video media space designs using our vocabulary and its discussion, a process described in detail by Boyle (2005). To summarize, designers and practitioners can analyze VMS designs using vocabulary terms from one or more of the sections reflected in Tables 7.1–7.5. They first select their focus in the table, and then systematically describe each aspect of their system in an unambiguous manner using the vocabulary terms from the descriptive theory. Subtle omissions or discrepancies between privacy as conceived in the descriptive theory versus privacy as embodied in the object of analysis highlight areas for future iteration on the design. It is not a checklist, as there could be good reasons for not attending to some of the phenomena implied by a particular vocabulary term. However, each term reminds the analyst about whether they have considered that phenomenon. Overall, this process should allow designers and practitioners to understand the merits and demerits of the design and any privacy safeguards found within it. This understanding can in turn indicate directions for further iterative or exploratory design. Boyle (2005) further applies this vocabulary to compare various privacy theories for completeness.

Naturally, there are limits to the work we have presented. It is not generative, i.e., it does not lead directly to design ideas, their implementation, or their evaluation. Rather, as a descriptive theory our work informs the analysis of video media space systems within their real world context. In particular, it is capable of revealing assumptions hidden in the design, or the implementation, or the evaluation (Boyle, 2005).

Although there has been a considerable corpus of work-relating privacy problems to the design of social technologies, there is tremendous work yet to be done. In particular, we still need to advance the state of our understanding from individual words that describe privacy, to axioms that explain what "privacy-preserving" means, to models that will drive the design and verification of privacy supporting social technologies. It is likely that each term in our vocabulary could generate a research investigation in its own right! Our work is a first step in this direction.

## References


Adams A (2000) Multimedia Information Changes the Whole Privacy Ballgame, in *Proceedings of Computers, Freedom, and Privacy 2000: Challenging the Assumptions*. ACM Press, Toronto, Ontario, Canada, pp. 25–32

Adler P and Adler P (1991) *Backboards and Blackboards*. Columbia University Press, New York

Altman I (1975) *The Environment and Social Behavior: Privacy, Personal Space, Territory, Crowding*. Wadsworth Publishing, Belmont, CA

Altman I and Chemers M (1980) *Culture and Environment*. Wadsworth Publishing, Stanford, CT

Bellotti V (1998) Design for Privacy in Multimedia Computing and Communications Environments, in *Technology and Privacy: The New Landscape*. Agre and Rotenberg eds., MIT Press, Massachusetts, pp. 63–98

Bellotti V and Sellen A (1993) Design for Privacy in Ubiquitous Computing Environments, in *Proceedings of the Third European Conference on Computer-Supported Cooperative Work (ECSCW'93)*. Kluwer, Milan, pp. 77–92

Boyle M (2005) Privacy in Video Media Spaces. Ph.D. Dissertation, Department of Computer Science, Calgary, Canada

Boyle M, Edwards C, and Greenberg S (2000) The Effects of Filtered Video on Awareness and Privacy, in *Proceedings of the CSCW 2000 Conference on Computer Supported Cooperative Work* [CHI Letters 2(3)]. ACM Press, New Orleans, pp. 1–10

Boyle M and Greenberg S (2005) The Language of Privacy: Learning from Video Media Space Analysis and Design. *ACM Transactions on Computer-Human Interaction (TOCHI)*. 12 (2), June, 328–370, ACM Press

Brierley-Newell P (1995) Perspectives on Privacy, in *Journal of Environmental Psychology*, vol. 15, Academic Press, New York, pp. 87–104

Brierley-Newell P (1998) A cross-cultural comparison of privacy definitions and functions: A systems approach, in *Journal of Environmental Psychology*, vol. 18, Academic Press, New York, pp. 357–371

Burkert H (1998) Privacy-Enhancing Technologies: Typology, Critique, Vision, in *Technology and Privacy: The New Landscape*, P Agre and M Rottenberg, eds. MIT Press, Cambridge, MA, pp. 125–142

Clarke R (1994) The digital persona and its application to data surveillance, in *The Information Society*, 10:2. Taylor and Francis, New York, pp. 77–92

Coutaz J, Bérard F, Carraux E, and Crowley J (1998) Early Experiences with the mediaspace CoMedi, in *IFIP Working Conference on Engineering for Human-Computer Interaction (EHCI'98)*, Heraklion, Greece

Crowley JL, Coutaz J, and Bérard F (2000) Things That See, in *Communications of the ACM*, ACM Press, 43(3), 54–64

Dourish, P (1993) Culture and Control in a Media Space, in *Proceedings of the Third European Conference on Computer-Supported Cooperative Work (ECSCW'93)*, Kluwer Academic Publishers, Milan, pp. 125–138

Duval S and Wicklund R (1972) *A Theory of Objective Self-Awareness*. Academic Press, New York

Gaver W (1992) The Affordances of Media Spaces for Collaboration, in *Proceedings of the Conference on Computer Supported Cooperative Work (CSCW'92)*, Toronto, pp. 17–24

Gavison R (1980) Privacy and the Limits of Law, in *Yale Law Journal*, 89:3 (January), The Yale Law Journal Company, New Haven, CT, pp. 421–471

Goffman E (1959) *The Presentation of Self in Everyday Life*. Doubleday Publishers, Garden City, NY

Grudin J (2001) Desituating Action: Digital Representation of Context, in *Human-Computer Interaction*, 16:2–4, Lawrence Erlbaum Associates, Hillsdale, NJ, pp. 269–286

Hall ET (1966) *Distances in Man: The Hidden Dimension*. Double Day, Garden City, NY

Harper RHR (1996) Why People Do and Don't Wear Active Badges: A Case Study, in *Computer Supported Cooperative Work: The Journal of Collaborative Computing* 4(4), 297–318, Kluwer

Harrison S and Dourish P (1996) Re-place-ing Space: The Roles of Place and Space and Collaborative Systems, in *Proceedings of the Conference on Computer Supported Cooperative Work (CSCW'96, Cambridge)*. ACM Press, New York, pp. 67–76

Hixon R (1987) *Privacy in a public society: Human rights in conflict*. Oxford University Press, New York

Hudson SE and Smith I (1996) Techniques for Addressing Fundamental Privacy and Disruption Tradeoffs in Awareness Support Systems, in *Proceedings of the Conference on Computer Supported Cooperative Work (CSCW'96)*, Cambridge, MA, pp. 248–247

Jancke G, Venolia GD, Grudin J, Cadiz JJ, and Gupta A (2001) Linking Public Spaces: Technical and Social Issues, in *Proceedings of the ACM/SIGCHI Conference on Human Factors in Computing Systems (CHI 2001)*, Seattle, pp. 530–537

Junestrand S, Keijer U, and Tollmar K (2001) Private and public digital domestic spaces, in *International Journal of Human-Computer Studies*, 54, 5 (May), Academic Press, New York, pp. 753–778

Langheinrich M (2001) Privacy by Design—Principles of Privacy-Aware Ubiquitous Systems, in *Proceedings of Ubicomp 2001*, Atlanta

Lee A, Girgensohn A, and Schlueter K (1997) NYNEX Portholes: Initial user reactions and redesign implications, in *Proceedings of the ACM/SIGGROUP Conference on Groupware (GROUP'97)*, ACM Press, New York, pp. 385–394

Nardi BA, Whittaker S, and Bradner E (2000) Interaction and Outeraction: Instant Messaging in Action, in *Proceedings of the Conference on Computer Supported Cooperative Work (CSCW'00)*, Philadelphia 79–89

Neustaedter C (2003) Balancing Privacy and Awareness in a Home Media Space. Masters Thesis, Department of Computer Science, Calgary, Canada

Neustaedter C and Greenberg S (2003) The Design of a Context-Aware Home Media Space, in *Proceedings of UBICOMP 2003 Fifth International Conference on Ubiquitous Computing*. LNCS Vol 2864, Springer-Verlag, Seattle, WA, USA, 297–314

Neustaedter C, Greenberg S, and Boyle M (2006) Blur Filtration Fails to Preserve Privacy for Home-Based Video Conferencing. *ACM Transactions on Computer Human Interactions (TOCHI)* 13(1):1–36

Palen L and Dourish P (2003) Unpacking Privacy for a Networked World, in *Proceedings of the Conference on Human Factors in Computing Systems (CHI 2003, Ft Lauderdale)*, ACM Press, New York, pp. 129–137

Root RW (1988) Design of a Multi-Media Vehicle for Social Browsing, in *Proceedings of the Conference on Computer Supported Cooperative Work (CSCW'88)*, Portland, OR, pp. 25–38

Samarajiva R (1997) Interactivity as Though Privacy Matters, in *Technology and Privacy: The New Landscape*, P. Agre & M. Rottenberg, Eds. MIT Press, Cambridge, MA

Schwartz B (1968) The Social Psychology of Privacy, in *American Journal of Sociology*, 73(6), 741–752, University of Chicago Press, Chicago, IL

Smith I and Hudson S (1995) Low Disturbance Audio for Awareness and Privacy in Media Space Applications, *in Proceedings of the third ACM international conference on Multimedia*, San Fransisco, pp. 91–97

Suchman L (1987) *Plans and Situated Actions: The Problem of Human-Machine Communication*. Cambridge University Press

Tang JC, Isaacs EA, and Rua M (1994) Supporting Distributed Groups with a Montage of Lightweight Interactions, in *Proceedings of the Conference on Computer Supported Cooperative Work (CSCW'94)*, Chapel Hill, NC, pp. 23–34

Westin A (1967) *Privacy and Freedom*. Atheneum, New York

Zhao QA and Stasko JT (1998) Evaluating Image Filtering Based Techniques in Media Space Applications, in *Proceedings of the Conference on Computer Supported Cooperative Work (CSCW'98)*, Seattle, pp. 11–18

# Chapter 8
# Affect and Dyads: Conflict Across Different Technological Media

**Jamika D. Burge and Deborah Tatar**

**Abstract** Communication is as, or more, important under conditions of conflict or disagreement as when agreement prevails. An experiment looked at couples engaged in discussing a topic that they disagreed about, either face-to-face, over the phone, or via instant messaging. At least one member of a couple was more likely to suffer an above-median decline in mood in the mediated condition as compared to the face-to-face condition. Couples in the face-to-face condition used the most words, while those in the instant messaging used the least. Couples in the phone condition nearly covered the spectrum. Current indications suggest that while the answer to the question, "Does arguing via mediated means have worse effects than all the other things in relationships, known and unknown, that contribute to the outcome of an argument?" is "No," the answer to the question, "Does arguing via mediated means have bad effects compared to arguing face-to-face?" is "Quite likely." At the minimum, the course of the argument and the facial expressions differ from medium to medium.

Communication is as, or more, important under conditions of conflict or disagreement as when agreement prevails. If media space integrates audio, video, and computer technologies to "define new methods of communication" (Mantei et al., 1991), the question arises as to whether and how these methods differ under conflict, from unmediated methods.

Although some conflict may be dispassionate, it is most interesting, and perhaps most important, when emotions are also involved. Not surprisingly, given the history of the power of information theory, there have been many attempts in human–computer interaction and communication to characterize the communication of emotion in relatively simple information-theoretic terms. On the other hand, there have been criticisms of this approach that directly or indirectly emphasize

J.D. Burge
The Pennsylvania State University
e-mail: jburge@ist.psu.edu

D. Tatar
Virginia Polytechnic Institute and State University
e-mail: dtatar@cs.vt.edu

S. Harrison (ed.), *Media Space 20+ Years of Mediated Life*,
Computer Supported Cooperative Work,

the situated nature of emotion (Boehner et al., 2007; Suchman, 2007, 1987). These critical studies typically devolve from sociology and anthropology; however, modern psychology also backs them up to some degree. An enduring outcome that challenges any simple, purely information-theoretic account of emotion is the principle that *affect precedes cognition* (Zajonc, 1980). Additionally, from a psychological perspective, emotions are usually thought of as constituted of experiential, behavioral, and physiological components (Gross et al., 2006), a definition which ties the emotion to the communication of that emotion and to the situation. So, on this one point, these disciplines are not as opposed as might be imagined. Conflict involves emotion and emotion is tied to the communication and the setting.

The purpose of this chapter is to advance the understanding of the conduct of discussions involving conflict, across different kinds of media. We present an analysis of an experiment that involved couples discussing issues that they disagreed about in one of the three mediated situations: face-to-face (f2f), telephone, and instant messaging (IM). Our results suggest that there are differences in the experience and outcome of arguing in mediated as compared to unmediated circumstances; that is, while these differences may not trump other factors (i.e., couples "manage" or are basically "all right"), the media may change the ecology of the interaction. While the idea that mediation makes a difference may seem obvious to some, it has been, and ought to be, the subject of hot controversy in the field. The effects of media space are not only a matter of scientific fact, but also a complex and value-laden arena involving what appears to be the case through the examining lens, what might be the case some time in the future, and the culture that evaluates the apparent situation. What is the difference between media? What is an important difference?

We begin by discussing conflict in the laboratory and the workplace, with a mention of workplace interviews conducted by the first author. Then, we present a discussion of media and their effects on communication. Next, we present the design of the current study, describe some of the results of the study and end with important takeaway points that we hope will motivate further research in understanding conflict, understanding couples, and understanding communication across different media.

## Conflict

### In the Laboratory and the Workplace

Conflict is an inevitable component of social interaction and, in particular, of any kind of nonroutinized work. Conflict can be described as an "incompatibility" of opposing values between two people (Ting-Toomey, 1994).

In laboratory explorations of conflict, people have been asked to solve problems or agree on ratings or rankings within different media. For example, it is typical to ask people to come to a consensus on problems such as the Desert Island challenge in which participants are asked to rank the order in which they would remove items from a plane after a crash landing on a desert island in the few minutes before the plane explodes. Both the amount and kind of conflict have been shown to increase in computer-mediated communication (CMC) compared to face-to-face (f2f) under these circumstances (Hobman et al., 2002; Zornoza et al., 2002).

The conflict created in these paradigms may be characterized as "low-stakes" in that strangers are brought together to work on problems assigned by the experimenter, with little likelihood of further personal or social entailment. Furthermore, participants may decide on the importance of resolving the conflict to the experimenters by taking cues from the kind of tasks and media that they are offered and adjust their level of work accordingly.

These approaches also emphasize the ways in which conflict is a property of cognitive processes and rational actors. Yet it is more than that. Ting-Toomey's definition prioritizes values, and values are not optimized in a single-valenced process. This definition is in this way compatible with psychological theories of interaction that emphasize how we manage multiple issues in the course of communication, including the psycholinguistic perspectives that emphasize how we manage communicative intent, referential adequacy, attention, and politeness (e.g., Clark, 1996; and to a small extent, Tatar, 1998) and the interpersonal perspective, which claims that people will be satisfied with an interaction when one person's behavior matches the other person's intention (Horowitz, 2004). Interpersonal psychology suggests that conflict will be about the conduct of the interaction as well as its content. Thus, if both parties seek to dominate one another, and behave in dominating ways, they may be in conflict even if their words appear to agree. Even if one person acts in a submissive way, if his goal was to dominate, he will be in conflict with the other.

Participants in laboratory studies may not have a deep commitment to making progress on the issue. This is also true in other situations. Participants in real work-place conflicts may approach dispute resolution with little or no commitment to creating their desired outcome; however, the reasons are quite different. In semi-structured, ethnographic interviews conducted by the first author of this chapter at a major national research organization, workers were asked to talk about their own experiences of conflict. Most expressed considerable ambivalence about seeking resolution as compared to living with unhappiness, irritation, and anger. In some cases, they were not sure that they wanted resolution at the anticipated price; in others, they did not want to risk exposure of all aspects of the conflict necessary for resolution. There was considerable concern about how exposure would influence the esteem with which they were regarded by third parties. Often, instead of seeking resolution, people sought to avoid or downplay the situation, to avoid interaction altogether with the offending party, or to avoid the topic or person in situations that could threaten their regulation of the situation.

Media richness theory (MRT, Daft and Lengel, 1984, 1986) has been used as explanatory in studies of media *choice*. That is, the theory seeks to answer the question "given an array of possibilities, when do people communicate using one medium as compared to another?" It predicts that if resolution of workplace conflict is more consequential than lack of resolution, parties in workplace conflict may seek less rich rather than more rich media in order to maintain personal control and lower personal accountability to the other. They may choose not only different media, but also *no* media, avoiding the issue altogether. Aoki and Woodruff (2002) have even proposed to build system features based on conflict avoidance. Avoidance systems are certainly an important avenue for exploration, but often conflict is important, and sometimes we have no choice of media.

## *Conflict in Couples*

Couples may also be concerned about pursuing conflicts beyond a certain point. However, they have more reason than workplace partners or strangers to attempt to solve conflict proactively. Their disagreements have (by definition) different meanings and consequences than those in the workplace. Members of a couple have more knowledge of the hopes, dreams, and expectations of the other than do most colleagues. They also have more obligations towards the feelings of the other than do coworkers; indeed, their own self-regard and satisfaction may depend crucially on the ability to be held in the other's esteem. The maintenance of mutual trust may be more salient and significant in romantic relationships than in workplace ones.[1] Parties who have a romantic interest operate on the basis of optimizing shared rather than individual outcomes, that is, they take an extended *communal* as compared to an *exchange* approach to equity (Clark, 1984; Clark and Mills, 1979). Couples differ from one another; Gottman (1994) categorizes couples into three groups – conflict validating, volatile, and avoidant. However, conflict occurs and is significant in virtually all couples.

We argue that communication about conflict in couples is a comparatively high-stakes situation, of importance to participants in the moment and in the long-run. In this way, asking couples to engage in the discussion of a conflictual matter has ecological validity and may be examined from the point of view of what it reveals about the process and nature of conflict in media in general as well as in couples. In this way, the validity of asking couples to argue is comparable to asking researchers to engage in double-sided copying, despite the fact that the participants had no intrinsic interest in doing such copying at that moment, as Suchman did in her seminal work in anthropology and models of human–computer interaction (Suchman, 1987, 2007). Such work is important to undertake because it is likely to reveal conditions and factors that would be more masked in other conditions, which would be extraordinarily difficult to study outside the laboratory. From the point of view of psychological experimentation, what we give up in the appearance of control by allowing couples to choose their own topics, we gain in actual control by locating the phenomena more closely with the object of our investigation.

---

[1] Note that maintenance of trust and a collegial concern with other's happiness is also important in the workplace, and that friendship and loyalty are important components of a happy work life.

## Communication via Different Media

Theories of media fall into three general categories: those that believe that media affects communication, those that do not, and those that believe that the effects are a product of how underlying psychological factors manifest themselves in relationship to media. Starting from the assumption that there are differences between media and with roots in the study of print and broadcast media, Media Richness Theory focuses on media choice (Daft and Lengel, 1986, 1984). Other theories in mass media research focus on consequences of the use of particular media. The cues-filtered-out (Culnan and Markus, 1987), social information processing (SIP, Walther, 1992), and social identity/deindividuation (SIDE, Lea and Spears, 1991; Postmes et al., 2000) theories all characterize peoples' communications via computer-mediated communication at global levels in terms of their outcomes. More recently, there have been targeted explorations of how constructs of importance in the psychology literature manifest themselves in relationship to media. These works argue that the predicted outcomes indicate important factors in the process of media use.

The "cues-filtered-out" approach focuses on the fact that different media have different properties from an informational perspective. It emphasizes the ways in which social cues that are available in some media are reduced or absent in other media. In the context of couples discussing conflict, it suggests that people will be less able to conduct interaction in the restricted atmosphere of IM than in the richer atmosphere of face-to-face interaction. They will neither be able to present their own point of view adequately, nor will they be able to interpret the others'. Therefore, their arguments will be shorter and less conclusive in more impoverished media than in richer media. Consequently, their arguments may also be more distressing. Thus, less of a loss of positive mood and more of a gain in negative mood for arguers in less rich environments is predicted.

In contrast, Social Information Processing (SIP; Walter et al., 1994) argues for effective media equivalency. The idea is that people learn to manage and compensate for any lacking information. SIP predicts that engaging in nonroutine, high-stakes interaction (such as arguing) via different media will produce no media differences from engaging in routine, low-stakes interaction.

A third approach argues that there are media differences, but that they are really quite subtle. SIDE points out that people rely on stereotypes to judge behaviors and calibrate appropriate responses in the absence of information (Lea and Spears, 1991; Postmes et al., 2000). A stereotype is a "generalization about a group of people in which identical characteristics area assigned to virtually all members of the group regardless of actual variation" (Aronson et al., 1994, p. G-11). As important as the SIDE theory is in general, when the interactants are already individuated and well-known, as in a couple, SIDE is unlikely to be predictive.

If one extends SIDE slightly to argue that people will use their personal model of the other in the absence of information, then one argues that precisely the growth in understanding that is crucial to solving difficult interpersonal problems is unlikely in less rich media compared to richer media. This predicts that arguments will be stalemated or unproductive and that interactant behavior and understanding will reflect this. Again, this predicts shorter, less conclusive arguments in more impoverished media than in richer. It also suggests that, in the more impoverished communication outlets, participants may be frustrated with the other person's lack of acknowledgement of them as a unique individual rather than as an abstract model. This may cause the arguments to be more distressing, increasing the loss of positive mood and the gain of negative mood.

A fourth take on Internet communication may be seen as an extension of the third and likewise shares with the cues-filtered-out perspective a focus on human behavior in the absence of information; however, it suggests a more complex mechanism and a different evaluative stance. Like Lea and Spears (1991), Bargh, McKenna, and Fitzsimons (2002) argue that Internet communication is relatively anonymous. They further argue that anonymity enables communicators to engage in self-disclosure, revealing their *true self* more than they would in face-to-face discourse. The true self consists of those aspects of the self that are usually unexpressed, but which are felt by the person to be important to their identity. Because communicators express their true selves more clearly, there is increased liking between communicators compared to face-to-face communicators. This state of liking permits idealization of the other. Like the SIDEs analysis, this analysis is concerned with how people make inferences about one another in the absence of information; however, the information that is filled-in derives from the person's ideals rather than their stereotypes. This line of thought does not make clear predictions about relationships between intimates because anonymity is the crucial feature.

More specific predictions about the relationship between media and circumstances are consonant with lines of work that start with the structure of interaction and point to potentially relevant properties of different media. While remaining neutral about the communicative consequences, Clark and Brennan (1991) outline constraints inherent in different media on communication, pointing out that the nature of communication work in synchronous and asynchronous contexts differs. More recently, Voida, Newstetter, and Mynatt (2002) have identified tropes in IM communication that they attribute to tensions between face-to-face and written genres of communication. Genres are the sets of expectations that readers and writers have for a given kind of communicative production, independent of actual media. Thus, newspapers and novels may both be produced via the same media, but only writers of newspaper articles put the most important information first and only readers of newspaper articles expect that information first. Likewise, different media (i.e., news articles in print or on the web) may share genre-based expectations as when both put the most important information first. Voida et al.'s analysis of genres opens up inquiry because, by existence, it pushes Clark's analysis of the inherent challenges of the media to the question of actual uses in practice. Additionally, Voida et al.'s (2002) analysis is consistent with McLuhan's (1964) observation that first the content of new media are made from the content of old media, then new media finds a new form, and finally aspects of that form are adopted into the old media. Thus, their analysis points the way toward the identification of new forms.

In the current case, we have an important societal phenomenon: that of people engaging in conflict using media. The phenomenon exists in the everyday world but is illusive. It presumably has significance in the workplace, where it is extremely difficult to study, and may be even more significant in interpersonal relationships. Some theories predict that there are no effects of employing different media, others predict that there may be global effects, and yet a third class predicts complex differences that may not obtain in the case of argumentation and people who know one another. Insofar as any of these theories are predictive, they predict an advantage for face-to-face media in the case of known participants and high-stakes conflict, but they also suggest a wealth of considerations at different levels of analysis.

## Study and Results

An experiment was conducted featuring couples arguing with each other using one of three technological media: face-to-face (f2f), phone, and instant messaging (IM).

Decline in mood is used in this study as a proxy for distress. Global measures were used as indicators of mood change by measuring participant states before and after the discussion. Additional global measures looked at feelings of closeness to the partner, participant depression, and preferences in interpersonal interaction. Since depression and interpersonal preferences are generally considered enduring states, they were only measured once. Additionally, participants wrote post hoc accounts of what happened during their arguments. The kind of measures of mood (PANAS, Watson and Clark, 1994), depression (Beck Depression Inventory, Beck, 1972), and interpersonal interaction (Inventory of Interpersonal Problems, Horowitz et al., 2000), descriptors of events and attitudes are common in personality and social psychological literature and might reasonably be expected to uncover differences at the scale of the current experiment.

Interactions were video- and audio-taped. Observational methods were used to characterize videotaped interactions. Face-to-face and phone interactions were transcribed at a rough level including restarts and word repetitions, but not, for example, characterizing overlaps. Observations and characterizations of observations were made by reference to videotapes. In the style of grounded theory (Corbin and Strauss, 1990), the first author of this article watched the videotapes repeatedly and noted phenomena.

Twenty-five self-described, mixed-gender couples were recruited by posters, listservs, and word of mouth on a university campus. All participants were between 18 and 40, with an average male age of 22.8 and an average female age of 22.4. Ten couples were white, nine were African-American, two were Asian, and four were mixed ethnicity/race. As measured by the Beck Depression Inventory, nearly all participants reported at least some signs of dysphoria or depression, excluding one female and four male participants. All couples were eligible for campus couple's counseling services. Working individually, participants were asked to fill out forms asking about their mood, disposition, and feelings about the other and the relationship. The researcher then helped the couples make a shared list of topics they disagreed about, and the couple jointly chose one as the topic to discuss. The couple discussed the topic for 20 min. Then, they were asked to report individually on their mood, their feelings about the other, and what happened during the interaction. Finally, the couple was brought together for a 10-min happy reminiscence session on a topic of their joint choice (usually they talked about when they first met). Their moods were measured separately again to ensure that no one was reporting extreme distress. Participants were informed about the counseling facilities available to them through the university and asked as a couple how they were feeling. Additionally, the researcher contacted each couple after three days to make sure that there had been no untoward effects from participation.

Asking people to discuss an area of conflict may raise ethical concerns. It is worth pointing out that the university counseling center was enthusiastic about the study, as discussion of difficult topics is a normal part of being in a relationship. In this case, because the participants already knew that they had a disagreement about the topic, they had advanced warning, and the territory was already well-trod, they were able to gauge the level of discussion they were willing to hold in the laboratory. Participants were paid $20/each when they arrived, which is enough to buy a nice student dinner in the local community. The researchers were careful to emphasize that the compensation was for appearing, not for participation, that participants were in charge of their own participation, and that they were free to withdraw without explanation at any time. Unlike many arguments, the experiment was conducted during the day rather than late at night. We argue that this method, when used with respect and appropriate caution, brings felt conflict into the laboratory while minimizing the likelihood of damaging extremes.

Couples chose a range of topics. Most couples talked about *how to live*, that is, differences in their attitudes, aspirations, and personal life influences. Many couples also argued about their *home life*, that is, practicalities of chores, and taking care of household responsibilities. The *relationship* itself was often a focus. Last some discussed *politics* and *money*. Figure 8.1 shows a breakdown of the topics discussed.

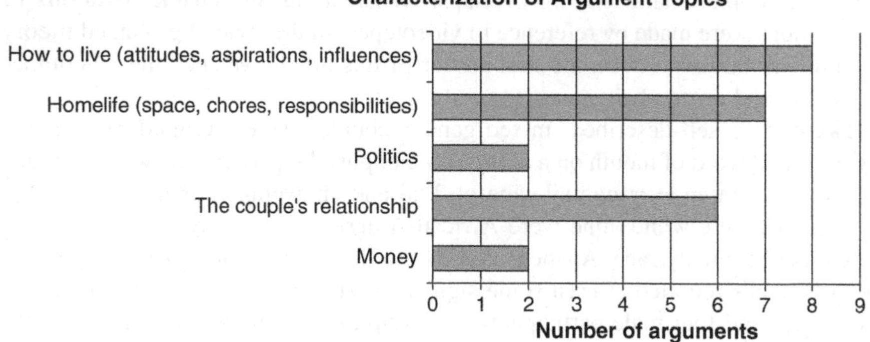


**Fig. 8.1** Characterization of argument topics

## *Analysis of Self and Other Report Data*

### Extent of Conflict

On a five-point Likert scale running from "not a very big argument" to "a very big argument," couples in all conditions reported moderate arguments. On a similar scale, all reported on the average that they reached a moderate degree of closure.

Two undergraduate raters blind to our hypotheses were also asked to watch the video and (in the IM case) read the transcripts of the discussions and characterize them using the same scales as the participants. These characterizations also showed no significant difference between conditions.

Rater comments reflected a complex phenomenology in which arguments were explained in terms of metaphors and images. The idea that an argument involves what is hidden or revealed is reflected in comments such as "seems like a big argument because they are uncovering a lot of deeper issues." Additionally, raters often saw arguments as involving metaphors to pressurized or explosive situations, as "this was a big argument because it was something that had been brewing under the surface for some time."

The PANAS (Positive Affect, Negative Affect Schedule; Watson and Clark, 1994) has two components. Both an increase in negative affect from before to after the encounter and a decrease in positive affect could show elements of a decline in mood. That is, mood decline could reflect more bad feelings and/or fewer good ones after the argument than before.

Further evidence that the couples touched on difficult topics was gleaned from their reported changes in mood. In 22 out of the 25 couples, one or both participants showed a decline in mood from the beginning to the end of the discussion. Only one couple in the IM condition and two in the face-to-face condition reported no such decline. Twenty-one female participants reported a decline in positive mood, and 19 reported an increase in negative mood. Slightly fewer men reported mood changes: 17 and 15, respectively.

### Technological Condition and Mood Change

A relationship between technological condition and decrease in reported mood state from before to after the discussion was anticipated. This was not found in a simple way. That is, an analysis of variance (ANOVA) was run using the three technological conditions (f2f, phone, and IM) as predictors of decline in mood state for a couple. Based on the grounds that the largest decrease in positive or increase in negative mood for either a partner in a couple has the most importance, a decline in mood state for a couple was calculated by taking the absolute value of the largest reported decline in positive or increase in negative mood for either the man or the woman in the couple. The results are nonsignificant ($F(20, 1) = 0.0018$, $p < .91$), strongly suggesting that the level of mood change was *not* related to technological condition.

**Table 8.1** Large declines in couple mood state by whether the couple's interaction was mediated

| | Low distress – neither partner had an above median decline in mood | High distress – at least one partner had an above median decline in mood |
|---|---|---|
| Unmediated interaction | 4 | 4 |
| Mediated interaction | 2 | 15 |

However, a small variation in the way the question is posed suggests the presence of an underlying relationship between technological state and argument process. When we divide couples into mediated – those that conducted their discussions using media (e.g., in the phone and IM conditions) – and unmediated – those that conducted their discussions without mediation (e.g., the f2f condition) groups, we see that a far greater proportion of those in the mediated condition was above the median for distress than those in the unmediated condition ($\chi^2(1) = 4.14$, $p < .05$). That is (Table 8.1), for the f2f condition, the couples are equally split between those couples for whom neither partner reported a substantial decrease in mood and those in which at least one partner did report such a decrease. But both the phone and IM conditions contained only one couple each in which both partners fell below the median. The other seven or eight couples all had at least one particularly distressed partner.

## *Expression*

So far, we have reason to believe that most of the couples actually did argue or at least discuss a difficult topic. Couples by-and-large suffered a decline in mood. It is possible, perhaps likely, that media is associated with mood change.

Mood change can be considered an outcome of importance in its own right. Additionally, reported mood change indicates a change in the cognitive component of emotion, that is, in people's beliefs about their internal states. Reported mood may also indirectly reflect other components of emotion, such as differences in physiological state at the time of the measurements (immediately before and after the actual discussions) or memory of such differences. However, video and audio recordings provide more direct indicators of expression and a more complete story about the emotional experiences of the participants.

Expression may be at once an important component of the emotional experience of the individual and a communicative influence on other people. Bavelas (Bavelas et al., 1986), for example, showed such a dual role for body motion by demonstrating that when people witness others in danger of being hurt, they wince in either direction if the other person cannot see them, but mirror the direction of avoiding the danger if the other person can see them. That is, the wincing movement appears to be an expression of an emotional reaction to witnessing another's harm, but it may also be overlaid with useful information.

In general, the discussions started with a similar pattern: greeting, initiation, and presentation of one point of view. Participants in the phone and IM conditions had been separated physically and had to reinitiate contact via the media, which made a greeting expected. However, the departure of the researcher and the closing of the door seemed to evoke a need for greeting even in the f2f condition, where participants would turn back towards one another (from the door) and often say "hello." In the phone condition, they always greeted one another. However, in IM, sometimes participants omitted the greeting.

Sometimes participants initiated discussion directly by jumping in with a position, but a typical discussion initiation was to comment on the oddity of the situation ("this is weird"), talk about the cameras ("we're supposed to be natural"), and speculate about whether they would be able to hold the discussion.

Then there was a topic switch. Many people started commenting on how stupid (their word, not ours) their topics were. Discussion of the topic typically involved presentation of the first speaker's point of view. However, sometimes the first speaker attempted to present the issue in overview or attempted to present the other person's point of view.

Subsequently, discussion patterns became more difficult to characterize. Discussions were wide-ranging and, not surprisingly, brought in factors whose connection and relevance to prior discussion was impossible for outsiders to assess meaningfully. In part, because of this, discussions were not easily decomposable by logical means or by such discourse-oriented means such as Toulmin structures (Toulmin, 1958).

We consider two aspects of expression in the following discussion: (1) number of words used, and (2) displays, both metalinguistic and paralinguistic.

## *Words Used*

Phone and f2f interactions were transcribed, noting repetitions and restarts in speech. IM interactions were captured via printed transcripts. One way of characterizing the interaction is in terms of the number of words used during the 20-minute encounter and these transcripts were used as a mechanism for counting words. As with mood change, the findings here are also complex.

Dividing the couples into those above and below the median of exchange, there was a strong difference in the number of words used by media ($\chi^2$ (2) = −21.26, $p < .0001$). On the average, all the couples in the unmediated (f2f) condition used more than the median number of words. Not surprisingly, couples in the IM condition always used less than the median number of words. However, the phone condition was split, with five couples using less than the median and four using more.

There was nothing to suggest that this range of word use in the phone condition turned the phone into an instrument more like face-to-face or IM. There was no hint of a correlation between number of words used and mood change in general ($r = .12$, $p = .59$) or within the phone condition ($r = .22$, $p = .60$). Indeed, the two couples with the lowest number of words in the phone condition (281 and 268 words) were well below the mean number of words (464) for the IM condition and both couples reported mood loss through the encounter. The two couples with the highest number of words in the phone condition (1,518 and 1,243) spanned the mean number of words for the f2f condition (1,273) and also both showed loss of mood.

Recent findings have suggested equating IM conditions with phone and f2f conditions in experiments by giving the interactors in IM more time (Connell et al., 2001), on the grounds that conversation is simply slower in IM than via other media and that, given enough time, it will catch up. This is an intriguing idea that addresses a thorny problem. It builds on the real-self literature. However, we believe that it is premature to conclude that any simple mechanism creates meaningful equality without reference to a multifaceted analysis of meaning.

## *Displays: Metalinguistic and Paralinguistic*

Metalinguistic and paralinguistic displays differed obviously by condition in amount, kind, and nature, with generally more quantity in the face-to-face condition than the phone and almost none in the IM. Some behaviors may be particularly important because the couple is engaged in conflict. Additionally, there are behaviors that occur in the mediated conditions that are not particularly expected.

### Face-to-Face

In addition to facial animation, participants in the face-to-face condition made large and small gestures, rocked in their chairs, leant forwards and backwards, and showed a range of vocal intensities (Table 8.2).

Although not everyone raises voice when they argue, one might expect raised voices in association with conflict. Indeed, participants often raise their voices, even to the extent that we might ordinarily describe them as “shouting.” Figure 8.2 shows a transcript in which the woman moves between softer vocalizations and markedly louder ones.

**Table 8.2** Behaviors prominent in face-to-face interaction during discussions

| |
|---|
| Facial Animation |
| Smiling (social and genuine) |
| Large body movements |
| Small body movements |
| Rocking side to side |
| Leaning forward and backwards |
| Range of vocal intensities |

| | |
|---|---|
| Female: | OK, but, when? I do that on purpose. When I turn on my radio, I turn the loud down and the bass out. |
| Male: | Why?! |
| Female: | **Not as loud as you**. Not as loud as you! |
| Male: | Yes you do. |
| Female: | You have to have the big amps, so you can make it sound louder. **You do! Yes you do!** |

**Fig. 8.2** Couples raised their voices in the face-to-face condition (Couple 6). **Bold** shows increased volume. Underlines show word emphasis

Thus, the experimental situation can evoke volume, and the presence of volume increases confidence that the couples are in fact conducting arguments.

Also notable was the ubiquitous presence of smiling in the face-to-face condition. The personal and interpersonal power, and the ambiguous status of the smile in this context are demonstrated by one participant who appears to resent that power: "It pisses me off. You're laughing and I'm smiling, but I'm really upset. I'm not playing with you!" (Couple 26).

Drawing on ethiological work with apes, Ekman (Ekman et al., 1972) remarks that there are different kinds of human smiles. Felt, genuine (so-called Duchenne) smiles involve not only the mouth and cheeks, but also a tightening of the orbicularis oculi muscles around the eyes. Fake smiles (those without this tightening) may include both those intended to deceive and those intended to convey a mix of emotions. Both fake and felt smiles occur frequently in the face-to-face condition.

## Phone

In general, displays are more subdued in the phone condition than in the face-to-face; however, a wide range of displays does occur. Indeed, we find that a wider range of facial displays of emotion occurs in the phone condition than in the face-to-face.

The first author of this article examined each of the videotapes for facial expressions, following a modified version of Ekman's rubric for identifying facial display of emotions (Ekman, 1982). Table 8.3 shows that disappointment, confusion, and sadness/upset were displayed over the phone but not face-to-face.

Phone displays are not confined to the face. They include large body movements, small body movements, and loud vocalizations. There were fewer large body movements than in the face-to-face condition, but these also occur. Indeed, on one occasion a participant, protesting her boyfriend's failure to put sufficient effort into his job search, stood up and put her foot on the chair as her vocalizations got louder and then softer again as she leant over her leg (Couple 3). More surprisingly, the phone condition displays also includes gestures that appear to be for interpersonal emphasis. Figure 8.3 shows a man extending his arm out to his side while arguing about whether the current war in Iraq is a good idea or not.

**Table 8.3** Occurrence of facial display by technological condition

| Displays | Face-to-face | Phone | IM |
|---|---|---|---|
| Contempt/disgust | X | X | X |
| Excitement | X | X | |
| Relief | X | | |
| Happiness | X | X | X |
| Disappointment | | X | |
| Confusion | | X | X |
| Surprise | X | X | X |
| Sadness/upset | | X | X |

**Fig. 8.3** Man making large gesture while arguing over the phone about the United States' role in the war in Iraq (Couple 50)

Some behaviors occur but are quite different over the phone than face-to-face. Most notable is the reduction of social smiling. An almost constant factor in the face-to-face becomes a rare or nonexistent event over the phone. Other smiles are also rare in the phone condition, but they do occur, as indicated in Fig. 8.4.[2]

Other behaviors occur over the phone that we never see in the face-to-face condition. First, people engage in distraction activities such as twisting the phone cord and playing with pens or pencils. They doodle on their informed consent copies.[3]

[2] We cannot show the distinction between social and genuine smiles while disguising the faces of the participants, which we feel is necessary.

[3] To speculate further, we note recent work suggesting that when people hear an angry voice, they fixate visually in the direction of the voice (Brosch et al., 2007). What happens when there is nothing on which to fixate? Perhaps the phone cord and doodles create a focus, curtailing a persistent search impulse.

**Fig. 8.4** Woman smiling while the couple, the most wordy of all phone participants, discusses whether a television show she likes has the proposed deleterious effect on her (Couple 39)

**Fig. 8.5** Man rubbing his forehead as if in pain while arguing over abortion (Couple 12)

Second, there are displays of pain or distress that do not occur in the face-to-face condition. One of the most vocal of the men (as measured by word numbers), in the course of an argument about abortion, rubbed his forehead persistently as if in pain (Fig. 8.5).

Third, we see behaviors in the phone condition that seem to signal a level of withdrawal from the situation. Indeed, one participant hung up the phone (and then called back). One of the least wordy men, in the course of an argument about his relationship with an ex-girlfriend, covered his head with his hood.

## IM

Not only are all displays rare in the IM condition, but participants show less variety of expressions than in the other conditions. Furthermore, their motions are discrete rather than blending into one another. Large body movements are confined to two types: (1) leaning back in the chair away from the keyboard and screen, while keeping the eyes trained on the screen and then leaning forward again, and (2) one participant turns his head and rolls his eyes at the camera. The fidgiting and small body movements found in phone conversations are also rare, as are adjustments in the chair, and overt facial displays.

However, some behaviors do occur: jaw tightening, raised eyebrows and upper lips (Fig. 8.6), and laughter (once) followed by a prolonged smile (Fig. 8.7), furrowed eyebrows, frowning, and eye narrowing. Using Ekman's characterizations, we classified these as expressing contempt or disgust, happiness, confusion, surprise, and sadness/upset (Table 8.3). Additionally, sometimes participants exhale sharply making "shhh" (as if disgusted), "whew" (as if relieved), or "whoa" sounds (as if backing away). Participants occasionally glance at the camera after these displays.

With the exception of relief and happiness, these behaviors are associated with negative emotions: frustration, skepticism, and annoyance (or boredom).

**Fig. 8.6** Woman narrowing and raising eyebrows and tightening lips (Couple 14). This expression can be characterized informally as skepticism, and more formally as a kind of mild disgust

**Fig. 8.7** A smile lingers on this woman's face after laughing while discussing her partner's wish that she would exercise more (Couple 48)

## Discussion

We asked people to argue, and the indications are that they did. They said that they had argued. They reported a decline in mood. They looked like they were arguing.

We presented experimental-style quantitative data with respect to mood. Our mood data show the importance of asking precisely the right question in the context of experimentation. A nonparametric statistical test, the chi-square, showed results, while the more usual parametric test, the ANOVA, did not. There are technical reasons to use a nonparametric. Nonparametric tests such as the chi-square are used in situations in which the underlying distribution may not be normal, which can be due to lack of power (in this case, not having enough participants). However, in this case, the chi-square can be conceptualized as posing a slightly different question than the ANOVA. The question associated with the ANOVA is, in essence, "how do we model mood change in couple's arguments?" with media as our only three-level predictor. The answer to that appears to be "it does not." The question posed by the chi-square is "does media have an effect on mood change in couple's arguments?" and the answer to that appears to be "quite possibly."

In fact, we do not and would not claim that the media was the unique or most important predictor of the outcome of a conflict. There are presumably many factors about the people, their relationship, the particular disagreement, the setting in which the argument took place, and the kind of measurement of mood change that we are not modeling in the current experiment.

Conventional thinking in experimentation would say that if media does not emerge as a significant predictor in relationship to that which we do not know about situational variation, it is unimportant. In fact, the judgment about whether a cause is likely depends on why we are asking the question and what we already know about the situation. As designers of technology, policy makers, or individuals in a relationship, we may be concerned about the impact of our technology even with the knowledge that other factors that are not currently possible to characterize well may be more important.

The phenomena that we control for and consider in experimentation depend on pre-extant theory of what constitute important phenomena. Bargh and his colleagues argue that "we need less description of the effects of Internet use and more theory about underlying processes" (Bargh, 2002, p 7). But our notions of theory are themselves tied to notions of what is important or of value. These theories of value assume that our phenomenology is sufficient for the task. By analogy, a recent study of the effects of living near highways on prenatal health showed deleterious effect, but only for women in affluent neighborhoods (Généreux et al., 2008). The effect did not show up statistically against the many problems faced by women in poorer circumstances. If the question is "how can we help poor mothers?" the answer is probably not "reduce highway emissions." But if the question is "should we reduce highway emissions?" the answer is probably "yes." The researchers were able to detect the importance of affluence to their study because their theory of the situation linked to an oft-studied and well-conceptualized covariate.

In the current case, that of couples arguing, it is easy to see how both the effects and no-effects findings about mediated communication came into being. It only takes a slight step to either side to see the media as important or not important. To take the argument about what we do not know one step further; we do not in fact know that a decline in mood state while arguing is a bad thing. Though undoubtedly unpleasant, it may be extremely functional. We do not currently have a scientific theory of variation in conflict in couples. (Gottman [1994] claims to be able to predict which couples will stay together, but this is a theory of catastrophic conflict.) Nonetheless, we still seek to investigate the role of media.

In the introduction, we used the term "ecology" to describe the interactions. The choice of the analogy "ecology" is deliberate. It suggests not only that the systems are complex, with many interrelated, moving parts, but also that at any given point in time, it is difficult, maybe impossible, to tell whether the system is truly in balance. While balanced systems may exhibit an ability to right themselves, there may also be points of no return that are enormously and unexpectedly destabilizing. As we know from the physical environment, apparently small changes in the ecology of a system should not be dismissed. These systems require careful thought. In particular, the phenomena themselves require elaboration and description. We may not yet know the terms of the required description. Years of patient phenomenology lie behind theoretical insights such as the Copernican revolution, the Mendelian laws of inheritance, and the notion of evolution through natural selection. This may not have the same importance as those topics to the history of thought, but there is no particular reason to expect that accounting for human behavior is less complex than any other element of nature.

When we turn to the behavioral phenomena in this case, we see that arguments in the three conditions unfold differently. We note three possibly important aspects of these data.

By-and-large research has focused on what people are missing in different media connections. An interesting question raised by the current research is "what is present?" We raise the question of what kinds of things occur when they cannot be seen and why. Clark and Brennan's work (1991) suggests that phone will be importantly similar to IM in their shared lack of visual co-presence and importantly different in the degree of simultaneity, audibility, reviewability, and amenability to revision. However, it is not clear that these factors account for the differences in what we see occurring in the privacy of the rooms. Perhaps other factors are also important. Some of these, like Bavelas' (Bavelas et al., 1991) motor mimicry, might be psychological factors. Others might be amenable to design; perhaps the need to sit still while typing and reading is as responsible for the lack of facial movement in IM as are the formal properties of the medium. Suppose people could dictate their words, which would be automatically transcribed and sent to the other, while the other person's words appeared on a big screen – would we then see animation similar to that over the phone, and if so, to what extent would that be a good outcome? If suppression of expression is a resource (Gross et al., 2006), IM might be better than SMS (Short text Messaging Systems).

An additional concern is that these behaviors are present because there are in fact potential witnesses to the interaction. The interaction is recorded. From an experimental perspective, recording is thought to make no difference as long as it is thought to affect all conditions similarly. From a quantitative, observational perspective, there is a widespread belief that people get used to the camera or do not notice it (Jordan and Henderson, 1995). However, in fact, noticing the camera may be part of a complex ecology. People might, for example, find it easier to remember the camera when in the relatively low stimulus IM situation as compared to the higher stimulus face-to-face situation. It may be that rather than assuming that researchers can ignore the effects of the camera, we must account for its interaction with different conditions.

In general, we must be careful in generalizing results pertaining to new forms of media. Internet communications are characterized by a high degree of anonymity today and have been lauded for the democratizing possibilities thought to be inherent in such freedom (Curtis, 1997; Cherny, 1999). Tomorrow, communications may rarely be anonymous. The results of today's experiments may, in that case, tell us something about anonymity, but not about the Internet per se or the effects of our design decisions on the Internet.

In discussing these data, we have focused on the couple as the unit of analysis, and we simplified our consideration of couples to mixed-gender couples. Gender differences are of interest in modeling couple's interaction and in modeling argumentation. It is also possible that there are interactions between gender and technology, or that the use of technology expresses something about the power relations within the couple. Differences between media may be significant for the goals and processes typically associated with women's roles in relationships.

One issue that we touched on in passing is that there were differences in greeting practices between different couples. It is impossible to know the extent to which these differences are a condition of the technology as compared to a side effect of this historical moment. At the first level of analysis, people greet one another or fail to greet one another because they feel a need to do the business that greeting accomplishes (or do not). Yet, the constitution of the activity as involving the business of greeting or not involving may have entailments. Thus, while greeting may not be required, its presence might (for example) provide better evidence of affiliation to the parties than failure to greet. An assumption of such affiliation may not be the same as a demonstration.

The degree of confidence that we need to consider a result as fixed is also influenced by the kind of decisions and characterizations we might make as a response. In the case of mediated conflict, we may be concerned as scientists, designers, and ordinary people. We may wish to do all in our power to protect the relationship (or not), or to maintain personal emotional balance, and the thought that phone or IM *might* have negative entailments for mood may be worth attention, if it causes participants to exercise more care when arguing, or if it causes them to avoid a deleterious component to the conversation.

As important as methods and theories are in understanding, Bargh's call to premiate their study omits the importance of continuing to note phenomena. Communication via technology is a vast and changing social experiment. It is important to note phenomena that may pose societal problems and ask important questions even when our theory is lacking or inadequate. You can avoid fighting with some people all of the time, with all people, some of the time, but you cannot avoid fighting with all of the people all of the time. So, the question remains "How do you want to hold your arguments?"

## References


Aoki, P. & Woodruff, A. (2000). "Improving Electronic Guidebook Interfaces Using a Task-Oriented Design Approach," Third Conference on Designing Interactive Systems, New York.

Aronson, E., T. Wilson, & Akert, R. (1994). *Social Psychology: The Heart and the Mind.* New York: Harper Collins.

Bargh, J. A. (2002). Beyond simple truths: the human-Internet interaction. *Journal of Social Issues* 58(1): 1–8.

Bargh, J. A., McKenna, K. Y. A., & Fitzsimmons, G. M. (2002). Can you see the real me? Activation and expression of the "true self" on the Internet. *Journal of Social Issues* 58: 33–48.

Bavelas, J. B., Black, A., Lemery, C. R., & Mullett, J. (1986). I show how you feel: motor mimicry as a communicative act. *Journal of Personality and Social Psychology* 50: 322–329.

Beck, A. T. (1972). *Depression: Causes and Treatment.* Philadelphia, PA: University of Pennsylvania Press.

Boehner, K., DePaula, R., Dourish, P., & Sengers, P. (2007). How emotion is made and measured. *International Journal of Human-Computer Studies* 65(4): 275–291.

Brosch, T., Grandjean, D., Sander, D., & Scherer, K. (2007). Behold the voice of wrath: cross-modal modulation of visual attention by anger prosody. *Cognition* 106(3): 1497–1503.

Cherny, L. (1999). *Conversation and Community: Chat in a Virtual World*. Stanford CA: CSLI Publications.

Clark, H. H. (1996). *Using Language*. New York: Cambridge University Press.

Clark, H. H. & Brennan, S. E. (1991). Grounding in communication. In L. B. Resnick, J. Levine, & S. D. Behrens (Eds.), *Perspectives on Socially Shared Cognition.*, Washington, DC: American Psychological Association, pp. 127–149.

Clark, M. (1984). Record keeping in two types of relationships. *Journal of Personality and Social Psychology* 47: 549–557.

Clark, M. S. & J. Mills (1979). Interpersonal attraction in exchange and communal relationships. *Journal of Personality and Social Psychology* 37: 12–24.

Connell, J. B., Mendelsohn, G. A., Robins, R. W., & Canny, J. (2001). Effects of Communication Medium on Interpersonal Perceptions: Don't Hang Up on the Telephone Yet!, *Proceedings of GROUP 2001, pp.* 117–124.

Corbin, J. & A. Strauss (1990). Grounded theory research: procedures, canons, and evaluative criteria. *Qualitative Sociology* 13(1): 3–21.

Culnan, M. J. & Markus, M. L. (1987). Information technologies. In F. M. Jablin, L. L. Putnam, K. H. Roberts, & L. W. Porter (Eds.), *Handbook of Organizational Communication: An Interdisciplinary Perspective*. Newbury Park, CA: Sage, pp. 420–443.

Curtis, P. (1997). MUDDING: Social phenomena in text-based virtual realities. In S. Kiesler (Ed.), *Culture of the Internet*. Mahwah, NJ: Lawrence Erlbaum, pp. 121–142.

Daft, R. L. & Lengel, R. H. (1984). Information richness: a new approach to manager information processing and organization design. In B. Staw and L. L. Cummings (Eds.), *Research in Organizational Behavior*. Greenwich, CT: JAI Press.

Daft, R. L. & Lengel, R. H. (1986). Organizational information requirements, media richness and structural design. *Management Science* 32: 554–571.

Ekman, P. (1982). Methods for measuring facial action. In K. Scherer & P. Ekman (Eds.), *Recent methods in nonverbal behavior research*. New York: Cambridge University Press, pp. 45–90.

Ekman, P., Friesen, W. V., & Ellsworth, P. (1972). *Emotion in the human face*. Elmsford, NY: Pergamon.

Généreux, M., Auger, N., Goneau, M., & Daniel, M. (2008). Neighbourhood socioeconomic status, maternal education and adverse birth outcomes among mothers living near highways, *Journal of Epidemiology and Community Health* 62: 695–700.

Gottman, J. (1994). *Why Marriages Succeed or Fail, and How You Can Make Yours Last*. New York: Simon & Schuster.

Gross, J. J., Richards, J., & John, O. (2006). Emotion regulation in everyday life. In D. K. Snyder, J. A. Simpson, & J. N. Hughes (Eds.), *Emotion Regulation in Families: Pathways to Dysfunction and Health*. Washington DC: American Psychological Association, pp. 13–35.

Jordan, B. & Henderson, A. (1995). Interaction analysis: foundations and practice. *Journal of the Learning Sciences* 4(1): 39–103.

Hobman, E. V., Bordia, P., Irmer, B., & Chang, A. (2002). The expression of conflict in computer-mediated and face-to-face groups. *Small Group Research* 33(4): 439–465.

Horowitz, L. (2004). *Interpersonal Foundations of Psychopathology*. Washington, DC: American Psychological Association.

Horowitz, L. M., Alden, L. E., Wiggins, J. S., & Pincus, A. L. (2000). *Inventory of Interpersonal Problems*. San Antonio, TX: The Psychological Corporation.

Kiesler, D. J. (1996). *Contemporary Interpersonal Theory and Research*. New York: Wiley.

Lea, M. & Spears, R. (1991). Computer-mediated communication, de-individuation and group decision-making. *International Journal of Man-Machine Studies* 39: 283–310.

Mantei, M. M., Baecker, R. M., Sellen, A. J., Buxton, W. A. S., Milligan, T., & Wellman, B. (1991). Experiences in the use of a media space. *Proceedings of the SIGCHI conference on Human factors in computing systems, CHI'91*. New Orleans, LA, pp. 203–208.

McLuhan, M. (1964). *Understanding Media: The Extensions of Man*. London: Routledge.

Postmes, T., Spears, R., Lea, M., & Reicher, S. (2000). *SIDE-Issues Centre-Stage: Recent Developments in Studies of De-individuation in Groups*. Amsterdam: KNAW.

Reeves, B. & Nass, C. (1996). *The Media Equation*. New York: CSLI Publications/Cambridge University Press.

Suchman, L. (2007). *Human-Machine Reconfigurations: Plans and Situated Actions*. New York: Cambridge University Press.

Suchman, L. A. (1987). *Plans and Situated Actions*. Cambridge: Cambridge University Press.

Ting-Toomey, S. (1994). Managing intercultural conflicts effectively. In L. Samovar & R. Porter (Eds.), *Intercultural Communication: A Reader*, 7th ed. Belmont, CA: Wadsworth, pp. 360–372.

Toulmin, S. (1958). *The Uses of Argument*. Cambridge: Cambridge University Press.

Voida, A., Newstetter, W. C., & Mynatt, E. D. (2002). When conventions collide: The tensions of instant messaging attributed. In *Proceedings of the ACM Conference on Human Factors in Computing Systems (SigCHI)*. New York: ACM Press, pp. 187–194.

Walther, J. B. (1992). Interpersonal effects in computer- mediated interaction: a relational perspective. *Communication Research* 19(1): 52–90.

Walther, J. B., Anderson, J. F., & Park, D. W. (1994). Interpersonal effects in computer-mediated communication. *Communication Research* 26: 460–487.

Watson, D. & Clark, L. A. "The PANAS-X: Positive and Negative Affect Schedule – Expanded Form," http://www.psychology.uiowa.edu/Faculty/Clark/PANAS-X.pdf, University of Iowa (Copyright 1994).

Zajonc, R. B. (1980). Feeling and thinking: preferences need no inferences. *American Psychologist* 35: 151–175.

Zornoza, A., Ripoll, P., & Peiro, J. M. (2002). Conflict management in groups that work in two different communication contexts: face-to-face and computer-mediated communication. *Small Group Research* 33(5): 481–508.

# Chapter 9
# The Watcher and the Watched: Social Judgments about Privacy in a Public Place*

**Batya Friedman, Peter H. Kahn Jr., Jennifer Hagman, Rachel L. Severson, and Brian Gill**

**Abstract** Digitally capturing and displaying real-time images of people in public places raises concerns for individual privacy. Applying the principles of Value Sensitive Design, we conducted two studies of people's social judgments about this topic. In Study I, 750 people were surveyed as they walked through a public plaza that was being captured by a HDTV camera and displayed in real-time in the office of a building overlooking the plaza. In Study II, 120 individuals were interviewed about the same topic. Moreover, Study II controlled for whether the participant was a direct stakeholder of the technology (inside the office watching people on the HDTV large-plasma display window) or an indirect stakeholder (being watched in the public venue). Taking both studies together, results (showed the following): (a) the majority of participants upheld some modicum of privacy in public; (b) people's privacy judgments were not a one-dimensional construct, but often involved considerations based on physical harm, psychological well-being, and informed consent; and (c) more women than men expressed concerns about the installation, and, unlike the men, equally brought forward their concerns, whether they were The Watcher or The Watched.

## Introduction

Few would disagree that privacy represents an enduring human value and in some form should be protected in private contexts, such as the home. Some measure of privacy also exists in public places. For example, before the advent of digital information systems, in a city, relatively few people knew when or where you went

*This chapter originally appeared as an article in the journal, *Human-Computer Interaction*, volume 21, pages 233–269. It appears here with permission of the publisher, Taylor & Francis.

B. Friedman, P.H. Kahn Jr., J. Hagman, and R.L. Severson
University of Washington
e-mails: batya@u.washington.edu; pkahn@u.washington.edu

B. Gill
Seattle Pacific University

S. Harrison (ed.), *Media Space 20+ Years of Mediated Life*,
Computer Supported Cooperative Work,

shopping or what you bought, even though the activity occurred in public purview. Yet such forms of privacy can be undermined by the technological capture and display of people's images.

In the United States, a version of this problem surfaced as far back as the late 1800s with the introduction of photographic equipment. For example, Warren and Brandeis (1985) wrote in 1890 that although in earlier times

> the state of the photographic art was such that one's picture could seldom be taken without his consciously "sitting" for the purpose, the law of contract or of trust might afford the prudent man sufficient safeguards against the improper circulation of his portrait; but since the latest advances in photographic art have rendered it possible to take pictures surreptitiously, the doctrines of contract and of trust are inadequate to support the required protection. (p. 179)

Warren and Brandeis argued that "the protection granted by the law must be placed upon a broader foundation" (p. 179).

With today's technologies – such as surveillance cameras, webcams, and ubiquitous sensing devices – there is all the more cause to be concerned about privacy in public places (Nissenbaum, 1998).

In the human–computer interaction and computer-supported cooperative work communities, researchers have partly explored this topic through real-time video collected in one part of a work environment and displayed in another. Some studies have involved "office-to-office" video connections on desktop systems (Adler and Henderson, 1994; Dourish et al., 1996; Dourish and Bly, 1992; Mantei et al., 1991; Root, 1988; Tang and Rua, 1994). Other studies have involved linking common rooms in research organizations by video (Fish et al., 1990; Jancke et al., 2001; Olson and Bly, 1991). For example, Jancke et al. (2001) linked three kitchen areas within a workplace by means of video cameras and semipublic displays. Unsolicited responses to their announcement about this proposed application alerted the researchers to privacy concerns. Despite the addition of an Off switch, roughly 20% of the individuals continued to voice concerns about privacy throughout the system's deployment.

As telecommuting became popular, researchers moved from linking offices within the workplace to linking home offices with workplace offices. Hudson and Smith (1996) spoke about the resulting privacy issues that can ensue:

> The home is often thought of as a protected and private space and part of the advantage of working at home is being able to operate in that more relaxed and informal setting. For example … home work spaces are often shared by family members who are not part of the work group and who have important expectations of privacy in their home.… Turning an otherwise private physical space into part of a very public virtual space (e.g., with a live video feed) is really not acceptable. On the other hand, working at home can easily cut one off from the rest of a (distributed or co-located) work group if no awareness support is provided. (p. 250)

Hudson and Smith offered various technical solutions, such as the blurring of the video images so that people's presence could be noticed but not their specific activities (see also Boyle et al., 2000).

More recently, researchers have begun to investigate real-time images and video within home environments in and of themselves. Junestrand et al. (2000), for example, presented a scenario using comTABLE, a video screen and camera in the kitchen that would allow a virtual guest to come to dinner through video-mediated communication. Elsewhere, Hutchinson et al. (2003) described a video-Probe that provided a simple method for sharing impromptu still images among family members living in different households. The images were displayed on a screen that could be mounted on the wall or sit on a desk, much like a picture frame. "Images fade over time and eventually disappear, to encourage families to create new ones" (p. 21).

In all of the aforementioned contexts, people are largely known to one another; people have reasons to be seen by others; and the nature of the interaction is largely reciprocal (e.g., Office Worker A sees Office Worker B, and vice versa). However, what happens when cameras are pointed at the public at large? What do people think about having their images captured by video cameras when they (the people) are out in public and where the purpose is not for maintaining security (e.g., to prevent shoplifting in a store or physical violence in a subway station) but for the enjoyment of the viewer, as occurs all the time with the multitude of webcams in public places across the globe. More recently, Goldberg (2005) created an installation where multiple remote users controlled the view and zoom of a camera set up over Sproul Plaza on the University of California, Berkeley, campus. The installation allowed the remote users visual access to a good deal of information about a person (e.g., the title of the book that a person was reading while sitting alone on the steps of the plaza or the patterns on a woman's dress). As cameras become more pervasive and powerful in public spaces, do people think that the cameras violate their privacy? Does it matter to people if their images are recorded or not, displayed locally or internationally, or displayed in a single location or in many locations? What if people could be in the position of directly using (benefiting from) the captured video themselves – would that change their views on some or even all of these issues? Do men and women bring different perspectives to bear on the judgments about privacy in public? Our current research sought to address these questions.

Our research draws on principles of Value Sensitive Design: a theoretically grounded, interactional approach to the design of technology that accounts for human values in a principled and comprehensive manner throughout the design process (Friedman, 1997a; Friedman, 2004; Friedman and Kahn, 2003; Friedman et al., 2009). One principle of Value Sensitive Design that is central to our investigation entailed consideration of both direct and indirect stakeholders. *Direct stakeholders* are parties, individuals, or organizations who interact directly with the computer system or its output. To date, the majority of work in human–computer interaction considers direct stakeholders, often taking the form of user studies and user experience in experimental settings as well as the home and workplace. *Indirect stakeholders* are all the other parties who are affected by the use of the system. Often, indirect stakeholders have been ignored in the design process. For example, computerized medical records systems have often been designed with many of the direct stakeholders in mind (e.g., insurance companies, hospitals, doctors, and nurses) but with too little regard for the values, such as the value of privacy, of a rather important group of indirect stakeholders: the patients.

To investigate direct and indirect stakeholders' judgments about privacy in a public place, particularly when the application is not primarily one for security, we installed a HDTV camera on top of a university building (Fig. 9.1a) that overlooked a scenic public plaza and fountain area on a university campus. Then we set up a room in an academic office approximately 15 ft (4.57 m) below the camera, with its window also facing the plaza and fountain area. On the inside of the window, we installed a 50-inch (127-cm) plasma display vertically covering up the real window. Thus, we displayed on the plasma screen virtually the identical real-time image of the plaza and fountain area as would be viewed from the real window (Fig. 9.1b).

One purpose of this installation was to investigate whether a real-time plasma "window" could garner some if not all of the psychological benefits of working in an office with a real window. Thus in a "classic" direct-stakeholder user study not reported here (manuscript in preparation), we involved participants in one of three conditions. The first condition involved the office that had the real view of the public plaza and fountain area. The second condition involved the same office but with the technical installation described earlier. The third condition involved a blank wall created by covering the real window with light-blocking curtains. Measures during a 2-h experiment included participants' physiological recovery from low-level stress, eye gaze (coded on a second-by-second basis to ascertain the type and duration of participants' looking behavior), performance on cognitive and creativity tasks, mood, and self-reflective judgments.

To investigate the effects vis-à-vis privacy on indirect stakeholders, we asked ourselves, who else would be affected by the technical installation? Granted, diffuse effects can percolate in many different ways, making it difficult to establish firmly the class of indirect stakeholders; and granted, potentially everyone (including future generations) could be considered an indirect stakeholder. That said, some categories of indirect stakeholders are more significantly affected (positively or negatively) than others, and it is to these that Value Sensitive Design draws focus. Specifically, one group seemed obvious: those people who, in the course of their regular business on the university campus, pass through the scene and would now have their images captured by the HDTV camera and displayed in an adjacent office (Fig. 9.1c). Thus, we sought to bring the perspectives of this group of indirect

**Fig. 9.1** The technical installation in context

stakeholders into our research. Accordingly, we conducted two additional studies, which are the focus of this article. In Study I, we surveyed 750 people (indirect stakeholders) as they walked through a public plaza that was being captured by the HDTV camera and displayed in real time in the office of a building overlooking the plaza. In Study II, we interviewed 120 individuals about the same topic. Moreover, in Study II we controlled for whether the participant was a direct stakeholder of the technology (inside the office watching people on the HDTV large-display window) or an indirect stakeholder (being watched in the public venue).

We sought to address four central issues. The first issue derives from the complexity of privacy as a social construct, one still being substantively negotiated in current society. Long-standing philosophical and legal discussions have sought, for example, to establish a basis for privacy as a right in and of itself, as derivative from other rights, such as property, as being essential for human autonomy and development and critical for social functioning (see Schoeman, 1984, for a discussion). In turn, with the design of information systems with widespread privacy implications, the field of human–computer interaction has begun to respond with emergent models for privacy management that in various ways engage aspects of this complexity (Abowd and Mynatt, 2000; Ackerman et al., 2001; Jiang et al., 2002; Langheinrich, 2001; Palen and Dourish, 2003). All such models, however, need to take into account how people understand the construct of privacy in public. Thus, we sought to systematically characterize how direct and indirect stakeholders conceptualize privacy in public. We expected that people's privacy judgments would be multidimensional, accounting, for example, for the legitimate use of information, anonymity, technical functionality, and conventional expectations of current social practices (both local and cultural), as well as other values of import, such as welfare, property, and informed consent.

The second issue builds on previous research that suggests that people's moral behavior and judgments sometimes depend on their spheres of power within hierarchical systems (Hatch, 1983; Wainryb and Turiel, 1994; Wikan, 2002). Typically, people who benefit from societal injustices – such as discrimination on the basis of race, gender, or religion – are more inclined to support the existing social practices than are its victims (Turiel, 2002). Thus in the current study we examined whether people's social judgments about privacy in public shifted whether they were in the vulnerable position (the Watched) or not (the Watcher).

The third issue builds on literature that suggests that judgments of moral harms are often sensitive to where the harm occurs (location) and the severity of the harm (magnitude). In terms of location, think, for example, of how neighborhood groups can rise in opposition to the proposed construction of a garbage dump or nuclear power plant – thus the expression *NIMBY* ("not in my back yard"). Location can also be a factor when people judge what morality demands of them in terms of helping others. For example, people often judge it a moral obligation to help people in need within one's immediate location (e.g., a starving child outside one's home) compared to a far off place (e.g., a starving child in another country; cf. Kahn, 1992, 1999). In terms of magnitude, Friedman (1997b), for example, found that adolescents less often judged that it was morally acceptable to copy software if the magnitude increased from making one copy to many copies. Such a finding is congruent with Milgram's classic study (1963, 1974) on obedience to authority where many participants administrated what they believed to be electric shocks to another person (a confederate of the experimenter), under the guise of a learning experiment. Milgram found that fewer participants continued to administer shocks when the magnitude of the voltage increased or when the magnitude of the confederate's suffering either appeared to increase or was made more visible to the participant. Thus, in our current study, we expected that both location and magnitude would play pivotal roles in people's judgments about privacy. It was an open question, however, whether magnitude and location would interact and, if so, how. For example, it is plausible that although people deem it worse for their images to be viewed by many versus one, that distinction diminishes when those many others live a long way away, perhaps because of greater anonymity given increased distance.

The fourth issue focuses on whether gender differences exist in people's judgments about privacy in public. The implications of gender for people's understandings and need for privacy has been of long-standing interest and concern within the social sciences. For example, legal scholar Allen in her 1988 book *Uneasy Access: Privacy for Women in a Free Society* called attention to gendered dimensions of privacy and devoted a chapter to the legal basis for women's privacy in public. Key issues for Allen entailed unreasonable intrusion, sexual harassment, public display of pornography, and exclusion and group privacy. Sociologists, public health researchers, and psychologists empirically investigated dimensions of privacy preferences, often with a focus on interpersonal relationships, personal space, and commerce. Results from this body of research suggest that on some dimensions men and women view privacy similarly (e.g., functions of privacy, judgments of abstract privacy rights), but on other dimensions women tend to be more concerned about privacy than men or may achieve privacy through different means than those of men (e.g., Friedman, 1997b; Idehen, 1997; Marshall, 1974; Newell, 1998; Pedersen, 1987, 1999; Rustemi and Kokdemir, 1993). Pedersen (1987), for example, suggested that women and men may differentially experience the social reality of public space. Moreover, other research suggests that women's greater sensitivity to issues of privacy in public may extend beyond security concerns. For example, a recent study conducted in the semipublic venue of an emergency room (Karro et al., 2005) found that significantly more women than men (a) judged their privacy to be important to them while in the emergency department and (b) were likely to perceive both auditory (e.g., overhearing other's medical or personal information) and visual (e.g., seeing other's body parts) privacy incidents in the emergency department.

What, then, does the literature in human–computer interaction show with respect to privacy and gender? To answer this question, we conducted a systematic search of that literature from 2000 to 2004 for gender findings related to privacy. A total corpus of 1,574 journal articles and conference papers were examined, by searching for relevant content terms and then reading the papers that contained them. Sources included *Human–Computer Interaction* (59 articles), *ACM Transactions on Computer–Human Interaction* (72 articles), *Proceedings and Extended Abstracts of CHI Conference* (370 full papers, 752 extended abstracts), *Proceedings of CSCW Conference* (150 full papers), *Proceedings of ECSCW Conference* (41 full papers), and *Proceedings of Ubicomp Conference* (and its predecessor, the *Handheld and Ubiquitous Computing Conference*; 130 full papers). There were 32 papers reporting empirical findings on privacy. Surprisingly, not a single paper analyzed gender effects. Thus the current study sought to provide empirical data on similarities and differences, by gender, on people's social judgments of privacy in public.

## Study I: "The Watched" Survey

### *Methods*

#### Participants

In sum, 750 individuals participated in this study (384 males, 364 females, 2 gender no response; age ranges: 18–25, 56%; 26–40, 26%; 41–55, 14%; 55+, 4%). Participants were solicited by research staff sitting at a card table in the plaza of the university.

#### Procedures and Measures

Participants completed a brief paper-and-pencil survey. The introductory text read as follows: "Currently there is a camera in M[…] Hall [the name of the university building] that is pointed toward the fountain. What the camera sees is being displayed live on a screen in someone's office in M[…]Hall. People's faces and gestures are recognizable."

The first set of questions were designed to get at participants' evaluations of the camera installation prior to introducing the term *privacy*: (1a) "Are you surprised to learn that your live image is being displayed in someone's office in M[…] Hall?" (1b) "How do you feel about this happening? Circle as many as apply: shocked, that's cool, so what?, curious, embarrassed, delighted, glamorous, worried, violated, puzzled, doesn't hurt anyone, excited." Thus the latter question (1b) equally encouraged responses that were positive ("that's cool," "delighted," "glamorous," "excited"), *neutral* ("so what?," "curious," "puzzled," "doesn't hurt anyone") and *negative* ("shocked," "embarrassed," "worried," "violated").

The next set of questions focused directly on participants' evaluations of the installation in terms of a privacy violation and, if so, what they thought about a legal remedy or of being informed as a remedy: (2) "As stated above, right now the fountain area is being displayed live on a screen in a nearby office. Do you think this violates your privacy?" (2a) "If you said 'yes' to Question 2 above, do you think there should be some sort of law that restricts displaying live video from public places like the fountain?" (2b) "If you said 'yes' to Question 2 above, let's say there was a big sign posted in the fountain area that said: 'A camera continually films this fountain area and displays the live image in nearby offices.' In this case, do you think your privacy would be violated?"

Next, we offered participants two equally balanced reasons for judging the installation as not a problem or as troubling: (3) "Here are two ideas. Idea 1: Some people say it's OK to have a camera pointed at the fountain and display the live image in someone's *interior* office (an inside office without windows) in M[…] Hall. After all, the fountain is a public place. Anyone can see you. There's really no problem. Idea 2: Other people find it troubling to think that when they walk by the fountain, their image is being collected by a video camera and displayed live in someone's *interior* office (an inside office without window). After all, they can't see the person, they don't know who is seeing them. They don't even know that their image is being collected. Do you tend to agree with Idea 1 or with Idea 2?"

Finally, we asked seven context-of-use questions that assessed judgments that might be sensitive to location (where the image is displayed) and magnitude (the number of people viewing the image): (4a–g) "For each of the 7 situations below a camera is pointed at the fountain area. Images are not recorded [for this version of the survey]. For each situation, please put an 'X' in one of the columns to indicate if you think the situation is 'all right' or 'not all right': (a) in an office with an *outside* window in M[…] Hall. (b) in an *inside* office with no windows in M[…] Hall. (c) in an apartment on University Ave [half mile away]. (d) in an apartment in a residential neighborhood in Tokyo. (e) in the homes of thousands of people living in the local area. (f) in the homes of thousands of people living in Tokyo. (g) in the homes of millions of people across the globe."

To assess whether participants' responses substantially depended on whether the survey said that their images were being recorded or not, we administered three versions of the survey, 250 of each version. The versions differed in only one respect: Version 1 specified that the live video from the installation was not recorded; Version 2 specified that the live video was recorded; and Version 3 made no reference about the matter one way or another (the "ambiguous" version).

## *Results*

### Similarities Among the Three Versions of the Survey

Using logistic regression models, no differences were found between the "ambiguous" and "not recorded" versions of the surveys, whereas one difference was found with the "recorded" version. Specifically, more participants agreed with the statement that the installation violates privacy in the "recorded" version (28%), compared to the "ambiguous" version (20%) and the "not recorded" version (22%; $p$ =.018, based on a likelihood ratio test in the logistic regression model). Given

| Survey response | Male<br>N = 384 | Female<br>N = 364 | | All<br>N = 750 |
|---|---|---|---|---|
| 1a. Surprised to learn your live image is being displayed in an office in M[…]. | 61 | 43 | * | 53 |
| 1b. Feel … | | | | |
| … positive about displaying your live image in an office in M[…] (1+ positive adjective). | 18 | 10 | * | 14 |
| … neutral about displaying your live image in an office in M[…] (1+ neutral adjective). | 87 | 83 | | 85 |
| … negative about displaying your live image in an office in M[…] (1+ negative adjective). | 25 | 31 | * | 28 |
| 2. Displaying live video from the fountain area on a screen in M[…] violates privacy. | 17 | 27 | * | 22 |
| a. … If a privacy violation ("yes" to 2; n = 165), then there should be a legal remedy. | 77 | 68 | | 72 |
| b. … If a privacy violation ("yes" to 2; n = 165), then even with a sign, still a privacy viol. | 42 | 32 | | 36 |
| 3. Agree with Idea 2: Find displaying the live video troubling. | 17 | 31 | * | 23 |
| 4. It's "not all right" if the camera displays live video from the fountain area on a screen in … | | | | |
| a. … Office with outside window M[…] | 19 | 28 | * | 24 |
| b. … Office without a window in M[…] | 21 | 35 | * | 28 |
| c. … Apartment on University Ave. | 37 | 59 | * | 47 |
| d. … Apartment in Tokyo | 35 | 57 | * | 46 |
| e. … Thousands of homes in the local city | 32 | 52 | * | 42 |
| f. … Thousands of homes in Tokyo | 34 | 55 | * | 44 |
| g. … Millions of homes across the globe | 33 | 54 | * | 43 |

(1) Values in the table are the percentage of participants who gave the indicated response. (2) Two participants did not provide their gender on the survey, so the total *n* from the male and female columns does not add up to 750. (3) Asterisks indicate questions with significant gender differences (Fisher's exact test, $\alpha$=.05). (4) M[…] Hall stands for the name of the building on which the HDTV camera was mounted. (5) Questions 2a and 2b were only asked of the 165 participants who judged the live video to be a privacy violation (question 2).

**Fig. 9.2** Study I: Percentage of The Watched Survey Responses by Gender

the small difference in percentages on this one question and the lack of any other statistical differences among the three versions of the surveys, the survey data were combined for further analyses (see Fig. 9.2).

### Initial Reactions to the Installation

The first set of questions tapped participants' initial reactions to the camera installation. Based on Question 1a, approximately half (53%) of the participants were surprised to learn about the camera and large display. Overall, 85% of participants selected at least one of the neutral responses on Question 1b, whereas only 28% selected at least one of the negative responses and 14% selected at least one positive response.

## Judgments of Privacy in Public

When asked explicitly about the installation in terms of privacy, roughly one quarter (22%) of the participants judged the display of real-time video from the fountain area to be a privacy violation. In addition, of those men and women who judged the display of real-time video from the fountain area to be a privacy violation (Question 2), 72% believed there should be a law against it (Question 2a) and 36% believed that even if there were a sign informing them of the video camera, it would still be a privacy violation (Question 2b).

## Effects of Location and Magnitude

For the majority of participants, neither location nor magnitude affected their privacy judgments about the installation. Specifically, more than half of the participants (61%, $p = .000$, binomial test) held to a consistent view of privacy across all the context-of-use questions (4a–g), answering all these questions in the same way (16% of all items, “not all right”; 45% of all items, “all right”) regardless of location (where the image was viewed) or magnitude (how many people viewed the image).

For the roughly 40% of participants whose privacy judgments were sensitive to location and magnitude, location (on the university campus versus elsewhere) was the greatest demarcation, with other nuanced interactions among location and magnitude thereafter. Specifically, the remaining 39% of the participants who did not hold a consistent view of privacy across the seven context-of-use questions more often indicated that it was not all right to display the image in a remote location (4c–g) than in a local location in M[...] Hall (4a–b). All pairwise comparisons between either of questions 4a and 4b and any of questions 4c through 4g yielded *p* values smaller than .0005 in a McNemar test. Furthermore, although the difference was smaller in magnitude, participants who did not hold a consistent view across questions were also significantly more likely ($p = .003$, McNemar) to indicate that it was not all right to display the image in an office without a window in M[...] Hall (4b, 30%) than in an office with a window in M[...] Hall (4a, 19%).

To further explore the patterns of acceptability within the seven parts of Question 4, a cluster analysis was conducted using a dendogram (see Fig. 9.3) that clustered together questions based on similarity of responses (within subject) among the 294 participants who did not provide the same answer to all seven of the context-of-use questions. Questions linked together low in the graph (with smaller roman numerals) had similar responses, whereas questions linked together high in the graph had different responses. The dashed line in Fig. 9.3 indicates a reasonable cut point in the data. This cut visually shows that responses to questions 4a and 4b were quite different, both from each other and from the five other questions (4c–4g). Thus Fig. 9.3 visually illustrates the statistical differences in acceptability noted earlier between a remote location (4c–4g) and a local location in M[...] Hall

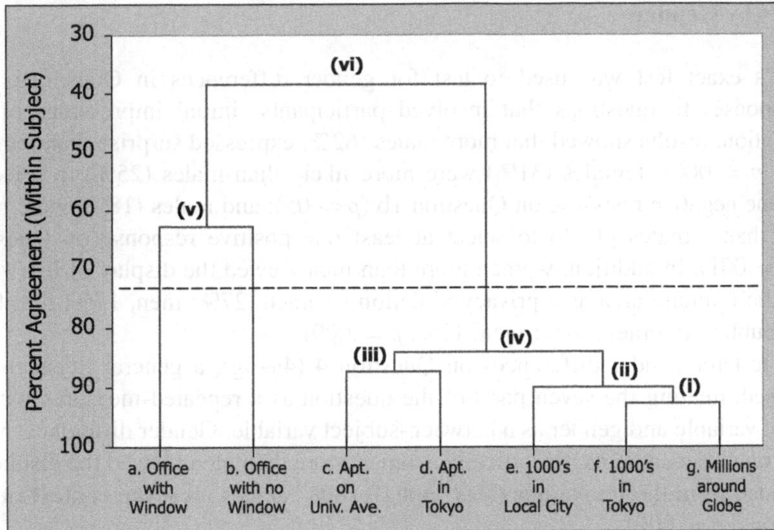


**Fig. 9.3** Study I: Clustering of the Watched survey responses to the seven context-of-use questions. This graph represents only the 294 individuals who did not give the same response for all seven context-of-use questions. Percent agreement (within subject): The lines represent links between questions or clusters of questions; the roman numerals represent the order in which the links were established. When two individual variables are linked together, the values on the vertical axis represent the percentage of individuals who gave the same answer (within subject) to the two questions. When two clusters of questions are linked together, the values represent the percentage of within-subject agreement for the two most similar questions from the two clusters

(4a–4b) as well as between offices in M[…] Hall with a window (4a) and without a window (4b).

The patterns of acceptability within the five remote locations (4c–4g) were somewhat more subtle. The cluster analysis in Fig. 9.3 indicates that responses to 4c and 4d formed one cluster and 4e, 4f, and 4g a separate cluster.

There is also some statistical support for this observation. Based on Cochran's *Q* test ($p < .0005$), there were statistically significant differences in acceptability among these five questions. This test was followed with pairwise comparisons among the five questions using McNemar tests, with the significance levels of the tests adjusted using Holm's sequential Bonferroni method to account for multiple comparisons. Significant differences were found in 5 of the 10 pairwise comparisons. Specifically, displaying the image in a single apartment on University Avenue was less acceptable (80%, "not all right") than displaying the image in thousands of homes in the local city (66%, $p < .0005$), millions of homes across the globe (69%, $p < .0005$), or thousands of homes in Tokyo (71%, $p = .006$). A single apartment in Tokyo (76%) was also deemed less acceptable than thousands of homes in the local city (66%, $p = .001$). Finally, thousands of apartments in Tokyo was less acceptable than thousands of apartments in the local city ($p = .007$).

### Effects by Gender

Fisher's exact test was used to test for gender differences in Questions 1–3. In responses to questions that involved participants' initial impressions of the installation, results showed that more males (62%) expressed surprise than females (43%; $p = .000$); females (31%) were more likely than males (25%) to select at least one negative response on Question 1b ($p = .05$); and males (18%) were more likely than females (10%) to select at least one positive response on Question 1b ($p = .001$). In addition, women more than men viewed the display of live video from the fountain area as a privacy violation (women, 27%; men, 17%; $p = .000$) and troubling (women, 31%; men, 17%; $p = .000$).

To test for gender differences on Question 4 (4a–4g), a general linear model was used, treating the seven parts of the question as a repeated-measures within-subject variable and gender as a between-subject variable. Gender differences were found on all seven items. Specifically, women more than men viewed the display of live video from the fountain area as "not all right" across all seven context-of-use questions ($p = .000$).

## Study II: "The Watcher and The Watched" Interview

Surveys readily allow for large sample sizes and thus provide greater confidence in the generalizability of one's findings. Yet surveys also represent a blunt instrument for exploring the complexities of how people understand the topic at hand (Kellert, 1996; Krathwohl, 1998). Thus this second study, in the context of the same installation, used a semistructured interview methodology (Damon, 1977; Helwig, 1995; Kahn, 1999; Killen, 1990; Piaget, 1929/1960; Turiel, 1983) to investigate in more depth the issues uncovered in the survey study. In addition, this second study examined possible differences in the social judgments about privacy in a public place between direct and indirect stakeholders – the users of the technology (the Watcher) and those individuals whose images are captured by the technology (the Watched).

### *Methods*

#### Participants

In sum, 120 people, with equal numbers of males and females, participated individually in a 20-minute semi-structured interview (age range: 18–25, 90%; 26–40, 8%; 41–55, 2%; 55+, 0%). Participants were recruited by local flyers and research staff sitting at a card table in the plaza of the university.

## Procedures and Methods

As described in the Introduction, a HDTV camera was mounted on the roof of a building overlooking a public plaza, and the real-time image was displayed in an office in that building. The four conditions in this study entailed: (a) the Watched – 30 individuals like those in the survey who walked across or briefly inhabited the public plaza in the course of their daily activities; (b) the Watcher large display – 30 individuals in an office in M[...] Hall with a large display showing the real-time image of the public plaza; (c) the Watcher real window – 30 individuals in the same office of M[...]Hall with a window overlooking the public plaza wherein participants were asked to imagine a large-display window; and (d) the Watcher blank wall – 30 individuals in the same office in M[...] Hall with a closed curtain covering the window wherein participants were asked to imagine a large-display window.

The interview included a question about the technological installation ("Currently there is a camera in M[...] Hall that is pointed toward the fountain. What the camera sees is being displayed live on a screen in someone's office in M[...] Hall. Do you think this it is all right or not all right that this is happening?"); 9 of the questions found on the survey (Questions 2, 3, 4a–g); and an 11th question, about the impact of recording the video ("Let's say that in addition to your live image at the fountain being shown on a screen in someone's office in M[...] Hall, your image was also being recorded. Would that be all right or not all right?"). For participants in the Watched condition, this later question and Question 2 were asked in terms of "your image" and "your privacy," but the questions were rephrased for participants in the Watcher conditions in terms of "people's images" and "people's privacy." In addition, participants in the Watched condition were asked three non-video-based questions about privacy expectations ("Do you think a handwritten diary is private?" "Do you think the same diary online is private?" and "Do you think that a whispered conversation in an outdoor café is private?").

The interviews were tape-recorded and then transcribed for analysis. Individual interviews averaged approximately ten single-spaced transcript pages. In total, the data set comprised approximately 1,160 single-spaced transcript pages.

## Coding

A detailed coding manual was developed from half of the data (approximately 550 transcript pages) and then applied to the entire data set. By *coding manual* we mean a systematic document that explicates how to interpret and characterize (and thereby "code") the qualitative data. Our approach followed well-established methods in the social–cognitive literature (Damon, 1977; Kahn, 1999; Kohlberg, 1984; Turiel, 1983). We began with close textual readings of interviews, seeking to characterize not only forms of reasoning but their interrelationships. We also moved back and forth between the empirical data and conceptual coherence, in part driven by philosophically informed categories, but always tested and often modified by the data itself. In addition, our coding manual drew – as most do in this line of work, when appropriate – from other coding manuals (Davidson et al., 1983; Friedman, 1997b; Kahn, 1992; Kahn et al., 2003; Nucci, 1981; Turiel et al., 1991).

As our coding manual took shape, we discovered, as is also typical, that some of our qualitative data resisted single interpretations. Such difficulties often emerged in one of three ways. First, the difficulty sometimes arose because the segment contained two or more independent justifications. We solved this difficulty by coding multiple justifications for a single evaluation. Second, the difficulty sometimes arose because two categories were conceptually intertwined. We often adjudicated this situation by moving forward with the conceptually dominant category while retaining their interconnections within the hierarchy. Third, the difficulty sometimes arose when there was more than one legitimate way to code the data. In this situation, the coding categories were driven not only by the data but by our theoretical commitments and research questions (see Kahn, 1999, Chapter 5, for a chapter-length discussion about the interview methodology and coding manual development). The complete version of our coding manual can be found as a technical report (Friedman et al., 2005).

### Reliability

Interviews from 24 participants (20% of the data) were recoded by a second individual trained in the use of the coding manual, 6 randomly chosen from each of the groups. Intercoder reliability was assessed through testing Cohen's kappa at the $\alpha = .05$ significance level. All tests were statistically significant. For evaluations, $\kappa = .92$ ($Z = 17.92$), and for justifications, $\kappa = .82$ ($Z = 38.94$). Reliability for justifications was established on the subcategory level as reported in Fig. 9.5.

## *Results*

Figure 9.4 reports the percentage of participant responses to the evaluation questions in both the survey and the interview. For Questions 1–3 and 5, Fisher's exact test was used both for gender comparisons and for pairwise comparisons between different conditions in the study. On Question 4, general linear models were used, treating the parts of the question (4a–4g) as a repeated-measures within-subject variable and treating condition and gender as between-subject variables.

### The Surveys Versus the Interviews

On Questions 2, 3, and 4a–4g, there were no statistically significant differences in the evaluation responses of the Watched between the 750 survey participants and the 30 interview participants. Thus there is no evidence of a difference between the views of the people in the interview compared to the views of the people in the larger population of those surveyed. As a result, for the remainder of this study, the interview data were used when comparing the views of the Watcher and the Watched.

**Fig. 9.4** Study I and II Combined: Percentage of The Watcher and The Watched Interview and Survey Responses by Gender

| | The Watcher | | | | | | The Watched | | | |
|---|---|---|---|---|---|---|---|---|---|---|
| | Display interview | | Window interview | | Wall interview | | Plaza interview | | Plaza survey | |
| Interview/Survey Response | *M* $n=15$ | *F* $n=15$ | *M* $n=15$ | *F* $n=15$ | *M* $n=15$ | *F* $n=15$ | *M* $n=15$ | *F* $n=15$ | *M* $n=384$ | *F* $n=364$ |
| 1. Live video from the fountain is displayed in someone's office in M[…] Hall. It's not all right this is happening. | 0 | 13 | 13 | 13 | 7 | 27 | 13 | 42 | – | – |
| 2. Displaying live video from the fountain are on a screen in M[…] Hall violates privacy. | 23 | 36 | 20 | 27 | 50 | 47 | 21 | 21 | 17 | 27 |
| 3. Agree with Idea 2: Find displaying the live video troubling. | 13 | 40 | 13 | 27 | 13 | 33 | 20 | 36 | 17 | 31 |
| 4. It's "not all right" if the camera displays live video from the foundation area on a screen in … | | | | | | | | | | |
| a. … Office with outside window M[...] Hall | 0 | 27 | 27 | 40 | 7 | 46 | 27 | 33 | 19 | 28 |
| b. … Office without a window M[...] Hall | 0 | 27 | 13 | 20 | 0 | 7 | 13 | 29 | 21 | 35 |
| c. … Apartment on University Ave. | 0 | 53 | 40 | 67 | 47 | 69 | 21 | 47 | 37 | 59 |
| d. … Apartment in Tokyo | 0 | 53 | 33 | 67 | 33 | 67 | 27 | 50 | 35 | 57 |
| e. … Thousands of homes in the local city | 7 | 47 | 33 | 53 | 47 | 67 | 27 | 50 | 32 | 52 |
| f. … Thousands of homes in Tokyo | 7 | 40 | 40 | 73 | 53 | 80 | 27 | 57 | 34 | 55 |
| g. … Millions of homes across the globe | 0 | 47 | 33 | 73 | 47 | 73 | 40 | 50 | 33 | 54 |
| 5. It's not all right if the video is recorded. | 53 | 79 | 73 | 87 | 67 | 87 | 60 | 93 | – | – |

*Note*. Values in the table are the percentage of participants who gave the indicated response. M[...] Hall stands for the university building on which the HDTV camera was mounted.

| | All Right | | | | Not All Right | | | |
|---|---|---|---|---|---|---|---|---|
| | W'er | | W'ed | | W'er | | W'ed | |
| Justification | *M* | *F* | *M* | *F* | *M* | *F* | *M* | *F* |
| 1. Personal interest | 26 | 34 | 35 | 27 | – | 3 | 11 | 4 |
| 1.1 Unelaborated | 4 | 0 | 1 | 2 | – | 3 | 4 | 0 |
| 1.2 Indifference | 5 | 11 | 10 | 11 | – | 0 | 0 | 0 |
| 1.3 Connection through info. | 3 | 11 | 18 | 4 | – | 0 | 0 | 2 |
| 1.4 Personal enjoyment | 9 | 8 | 4 | 2 | – | 0 | 7 | 2 |
| 1.5 Aesthetics of view | 3 | 15 | 4 | 11 | – | 0 | 0 | 2 |
| 2. External sanctions | 0 | 3 | 8 | 0 | – | 11 | 0 | 0 |
| 2.1 Unelaborated | 0 | 0 | 0 | 0 | – | 11 | 0 | 0 |
| 2.2 Punishment avoidance | 0 | 0 | 0 | 0 | – | 0 | 0 | 0 |
| 2.3 Social condemnation | 0 | 2 | 8 | 0 | – | 0 | 0 | 0 |
| 2.4 Rules and laws | 0 | 2 | 0 | 0 | – | 0 | 0 | 0 |
| 3. Functionality | 23 | 21 | 34 | 47 | – | 53 | 22 | 27 |
| 3.1 Biology | 1 | 2 | 3 | 13 | – | 0 | 4 | 0 |
| 3.2 Tech. isomorphism | 12 | 18 | 21 | 16 | – | 17 | 0 | 4 |
| 3.3 Tech. augmentation | 12 | 3 | 12 | 27 | – | 39 | 19 | 24 |
| 4. Social expectations | 29 | 23 | 32 | 11 | – | 28 | 30 | 31 |
| 4.1 Unelaborated | 0 | 2 | 0 | 4 | – | 17 | 7 | 11 |
| 4.2 Socio-tech. isomorphism | 3 | 0 | 4 | 4 | – | 0 | 0 | 0 |
| 4.3 Biological capabilities | 0 | 10 | 0 | 2 | – | 0 | 0 | 0 |
| 4.4 Place | 25 | 21 | 23 | 5 | – | 6 | 4 | 7 |
| 4.5 Current tech. practice | 0 | 0 | 5 | 0 | – | 0 | 0 | 0 |
| 4.6 Work practice | 8 | 2 | 0 | 2 | – | 11 | 19 | 16 |
| 5. Welfare | 8 | 2 | 14 | 5 | – | 22 | 26 | 28 |
| 5.1 Unelaborated | 1 | 0 | 1 | 2 | – | 3 | 4 | 0 |
| 5.2 Physical | 2 | 0 | 4 | 2 | – | 0 | 4 | 7 |
| 5.3 Material | 3 | 0 | 5 | 0 | – | 11 | 7 | 13 |
| 5.4 Psychological | 1 | 2 | 1 | 2 | – | 8 | 11 | 20 |
| 5.5 Educational | 1 | 0 | 3 | 0 | – | 0 | 0 | 0 |
| 6. Privacy | 8 | 15 | 3 | 0 | – | 8 | 37 | 16 |
| 6.1 Unelaborated | 4 | 2 | 0 | 0 | – | 6 | 4 | 16 |
| 6.2 Private Content | 0 | 0 | 0 | 0 | – | 0 | 0 | 0 |
| 6.3 Legitimate use | 3 | 0 | 0 | 0 | – | 3 | 19 | 0 |
| 6.4 Maintain anonymity | 5 | 13 | 3 | 0 | – | 0 | 7 | 0 |
| 6.5 Control | 0 | 0 | 0 | 0 | – | 0 | 7 | 0 |
| 7. Property | 0 | 2 | 0 | 0 | – | 0 | 0 | 0 |
| 8. Informed consent | 0 | 0 | 0 | 0 | – | 61 | 22 | 31 |
| 8.1 Informed | 0 | 0 | 0 | 0 | – | 44 | 4 | 22 |
| 8.2 Consent | 0 | 0 | 0 | 0 | – | 17 | 4 | 4 |
| 8.3 Informed consent | 0 | 0 | 0 | 0 | – | 0 | 15 | 4 |
| 9. Fairness | 1 | 7 | 1 | 0 | – | 2 | 7 | 0 |

**Fig. 9.5** Study II: Percentage of Justification Use (Averaged Across the 7 Context-of-Use Questions) for The Watcher Large Display and The Watched Interview Responses by Evaluation, Stakeholder Role [W'er = Watcher; W'ed = Watched] and Gender.

| | All Right | | | | Not All Right | | | |
|---|---|---|---|---|---|---|---|---|
| | W'er | | W'ed | | W'er | | W'ed | |
| Justification | *M* | *F* | *M* | *F* | *M* | *F* | *M* | *F* |
| 10. Nonissue | 7 | 8 | 0 | 7 | – | 0 | 0 | 0 |
| 10.1 No harm | 5 | 8 | 0 | 2 | – | 0 | 0 | 0 |
| 10.2 No privacy | 1 | 0 | 0 | 0 | – | 0 | 0 | 0 |
| 10.3 Implied consent | 1 | 0 | 0 | 5 | – | 0 | 0 | 0 |

The number of the participants by evaluation, stakeholder role, and gender (each column) who provided justifications for each of the questions is as follows. All Right Evaluations: W'er, M, 102; W'er F, 61; W'ed, M, 77; W'ed, F, 55. Not All Right Evaluations: W'er F, 36; W'ed, M, 27; W'ed, F, 45. Because virtually no men in The Watcher Large Display condition provided negative "not all right" evaluations, no justification data for this group is reported. Percentages of subcategories may not equal those of overarching categories due to (a) rounding and (b) collapsing multiple justifications.

**Fig. 9.5** (continued)

## The Watcher and the Watched

One central question of this study was whether there were differences between the social judgments about privacy for participants in the Watcher large display condition (i.e., people who were directly using and potentially benefiting from the technology) and the Watched condition (i.e., people who had no voice in and potentially incur harms by the technological installation). Results revealed an interesting interaction between condition and gender: The males (but not the females) expressed less concern about the installation when being the Watcher rather than the Watched. Specifically, as shown in Fig. 9.4 across all the seven context-of-use questions (Questions 4a–4g), results showed the following: First, in the Watcher large display condition, more women than men expressed concerns about the HDTV camera ($p = 0.002$); second, more men in the Watched condition expressed concerns about the HDTV camera than men in the Watcher large display condition ($p = 0.014$).

Interestingly, there were no gender differences for the three questions in the Watched condition that represented canonical examples of private and semiprivate information. Specifically, all of the Watched interview participants considered a handwritten diary as being private (males, 100%; females, 100%); virtually all of them viewed that same diary as being public when it is placed online (males, 93%; females, 93%); and slightly more than half viewed a whispered conversation in an outdoor café as being private (males, 53%; females, 60%).

As with the survey data, at least half of the interview participants in both the Watcher large display condition (77% overall; 10% of all items, "not all right"; 67% of all items, "all right") and the Watched condition (50% overall; 10% of all items, "not all right"; 40% of all items, "all right") held a consistent view about privacy in a public place that applied across all of the seven context-of-use questions (Questions 4a–4g). Moreover, for those participants (the Watcher large display, 23%; the Watched, 50%) who did not hold a consistent view, the pattern of evaluations was similar to that found in the survey data, with more participants saying it was "not all right" to display the image in a remote location (in the participants' city, in Tokyo, and across the globe; Questions 4c–4g) than in a local location (outside and inside offices in M[…] Hall; Questions 4a–4b).

Using the McNemar test, results showed that participants more often objected to the recording of the live video (Question 5) as compared to not recording the live video (Questions 1 and 4a–4g) in both the Watcher large display condition ($p \leq .001$ for all tests) and the Watched condition ($p \leq .004$ for all tests).

## The Watchers: In Situ Condition Versus Hypothetical Conditions

Another question of interest was whether participants' social judgments differed while actually looking at the real-time images on the large display (in situ) compared to imagining the comparable circumstance while physically in the office overlooking the plaza (as a hypothetical scenario). Two conditions involved participants in such a hypothetical situation: the Watcher real window condition and the Watcher blank wall condition. Results showed no significant differences between these two hypothetical conditions; thus, these data were combined and then compared to participants in the Watcher large display condition. These results showed differences for males but not for females. Specifically, fewer males in the Watcher large display condition expressed concerns about the HDTV camera for the seven context-of-use questions (Questions 4a–4g) compared to males in the Watcher real window condition and the Watcher blank wall condition ($p = .003$). The same comparison for females showed no statistically significant differences ($p = .347$).

No significant differences were found for males ($p = .675$) or females ($p = .349$) in comparing the responses to Questions 4a–4g for the Watchers in the hypothetical conditions (the real window and blank wall conditions combined) versus the Watched condition. In other words, the aforementioned interaction between gender and condition disappeared when the questions were asked hypothetically (in the Watcher real window and blank wall conditions) rather than in situ (in the Watcher large display condition). Females responded similarly to these questions regardless of condition (Watcher or Watched) and regardless of whether the questions were asked hypothetically or in situ. Males also responded similarly when they were in the Watched condition or when they were asked hypothetically about being a Watcher, but males showed significantly fewer concerns when they were actually in the situation of being the Watcher.

## Reasoning About Privacy in Public

One major thrust of this study was to characterize people's reasoning about privacy in public. Toward this end, we asked participants to explain why they judged the above activities as "all right" or "not all right" – and through this process engaged them in substantive discussion. Then, through extensive systematic qualitative analyses of the transcribed interviews (discussed in Methods), we generated a hierarchical typology of reasoning about privacy in public. Figure 9.5 summarizes the ten overarching categories. In this section, we report on each of these categories in more depth so as to explicate more of the complexity of the ideas and the context within which they emerged. Each category description contains a concise definition of the category (with brief illustrative examples from the interviews in parentheses) followed by one somewhat longer segment from an interview that provides a fuller sense of participants' thoughts and means of expression. The goal here is to provide a "thicker" (Geertz, 1984; Spradley, 1970/2000) description of people's reasoning, before moving forward with reporting on the quantitative reasoning results. In the qualitative protocols that follow, participants' verbatim words are in regular font, and the interviewer's words are in italics.

**Personal Interests**. Personal Interests refers to an appeal based on individual likes and dislikes, including personal indifference (e.g., "It doesn't really matter to me"), connection through information (e.g., "People can see a different part of the world and feel connected across the globe"), personal enjoyment (e.g., "It'd be interesting to watch … fun for people"), and aesthetics of view (e.g., "just to add a little more ambience to the room … a little touch of nature").

One of the most direct forms of the Personal Interest justification category is an appeal to "fun."

> *Do you think that it is all right or not all right that this is happening?* I think it's all right. *Why?* Because we're people and we have eyes and we're gonna end up watching other people. We're interested in other people so if we weren't interested in other people you'd just sit there by yourself and that's not fun.

This response also received a second code for "biological naturalism" wherein the participant says that given the nature of human biology (that "we have eyes") it is in effect natural to use one's eyes to watch other people through a window.

**External Sanctions**. External Sanctions refers to an appeal based on consequences, rules, and norms established by others, including punishment avoidance (not found in this data set), social condemnation (e.g., "I won't do anything that weird out here"), and rules and laws (e.g., "Certain things are allowed when they're contained within the university, but once you get out of it, there's different rules that apply").

In the moral developmental literature as framed by Kohlberg and colleagues (e.g., Colby et al., 1983; Kohlberg, 1969, 1984; Power, 1991), avoidance of punishment – a canonical external sanction – is a common early form of moral reasoning. Typical examples include "because I could get in trouble," "because you could get caught by the police," "because one could be put in jail." In the current study, one might imagine an individual's objecting to the installation because he or she might be seen doing something improper if not illegal and does not want to be caught and potentially punished. However, not a single individual used this form of external sanction reasoning. Perhaps the closest that emerged from the data was in the following passage:

> *Let's say the screen's in an apartment in a residential neighborhood in Tokyo. Is that all right or not all right?* It's starting to feel stranger and stranger the more I think about this. Umm, I don't see any difference between putting it in Tokyo or putting it here. But the more I think about it, you know I don't like the idea of not being able to sneak around, when I think no one's looking.

Here the participant objects to the installation because it would prevent him from "being able to sneak around" – an idea that seems more aligned with a concern with what others might think of him, in terms of socially condemning the sneaking, rather than in terms of being directly punished for it.

**Functionality**. Functionality refers to an appeal based on how the technology mimics or augments human biology, the physical world, or other technology, including biology (e.g., "Yeah that's fine. … They could probably see down here anyway"), technological isomorphism (e.g., "because [the large display] is just like another window"), and technological augmentation (e.g., "Not only are your actions viewable to anyone here … they'd be viewable to anyone there").

Perhaps the clearest examples of functionality involve technological isomorphisms, wherein the technical installation is viewed to function like other existing technologies. One technology was a webcam ("It's just like looking at the webcam on K[…] Hall on your computer so I don't see the difference"). Another involved television, videos, and movies ("I don't know how it's gonna be viewed any different than TV"). And another involved a window itself ("You can watch people out a window and this is the same thing"). Yet for some participants the technology also functioned as a means to extend features of the physical world:

> *Let's say the large screen is in an apartment on University Avenue. Is that all right or not all right?* Hmmm, that's fine. *Okay, how come?* It opens up the publicness of the space so that not only are your actions viewable to anyone here, they'd be viewable to anyone there. But it's still a public place.

Here the technology is conceptualized as extending the boundaries of public space ("It opens up the publicness of the space") to include remote watchers. Other times, the technology was conceptualized as extending the boundaries of time beyond what was biologically normal ("It wouldn't be all right [to record] because then you'd be able to watch it over and over and over again whereas if it's just a live feed, you just watch it once and that's pretty much it").

**Social Expectations**. Social Expectations refers to an appeal based on current and expected practices in socially situated contexts, including sociotechnical isomorphism (e.g., "People do it anyway on TV so it's not like it's new"), biological capabilities (e.g., "Everybody does it. … I mean it's part of life, seeing people"), place (e.g., "Well you're out in public and it's showing a public image of a fountain at a public university"), current technological practices (e.g., "Technology's all around us. … They come in many tiny forms"), and work practice (e.g., "When you're in an office … there's certain things that you do and you don't do").

The main idea here is that for some participants their social judgments (and potentially their corresponding behaviors) drew heavily on how they understood conventional practices. In its unelaborated form, this category characterizes how participants spoke about the way that social life is ("We're watched a lot more than we know, everywhere we go, so it's just one of those facts of life"). Along these lines, another participant made the following analogy: "Like in your home, you don't expect anybody to be watching you, even through your windows." Because participants sometimes assumed that different social contexts engendered different moral practices in terms of publicity and privacy, the same technical installation appropriate in one place may not be appropriate in another. Here is an example:

> *Let's say the screen is in an apartment on University Avenue. Is that all right or not all right?* Kind of interesting question. … When you're in your personal apartment, there's no-holds-barred. Like you can do anything you want to. … there's no supervision, there can be a lot of exploitation. Whereas in the work environment, there's no exploitation, there's no chance of it, there's no chance of like any kind of stalking behavior.

For this participant, work environments are considered free of exploitation. Presumably if at some point this participant became convinced that in his location, or in a location elsewhere, work environments were rife with exploitation, his judgment about the appropriateness of the installation would change accordingly.

**Welfare**. Welfare refers to an appeal based on people's well-being, including physical welfare (e.g., "Safety is a good reason"), material welfare (e.g., "It's a waste of money and time … [to have] two of the same pictures"), psychological welfare (e.g., "There are some people who are going to be uncomfortable with this"), and educational welfare (e.g., "There might be some educational value … learn about different places").

Participants sometimes sought to balance what they perceived as potential harms and benefits, as in the following example:

> *Let's say in addition to your live image at the fountain being shown on a screen in someone's office in M[…] Hall, your image is also being recorded. So would that be all right or not all right?* It'd be better for security reasons, better for the safety of us the students. Otherwise I would have a problem with that because that's something they can replay and replay, and they can put that stuff on the Internet; they can do stuff with that that can really, you know, damage people. Say you're walking down the street and you know you pick a wedgie and someone could like blow that up on the Internet, and the next thing you know you're just the hot spot next to the hamster dance in Napster. That's embarrassing, and nobody needs to see that sort of thing. Um so yeah, if it were for security reasons, then yeah sure I would not have a problem with that at all. Otherwise I think I might.

This participant recognizes that recording the public images could cause psychological harm ("Someone could like blow that up on the Internet, and the next thing you know you're just the hot spot next to the hamster dance in Napster") but could also "be better for security" for students. In this particular segment, it is not clear whether the participant would judge in favor of the installation if it could be used for both purposes (psychological harm and physical security). What is clear is that both considerations are central to this person's orientation.

**Privacy**. Privacy refers to an appeal based on a claim, an entitlement, or a right of an individual to determine what information about himself or herself is communicated to others, including private content (not found in this data set; retained as a canonical example of the Privacy category; Margulis, 2003), legitimate use (e.g., "There's absolutely no reason for anybody … to need to know"); maintain anonymity (e.g., "Because we can't pick up details of people's faces. I mean, you get body shapes, that sort of things. … It's all very anonymous"), and control (e.g., "It depends on how closely you guard it").

Often privacy justifications were overlaid with multiple considerations.

> *Let's say the screen is in an apartment on University Avenue. Is that all right or not all right?* Oh no. No, no, no, no, no. *Why is it not all right?* It's footage of public place. Because if I chose to be on the five o'clock news and I put myself in the path of the camera, then that would be my choice. But if I walked by the fountain and had no idea that I'd be, effectively speaking, on the five o'clock news, I would resent it. … That would be problematic for me … just seems like an invasion of privacy.

This participant begins with a statement about context: "It's footage of public place." Then she asserts a claim or entitlement to determine what information about her may be communicated to others in that context ("if I chose to be on the five o'clock news and I put myself in the path of the camera"). She also touches on the idea of the need to be informed when public places are being filmed (see the justification category Informed Consent). Only then does she end with a straightforward claim to privacy ("just seems like an invasion of privacy").

**Property**. Property refers to an appeal based on a concept of tangible property (e.g., "[The] university … is owned by somebody … and they have the same right that someone who owns a store does when someone is on their property so it's all right") and intangible property (e.g., "My image is a different property right").

> *Let's say in addition to your live image at the fountain being shown on a screen in someone's office in M[…] Hall, it was also being recorded. In that case would it be all right or not all right?* Not all right. *Why?* For the same reason that it's not all right even to flash it up there, because of nonconsent. And because of property rights. My image, if I'm being looked at is a different, I feel a different property right even then if I'm being recorded. Because if I'm being recorded it's like any recording, a song or a book, you have copyright laws and intellectual property laws and those kinds of things. For someone to take that image and record it without my consent, it violates my privacy.

This example illustrates a prototypic property justification ("I feel a different property right") with a clear analogy of one's image in public being like other forms of intellectual property ("Because if I'm being recorded it's like any recording, a song or a book, you have copyright laws and intellectual property laws"). This example also illustrates how closely intertwined many of these justifications are in participants' reasoning insofar as this participant's property reasoning led readily into a consideration based on informed consent ("For someone to take that image and record it without my consent …") and privacy ("… it violates my privacy").

**Informed Consent**. Informed Consent refers to an appeal based on being informed of the risks and benefits of an activity and the opportunity to choose to participate, including being informed (e.g., "It's okay with me if it's disclosed"), providing consent (e.g., "It kinda reminds me of like the reality TV, but you didn't sign up for anything like that"), and providing informed consent (e.g., "Outright consent like not even just a sign saying this is being recorded but opting in rather than opting out").

As noted, there are close linkages between informed consent and privacy:

> *Do you think this violates your privacy?* Because it's not disclosed, it violates my privacy—again because it's a form of observation, private observation without any consent.

This participant succinctly captures both the idea of being informed ("It's not disclosed") and the need for individuals to provide consent ("It's a form of observation … without any consent"). Moreover, this passage shows that the identical act can invade privacy or not depending on whether individuals have been informed about the act and given a meaningful opportunity to opt out.

**Fairness**. Fairness refers to an appeal based on freedom from misrepresentation (e.g., "There have been a number of cases where recorded images matched up with facial profiles of [innocent people apprehended for crimes])" and reciprocity (e.g., "They can see us, I can possibly see them, so yeah I don't mind").

One of the distinguishing features of someone's looking out a window and observing others in a public place is that, at least usually, others in the public place can reciprocally look back through the window and look at the person who is looking at them. Thus, the person in the public place can both know that someone is looking and, reciprocally, be able to see (to some extent) the person who is looking. For some participants, this feature established conditions of fairness, which this large display could not duplicate.

> *Let's say the screens are in homes of thousands of people living in the local area. Is that all right or not all right?* It's not all right. *How come?* Mostly because I'm starting to feel weirder and weirder that people are looking at me when I can't tell if anyone's looking or not. … If everyone in [this city] has a view … chances are, someone I know is [watching], but I have no way of knowing. It's a little disconcerting.

This participant feels "weirder and weirder" that the large display could allow acquaintances to look at him without his knowing. Moreover, the reciprocity afforded by real windows appears to check perceived harms that can occur through watchers' watching others on a large display.

**Nonissue**. Nonissue refers to an appeal based on a belief that the issue under discussion is irrelevant or does not occur, including no harm (e.g., "It's not being used for any malicious purposes"), no privacy (e.g., "Privacy, that's such an old concept; that doesn't exist anymore"), and implied consent (e.g., "It would become a knowledge that this area is being filmed, and … I can choose to avoid this place if I don't want to be on somebody's screen").

The "no harm" consideration sometimes emerged when participants were considering the lack of access that remote viewers had to the individual being viewed:

> *Let's say that the screen's in an apartment in a residential neighborhood in Tokyo. Is that all right or not all right?* Again, I'd have to ask why do they want to see it? In a way it's not quite as creepy as the guy on University Ave., because they can't come here. … That doesn't bother me quite as much actually. … Because it's far away, they couldn't come here anyway; then it's not quite as bad. Because somebody at an apartment implies that they want to watch here without being there physically, which implies that maybe there's something. You know.

It is in this way that, for some participants, people watching the large screen could increase in number without increasing the risks as long as those people watching were in far-off locations such that they could not physically access the public area and harm individuals there. It is also worth highlighting that the "no privacy" justification was used in three ways, each increasing in scope. The first focused on the lack of a privacy violation in the instance at hand ("You're not really invading on their privacy if you're just kind of like filming them walking"). The second argued that privacy does not exist in public spaces ("Just because this is a public place, you don't require privacy in a public place"). And the third argued that privacy no longer exists ("Privacy, that's such an old concept; that doesn't exist anymore"). Note, finally, that we placed the Implied Consent subcategory here under Nonissue rather than Informed Consent. Our reason is that participants used this justification as a means to establish that they could have chosen otherwise, and thus the potential concerns raised at this point in the interview were to them actually not of concern.

## Quantitative Results of Justification Use

We quantitatively analyzed the Watched and the large display Watcher participants' justification use, averaged across the seven context-of-use questions (4a–4g). Given the numerous categories used and the comparatively small number of participants in each category, it was not possible to perform inferential statistics on this segment of results. Nonetheless, by visual inspection of the quantitative results, certain trends can be seen.

Across condition and gender, at the overarching level of the categories, participants provided a consistent pattern of justification use to support their "all right" evaluations. Specifically, as shown in Fig. 9.5, participants on average primarily drew on three forms of justifications: personal interest (31%), functionality (31%), and social expectations (24%). Two of these same categories played an important role in supporting participants' "not all right" evaluations: functionality (34%) and social expectations (30%). More specifically, functionality understood in terms of a technological isomorphism (e.g., that the large screen functioned analogously to an existing technology) more often supported affirmative evaluations for the use of the display (17%) than not (5%); yet, functionality understood in terms of an augmentation (e.g., that the large screen extended the capabilities or features of one's biology, the physical world, or existing technologies) less often supported affirmative evaluations for the use of the display (14%) than not (27%). In turn, social expectations understood in terms of place (e.g., what one expects being in a public place) more often supported affirmative evaluations for the use of the display (18%) than not (6%); yet, social expectations understood in terms of work practice (e.g., what one expects being in a work environment) less often supported affirmative evaluations for the use of the display (3%) than not (15%).

In addition to functionality and social expectations, three other overarching justifications played, on average, an important role in supporting participants' "not all right" evaluations: welfare (25%), privacy (29%), and informed consent (38%). Under welfare, the most often used subcategories were psychological welfare (13%) and material welfare (10%). Under privacy, the most often used subcategory (not counting "unelaborated") was legitimate use (7%). Under informed consent the most often used subcategory was informed (23%).

Notably, certain justifications averaged across questions played little role in participants' "all right" or "not all right" evaluations: external sanctions (3%, "all right"; 4%, "not all right"), property (1%, "all right"; 0%, "not all right"), fairness (2%, "all right"; 3%, "not all right"), and nonissue (6%, "all right"; 0%, "not all right").

## Discussion

Some scholars have argued that privacy no longer exists, or, if it does, it is quickly disappearing with the advent of new technologies that increasingly make people's activities public (Gotlieb, 1996). Moreover, it could be said that as a society people should stop worrying about long-lost ways of being and, instead, adjust to the new world. Yet the results from these two studies support a different conclusion.

All (100%) of the participants in the Watched interview condition conceptualized the canonical privacy item (a handwritten diary) as being private, and a majority (57%) said that a whispered conversation in an outdoor café was also private. Against this backdrop, over half (55%) of the participants we surveyed expressed some concern for having their images in a public place collected and displayed elsewhere. In turn, 53% to 93% of the participants we interviewed (depending on gender and condition) judged that it is not all right to record a live video image in a public place. These results are consistent with related literature on attitudes about online privacy (Cranor et al., 1999; Privacy and American Business, 1997, 1998) and privacy concerns and consumer choice (Taylor, 2003). In addition, 16% of the participants we surveyed expressed strong and consistent concerns about having their images in a public place collected and displayed elsewhere. These results are in line with those by Jancke et al. (2001), who found that roughly 20% of people in their study expressed strong privacy concerns about linking a workplace through real-time video. The results are also roughly compatible with those found over the years in Harris Polls where approximately 25% of the population in the United States has been characterized as "privacy fundamentalists" (Taylor, 2003). Taken together, our results extend previous research by providing evidence that people have concerns for their privacy even while walking through a public plaza.

The results of the interview study (Study II) provide a deep and broad understanding of the ways in which participants understood privacy. In terms of depth, participants' privacy conceptions were often more than a mere restatement of the word privacy (e.g., "because it's an invasion of my privacy"). Rather, participants brought to bear privacy considerations based on whether there are legitimate uses of the information (e.g., "I just don't feel like people in Tokyo, and I'm sure they're all very nice, need to be privy to what I look like"), ways of maintaining anonymity through technical mechanisms (e.g., "Because [of the way the technology works], we can't pick up details of people's faces"), and people's control over information (e.g., "They don't want other people to know"). The results also show that people's privacy judgments are multifaceted and overlap with broader considerations based on physical harm (e.g., "If there is an accident, you can see them and then you can help them"), psychological well-being (e.g., "At this point, it's getting kinda scary as to why in the world they're doing this"), and informed consent (e.g., "It's okay with me … if it's disclosed"). It was also the case that participants' privacy evaluations depended, in part, on how they viewed the local and cultural practices. Thus participants drew on their differing understanding of social expectations to support both positive evaluations (e.g., "It just seems fine; there's hundreds of cameras all over the place, you know, watching you constantly") and negative evaluations (e.g., "I don't feel the same way about it [the large display in an apartment on University Ave.] because when you're in an office, you're in a professional environment, you know, there's certain things that you do and you don't do"). Thus future studies of information technologies and privacy in public places would do well to engage people with these deeper and broader considerations.

As shown in the introduction, in the field of human–computer interaction (as represented by its major publication venues during 2000–2004), we did not find a single empirical publication about privacy that reported analyses with respect to gender. Thus one of the goals of this study was to examine potential gender differences in people's judgments about privacy in public. We found across both the surveys (Study I) and the interviews (Study II) a clear pattern in which more women than men expressed concerns about the display of real-time images from a camera in a public place. In addition, a greater percentage of men expressed concerns about privacy when they were in the more vulnerable position of being the Watched compared to the Watcher. This latter finding is not surprising insofar as people typically become more concerned about an issue when it affects them directly. What is surprising is that the percentage of women who expressed concerns did not change across conditions. Our interpretation is that, compared to men, women feel more vulnerable, especially in terms of physical safety and psychological well-being (such as being stalked) and that women bring these concerns into a greater variety of roles in life. One implication of our results is that when designing systems that may implicate privacy, it is important to bring a representation of perspectives (in this case vis-à-vis gender) to the design table, in terms of the user perspective, indirect stakeholders, and the design team itself.

In terms of the effect of location of the large display (in an office adjacent to the public plaza, within the same town, in Tokyo, across the globe) and the number of people watching (one person, thousands, millions), the majority of participants (61%) held consistent views about privacy across the seven context-of-use questions. Of the 39% of the participants who expressed differing views about privacy across the seven context-of-use questions, a cluster analysis revealed two overarching patterns. First, these participants more often said that it was all right to display the image in the building adjacent to the public plaza than elsewhere. Second, these participants more often said that it was all right to display the image in an office with a window view of the public plaza compared to an inside office in the same building. In addition, our results show some indication that for the participants who did not hold a consistent view of privacy across the seven context-of-use questions, displaying the image in a large number of remote locations was more acceptable than displaying the image in a single remote location. This finding runs counter to a good deal of literature that shows that when the magnitude of a problem increases, so does the judgment against it. Why, then, the different pattern of results regarding magnitude in our current study? One explanation emerged from the interview justification results. Namely, by increasing the number of people watching one's image on a large display, personal security could be enhanced by virtue of the increasing number of people who would be in a position to come to one's aid in time of trouble.

There are at least two substantial concerns that can be raised about the studies reported here. One concern entails our approach to the qualitative interview data. Specifically, it could be argued that through a systematic treatment of the qualitative data, we have lost a rich, textured account of people's experiences and judgments about privacy and that a narrative-like approach to the data would have yielded a more cohesive account of each person's unique circumstance and perspective. We agree that such narrative analyses are valuable, particularly when the research goals emphasize the detailed perspectives of a limited number of individuals (see, e.g., in our own work, Friedman et al., 2005; also Dourish et al., 2004). At the same time, such narrative methods are less well-suited to identifying more general patterns across larger data sets, as was the case here with the patterns that we sought with respect to the multidimensional elements of people's privacy judgments. Thus, we drew on well-established methods for analyzing social–cognitive data (Damon, 1977; Kahn, 1999; Kohlberg, 1984; Turiel, 1983). Like the narrative analyses, these social–cognitive methods entail a careful reading of every interview in its entirety (over 1,100 single-spaced transcript pages from 120 individuals). Then, as we have described in the Methods section, coding categories were generated from half of the data, staying close to how people spoke about their views. Those categories were then applied to the entire data set. Thus, although giving up some on a rich narrative account, we believe that our systematic coding of the qualitative interview data at the level of people's reasons positioned us to speak to the research questions at hand.

A second concern entails that of potential bias in the survey and interview questions. Granted, the questions directed participants' attention to some issues – in this case, that of privacy in public – and not to other issues, such as security. Thus it could be argued that our survey and interview questions led participants to identify privacy concerns. There is some merit to this argument, and in this sense our results may represent an upper bound on participants' concerns and that other benefits from the installation, such as increased security, may be underrepresented in the data. That said, we want to emphasize the many ways that we were able to limit bias in the research methods: First, there was no mention of privacy in the recruitment of participants. Second, there was no mention of privacy in the initial questions in both the survey and the interview. Third, when privacy was introduced, participants were free to say that their privacy was not violated. Indeed, many did. Recall that 50% to 83% of the participants we interviewed (depending on gender and condition) said that their privacy was not violated (see Fig. 9.4). Fourth, the semistructured-interview methodology allowed participants to expand on topics of import to them and to bring more than one type of issue to bear in responding to a single question. As illustrated in the discussion of the qualitative data, participants often did so, and all of their reasons were coded and analyzed. Thus, the range of justifications reported in Fig. 9.5 emerged, including not only references to privacy but to nine other overarching categories: personal interest, external sanctions, functionality, social expectations, welfare, property, informed consent, fairness, and nonissue. Finally, it is important to recognize that the key gender findings of this study stand in the sense that men and women were asked the same questions but responded differently.

We turn finally to some larger biological and cultural reflections on privacy in public. From a biological perspective, it seems reasonable to assume that the human experience of privacy has grown out of biological capacities as a species to sense and to be sensed (Arendt, 1958/1998; Barkow et al., 1992; Wilson, 1975, 1998). Imagine, for example, a social group some tens of thousands of years ago: A person's presence in public was known by people who could directly sense (such as in see or hear) the other. Vice versa, the sensed person could, in virtually all situations, equally well sense the sensor. In the current study, we saw evidence of such biological reasoning. For example, when participants distinguished among the seven context-of-use questions, they primarily did so on the basis of what they could see (the university building) versus what was out of sight (locations in the local city, in Tokyo, and across the globe). Moreover, participants brought considerations of biology into their reasoning about personal interests (e.g., "We're people, and we have eyes, and we're gonna end up watching other people; we're interested in other people"), social expectations (e.g., "Since you're in a public place, you know that somebody's going to watch you. ... Somebody will be watching you"), and how the technology mimics or augments human senses (e.g., "[The large display is] the same as someone looking across the fountain"). Future research could further explore how people's conceptions of privacy in a technological context are at times tethered to human biology.

From a cultural perspective, most new technologies take time to become integrated into – and change – existing patterns of social life (Friedman, 1997b; Grudin, 2001; Pelto, 1973; Sharp, 1980/1952). Thus it remains to be seen to what extent people will allow and adapt to emerging conventional practices that involve web cameras and surveillance technologies that usurp privacy in public places. On the one hand people may well accept greater erosion of privacy, as much due to the benefits accorded by increased personal security as to the juggernaut of technological progress that is difficult to stop. On the other hand, the research literature suggests that children and adults need some privacy to develop a healthy sense of identity, to form attachments based on mutual trust, and to maintain the larger social fabric (Fried, 1968; Newell, 1998; Palen and Dourish, 2003; Reiman, 1976; Schoeman, 1984). The literature also shows that privacy in some form exists cross-culturally (Briggs, 1970; Moore, 1984; Westin, 1967).

As technologies continue to augment the senses and decrease the limitations of physical space and time, there may become fewer and fewer mechanisms by which to maintain privacy in the public realm. Moreover, if it is true – and we believe it is – that some modicum of privacy in public is part of our biological heritage and necessary for healthy psychological and societal functioning, then the private in public needs to be accounted for and supported in system design.

## Notes

**Background** An earlier version of this article appeared in *Online Proceedings of CHI Fringe 2004*.

**Acknowledgments** We thank Stephanie Collett and Peyina Lin for assistance with the privacy and gender literature review, Daniel Dethloff, Brandon Rich, and Anna Stolyar for assistance with data collection, Annie Jo Cain for assistance with transcribing, Anna Stolyar for assistance with data entry, Nathan G. Freier for assistance with data analyses, Donald Horowitz for discussions about power relationships, privacy and gender, and our study participants. We also thank Action Editor Terry Winograd and three anonymous reviewers for their thoughtful comments.

**Support** This material is based upon work supported by the U.S. National Science Foundation under Grant Nos. IIS-0102558 and IIS-0325035. Any opinions, findings, and conclusions or recommendations expressed in this material are those of the authors and do not necessarily reflect the views of the National Science Foundation.

## References

Abowd, G. A. and Mynatt, E. D. (2000). Charting past, present, and future research in ubiquitous computing. *ACM Transactions on Computer–Human Interaction, 7*(1), 29–58.

Ackerman, M., Darrell, T., and Weitzner, D. J. (2001). Privacy in context. *Human–Computer Interaction, 16*, 167–176.

Adler, A. and Henderson, A. (1994). A room of our own: Experiences from a direct office-share. *Proceedings of the CHI 94*. New York: ACM Press.

Allen, A. L. (1988). *Uneasy access: Privacy for women in a free society*. Totowa, NJ: Rowman & Littlefield.

Arendt, H. (1998). *The human condition*. Chicago: University of Chicago Press. (Original work published 1958).

Barkow, J. H., Cosmides, L., and Tooby, J. (Eds.). (1992). *The adapted mind: Evolutionary psychology and the generation of culture*. New York: Oxford University Press.

Boyle, M., Edwards, C., and Greenberg, S. (2000). The effects of filtered video on awareness and privacy. *Proceedings of CSCW 2000*. New York: ACM Press.

Briggs, J. L. (1970). *Never in anger: Portrait of an Eskimo family*. Cambridge, MA: Harvard University Press.

Colby, A., Kohlberg, L., Gibbs, J., and Lieberman, M. (1983). A longitudinal study of moral judgment. *Monographs of the Society for Research in Child Development, 48*(Serial No. 200), 1–124.

Cranor, L. F., Reagle, J., and Ackerman, M. S. (1999). Beyond concern: Understanding net users' attitudes about online privacy. *AT&T Labs-Research Technical Report TR 99.4.3*. Retrieved from http://www.research.att.com/library/trs/TRs/99/99.4/99.4.3

Damon, W. (1977). *The social world of the child*. San Francisco: Jossey-Bass.

Davidson, P., Turiel, E., and Black, A. (1983). The effect of stimulus familiarity on the use of criteria and justifications in children's social reasoning. *British Journal of Developmental Psychology, 1*, 49–65.

Dourish, P., Adler, A., Bellotti, V., and Henderson, A. (1996). Your place or mine? Learning from long-term use of audio-video communication. *Computer-Supported Cooperative Work, 51*, 33–62.

Dourish, P. and Bly, S. (1992). Portholes: Supporting awareness in a distributed work group. *Proceedings of the CHI 1992* (pp. 541–547). New York: ACM Press.

Dourish, P., Grinter, R. E., Delgado de la Flor, J., and Joseph, M. (2004). Security in the wild: User strategies for managing security as an everyday, practical problem. *Pers Ubiquit Comput, 8*, 391–401.

Fish, R. S., Kraut, R. E., and Chalfonte, B. L. (1990). The VideoWindow system in informal communications. *Proceedings of the CSCW 1990*. New York: ACM Press.

Fried, C. (1968). Privacy: A moral analysis. *Yale Law Journal, 77*, 475–493.

Friedman, B. (Ed.). (1997a). *Human values and the design of computer technology*. New York: Cambridge University Press.

Friedman, B. (1997b). Social judgments and technological innovation: Adolescents' understanding of property, privacy, and electronic information. *Computers in Human Behavior, 13*, 327–351.

Friedman, B. (2004). Value sensitive design. In W. S. Bainbridge (Ed.), *Berkshire encyclopedia of human–computer interaction* (pp. 769–774). Great Barrington, MA: Berkshire.

Friedman, B., Freier, N. G., Kahn, P. H., Jr., Lin, P., and Sodeman, R. (2008). Office window of the future? Field-based analyses of a new use of a large display. *International Journal of Human Computer Studies, 66*, 452–465.

Friedman, B. and Kahn, P. H., Jr. (2003). Human values, ethics, and design. In J. Jacko and A. Sears (Eds.), *Handbook of human–computer interaction* (pp. 1177–1201). Mahwah, NJ: Lawrence Erlbaum.

Friedman, B., Kahn, P. H., Jr., and Borning, A. (2006). Value sensitive design and information systems. In P. Zhang and D. Galletta (Eds.), *Human–computer interaction in management information systems: Foundations* (pp. 348–372). Armonk, NY: M. E. Sharpe.

Friedman, B., Kahn, P. H., Jr., Hagman, J., and Severson, R. L. (2005). *Coding manual for "The watcher and the watched: Social judgments about privacy in a public place"* (University of Washington Information School Technical Report IS-TR-2005–07–01). Seattle: Information School, University of Washington.

Geertz, C. (1984). "From the native's point of view": On the nature of anthropological understanding. In R. A. Shweder and R. A. LeVine (Eds.), *Culture theory: Essays on mind, self, and emotion* (pp. 123–136). Cambridge: Cambridge University Press.

Goldberg, K. (2005). *Demonstrate project*. Retrieved from http://demonstrate.berkeley.edu.

Gotlieb, C. C. (1996). Privacy: A concept whose time has come and gone. In D. Lyon and E. Zureik (Eds.), *Computers, surveillance, and privacy* (pp. 156–171). Minneapolis: University of Minnesota Press.

Grudin, J. (2001). Desituating action: Digital representation of context. *Human–Computer Interaction, 16*, 269–286.

Hatch, E. (1983). *Culture and morality*. New York: Columbia University Press.

Helwig, C. C. (1995). Adolescents' and young adults' conceptions of civil liberties: Freedom of speech and religion. *Child Development, 66*, 152–166.

Hudson, S. E. and Smith, I. (1996). Techniques for addressing fundamental privacy and disruption tradeoffs in awareness support systems. *Proceedings of the CSCW 1996*. New York: ACM Press.

Hutchinson, H., Mackay, W., Westerlund, B., Bederson, B. B., Druin, A., Plaisant, C., et al. (2003). Technology probes: Inspiring design for and with families. *Extended Abstracts of CHI 2003*. New York: ACM Press.

Idehen, E. E. (1997). The influence of gender and space sharing history on the conceptions of privacy by undergraduates. *IFE Pscyhologia, 5*(1), 59–75.

Jancke, G., Venolia, G. D., Grudin, J., Cadiz, J. J., and Gupta, A. (2001). Linking public spaces: Technical and social issues. *Proceedings of the CHI 2001*. New York: ACM Press.

Jiang, X., Hong, J. I., and Landay, J. A. (2002). Approximate information flows: Socially-based modeling of privacy in ubiquitous computing. *Proceedings of Ubicomp 2002*. Berlin: Springer-Verlag.

Junestrand, S., Tollmar, K., Lenman, S., and Thuresson, B. (2000). Private and public spaces—The use of video mediated communication in a future home environment. *Extended Abstracts of the CHI 2000*. New York: ACM Press.

Kahn, P. H., Jr. (1992). Children's obligatory and discretionary moral judgments. *Child Development, 63*, 416–430.

Kahn, P. H., Jr. (1999). *The human relationship with nature: Development and culture*. Cambridge, MA: MIT Press.

Kahn, P. H., Jr., Friedman, B., Freier, N., and Severson, R. (2003). *Coding manual for children's interactions with AIBO, the robotic dog—The preschool study* (UW CSE Technical Report 03–04–03). Seattle: Department of Computer Science and Engineering, University of Washington.

Karro, J., Dent, A. W., and Farish, S. (2005). Patient perceptions of privacy infringements in an emergency department. *Emergency Medicine Australasia, 17*, 117–123.

Kellert, S. R. (1996). *The value of life*. Washington, DC: Island Press.

Killen, M. (1990). Children's evaluations of morality in the context of peer, teacher-child and familial relations. *Journal of Genetic Psychology, 151*, 395–410.

Kohlberg, L. (1969). Stage and sequence: The cognitive-developmental approach to socialization. In D. A. Goslin (Ed.), *Handbook of socialization theory and research* (pp. 347–480). New York: Rand McNally.

Kohlberg, L. (1984). *Essays on moral development: The psychology of moral development: Vol. 2*. San Francisco: Harper & Row.

Krathwohl, D. R. (1998). *Methods of educational and social science research: An integrated approach*. Reading, MA: Addison-Wesley.

Langheinrich, M. (2001). Privacy by design—Principles of privacy-aware ubiquitous systems. *Proceedings of Ubicomp 2001*. Berlin: Springer-Verlag.

Mantei, M., Baecker, R., Sellen, A., Buxton, W., Milligan, T., and Wellman, B. (1991). Experiences in the use of a media space. *Proceedings of CHI 1991*. New York: ACM Press.

Margulis, S. T. (2003). On the status and contribution of Westin's and Altman's theories of privacy. *Journal of Social Issues, 59*, 429–441.

Marshall, N. J. (1974). Dimensions of privacy preferences. *Multivariate Behavioral Research, 9*(3), 255–271.

Milgram, S. (1963). Behavioral study of obedience. *Journal of Abnormal and Social Psychology, 67*, 371–378.

Milgram, S. (1974). *Obedience to authority*. New York: Harper & Row.

Moore, B., Jr. (1984). *Privacy: Studies in social and cultural history*. Armonk, NY: M. E. Sharpe.

Newell, P. B. (1998). A cross-cultural comparison of privacy definitions and functions: A systems approach. *Journal of Environmental Psychology, 18*, 357–371.

Nissenbaum, H. (1998). Protecting privacy in an information age: The problem of privacy in public. *Law and Philosophy, 17*, 559–596.

Nucci, L. P. (1981). The development of personal concepts: A domain distinct from moral and societal concepts. *Child Development, 52*, 114–121.

Olson, M. and Bly, S. (1991). The Portland experience: A report on a distributed research group. *International Journal of Man-Machine Studies, 34*, 211–228.

Palen, L. and Dourish, P. (2003). Unpacking "privacy" for a networked world. *Proceedings of the CHI 2003*. New York: ACM Press.

Pedersen, D. M. (1987). Sex differences in privacy preferences. *Perceptual & Motor Skills, 64*, 1239–1242.

Pedersen, D. M. (1999). Model for types of privacy by privacy functions. *Journal of Environmental Psychology, 19*, 397–405.

Pelto, P. J. (1973). *The snowmobile revolution: Technology and social change in the Arctic*. Menlo Park, CA: Cummings.

Piaget, J. (1960). *The child's conception of the world*. London: Routledge & Kegan Paul. (Original work published 1929).

Privacy and American Business. (1997, April). *Commerce, communication, and privacy online*. Retrieved July 24, 2003, from http://www.pandab.org/compsurv.html

Privacy and America Business. (1998, December). *Executive summary*. Retrieved July 24, 2003, from http://www.pandab.org/1298execsum.html

Power, C. (1991). Democratic schools and the problem of moral authority. In W. Kurtines and J. Gewirtz (Eds.), *Handbook of moral behavior and development: Vol. 3* (pp. 317–333). Hillsdale, NJ: Lawrence Erlbaum.

Reiman, J. H. (1976). Privacy, intimacy, and personhood. *Philosophy & Public Affairs, 6*, 26–44.

Root, R. W. (1988). Design of a multi-media vehicle for social browsing. *Proceedings of the CSCW 1988* (pp. 25–28). New York: ACM Press.

Rustemi, A. and Kokdemir, D. (1993). Privacy dimensions and preferences among Turkish students. *Journal of Social Psychology, 133*(6), 807–808.

Schoeman, F. D. (Ed.). (1984). *Philosophical dimensions of privacy: An anthology*. London: Cambridge University Press.

Sharp, L. (1980). Steel axes for stone-age Australians. In J. P. Spradley and D. W. McCurdy (Eds.), *Conformity and conflict* (pp. 345–359). Boston: Little, Brown, & Company. (Reprinted from *Human Organization*, 1952, *11*, 17–22).

Spradley, J. P. (2000). *You owe yourself a drunk: An ethnography of urban nomads*. Prospect Heights, IL: Waveland Press (Originally published 1970).

Tang, J. C., & Rua, M. (1994). Montage: Providing teleproximity for distributed groups. Proceedings of *the CHI 94*. New York: ACM Press.

Taylor, H. (2003). Most people are "Privacy Pragmatists" who, while concerned about privacy, will sometimes trade it off for other benefits. *The Harris Poll #17*. Retrieved August 28, 2003, from http://www.harrisinteractive.com/harris_poll/ index.asp?PID=365

Turiel, E. (1983). *The development of social knowledge*. Cambridge: Cambridge University Press.

Turiel, E. (2002). *The culture of morality: Social development and social opposition*. Cambridge: Cambridge University Press.

Turiel, E., Hildebrandt, C., & Wainryb, C. (1991). Judging social issues: Difficulties, inconsistencies, and consistencies. *Monographs of the Society for Research in Child Development, 56*(2, Serial No. 224), 1–103.

Wainryb, C. and Turiel, E. (1994). Dominance, subordination, and concepts of personal entitlements in cultural contexts. *Child Development, 65*, 1701–1722.

Warren, S. D. and Brandeis, L. D. (1985). The right to privacy. In D. G. Johnson and J. W. Snapper (Eds.), *Ethical issues in the use of computers* (pp. 172–183). Belmont, CA: Wadsworth (Originally published in *Harvard Educational Review 4*, December 5, 1890, 193–220).

Westin, A. (1967). *Privacy and freedom*. New York: Antheneum.

Wilson, E. O. (1975). *Sociobiology: The new synthesis*. Cambridge, MA: Harvard University Press.

Wilson, E. O. (1998). *Consilience*. New York: Knopf.

Wikan, U. (2002). *Generous betrayal: Politics of culture in the new Europe*. Chicago: University of Chicago Press.

# Chapter 10
# (Dis)connecting Cultures: The Diary of a Short Lived Media Space

**Sara Bly and Steve Harrison**

**Abstract** Most media space projects were reported as "successes" in that the participants developed or maintained close working relationships. A few reported problematic social results, but were created wholesale with groups with no media space experience. This chapter reports a case where media space users tried and failed to extend the media space to new user communities, building in part on experiences gained in the earlier "successes" and, in part, ignoring the key elements of those successes.

## Introduction

*During the existence of the link described here, the first author kept an e-mail-based diary of the project and drafted an initial report; this chapter consists of a version of that report and the diary with our reflections (in italics) to guide the reader.*

We report one particular example of the use of a Media Space to connect two different group areas within PARC. This is an unusual example in that it was not motivated either by an existing workgroup or by the study of distributed technologies. It was an attempt to connect two diverse groups who were being linked administratively. The purpose of this report is to document the experience and suggest findings that might be applied to future media space connections.

The Media Space was created in the Systems Concept Laboratory (SCL) of Xerox PARC (with an early connection to an SCL group in Portland, OR). This version of the PARC Media Space has been described in a number of publications as well as in other chapters of this book (Stults, 1986; Olson and Bly, 1991; Bly

S. Bly
Sara Bly Consulting

S. Harrison
Virginia Polytechnic Institute and State University
e-mail: sHarrison@vt.edu

S. Harrison (ed.), *Media Space 20+ Years of Mediated Life*,
Computer Supported Cooperative Work,

et al., 1993; Harrison, et al., 1997). Media Space development followed an iterative molding of activity and technology; the work and design evolved together. At the same time, the Media Space focused on supporting a working *group* rather than a particular work *task*. The group easily moved to new devices and behaviors, accepting those that worked and discarding those that did not. There were cross-site reporting relationships and cross-site projects. People were encouraged to meet face-to-face regularly and Media Space equipment was constantly in flux, always available to everyone to reconfigure as desired.

The project described here was an attempt to extend the Media Space into another area of the Xerox PARC facility itself, rather than across geographic distances. The Xerox PARC facility holds approximately 300 people with offices arranged around common areas. A set of offices and the corresponding common area are typically called *a pod*. Within PARC, there are three floors, each consisting of six pods. Pods on a single floor are separated from each other by large landscaped light wells. Pods are numbered by the floor (1, 2, or 3) and by the location on the floor (1 is nearest to the entrance of the building, 6 is farthest from the entrance).

## Linking Pods 16/26

After closing the link to Portland in 1988, the researchers in Pod 26 (housing Media Space) were reorganized to work with researchers in another lab, including those in Pod 16. This report describes extending Media Space into Pod 16, thus linking together folks working in Pod 26 with folks working in Pod 16, directly below in the building. The Pod 16 link into the Pod 26 Media Space existed for 7 weeks, beginning August 22 and ending October 10, 1988. The majority of people in both locations were researchers although administrative staff members were also present and participated in the lives of the two pods.

This report will focus on the issues that arose in Pod 16 and changes to the configuration of equipment there. The configuration of equipment in Pod 26 did not change during the period. In fact, Media Space equipment continued in use for some years after this Pod 16/26 link, moving with some of the Pod 26 researchers as they changed organizations and offices throughout PARC.

The motivation for linking the two pods had come up earlier in the year. Two PARC laboratories, the System Concepts Laboratory (SCL, a lab of 20 members, all of whom had participated to some degree in the Media Space and who were in Pod 26) and the Integrated Systems Laboratory (ISL, a lab of about 80 members spread across Pods 15, 16, and 25), were asked to reorganize. There were complex history and divisive internal politics behind this reorganization: most obviously, with the recent shut down of SCL's Portland facility, most of those researchers – nearly half of SCL – choose not to relocate. This eliminated the driving force in SCL's remote-site collaboration research including the Media Space. Other historical factors were as arcane as the attribution of development of garbage-collection techniques and the correct model of class inheritance.

Some individual Pod 25 members of ISL had recently become part of the Media Space. This indicated to people in SCL/Pod 26 a willingness of those in ISL to participate in the Media Space method of experimentation and an interest in the Media Space for potential utility with respect to their own projects and collaborations. (We discovered later that this was, in part, an expression of the internal disconnect the various research groups had within ISL, in contrast to the strong sense of community that typified SCL.)

A member of ISL suggested that a media link between the two labs might help the process of getting to know each other. Two members from each lab immediately embarked on a tour of ISL space to find a location for a link. Administrators were contacted, including a request to provide the necessary telephone connection. The telephone line appeared as did the new lab organization, a merging of the two labs into a single System Sciences Laboratory (SSL). As a result of the latter, the newly formed SSL staff decided that they would like to participate in the Media Space for their own communication although the necessary node equipment for both was unavailable at that time.

In July 1988, the equipment became available and two of the Pod 26'ers decided to move ahead with connecting Pods 16 and 26. On Monday, August 22, Pod 16 was linked into the Media Space already existing in Pod 26. The Pod 16 node consisted of a camera, a 19′ monitor, a remote control of the Pod 26 Commons camera, and a Quorum half-duplex audio link to the Pod 26 Commons. The Pod 26 Commons was left as usual with a camera, a 45″ large-screen display, and a Quorum half-duplex audio microphone. A remote control for the camera in Pod 16 was added to the Pod 26 configuration.

The link in Pod 16 was placed in a public kitchen/couch area with the camera and monitor in three different locations over the 7-week period. Figure 10.1 shows the initial configuration of the node in Pod 16.

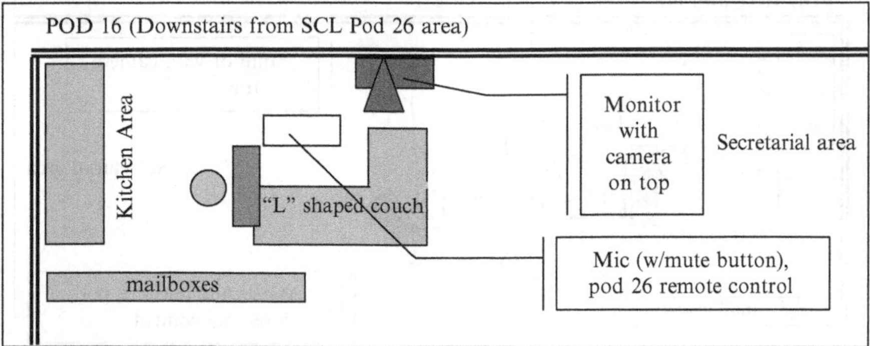


**Fig. 10.1** Initial location of camera, monitor, remote control of Pod 26 camera, and microphone

## Evolving the Pods 16/26 Link

Very few people knew that a Media Space node was being added in Pod 16, so its appearance was a surprise. The link was connected to the Pod 26 Commons area but other nodes of the Media Space could also receive the Pod 16 link signal. There was an initial strong negative reaction from members of Pod 16, resulting in many small group discussions of the Media Space as well as a presentation and open discussion of the link at the biweekly laboratory meeting. At the same time, a few people did begin using the new Media Space node, suggesting that the media connection did have potential utility in connecting Pods 16/26. Feedback centered around two concerns: privacy issues and intrusion on space.

We informally gathered four types of data about the effects of the Pod 16 node: attendance at the open Pod 26 tea time for a week before the link and for 2 weeks following the addition of the link, a diary of events for the first 3 weeks of the link, a videotape of a laboratory discussion about the link, and a collection of mail messages reacting to the link.

*While the diary follows the body of this chapter, it is meant to be read in parallel with it.*

After gathering input from the lab meeting discussion and from individual feedback, a small volunteer group met 3 weeks after the initial installation to consider changes to the placement of the node. The general consensus seemed to be that the camera would be better focused on the kitchen area rather than on the couch area. In addition, the remote camera control was a major factor in feeling out of control and spied upon. The group implemented a second configuration of the Pod 16 node, shown in Fig. 10.2, that was intended to solve the major issues while providing maximum flexibility in use of the node and a reasonable view of the area.

Configuration 2 was quite unusable; it was not satisfactory for either folks in the kitchen or for folks on the couches. A week later a third configuration was implemented, shown in Fig. 10.3, that attempted to follow more closely the original

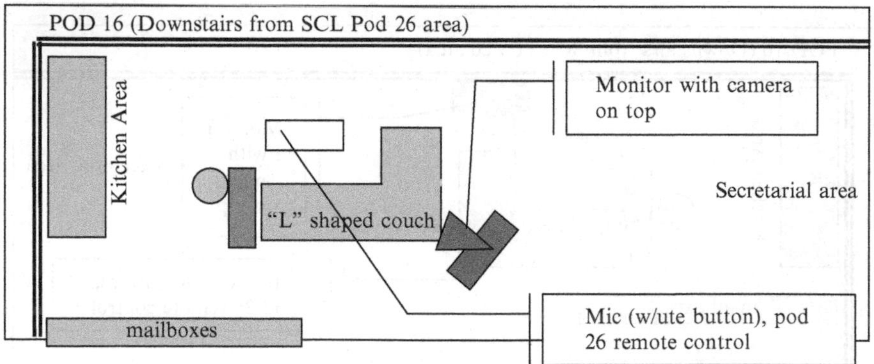


**Fig. 10.2** Second location of camera, monitor, remote control of Pod 26 camera, and microphone

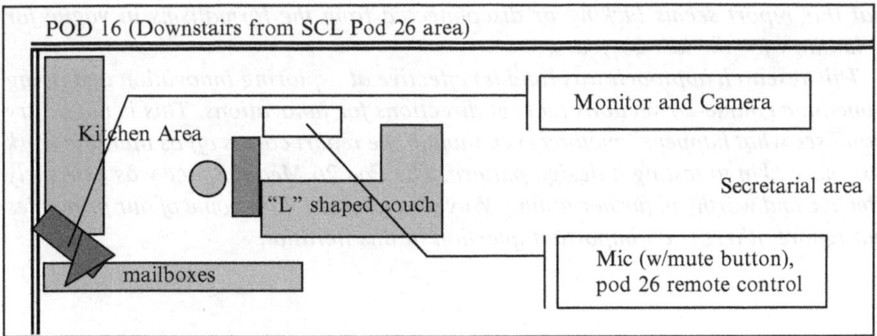


**Fig. 10.3** Final location of camera, monitor, remote control of Pod 26 camera, and microphone

feedback on placement (i.e. less intrusion on the couch and secretarial areas). Tea was planned and announced for both pods the next day to include a demo of the various equipment components. The event was very well attended, particularly by folks in the Pod 16 area. Nevertheless, the node was rarely used for interactions between folks in the two pods. Three weeks later when the equipment had to be dismantled for office construction work, the node was completely removed.

During the 7 weeks of the Pods 16/26 link, the node was used both interactively and passively. The initial configuration provided the most interactive use of the node but was limited by the lack of always-on audio. However, all configurations provided some passive use; folks were aware of the presence of folks in the other pod area.

In addition to the discussions and e-mail feedback, two other effects of the Pods 16/26 link were noted. One, the attendance at tea in Pod 26 increased dramatically and two, the folks in Pod 16 began to use the node in ways that are similar to more experienced use of remote media spaces (e.g., the Portland link).

A primary effect that was hoped for in the introduction of the Pod 16 node was to increase the informal interactions between folks in ISL and folks in SCL. The sidebar contains events gathered from an informal diary kept during the first 3 weeks of the Pods 16/26 link. As in more experienced use of a remote media space, folks used the link to make connections (e.g., Day 5), to share culture (e.g. Day 3, Day 26), and to exchange information (e.g., Day 9, Day 11).

*A reader schooled in HCI or CSCW research will, by now, be wondering about our methodology: our research questions, our hypotheses, our experimental design. To many, this will not seem like an adequate research report. Actually, this document is the shadow – the barest outline of – what is referred to in a few places as "designerly research." Loosely, that form of research is driven out of the designer's impulse, the tension between what is and what ought to be. You can see that neither "what is" nor "what ought to be" were well expressed or reflected upon before embarking on the project.*

*This same set of impulses and quick, evolving trials also show up in Bob Stults' original Media Space Report (Stults, 1986) – but may be lost for the same reason that this report seems lacking or disconnected from the formalisms in vogue for technology for the last 20 years.*

*This research approach was (and is) effective at exploring innovation and doing immediate course-corrections that set directions for innovations. This is not a "try it and see what happens" method even though the report comes off as that; the work was more akin to testing a design pattern. The Pod 26 Media Space was extremely effective and worthy of further testing. Why we chose to follow some of our principles and ignore others is an important question in this iteration.*

## Discussion

Several problems existed with the Pods 16/26 link that can be instructive for the use of Media Spaces. Understandably, the way in which the Pod 16 node was introduced caused many hard feelings and generated heated discussions. The introduction of new technologies into organizations is a well-studied area and will not be addressed here. Why we ignored our own practice of involving others in decisions probably has more to do with our enthusiasm for continuing to explore the design of the Media Space and our desire that other groups would work much like the group in Pod 26 worked. However, other problems were probably at least as significant in contributing to the lack of effectiveness of the link. An understanding of the use of space, the availability of audio as well as video connection, the control of the equipment, and the relationship between the nodes were all areas that deserved more careful planning.

The space into which a public media space node is placed needs to allow a monitor and camera combination that is easy to see, has a reasonable view of the space for the other end, collocates the camera and monitor, and contributes to informal conversations as well as interactions. In some sense, the camera and monitor need to occupy a position that might as well be occupied by 2–3 people. When the node was placed in Pod 16, these criteria were met. As shown in Fig. 10.1, the monitor and camera were across from the couch area, allowing folks on the couch to include folks in Pod 26 "naturally" or not depending on whether or not they were present. The camera provided a view of the couches and peripheral areas. However, the accustomed use of the space in Pod 16 had been incorrectly assumed rather than observed and studied. Although the couch area appeared to be a public area, in fact it was used fairly specifically for individual relaxation and small group meetings. The additions of a quite public space (the Pod 26 Commons) made both these uses much more difficult.

In addition to the camera and monitor in the space, a microphone was also available for conversing between pods. However, in Pod 16, the couch area was adjacent to administrative office space and acoustically not separated from it. Thus, any constant audio became part of the administrative staff's working areas. This was unacceptable, and the audio connection was left off unless a specific interaction was desired between the Pods. This made it impossible to walk by the area casually and say "hello" to anyone in the other space. As a result, informal interactions were limited. Furthermore, since the controls on the microphone were not intuitively easy to use, the chore of merely turning the microphone on and off increased frustration with the link communication and with the feeling of being out-of-control. Further, folks often thought that turning off the local mike would eliminate the sound from the other node. In fact, it turned off the transmission of sound, not the receipt of sound thus exacerbating the problem.

A remote camera control was a relatively new addition to the Media Space, and one was installed in Pods 16 and 26. The expectation was that the remote control allowed a person to have *more* control over what she/he saw and greater knowledge of who was watching. In fact, this was the one piece of equipment that most folks tended to experiment with in Pod 16. However, watching the camera move because someone else was controlling it remotely added significantly to the feelings of being spied upon. (Note that although cameras could be easily moved in the Portland Media Space, they were always moved by people at the local site.)

The equipment itself provided some obstacle to the use of the Pods link. Since folks in Pod 16 felt little or no ownership of the monitor and camera (given that it was in fact not their equipment and they had not participated in its installation), people tended to manipulate it very rarely. Only occasionally did someone choose to put on the lens cap or to turn the camera to a particular view of the room. Given the complexities of the remote camera control and the difficulties of the audio connection, the result seemed to be very little use of the equipment and perhaps a feeling of being in control of the environment.

*These "findings" are useful as guidelines. The simple message of the project is "Don't do this!" Don't intrude on another's space and way of working. Don't force unwanted connections. Nevertheless, the Pods 16/20 connection does support earlier findings reported in (Bly, Harrison and Irwin, 1999): the value of a commonality of purpose and an openness about work, control interfaces that are easy to use, a technological set-up based on understanding the uses of the particular space.*

## Conclusions

So, what did we learn – or perhaps, relearn? Two factors are critical to the success of media spaces in new areas.

One, **the expansion of the existing space into a media space should be an expansion, not an intrusion**. The folks in the space should have reason to interact with others in the space, and it should be comfortable to have "newcomers" entering the area. The media space is an addition to space, and just as one wouldn't open up one's living room to all families in the town, one probably shouldn't expand a media space to include more than a meaningful working group.

Two, **the use of the media space should require as little overhead as possible**. In general, folks should be able to see and converse freely without regard to the equipment. Folks should feel they control the equipment, not that they are controlled by the equipment.

We were and are both embarrassed and frustrated that we created a negative set of interactions between Pod 16 and Pod 26 around the Media Space. It appears to verify the initial hypotheses of the Burge and Tater work that more impoverished media connections lead to more impoverished communication (Burge and Tatar, 2008). But they show that these results do not show up with couples who know each other well and "the person being interacted with is already quite individuated and well-known, making it unlikely for general stereotypes to be invoked."

Our only at-hand model of successful use of a public media space was the one that SCL had used when it was connected between Palo Alto and Portland. That model was one of close working relations built upon carefully constructed and maintained social relations. As Harrison (2008) says, "media space was (is!) not a general solution to putting remote co-workers together but a means of conjoining spaces for people with close working relations." People worked hard in SCL to get along, to know what others were up to, and to be part of community. That is probably very unusual. It certainly is not a reasonable assumption for all remote (or even local) collaboration to rest upon.

## References

Bly, S., Harrison, S., and Irwin, S. (1993) "Media Spaces: Bringing people together in a video, audio, and computing environment." *Communications of the Association of Computing Machinery*, New York; 36(1), 28–45, January

Burge, J.D. and Tatar, D. (2008) "Affect and Dyads: Conflict Across Different Technological Media" in Media Space 20+ Years of Mediated Life, Chapter 8

Harrison, S. (2008) "Big Brother's Other Sibling" in Media Space 20+ Years of Mediated Life, Chapter 10.2

Harrison, S., Bly, S., Anderson, S., Minneman, S., (1997) "The Media Space," *Video-Mediated Communication* (Finn, K., Sellen, A., & Wilbur, S. eds.), Mahwah, NJ, Lawrence Erlbaum, pp. 273–300.

Olson, M., Bly, S. (1991) The Portland experience: a report on a distributed research group, *International Journal of Man-Machine Studies*, 34(2), 211–228, February

Stults, R. (1986) *Media Space*. Xerox Corporation, Palo Alto

## Appendix: Diary of The Pods 16/26 Link

*The first author's annotated notes made during the media space link between Floors One and Two at Xerox PARC.*

## Day 1 – August 22, 1988 (Monday)

The link was first up with *video* and audio about 11 am. New users seem to try a fairly typical set of actions: making faces, panning and zooming the camera *in* the other Pod, and coming up close to the camera so that the camera view *is* not recognizable. Negative reactions included turning off the mike (usually *in* an unsuccessful attempt to cut down on the *noise* heard from the other end), running whenever the camera moved toward them, and being disturbed by the *noise*.

Tea [*in* Pod 26] included an unveiling of the 1949 Zenith television set. A few folks *in* Pod 16 noted the action and "looked *in*". One person seemed particularly interested *in* the link and joined us for tea (perhaps for the first time?).

*SCL had a regular tea time so that researchers would socialize. During the time SCL was connected between Palo Alto and Portland, tea was an important time for Lab members to reassert their relationships outside their research areas. Thus, we see that this tea-over-media space concept was an attempt to reach out to members of ISL, a means to hold onto valued aspects of the old lab culture, and a setting for discussion of the link (and of the new power alignments).*

Several folks remarked about the need for two sets of camera controls; one for the local camera and one for the camera *in* the other pod.

A meeting was scheduled *in* the [Pod 16] common area for the end of the day. A visitor to PARC attending the meeting was said to have cast many curious looks at the camera before interrupting the meeting to ask "where IS that?"

The location appears to be unfortunate, since several administrative folks have desks *in* the area and feel that their individual spaces are being violated by the camera and the *noise*.

## Day 2 – August 23, 1988 (Tuesday)

This day seemed to get started with great concern about the noise coming from Pod 26 into Pod 16, A secretary in Pod 16 appeared quite upset and forcefully hit the "off" button on the mike (not only failing to eliminate the noise from Pod 26 but adding a disconnected phone line to the confusion).

One Pod 16'er had put instructions on the wall near the equipment. At the end of the day, we traded Quorum mikes between pods (the one that had been in pod 26 seemed particularly loud and had no volume control). We then placed new instructions on the wall.

Folks continued to play with various "video effects," particularly with the remote camera control. The "negative/positive" switch came into use. When I saw that someone in Pod 16 was playing with the Pod 26 camera, I came into video view (with the intent of interacting with the person). When I panned the Pod 16 camera to find the person, he jumped up and ran away.

**12:05:56 PDT:** When the video link to Portland was first implemented, the first week saw a number of video-feedback experiments (i.e. explorations). Last night, the first day the 16/26 link was operational, I saw 2 people were experimenting with video-feedback using the Pod 16 gear.

**14:57:24 PDT:** An MIT summer student had a couple hardware suggestions after watching the link for a bit:

1. One might want to "zoom" the audio as well as the video (i.e. so that the audio "follows" the video). A possible method might be to hang mikes in the ceiling in various places. Depending on where the visuals are pointed, then the system figures out which mike to turn on.
2. Set up additional cameras *in* a manner so that as one uses the remote control to move toward a position, the system automatically switches to the next nearest camera.

## Day 3 – August 24, 1988 (Wednesday)

The morning was mostly quiet with very little action (not to mention interaction) at either end. About 1:30 pm there was a good interaction between the MIT student (in Pod 26), who was himself a newcomer to Media Space, and a new user in Pod 16.

**About tea time**, one of the individuals with a link in Pod 25 and her visitor saw (on her newly installed Media Space link) that there were the remains of a cake in Pod 16. The two promptly hurried downstairs for cake and were then seen by folks having tea in Pod 26. The folks in Pod 26 called the two to come up to tea (with cake!). They then came upstairs to Pod 26 (with the remains of the cake) and joined us at tea.

*Coupled with the person running away episode of the previous day, it is tempting to speculate about the complex sense of ownership and permission amongst the members of ISL. In the cake story, the folks were members of ISL and felt that they had legitimacy to retrieve the remaining cake. Interestingly, it was brought to the SCL/Pod 26 tea. It would seem that the tea time inculcation attempt was reaching some members of the other Lab – or perhaps, they were feeling (and expressing) both permission and disconnect.*

*In the running away story, the equipment was an intrusion into the ISL Space, but held enough of a power that the person felt they must not confront the equipment "owners" directly. (Others will act much less inhibited in the next few days.)*

## Day 4 – August 25, 1988 (Thursday)

Again, the morning was mostly quiet. About 1:30 pm, a researcher in Pod 16 could be seen playing with the remote camera control.

At least one person seemed to have joined us for tea as a direct result of seeing us over the link. Also, the secretary in the open area of Pod 16 seems to be more comfortable with the link. She's played with the remote camera control and spoken to us a bit at tea-time.

## Day 5 – August 26, 1988 (Friday)

This afternoon, the head of Xerox's electrical component design group dropped in to see a member of SCL/Pod 26. The visitor was at PARC as part of the Chief Engineers junket. A group gathered to talk in the Pod 26 Commons. The discussion centered on possible joint projects (some real-time, some recorded video). The mike was off during most of the conversation, but [the group] was visible.

EVENT ONE (**approximately 2:30**)

An ISL member walked through 16 and noticed the discussion. The visitor [in Pod 26] was introduced to the ISL member. A brief conversation ensued that turned to an invitation to a possible project: an "early-warning system" for service techs.

EVENT TWO (**2:35**)

At the point where the visitor asked what anthropologists had to do with service, the ISL member decided to come upstairs to become fully part of the conversation. He said he had to raise his voice to be heard (there was background conversation and some construction noise in Pod 16.) During the interval that he used to walk upstairs, the direction of the conversation returned to the subject it was on before he had entered (event one). Upon arriving in Pod 26, the conversation did not again return to the subject that they had been discussing over the link and was never reintroduced.

EVENT THREE (**2:50**)

An administrator entered the Pod 16 coffee area, obviously looking for someone.

Although (to my knowledge) she has never used the link before, she walked directly to the camera. Because of the deliberateness of her actions, the conversation in Pod 26 was interrupted. She was looking for the ISL member who had joined the Pod 26 conversation and who was visible on the Pod 16 monitor. The ISL member was called back downstairs to assist in restoring a machine. Both exit.

EVENT FOUR (**3:15**)

A manager walked by in Pod 16 and interrupted the conversation in Pod 26 to say hello to the visitor. The conversation proceeds as if they are present in the hallway together.

Later, the ISL lab member writes: Actually, at Event One, I had the impression you were trying to get my attention, presumably in order to introduce me to the visitor. Egocentric, what?

*A lot is happening in this vignette: the shared space encounter is a trope often used to describe the media space. In this case we have two – the ISL member and the manager. More interestingly, notice that the ISL member has one kind of focused meeting with the visitor over the media space connection. A project was even proposed. But when they meet in person, the subject does not come up again.*

*Another noteworthy aspect is that the performance of the meeting with this visitor takes place in a very open area that is extended with the media space connection. Thus, the administrator could freely interrupt in the same way that the manager did. In the hallways of the main engineering facilities of Xerox, executives in conversation might be acknowledged with a wave of the hand or a "Hi – how are you?" but would rarely have a conversation interrupted so freely.*

Again the day was fairly quiet. There were interesting interactions in the afternoon; see above description. We saw two researchers in Pod 16 during tea (in Pod 26) and invited them to join us (which they did). We disconnected the telephone connection about 6 pm; left the video on in both locations.

Folks in DIAL [a cross-lab research working group] spent about 30 min discussing the link. People were concerned about privacy issues but also seemed to wish for tapes of the events occurring across the link. At some point, an ISL/Pod 16 researcher expressed great surprise when he discovered that folks could see the pods (16/26) in their offices.

*DIAL ("Design Interaction Analysis Lab") was a research group based in ISL, but with some participation by members of SCL. It was probably the only regular meeting across the boundary of the two laboratories. Anthropologists and socio-logists provided the analytic methods (close observation of video tapes of work situations), ethical and investigational aesthetic values. This setting for discussion of the ethics raised quite a number of issues about the "design" of the research and the intrusion into personal privacy.*

*In both Pods 16 and 26, offices faced public areas; what was said and the appearance of people in the hallways and open areas of both pods was available to anyone with an adjoining office. Thus, the Pod 26 people asserted/believed that the mediated extension of the public space into their offices was no different. The Pod 16 people asserted/believed that it was quite different in that no one knew about it – it was invisible.*

*It seems ironic that the concerns raised did not completely dissuade the impulse of the DIAL community to study this event and the technology. In some ways this opportunistic approach builds upon the designerly approach that put the 16/26 link in place.*

## Day 8 – August 29, 1988 (Monday)

We established the audio connection about 9:30 am. The secretary in the Pod 16 open area explained how the link is seriously disrupting her work: increased activity in the Pod 16 area, noise from Pod 26, and questions (about the link) from folks wandering by.

*One fact noted by the secretary seems to have gone unnoticed at the time: the note says the secretary was disturbed by increased activity in the Pod 16 open area. What new activity? Was it actually in the 16 open area or was it virtual – coming over the link? Why would anyone come to the space who would not have otherwise come there if they did not use the link?*

Those *of* us who had installed the link met to discuss its general status. We decided to leave it another few days, then send a question set to SSL *[that is the combined SCL + ISL]* including – shall we continue with a link? *if* so, where?; what are the problems? the advantages?. Whatever else, we definitely need to get back to the secretary in the open area within a few days.

A couple *of* us discussed a possible shared drawing tool for the Pods 16/26 link.

**A bit later**... Not much happened during tea. A friend *of* R's was looking for her, saw her on the monitor, then came up to join us. Apparently the secretary in Pod 16 was bothered by the noise (presumably from Pod 26 during tea) so asked someone (R's friend) to turn off the mike (in Pod 16). The person turned "off" the mike but we didn't realize it upstairs. Only after tea did we know there was a problem and reestablished the phone connection. I explained to the secretary that she probably doesn't want the Pod 16 mike off, but rather the Pod 26 mike off.

During the process of "playing" with the controls in Pod 26 at teatime, the video disappeared on the big monitor. One Pod 16 member thought it was related to his playing with the remote camera control. Subsequently, all looked fine downstairs. Finally at about 5:45 pm we attacked the problem, realized it was the state of the PIP *[picture-in-a-picture unit]*, and fixed everything.

## Day 9 – August 30, 1988 (Tuesday)

I was gone much of the day but interactions seemed minimal, This may have been the day in which two Pod 16 researchers were having a discussion on the couches in Pod 16. Meanwhile, the audio connection had been broken and someone had asked to have it fixed (it was initially loud in Pod 16 – the dial tone).

A few of us gathered to check it out in Pod 26. When I went downstairs (and interrupted the researcher conversation), I asked if they would like to have their mike turned off. One said "no," he assumed the Pod 26 person might want to listen in. Others in Pod 16 saw tea occurring and came up for a brief time. Some made a tape of the link for a PARC-o-gram. *[videotaped messages exchanged with EuroPARC in Cambridge]*

## Day 10 – August 31, 1988 (Wednesday)

I was gone (as was most of Pod 26 after 10:30 am). A Pod 16 member sent a well-written commentary on his reactions (primarily negative) to the link.

## Day 11 – September 1, 1988 (Thursday)

A large crowd gathered at tea, and I started to talk with H *[a computer scientist from ISL]* about reactions to the link. Others joined us so that we had a 30–45 min discussion of media space issues. The primary problems seem to be:

1. Noise
2. Intrusion on secretarial space
3. Intrusion on Pod 16 space that folks consider their own
4. Not knowing who is seeing whom

Practical suggestions have included moving the node (to a "new" Pod 15 common area or to a corner nearer the kitchen), fixing the camera angle at both ends, and removing the node. A major issue in many folks' minds is that the node appeared in Pod 16 without warning.

Later in the evening, I decided to take advantage of the fact that the Pod 26 common area node was easily connected to a video tape recorder. I wanted to add 5 min to a videotape I was making for a colleague in England. Thus, I was sitting in Pod 26 talking into the camera when someone wandered through Pod 16.

Seeing me talking to the camera, he motioned that he couldn't hear me. I just went on talking (to my English colleague via a recorder, of course), The person in Pod 16 made more "can't hear you" motions until finally I made a shrugging "oh well" motion (and then continued to talk onto my tape). He walked out of the pod – but appeared a couple minutes later in Pod 26, No doubt he was confused!

## Day 12 – September 2, 1988 (Friday)

The audio was off most of the day; finally it was connected at tea-time. The secretary in the open area said that the experience with the link was much less distracting this week than last; folks don't play as much.

I started talking with various folks about the next steps to take with the link. Folks had been discussing the link during lunchtime. Several of the administrative staff seem to be upset even though their office areas are not part of the Pod 16 Commons. I suspect that they may identify with and "protect" the two who are in the area. My take on the general feeling is that several people are upset and that a public discussion would be useful. There was some question as to whether or not the biweekly lab meeting was an appropriate forum, but I finally decided to do it then. A message went out to SSL at the end of the day.

**During tea**, a Pod 16 researcher first interacted with Pod 26 folks over the link (and fixed the camera and audio connection). He then joined us in Pod 26. The secretary in the Pod 16 open area then began interacting with us over the link, making faces. When asked if she would like our mike off, she said that "nobody's down here, so it's okay." At some point, another person joined her in the interaction.

# Day 13 – September 3, 1988 (Saturday)

Two of the Pod 16'ers got into serious playing with video feedback ~ effects. They spent some time with the Pod 16 camera, then ventured up to Pod 26 to create double feedback loops. In process, one of them turned on the audio in Pod 16 so that audio connection was also alive. The other suggested to leave the effects but that he expected folks to be unhappy – i.e., those of us who were considered "media space" folks. I encouraged him to leave the cameras in whatever state he wished (pointing out that the Pod 16 folks might be most frustrated since they are less familiar with the equipment).

# Day 16 – September 6, 1988 (Tuesday)

The Pod 16 camera was initially turned toward the wall (the light switch was showing). Someone did turn the camera back to the "normal" position. The day seemed generally uneventful over the link; audio was up and on in both sites a couple times (I think).

I talked with D *[an SSL manager]* about the link. He had lots of questions about what we really thought we could gain by this research. He suspects that there are more effective ways to increase communication between the two areas. And if Media Space is a useful concept for this sort of communication, the technology needs serious attention. He did say that he thought it worth leaving the link connected in some way….

The discussion at the laboratory meeting focused entirely on the link. I don't think there were any really new ideas that emerged. The primary problems seem to be:

(a) Noise
(b) Invasion of a space that is frequently used privately

- The secretarial office space
- The "pacing", "lounging" space (comments from two folks in particular)

(c) Being seen without seeing

- The angle of monitor viewing is wider than the camera angle
- The Media Space allows any node to "see into" the Pods

I suspect that feelings of control are also an issue – in general, folks outside Pod 26 don't seem to feel free to manipulate the equipment (beyond the remote camera control). I'd suggest that we

- Make sure everyone knows how to use the equipment (particularly the tricks for carrying on a two-way conversation)
- Take away the remote camera controls (seems that what adds control for "us", constrains control for "them" – i.e., the remote camera control gives Pod 16'ers less feeling of controlling their own space)
- Move the monitors and cameras to the space currently occupied by the small table in Pod 16; move the small table near the bulletin board (and move the plant to the right as needed)
- Leave the audio connection "on" at low volume but be sure that everyone knows how to toggle off the mike to protect the privacy of their own conversations
- Propose these steps (plus leaving "as is" plus "removing it") to SSL ~ with a definite discussion time (say next Monday after tea)
- Establish a regular "evaluation" period (say each month) in which we publicly request feedback

I think these steps solve (a) and (b) of the problems. I don't think they think they address (c). J1 *[a social scientist in ISL]* and others suggest that we not allow the Pod 16 commons picture/audio in individual offices.

I think we need to send out some message today to eliminate any fears that we don't plan to respond.

## Day 17 – September 7, 1988 (Wednesday)

In Pod 16 the monitors were turned off, the camera lens cap was on, and the audio was disconnected. No one seems to know who did it. I'd like to see it as an expression of someone in Pod 16 "taking control"; many people saw it as a Pod 26 action. We turned everything back on about 10:30 am.

The secretary in the Pod 16 open area felt that everyone was just being nice to each other at the lab meeting. Another secretary who had voiced earlier complaints felt that folks got to air complaints in the meeting (second-hand information).

## Day 22 – September 12, 1988 (Monday)

We had a meeting for any interested SSL'ers *[members of the combined SCL + ISL]* to discuss the next steps of the Pods link. Six folks attended: one from Pod 16, one from Pod 25, and the remainder from Pod 26. After some discussion, we went to the Pod 16 node and five others from there entered into the talk.

See message to SSL for the decision.

- It was felt by many in the group that having the camera in the kitchen itself offered too narrow a field of view.
- Steve pointed out that as long as cameras are in the Pod 26 Commons and surrounding offices, it is impossible to decouple the Pod 16 link from the Media Space.
- Folks at the meeting seemed to agree generally that the Pods.
- Link was of some value and should not be taken away.
- G *[an ISL computer scientist]* to a great extent, and J [an ISL social scientist], to a lesser extent, felt strongly that the link node should not be a part of the couch space in Pod 16 at all (despite the field of view issues – G suggested placing the camera back by the mailboxes to offer a broader picture).

*SCL media space researchers* rearrange the equipment after the group's vote on location. A monitor was added to give L *[an admin in SCL]* a view of the link between commons.

## Day 23 – September 13, 1988 (Tuesday)

The Pod 16 camera lens was on for a good part of the morning and again in the afternoon. Pod 26'ers did not modify the state; those in Pod 16 both put on and removed the lens cap.

## Day 24 – September 14, 1988 (Wednesday)

I have noticed no interactions occurring over the link (my impression is that this is a change from the previous position in which occasional waves/"passing in the hall acknowledgements" occurred and at least once or twice a day someone would actually talk with someone at the other end. B *[an SCL media space researcher]* did initiate an interaction with J2 *[an ISL researcher]* (no speech), and J3 *[an ISL HCI scientist]* and I had a "wave" plus conversation about UIs in the afternoon. The audio itself has been a problem – disconnected in a way that doesn't make for an easy fix.

Again the lens cap was put on the Pod 16 camera (and monitors turned off) a couple times when people seem to want to use the couch area.

General comments:

We seem to be generating some interest from other Pods (EDL/CSL).

I would like to ask SSL's permission to tape a couple days of the link as "hard" data about its use.

I'm curious about what we think we've learned from this trial. I don't think much (I know that introducing technology without involving users always creates negative reactions). I do think that the use of the Pod 16 Commons is more different from the Pod 26 Commons than we may have realized.

In particular, what appears to be a public [space is] thought by many to be a private place. And the benefits of "greater peripheral vision interactions" to outweigh the costs, doesn't seem to be so.....

I think I made a mistake in having an open meeting to discuss the next steps of the Pods link without being sure that various factions would be represented. Perhaps I should have gotten a "committee" together at Circus *[the SSL Lab meeting]* (and still left the meeting open to additional participants) so that everyone could know who would be coming.

I'm not sure how to get out of the current situation (if it's a bad one – which I think it is) in a positive way....

## Day 26 – September 16, 1988 (Friday)

Humor over the link: Someone this morning put MM's nameplate on the door to the freezer in the 16 Commons. The camera was then trained on it. (Explanation for those not in the know: MM often talked about having his head frozen when he dies.)

I think it's the first example of deliberate video link humor from Pod 16. And then S [an ISL computer scientist in Pod 25] and M *[an ISL admin also from Pod 25]* got into a non-verbal interaction with B [an ISL system scientist from Pod 16] and/or D *[a senior ISL scientist who worked closely with people in Pods 15, 16, and 25]*.

**Some final reflections culled from an e-mail to a former SCL colleague:**

We've had a Loooooong three weeks of media link between Pods 16 and 26. And no, I didn't need to learn that you can't please all the people all the time or that folks don't like changes of which they weren't a part. The Circus *[the SSL Lab meeting]* discussion went fine (we'd done our "homework", talking to all the concerned folks first so there were no surprises and we could remain non-defensive).

Then I goofed and had an open meeting to decide on changes. I'd had lots of the negative feedback but those folks didn't come to the meeting. So of course, the changes weren't the ones they wanted (and I knew that phase 2 wouldn't be too successful either). Now we're in phase 3 – a weird location but few screams. We'll decide after CSCW [*conference*] what to do with this particular link in the long term.

Meanwhile, I actually believe that several things have happened as we might expect. There have been a couple shared "jokes" from Pod 16 to Pod 26. And obviously, folks "down there" are now much more video-aware. And I've seen a few folks in our Pod that hadn't wandered in before. And for a couple weeks, the tea attendance was up considerably, Since I think a lot of this is about folks connecting, I think it helps (but I doubt that this is a widely held opinion). (There have also been long discussions about all the "usual" issues – privacy, being seen without seeing, etc.).

# Anecdotes About Recording

*The following are short anecdotes about recording that, like the Pod 16/26 exploration, highlight the opportunity of media space -- and the ease with which it could become problematic.*

## Early Video Mail

**Bill Buxton**
Principal Researcher, Microsoft Research

I have always characterized the approach that we took with our various media spaces as doing smart things with stupid technologies. That is, the way we got to live the future yesterday, so that we could better understand the human requirements of what we might build in the future, was to implement everything with well-known technologies. In other words, we faked the digital future with old analogue video technology – albeit technology that we could control by computer.

Let me give one of my favorite examples.

We set up EuroPARC in Cambridge, England, in 1987. As the name suggests, however, we were supposed to be part of PARC, that is, the Palo Alto Research Center – as literally as the laws of physics would permit.

We had a video codec that let us bridge the EuroPARC and PARC media spaces for synchronous meetings. However, there was this little problem of the 8-h time difference. This stressed the reliance on synchronous communication. So we decided that we needed to support video mail. The problem was that there was no broadband Internet back then, and getting a dedicated line capable of shipping the video back and forth was prohibitive – especially at UK pricing. So we resorted to stupid technologies.

What we did is take a leaf out of the old-school audio-cassette-driven answering machine playbook. We added a special node to the media space switch, along with appropriate software. What we connected to it was a conventional VHS VCR that was capable of two things:

1. Handling SMPTE time code
2. Capable of being controlled from a computer

With this we were able to develop software that enabled one to lay down a message on the cassette that followed the previous one, and by using the time-code as a kind of index, keep track of where that message started and stopped, and whom it was for.

We then used the world's highest bandwidth, cheapest, and – at the time – fastest unregulated telecommunications carrier to convey the video messages to Palo Alto: Federal Express.

Within 24 h of transmitting the mail, the folks at PARC could mount it in the appropriate VCR on their media space, so that the intended recipients could access their messages from their office.

Did it work? Yes, sort of. Was it used? No, not really. Just for some demos. Why? Because it turns out that there was not a pent up demand for video mail after all. Would there have been if we had improved the flow? Well, perhaps. But we were not at all convinced, and now that it is practical and still not prevalent, we were probably right.

But that is only half the truth. What that infrastructure *was* used for, was as a kind of video server from which one could access video clips and demos.

So did we learn the importance of that message? Well, sort of. But then, not really. How do I know? Well, none of us invented YouTube.

Damnn!!!!

## Big Brother's Other Sibling

**Steve Harrison**
Virginia Polytechnic Institute and State University

PARC had (and still has) tremendous fascination for outside visitors as the birthplace of many important technology ideas. But as a research facility, visitors would mostly just see hallways, a few bean-bag chairs, and offices. Looking into the offices, they would see computers, of course. By the early 1990s, even the vaunted prototype desktop computers like the Dorado had been replaced by commercial workstations that were not particularly impressive. So any tour-guide would desperately look for something visual to show off.

At the other end of the building from the System Concepts Laboratory (where the media space was located) was a decidedly more gadget-centric Lab – the Computer Science Lab. In it, Roy Want was working with a technology called Active Badges. Originally developed by Olivetti's Cambridge Research Lab, these badges had unique ids that would allow the environment to track the wearer. Thus, it was possible to write systems that would tell when people arrived and left work, in their offices, in meetings, etc. In one application, the system automatically would set the temperature and lighting levels for a wearer when they were present. When Mark Weiser arrived to begin work on what became Ubiquitous Computing, the Active Badge technology and applications were incorporated into it. So for a while the Active Badges were one of the most visible projects that could be shown to visitors.

The media space at Xerox PARC was an enduring project. It endured in that it was used long after PARC management had terminated the research about it and it, too, was "on the tour." It gave the tours a reason to walk to the far end of the building. The cameras and monitors were in place in many offices. Even without a formal demo, it was possible to look into an office and see how people were working with remote colleagues. Thus, offices with cameras and monitors – even vacant ones connected to other vacant ones – were more interesting than those with just computers.

But there was a problem of what PARC was saying about technology: taken together, the Active Badges and the Media Space produced one obvious question from nearly every visitor: "Aren't you just doing research to create 'Big Brother'?" The PR people would try to change the subject, but by that point, the topic had been raised and it was often impossible to get anyone to see the usefulness of either idea. This would open the door to a whole host of questions that made the media space hard to understand.

The next question would inevitably be, "How are you going to avoid fumbling the future?" – a reference to a book of the same name that described how Xerox had lost the PC to IBM and the graphical user interface to Apple. The best response was, "We have filed a patent on the system and its interface." But this would bring us back to the question of "Big Brother" and was not this just a method of monitoring employees.

A variation of the "fumbling the future question" was, "How are you going to commercialize Media Space?" The patent was a good opening gambit in a response, but it did not get to the heart of the problem – we were always careful to point out that the media space was not a general solution for putting remote coworkers together, but a means of conjoining spaces for people with close working relations. The only way we knew to design an appropriate media space was to use a form of fairly intense participatory design and avoid placing mediated connection in situations of radically differing power relations or differing work cultures.[1]

In the intervening years, concern over privacy seems to focus more on the practical than the ethical, political, or psychological. "Big Brother has been replaced by the identity thief. And many new forms of mediation have arisen – e.g., ubiquitous cell phones, WiFi, and iChat. It would be interesting to imagine revisiting the PARC of 1991 and whether or not anyone today would jump on the "Big Brother" issue. What sort of mechanisms would ensure the kind of care that was taken with creating media spaces (and explaining them to visitors, regardless of whether they could hear it) that would still be viable and central to their creation? Perhaps that is one of the central lingering research questions of Media Space.

---

[1] See the section on the Pod 16/26 Media Space "experiment" for more about how differing cultures did not come together in a mediated presence.

## Recoding Ethics, Then and Now

**John C. Tang**
Microsoft Research

"S" (another PARC researcher) and I were setting up to record a demo using a video camera in the Media Space node in the Commons, so we hooked it up to a video deck. We were just about to start recording our demo when "L," a manager from facilities, comes walking into the Commons. Coincidentally, other researchers had removed a large number of ceiling tiles in the common area of the Lab earlier in the day. For some reason, no one else was in that part of PARC at the time, so I do not think anyone else witnessed it. "L" looks around a bit, particularly at the missing ceiling tiles, and starts a lecture to us (as the only targets within range) about unauthorized modification to the building and gets increasingly agitated. "S" and I mainly listen, directing him to more senior members of the Lab (since we were both graduate students at the time). As "L" leaves angrily, I realize that this entire interaction has been recorded on tape – he was not directly on camera, but since the mic was on to record our demo, it recorded the conversation.

Despite how annoyed I was at the interaction, I felt compelled to immediately erase the tape. Clearly, he was unaware that he was being taped (we had no active signal for recording at the time). Using the tape, even to show others in the Lab who were not present at the time, seemed like a blatant ethical violation that would have ultimately harmed the reputation of Media Space, especially during that early phase of the research. So, the video was immediately erased, and I am not sure who else ever knew about that incident.

What is curious to me is that a major concern in the early Media Space-days was about unintended recording and ethics about recorded video. Yet, today, recorded video seems to be commonly accepted – even relied on – to prosecute criminal activity, and furthermore glorified in the many funny clips shared on YouTube and the like. It seems ironic to me that one of the primary privacy concerns of the early stages of Media Space has been swept aside by common-use practices of recorded video

# Chapter 11
# Section 2: The Space of Media Space

**Steve Harrison**

## Introduction

We began our study of media space with the social aspects of mediated communication because many in the computer-supported cooperative work (CSCW) realm are familiar with models, theories, frameworks, issues, and design approaches related to sociality. But the first media space research came from another set of traditions – the ordering of space and the making of place. Formally, these are the professional and intellectual provinces of architecture, which are probably remote from the disciplinary backgrounds of most readers. However, remoteness in terms of rhetoric and training does not prevent proximity to everyday human experience. The meaning of media space with respect to human experience is the focus of the articles in this section. The spaces are designed to have meaning, and the meaning of the design derives from spatial experience.

The notion of "space" is half of "media space." What does it mean to think of media space as fundamentally "a space"? What is a space anyway? The chapters in this section all proceed from the idea that space has metaphoric power and power as a metaphor. In addition, they consider a number of spatial conceits: (1) that the presence of media in physical space alters and extends the space it is in, (2) that the means of understanding experience in space is through the screen and out of the speaker, (3) that place can be constructed in mediated space as well as physical space, and (4) that the affordances of space and place are significant elements in the construction of sociality and of interpersonal communications. No single chapter tackles all these issues; in fact, none tackles any one of them as a single independent theme. Instead, they draw upon elements of these themes in a networked fashion.

S. Harrison
Virginia Polytechnic Institute and State University
e-mail: sHarrison@vt.edu

S. Harrison (ed.), *Media Space 20+ Years of Mediated Life*,
Computer Supported Cooperative Work,

## The View from Space

First, let us consider the phenomenology of space and then of place. As the geographer Tuan and Hoelscher (2001) points out, the term space applies to an organization of experience (Dreyfus, 1990) shaped by the physicality of our bodies, gravity, and the surface of the earth. Our eyes are on one side of our body, giving rise to a notion of front and back; our eyes are about 1.8 m above the ground so that open space extends to a horizon. We pick up things that rest on the ground and drop them; they fall, giving us the concept of up and down. Looking and reaching, we get additional lateral relative directions of left and right. Our legs propel us forward, giving motion through space that plays out over time; this motion-over-time gives rise to metaphors of "forward progress" that apply to activities, concrete or abstract.

Because of this view, the bodily experiences of action and observation translate into the idea that there is an enabling "medium." That medium is called space. Thus, "media space" augments and changes the normal medium with electronic properties. But both media and space are high-level abstractions with the potential to subsume one another intellectually.

The notion of space is deeply tied to the notion of place. Although both these terms are surprisingly controversial, in my view, space is the opportunity and place is the experienced reality (Harrison and Dourish, 1996; Harrison and Tatar, 2008). The social construction of space and place, the organization of physical space for human ends – to create shelter from the elements, to be secure from threats, to store and prepare food, to exchange and trade foodstuffs, tools, and items of power, to celebrate, to mourn, to sleep, to eat, etc. – creates locations in space with meaning. Additionally, events that occur at locations regardless of this human organization load locations with meaning. Human ability to recognize locations leads to human facility to name locations, to mark locations, to own, and to control. These capacities and processes create "places."[1] Activity around the concrete and literal lead to auxiliary concepts such as inside and outside, public and private, hierarchy, and shared.

This section progresses through ideas about space (abstraction, affordance, and meaning) and then shifts to specifics of place.

### *Abstractions of Space*

#### Henderson

In this chapter, Henderson describes approaching media space first as a kind of video, the extension of other video-based capture techniques. The two-way connectivity of media space is initially presented as a natural and unproblematic

[1] My apologies to dash through this aspect of social construction of space. The reader is invited to revisit "Re-Placeing Space" and other works that argue different phenomenologies of space and place with this author's admonition to try to get beyond the corollaries.

extension of everyday experience is drawn through the lens of video technology. Only over time and through exposure and experimentation with various forms and implementations of media space did he develop a sense of the connection or unification of disparate spaces.

While not the first PARC user of media space, he was an early adopter. Furthermore, he was an important "ambassador" in that he mediated between the parts of PARC using the media space and those not, between PARC and its Cambridge, UK branch, EuroPARC, and among those who frame interaction in cognitive terms and those who frame it in phenomenological terms. So, too, in this book, Henderson mediates between readers who are used to thinking of space and place in pragmatic and Cartesian terms, and authors who think and design in terms of spatial metaphors and meaning.

## *Affordances of Space*

### Buxton

Where Henderson commits works of bricolage, appropriation, and reconfiguration that is analogous to the world of software development, Bill Buxton advances the interaction designer's perspective that physicality is primary. Buxton designed and designs the world about him with a mix of actual and mediated presences, signals, and gestures.

Buxton starts with the idea of extending the capability of everyday by backing technology into situations that leverage aspects of everyday. He describes how arranging visual and acoustic simulacra of physical configurations – in physical configurations – supports socially appropriate behavior. For example, the semantics of office doorways as sites of negotiation for conversation are reused with a monitor–camera pair placed on the door for the purposes of negotiating the initiation of mediated conversation. Suddenly, people can come to his office door (not the metaphorical one on the desktop – but the hinged slab of wood that separates him from the hallway) whether they are walking down the hall or connecting across the Atlantic. J.J. Gibson (1976), the ecological psychologist, might say that the physical/technological arrangement *affords* or invites the social interaction.

## *The Meanings of Space (and Place)*

### Stults

In the third chapter in this section, Robert Stults, the originator of PARC's first media space, revisits it with the perspective of the professional place maker, the architect. What does an architect see? What actions or "moves" does an architect take to make places? A major concern of architects, in the design of media spaces as well as in other built environments, is the balance between what the second-century Roman architect, Vitruvius, called *commodity, firmness*, and *delight*. "Commodity" – in this nineteenth century poeticized translation – means "function." "Firmness" means engineering, and "delight" is just an engaging experience, the sensual aspects of the creation. Those who, like Simon (1996), characterize design as problem solving are usually focusing on commodity and firmness. In contrast, Stults focuses primarily on "delight." Therefore, he asks how architects create and manipulate meaning.

For example, the front door of a house might have a folksy porch or a formal pediment supported by columns. Both approaches celebrate arrival and entry to the private realm of the house. But why choose one over the other? What is the right meaning to intend? Architects appropriate experiential or symbolic elements just as they collect ways to solve technical, utilitarian problems. The architect "reads" the moves or design decisions, and the coincidences that create experience. This reading is often accompanied by an implicit mental redrawing of plans. Reworking of form, drawing over previous plans, and trying new variations are simultaneously forms of rewriting experience and meaning.

Media spaces are designed in the same sense as porticos, with intentionality, reference to the past, and concern for the balance of commodity, firmness, and especially delight. Media space has been operationally defined as persistent video connections. This is a quality of firmness – and also delight. The decision to leave locations visually linked regardless of use or occupancy makes visible the social construction of space.[2] So how does the architect understand this and construct place from it? With this decision, the architect can utilize in media space the conventions of a framed view such as a well-placed window affords. Similar decisions can influence the social affordances of the place. In the cartoon series, the Jetson's, the video phone displaying George Jetson's boss was always high up in the room – dominating George, the employee and so on.

Stults leads us through the construction of a number of structures that create specific experiences; in turn, their appearance stands for the aggregation of the experiences and readings vis-à-vis media spaces.

## *Giving At the Office*

### Roussel

Stults talks in architectural abstractions, but Roussel brings the discussion down to brass tacks. When we become pragmatic, what differentiates the place of the office

[2] This definition is deeply problematic since living the mediated life does not always mean having persistent location-to-location connection, that locational relations do not change, or even that to be present means that a particular connection must persist. (In fact, a chapter in the next section describes media space places that exist only to resolve emergency situations; when the emergency is over, the media space and the place disappear.)

from the place of the home? And what makes Nicolas Roussel to use a media space at work but not at home?

Roussel's account of the pragmatics of distributed work places uncovers dislocation and seamfulness as intrinsic, useful, and important parts of work that are also uncomfortable and alienating. On this view, private life is in deep contrast to work life, and media space, essential for one, is anathema to the other. Though his experiences with media space include 5 plus years, Roussel's first experiences with mediated space are in the context of more contemporary computing systems and ideas about connectivity. Just as computing has moved into more realms of being over the past 20 years, it is not surprising that the understanding of computing would become more nuanced.

## *Playing At Home*

### Gaver

Yet, other views of home mediation are possible. The last chapter in this section is a report by Bill Gaver about his relationship with a small media space in his London house. The arc of Bill Gaver's research, from appropriation of Gibsonian psychology (Gibson, 1976) to the appropriation of technology for cultural interpretation (Sengers and Gaver, 2006; Gaver et al., 2003), is remarkable. His playful relationship with media space is well reflected in "The VideoWindow: My Life with a Ludic System." In contrast to Roussel's practical and ethical concerns, Gaver treats the media space as a play space. A little camera waving on the end of a flexible rod brings bits of London into the corners of his house. The idea and the camera bring us all a bit closer to another Hole in Space.

The observant reader will have noticed that all chapters in this section have but one author each. Why? Coincidence or is it that spatial qualities result in more singular experiences and singular design approaches? Some play more than others, some play with ideas and abstractions more than others, but, crucially, all authors in this section see space as important to media space and see both dislocation and relocation as central affordances of media spaces.

## References

Dreyfus, H. (1990). *Being in the World: A Commentary on Heidegger's Being and Time*. MIT Press, Cambridge.

Gaver, W., Beaver, J., and Benford, S. (2003) "Ambiguity as a resource for design," *Proceedings of the SIGCHI conference on human factors in computing systems*, April 05–10, 2003, Ft. Lauderdale, Florida, USA.

Gibson, J.J. (1976) *The Ecological Approach to Visual Perceptual Systems*. Allen & Unwin, London.

Harrison, S. and Dourish, P. (1996) "Re-Placing Space: The Roles of Place and Space in Collaborative Systems." *Proceedings of ACM CSCW 96*. November 18–21, 1996, Addison-Wesley, Reading, MA, pp. 67–76.

Harrison, S. and Tatar, D. (2008) "Places: People, Events, Loci. The relation of semantic frames in the construction of place" *Journal of Computer Supported Cooperative Work*, Springer, 17(2–3): 97–135.

Sengers, P. and Gaver, B. (2006) "Staying open to interpretation: engaging multiple meanings in design and evaluation", *Proceedings of the 6th ACM conference on designing interactive systems*, June 26–28, 2006, University Park, PA, USA.

Simon, H. (1996). *The Sciences of the Artificial*. MIT Press, Cambridge.

Tuan, Y. and Hoelscher, S. (2001) *Space and Place: The Perspective of Experience*. University of Minnesota Press, Minneapolis, MN.

# Chapter 12
# Constructing Space

**Austin Henderson**

**Abstract** This chapter chronicles the growth of the author's understanding of Media Space through his 20-year experience with coupling spaces, using video. It is a "technology-first" understanding of the construction of space. Key ideas from research studies and practice are presented, and contrasts with other genres of communication are made. The implications for distributed collaboration are explored.

## Introduction

This chapter sketches my experience with Media Space over the years, and the conceptual discoveries I have made in the process. These ideas are not new, but they were to me at the time, and they may surprise you as much as they did me.

## A Brief History

In the early 1980s, in the Cognitive and Instructional Sciences group at Xerox Palo Alto Research Center, as part of my work with Lucy Suchman on what it is to operate a machine, I was using video to make records to help analyze people interacting with copiers (Suchman, 1987). We used the perspectives and methods of ethnomethodology (Heritage, 1984) and interaction analysis (Jordan and Henderson, 1995), based on careful observation and fine-grained analysis of the workings of human activity (Suchman, 1983). This was a video record of human activity for the purpose of analyzing that activity later.

At the same time, Bob Stults and Steve Harrison in the Design Research Group of the Systems Concept Lab were working on a different problem that also involved video. I remember them showing me, as someone also interested in both video and

A. Henderson
Rivendel Consulting and Design
e-mail: austin.henderson@pb.com

S. Harrison (ed.), *Media Space 20+ Years of Mediated Life*,
Computer Supported Cooperative Work,

human interaction, various experiments that, in retrospect, I now think of as the roots of Media Space. They were recording designers designing, less for the purpose of analysis, and more with the intent of enabling designers to pick up the thread of an interrupted design session and continue from where they had left off.

A thread that these different, but co-informing, uses of video had in common was an appreciation of the fact that human activity takes place in physical space. Further, space matters in understanding activity. My discipline, Human–Computer Interaction (HCI), arose from the study of technology (computer science) and cognition (psychology), and tended to locate the interesting action between the thinking and interaction devices of humans and machines. Not really much place for space there. Yet our video observations of people operating copiers had to capture the full space surrounding the machine, or we missed not only the work of managing paper (originals, supplies, and copies), but also of fixing paper jams. Similarly, the study of designers designing involved paper on tables and sketches on whiteboards. Most importantly, we learned that both making copies and designing were social activities; here again, space was essential. Our sharing of experiences and arguing over lunch were probably important to the subsequent courses of both these pieces of work.

The first encounter with Media Space itself was a couple of years later, in 1985. Now the video was live, used to connect designers who wanted to work together, but were not physically together. The original motivation was to "fix" PARC's beautiful, personal, but isolating offices; designers wanted to be able to work together without having to get up and hike to other offices. With Media Space, people had video connections between offices; using controls on their workstations, they could quickly connect to any office on the system.

By 1986, PARC's Palo Alto Media Space had gotten coupled over continuously operating (24/7) video connections to the Media Space at the PARC's Portland site. This interconnecting of Media Spaces was important to me because it showed that the practices of local Media Space could be extended without significant change to offices at multiple sites.

In 1987, when opening PARC's site in Cambridge, England, we decided to install Media Space throughout. This decision was driven by three factors: the successful experience with coupling other PARC labs (specifically Palo Alto and Portland), space connectivity problems (six fairly separate pods on three floors), and the desire to observe ourselves as part of our research. PortHoles, an application using images from Media Space, provided snapshots of all Media Space ports at once, yielding a sense of the EuroPARC offices as a single space. For research observation, Media Space could support observation within EuroPARC.

However, we faced a new challenge: EuroPARC and PARC were separated by eight time zones. On the face of it, this time offset rendered the 24/7 coupling of the sites with Media Space less valuable for working together. More importantly, however, for folks at both sites, the Media Space supported a constant presence of "the rest of PARC," producing the extraordinarily valuable sense of being part of a single whole. Perhaps this was particularly important for me, because, as liaison between the sites, I was living in both places; wherever I was physically present, I had strong reason to be engaged with what was happening at my other office.

In addition, the Media Space not only supported the work at EuroPARC, but also became the subject matter. In particular, the Khronica event manager (a sort of calendar application on steroids) system used the Media Space to deliver its alerts, for example, by slowly increasing the sound of the tinkling of teacups as afternoon tea time approached and showing the Commons filling (or not!) with people.

In the early 1990s, back at PARC, I was working with Annette Adler whose office was remote from mine in the building. Because moving offices at PARC often required an act of god or more, we solved the problem by making a private Media Space. We coupled our offices by directly connecting a camera in each of our offices to a monitor in the other office using a pair of coax cables. This "direct office share" configuration lasted for nearly a year (Adler and Henderson, 1994). We came to think of ourselves as working in a single room having two doors onto two different hallways, with a funny problem in handing things to each other. Colleagues, managers, visitors, and cleaning staffs all experienced this direct office share differently, often with amusing results. People came to my door to talk to Annette. When my office was empty, people who came in looked at things, and even adjusted clothing, being unaware or forgetting that the other "half" of the office was still occupied. Simultaneously, with a somewhat different implementation, Victoria Bellotti and Paul Dourish were running a similar experiment at EuroPARC; their experiences aligned with, and complemented, ours (Dourish et al., 1996).

From 1991 to 1994, I led a Xerox-wide architecture project. For the first 2 years, we gathered for a week to work together to negotiate and align understanding and plan the next segment of work. This involved large groups of people flying somewhere in the world every few months, staying in hotels, and driving on strange sides of the road. In January 1993, Media Space began to change all that. At Bill Buxton's urging, we got the first video codecs that worked at dial-up ISDN-line speeds, and connected spaces instead of jumping on airplanes. Delayed, and a little choppy, the images created havoc with fine-grained interactions, like interruptions and restarts. But being connected was great. At first, we worked in conference rooms equipped with videoconference equipment; all project members attended, but some attended remotely. Soon, however, most sites installed Media Spaces, and people held working sessions over this dial-up Media Space between the get-togethers. The rhythm of interaction on the project changed from months between in-person workshops to days between Media Space meetings. The work moved much faster, with less need for long-range planning, and with quicker response to outside change. Toward the end of the project, workshops had dropped to once or twice a year.

Around 2000, I did some consulting for Sun Microsystems on videoconferencing based on my experience with Media Space. Sun was spilling out of Silicon Valley and the Worksplace Effectiveness Group (a research group in Sun's facilities organization) was concerned with how Sun employees would work together at a distance. At Sun it was generally felt that videoconferencing was a pretty bad way to work, to be avoided if at all possible. However, certain groups were using it with singular success and loving it. It did not take long to discover that what the successful groups were doing was using videoconferencing equipment to create dial-up Media Space. They were connecting small conference rooms and sitting around a virtual table spanning the rooms. Working with psychologist Lynne Henderson, we studied what made this so successful (see Chapter 21). Based on our resulting understanding, and our Media Space experience, we adjusted the videoconferencing equipment to support the Media Space notion of coupling rooms. We were successful enough at this that the groups asked whether we could extend this practice to their all-hands meeting. This led to a number of large-room trials, resulting in a configuration that placed the rooms in a kind of ring in virtual space, each room both in front of and behind the other. Although this configuration is unrealizable in physical space, it directly supports extending the practices of an all-hands meeting held in a single room to the larger virtual room.

## Some Discoveries

As a result of, and in the midst of, these encounters with Media Space in a number of different forms, I continued to be surprised by Media Space. New aspects of the practices of coupling spaces continued to emerge, long after I thought I understood what Media Space was about. Despite its apparent conceptual simplicity, for me Media Space has become a very rich idea. Here is the way I see it.

### *Bridging Distance*

At the heart of the matter, Media Space lets people work with other folks who are some distance away. It is interesting to note that the distances that were bridged in the earliest Media Space were often only a few yards. The designers felt that walking between private offices was a real pain; you ought to be able to simply adjust your position to open – usually continue – an interaction with a coworker. The direct office share configuration was used to connect spaces that were hundreds of feet and floors apart; and I have worked in offices that are part of Media Spaces that spanned many time zones. However, I believe that it is the existence of a distance to be bridged, rather than the extent of that distance, that is at the heart of Media Space's offering.

### *Bridging Time: NOT!*

Media Space for me has not been about time-shifting activity, making experiences available later. On occasion, I have used the fact that I was in Media Space as a cheap way to make records of the activity taking place; after all, the video was there, and simply connecting a recorder (or two) was conceptually and often technically easy.

However, the move to making recordings is not socially easy. Working on-camera with a record is a different experience than working without one, in that with a record the work may possibly become available for someone other than those present. My experience has been that making a record may distort the activity being recorded, and unless getting a record is required, it is usually not worth doing.

It is also the case that the images used to implement Media Space are not necessarily those you would want as the record. For example, this brings pressure to compromise the positioning of the Media Space cameras, often making neither the Media Space nor the recording work well. All the Media Spaces that I have found effective have been entirely about connection in real time.

## Bridging People: Not Necessarily

Because Media Space enables people at a distance to work together, we often tend to imagine that the people using the Media Space have to be there for Media Space to be useful. One of the earliest learnings was that Media Space was also helping people to know when other people were *absent*. I remember a manager challenging me whether Media Space was really necessary to talk to someone whose office was just down the hall. I reminded him that saving the time and effort of all the trips down the hall when the other person was either not there, or was busy on the phone, or was with someone else, was very effective indeed.

With PortHoles, seeing dark rooms was as important as seeing lighted ones. An unoccupied yet lighted room suggested that checking again soon might be rewarded. That knowledge was invaluable over eight time zones; and it was also valuable with spaces just down the hall.

## Connecting Spaces

What Media Space connects is spaces. The camera captures everything in the space; the monitor presents it in the space at the other end. The microphones convey sound to the remote audio output. As a result one space is accessible from the other.

However, the connection is partial. Access is visual and aural. Handing something physical across Media Space does not work. You cannot smell. You cannot touch. The connection is limited in its reach. Some places in most rooms with Media Space are off-camera. The sound may be better or worse in different parts of the room. And visual space is not the same as aural space. People call out to people they cannot see, both in the room, and also down the hall outside the room. Sound from down the hall is available at the remote end. I was amazed when people came to my door to find out if the Jazzercise class had started in the Health Center, which was down the hall from Annette's office.

Non-office spaces were also important. The Commons was an important space in PARC's Pod 26, and also at EuroPARC. It was no one's office, but was a place where people gathered. At times I have seen people point a Media Space camera down a hallway. (Cruiser, an exploration of enabling walking remote hallways, was entirely based on that idea [Root, 1988]).

Although it is tempting to think of Media Space as connecting people, in my view, Media Space is best understood as being about connecting space.

## *Constructing Spaces*

Although it is natural to focus on connecting spaces, I think it is better to think of Media Space as a way of making a single virtual constructed space out of a number of component spaces. This is like the virtual space created by a phone call: the "there" in "Are you there?" refers not to the place where the other person is, but rather to the virtual space of the phone call. This constructed space is created in people's minds by the telephone connection and the practices of talking. The constructed space vanishes when the connections are broken. All players in the component spaces are in the constructed space; they share the space.

One of the things that makes videoconferencing difficult is that its facilities (the component spaces) and practices do not lend themselves to the easy mental creation of a single constructed space. Everything keeps one focused on "we here" and 'they there." Media Space can be much more powerful because it provides for treating all the spaces as extensions of every component space.

## *Constructed Spaces*

Some connected spaces are "always on," and make the beginning of interactions easy. In the Direct Office Share, Annette would ask a question ("Lunch?) and I'd respond ("Meet you upstairs in five minutes."). No "hello" to get started, and no need to say "goodbye"; we were both aware of the other in the space and could just use the space for talking.

However, when using Dial-up spaces (e.g., for meetings in the Xerox architecture work, or in our distance collaboration study at Sun), there is active work required to make the connection and construct the space. At Sun, the study group had automated the whole start-up process, so that flipping a single switch would set up the connection to the other space. More notable yet was the timing of when this switch was flipped: the first person into the room at either end was expected to flip the switch on; and the last person out at either end would flip it off. This practice might increase the cost of technical communications, but it also ensured that the constructed space was in place for everyone, not only during the formal discussion, but also during the informal yet critical socializing before and after the meeting where the work of the meeting is also done.

It is interesting to note that this practice of supporting the whole meeting broke down when the rooms were being used continuously: then the socializing tended to happen in the halls outside the room at each end independently. When the meetings started, the only people who had any sense of completeness were those who had been in the previous meeting and were staying on for this one. We recommended scheduling time between meetings.

As part of setting up, what should the camera see? In a single physical space, you can usually tell who is present, and can hear them speak. A constructed space has to be created to provide the same capabilities. If the door into the room is off-camera, someone arriving or leaving may not be visible. Sometimes people think this is good because it prevents interruptions from propagating to the other end. I think it is bad, for exactly the same reason. With practiced Media Space users, when people arrive or leave it is often noted – even announced – to the other end. When possible, it is best to have the door on-camera, that is, toward the presentation end of the room.

Similarly, hearing in even a single physical space may not be uniformly good, and people develop practices for working around it. For example, people learn to ask for repeats when they cannot hear. Similar work-arounds must be developed in constructed spaces. For example, one of the most disruptive practices in meetings is for people to "sub-group" – hold conversations that are not available to everyone. In a local room, subgrouping is always visible, and social practices can be put in place to manage it. In constructed space, subgrouping may be invisible to those who are remote. This is particularly bad: the goal should be that everyone has access to everything. By maintaining awareness of group interaction, equal access can be provided ("Is there something you want to share, John?"). By leveling the playing field, everyone gets all the information, and everyone feels included.

## *Arranging the Rooms*

It takes thought to arrange the component spaces so that they contribute effectively to the constructed whole. The constructed space needs to be shaped by the activity in which one is engaged (e.g., a chat, a working session, a presentation, an all-hands meeting).

When connecting my office to others in Media Space, I found that I often wanted the camera to be in different places: looking at my whiteboard, looking at my screen, looking at a small working table around which a small number of us would gather, and looking down on a document. I set up a number of cameras and a switcher in my office so that I could quickly switch the view that I was providing to others.

When connecting small conference rooms, the conference room practices to extend to the connected room are sitting around the table and discussing, or listening to a presentation. Because it takes effort to move video equipment around a room, and because doing so is disruptive, getting a single configuration is desirable. I have found that most videoconferencing rooms are set up so that the monitor (with the camera perched on top) are at the "presentation end" of the room, the end where the screen and other presentation equipment is positioned. For Media Space, I have found that I want the monitor and camera at the other end of the room, the end opposite to the presentation end, with the table between. The video equipment thus couples the tables in the two small conference rooms end to end, with presentation ends at the "outboard" ends of the constructed room. This often requires long cables because meeting support people usually do not think of putting the videoconferencing equipment there. It also requires having a long cable to permit the "document camera" to be at the presentation end of the room. In my experience, document cameras come with a 10 ft cable, indicating how deeply the idea of the video as presenter is built into the videoconference thinking (see Chapter 21).

When connecting large rooms, the practice for all-hands meetings was to set large rooms with a stage (the presentation area) at one end, and lines of chairs facing it. Most interaction was presumed to be between the "presenters" on the stage and the "audience" in the chairs. However, in reality, people in the audience also interacted with each other. This was generally achieved by turning to face each other. To extend these practices with Media Space required letting audiences in each site see both stages, presenters on both stages see all people in audiences at all sites, and somehow let people in audiences at all sites turn to see everyone. To achieve this, we also wanted to use the same small-room video equipment, both for reasons of cost and for being able to use both small and large rooms as part of the arrangements for both small- and large-group meetings.

Through a number of attempts, we developed a configuration that did the job pretty well; interestingly, it cannot be achieved in physical space. As in the small rooms, put the videoconference equipment at the "back" of the room, facing the stage. Allot half the stage for the second screen and project onto it the video image coming from the remote end. Unless you have a very large monitor as part of the videoconferencing equipment, also project the remote image on a screen at the back of the room. Each room is then conceptually behind the other, in a virtual ring. People look forward to see both the live local stage, and – through the screen – the remote stage. People can talk to other people in the local or the remote room by turning either forward or backward to face each other.

## *Hosting*

Media Spaces often span sites. When continuously operating Media Spaces break, or when intermittent Media Spaces are started and stopped as at the beginning and end of a meeting, coordination support is needed. Additional channels of communication are required, and people are needed to make it happen. One good way of arranging this is to identify and publish contact information for "hosts" for each site, people who can be contacted when help is needed.

These arrangements have practical implications. In addition to all the communications equipment needed for videoconferencing, it is important to make sure that there is a telephone in the meeting room at each site. A fax machine to ship physical documents quickly between sites is also a plus. Telephone numbers for the remote hosts should be easily accessible.

Hosts provide two sorts of support: that occuring outside the meeting and that occuring within the meeting. Before and after the meeting and in the hallways during the meeting, hosts handle such everyday difficulties as rescheduling (changes at one end must be coordinated with folks at the other), interrupting (the meeting must be cut short, or messages need to be interjected), and providing supplies. Within the meeting, hosts handle difficulties with the technology and communications with remote hosts. Hosts should not be leading the meeting, as they must be able to fix things while the leader directs the activity.

The hosting role provides the connectivity and continuity between meetings that are part of a series. Each meeting produces information that informs the next: schedule, people who should be there, and documentation that will be important. Further, because hosts are in the hallways after the meeting they can hear further thoughts about the meeting and use that in setting up the next.

The studies I did with Lynne Henderson at Sun showed how important these roles were. We discovered this because, as observers, we could see the needs, and as people not participating in the work of the meeting, we could meet those needs without disrupting the activity (e.g., taking a document out to fax it to a remote site, or alerting hosts to changes in scheduling).

Our experience indicated how important these often-invisible – even forgotten – roles are. Hosting is an essential part of Media Space.

## *Nonuniform Spaces*

Although uniformity is desirable in the constructed room, in practice there are many things that will inevitably be different at the different sites, and the constructed room will reflect these. Working in a constructed room requires taking these inevitable differences into account and adjusting joint practice accordingly. Over the years, experience revealed more and more of these. Here are some examples.

You cannot do much about time zones. When trying to find a time for meetings between PARC (usually GMT – 8) and EuroPARC (usually GMT), a one hour meeting at 9:00 in the morning in California was one hour before all could be relied upon to have gotten to work in Silicon Valley, and finished one hour after most people would be headed for the pub in the UK. And even at that, biological and social rhythms were not aligned: people on one end were bright-eyed and bushy-tailed, ready for the work of the day, where those at the other were ready for a pint. We also tripped over exactly when it was that Daylight Savings time (Summer time) came in and went out; it differs with country and state, and countries are aligned differently with each other in spring and fall.

You cannot do much about weather: Outside the windows of the rooms, or in people's minds if the room has no windows, the reality of a blizzard in Rochester, New York had to be made clear to the spoiled residents of Palo Alto. Meetings were cancelled early, so people could drive home. Correspondingly, the reactions of people to earthquakes shook up a number of meetings I was in: suddenly half the people in the (constructed) room were looking around at the lights and each other, checking whether it really was an earthquake and speculating on the size. Also, what constitutes a blizzard or a heat wave is a matter of negotiation: a foot of snow in Cambridge, UK is unremarkable in upper New York state, but surely it will be remarked upon in the constructed room.

You also cannot fix culture: Any number of meetings have been scheduled only to discover that others will not be there because it is a holiday of one form or another (national, state, city). Corporate activities differ by location, even for the same corporation. People are embedded in their cultures and until they are practiced at it, forget that what's unremarkable to them may not be to others. Dress codes, speaking practices, and punctuality all require awareness and negotiation. "Wow, that's tough; go have your cold beer!" "Cold?"

There may be nothing particularly new here for those who have worked with others at a distance. What struck me as interesting, however, was how much these nonuniformities between locations make the ends of the room different. When well constructed, the virtual room becomes one space. The trick is to remain aware of the nonuniformities without losing the sense of being in a single space.

## *Moving Spaces*

It seems to me that Media Space's constructed spaces are taken apart and created out of pieces. Just as I walk down the hall carrying the thread from previous work, my space carries with it a richer thread from meeting to meeting.

Particularly during the Xerox architecture work, I often attended meetings back to back. Some of these were with people at different sites. What we all learned was that sitting in Palo Alto, I could "drive" across Rochester (where most of Xerox was located) much faster than those in Rochester could. Allen would leave a meeting in Henrietta (one of Xerox's sites near Rochester) a little early, saying that he was headed for Webster (on the other side of Rochester). After the Henrietta meeting finished, I'd connect to the Webster meeting and tell them that Allen was on his way.

What I particularly liked was the ability to take with me to a meeting everything that I might possibly need there. Sitting in my office, my filing cabinets were at hand, as was my whiteboard with the work from other meetings.

## *Value of Media Space*

Over the years, I have been part of many discussions on whether Media Space provided better communication than using telephones. Why pay the price of video when you can just use a conference phone?

The common argument, that video provides facial expressions, does not make sense to me, since the resolution is too low, particularly for the wide-angle, fixed-direction "room" camera positioning that is used in Media Space. Similarly, I have found that the argument for supporting heavy use of graphics is weak: rich documents are better supported with paper, because the video resolution is too low.

Instead, I believe that the value of Media Space is that it makes possible the distributed remote social construction of meaning, particularly agreements. You can tell who is in the room, and you can tell from body language the nature of their engagement. You can use the visual channel as a back-channel and not interrupt the speaker (e.g., give him a thumbs up). You can show disagreement, form coalitions, and give support using the visual concurrently with speaking (e.g., waving hands, jumping up and walking around, leaning back in disapproval or forward in engagement).

At the end, when agreement is reached, you can know that all agreed, and who agreed with reservations, and that they know that you know. Media Space supports the undeniable understanding that "you" were there and that you were part of the "we" that had the discussion and made the decision.

## Conclusion

Media Space supports the construction of complex compound spaces out of distributed sets of local physical spaces. These spaces can be created with relatively simple usages of standard videoconferencing technology. And the practices that work in physical spaces can be extended with manageable effort and minimal change to enable similar work to be done together at a distance.

## References

Adler A, Henderson A (1994) A room of our own: experiences from a direct office share. Proceedings of CHI'94, Human Factors in Computing Systems. ACM Press, New York.

Dourish P, Adler A, Bellotti V, Henderson A (1996) Your place or mine? Learning from long-term use of audio-video communication. Journal of Computer Supported Cooperative Work 5(1) 33–62.

Heritage J (1984) Garfinkel and Ethnomethodology. Blackwell, London.

Jordan B, Henderson A (1995) Interaction analysis: foundations and practice. The Journal of Learning Sciences 4(1), 39–103.

Root R (1988) Design of a multi-media vehicle for social browsing. Proceedings of the 1988 ACM conference on Computer-supported cooperative work. ACM Press, New York.

Suchman L (1983) Office procedures as practical action: models of work and systems design. ACM Transactions on Information Systems 1(4), 320–328.

Suchman L (1987) Plans and Situated Actions: The Problem of Human/Machine Communication. Cambridge University Press, Cambridge.

# Chapter 13
# Mediaspace – Meaningspace – Meetingspace

**Bill Buxton**

*Thoughts exchanged by one and another are not the same in one room as in another.*

Louis I. Kahn

**Abstract** As technology becomes ever more pervasive in our lives, one of the fundamental questions confronting us is how to resolve the increasing complexity that too often accompanies it – complexity which threatens to prevent us from reaping the potential benefits that it offers. In addressing this question, much of the literature has focused on improving the design and usability of the interface to the technologies. In this chapter we investigate another approach, one in which some of the complexity in using the devices is eliminated by exploiting some of the key properties of architectural and social space. Our work is based on the observation that there is meaning in space and in distance. Hence, we can relieve users of the complexity of having to explicitly specify such meaning, as – through appropriate design – it can be implicit, given its spatial context.

## Introduction

When you walk into a lecture hall at a university, even one that you have never been in before, and where you know nobody, you still know who is the professor and who are the students. If you see a photo of a dinner party, with everyone sitting around the dining table, you know who are the hosts and who are the guests. Walking in the park, you can tell if two people are in love, even if you see them only from a distance.

In each of these examples, we know what we know because of our literacy in the meaning of space. In the lecture hall, the professor is at the front, and the students in the chairs. We gain our understanding from the position of the people relative to the architectural space. With the dinner party, we can infer who are the hosts because

B. Buxton
Principal Researcher, Microsoft Research
e-mail: www.billbuxton.com

they typically sit at the head of the table. In this case, it is position relative to a fixed object in the architectural space that provides the cues for interpreting the social relationship of the party. And finally, with the lovers in the park, it is their physical proximity relative to each other – regardless of if they are in the park, on a bus, or on a boat – which leads to our conclusion about their emotional closeness.

What all these examples illustrate is that from a lifetime of living in the everyday world, we have all built up a phenomenal depth of knowledge about the conventions of space and its meaning – both absolute and relative, and physical and social. This is knowledge that we exploit every day, in almost everything that we do, in order to make sense of, and function in, the world.

It is also something that can be exploited to reduce the complexity and intrusiveness of the technologies that we introduce into our world. This is something that the examples discussed in this chapter are intended to illustrate.

The examples discussed have been implemented and used in practice. The approach was opportunistic: to do smart things with stupid technologies. Rather than make engineering breakthroughs, our objective was to create an opportunity to gain experience living with these technologies *before* they were commercially viable. Our hope was that the human insights gained might help inform future design practice and development. Our mantra while doing this work was as follows:

*The only way to engineer the future tomorrow is to have lived in it yesterday.*

## Background

In the 1980s I was involved in two projects at Xerox PARC. One was the *Ubiquitous Computing* project led by Mark Weiser, which was to have a major impact on our thinking about the future of computation (Weiser, 1991). The other was the *Mediaspace Project*, initiated by Bob Stults, Steve Harrison, and Sara Bly (Stults, 1986; Bly et al., 1993).

The former had to do with digital computers, and as manifest at PARC at the time, primarily pen-based computing on three scales: palm-sized "tabs," slate-sized tablets, and whiteboard-sized panels. All were networked using (then) uncommon wireless technologies (infrared and packet radio), and had high levels of interoperability.

On the other hand, the Mediaspace work had to do with audio/video technologies that let designers, in particular, to better collaborate from a distance. The idea was to use the technology to establish a persistent sense of presence among a community that was geographically distributed. The technologies used were decidedly "old school" in that conventional analogue video gear (albeit controlled by a novel computer interface) formed the foundation of the system.

Despite both existing at PARC, these two projects were very far apart, physically and intellectually. Yet, in my mind, the two were actually two sides of the same coin. Both dealt with technologies that were destined to become pervasive. At the meta-level, the only difference was that the slant of one was computation and the other remote collaboration.

Between 1987 and 1989 I had the opportunity to design the media infrastructure for the new EuroPARC facility in Cambridge, what became known as the "IIIF" or "RAVE" system (Buxton and Moran, 1990; Gaver et al., 1992). This gave me the chance to take an initial step in integrating some of these concepts. Then, from 1989 to 1994, I got a chance to go through another iteration when I set up the Ontario Telepresence Project in Toronto (Mantei et al. 1991).

It is work undertaken as part of this latter project that forms the basis for this chapter. However, it is important for me to provide the above historical context since it is hard to separate what we did in Toronto from what was being done at PARC. In many ways they *were* the same project, since while I was scientific director of the Telepresence Project in Toronto, I was also working half time at PARC as part of both the UbiComp and Mediaspace projects. Furthermore, the software which provided the foundation for the Telepresence project was first developed at EuroPARC, then further developed in Toronto, and subsequently installed at PARC.

## The Social–Spatial Anatomy of My Workspace

Let's start with my old office at the University of Toronto, which is shown schematically in Fig. 13.1. Even within this relatively simple space, very different social interactions or protocols are associated with each of the various locations identified in the figure:

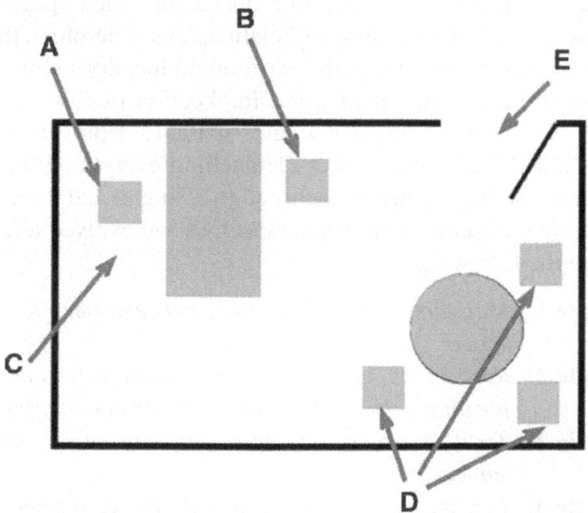


**Fig. 13.1** Schematic of my office. A number of distinct locations in the office are indicated, including the chair behind my desk (A), the chair across from my desk (B), standing space behind my desk (C), and chairs around the coffee table (D) and the door (E). Different social functions are associated with each location. The deployment of any technology in the office to support collaboration or social activities should reflect and respect these differences

(A) My chair behind the desk.
(B) The chair across from my desk.
(C) The position beside my chair.
(D) The chairs around the coffee table.
(E) The doorway.

To get a taste of what I mean, consider a meeting with a student.

First, I might sit in my chair (A) and have the student sit across the desk from me in position (B). In this case, I am Professor Buxton, and they are not. This would likely be the situation if I were telling a student that they had failed, or if I was formally congratulating them on a great job.

Second, if I was working closely with the student on something, they might come behind my desk to position (C), while I sat in my chair. However, it would be very unusual for a stranger or someone with whom I was not working closely, or did not know, to stand there.

Third, if I was having a casual meeting, or just chatting, we may sit around the coffee table in the chairs labelled (D). This would occur if the meeting was informal, and it would indicate that the relationship was more collegial than subordinate. It would be a meeting with "Bill" rather than "Professor Buxton."

Fourth, while I was working at my desk a student might pop their head in the door to ask something. If I do not ask them in, the student would know that I was busy, not be offended, and the conversation would be brief.

Finally, if a meeting involved a number of students, rather than use my office, it would likely take place in a conference room – a space which has its own set of conventions around space.

Our premise is that any technology introduced into such spaces must reflect and respect these space–function–distance relationships. Therefore, the appropriate technologies need to be distributed at the appropriate locations within that space.

Mies van der Rohe notwithstanding, the implication of this is, *More is Less*: interaction with *more* of the right technologies spatially deployed in the appropriate locations is much *less* intrusive than channelling everything through a single general-purpose technology typically anchored to a single, and therefore generally wrong, location. In designing from this perspective, we evolved a few basic principles, including the following:

**Design Principle 1:** *Maintain a clear distinction between person space and task space.*
**Design Principle 2:** *Respect the function–location relationships and conventions for all present, either physically or via telepresence.*
**Design Principle 3:** *Treat electronic and physical "presences" or visitors the same.*
**Design Principle 4:** *Use the same social protocols for electronic and physical social interactions.*

We will now work through some examples that illustrate how we approached supporting scenarios such as those discussed above for those who were not physically present.

### Example: At the Desk

Let's start with the scenario of working closely with someone at the desk. The typical configuration here is for the remote person to appear on a monitor by the desk that has a video camera placed on top of, or beside it. In our implementation, illustrated in Fig. 13.2, we already see Principle 1 kicking in, resulting from a departure from the norm. The monitor used is physically distinct from the computer screen on which the work being discussed would appear. Among other things, this prevents any contention for screen real-estate on the computer monitor. Documents and people have their own distinct place – just as in the physical world (Buxton, 1992).

Apart from the problems of approach, which we will discuss later, this configuration could be fine for some meetings, such as those where it would be appropriate for the visitor to be positioned at location B or C in my office. But what if I am sitting at my coffee table, position D, a not uncommon thing? How do I interact with the remote person if the monitor on which they appear and the camera which they see me by is by my desk pointing at my chair at location (A)? I could get up and reposition either myself or the video set-up, but that would be a disruption that need not happen.

### Example: Around the Coffee Table

Design Principle 2 leads us to our solution. Just as there are different places where those physically present can sit for different purposes, so should it be for the remote participant. Hence, besides the video system at my desk (Fig. 13.2), there was also a system at the coffee table (Fig. 13.3) where a visitor could "sit" and participate in around-the-table conversations.

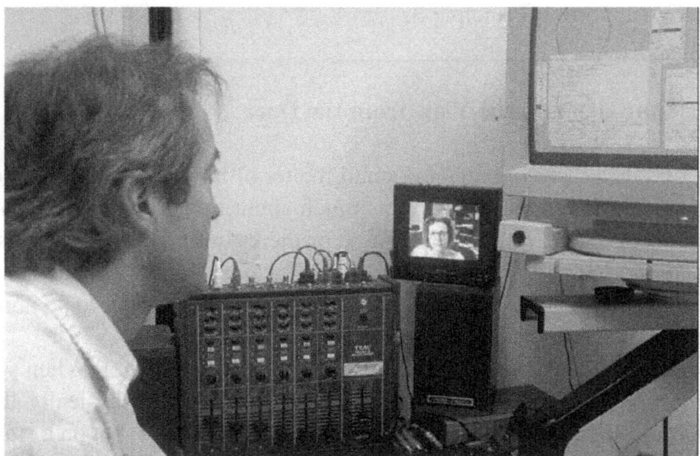

**Fig. 13.2** A typical desktop video conferencing configuration. Conferencing is typically channelled through a video camera on top of a monitor on the user's desktop. However, that monitor is distinct from the computer monitor so as to differentiate "person space" from "task space"

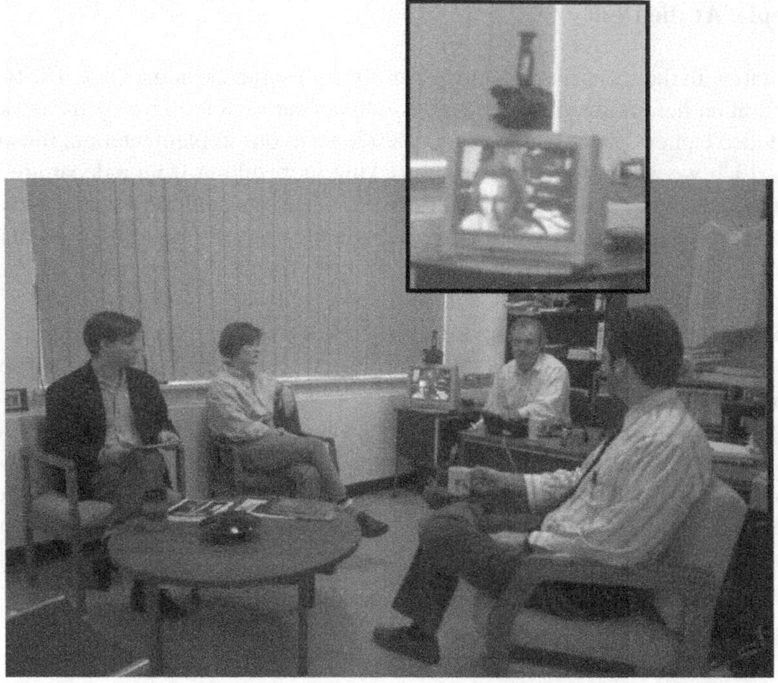

**Fig. 13.3** Remote participation in an informal group. Here a group, including a remote participant (detail in inset), are sitting around the coffee table in my office having a casual meeting. (In position "D" relative to the schematic in Fig. 13.1.)

The visitor is able to sit at the location physically appropriate for the social function of the meeting, regardless of whether they are there physically or electronically, thereby supporting Principle 3.

## Example: Approach and the View from the Door

So far so good. But there remains the small matter of how you entered my office in the first place. Social conventions are as much about transitions, such as approach and departure, as they are about being here or there. In the desktop video situation illustrated in Fig. 13.2, for example, you are either there or not. When you are there, you are right in my face. Worse than that, when you arrive, you do so abruptly, in a way that violates normal social conventions of approach.

Figure 13.4 illustrates our approach to addressing this problem. When you come to my office, you come via location (E), the door. If you come physically, then all is normal. If you come electronically, you also appear by the door, but on a small video monitor mounted above it. In a manner analogous to hearing your footsteps coming down the physical corridor outside my office, I hear your approach *via* an emitted "earcon" which emanates from a speaker by the door monitor. And, I hear you *before*

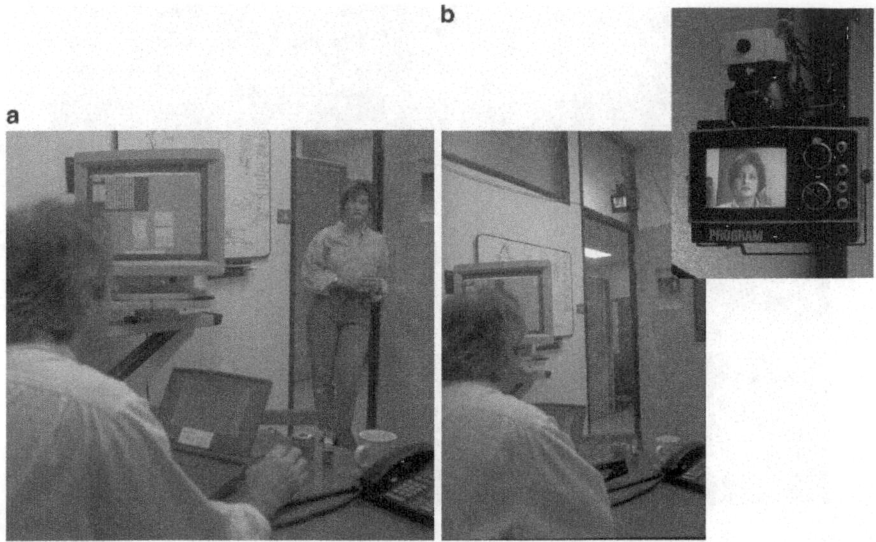

**Fig. 13.4** Maintaining social distance. In establishing contact, one appears by the door and has a from-the-door view via the camera, regardless of whether one approaches from the physical corridor (left image) or the electronic corridor (right image). People approaching electronically do so via a monitor and speaker mounted above the door (inset on right image). The social graces of approach are preserved, and the same social conventions are used for both physical and electronic visitors

you appear or can see me. When you do see me (which is at the same time I can see you), you do so from a wide-angle low-resolution camera that is integrated with the monitor that I see you on and the speaker from which I hear you. Thus, the glance that you first get is essentially the same as what you would get through the door. If I am concentrating on something or someone else, I may not see you or pay attention to you, just as would be the case if you were walking by in the hall (even though I may well hear that someone is there or has passed by). Appropriate distance is maintained. If you knock or announce yourself, I may invite you in, in which case you could take a place at my desk, or around the coffee table, whichever is more appropriate.

## Example: Front-to-Back-to-Front Videoconferencing

As stated previously, not all meetings happen in my office. So let us now look at how some of these ideas apply in a small conference room. Most such rooms equipped for videoconferencing that I have used are set up more-or-less like the one shown in Fig. 13.5.

The videoconferencing technology is at the front of the room, which is the location from which one typically presents. The problem arises when the remote person is actually just one of the attendees, rather than the speaker. In this case, the remote attendee is clearly in the wrong place, especially if a physically present person is

**Fig. 13.5** Front-to-back videoconferencing. Here the remote person is located at the front of the room. Hence, one could reasonably infer that he is presenting, since the front is the place that one presents from

making a presentation from the front. All that the remote person will see is the back of the head of the presenter, while at the same time being a visual distraction for all of the other attendees. In this situation things are socially broken just because of where the technology is placed.

The wrong way to fix this, however, is to move the conferencing gear to the back. This just reverses the problem. What we did instead is enable remote participants to "take a place at the table" like any other participant when not presenting. An implementation of this "back-to-front" videoconferencing is illustrated in Fig. 13.6.

Here, a presentation is being made to one remote and four local participants. Due to the maintenance of audio and video reciprocity coupled with the appropriate use of space, the presenter uses the same social mechanisms in interacting with both local and remote attendees. Stated another way, even if the presenter has no experience with videoconferencing or technology, there is no new "user interface" to learn. If someone raises their hand, it is clear they want to ask a question. If someone looks confused, a point can be clarified – no matter where they are.

**Example: Hydra: supporting a four-way roundtable meeting**

Underlying our work was a kind of mantra that reflects the attitude of ubiquitous computing: one size doesn't fit all. We experimented with different designs for different types of meetings. One of these was a technique to support a four-way meeting, where each of the participants is in a different location. It was designed to capture many of the spatial cues of gaze, head turning, gaze awareness (Ishii et al., 1992)

**Fig. 13.6** Back-to-front videoconferencing. Remote attendees to a meeting take their place at the table by means of video monitors mounted on the back wall. They see through the adjacent camera, hear via a microphone, and speak through their monitor's loudspeaker. The presenter uses the same conventional skills in interacting with those attending physically and those attending electronically. No new skills are required

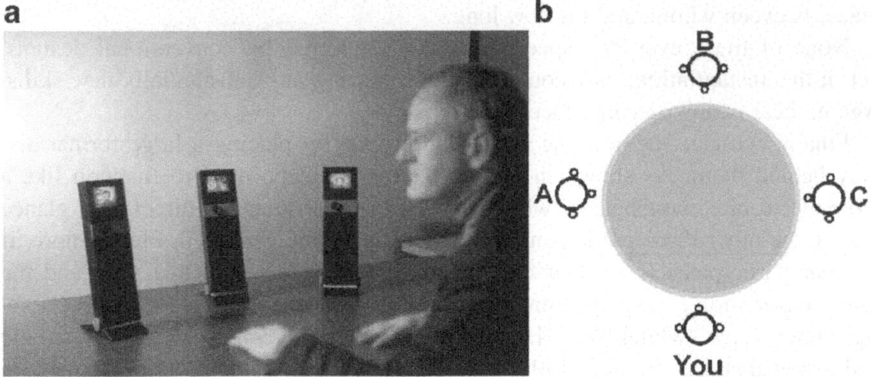


**Fig. 13.7** Using video "surrogates". The photo on the left shows a four-way video conference where each of the three remote participants attends via a video "surrogate." By preserving the "roundtable" relationships illustrated schematically on the right, conversational acts found in face-to-face meetings, such as gaze awareness, head turning, etc. are preserved

and turn-taking that are found in face-to-face meetings. Consistent with the design principles outlined above, we do this by preserving the spatial relationships "around the table".[1] This is illustrated in Fig. 13.7.

[1] This idea of using video surrogates in this way for multiparty meetings turns out not to be new. After implementing it ourselves, we found that it had been proposed by Fields (1983).

Each of the three remote participants is represented by a small video surrogate. These are the small Hydra units seen on the desk (Sellen et al., 1992; Buxton et al., 1997). Each provides a unique view of one of the remote participants, and provides each remote participant a unique view of you. The spatial relationship of the participants is illustrated by the "roundtable" on the right. Hence, relative to you, person A, B, and C appear on the Hydra units to your left, front, and right, respectively. Likewise, person A sees you to their right, and sees person B to their left.

Collectively, the units shown in the figure mean that the user has three monitors, cameras, and speakers on their desk. Yet, the combined footprint is less than that of a conventional telephone. These Hydra units represent a good example of transparency through ubiquity. This is because each provides a distinct location for the source of each remote participant's voice. As a result, due to the resulting "cocktail party effect," the basis for supporting parallel conversations is provided. This showed up in a formal study that compared various technologies for supporting multiparty meetings (Sellen, 1992). The Hydra units were the only technology tested that exhibited the parallel conversations seen in face-to-face meetings.

The units lend themselves to incorporating proximity sensors that would enable aside comments to be made in the same way as face-to-face meetings: by leaning towards the person to whom the aside is being directed. Because of the gaze awareness that the units provide, the regular checks and balances of face-to-face meetings would be preserved, since all participants would be aware that the aside was being made, between whom, and for how long.

None of these everyday speech acts are supported by conventional designs, yet in this instantiation, they come without requiring any substantially new skills. Again, there is no "user interface."

Finally, we can augment the basic Hydra units by placing a large format display behind them. As shown in Fig. 13.8, this could be used to function like a large electronic "whiteboard," which enables the user to easily direct their glance among the other three participants and the work being discussed. Furthermore, if all four participants have their environments configured the same way, and the same information is displayed on each of the large displays, then each has optimal sight lines to the "whiteboard." Here is a case where the combination of electronic and physical space (Buxton, 1992) provides something that is an improvement on the traditional physical world where, if the physical whiteboard were across from you, it would be behind person "B" sitting opposite you. Furthermore, note that the awareness that each participant has of who is looking at who ("gaze awareness") extends to the "whiteboard."

## Example: Size Matters

Scale, as well as location, is important in terms of its ability to affect the quality of interaction in a Mediaspace. Consider the impact of electronically sitting across the desk from one another, as illustrated in Fig. 13.2 compared to Fig. 13.9, where,

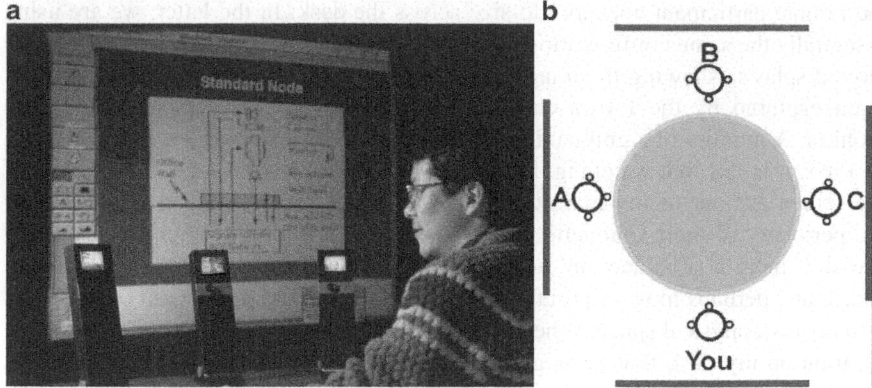


**Fig. 13.8** Seamless integration of person and task space. The photo on the left also shows a four-way video conference using the Hydra units. However, this time, a large electronic "whiteboard" containing the information being discussed appears behind the units. As illustrated in blue in the schematic on the right, the same display can appear behind the units at each of the four sites, thereby giving each participant ideal sight lines to the" "same"" whiteboard (something that does not occur in same-place roundtable meetings.) Furthermore, gaze awareness now extends to whether one is looking up at the "whiteboard" or at a person, thereby seamlessly blending person and task space

**Fig. 13.9** Face-to-face. In this scenario, each participant has a computerized desktop on which the same information is displayed. The intention is to capture the essence of working across the desk from one-another. Each sees the remote participant life-size. The video camera (from a Hydra unit) is unobtrusive on the desk. Participants interact with the computer using a stylus. When one participant looks down to their desktop, their eyes seem to project into the space of the other, thereby strengthening the sense of telepresence. While there is a considerable amount of technology involved, it is integrated into the architectural ecology. What one gets is lots of service and lots of space, not lots of gear and appliances

the remote participant appears life-size across the desk. In the latter, we are using essentially the same configuration as we saw in Fig. 13.8; however, in this case the large display is showing the image of the remote person in a 1-on-1 conversation. I am captured by the Hydra camera, but the large display replaces thc Hydra monitor. A number of significant points arise from this example.

First, it is not like watching TV. Due to the scale of the image, the borders of the screen are out of my main cone of vision. The remote person is defined by the periphery of their silhouette, not by the bezel of a monitor. Second, by being life-size, there is a balance in the weight or power exercised by each participant. Third, and perhaps most important, the gaze of the remote participant can traverse into my own physical space. When he looks down, my eyes are directed to the same location on my desk that he is gazing at on his. Our gaze traverses the distance, thereby strengthening the sense of presence. What is central to this example is the contrast between the simplicity and naturalness of the environment and the potency of its functionality. In keeping with the principle of invisibility, a powerful, nonintrusive work situation has been created.

## Recapitulation: From the Macro to the Micro

Throughout this chapter, and elsewhere (Buxton, 1995; Buxton, 2006) I have referred to the notion of "task space" and "person space" and emphasized the importance of keeping them separate. Before concluding, I want to drill down on this because something is missing, a bridge, which emerges if we look at things at finer granularity.

The heart of what I am getting at is that there is a place where the space of the person and the task overlap, and this is what I am going to call *reference space*. This is perhaps best explained by referring to Tang and Minneman's (1991) *Videowhiteboard* system, illustrated in Fig. 13.10. Contrast this to the photograph in Fig. 13.8. In both cases one can see the remote participant(s) and the work being done – in both cases on a large rear projection screen. But here the similarities disappear rather quickly. In Fig. 13.10, one can see no details of the remote person's face, such as their eyes or where they are looking. On the other hand, in Fig. 13.8, the only way that people can point or gesture is with a single point, controlled by a mouse or stylus. This restricts them to the gestural vocabulary of a fruit fly. What a contrast to Fig. 13.10 where one has the full use or both hands and the body to reference aspects of the work through gestures. In addition, the sharpness and contrast of the shadows provide strong cues that help one anticipate what the remote person is about to do, and where.

To summarize, I would identify three distinct types of spaces that need to be considered at the microlevel of collaboration:

1. *Person space*: this is the space where one reads the cues about expression, trust, and gaze. It is where the voice comes from, and where you look when speaking to someone.

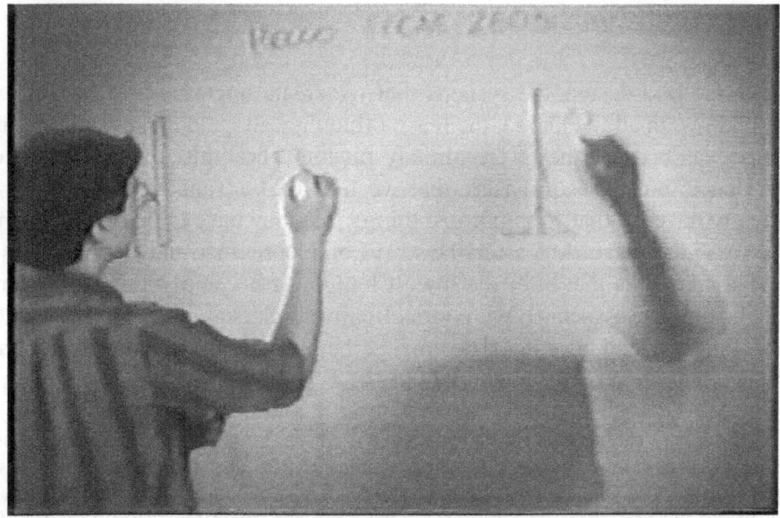

**Fig. 13.10** Referencing with shadows. In this example from Tang and Minneman's (1991) *Videowhiteboard*, one sees the remote person, but not like we have seen in the other examples. Here what is important is the relationship between shadow relative to the work

2. *Task space*: this is the space where the work appears. If others can see it, it is shared. If not, it is private. Besides viewing, this is the space where one does things, such as marking or creating. One changes things here.
3. *Reference space*: this is the space within which the remote party can use body language to reference the work – things like pointing and gesturing. It is also the channel through which one can sense proximity, approach, departure, and anticipate intent. Like the task space, there are different types. In this case, the types vary according to richness, with a telepointer being pretty low on the scale, and the shadows of Tang and Minneman fairly high.

The reason that I make these distinctions is to emphasize that person space and reference space need not be the same thing. The most interesting evidence of this is that one can have both, yet disconnected. For example, in Fig. 13.10, if there was a high-quality video image of the remote person's head hanging like a rearview mirror of the left of the frame, there would be no disorientation in seeing the shadow of the body, including the head superimposed on the work surface, and the video image of the face to the left. The reason is that they serve different purposes, even if they are the same person. In some ways, this is similar to our ability to "point" with a mouse, where our hand is on the desk, while our eye tracks the cursor.

The importance of this is directly related to the importance of being able to effectively frame and make reference to things that we are working on in the everyday world. It is a rich form of communication, and telepresence systems that do not support it well will be impoverished as a result – no matter how good the audio and video might otherwise be.

## Summary and Conclusions

Even with the best design, the systems that we create impose a load on our users. The problem is, in all likelihood, the reason that they adopted the technology in the first place was because they were already pushing the limits of what they could handle. Hence, our job is to ensure that we take best advantage of the skills that they already have, so that we minimize things that they have to do or learn, simply because we didn't do so. At least in the world of telepresence and media spaces, the knowledge and skills that offer the lowest hanging fruit, and yet among the most neglected, are those associated with our collective understanding of place, location, distance, function, and meaning. The hope is that the work described in this chapter helps shed some light on this potential.

**Acknowledgments** The ideas developed in this essay have evolved over countless discussions with colleagues at Rank Xerox EuroPARC, Xerox PARC, and the Ontario Telepresence Project. To all of those who have helped make these such stimulating environments, I am very grateful. I would like to especially acknowledge the contributions of Abi Sellen, Sara Bly, Steve Harrison, Mark Weiser, Brigitta Jordan, and Bill Gaver. Finally, I would like to acknowledge the contribution of my wife, Elizabeth Russ, who made many helpful comments on the manuscript. The research discussed in this chapter has been supported by the Ontario Telepresence Project, Xerox PARC, and the Natural Sciences and Engineering Research Council of Canada. This support is gratefully acknowledged.

## References

Bly, S., Harrison, S. and Irwin, S. (1993). Media Spaces: bringing people together in a video, audio and computing environment. *Communications of the ACM*, 36(1), 28–47.

Buxton, W. (1992). Telepresence: integrating shared task and person spaces. *Proceedings of Graphics Interface '92,* 123–129. Earlier version appears in Proceedings of Groupware '91, Amsterdam, Oct. 29, 1991, 27–36.

Buxton, W. (1995). Integrating the periphery and context: a new model of telematics. *Proceedings of Graphics Interface '95*, 239–246.

Buxton, W. (1997). Living in augmented reality: ubiquitous media and reactive environments. In K. Finn, A. Sellen and S. Wilber (Eds.). *Video Mediated Communication.* Hillsdale, NJ: Lawrence Erlbaum, 363–384. An earlier version of this chapter also appears in *Proceedings of Imagina '95*, 215–229.

Buxton, W. (2006). Space-function integration and ubiquitous media. In M. Shamiyeh (Ed.). *Towards and Interactive and Integrative Design Process*. Linz, Austria: DOM Publications, 248–271.

Buxton, W. and Moran, T. (1990). EuroPARC's Integrated Interactive Intermedia Facility (IIIF): early experience. In S. Gibbs and A.A. Verrijn-Stuart (Eds.). *Multi-user Interfaces and Applications, Proceedings of the IFIP WG 8.4 Conference on Multi-user Interfaces and Applications*, Heraklion, Crete. Amsterdam: Elsevier Science B.V. (North-Holland), 11–34.

Buxton, W., Sellen, A. and Sheasby, M. (1997). Interfaces for multiparty videoconferencing. In K. Finn, A. Sellen and S. Wilber (Eds.). *Video Mediated Communication.* Hillsdale, N.J.: Lawrence Erlbaum, 385–400.

Fields, C.I. (1983). Virtual space teleconference system. *United States Patent 4,400,724*, August 23, 1983.

Gaver, W., Moran, T., MacLean, A., Lövstrand, L., Dourish, P., Carter, K. and Buxton, W. (1992). Realizing a video environment: EuroPARC's RAVE System. *Proceedings of CHI '92, ACM Conference on Human Factors in Software* 27–35.

Ishii, H., Kobayashi, M. and Grudin, J. (1992). Integration of inter-personal space and shared workspace: Clearboard design and experiments. *Proceedings of CSCW '92*, 33–42.

Mantei, M., Baecker, R., Sellen, A., Buxton, W., Milligan, T. and Welleman, B. (1991). Experiences in the use of a media space. *Proceedings of CHI '91, ACM Conference on Human Factors in Software*, 203–208.

Sellen, A. (1992). Speech patterns in video mediated conferences. *Proceedings of CHI '92, ACM Conference on Human Factors in Software*, 49–59.

Sellen, A., Buxton, W. and Arnott, J. (1992). Using spatial cues to improve videoconferencing. *Proceedings of CHI '92, ACM Conference on Human Factors in Software*, 651–652. Also videotape in CHI '92 Video Proceedings.

Stults, R. (1986). Media Space. *Systems Concepts Lab Technical Report*. Palo Alto, CA: Xerox PARC.

Tang, J.C. and Minneman, S.L. (1991). Videowhiteboard: Video shadows to support remote collaboration. *Proceedings of the ACM-SIGCHI Conference on Human Factors in Computing Systems (CHI'91)*, 315–322.

Weiser, M. (1991). The computer for the 21st century. *Scientific American*, 265(3), 94–104.

# Chapter 14
# Media Space, After 20 Years

**Robert Stults**

*But I can say this of myself: I have often conceived of projects in the mind that seemed quite commendable at the time; but when I translated them into drawings, I found several errors in the very parts that delighted me most, and quite serious ones; again, when I return to drawings, and measure the dimensions, I recognize and lament my carelessness; finally, when I pass from the drawings to the model, I sometimes notice further mistakes in the individual parts.... Alberti, On the Art of Building in Ten Books, IX, 10*

*[C]ulture that is engaged in translating itself from one radical mode such as the auditory, into another mode like the visual, is bound to be in a creative ferment, as was classical Greece or the Renaissance. But our own time is an even more massive instance of such ferment, and just because of such "translation."* Marshall McLuhan, *The Gutenberg Galaxy*

**Abstract** One origin of Media Space was research in design during the 1970s that sought to integrate design models with design processes. An approach was demonstrated in the 1980s to represent design processes in Media Space. The approach extended the concepts and vocabulary of physical design, centered on physical space, to organize emerging technologies for capture, transmission, storage, and indexing of video and audio, in combination with digital information systems. That approach juxtaposed video and audio to represent process with design representations, but did not integrate them. With the maturing of technology over the past 20 years, and with nonphysical design increasingly replacing the primacy of physical design, technical possibilities for integrated technology in Media Spaces have increased, and, at the same time, the concepts and vocabulary of physical space have become misleading in their development and use.

S. Harrison (ed.), *Media Space 20+ Years of Mediated Life*,
Computer Supported Cooperative Work,

## Design in Media Space

Looking back to my initial involvement with Media Space, I find a personal origin in architecture, architectural practices, and architectural space, first, as they appeared at the beginning of the Italian Renaissance, and then, as they were transformed by the electronic media. My canonical reference for the first is Leon Battista Alberti's *On the Art of Building in Ten Books*[1]; and for the second, Marshall McLuhan's *The Gutenberg Galaxy*.[2]

Alberti, in his architectural writings and other writings, as well as in his buildings, touches upon components of architecture, design, and space that later coalesced into a primacy of spaces and places of Western architecture. While Alberti's work is incomplete, anticipatory, and suggestive, it is not fragmented; rather it manifests a unified but not fully articulated approach, a bundle of techniques and knowledge, to shape and realize a built and visual world. The arena for this is space – measurement, uniformity, and geometry – brought under the order of perspective construction, which he was the first to document.[3]

The components that Alberti brought together were part of the constellation of thinking, awareness, and practices that coalesced into design and design media, and developed through the Early Modern Age in Europe to the twentieth century – not to mention the twenty-first century – design. It was Alberti's position early in the formation of a long primacy of physical architecture that was so suggestive in approaching electronic media as an emerging primacy, something like architecture, with its own approaches, techniques, and knowledge, in which we might shape and realize spaces … Media Spaces.

The second personal origin for Media Space, McLuhan, for me articulated the replacement of a typographic/print world by electronic media; and by extension, this also meant to me the undermining of the primacy of physical spaces and places of Western architecture by electronic replacements. If Alberti brought us practices and spaces of physical architecture, McLuhan heralded their replacement with electronic media.

So approximately: Alberti + McLuhan = → Media Space

From this approximate origin of Media Space there is a long hop to its more specific origin: not just the extrapolation of Alberti's practices and meanings of architecture, but representations, processes, and meanings of architectural, civil, and mechanical design in the 1980s; and not just the analog electronic media

---

[1] Leon Battista Alberti, *On the Art of Building in Ten Books*, translated by Joseph Rykwert, Neil Leach, and Robert Tavenor (MIT Press) Cambridge, MA, 1988 is now the standard translation, although it was not available at the time of the reported work.

[2] Marshall McLuhan, *The Gutenberg Galaxy, the making of typographic man* (University of Toronto) Toronto, 1962.

[3] Leon Battista Alberti, *On Painting*, translated by John R. Spencer (Yale University Press) New Haven, CT, 1956.

of McLuhan, but the digital media, encompassing computing, video, audio, and networks. Within this context, Media Space began for me, and did so with a search for design media.

The design media that we searched for were representations of the processes of architecture, civil, and mechanical design, commensurate with the geometric representations of design media. Geometrically based design media had long provided flexible and authoritative means for representing the objects of design, flexible in the sense the geometrically based representations encompassed multiple, specialized meanings, and authoritative in the sense that representations could serve as referential bases for responsibility, action, and other aspects of design and realization. Flexibility and authority of representations enable individual designers and primary-level design groups to think and act informally and independent of structure; the representations account for coordination of actions, and for recording outcomes. But the representations did not account for participation in more complex process. These had been carried in process representations, usually encoded in methods of practice, which in turn were embedded in organizations. With computing systems, geometrically based models improved the flexibility and authority of design media, and at the same time increasingly explicit representations of process marginalized informal studio process in design projects.

The idea of Media Space for design was to fix the imbalance, by providing process representations that were as comfortable and as effective as the design media, and as capable of containing design activities as design studios. In Media Space activities at Xerox PARC,[4] we asked the questions, Can we find representations for design that enable designers to work in parallel between objects and processes of design? and to work among themselves, as cooperating members of design groups?

We approached these questions through examples: an impeller for a propulsion turbine; a spar for an aircraft wing; and, a pipeway between vessels of a process plant.[5] In these examples, engineering groups designed physical objects or systems, using digital representations. An example of a digital geometric model comes from the example of a propulsion turbine. In an engineering process, engineers model an impeller as a solid body, based on computed surface geometry for its blades. The geometric model can be displayed to an engineer through a display device; can be used to define a model for finite element analysis; and can be used to generate milling machine instructions for its manufacture (Figs. 14.1, 14.2, and 14.3).

[4] The Media Space work discussed here was carried out in the Software Concepts Laboratory of Xerox Palo Alto Research Center, in the Design and Media Spaces Area. We formed the Area in 1985; I was the leader, and Steve Harrison was my partner in research.

[5] The examples of impeller, spar, and pipeway were developed with customers of the Evans & Sutherland Computer company during 1976–1979.

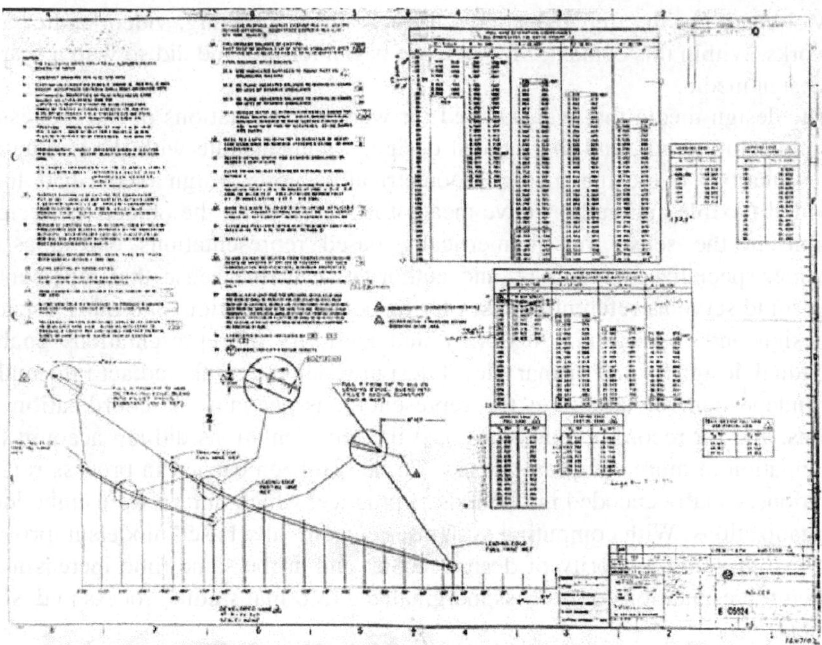

**Fig. 14.1** Engineering drawing of impeller, surface geometry of Vanes, 1978
*Source*: Stults, photo of engineering drawing, 1978.

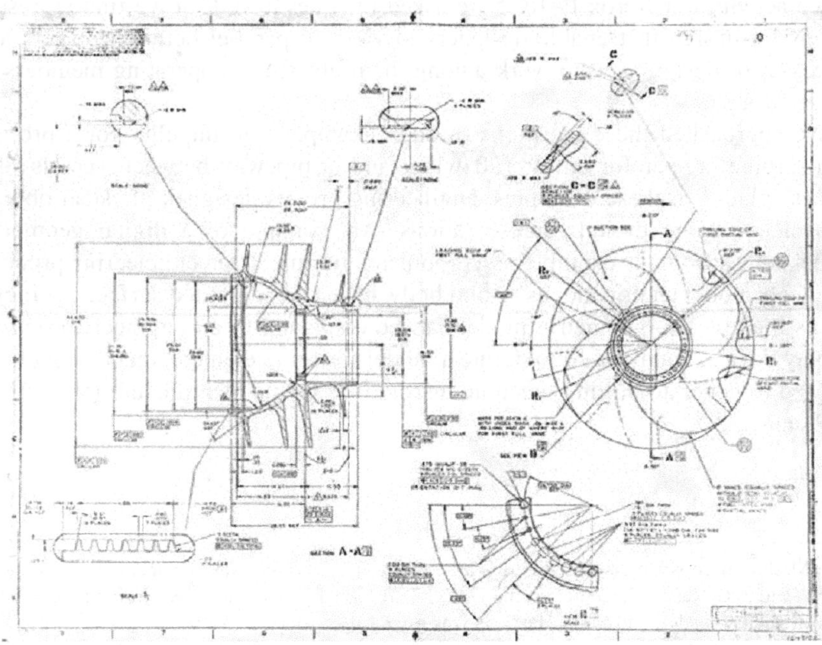

**Fig. 14.2** Engineering drawing of impeller, dimensioned drawing, 1978
*Source*: Stults, photo of engineering drawing, 1978

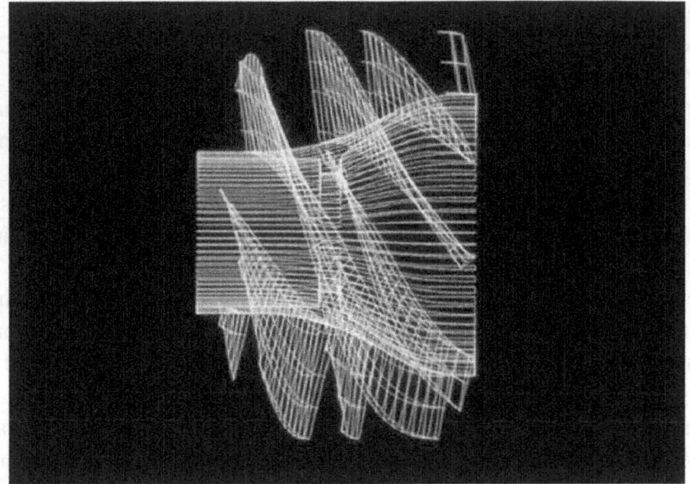

**Fig. 14.3** Displayed image of impeller, Evans & Sutherland Picture System 2, 1978
*Source*: Stults, photo of display screen showing model constructed by Stults, 1978.

## Designer-and-Design-Medium

In the examples of impeller, spar, and pipeway, a designer works with a representation, called a design medium, as a substitute for working directly with the physical object or system. In our approach, Designer-and-Design-Medium was a condition of design; initially the primary condition; and as developed below, one of two primary conditions of design. Working in a design medium, a designer defines form in cycles of action, perception, understanding, action, and so on. For static, physical systems, geometrically based representations constitute the central design media, and designers interact with them. These might be physical models, perspectives or isometric projections, or measured drawings. The designer uses the representations as surrogates that are easier to understand and manipulate than the actual objects or physical systems. To serve as a serviceable surrogate, a representation simulates enough of the replaced object of design that interaction with the medium is meaningful.[6] Static three-dimensional space serves in the studio for models and drawings of design, and scaled and displaced, as the site of the realized building. For static physical systems and objects, geometry underlies the successful substitution of medium for the object of design.

[6] The argument made here that the medium can substitute for the thing being designed echoes the argument by John Dewey, *Art as Experience* (Minton, Balch & Company) New York, 1934, pp. 195f that an artistic medium is not an external means for a work, but is intrinsic to the work. While a design medium serves as an external surrogate, i.e., does not have a completely intrinsic binding, the medium is also bound with its content. Without this binding, the vision and actions on the medium would not be meaningful when translated back to the thing being designed; with the binding, a designer works in the medium as if he/she is working on the thing itself.

Geometric modeling is a canonical representation in design, but in itself does not constitute a medium. It is part of a larger configuration of Designer-and-Design-Medium that accounts for practices in which a designer defines, understands, and realizes form. In the Italian Renaissance, Alberti's *On the Art of Building*[7] regularized architecture into design practices by a combination of theoretical principles, references to antique buildings, and considerations of siting and construction. Regarding design media, the text refers to sketches, and is explicit in recommending small-scale physical models, for the understanding of both architects and clients.[8]

Geometrically based perspective representations expressed the primacy in design of the eye viewing a framed scene, orderly within the frame, and messiness out-of-frame and invisible. An early example of this is the beautiful and visually compelling *Ideal City* panel from Urbino, *c.*1470 (Figs. 14.4 and 14.5). We can look at the image and comprehend the buildings and spaces that it shows, and from it we can project through a perspective transformation to a static, three-dimensional model of a town. Perspective projection is one representation of static geometry. Another representation is a scaled map, for example, Alberti's map of the enclosing wall of Rome.[9]

The painting in Fig. 14.4 represents an imagined *Ideal City*, projected by perspective transformation onto a framed surface. The city plan and its buildings are laid out in a grid in three-dimensional Cartesian space: the ground is a

**Fig. 14.4** Unknown Italian Painter, Ideal City, *c.*1470 (Palazzo Ducale, Urbino)
*Source*: Stults, photo, 2004.

[7] Alberti, *On the Art of Building*, op.cit.

[8] Alberti, *On the Art of Building*, op.cit., II, 1, pp. 33–34. Alberti is a central figure in the definition of perspective construction, using an example from the viewing of a building. But there is no evidence that he applied perspective to the other direction from viewing, i.e., to definition of form. That emerged with painters in the decades after Alberti, and then in architecture by Bramante, perhaps following Leonardo, Rudolph Wittkower, *Architectural Principles in the Age of Humanism* (Harper) New York, First American Edition, 1963, pp. 18, 20.

[9] Leon Battista Alberti, *On the Art of Building*, op.cit., Book X, section 7, pp. 337–338 describes a method for map making using polar coordinates. A map of the walls of Rome made by Alberti's method is reproduced in Franco Borsi, *Leon Battista Alberti*, translated by Rudolf G. Carpanini (Harper & Row) New York, 1977, p. 34.

**Fig. 14.5** Leon Battista Alberti, Tempio Malatestiano, Rimini, 1450 and After
*Source*: Stults, photo, 2004.

horizontal plane, gridded into squares; the buildings are placed parallel with the grid lines; the floors of the buildings are horizontal; and the buildings (except for the central temple) are organized into rectilinear cells. With respect to the space of the city, the picture plane is vertical and parallel to one of the principal grid directions.

The Designer-and-Design-Medium of the impeller example shows the main features of Renaissance architectural design, but modernized: the principles of metaphysics and aesthetics of earlier practice have been succeeded by principles of Newtonian physics[10]; historical references have been replaced by catalogs of solutions, organized by discipline, function, and morphology[11]; and construction and manufacturing processes have been industrialized.[12] The representations of the objects of design have also been modernized, with extensions from framed perspective to specialized representations, each framed in its own way, all unified by underlying geometric models, and all performed in studio or lab settings organized for working on the models.

---

[10] An example of metaphysics (in the guise of artistic expression, *künstlerische Ausdruck*) meeting structural statics, is Max Bill's comparison of a Mondrian painting and a Maillart layout of steel reinforcing, Max Bill, *Robert Maillart, Bridges and Constructions*, translated by W.P.M. Keatinge Clay (Praeger) New York, 1969, p. 25.

[11] Nikolas Pevsner, *A History of Building Types* (Princeton University Press) Princeton, NJ, 1976.

[12] For example, the combination of standardized rolled steel shapes and methods of computation for steel frame structures.

Since Alberti and before computers, extensions of design media included improved two-dimensional drawings of implicit three-dimensional models – axonometrics, measured drawings, and other systematic, geometrically based representations – for architecture, shipbuilding, and other fields of physical design. With these developments, Designer-and-Design-Medium continued as the means for designers to define and understand forms during their process of emergence. These maintained a focus on the thing being designed, and did not explicitly represent practices, such as involvement of multiple participants, development from concept to completion, focus of activities onto specialized topics, and the purposes and rationale for the thing being designed.

Figure 14.6 shows Alberti's personal logo as an eye, disembodied, and repackaged with wings for mobility. The eye has freed itself from fixed and framed images, but is still operating in a thoroughly optical world.

The image of the *Ideal City* in the Urbino panel suggests buildings, spaces, and places of an Ideal City, as projected onto a framed surface. While looking at the painting, the fixed eye substitutes for the viewer in the imagined city; vision is the surrogate for presence. Rationally and optically the image replaces the Ideal City, through the geometry of the perspective projection applied to the regular, gridded space of the city, and through the geometry of the eye – lens and retina – that are closely modeled by the perspective geometry. And within a studio, designers use the same mechanisms to view the models and images that represent the objects of design.

**Fig. 14.6** Impresa of Leon Battista Alberti, *c.*1446 (London, British Museum)
*Source*: http://www.britishmuseum.org/explore/highlights/highlight_image.aspx?image = ps228436.jpg&retpage = 17256

## Extensions and Limitations to Designer-and-Design-Medium

The powerful method of image creation and viewing of the *Ideal City* in the Urbino panel, however persuasive we find it, is a narrowing of the architecture that it represents. Referring to imaginative architectural drawings of the 18th century, Walter Benjamin noted the limitations of images of architecture from a broader "architecture … not primarily 'seen,' but rather … imagined as an objective entity and … experienced by those who approach or even enter it as a surrounding space sui generis, that is, without the distancing effects of the frame of pictorial space."[13] Other drawing types remedy aspects of the limitations of the framed images by providing alternative visioning, operating by different rules from those of perspective, yet still part of Designer-and-Design-Medium.

In the examples of impeller, spar, and pipeway as described so far, static geometry provided the canonical representation of the object of design, and optical vision provided the means of engagement for the designer. But in our work with design, examples from manufacturing and software became increasingly frequent in which optical geometry of the referent design medium was secondary or even irrelevant.[14] This appeared in problem-solving activities embedded within the design of the physical systems, in the irrational foundations of many projects, in systems in which static geometry was not an important concern, and in the persistence of the body as participant in design and with the things being designed.

**Problem Solving**. Instead of optical engagement, a designer or engineer can define form by applying understanding to problem solving.[15] This appeared in several examples: a successful designer of hot gas turbines told me that many engineers can solve differential equations, but few (he actually said no one other than him) understand how the flows define the surfaces of the blades; the manager of an airfoil design group in an aerospace company, after introducing me to a staff of applied mathematicians and specialized engineers, introduced me to the one person in the group without specialized skills, the group's thought leader, who "knows why planes fly" and specifically how the wings and tail provide lift and control; the lead engineer of a testing company told me that he used the same test stands, instrumentation, and computing systems as the automobile companies, but that those companies hired him to do testing because he could use data from instrumentation and Fourier transform boxes to understand how the cars vibrated. These three examples were about problem solving, guided by understanding, absent engagement with

[13] Walter Benjamin, "Rigorous Study of Art," translated by Thomas Y. Levin, *October 47* (MIT Press) Cambridge, Winter 1988, originally published in the *Frankfurter Zeitung*, 1933.

[14] From 1980 to 1990 important examples came from engineering divisions of Xerox Corporation.

[15] Perhaps parallel with the meeting of design and metaphysics, noted above, is the meeting of design and problem solving, for example, as noted by Horst Rittel as wicked problems, which might be open-ended in a way similar to theoretically solvable but computationally intractable problems (e.g., travel salesperson problem of graph theory).

optical geometry. In these, specialized representations for problem solving serve as design media, within a predefined framework of form.

**Beneath the Rationalist Cover Story**. The imagined architecture of the *Ideal City* is represented in rational layers: the balanced, symmetrical image in the painting; the imagined three-dimensional city, with its harmonious and orderly buildings and spaces, from which the painting image was projected; the three-dimensional grid that gave order to the buildings and spaces of the city; and across all of the layers, continuities, laws, and projections of static geometry. Within this geometric system, vocabularies were defined from the precedents of Antiquity; layout, and measurements from metaphysics; building types from social uses. The geometry, metaphysics, precedents, and types represent as overtly comprehensive the concerns of architecture, and permit Designer-and-Design-Medium to proceed in a broad variety of projects using an orderly, seemingly rational framework. The reality, however, was messier than this, with the principal determinants largely irrational.[16] Examples are: the pagan, self-memorializing impulses, and the late medieval military scene that stood behind Alberti's *Tempio Malatestiano* (Fig. 14.5); and, the religious and political programs that stood behind Bramante's reconstruction of *Saint Peter's*. None would claim an orderly, rationalist footing for either of these projects of Renaissance architecture, though both projects are great achievements of rational, humanist architecture.

In the extensions of Designer-and-Design-Medium from the imaginary architecture of the *Ideal City* to the modern examples of impeller, spar, and pipeway, comparable orderly, rational configurations guided creation of form; and similarly, these represent, and also render invisible, underlying, mainly irrational, foundations for the projects. At the time of our design studies, we addressed the importance of their irrational foundation under the topic, "Tailfins, Getting Beyond the Rationalist Cover Story."[17] The argument was that computer applications, though widely discussed in terms of their utility, can be understood more fully as means of identity. The analogy was with tailfins, as the emblem of styling in American automobiles of the 1950s. Styling had been introduced into mass-market automobiles by General Motors before World War II, under the direction of Harley Earl. These cars were placed into a mass market created by Henry Ford for transportation-only vehicles, and then extended to a new one for vehicles of personal identity. While the utility of the vehicles for transportation never went away, styling, branding, and identity dominated the automobile market of the

[16] McLuhan, op.cit., pp247, "the influence of unexamined assumptions derived from technology leads quite unnecessarily to maximal determinism in human life." In the argument here, this suggests that the technology and other aspects of conventional framing for a project, if unexamined, neuters design and restricts outcomes. The conventional framing, often unexamined, is labeled here as "irrational."

[17] Robert Stults, "Tailfins for the Users: Getting Beyond the Rationalist Cover Story", unpublished, 1979, revised 1983.

1950s. The argument in the Tailfins essay was that computer applications should be understood like cars, with a basic, commodity-like function embedded in styling that provides identity. And styling and identity, both central to design, are not the province of rationality.

**Non-physical Systems**. In contrast with impeller, spar, and pipeway, which can be designed largely as physical systems, we increasingly encountered systems in which geometry was secondary or even absent. In servo-mechanical systems, electronic servos replaced mechanical assemblies during the 1970s and 1980s. With the vanishing mechanical servos the primacy of geometry in servo design also vanished. If geometry lost primacy in servo-mechanical systems, it was altogether absent in the software systems, which were the primary technology interest of the group that carried out the Media Space project. For example, one software structure developed by the group was Model-View-Controller (MVC),[18] which was explained, discussed, and diagramed with quasi-spatial concepts and vocabulary, in fact has no geometric existence. For these and other examples, geometry was secondary or absent, and relevance of Designer-and-Design-Medium was questionable. Moreover, the objects of design, no longer physical, did not bring with them the need for static, three-dimensional space of a studio or lab in which to view them, but in principle, were viewable wherever electronic networks and workstations made them accessible.

**When the Body Vanishes**.... The winged eye in Alberti's Impresa is largely disembodied, except for its packaging with wings, and with appendages fore and aft. The disembodied eye can move from the fixed viewing point for the *Ideal City*, to become a mobile viewer in Cartesian three-dimensional space, and looking at objects deployed in the space: observer and observed; subject and object. Insofar as a body is placed in the space, it too is an object. As already discussed, Walter Benjamin noted absence in image of the experience of architecture, and also as noted, specialized representations extended design media and mitigated the shortcomings of images in providing experience. The limitation that Benjamin noted can be understood as proceeding from fundamental differences in the mechanisms of engagement for designer with design medium from those of a person with the physical object or system. We can disembody ourselves into an eye, and substitute optical space for our multifaceted surroundings when looking at buildings. But in our multifaceted surroundings, we are more than moving eyes: we touch, feel, move, gesture, and physically engage. We have bodies, and so do designers, even in the presence of their design media. This fact, at times seemingly a pesky footnote to architects, is an ineludible fact, and a fundamental shortcoming of Designer-and-Design-Medium, as developed here from the perspective representations in three-dimensional Cartesian space.

[18] The initial development of MVC by Trygve Reenskaug undoubtedly benefited from his experience and conceptualization of physical systems and associated construction processes of off-shore oil drilling at the Institute for Industrial Research, Oslo; but the geometric concepts and vocabulary did not model MVC, but provided a metaphor.

## Social Process of Design

In approaching examples from manufacturing and software, and revisiting architectural design, Designer-and-Design-Medium did not adequately account for things that we saw and heard in the organization of designers and their work, in the representations that they used, and in the processes that they performed. These constituted gaps between Designer-and-Design-Medium and practices of design. Several of the gaps are summarized as topics in this section. The list is not comprehensive, but illustrates gaps that we articulated at the time of the examples. Together they indicate a different condition for design from the condition of Designer-and-Design-Medium, the condition of the *Social Process of Design*.

**Design Groups**. In performing large projects individual designers organize themselves into groups; or an organization responsible for a project staffs itself with designers. In either case the group permits people to perform large and more complex projects, through division of labor, specializations of knowledge and responsibility, and other familiar features of an industrialized activity. Participation of multiple designers under specific roles and responsibilities employs schemes for organizing, naming, signing, release control, and so on, as discussed below in *Managed Design Representations*.

At a primary level of design organization, responsibilities for interacting with representations can be defined and changed in on-going activities that cross between project content and role-in-group, perhaps directly negotiated among group members or defined by a project lead or manager. In more complex design organizations, for example, with multiple levels of hierarchy, or with reporting matrixed by domain and by subassembly, the impacts of changing responsibilities for interacting with the design representations are usually complex, and are explicitly managed at a distance from Designer-and-Design-Medium. The former, primary design group has a high affinity for Designer-and-Design-Medium; the latter, higher-level design organization is performed at a distance from Designer-and-Design-Medium, and is discussed below in *Design Processes*.

**Managed Design Representations**. Large, structured engineering projects developed methods in CAD and CAE systems, in order to provide for orderly performance of engineering activities on coordinated sets of design representations. For example, a CAD system representation for an architectural project uses layers to represent subsystems, such as foundation, structure, electric, and HVAC, within roles and responsibilities noted above for *Design Group*. Access to and responsibility for the layers are assigned by engineering discipline, versions are coordinated among disciplines, and geometric placement and interference is managed by reconciling layers. Long-established practices of drafting rooms were the primary sources for these methods of managing design documents, and the Designer-and-Design-Medium was only of secondary importance. Conversely, Designer-and-Design-Medium, in and of itself, provides little help in managing representations in large projects.

**Design Processes**. An important source for process modeling in engineering is Frederick Taylor's modeling of manufacturing processes.[19] While initially applied to manufacturing and not to the engineering process itself, these models provided for both reasoning about the processes and performing them. Like the geometric model of Designer-and-Design-Medium, they serve as surrogates and also bridges to the actual. By the mid-twentieth century, specialized process models were widely used in engineering projects, for example, in PERT charts of the 1960s. In the 1980s there were many forms of process representations for projects. These were not spatial, but were usually in a time-and-resource domain.[20]

## Design Medium, Design Process, Design Space: Media Space

The question that we addressed in 1985 was, "In what ways can we use computational systems to support design?" Two conditions circumscribed the question.

**Condition 1, Designer-and-Design-Medium**. Design is performed by designers, working in a studio, within a field, which provides scope for the project and which receives its outcomes, interacting with a surrogate representation of the thing being designed, a *design medium*. The medium is a good-enough replacement for the thing being designed that the designers can look at and act on it in the studio as if they are acting on the thing in its actual location.

**Condition 2, Social Process of Design**. Design is performed in social processes by groups of designers, with specialized knowledge and responsibility, organized with more or less formalized structure. Yet even within an organization with defined roles and scope for action, informal and often transient groups carry out integration, form creation and related fundamentals of design that are beyond access to the formal structures.

The central issue in 1985 was the gap in concepts, vocabularies, and means of engagement in established design practices, when approached in terms of Condition 1, Designer-and-Design-Medium versus Condition 2, Social Process of Design. This was important because it separated understanding and action regarding objects of design from the process of performing design. At best the separation was cumbersome; and at worst a separation of ends and means. With these considerations, the question became, "Can we find representations for design that enable designers to work in parallel between objects and processes of design?"

[19] Sudhir Kakar, *Frederick Taylor, a Study in Personality and Innovation* (MIT Press) Cambridge, MA, 1970.

[20] Anatol W. Holt, *Organized Activity and Its Support by Computer* (Kluwer) Dordrecht, 1997, reports work from before 1980 on modeling of *social machinery*, and introduces a graphical notation to represent organized activity.

To address the question of representations, we adopted concepts and vocabulary of architectural design. Not just applicable to architecture, these concepts and vocabulary fit with design of physical systems, like the impeller, spar, and pipe-way. With these, we addressed both conditions, Designer-and-Design-Medium and Social Process of Design. In adopting concepts and vocabulary of architecture, we consciously engaged in a tension between technology that seemed to be accelerating us into something resembling a Brave New World, and at the same time, realizing that There Is Nothing New Under the Sun. From one side, we promoted technology and from the other amplified historically based practices and meanings of design.

The organizing word and concept from architecture for the parallel representations is *space*, meaning the space of design media and design studios: static space occupied by a physical building and the design group that uses it; optical space in which images of the building are constructed; and design–time space of a studio in which designers work together on media that represent the thing being designed. Within the condition of Designer-and-Design-Medium, the design space of a studio replaces the larger space of the building and its users through drawings, models, and other design media that stand for the physical building. Thus, abstraction appears in the studio, as it bridges from being a literal *design space* to the metaphoric *design space* represented in design media. To complete the parallel, for properties and activities of the building or physical system at *use time* we substitute the activities in the design space during *design time*. The design space of architecture and physical systems brought with it concepts, vocabulary, and practices that spanned from the activities of design to the physical system in use.

A design studio is proposed here as the locus for design space. It realizes the in-betweenness of a design medium: between designer and the object of design; between representations and the objects of design; between organizational structures and in form design groups; between well-defined, structured, repeatable process and irregular, impulse-driven, spontaneous, primary activities of discovering, understanding, and making form. As used here, the studio, as a locus, is a place as well a space: a place for designers to come together, and act, not in the domains of engineering, manufacturing, maintenance, use, and so on; but adjacent to those domains. In the language used here, place in its referential meaning is not virtualized, is not places. Practically, the referent means: a physical studio; a common room, perhaps surrounded by personal workspaces; and a laboratory, perhaps with common lab benches and with adjacent personal offices.

Virtualization of design space appears as constituting a place for design from multiple places. These can be fixed – a main studio space, with an ancillary working area located out of adjacency; design studios in nearby buildings maintained in tandem by architects collaborating on a project. The places from which design spaces can be constituted can also be transient. Our social practices, without electronic technology, admit extensions to the defined, fixed place of studio through interactions and conversation: in stairwells, parking lots, hallways, sidebar conversation at meetings, and so on. We practice informal social construction of transient places as part of all sorts of activities, not just design; and we have complex, inconsistent, conventions for incorporating these "outside the game," "off the record" places and activities into legitimate places and activities. For design, incorporation of these transient spaces into a place of design fits easily within the in-betweenness of design medium and design space, so long as technology is available. Knitting together a small number of predefined, fixed locations is technically simpler than knitting together transient places. But in either case, the human and social engagement from multiple, separate locations as if they were a single place for design, extends the as-if-ness that is at the heart of design media and spaces.

In 1985, we looked for a computable representation that could implement a design space, and to serve both conditions. But no unifying formulation appeared, and the prospect for pursuing a computable solution head-on seemed too big to take on. Rather, we simplified, and asked, Does the representation of process need to be computable? An electronic, non-computable representation appeared to be achievable: represent the non-computable appearance of the social processes of design in audio and video. The appearance of the processes in audio and video could then be transmitted, stored, and accessed in parallel with computable content. This could establish commensurability between design media and representations of design process, under the organizing principle of design space.

The 1985 video, *Shoptalk, Representing the Process of Design*, outlined a program for coordinated use of video/audio with computing systems in support of design, "As a medium for representing process, both computing and video have a part, computing because it is now used so widely in modeling and analyzing the artifacts of design, and because it allows us to organize and access information; and video because it conveys the appearance of social activity." (Fig. 14.7).[21] This was a pragmatic strategy that sought to close the gaps between the two conditions, Designer-and-Design-Medium and Social Process of Design, by inserting video and audio representations of design process into the design settings, which were organized around geometrically based representations. With this approach, support for design became involvement with Media Space. The processes of design would be contained in, captured, transmitted, stored, and retrieved in non-computable, electronic form.[22]

[21] *Shoptalk, Representing the Process of Design*, Video, 24 minutes (Xerox Palo Alto Research Center) Palo Alto, CA, 1985.

[22] A parallel effort to Media Space was carried out within the Design and Media Spaces Area at PARC by Ranjit Makkuni. It directly addressed a computable representation of a design artifact and the process of its design. Ranjit's work extended William Mitchell's work on generative grammars in architecture, in the *Sketchbook of Tibentan Thanka Painting* and other projects. It also reintroduced the body to the process, through a gestural interface, Ranjit Makkuni, Frank Zdybel, Jr., Robert Stults, *Gesture-modified diagram for retrieval of image resembling diagram, with parts selectable for further interactive retrieval*, United States Patent 5010500, issued April 23, 1991.

**Fig. 14.7** Diagram of video and computing from Shoptalk Video, 1985
*Source*: Stults, scan of drawing made by Stults, 1985.

## Media Space for Design

We intended that use of Media Space for support of design processes should demonstrate closing of a gap between Designer-and-Design-Medium and the Social Process of Design, by juxtaposing representation of process with audio and video with studio-based representations of the things being designed. The demonstration was to show ourselves and other designers, who were experienced in using nonelectronic media, that these new media offered possibilities for organizing and carrying out design projects by primary design groups, especially discovery and articulation of form through engagement of designers working informally together. The demonstration was not about showing specific tools, whether for visualization, analysis, or managed creation of design documents; but was about demonstrating that a process, heretofore experienced in design studios, could be carried out in synthetic, replacement spaces, with many of the same capabilities to support a social process of design, plus new capabilities that physical studio space could not provide.

The demonstration was to be partial and suggestive, containing major features of a Media Space, but not constituting a comprehensive solution. It would demonstrate something of the social process of design, by opportunistic use of computable representations and video/audio technology, under principles:

1. Concepts and vocabulary of design and engineering, initially based on established practices in physical spaces of labs and studios.
2. Open-ended and ill-defined activities, such as project and concept definition, as well as defined, problem-solving activities; these would include orderly and factual

content, structured and unstructured argument, as well as expression of irrational content, as they appear in video and audio of participants and their activities.
3. Informal social processes of design, initially based on experience in physical spaces of labs and studios, in which members of design relate and interact with each other, especially in unplanned interactions.
4. Compatibility with electronic design artifacts, CAD drawings, and CAE models, for transmission, storage, and retrieval.
5. Indexable, with indexing created by and useable from computing systems in order to discover reference and relationship carried in the video/audio representations, and as a starting point for integration with anticipated models of design processes.

Prototype Media Spaces were developed by these principles, and used for design. We assembled the first prototype Media Space across the personal offices of three researchers, all trained professionally as traditional architects, all working on methods and technologies of design. The offices were all located on the same floor, but did not open onto a shared space. The original impulse was to create a studio-like space among the offices to substitute for absence of adjacency to a studio space. This provided for real-time connection, and also for recording and playback for across-time connection.[23] Later, a Media Space was included as part of a larger project to distribute and integrate research activities across multiple sites, nationally and globally. This Media Space was constructed across personal and common spaces at facilities in Palo Alto, California and Portland, Oregon.[24]

Figure 14.8 is a stillframe from a recording in an early Media Space. It shows hands of a designer sketching a layout. The hands and their actions in time domain represent the process of design, as the designer works as Designer-and-Design-Medium. The video/audio demonstrates capture, transmission, storage, and retrieval of a non-computable representation that spans process and design medium.

**Indexing and Retrieval of Records**. From our experience with Media Space for design, one topic is revisited here, indexing and retrieval of records.

For well-defined activities, such as bank transactions, record structures were subjected to predefinition; occurrence of transactions could be detected, and data from a transaction could be captured and stored into the predefined structures; and means for finding and retrieving records could, in principle, be easily defined.[25] But

[23] Bob [Robert] Stults, *Media Space*, Technical Report of the System Concepts Laboratory (Xerox Palo Alto Research Center) Palo Alto, CA, 1987.

*Shoptalk 3, Design and Media Space*, Video 13 minutes (Xerox Palo Alto Research Center), Palo Alto, CA, 1987.

Robert Stults, *Experimental Uses of Video to Support Design Activities*, Technical Report SSL-89–19 (Xerox Palo Alto Research Center) Palo Alto, CA, 1988.

[24] Sarah Bly, Steve Harrison, Susan Irwin, "Media Spaces: Bringing people together in a video, audio, and computing environment," *Communications of the Association of Computing Machinery*, New York, vol 36, no 1, January 1993, pp. 28–45.

[25] Application systems of the 1980s, typically implemented in COBOL, provided for handling and reporting on transactions and accounts. These applications are "easy" in the sense they cover relatively simple, well-defined activities; scalability to high transaction rates, reliability, and security were not easy to achieve.

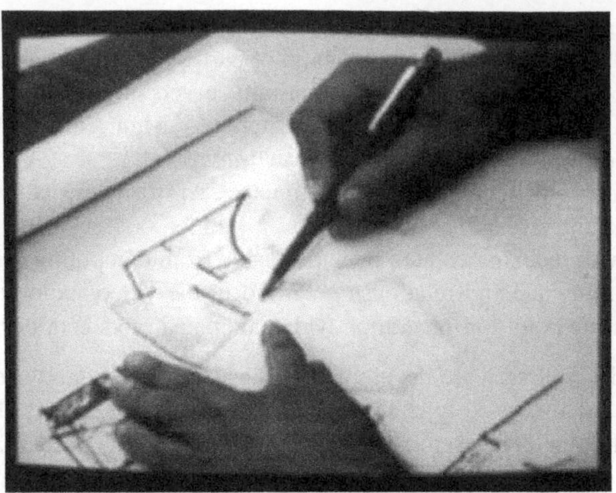

**Fig. 14.8** Stillframe from a design project in Media Space
*Source*: Stults, photo of montior display of VHS video recorded by Stults/Harrison, 1985.

for the records of diverse, open-ended, ill-defined activities of design, meaningful, and comprehensive definition of record structures was not within reach: means to populate records with data from the social processes of design were not feasible; and still less feasible were means to represent relationships among the records and to represent external references from them. Rather, only a simple structure for design records was feasible: identify their sources, and accumulate them into time-based structures, absent connection between the record structures and the video/audio content with which they were associated. Within this simple approach, there was still a problem of indexing and retrieval of the records, first of defining a structure, which we would now call metadata, in which to represent meaningful, computable data about the video/audio data, second, to populate that structure with data that pointed to the video/audio content, and third to review, select, and redact the content in a process of establishing meaning.

The approach to indexing in order to establish meaning was derived from John Cage[26] and called *Design Journal*. Cage had addressed selection of excerpts from texts and had noted that the main question was the granularity of the excerpts – where to begin and end them. He also noted that the actual selection did not matter very much: random selection provided as good a synopsis as selection informed by analysis of the text. The Design Journal transferred Cage's approach from text to recorded video/audio, with granularity set to the length of an uttered phrase, nominally 5 seconds. Selection was performed in three ways: at random, at regular intervals, and by informed selection. Use of random selection showed promise for

[26] I first heard the idea of random selection from texts from John Cage, while he was a visiting artist in 1970 at the University of Pennsylvania, Graduate School of Fine Arts. The technique is partially documented and is applied in John Cage, *M, Writings'67–'72*, First Paperback Edition (Wesleyan University Press) Middletown, CT, 1974.

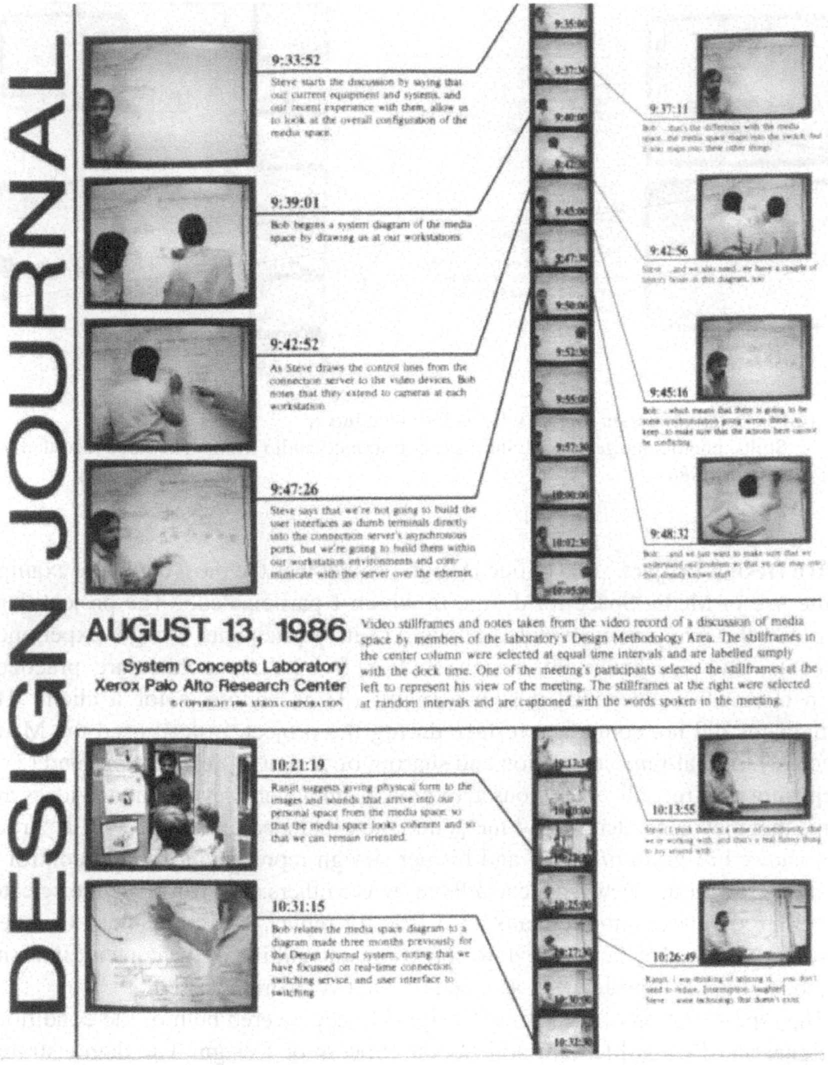


**Fig. 14.9** Design Journal schema for video index
*Source*: Stults, photomontage of stillframes and transcribed audio from VHS video recorded by Stults/Harrison, 1986.

initial indexing, especially if used with indexing clues provided by participants at time of recording.[27] We investigated this approach, but did not implement a usable prototype (Figs. 14.9 and 14.10).

[27] In an early form of the Design Journal at Evans & Sutherland, we contemplated, but never implemented, a foot pedal that a designer could use during a design activity simply to indicate "something has happened." Use of the pedal would be recorded and used as an index into a process context that would have a higher-than-random chance of being of interest in the future.

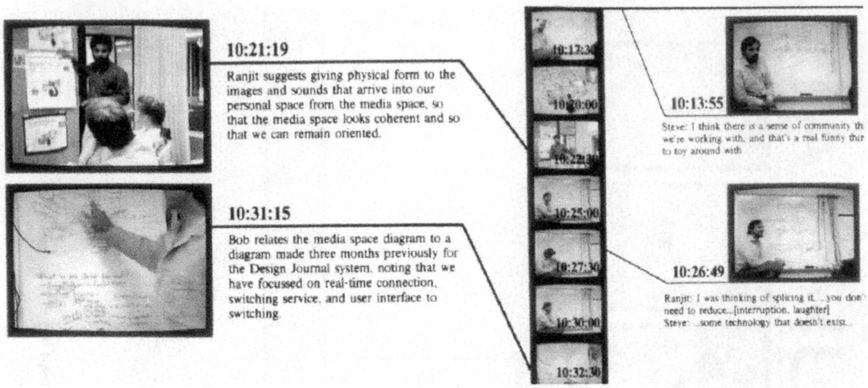


**Fig. 14.10** Detail of Design Journal schema for video index
*Source*: Stults, photomontage of stillframes and transcribed audio from VHS video recorded by Stults/Harrison, 1986.

**Office Design Project**. The Office Design Project was the most complete example of the use of Media Space for design in which I participated.[28] The project demonstrated the five principles noted above: (1) its participants brought experience, concepts, and vocabulary of design studios from their architecture practices; (2) performed a conceptual design activity; (3) as architects for a client. The participants did not come face-to-face during the project, instead used the Media Space (4) for real-time connection and sharing of design representations, and (5) as a repository for records of previous activities, from which they articulated ideas and forms that they generated. Real-time connection included control of what a participant showed of himself/herself and his/her design representations, and control of what one saw of the views made available by the others. The records were selected and indexed video/audio segments, available for replay. The critical task of indexing was performed by human review, selection, and editing of the content; indexing methods of the Design Journal, as discussed above, were not used.

The representation of the Office Design Project covered both of the conditions, Designer-and-Design-Medium and Social Process of Design. The demonstration was limited, first, because use of the representation was only partially automated with human handlers overcoming shortcomings in user interface and in information management; and second, because the underlying system was more a collection of functionality than a prototype system, and not ready for scaling from the limited context of the example to anything like actual conditions that spanned more participants, time, and content.

[28] Karen Weber and Scott Minneman, *Office Design Project*, Video (Xerox Palo Alto Research Center) Palo Alto, CA, 1987.
Steve Harrison, *The Office Design Project, a paper video tape* (Xerox Palo Alto Research Center) Palo Alto, CA, 1988.

## After 20 Years, Still Design? Still Media Space?

The starting point for Media Space of 1985 was the concept and the word *space*, to span the two conditions of Designer-and-Design-Medium and Social Process of Design. This was a pragmatic approach, to bring technology components to bear, short of a coherent solution for design and participation. Coupled with *space* was the concept and the word *media*, which referred to electronic systems as means and ends for design. *Space* brought under control of perspective for architecture following Alberti,[29] and *media* characterizing the post-typographic, post-physical world suggested by McLuhan.[30]

The source of concepts and vocabulary of Media Space in 1985 were physical architecture, its practices, settings, and buildings. Now physical architecture, especially the physical spaces of architecture, in all their variety, is less relevant. This declining relevance is part of the continued ascent of nonphysical systems, and the corresponding loss of primacy of architecture as the setting, subject, and object of design. Certainly physical systems and their design have not vanished; airplanes, cars, buildings, roads, subdivisions, and so on still provide our physical environment. But these physical systems have nonphysical content not found in their counterparts 20 years ago. Moreover, we are increasingly constituting our world with nonphysical systems, notably the Internet and its many faces, as well as cell phones. These are implemented through physical devices – laptops, routers, cell phone towers, iPhones, and so on – not in themselves the nonphysical systems, but physical instrumentalities serving as components within systems that interpenetrate physical spaces.

In parallel with the ascent of nonphysical systems, my personal reference examples have shifted during the past 20 years from building, impeller, spar, and pipeway to a new example set: on-line shopping, ordering and customer support; Internet access to professional information and community; delivery of health awareness through the Internet and on-location presence; in-the-field regulation and law enforcement; and operation of emergency medical departments.

Figure 14.11 illustrates aspects of the example of Emergency Medicine.[31] The center of the figure is a simplified flow for delivery of care to a patient in an Emergency Department of a medical center. The thumbnail images at the bottom show activity centers of care delivery, and the images at the top show representations of care delivery operations.

In the design examples for the earlier Media Space, *design* emerged from representation of physical objects in a surrogate *design medium*, more easily visualized, defined, manipulated, analyzed, assessed, and so on than the actual object. As we

---

[29] Alberti, *On the Art of Building*, op.cit.

[30] McLuhan, op.cit.

[31] The emergency medicine project referenced here is in progress at the time of this writing. The thoughts presented here are my own; but the project is not. It was created and led by Gary Tyndall, M.D., National Director of Emergency Medicine, Veterans Health Administration.

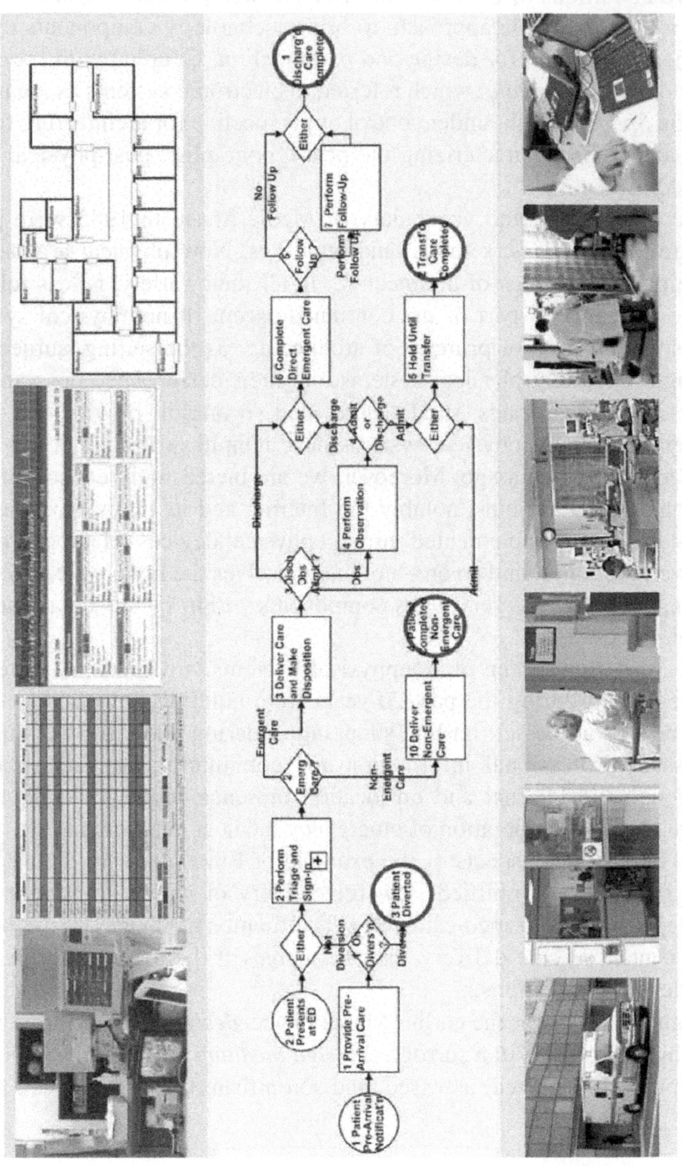


**Fig. 14.11** Example of emergency medical care
*Source:* Stults, photomontage of photos and diagrams by Stults, 2007.

pursued *design* and *design media* we progressively and incrementally extended the surrogate role of the medium, especially from the original static three-dimensional space projected through perspective into two dimensions, to *design space*; and we provided *design space* within Media Space. With further shift from the physical systems to nonphysical systems, do we continue to extend this as metaphor? Does it still make sense to speak of *design, design medium? design space? Media Space*?

To proceed with *design, design media, design space, and Media Space*, we are repurposing *space*, but are we doing so without recognition of the baggage of *physical space*? When we use the language of physical space for the nonphysical we bring along illusory meaning that is actually absent. Two indicators of absence are noted here: absence of coherence of physical space; and absence of body.

Coherence of physical space can be the constructed coherence of three-dimensional space of the *Ideal City*, and can be simulated, at least partially, in nonphysical systems. But coherence in the representation is optional: connection topology among simulated spaces can mimic physical, terrestrial adjacency, or can implement worm holes that we do not encounter with our terrestrial bodies. The metaphor of windows, initially suggestive and inventive, has exhausted any meaning that it initially brought from its physical world referent. But just because the coherence of physical space is optional and necessarily incomplete does not mean that coherence is or should be absent. If we look beyond the mask of these physical metaphors, can we find coherence that fits with Media Spaces as design media and design spaces?

At the time of the Media Space of 1985, we recognized the narrowing of architectural experience when replaced by eye and image, discussed above as *When the Body Vanishes*.... In the Office Design Project, we glossed over the absence of the body by using video and audio to capture and convey representations – video and audio – that we accepted as substitutes for actual bodies and presence, aware that the audio and video renderings in fact were substitutes for something. Now, with nonphysical spaces, such as Myspace and YouTube established as an experience base, audio and video are distanced from referent bodies and presence; and more broadly, action and perception are narrowed onto keyboards and mouses, luminous screens, display-mounted cameras, and desktop speakers. Whatever actualities underlay suggested and recalled haptic experiences of the Office Design Project, they have receded; and modalities for design, formerly embedded with the body in physical presence and perception in physical space – in *design space* – have narrowed.

We can in our imagination move the Office Design Project from 1985 to the present; substitute for original participant members (in organizational roles) of a structured project; replace informal and haptic media with design documents within a systematic framework, like Zachman[32]; and replace the original laboratory setting with meeting rooms connected by Live Meeting or similar technology. The new setting does not constitute a *design space*; does not provide coherence across and

[32] The Zachman Institute for Framework Advancement, http://www.zifa.com/

around structured representation, relations, and processes; and does not provide for participation of person and body. If little survives in the new setting that responds to the original impulse for design, how can we adjust the setting and its use? Perhaps we can bundle adjustments and correctives, by resurrecting and reconstituting a now largely discredited ground of design, aesthetics.

*Aesthetics* is meant here to label a comprehensive principle for design that complements the orderly techniques by which we organize projects and activities. For the architecture of optical, Cartesian space, aesthetics has a relatively precise historical meaning, as in the aesthetics of Kant, who situated Judgment, that is Aesthetics, next to Reason and not subordinate to it.[33] And in a later focused meaning, Croce developed aesthetics as intuition, and allowed for its selective use beyond fine arts.[34] The concept and term *aesthetics* is now out of fashion; and its older meanings, aligned strongly with beauty, are supplanted by post-beauty and post-art concepts, to which no single concept or word has received currency.[35] Thus, *aesthetics* is used here as a placeholder for the essential ground of design that is an independent source for action and identity.

Aesthetics, as meant here, is essential to design; avoids devolution of reason-based methods into mechanistic engineering; keeps poetry in Le Corbusier's *machine for living*; and keeps tailfins – styling – as part of cars. Design is constituted on one side by mechanistic engineering, classification, bureaucracy, and repeatable processes; and on the other by a non-methodical, nonclassified ground of *aesthetics*.[36] A Media Space for Design admits unplanned, participatory action, experimentation, understanding, speculation, and legitimizes them against methodical, structured, mechanistic engineering; and it admits participation of people – not as roles and positions, and not as disembodied analysis and assessment – through available modalities for meaningful bodily presence and awareness – touching, forming, gesturing, sensing, and so on – closing the haptic gap built into structured use of workstations and other media of organized design. In approaching Media Space for Design in this way, perhaps we can decouple ourselves from baggage of physical space, as needed to work with current conditions; but not lose continuities with the past that can enliven design projects that otherwise seem predetermined to increasingly mechanize our lives.

[33] Immanuel Kant, *Critique of Judgment*, Translated by Werner S. Pluhar (Hackett) Indianapolis, 1987.

[34] Benedetto Croce, *Aesthetic as Science of Expression and General Linguistic*, Translated by Douglas Ainslie (Macmillan) London, Second Edition, 1922, p117.

[35] Thierry de Duve, *Kant after Duchamp* (October) Cambridge, MA, 1996 is an example.

[36] This argument is similar to one made about science by Paul K. Feyerabend, *Against Method* (Schocken) New York, 1976.

The following is an argument to seek out Bob Stults' original visionary report on PARC's media space

# The Unknown Media Space Report*

**Steve Harrison**
Virginia Polytechnic Institute and State University

Bob Stults and I were the founders of the first Media Space. He wrote the first report about the project, describing the open, always-on video, shared computing environments, and reconfigurable audio environments that created connected office and public spaces. We all knew that we were engaged in something radical, but it has taken years to realize how much more Bob saw in the project than we did at the moment. This is the story of that report, *The Media Space* (Stults, 1986).

Bob's report – an internal Xerox PARC Technical report – is not well known. We thought it reported the essence of what we were experiencing and in the early years, cited it whenever we were writing about the project. Bob Stults prided himself on making slow but steady progress, yet he was intellectually restless. Moving on from PARC before the Media Space research became widely known by the HCI or CSCW communities, Bob left behind a box of the reports. While we would send out occasional copies when colleagues requested them or hand them out to visiting corporate types, it had almost no impact.

Shortly before Bob left PARC, he gave a presentation on Media Space to a Xerox executive who was reported to have said, "I don't understand what Bob was saying, but I am really pleased he is working for us." My colleagues and I, on the other hand, thought we knew what Bob was saying – but I am getting ahead of our story.

## Media Space

At the time of its writing, PARC technical reports were almost exclusively about the utility and implementation of the technology. Whether reading about Alan Kay's vision for the Dynabook or the technical specifications of Interpress (the

* The following is an argument to seek out Bob Stults' original visionary report on PARC's media space.

Xerox-proprietary forerunner to Adobe's Postscript), the reports were supposed to leave a "gee-whiz" impression on readers. Many of the technical reports have been widely read and cited in HCI.

"Media Space" does not follow that mould. It is written in an idiosyncratic elliptical prose style. It is formatted horizontally, like a promotional brochure for a real-estate development. It has no system diagrams or specifications. It has pictures of people looking at television sets. Going back to Alberti, it discusses the representations of space and the impact of the development of perspective. It reports on one of David Letterman's shows and reminisces about the 1950s children show, *Howdy Doody*.

## The We-Saw, He-Saw SeeSaw

All of us saw:

- That thinking in terms of "space" instead of tasks and applications creates a continuum from casual social interaction to task-focused work
- People as legitimate creators of their own places
- People acting through the media as though they were together
- People acting through the media in ways that were impossible in physical space, but always building from the experience of physical space
- That the media space could become continuous with our physical space

The Media Space report saw more:

- That there was a tradition of representing space that media space built upon
- Further, that the representations of space were constructions – and that the idea of space that was represented was itself a construction
- That all of this worked in large part because they were on-going in-the-moment social constructions (the report calls this human mediation)
- And that we could conduct and report research in a designerly fashion.

## Constructing Space, Mediating Mediation

Why are we arguing that the reader should seek out the report even though there are a number of very good descriptions of Media Space that are more accessible? The main reason is the effort required to see what it is that is being said. By asking why the report pulls together the construction of perspective space and David Letterman's construction of his television show, the reader will begin to really see how complex the social construction process is. Bob's first-person description of how he was made to feel that he was in the studio audience when he was at home while he watched *Howdy Doody* is amusing. More importantly, it is a first-hand reconstruction of the experience of the social construction of virtualized space.

This is different from enumerating phenomena or showing five different ways that people can use such a space.[1] While his could be argued on instrumental grounds, we would argue that there is more. Just as Paul Dourish (2006) has argued that finding "design implications" is not the only reason to conduct HCI research, we would argue that spending time with a unique perspective is its own reward.

## References

Bly, S., Harrison, S., and Irwin, S. (1993) Media Spaces: bringing people together in a video, audio, and computing environment. *Communications of the Association of Computing Machinery*, vol. 36, no. 1, January 1993, pp. 28–45.

Brand, S. (1972) "Spacewar: Fanatic Life & Symbolic Death Among the Computer Bums." *Rolling Stone*. #7 December 1972. http://www.wheels.org/spacewar/stone/rolling_stone.html

Dourish, P. (2006) Design Implications. *Proceedings of the SIGCHI Conference on Human Factors in Computing Systems*. New York: ACM Press, pp. 541–550

Harrison, S., Bly, S., Anderson, S., Minneman, S. (1997) "The Media Space" *Video-Mediated Communication* (Finn, K., Sellen, A., Wilbur, S., eds.) Mahwah, NJ: Lawrence Erlbaum, pp. 273–300.

Stults, R. (1986) *Media Space*. Xerox Corporation, Palo Alto, CA.

[1] Other than Stewart Brand's "Fanatic Life & Symbolic Death Among the Computer Bums" article in *Rolling Stone Magazine* (Brand, 1972) this is the only experientially based report of technology that springs to mind.

# Chapter 15
# From Analog to Digital, from the Office to the Living Room: Why I Happily Worked in a Media Space but Don't Live in One

**N. Roussel**

**Abstract** I first got interested in media spaces in 1995 when I was asked to design the user interface of an analog audio-video system at Paris-Sud University. Having since designed, implemented and used various other systems inspired by early media spaces, I have witnessed the transitions from analog to digital, and from office settings do domestic ones. This chapter describes what I learned from media spaces in this context, how I built upon them, and what I think remains to be done.

## Introduction

CSCW researchers have long investigated the reasons for the failure of traditional videoconferencing (Egido, 1988) and proposed alternative uses of video for mediated communication. Media Spaces, particularly, showed the value of persistent connections to support activities ranging from casual awareness and informal talks to focused collaboration (Bly et al., 1993). This research somehow culminated in 1997 in the book *Video-mediated Communication* edited by Finn, Sellen and Wilbur. Strangely, however, the interest in innovative uses of video and Media Spaces dropped off, just as digital media and fast large area networks were becoming ubiquitous. As partly prophesied by Karam (Riesenbach et al., 1995), the information superhighways killed most of the existing projects based on analog media, just as the US interstate system killed Route 66:

> People were not so likely to seek their fortune on the edge of a doomed road, and of those who were already there, fewer and fewer saw any value in upgrading or expanding or – sometimes – doing basic maintenance. After 1956, Route 66 remained important, but its importance was slowly moving away from the concrete toward the glorification of what the highway had been (S.C. Kelly in Route 66 – The highway and its people, cited in Riesenbach et al., 1995)

Over the last 10 years, I have myself designed, implemented, and used several video communication systems, inspired by early Media Spaces. I am personally

N. Roussel
LRI (Univ. Paris-Sud – CNRS) & INRIA
e-mail: Nicolas.Roussel@lri.fr

S. Harrison (ed.), *Media Space 20+ Years of Mediated Life*,
Computer Supported Cooperative Work,

convinced that Media Spaces remain an interesting research topic and that they deserve more than just a souvenir ceremony. In this chapter, I will briefly describe what I learned from these systems, how I built upon them, and what I think remains to be done.

## From Analog to Digital

I first got interested in video-mediated communication in 1995. Michel Beaudouin-Lafon was then looking for someone to design the user interface of what would be the first French Media Space at Paris-Sud University. Michel had visited the Telepresence Project in Toronto and Rank Xerox EuroPARC. He had notably implemented *xcave*, a control interface for *Kasmer*, the system used at PARC. I had no particular experience in audiovisual communication but happily started reading papers, playing with the analog 8 × 8 crossbar switch and pulling wires through the building.

*Lascaux* (Roussel, 1997) was the first application I created to control our Media Space. It allowed us to glance at other people or connect with them for an undefined period of time. It provided a simple available/do-not-disturb switch for privacy protection. It also implemented a basic session model which supported multiuser conferences using a push-to-talk approach and the association of shared applications (e.g., a whiteboard) to the current session. Lascaux, however, was far from successful. It was hard to maintain and distribute. As we were all in the same building, people saw little interest in the multiuser conferences and the shared tools. Many of them often "forgot" to run the software. The only service that was really used was a Web gateway that captured snapshots from the nodes of our analog network and presented them on our group's Web page in a way similar to NYNEX Portholes (Lee et al., 1997).

A closer look at early Media Space literature made me realize I had underestimated several essential aspects of these environments. Successful Media Spaces were designed to support existing practices and tools rather than impose new ones. They were designed to be flexible, making it possible for users to repurpose them with little effort. They provided sophisticated notification and control mechanisms. As the Web gateway was the only popular component of our Media Space, I decided to make the analog services also available through a Web-based interface. I implemented a custom HTTP server to control the crossbar switch. This server supported the old glance, and connect and snapshot services, as well as a new one that allowed users to leave messages on other people's computer screen. It also implemented more refined control mechanisms inspired by CAVECAT's door states (Riesenbach et al., 1995). The resulting system, named *Mediascape* (Roussel, 1999), made it possible to easily create interfaces to our Media Space by using simple HTML code such as:

```
< a href="http://mediascape/connect.michel" >
< img src="http://mediascape/grab.michel" >
< /a >
```

Duplicating these lines and replacing michel with other users' name was enough to create an HTML awareness view that could also be used to establish analog con-

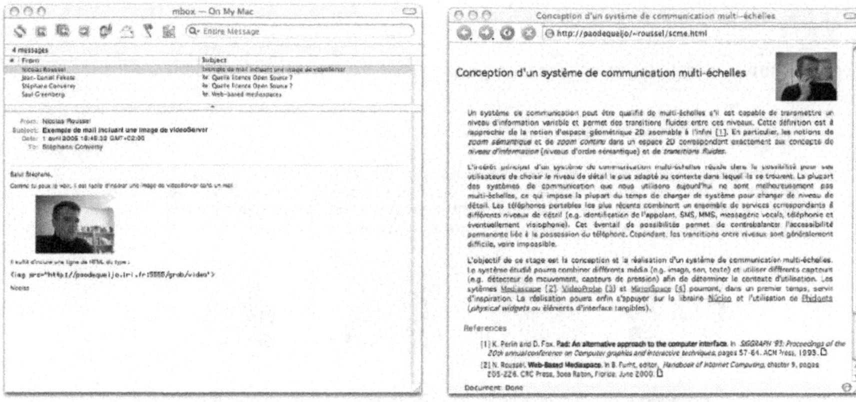


**Fig. 15.1** Live snapshots displayed in an email message and a traditional HTML document. Images are captured and transmitted every time the message or document is rendered by the application

nections. The same code could also be used to integrate live snapshots into email messages (Fig. 15.1, left) and existing or new HTML documents (Fig. 15.1, right). An interesting use of this feature was to include a live snapshot of one's office in one's email signature or in a Web page showing contact information so that people who wanted to reply to an email or talk with someone could see if that person was available for discussion.

The snapshot service of Mediascape made it possible to send live pictures from our offices to distant colleagues, friends, or relatives. In order to share the Media Space experience with them, I designed and implemented *videoServer* (Roussel, 1999), a personal HTTP server that could make live images or video streams captured from a local digital camera accessible through simple URLs similar to the ones presented above. As webcams were becoming more common, we started adding videoServer images to the awareness views of our analog Media Space. At some point, the room hosting the analog equipment had to be cleared for maintenance. This equipment was never put back in order after that. But although we stopped using the Mediascape system, videoServer still runs on some machines around the world.

VideoServer has no support for audio communication. But it allows people to see live images from a distant camera by simply pointing a standard, unmodified Web browser to the appropriate URL. As a group communication tool, it quickly became an invaluable add-on to the telephone, as a way of checking the availability of someone before making a call and seeing that person while talking to her. Obviously, digital video makes it possible to communicate with people much farther away. But it also allows more dynamic forms of communication. A few lines of JavaScript, for example, can simply turn a snapshot into a medium frame-rate video when the mouse moves over it and pop up a new window displaying a high frame-rate and resizable stream when one clicks on it (Fig. 15.2). These three levels of details proved very useful to resolve ambiguities related to the small size

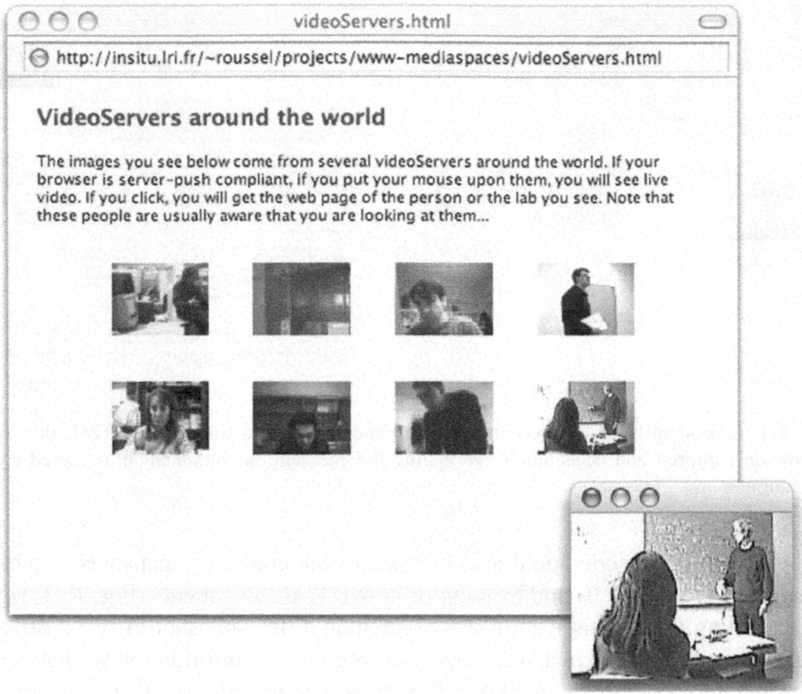


**Fig. 15.2** Gradual engagement: from a low resolution snapshot in a Portholes-like awareness view to a high frame rate independent video that the user can freely move and resize

of awareness views and accompany the transition between the moments when a user checks for the availability of another person, picks up the phone, and starts calling that person.

As most Media Spaces, and unlike webcam software, videoServer provides users with customizable notification and access control mechanisms. For every request it receives, it executes a control script with arguments indicating the name of the remote machine, possibly the remote user's login name, the resource that led to the server (the HTTP referrer) and a description of the requested service. The script uses this contextual information to generate auditory or on-screen notifications and sends back to the server a description of the service to be executed. This description can be inferred from a set of predefined rules or negotiated with the user through some interactive dialog. An important feature is that the script is not limited to a binary accept/refuse choice but can freely redefine the service to be executed, supporting selective accessibility. It might request that a spatial filter be applied on the images, which the remote person will probably notice. It might redirect the client to another server. But it might also substitute a prerecorded sequence to the live stream, supporting the creation of ambiguities and stories (Aoki and Woodruff, 2005).

I lived in a Media Space constantly accessible from the Internet for about 5 years and this was great. But to be more precise, I should probably say "I worked in a Media Space," since I only had access to it in my office. To be even more precise, I might even say that I worked in a Media Space, which was nice, and that I took advantage of this situation to keep in touch with my girlfriend and other close friends during office hours, which made it great. This might sound anecdotal but I somehow suspect that every successful Media Space built on similar close relationships, although they're rarely mentioned in scientific papers.

## From the Office to the Living Room

Domestic environments pose a number of interesting challenges for Media Space designers. While most Media Space studies probably dealt with relatively predictable office configurations and uses, homes are highly dynamic places that host a wide range of activities, many of which the inhabitants might not want to expose. In the context of the *interLiving* project, I participated in an effort to adapt some of the Media Space concepts to support communication among distributed, multigenerational families. Together with other colleagues, I designed and implemented *videoProbe*, a *technology probe* that allows a group of people to share their daily lives by exchanging pictures (Hutchinson et al., 2003; Conversy et al., 2003).

The system physically consists in a screen, two speakers and a camera connected to a networked computer. A specific software analyzes the images captured by the camera in real-time and automatically transmits a picture to similar systems in other households when it detects a persistent scene change (only pictures are exchanged, not video streams). The screen normally operates in mirror mode, showing the camera images, but can be switched (using a remote control) to a browsing mode that shows the pictures taken by all the connected systems.

VideoProbe was designed as a kind of portable Media Space node: it had to be compact, nonintrusive, simple to handle, and usable in a variety of spatial configurations (Fig. 15.3). As a result, it can stand alone on any item of furniture or

**Fig. 15.3** VideoProbe

be mounted onto a wall like a picture frame. The interaction with the system was also carefully designed to be as simple and direct as possible without imposing physical proximity. Motion-based scene change detection was chosen to allow users to interact with the device at a distance in order to trigger or prevent the transmission of a picture. Graphical and auditory feedback are also used to indicate transitions between the various states of the system (e.g. asleep, awake, about to take a picture, transmitting).

VideoProbe supports both explicit and implicit forms of communication. The explicit form takes place when the user is consciously using the system to transmit a particular image. The implicit form typically takes place when someone enters the room, stays there for some reason but doesn't pay attention to the device. This implicit form proved very useful for maintaining group awareness as it usually produces pictures showing day-to-day activities that users would not or could not take themselves.

But choosing the right place to install the videoProbe in a home (or any other communication device) is quite difficult. Lightweight wireless devices that people could move around might partially solve this problem. Yet, my experience with wireless phones indicates that these devices seem to always be in the wrong place when they're needed, no matter how many you have got... Another problem, in the case of videoProbe, is that windows, doors and corridors make it difficult to limit the field of view to a unique room.

This problem got me interested in the use of space in video-mediated communication and lead to the design of *MirrorSpace* (Roussel et al., 2004). As the name suggests, this system relies on a mirror metaphor (Fig. 15.4). Live video streams from the places connected through the system are superimposed on a single display at each site. In order to support intimate forms of communication, the camera has been placed right in the middle of the screen. This setup allows users to come very close to the camera while still being able to see the remote people and interact with them.

**Fig. 15.4** MirrorSpace

MirrorSpace also includes a proximity sensor. A blur filter applied on the images visually expresses a distance computed from the local and remote sensor values.

Blurring distant objects and people allows one to perceive their movement or passing with minimum involvement. It also offers a simple way of initiating or avoiding a change to a more engaged form of communication by simply moving closer or further away. A recent study showed that blur filtration fails at providing an obfuscation level that could balance privacy and awareness for home situations (Neustaedter et al., 2006). Yet, I strongly believe that this type of filtering is still valuable. Not because of what it tries to remove, but because of what it adds: the filter shows the remote person that we don't want them to observe. The fact that it does not necessarily enforce this leaves room for negotiation and social regulation, two concepts traditionally associated with Media Spaces.

## What Remains to be Done

A lot! As I said in the introduction, I believe that the concepts that originated from early Media Space studies still offer many opportunities for research.

As I hope to have illustrated, I think that digital technologies can provide ways of enriching or impoverishing audio and video communications to create a wider range of services corresponding to more degrees of engagement. I believe that a key aspect of future Media Space research will be to find ways to ease transitions both ways between low levels of engagement (i.e., awareness services) and higher ones (e.g., synchronous chat, telephony, videoconferencing). The general idea is to move towards the notion of *multiscale communication*, a concept I am currently investigating (Gueddana and Roussel, 2006; Roussel and Gueddana, 2007).

I would love to see more work done on the adaptation of Media Space concepts to domestic environments. One aspect that seems particularly interesting to me is the use of Media Space technologies for in-house communication. Asynchronous communication, for example. Domestic environments also pose the problem of shared always-on communication resources, a problem that already existed but wasn't really solved in office settings.

Finally, Media Spaces in mobile contexts also seems an interesting topic. One of the reasons why I don't run videoServer on my laptop anymore is that I skip from one network to another with long periods of unreachability. Again, simple, unobtrusive asynchronous communication services (other than text-based) would be greatly appreciated.

## References

Aoki P M, Woodruff A (2005) Making space for stories: ambiguity in the design of personal communication systems. In *Proceedings of CHI '05*, pages 181–190, April 2005. ACM Press, New York.

Bly S, Harrison S, Irwin S (1993) Mediaspaces: Bringing people together in a video, audio and computing environment. *Communications of the ACM*, 36(1):28–47, January 1993.

Conversy S, Roussel N, Hansen H, Evans H, Beaudouin-Lafon M, Mackay W (2003) Partager les images de la vie quotidienne et familiale avec videoProbe. In *Proceedings of IHM 2003*, pages 228–231, Novemebr 2003. ACM, International Conference Proceedings Series.

Egido C (1988) Videoconferencing as a technology to support group work: A review of its failure. In *Proceedings of CSCW'88*, pages 13–24, September 1988. ACM Press, New York.

Gueddana S, Roussel N (2006) Pêle-Mêle, a video communication system supporting a variable degree of engagement. In *Proceedings of ACM CSCW'06 Conference on Computer-Supported Cooperative Work*, pages 423–426, November 2006. ACM Press, New York.

Hutchinson H, Mackay W, Westerlund B, Bederson B, Druin A, Plaisant C, Beaudouin-Lafon M, Conversy S, Evans H, Hansen H, Roussel N, Eiderbäck B, Lindquist S, Sundblad Y (2003) Technology probes: inspiring design for and with families. In *Proceedings of CHI 2003*, pages 17–24, April 2003. ACM Press, New York.

Lee A, Girgensohn A, Schlueter K (1997) NYNEX Portholes: Initial User Reactions and Redesign Implications. In *Proceedings of GROUP'97*, pages 385–394, 1997. ACM Press, New York.

Neustaedter C, Greenberg S and Boyle M. Blur filtration fails to preserve privacy for home-based video conferencing. *ACM Transactions on Computer–Human Interaction*, 13(1):1–36, 2006.

Riesenbach R, Buxton W, Karam G, Moore G (1995) Ontario Telepresence project. final report, Information technology research centre, Telecommunications research institute of Ontario, March 1995.

Roussel N (1997) Au-delà du mediaspace: un modèle pour la collaboration médiatisée. In *Proceedings of IHM'97*, pages 159–166, Septembre 1997. Cépaduès.

Roussel N (1999) Mediascape: a Web-based Mediaspace. *IEEE Multimedia*, 6(2):64–74, April–June 1999.

Roussel N, Evans H, Hansen H (2004) Proximity as an interface for video communication. *IEEE Multimedia*, 11(3):12–16, July–September 2004.

Roussel N, Gueddana S (2007) Beyond "Beyond being there": towards multiscale communication systems. In *Proceedings of ACM Multimedia 2007*, pages 238–246, September 2007. ACM Press, New York.

# Chapter 16
# The Video Window: My Life with a Ludic System

**William W. Gaver**

**Abstract** The Video Window is a video screen hanging next to a window on my bedroom wall, showing the image from a camera mounted to show the skyline from outside the same window. This chapter describes the appeal of living with such a system, and the intermingled aesthetic, utilitarian and practical issues involved in its creation and the experience it offers.

## Introduction

About 6 months ago,[1] I mounted a small video camera on a mast outside our bedroom window, oriented to pick up a view of the skyline down the hill from our house (see Fig. 16.1). The camera output is wired directly to a small flat-screen display hung on our bedroom wall, across from our bed, and is always left on.

The result is a 'Video Window' hanging close to the real window of our bedroom (see Fig. 16.2). It is a very simple configuration of technology, and is not really 'for' anything. Instead, it encourages a ludic experience (Gaver, 2002) of curiosity, exploration, and aesthetic enjoyment that my wife, child and I have found surprisingly compelling. And though the system was not designed as a part of my research, living with it has taught me both the value of this sort of device and issues in its design. In this chapter, I reflect on our experience of living with the Video Window to uncover factors in its appeal, and more generally, lessons for designing everyday technologies.

---

W.W. Gaver
Goldsmiths, University of London
w.gaver@gold.ac.uk

[1] This originally appeared under the same title at the 3AD International Conference of Appliance Design in 2005, and in 2006 in Personal and Ubiquitous Computing 10(2–3): 60–65. I have chosen not to update the experiences described here, but am happy to report that the Video Window is still in place in our bedroom, more than 3 years after I wrote this original account.

S. Harrison (ed.), *Media Space 20+ Years of Mediated Life*,
Computer Supported Cooperative Work,

**Fig. 16.1** Camera on a mast extending above our roof

**Fig. 16.2** Video Window in our bed room

## *Origins of the Video Window*

This is actually our second Video Window. I built the first one a number of years ago, by leaning a pole with a small camera attached to it outside our bedroom window, and displaying the image on a monitor that I propped on a chair. It was a jerry-rigged, precarious and inconvenient system, but my wife and I enjoyed it for a few weeks before I dismantled it to use the camera for another project.

Playing with video in this way was influenced by my previous experience with media spaces and computer-controlled networks of audio and video equipment used to support collaboration among remote colleagues (Bly et al., 1993; Gaver et al., 1992). Though usually justified along utilitarian lines, media space systems were often used in more playful ways as well – for instance, to view a nearby public green, or to watch a bird's nest being built outside an office. Such activities were never taken very seriously, but were a continual feature of the media spaces I experienced.

I never took the first Video Window very seriously either, and though we missed it when we took it down, my wife and I never seriously considered replacing it. Then in 2003, one of our students, Sebastian Irrgang, attached a video camera to a weather balloon and tethered it to his roof, displaying the image in his home to alleviate the claustrophobia of living in a basement flat. His configuration was quite different from ours – most notably, the image spun and swayed wildly as the balloon was buffeted by the wind – but seeing his project reawakened my interest in making a new Video Window for our own home.

However, it took another year before I finally installed our current Video Window, and when I did it was because of a fishing pole. Tobie Kerridge, a researcher in our studio, found a source for long (6.7m), lightweight (800g), telescopic fishing poles while looking for a way to mount a weather station outside the home (http://www.sotabeams.co.uk/sotapole.htm). As soon as he unpacked the pole and we started playing with it, I knew it would be perfect for a Video Window. I ordered my own later that day, and when it arrived set about collecting the equipment for a new installation.

## Living with the Video Window

Because the Video Window is in our bedroom, we usually encounter the view in the mornings and evenings. This makes the experience very different from similar systems found in workplaces or even other areas of the home. For instance, the view 'out' the Video Window is one of the first things we see in the morning (see Fig. 16.3). While we drink coffee and read paper (or children's stories), we find ourselves staring at the skyline, admiring a pretty sunrise, assessing the weather, or simply enjoying the view.

At night, most of the interest is in seeing our urban neighbourhood, rather than the sky – particularly the lights of nearby office buildings and glimpses of moving traffic we catch on the corners of the screen (see Fig. 16.4). Sometimes we see

**Fig. 16.3** Sunrise on the Video Window

**Fig. 16.4** The Video Window by night

the moon or particularly bright stars, the lights of a passing plane, or even, on one occasion, fireworks in a nearby park, but these are special events and greeted as such. Usually, the scene is much less dramatic: a view of the city slowly settling for the night.

Because we are usually out of the house, or at least not in our bedroom, we see the Video Window much less often during the day. Sometimes when we see it, the view seems flatter and more prosaic than during the mornings or evenings – though this could be a function of our being occupied with other activities. But other times, it can suddenly bring moments of new appreciation, as when the buildings are painted red by sunset, lights come on before the evening sun has faded from the sky, or the moon slowly rises over the cityscape (see Fig. 16.5).

Often the view from the Video Window is apparently static and unremarkable. Still, it is almost always interesting. The clouds and lights change slowly but continuously, punctuated by the small drama of a bird flying past or a plane on its decent into Heathrow. The Video Window is not distracting or entertaining, but it is endlessly fascinating, and we often find ourselves watching it rather than looking out the real window directly beside it.

A central value of the Video Window is in increasing the view from our bedroom. This might seem odd, as the display hangs next to a much larger, physical window. But the view through our real window is relatively constrained, not least

**Fig. 16.5** A pretty twilight

because we hang a shade over its lower half for privacy. Moreover, the outlook it affords is unequal from the two sides of our bed. My wife's view is dominated by a modern university building, while from my side one can see between this building and a neighbouring Victorian hospital down towards our neighbourhood's shopping district. The Video Window has equalised our outlook from the bedroom, and allows us to see a much larger panorama as well. My wife likes to compare it to a room with an ocean view, in which the sheer scope of the scene seems to extend one's feeling of living space to include the landscape and its subtle changes.

## Constructing the Video Window

The Video Window is a very simple arrangement of technology, but it took a surprising amount of work to 'get it right'. In retrospect, 'getting it right' involved both practical and aesthetic issues. But at the time I did not differentiate the two. Instead, they were intertwined in creating an experience we wanted to live with.

### *Choosing a Camera*

The most notable issue in crafting the Video Window was finding an appropriate video camera (see Fig. 16.6). The camera I am using currently is my fourth, and I am considering trying yet another one.

The first camera was a relatively small 'bullet camera'. It gave a very acceptable image, but was not completely waterproof. Moisture condensed inside the lens at night, blurring the image completely in the morning. Next I tried a domestic security camera that enclosed a bullet camera surrounded by infrared light-emitting

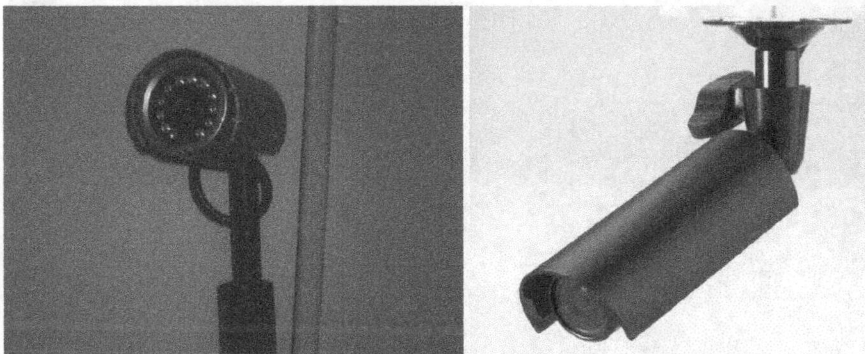

**Fig. 16.6** Cameras: *left*, security camera with infrared LEDs; *right*, current bulletcam

diodes (LEDs) (for night-time illumination) in a waterproof housing. The image was crisp and impervious to moisture, but the viewing angle was only about 50° and seemed too similar to the existing outlook to be interesting. It became apparent that one of the aesthetic values of the Video Window was in offering an enhanced view rather than a realistic one. The 100° field of view of the third camera, however, seemed too wide, producing a distorted image that emphasised technical mediation. In addition, the infrared lighting used by both the second and third cameras produced interesting effects at night – for instance, bright streaks across the screen as individual raindrops were illuminated – but ultimately these were too unnatural and even eerie to live with.

Our current camera is a waterproof one, without infrared lighting, sourced via the Web (www.rfconcepts.co.uk/). This has withstood rain- and snowstorms extremely well, and has what appears to be an optimal field of view (about 70°). In addition, it is designed for low-light conditions, and can show the surrounding scenery even in the middle of the night (the city's ambient light no doubt helps with this) without the distracting effects of infrared lighting. Nonetheless, the image is somewhat blurry, and at night there is a great deal of visual noise obscuring the image. This may be because the last metre of the video cable is unshielded, or may simply reflect the camera's struggle to cope with low-light conditions, but in any case I am considering trying yet another camera.

Weatherproofing, night vision and field of view were among the most important issues in finding an acceptable camera. Some of these seem to reflect clearly practical concerns (e.g. waterproofing), while others are aesthetic (e.g. field of view). Some (e.g. night vision), however, seem to involve both. In the end, distinctions between practicality and aesthetics are difficult to make for this system – an issue I will return to later.

## *A View of Our Own*

Deciding what to look at was another issue in configuring the Video Window. The camera's field of view is important here – in our situation, we value seeing a wider-angle view than that seems realistic, without using such a wide-angle lens that the image is obviously distorted. Beyond how much we can see, however, where the camera is focused also matters, and adjusting that view has been an important factor in configuring our system.

The Video Window's camera mast is mounted just outside our bedroom window, attached to our exterior wall with a couple of spring clips on a bracket. This affords easy removal for maintenance, and also allows the view to be panned 360° around our house (the camera is high enough to look over our roof). Despite the flexibility of our view, however, I tend to strongly prefer a very particular angle of view down the hill from our home (my wife is less adamant about this). This preference is unexpected and difficult to explain. One factor is that the camera extends the line of sight from our bed so that we look in the 'right' direction, rather than, for instance, seeing a landscape that is actually behind our backs. But my preference is more exact than this explanation suggests: I am sensitive to swings of as little as 1° or so from my preferred angle. On reflection, it seems that I frame the image to achieve a visual balance, much as photographers or painters compose their images. Thus, the view on the Window is determined both by its correspondence with our physical situation and the desire to compose it aesthetically.

Adjusting the pan of the Video Window is easy – sometimes too easy, as it tends to be perturbed by wind. More difficult is changing the tilt and vertical orientation of the camera, and I have spent long sessions readjusting these through in a laborious process of bringing the camera inside, adjusting the angles, remounting it outside and checking the results. This has made clear the importance of both precisely tuning the view and having the camera mounted in a way that is easily accessible – if it was mounted on the roof, for example, finding and maintaining a desirable view would be much more difficult.

## *Tinkering, Maintenance and Simple Use*

Evolving the current arrangement of the Video Window was pursued in odd moments over a number of months. The many tasks involved in configuring the equipment both as a technical system and one of the home's fittings combined the pleasures of design research and DIY home-improvement projects. They accounted for the majority of time I spent with the system for the first couple of months, and assessing the effects of recent changes was an integral part of my involvement with the view. For a while, it seemed that crafting the system was perhaps the most fundamental part of the pleasure it offered.

I stopped working on the system when I finally decided that the arrangement was good enough and that I would spend enough time on it. This was a fairly sudden shift from regular tinkering to almost no modifications: I simply gave up working on the Video Window as a hobby. At this point, I started to engage with the Video Window as a background amenity in our home, and found to my relief that I enjoyed it just as much as when I was continually trying to improve it. But the Window still requires periodic maintenance – particularly to readjust the viewing angle every few days when the wind shifts the camera slightly. This has become a chore, however, that has little intrinsic interest.

The differences among these forms of engagement – tinkering, maintenance, and simple use – are likely to appear for many systems, and particularly those developed for the home. Tinkering is enjoyable, but maintenance is not. On the one hand, this means that systems should be robust and require little adjustment once they have been tuned. On the other hand, requiring some work to achieve a desirable configuration may be intrinsically rewarding, and even a means to encourage initial engagement with a new system.

## Aesthetics, Utility and Practicality

The Video Window is a good reminder that aesthetics, utility and practicality are conceptual distinctions that may be difficult to isolate in practice. Practical concerns often have aesthetic implications. As I have discussed, some of the system's most beautiful features are also its most useful. But, conversely, some come from what might be considered flaws in the system.

### *Watching the Weather*

If the Video Window has any clear utility, for instance, it is in making us aware of the weather. This goes beyond a visual assessment of cloud cover to incorporate unexpected attributes of the system. On windy days, for instance, the image bucks and sways because the camera mast is relatively flexible and only secured at its base. This could be fixed, but we enjoy the visual effect both for what it tells us about the weather and for the giddy effect of seeing the landscape heaving onscreen like a ship on a stormy sea – an exciting counterpoint to the Window's normally peaceful view.

On rainy days, drops of water on the exterior of the camera lens create abstract shapes of pure colour that overwhelm the image. Snow, in contrast, tends to cause ugly grey shadows when it lands on the camera, but the sight of hundreds of flakes swirling in the sky is striking. In each case, it is difficult to say which we value more, the information or the visual effect.

Idiosyncrasies of the camera combine with monitor settings to create an image that is unrealistic, but enhanced. For instance, the camera is sensitive in low-light situations, so the scene very early in the morning is usually much lighter than what we see out our window. Waking in the middle of the night, for instance, to attend to a distressed 3-year-old, I have often seen the Video Window show the first glow of dawn despite the sky appearing black outside our window, and realised that I would have to get up sooner than I thought. We also have the colour and contrast on the monitor turned fairly high, which tends to make the sky appear quite dramatic. Only on the gloomiest of days do we see a uniformly grey sky on the Window, and such a sight can be depressing as it emphasises how unremitting the cloud cover must be. The Video Monitor usually reveals contours of cloud density that are quite lovely, buoying our mood even on overcast days, and having lasting effects on how we look at the sky on leaving home.

The Video Window could be seen as an ambient weather display. The fact that seeing the weather is a side effect of looking out of our room, however, and that features of the weather appear as unanticipated side effects of its configuration, makes seeing the weather through the Video Window particularly uncontrived and aesthetically pleasing. Moreover, the potentially utilitarian information we get from the window is completely interwoven with its psychological and aesthetic effects – there are no artificial boundaries between the various ways of engaging with the view it offers.

## *The Aesthetics of Technology*

Other characteristics of the technology can also have surprising and aesthetically pleasing effects. For instance, when the sun rises over the hospital building below our house, it causes a vertical white line to appear as it overloads the camera. Sometimes lens flare causes translucent, pastel-coloured circles to radiate diagonally from the sun, another effect that we enjoy (see Fig. 16.7).

In general, the aesthetics of the experience offered by the Video Window depend in part on characteristics of the technology as well as the scene. Many of these characteristics could be seen as limitations, insofar as they interfere with a veridical representation of the actual view. Some – for instance, the shadows caused by snow, or the blue static that appears in low-light situations – are genuinely irritating. Many, however, are integral to the appeal of the Video Window. This experience, that technological limitations can be resources for aesthetic appreciation, chimes with similar observations we[2] have made of people interacting with purposefully constrained research prototypes (e.g. Gaver et al., 2004): the very features that frustrate users at first can become the source of aesthetic appreciation with experience.

**Fig. 16.7** Visual artefacts can be aesthetically pleasing

[2] I am indebted to John Bowers for articulating this phenomenon.

## Lessons from the Video Window

The Video Window is a simple system. Considered merely as a concept, it seems hardly worth discussing as a design at all. Its value, and the variety of experiences it has offered, has only become clear because my wife, child and I have lived with it continuously over a period of time.

In describing the Video Window, I have tried to articulate some of the factors that appear to make it so compelling. To summarise these lessons:

- Technology can offer ludic pleasure during all our waking hours (even early in the morning!).
- New views on the existing environment can be fascinating.
- Slight distortion can augment experience without distracting from the 'natural' view.
- One's own, non-arbitrary view may engender strong feelings of engagement.
- Physical causation can convey information (e.g. about the weather) in uncontrived and aesthetically pleasing ways.
- (Some) technological artefacts and constraints can be aesthetically pleasing.
- Systems can seamlessly mix resources for task-based pursuits, ludic engagement and aesthetic pleasure.
- Tinkering is enjoyable, but maintenance is a chore.

In sum, the Video Window is a simple system offering a rich experience. Perhaps the best evidence for this comes from the degree of attachment we have formed to it. For instance, when the mast blew down in a windstorm, I remounted it within a day. I accidentally cut the video cable while trying to attach it more neatly to our wall, and shared a mild panic with my wife on realising that, because I was about to travel for a few days, it would remain broken unless I fixed it that evening (which I did manage to do). It is a compelling indication of the value we find in the Video Window that I probably attend to such problems more quickly than I would to other broken fixtures in our home – including burnt-out light bulbs – and that my wife concurs with this sense of urgency. Unlike many modern technologies, the Video Window is more than a luxury or delightful plaything: it has become an integral part of our experience of home.

**Acknowledgements** I am grateful to my wife, Anne Schlottmann, for her insights on the Video Window, and to John Bowers for his work on ludic technologies more generally.

## References

Bly, S., Harrison, S., and Irwin, S. (1993). Media spaces: Bringing people together in a video, audio, and computing environment. Communications of the ACM 36(1), 28–47.

Gaver, W., Bowers, J., Boucher, A., Gellerson, H., Pennington, S., Schmidt, A., Steed, A., Villars, N., and Walker, B. (2004). The drift table: Designing for ludic engagement. Proc. CHI'04 Design Expo. New York: ACM Press.

Gaver, W.W. (2002). Designing for Homo Ludens. I3 Magazine No. 12, June 2002.

Gaver, W.W., Moran, T., MacLean, A., Lövstrand, L., Dourish, P., Carter, K., and Buxton, W. (1992). Realizing a video environment: EuroPARC's RAVE system. Proc. CHI'92. New York: ACM Press.

# Chapter 17
# Section 3: Communications

**Steve Harrison**

The previous two sections laid out the social and spatial approaches to mediated connection. But is not mediated connection, fundamentally, just *communication*? A "communications-centered approach" subsumes a range of connected but widely different issues: information theory, media, genre, content, task, and activity.

Despite these differences, this approach shares a focus on evaluative frameworks and design metrics. Information processing has well-understood principles; other approaches move up a level from information to include content and meaning as part of their framework; other frameworks focus on the events as organizing the evaluative framework. Moving in a different direction, some are concerned with the characterization of embodied communication and presence, examining the range of communicative moves, gestures, and utterances that constitute the richness of meaningful transmission and understanding in conversation.

A communications-centered approach often rests on particular communication technologies. It encompasses not only the most immobile instantiation of media space, teleconferences, and the most mobile, but also those based on cell phones.

## Mobile Media Spaces

### *Signal and Noise*

Much of computer science and many of the foundational methods in human–computer interaction are derived from Shannon and Weaver's model of information (1949): sender creates a message, reduced to its basic signal; it is transmitted through a medium to a receiver where it is decoded and understood by the recipient. Along the way – and particularly in the mechanics of encoding, transmitting, and decoding – noise can occur, which reduces or alters the signal. Noise therefore should be reduced. This model also offered an engineerable metric for optimization:

S. Harrison
Virginia Polytechnic Institute and State University
sHarrison@vt.edu

S. Harrison (ed.), *Media Space 20+ Years of Mediated Life*,
Computer Supported Cooperative Work,

bandwidth utilization is most efficient when the minimal number of bits is used to transmit a signal. This is the underlying abstraction in all digital computing machines, and early attempts to understand communication media adopted it as a description of human communication.

### Aoki, Woodruff, and Szymanski

In the first of the two chapters that examine mobile media (i.e., cell phones), Paul Aoki, Allison Woodruff, and Peggy Szymanski look at media space as the construction of appropriate signaling in whatever context the people are. From their first commercial deployment, telephones have had a caller-biased initiation sequence. The caller causes the phone to ring at the receiver's end, regardless of receiver's situation. This is an efficient signaling system with little "noise" in the information-theoretic sense (regardless of how people may feel about ringtones). Their experiments develop a nuanced sense of the caller-and-receiver-signaling regime. This analysis is then used to push back on the long-standing but familiar minimalist design.

Early studies of the AT&T picturephone could not "justify" the manyfold increase in bandwidth necessary to add a picture to a telephone call.[1] As bandwidth became less expensive and real-time digital compression better, strictly information-theoretic analyses of the efficacy of ICT technology became irrelevant. But variations of the basic question it raised – "What does the extra bandwidth of multiple channels audio and video provide?" – still haunts those trying to create media spaces or even justify the acquisition of teleconferencing capability.

## *Signal and Noise and Semiotics*

One of the great strengths of information theory is that it ignores content and the systems of meaning associated with content. This permits us to create a simple metric, the ratio of signal-to-noise, to characterize performance. But with media space investigations, CSCW researchers began to wonder whether the abstraction overlooked important components of richness of face-to-face communications, deeply intertwined with particular content. As Scott Minneman, John Tang, Sara Bly, and Hiroshi Ishii discovered the works of conversation analysts such as Sacks, Schegloff, and Jefferson (1974) and psycho-linguists like Herb Clark (1996) and David McNeil (1992), they began to recognize the expression of meaning as a

[1] Interestingly, since multiplexing signals was a problem, even the audio range of telephony was greatly reduced from full range of human hearing.

whole-body process and its construction as a joint process. Particularly seminal were the years that Charles and Margaret Goodwin spent at Xerox PARC and the time that Christian Heath spent at EuroPARC – coinciding with media space research at both institutions. One of the early manifestations of this was the exploration of deixis, that is, indicating or pointing, as a rich activity that can involve language ("this", "that"), fingers that point, gaze, other body parts used to indicate or combinations of these all.

From a different philosophical basis, we note that the basic semiotic model of communication inserts intentionality into the information theory model; however, this perspective leads to the utter rejection of information theory, as it is impossible to measure the noise if the signal is taken as the sender's unknowable intent (Hall, 2007).

### O'Hara, Black, and Lipson

In the second chapter in this section, Kenton O'Hara, Alison Black, and Matthew Lipson extend mobile phones to mobile video phones with an early probe of the design space. The peculiar public-use-for-private-communications status of the cell phone becomes more problematic with the addition of a visual channel. The issues are not whether the technology is the optimal use of bandwidth or if the visual channel improves signal-to-noise, but what sorts of things can be communicated, in what situations, and with what entailments. The project shows the technology has some promise for deictic illustration and context-setting but does not afford the more direct deictic applications that Minneman and Tang (Tang and Minneman, 1990, 1991) noted and exploited in their earliest media space research, VideoDraw and Video WhiteBoard.

## *Signal and Noise and Semiotics and Task*

### Kristensen and Kyng

In the next chapter, Kristensen and Kyng consider a different form of mobile media space – the emergency response scene. Like O'Hara, et al., they report on the hybrid construction of disjoint places – in their case, the ones that span between the emergency room and the emergency site. In this situation, ambiguity can be a life or death matter. Content and context are as significant to the success of the communication as the signal and noise. That success is bound to the immediate set of tasks at hand and the overall activity.

All three of these chapters share the problem that space in which the communications occurs is an element of the system (albeit of only minor consequence to Aoki, Woodruff, and Symanski's system) but that mobile technology renders the space and its role as context and content problematic.[2] It cannot be measured in the same communicative terms as the other content. Let us then turn to other class of technologies that involve the space as content and context.

## Teleconferencing and Telepresence

To many, media space looks like teleconferencing – audio and video meeting technology. While the term media space is almost exclusively used to describe research audio and video environments, teleconferencing is used in commercial production and teleconferencing systems have been building in accessibility, ubiquity, and subtlety. The communication in teleconferencing is in terms of maintenance of the illusion of being the same event rather than signal-to-noise ratios, conveying of meaning, or direct relationships of gestures to speech of embodied communications. What is the central information of teleconferencing? The faces? The attentional resources of the participants? The room itself?

### *Henderson and Henderson*

Austin and Lynne Henderson have observed the teleconferencing situation and propose some interesting and eminently doable alternative configurations and interfaces. We start the teleconferencing collection with this since it is important to keep in mind how the form of teleconferencing is as much a construction of a short tradition of standard forms as it devolves from its first principles.

### *Gorzynski, Derocher, and Mitchell*

Mark Gorzynski, Mike Derocher, and April Slayden Mitchell are system designers who worked on the state-of-the-art Hewlett-Packard Halo system. Their description is framed on the issues that drive the market for their high-end systems. The aspect that matters to them and their competitors is the conceit that all parties

[2] Revisiting issues from the previous section on spatial approaches to media space, all three of these chapters ask, "How can media space be a space if it can be turned on and off?" It is here that the abstraction and the reality intersect. Space (the physical kind) may be bounded but it is persistent; it is one of the foundations of human development that space and the objects in it persist from moment to moment. In this chapter, the space is fundamentally a social construction – an agreement that the working relations of the emergency sites and the emergency rooms have problems, events, resources, and people that must work together moment-to-moment. This space-by-necessity is the foundation for constituting a new place out of the specifics of each emergency event.

are in (sort of) the same meeting room. Their particular measures are non-verbal communication (such as eye contact and gaze awareness, maintained within and between the rooms) and "presence" (that interesting cluster of phenomena that ranges from factual knowledge of another's presence in a location to the feeling of physical closeness).

## *Alem*

Leila Alem asks the question, so important to Halo's design, of how we can measure presence. To answer it, she appropriates metrics used in the world of virtual reality to assess "presence"[3] and examines telepresence systems, in particular, and media spaces in general. The idea of presence is, of course, deeply social; nonetheless, Alem's chapter is included in this section rather than the first, since she uses it to measure the quality of the communications; both this chapter and the previous one on Halo bring our attention to the question of what transmittable information serves to constitute an experience of presence.

## *Corrie and Zimmerman*

Last, Brian Corrie and Todd Zimmerman study the communicative practices of a group of scientists whose work is embedded in a collaboratory, a scientific media space. It is predominantly a study of meeting patterns in a "teleconferencing"[4] space. The space was a rigid room-like structure (like a traditional teleconference room) built for a specific purpose of supporting the scientific work at hand but with a strong orientation to the always-on and providing-presence aspects of a media space. They ask, "How do you support a specific purpose (i.e., scientific collaboration) in the context of a room that provides the flexibility of a media space in its more "pure" form? What do you do when you want both specific purpose and general flexibility?"

In this case, the communicative measures are framed in terms of the conduct of the science that was supported by the collaboratory. Where presence, sameroomness, optimal bandwidth, and the like that were salient features of the other chapters in this section are part of the story, the use of the resource itself is the fundamental metric here.

---

[3] Presence seems to have first been a CSCW phenomenon noted by Judy and Gary Olsen during a sabbatical visit to EuroPARC. It was subsequently investigated by PARC and EuroPARC researchers with still-image presence/absence monitors like "Portholes".

[4] "Teleconferencing" on this view is closer to the notion of audio- and video-mediated spaces in which meetings occur than the carefully constructed rooms described in the chapter on Halo. The author suggests perhaps "telepresence" – the term used by Bill Buxton – which includes the range of technologies and interventions from teleconferencing to task-specific systems.

## References

Clark, H. (1996) *Using Language*. Cambridge/New York: Cambridge University Press.

Hall, S. (2007). *This Means This. This Means That.* London: Laurance King Publishers.

McNeill, D. (1992). *Hand and Mind.* Chicago: University of Chicago Press.

Sacks, H., Schegloff, E., and Jefferson, G. (1974). A Simplest Systematics for the Organization of Turn-Taking for Conversation. *Language, 50*, 696–735.

Shannon, C.E. and Weaver, W. (1949) *The Mathematical Theory of Communication*. The University of Illinois Press, Urbana, IL.

Tang, J. and Minneman, S. (1990). "VideoDraw: a video interface for collaborative drawing", *Proceedings of the SIGCHI Conference on Human Factors in Computing Systems: Empowering People*, pp. 313–320.

Tang, J. and Minneman, S. (1991). "VideoWhiteboard: video shadows to support remote collaboration", *Proceedings of the SIGCHI Conference on Human Factors in Computing Systems: Reaching Through Technology*, pp. 315–322.

# Chapter 18
# Bringing Media Spaces Back to the Streets

## Notes on the Interplay of Research on Media Space and Mobile Communication

**Paul M. Aoki, Margaret H. Szymanski, and Allison Woodruff**

**Abstract** In this chapter, we argue for the mutual relevance of media space and mobile communications researches. Surveying the two literatures, we note that the findings of media space research are often echoed by later mobile communication research and discuss some of the ideas they hold in common. However, mobile phones are used in a more diverse environment, both organizationally and physically. As such, research on mobile communication can be seen as not only building upon, but also significantly extending media space research. We discuss a few cases where this is true, as well as our own attempts to explore these connections through design and prototyping.

## Introduction

Media spaces have had a tremendous impact on human-computer interaction (HCI) and computer-supported cooperative work (CSCW) research. The idea of conceptualizing "real-time visual and acoustic environments that span physically separate areas" (Stults, 1986) as flexible assemblages of people, technology, and practices (as opposed to technology alone) has been extremely productive. Hundreds of research papers cite the standard entry points into media space literature (e.g., Bly et al., 1993).

Given this positive impact, it is surprising to find little mention of media spaces in the fast-growing literature on mobile communication systems. For example, the standard media space references do not appear at all in the most prominent works on

P.M. Aoki
Intel Research Berkeley
e-mail: aoki@acm.org

M.H. Szymanski
PARC

A. Woodruff
Intel Research Berkeley
e-mail: Allison.Woodruff@Intel.Com

S. Harrison (ed.), *Media Space 20+ Years of Mediated Life*,
Computer Supported Cooperative Work,

everyday use of mobile phones.[1] This is undoubtedly due, in part, to the prevalence in this area of social science researchers whose expertise lies in areas other than HCI and CSCW. However, even in the HCI and CSCW literature on mobile communication, there are surprisingly few references to media spaces. Here, the issue is more likely that the standard mental formulation of a media space as an always-on, desktop-based audio/video environment does not seem to have much relevance to mobile phones – one imagines "mobile media space" to mean some kind of wearable computing system, something akin to WearComp and WearCam (Mann, 1997) or the always-on Nomadic Radio system (Sawhney and Schmandt, 2000).

Looking beyond such formulations, however, it is immediately clear that insights from media space research have much to offer to the design of mobile communication systems. After all, the *ur*-media space, Hole-in-Space, connected open public spaces rather than offices. We have tried to leverage these insights in our own research agenda, in which we have explored the question: *What does it mean to have an "off-the desktop" media space*?

In this chapter, we make a case for the mutual relevance of media space and mobile communications research. We first discuss the connections between media space and mobile communication research. We then describe how we have tried to take advantage of the legacy of media spaces in our own research agenda in mobile communication – to bring media spaces back to the streets of their origin.

## Media Spaces and Mobile Phones

We asserted above that media space research is relevant to research on mobile communication, and vice versa. This is based on two lines of argument. First, we observe that it is quite possible to use today's mobile communication technology in a way that essentially follows the original uses of media spaces. Hence, in these usage scenarios, one would expect the lessons of media spaces to carry forward. Second, we argue that there is demonstrable overlap between the findings of these two research areas – enough that it is clear that we should be looking for more connections between the two in any case.

### *Can a Mobile Phone Be a Media Space?*

Most descriptions of media spaces make it clear that they are configured through emergent collective practice rather than through preestablished policy, and this is typically true of mobile phone communication as well. But are not there obvious

[1] Interdisciplinary edited collections include Brown et al. (2001), Fortunati et al. (2003), Glotz et al. (2005), Goggin (2007), Hamill and Lasen (2005), Harper et al. (2005), Höflich and Hartmann (2006), Ito et al. (2005), Katz (2003, 2008), Katz and Aakhus (2002), Kavoori and Arceneaux (2006), Ling and Pederson (2005), and Nyíri (2003, 2005, 2006). Works from anthropology, communication, and sociology include Castells et al. (2007), Goggin (2006), Horst and Miller (2006), Kasesniemi (2003), Katz (2006), Kopomaa (2000), Koskinen (2007), Ling (2004), Pertierra (2006), and Pertierra et al. (2002).

key technical differences by which we can distinguish a media space from other systems? Why should we expect any similarity in use between the two?

Scanning the most frequently cited paper on media spaces (Bly et al., 1993) and other early work, one might get the impression that a media space can be technologically characterized as a system that

- Connects *fixed locations* such as office desktops
- Uses *continuous* audio and video media
- Enables both (1) awareness and (2) lightweight communication by providing *always-open channels*

Such a characterization (which does describe many uses of media spaces, such as "office shares" or "windows" between common areas) comes close to ruling out a mobile instantiation.

However, the characterization above is also an oversimplification. If one considers subsequent research on presence and awareness, a more accurate characterization of the key properties of a media space is that it

- Is associated with an *understood spatial/social context* (as opposed to fixed locations; see, e.g., the lightweight reconfigurability of the original media spaces [Bly et al., 1993]), or the mobile Awareness system [Tang et al., 2001])
- Uses *continuous or discrete media* (as opposed to continuous media alone; see, e.g., Portholes [Dourish and Bly, 1992])
- Enables (1) awareness by providing an *ongoing stream of awareness updates* and (2) lightweight communication by providing an *ongoing state of incipient interaction*

One might object that this characterization seems overbroad – after all, instant messaging, or even text messaging, one's friends frequently on a mobile phone fits this description. But again, the claim has been that the core properties of a media space lie in its use, not in the specifics of its "delivery" technology.

In considering this claim in the mobile context, it is useful to consider some of the basic ideas developed in conversation analysis (Sacks, 1984), a methodology for analyzing how human interaction is organized into sequences of action. The organization of taking turns at talk is fundamental to conversation. One of the ways in which turn-taking organization operates is by specifying opportunities for *speaker change* at *turn-constructional units* (TCUs) from which turns at talk are composed (Sacks et al., 1974). This enables listeners to monitor and project the completion of others' TCUs in order to time the initiation of their own turns properly. Completion of a TCU is often accompanied by a pause in speech, making a *transition-relevance place* (TRP) where speaker change may occur. Building on these basic concepts, conversation analysis describes additional mechanisms that underlie the unfolding of conversational encounters. Of particular relevance to us here is a concept of a "continuing state of incipient talk" (Sacks et al., 1974) that differs notably from a single, focused conversational encounter (Fig. 18.1, top). Once participants in physical copresence enter a state of incipient talk, they engage, disengage, and reengage (Szymanski, 1999) from talk-in-interaction without explicitly regreeting

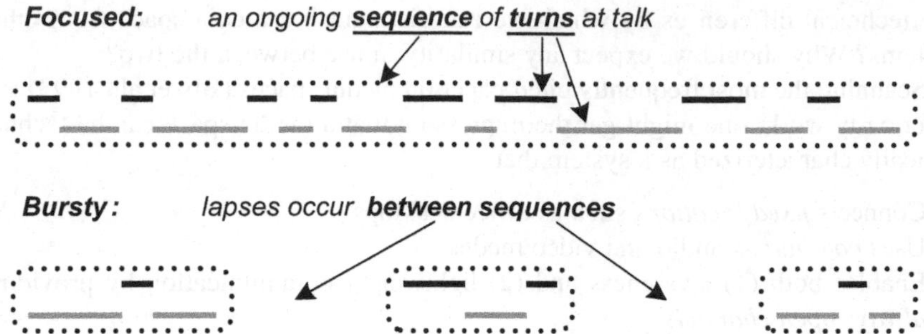


Fig. 18.1 Focused interaction versus interaction in a state of incipient talk

each other, reintroducing themselves, or otherwise re-"opening" the conversation. Interaction proceeds in a "bursty" fashion, with lapses occurring between spates of talk (Fig. 18.1, bottom).

Copresence is not necessary to a state of incipient talk. We know that physical copresence is not necessary as similar states are described in media space research such as that on the Interval Research series of audio-only media spaces (Ackerman et al., 1997). Indeed, virtual copresence (in the form of an always-on channel) is not necessary as similar states have also been observed in the use of instant messaging (Nardi et al., 2000) and mobile push-to-talk voice messaging (Szymanski et al., 2006). Open audio and video channels may make some aspects of the experience more lightweight, since one does not have to compose messages. However, in creating a sense of presence and awareness, it is more important for the network to be available than for data to be passing through it at all times. In other words, "always on" in the network-level sense (always connected to the network) is more critical than "always on" in the application-level sense (always running). It is important for mobile communication researchers to understand this point, because it makes clear why the experience gained from media space research often apply in this domain as well.

## The Interplay of Media Spaces and Mobility

If one accepts that media space research and mobile communication research ought to have mutual relevance, the natural question is: what is this relevance? We argue that the earlier research on media spaces serves as a useful conceptual foundation for a great deal of mobile communication research, and further suggest that many general phenomena described in the last 2 decades of media space research have in some sense been rediscovered in the last 5 years of work on mobile phones. However, it is also true that the understanding gained of the nuances of mobile communication practice extends and refines the insights gained from media spaces as well. It could hardly be otherwise when one considers how connectivity has extended from the workplace into everyday life, and the great increase in expectations of connectivity (Ito and Okabe, 2005; Ling and Yttri, 2002). By way of example, we detail a few areas of commonality below.

### Sustaining Relationships

One area of commonality is a predominance of use for coordination and awareness within relatively small, preexisting groups. It has long been clear that media space is a tool for *sustaining* relationships (Bly et al., 1993, p.42) – that initial trust is necessary for stable sharing practices to develop, and that this trust occurs most readily in already-formed groups. Given that, it is arguably unsurprising that, across societies, mobile communication is overwhelmingly used to maintain existing relationships within small groups (Habuchi, 2005; Ito and Okabe, 2005; Ling and Yttri, 2002; Matsuda, 2005; Woodruff and Aoki, 2003). Although one frequently sees empirical reports of overflowing contact lists, it is also typically found that the bulk of mobile phone interaction occurs within core groups of 10 or fewer. This is captured by notions such as "full-time intimate community" (Nakajima et al., 1999, cited in Matsuda, 2005), "tele-cocooning" (Habuchi, 2005), and "selective sociality" (Matsuda, 2005).

In both cases, what passes through channels is often classic "phatic" communication (Malinowski, 1922) – intermittent and often unimportant and uninformative in itself – but the commitment to availability in itself reinforces relationships (Simmel, 1950 [1910]). Further, even if awareness updates – seeing a coworker in an office, receiving a text message from a friend complaining, "I'm tired" – do not provide immediately relevant or actionable activity awareness, updates from members of the group over time can provide "local resources" for talk, material for "noticings" in subsequent interaction (Sacks, 1992, pp.87–97), and "arrangement tokens" that span multiple interactions (Button, 1991).

In the mobile case, notions such as "full-time intimate community" and "ambient virtual copresence" (Ito and Okabe, 2005) do differ from prior notions in degree. Mobile communication extends into everyday, on-the-street life, and core groups are typically made up of friends (as opposed to coworkers – who might be, but need not be, friends). Indeed, a key reported use of mobile communication is maintaining connections with friends who one no longer sees regularly at school or at work (Matsuda, 2005).

### Keeping Company

A second area of commonality is the ability to enable a particular kind of presence or "connectedness." Users of the original PARC media space – users who were not collaborators – were observed connecting their offices to keep each other company while working at night (Bly et al., 1993, p.39). Mobile phone users have been observed making periodic contact (e.g., updates by mobile e-mail) with selected friends to create a sense of connectedness as they go through their daily routine (which for city dwellers often involve extended periods of walking or travel on public transportation) (Ito and Okabe, 2005). In our own design fieldwork of users of mobile push-to-talk, we have observed what we termed "extended remote presence" (Woodruff and Aoki, 2003), or intermittent communication with a specific "companion" while in transit or doing errands – a way of creating an audible version of what Goffman (1971) called a "with" through the use of mobile communication.

In both cases, as in the previous subsection, the contact need not be continuous or particularly informative in a semantic sense. It is the implicit commitment by a specific person or persons to availability for an extended period (rather than a general sense of availability within a group) that creates this kind of connectedness.

In the mobile case, the sense of connectedness is threatened by several challenges that do not arise (or arise to a much more limited degree) in the media space case. One set of challenges has to do with obstacles to the use of mobile communication in different physical environments that arise from social sanctions, legal restrictions and physical safety implications (see, e.g., Paragas, 2005). These vary not only across societies, but also when one moves through (e.g.) a city. A second set of challenges has to do with finding suitable partners. A media space provides relatively simple mechanisms for browsing for active system participants; more abstract presence mechanisms, or an absence of presence mechanisms altogether, can reduce users to "polling" their friends to find "companions" (e.g., Woodruff and Aoki, 2003).

## Temporality

A third area of commonality relates to awareness of temporal rhythms and patterns. Such awareness is a key resource (along with explicit presence data) in knowing whether it is appropriate to make contact. This appears in at least two different forms that work on different time scales. The first involves synchronic events, typically on a diurnal scale. In the PARC media space studies, a wave and a "good morning" and "good night" would be sent through the media space (Bly et al., 1993, p.39). Similarly, "good morning" (Taylor and Harper, 2003) and "good night" (Grinter and Eldridge, 2001) messages are often reported in mobile phone studies, particularly those of text messaging. These let others know that one is "signing off" from contact. The second involves detailed understanding of daily routines. Individuals within work groups who are able to observe each other (whether through media or copresence) are able to form mental models of each others' schedules and potential availability (Begole et al., 2002). Similarly, in a college environment, students' schedules may be very structured in the sense that friends have detailed awareness of each others' class and work schedules (Woodruff and Aoki, 2003).

In both cases, users can gather information about each others' activities by passive observation (watching or listening) or active information sharing. Where awareness/presence information is ambiguous (as is usually the case with buddy-list-like presence mechanisms) or is updated on an infrequent or irregular basis, difficulties can arise in interpretation.

In the mobile case, practices around temporality may diverge from those seen in conventional media spaces. First, users may simply accept more interruptions. Because awareness in the mobile case is much less likely to be based on high-fidelity observation (e.g., video) and more likely to be irregularly updated (e.g., manual text messages, or presence information based on handset status), it is recognized that predictions of others' availability may be unreliable. Second, users may develop graduated contact strategies that involve communication media that are less "interruptive." In most societies, textual communication media are considered less of an interruption than a voice call; the practice often arises of texting before calling.

### Discussion

This section contributes nothing new in a strictly empirical sense. That is, the phenomena discussed – use for sustaining relationships, use for keeping company, and the role of temporality in activity awareness – are well known in media space research and visible to varying degrees in mobile communication research.

What we illustrate here is that there are many concrete connections between the two research areas that become evident when one views media spaces in the generalized sense described in the preceding subsection. Media space research identified some specific connections – e.g., the relevance of earlier desktop work on presence to mobile presence, as in Tang et al. (2001) – but the generalized view enables one to see how users of mobile communication systems have systematically produced many of the same emergent practices as did the users of media spaces.

## Social, Mobile Audio Spaces

Having discussed a few of the ways in which media space and mobile communication researches can interact in the context of empirical research, we now turn to the question of how this might be accomplished in the context of design. In this section, we provide an overview of our own mobile communication project. In doing so, we illustrate some of the ways in which this project has drawn inspiration from media space research.

From a design perspective, our point of departure becomes obvious from the project name: social, mobile, and audio spaces (http://www.parc.com/audiospaces/). From the beginning, we explicitly focused our design efforts in three ways:

- *Social.* Our design goal is to facilitate sociable interaction within small groups. This focus draws direct inspiration from the emergent uses of mobile communication described in the previous section rather than from workplace interaction alone.
- *Mobile.* A great deal of "mobile" technology use is actually portable technology use (consider the typical uses of laptop and handheld computers). However, choosing to enable mobile, "on-the-go" scenarios such as "talking while walking"

implies an emphasis on eyes-free and hands-free use and a prioritization of non-visual interaction modalities (e.g., of audio over text or video).
- *Audio spaces*. By alluding to the Interval Research series of "audio-only media spaces" or *audio spaces* (Ackerman et al., 1997), we indicate a common emphasis on lightweight audio interaction. That is, the desired interaction model should resemble an audio space in the degree of spontaneity that it enables rather than resembling a telephone call.

However, mobility on-the-go constrains this design space in the sense that exposing one's face-to-face interactions through wearable, always-on media streaming (Mann, 1997) is not desirable for most people as well as problematic in many social settings.

From a social science perspective, we explicitly framed our research in terms of interactional engagement, albeit at several levels of granularity. Our previous research on wirelessly connected museum audio guides (Aoki et al., 2002) had taught us the importance of managing transitions between levels of engagement. Our experience had been that we could design mobile systems that engendered states of connectedness and activity awareness within small groups through wireless audio sharing. However, it also showed us that it was difficult to get people "back" into a state of engagement once they began to pursue separate activities. These kinds of transitions would clearly be quite frequent in anything that aspired to be a "social, mobile audio space."

Drawing on our prior research and on our design fieldwork conducted using mobile push-to-talk "radios" as an approximation of a future lightweight audio communication system (Woodruff and Aoki, 2003), we engaged in a variety of design-oriented explorations of the processes of engagement, disengagement, and reengagement of interaction. These explorations included the following.

- Managing engagement of floor participation *within a given conversational encounter* (Aoki et al., 2003, 2006)
- Managing engagement *within a state of incipient talk* (Szymanski et al., 2006; Woodruff and Aoki, 2003; Yu et al., 2004)
- Managing engagement *within the context of a social relationship or association* (Aoki and Woodruff, 2005)

The first two were developed the furthest, and we discuss each in turn in the following sections.

## *Within a Conversational Encounter*

If multiple mobile users want to be able to "keep each other company" as described above, what needs to change in audio communication technology for such users to be able to hold spontaneous conversations in an audio space? Is sociable interaction within a small group, the kind that is such a key part of the "sustaining relationships"

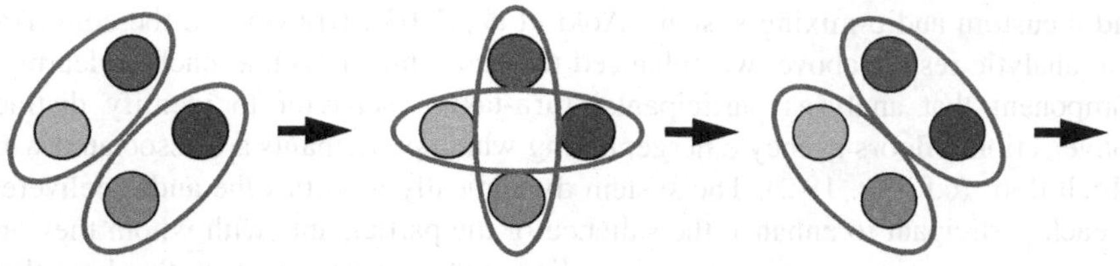

**Fig. 18.2** Participation in multiparty interaction changes over time

described above, different from other kinds of conversation – and if so, how can we support and facilitate such interactions?

In approaching these questions from a design perspective, we first needed to understand what kinds of sociable interactions might need to be supported. For example, consider the fluidity of casual conversation around a dinner table or at a cocktail party. A salient feature of such events is the occurrence of *multiple simultaneous conversations* (Egbert, 1997; Sacks et al., 1974) in which membership changes over time (Fig. 18.2). Anyone who has experienced a disorganized conference call knows that this is clearly not something that is well-supported by off-the-shelf conferencing technology, as simultaneous speech on a phone line is nearly unintelligible.

In addition to the previously mentioned design fieldwork (Woodruff and Aoki, 2003), we conducted a series of studies of small-group talk to identify key phenomena of sociable interaction (Aoki et al., 2003, 2006). We knew that detailed examinations of interactional practices in media spaces had been carried out in the past. For example, studies of interactions in the original PARC media spaces had uncovered problematic aspects of video mediation of collaborative activity (see, e.g., Heath et al., 1997). Casual workplace interactions in the interval audio spaces had been examined as well (Ackerman et al., 1997). However, the kinds of settings and problems in which we were interested had not been examined before; designing technology to facilitate phenomena such as multiple simultaneous conversations would clearly require very specific characterization of the phenomena in question.

Our studies drew upon the research and methods of conversation analysis. As mentioned above, conversation analysis is the study of the sequential organization of interaction. Empirical research has characterized the normative duration of pauses in two-party conversation and has also indicated that sustained periods of *simultaneous speech* are infrequent. Multiparty conversations of the kind with which we are concerned may have a single *floor* in which participants orient to each others' turn-taking behavior as just described. However, in casual multiparty conversation, s*chisms* (Egbert, 1997) may occur frequently, a dynamic process in which conversations merge and new conversations arise.

For our initial design exploration, we decided to focus on enabling multiple simultaneous conversations using only the capabilities of a conventional mobile phone. We built a prototype multiparty audio space using wireless handheld computers and a custom audio-mixing system (Aoki et al., 2003). Drawing on the conversation analytic results above, we enhanced the audio mixer with a machine learning component that analyzes participants' turn-taking behavior to identify distinct conversational floors as they emerge, noting which participants are associated with which floor (c.f. Fig. 18.2). The system dynamically modifies the audio delivered to each participant to enhance the salience of the participants with whom they are currently conversing and to reduce the salience of the participants with whom they are not currently conversing. Each participant therefore receives a customized mix of all floors, tailored to their current conversational status.

The main observation is that when two simultaneous conversational floors are on-going, participants associated with one do not orient to the turn-taking organization of the other. This has two implications: (1) speakers in one conversation no longer align the initiation of their TCUs with the TRPs of the other conversation, and (2) speakers in the distinct conversations overlap their talk much more than if they were participating in a single floor. These implications form the basis for the mixer's machine learning component. The floor assignment subsystem continually determines the most likely configuration of conversational participants from the content of the audio streams. It runs a voice activity detector on each incoming audio stream, producing binary classifications (speech/nonspeech). It then extracts temporal features from each pair of binary streams (TRP positioning for speakers A and B is the distance between the starting point of A's most recent utterance and the endpoint of B's utterance that mostly closely precedes A's utterance; simultaneous speech is the amount of overlap between A's and B's utterances during a given time period). A classifier outputs probabilities of mutual floor participation for each pair of users; it considers these probabilities in view of a model of valid floor configurations, choosing the most likely configuration. The chosen floor configuration is used to set how speaker A's audio is presented to speaker B. In the current system, if A and B are participating in the same floor, then they hear each other at a "normal" volume level. Otherwise, they hear each other at a "quiet" volume level (currently 20% of the "normal" level). As a result, every participant in the audio space hears a customized mix.

In summary, we found that detailed consideration of the processes of engagement, disengagement, and reengagement *within* a conversational encounter led us in interesting and fruitful directions, both in terms of producing new technical ideas for augmenting conventional media space designs (Aoki et al., 2003), as well as producing new results in social science (Aoki et al., 2003, 2006).

## *Within a State of Incipient Talk*

There is a growing array of mobile communication technologies – full-duplex voice, half-duplex push-to-talk voice messaging (Fig. 18.3), text messaging, etc. – each with its own uses and affordances. For example, mobile telephony is well-suited to bounded, relatively focused interaction between two participants

**Fig. 18.3** "Walkie-talkie" interaction over push-to-talk mobile voice

(as in Fig. 18.1, top); message-oriented systems such as instant messaging and push-to-talk voice messaging are well-suited to longer interactions that proceed in bursts (as in Fig. 18.1, bottom). How should users choose between them? As the degree of engagement changes over time, is the medium used to begin an interaction the right medium to continue, or is explicit "media-switching" (Nardi et al., 2000) always the right answer?

Our design fieldwork suggested that media-switching is more problematic than one might think. For example, in our studies of push-to-talk voice messaging, users continued interactions in the initial medium even when a "media switch" seemed warranted (Woodruff and Aoki, 2003). And indeed, analyses of interaction in prior media spaces provided some hints of relevant issues. In the original media space research, it had been noted that visual gestures intended to initiate interactions during a state of incipient talk often failed (Heath et al., 1997). (Working at PARC, we had also observed that long-time users of the Kasmer media space [Bly et al., 1993] made frequent transitions between video-only and audio/video communications but that, similarly, often failed).

The points above suggest that "smoothing" the media-switching process may be an opportunity for technological intervention. Research in pragmatics (Selting, 1994) and conversation analysis (Goodwin and Goodwin, 2000) suggests that there are prosodic elements of speech that indicate heightened conversational engagement. If we could construct a system to estimate the level of the users' engagement in an ongoing remote conversation, e.g., by drawing on research on detecting emotion in human speech (Cowie et al., 2001), we could use these estimates to modify the communication system in useful ways. For example, if two users are speaking in a push-to-talk audio session and become highly engaged, the system could switch over to a telephony (duplex audio) connection.

To understand some of the issues behind these questions, we have conducted machine learning experiments in which we attempt to differentiate between states of conversational engagement and nonengagement using acoustic features extracted from audio (Yu et al., 2004). These experiments, while preliminary, have had a degree of success comparable to that of similar studies of emotion recognition from audio (Scherer, 2003).

## *Discussion*

While we have discussed (briefly) some design, prototyping, and social science activities, the framing of the various problems has been rooted in the deep explorations of presence, awareness, availability, mediated communication, and small-group dynamics pioneered by the research on media spaces. We suggest two related areas that are open for additional research.

The first area concerns the evolution of one's social groups over time, as described in the preceding section. When mobile users wish to prune their contact lists, what resources are available to them? One's sphere of frequent social contact evolves over time, but once contact information has been exchanged, how does one disengage from such people? Our design fieldwork (as well as that of others) suggests that it is difficult to navigate the social process of avoiding unwanted interaction as one's social relations evolve. Research on workplace-oriented media spaces offers little explicit guidance. After reflection on some of the issues behind these questions, we have offered some preliminary thoughts on resources that system designers can provide to users that might be of use in such efforts (Aoki and Woodruff, 2005). Specifically, we point out that ambiguity can be a useful aspect of communication system design when it affords relevant resources for social interaction.

The second area concerns recent developments in mobility and scale. Hole-in-Space connected crowds in distant public locations and there have been countless recreations of this idea in semipublic spaces. However, the recent commoditization of data service over cellular networks has enabled video-based "lifecasting" of all of one's interactions over the Internet (a current commercial example being justin.tv). There is a sense in which lifecasting creates a somewhat covert and highly mobile version of Hole-in-Space – but one in which unidirectionality violates the communicative reciprocity that was so critical to the successes of media spaces (and unlike prior experiments in wearable computing [Mann, 1997], does so on a massive scale). Clearly, the ideas refined over the course of 2 decades of media space research can inform the debate over developments such as lifecasting.

## Conclusion

Because the uses of media spaces and mobile phones are often similar, the findings of media space research are often closely related to those of later mobile communication research. While we have pointed out that one should not dismiss media space research as being irrelevant to mobile communication research based on spurious technological distinctions, we have also described some areas where the findings of the earlier research have been echoed in those of the later. Some areas where common phenomena and practices have arisen include their use in sustaining relationships, in enabling remote "companionship," and in the employment of temporal patterns. However, mobile phones are used in a more diverse environment, both organizationally and physically. As such, research on mobile communication can be seen as not only building upon, but also significantly extending media space research. We have discussed a few cases where this is true, as well as our own attempts to explore these connections.

## References


Ackerman, M., Starr, B., Hindus, D., & Mainwaring, S.D. (1997): "Hanging on the Wire: A Field Study of an Audio-Only Media Space," *ACM TOCHI, vol.* 4, no. 1, pp. 39–66.

Aoki, P.M., & Woodruff, A. (2005): "Making Space for Stories: Ambiguity in the Design of Personal Communication Systems," in Proc. CHI 2005, ACM, pp. 181–190.

Aoki, P.M., Grinter, R.E., Hurst, A., Szymanski, M.H., Thornton, J.D., & Woodruff, A. (2002): "*Sotto Voce*: Exploring the Interplay of Conversation and Mobile Audio Spaces," in Proc. CHI 2002, ACM, pp. 431–438.

Aoki, P.M., Romaine, M., Szymanski, M.H., Thornton, J.D., Wilson, D., & Woodruff, A. (2003): "The Mad Hatter's Cocktail Party: A Social Mobile Audio Space Supporting Multiple Simultaneous Conversations," in Proc. CHI 2003, ACM, pp. 425–432.

Aoki, P.M., Szymanski, M.H., Plurkowski, L., Thornton, J.D., Woodruff, A., & Yi, W. (2006): "Where's the 'Party' in 'Multi-Party? Analyzing the Structure of Small-Group Sociable Talk," in Proc. CSCW 2006, ACM, pp. 393–402.

Begole, J., Tang, J.C., Smith, R., & Yankelovich, N. (2002): "Work Rhythms: Analyzing Visualizations of Awareness Histories of Distributed Groups," in Proc. CSCW 2002, ACM, pp. 334–343.

Bly, S., Harrison, S., & Irwin, S. (1993): "Media Spaces: Bringing People Together in a Video, Audio and Computing Environment," *CACM, vol.* 36, no. 1, pp. 28–47.

Brown, B., Green, N., & Harper, R. (Eds.). (2001). *Wireless World: Social and Interactional Aspects of the Mobile Age*. Springer, Berlin.

Button, G. (1991): "Conversation-in-a-Series," In D. Boden, & D.H. Zimmerman (Eds.): *Talk and Social Structure: Studies in Ethnomethodology and Conversation Analysis*. UC Press, Berkeley, pp. 251–277.

Castells, M., Fernández-Ardèvol, M., Qiu, J.L., & Sey, A. (2007): *Mobile Communication and Society: A Global Perspective*. MIT Press, Cambridge, MA.

Cowie, R., Douglas-Cowie, E., Tsapatsoulis, N., Votsis, G., Kollias, S., Fellenz, W., & Taylor, J.G. (2001): "Emotion Recognition in Human-Computer Interaction," *IEEE Signal Processing, vol.* 18, no. 1, pp. 32–80.

Dourish, P., & Bly, S. (1992): "Portholes: Supporting Awareness in a Distributed Work Group," in Proc. CHI 1992, ACM, pp. 541–547.

Egbert, M.M. (1997): "Schisming: The Collaborative Transformation from a Single Conversation to Multiple Conversations," *Research on Language & Social Interaction, vol.* 30, pp. 1–51.

Fortunati, L., Katz, J.E., & Riccini, R. (Eds.). (2003), *Mediating the Human Body: Technology, Communication, and Fashion*. LEA, Mahwah, NJ.

Glotz, P., Bertschi, S., & Locke, C. (Eds.). (2005). *Thumb Culture: The Meaning of Mobile Phones for Society*. Transcript, Bielefeld, Germany.

Goffman, E. (1971): "The Individual as Unit," In *Relations in Public*. Harper & Row, New York, pp. 3–27.

Goggin, G. (2006): *Cell Phone Culture: Mobile Technology in Everyday Life*. Routledge, Abingdon, UK.

Goggin, G. (Ed.). (2007). *Mobile Phone Culture*. Routledge, Abingdon.

Goodwin, M.H., & Goodwin, C. (2000): "Emotion Within Situated Activity," In N. Budwig, I.Č. Užgiris, & J.V. Wertsch (Eds.): *Communication: An Arena of Development*. Ablex, Stamford, CT, pp. 33–54.

Grinter, R.E., & Eldridge, M. (2001): "y do tngrs luv 2 txt msg?," In *Proc. ECSCW 2001*, Kluwer, Dordrecht, The Netherlands, pp. 219–238.

Habuchi, I. (2005): "Accelerating Reflexivity," In M. Ito, D. Okabe, & M. Matsuda (Eds.): *Personal, Portable, Pedestrian: Mobile Phones in Japanese Life*. MIT Press, Cambridge, MA, pp. 165–182.

Hamill, L., & Lasen, A. (Eds.). (2005). *Mobile World: Past, Present and Future*. Springer, Berlin.

Harper, R., Palen, L., & Taylor, A. (Eds.). (2005). *The Inside Text: Social, Cultural and Design Perspectives on SMS*. Springer, Berlin.

Heath, C., Luff, P., & Sellen, A. (1997): "Reconfiguring Media Space: Supporting Collaborative Work," In K.E. Finn, A.J. Sellen, & S.B. Wilbur (Eds.): *Video-Mediated Communication*. LEA, Mahwah, NJ, pp. 323–347.

Höflich, J.R., & Hartmann, M. (Eds.). (2006). *Mobile Communication in Everyday Life: Ethnographic Views, Observations and Reflections*. Frank & Timme, Berlin.

Horst, H.A., & Miller, D. (2006): *The Cell Phone: An Anthropology of Communication*. Berg, Oxford.

Ito, M., & Okabe, D. (2005): "Technosocial Situations: Emergent Structuring of Mobile E-mail Use," In M. Ito, D. Okabe, & M. Matsuda (Eds.): *Personal, Portable, Pedestrian: Mobile Phones in Japanese Life*. MIT Press, Cambridge, MA, pp. 257–273.

Ito, M., Okabe, D., & Matsuda, M. (Eds.). (2005). *Personal, Portable, Pedestrian: Mobile Phones in Japanese Life*. MIT Press, Cambridge, MA.

Kasesniemi, E.-L. (2003): *Mobile Messages: Young People and a New Communication Culture*. Tampere University Press, Tampere, Finland.

Katz, J.E. (Ed.). (2003). *Machines That Become Us: The Social Content of Personal Communication Technology*. Transaction, New Brunswick, NJ.

Katz, J.E. (Ed.). (2006). *Magic in the Air: Mobile Communication and the Transformation of Social Life*. New Brunswick, NJ: Transaction, New Brunswick, NJ.

Katz, J.E. (Ed.). (2008). *Handbook of Mobile Communication Studies*. MIT Press, Cambridge, MA.

Katz, J.E., & Aakhus, M.A. (Eds.). (2002). *Perpetual Contact: Mobile Communication, Private Talk, Public Performance*. Cambridge University Press, Cambridge.

Kavoori, A., & Arceneaux, N. (2006): *The Cell Phone Reader: Essays in Social Transformation*. Peter Lang, New York.

Kopomaa, T. (2000): *The City in Your Pocket: Birth of the Mobile Information Society*. Gaudeamus, Helsinki.

Koskinen, I.K. (2007): *Mobile Multimedia in Action*. Transaction, New Brunswick, NJ.

Ling, R. (2004): *The Mobile Connection: The Cell Phone's Impact on Society*. Morgan Kaufmann, San Francisco, CA.

Ling, R., & Pederson, P.E. (Eds.). (2005). *Mobile Communications: Re-Negotiation of the Social Sphere*. Springer, Berlin.

Ling, R., & Yttri, B. (2002): "Hyper-coordination via Mobile Phones in Norway," In J.E. Katz, & M.A. Aakhus (Eds.): *Perpetual Contact*. Cambridge University Press, Cambridge, pp. 139–169.

Malinowski, B. (1922): "The Problem of Meaning in Primitive Languages," In C.K. Ogden, & I.A. Richards (Eds.): *The Meaning of Meaning*. Harcourt, Brace & Co., New York, pp. 296–336.

Mann, S. (1997): "Smart Clothing: The Wearable Computer and WearCam," *Personal Technologies, vol.* 1, no. 1, pp. 21–27.

Matsuda, M. (2005): "Mobile Communication and Selective Sociality," In M. Ito, D. Okabe, & M. Matsuda (Eds.): *Personal, Portable, Pedestrian: Mobile Phones in Japanese Life*. MIT Press, Cambridge, MA, pp. 123–142.

Nakajima, I., Himeno, K., & Yoshii, H. (1999): "Ido-denwa Riyo no Fukyu to sono Shakaiteki-imi (Diffusion of Cellular Phones and PHS and its Social Meanings)," *Joho Tsushin Gakkai-shi, vol.* 16, no. 3, pp. 79–92.

Nardi, B.A., Whittaker, S., & Bradner, E. (2000): "Interaction and Outeraction: Instant Messaging in Action," in Proc. CSCW 2000, ACM, pp. 79–88.

Nyíri, K. (Ed.). (2003). *Mobile Democracy: Essays on Society, Self and Politics*. Passagen, Vienna.

Nyíri, K. (Ed.). (2005). *A Sense of Place: The Global and the Local in Mobile Communication*. Passagen, Vienna.

Nyíri, K. (Ed.). (2006). *Mobile Understanding: The Epistemology of Ubiquitous Communication*. Passagen, Vienna.

Paragas, F. (2005): "Being Mobile with the Mobile: Cellular Telephony and Renegotiations of Public Transport as Public Sphere," In R. Ling, & P.E. Pederson (Eds.): *Mobile Communications*. Springer, Berlin, pp. 113–129.

Pertierra, R. (2006): *Transforming Technologies, Altered Selves: Mobile Phone and Internet Use in the Philippines*. De La Salle University Press, Manila.

Pertierra, R., Ugarte, E.F., Pingol, A., Hernandez, J., & Dacanay, N.L. (2002): *Txt-ing Selves: Cellphones and Philippine Modernity*. De La Salle University Press, Manila.

Sacks, H. (1984): "Notes on Methodology," In J.M. Atkinson, & J. Heritage (Eds.): *Structures of Social Action*. Cambridge University Press, Cambridge, pp. 21–27.

Sacks, H. (1992): *Lectures on Conversation*, Vol. II. Blackwell, Oxford.

Sacks, H., Schegloff, E.A., & Jefferson, G. (1974): "A Simplest Systematics for the Organization of Turn-Taking for Conversation," *Language, vol.* 50, pp. 696–735.

Sawhney, N., & Schmandt, C. (2000): "Nomadic Radio: Speech and Audio Interaction for Contextual Messaging in Nomadic Environments," *ACM TOCHI, vol.* 7, no. 3, pp. 353–383.

Scherer, K.R. (2003): "Vocal Communication of Emotion: A Review of Research Paradigms," *Speech Communication, vol.* 40, no. 1–2, pp. 227–256.

Selting, M. (1994): "Emphatic Speech Style - With Special Focus on the Prosodic Signalling of Heightened Emotive Involvement in Conversation," *Journal of Pragmatics, vol.* 22, no. 3–4, pp. 375–408.

Simmel, G. (1950 [1910]): "Sociability," In K.H. Wolff (Ed.), *The Sociology of Georg Simmel*. Free Press, New York, pp. 40–57.

Stults, R. (1986): *Media Space*. Systems Concepts Lab, Xerox PARC, Palo Alto, CA.

Szymanski, M.H. (1999): "Re-engaging and Dis-engaging Talk in Activity," *Language in Society, vol.* 28, no. 1, pp. 1–23.

Szymanski, M.H., Aoki, P.M., Vinkhuyzen, E., & Woodruff, A. (2006): "Organizing a Remote State of Incipient Talk: Push-to-Talk Mobile Radio Interaction," *Language in Society, vol.* 35, no. 3, pp. 393–418.

Tang, J.C., Yankelovich, N., Begole, J., van Kleek, M., Li, F., & Bhalodia, J. (2001): "ConNexus to Awarenex: Extending Awareness to Mobile Users," in Proc. CHI 2001, ACM, pp. 221–228.

Taylor, A.S., & Harper, R. (2003): "The Gift of the *Gab*?: A Design Oriented Sociology of Young People's Use of Mobiles," *CSCW, vol.* 12, no. 3, pp. 267–296.

Woodruff, A., & Aoki, P.M. (2003): "How Push-to-Talk Makes Talk Less Pushy," in Proc. GROUP 2003, ACM, pp. 170–179.

Yu, C., Aoki, P.M., & Woodruff, A. (2004): "Detecting User Engagement in Everyday Conversations," in Proc. ICSLP 2004, pp. 1329–1332.

# Chapter 19
# Media Spaces and Mobile Video Telephony

**Kenton O'Hara, Alison Black, and Matthew Lipson**

**Abstract** In this chapter we examine everyday practices with mobile video telephony. Drawing on a diary study of video telephony users, we examine the social and practical aspects of mobile video telephony use and the ways it becomes part of people's everyday lives. We explore how particular characteristics of mobile video telephony afford these practices and then draw parallels and points of contrast with the traditional fixed video telephony and media spaces.

## Introduction

Since the early days of media space, video-mediated communication technology has moved on considerably. Technological advances and reductions in cost have meant that video-mediated communication is now in the hands of everyday consumers as opposed to being limited to large corporations and the world of work. Webcams are commonplace in many households and mobile phones are increasingly available with video telephony capabilities. Our particular concern in this chapter is with mobile video telephony, the social practices that take place around this technology, and the relationship with the original concepts of media spaces.

Historically, the relationship between media spaces and audio and video telephony has been a mixed one. A key aspect of a media space is that it promotes an ongoing presence and awareness that can lead to immediate casual interactions between the connected people. In this respect, while audio and video telephony are

K. O'Hara
CSIRO ICT Centre
email: kenton@gwork.org
A. Black
Alison Black Consulting
email: dtatar@cs.vt.edu
M. Lipson
Orange UK
email: matthewlipson@yahoo.co.uk

S. Harrison (ed.), *Media Space 20+ Years of Mediated Life*,
Computer Supported Cooperative Work,

important components of media space, some media space commentators argue that the call structure model of traditional telephony breaks the basic notions of always-on connectivity for awareness and casual interaction. From a purist perspective one can see some appeal to this argument but a quick look at some of the foundational media space work shows that the boundaries are a lot more fuzzy. For example, in EuroPARC's RAVE system, one of the archetypal media spaces, a fundamental part of the design was about exploring different levels of engagement and connectivity made possible by the technology and the social implications of these differences. So in addition to having an always-on-office share between two offices in which there was a continuous audio and video connection between two spaces, other models included glance, video phone, sweep, and background. These models have similar underlying technology but differ in terms of the social meaning behind them. Some of these also have the characteristics of traditional technology and call initiation. In the video phone example one essentially is initiating a temporary audio and video connection between two offices. With the glance model, a view into another office is deliberately initiated. While there is no need for an answer, the act of glancing is something that is deliberately initiated in the media space – this communicates a particular social meaning that is different from looking at the screen of an always-on-office share.

The relationship between media space and mobile video telephony is even more complex than the relationship between fixed line audio and video telephony. In some ways the mobile aspects of telephony move closer towards the media space model and in other aspects it moves away from some of the fundamental foundations underlying the media space concept. Through its mobility, the mobile phone and mobile video phone create a sense of continuous availability. In theory then this can provide some of the elements of spontaneous and casual interaction fundamental to the media space concept. By having the phone all the time, one can always make a call and one is always available to receive a call. From a social point of view, this ubiquitous availability of connection potential made possible by mobile phones has had a number of important consequences, both positive and negative (e.g., Licoppe and Heurtin, 2001). On the positive side, people can reach you all the time. On the negative side, people can reach you all the time. Such tensions too are present in the experiences with media spaces. On the one hand the media spaces provided support for awareness of colleagues but from another perspective the same technology could be construed as a form of monitoring. What is important is how these tensions are realized and managed through social action that happens with the technology.

Mobility of the phone also has its implications for the notions of space and place that are important underpinnings of the media space concept (Harrison and Dourish, 1996). For media space to work, the connections were between fixed architectural spaces. The knowable relationship between media space nodes and particular architectural spaces provided some of the foundations on which people made judgments about appropriate social action and interaction. With the mobile phone, the connection possibilities between people across distance are not bound to particular architectural space. On the one hand this provides an important flexibility and a fluid network of connections that is not bound to particular space. However, it can remove some of the significant cues necessary to make judgments about the appropriate levels of engagement to be had, as the context is inherently unpredictable. This is not to argue that place is not important for conducting mobile video telephony; on the contrary, it is an extremely important practical concern – one that can create problems and one that needs to be managed (cf. Brown and O'Hara, 2003).

In the remainder of the chapter, we explore these issues further. Drawing on an answerphone diary and interview study of 21 established mobile video telephony users (O'Hara et al., 2006) we examine the social and practical aspects of usage and the ways it becomes part of people's everyday lives. In our discussion we will attempt to draw parallels and points of contrast with the traditional video telephony and media space work (e.g., Bly et al., 1993; Bellotti and Sellen, 1993; Buxton and Moran, 1990; Dourish et al., 1996; Dourish and Bly, 1992; Finn et al., 1997; Gaver et al., 1993, 1992a, b; Mackay, 1999, Mantei et al., 1991; Sellen and Harper, 1997; Sellen, 1995; Tang and Isaacs, 1993).

## When and Where

Before entering into a deeper discussion about the social and behavioral practices surrounding mobile video telephony it is worth briefly noting how often people were making these calls and where they were doing it. Relative to audio calls, the average number of video calls over the 5-week period was low, with people making one video call approximately every 2 weeks and receiving one approximately every 3 weeks. While there are certain mitigating factors contributing to this low frequency such as difficulties with 3G network coverage in some locations, these do not tell the whole story. Rather, much of the reason for the low frequency of video calls lies in social issues and motivations surrounding the use of mobile video telephony in the variety of places where it could be used.

In terms of where video calls were made, almost half were made in circumstances and locations away from work and home locations that might traditionally be associated with media spaces and video telephony. A fifth of all the calls made were while people were "out and about", 14% from a retail environment, 8% from a car, 6% from public transport, and 4% from a public bar. Mobility was obviously an important part of enabling video calls in these spaces. But in the home and work environment too where respectively 30% and 19% of calls were made, the mobile nature of the video call had important implications for the ways calls were managed. We will discuss this further later.

### *Why Were People Video Calling*

One of the interesting properties of media spaces was the ability to move from awareness to more focussed functional talk – from outeraction to interaction. Surprisingly, mobile video telephony did not prove particularly useful for this. Less than a quarter (22%) of all mobile video calls were used for the functional purpose of achieving specific goals such as making arrangements for work, organizing nights out, or simply to discuss when and where to meet up for lunch. Even in those circumstances when it was used, invariably they said "just because they could" rather than due to something useful about the video channel. Such occasions tended to be when they needed to speak with someone who happened to have a video phone; they were just opportunities to use the technology with little to suggest this kind of talk would be a long-term feature of video call use. As PW says, *"you don't use it if you really have something important to talk about,"* a sentiment shared by the majority of participants who suggested it was not suitable for the purpose.

This reaction to the video in these circumstances was not neutral and, indeed, it was felt that mobile video calls detracted from the ability to have a serious conversational exchange. There was a video and connection quality issue here for which there was often a need for conversational repair work to be done. But there are additional properties of the mobile video channel where looking at the caller through the small window of the mobile device is deemed somewhat unnatural and attention demanding. It can be difficult to look away at other things during these calls and this can lead to a difficult, distracted and stilted conversation.

> "So just before the end of the [video] call I asked Raj when would be a good time for an audio call so that we could talk business. With audio only it is much less distracting and chaotic... Because you are concentrating so much on the video call you sometimes don't think about what you are saying too much and you sometimes lose the point you have actually phoned up for and you end up sort of staring and going "well, I'll call you some other time – I'll see you later"." SM

Some of these properties have also been reported in other video-mediated communication and indeed media spaces. But there is a difference here. With the traditional media spaces such as RAVE (Gaver et al., 1992) there was a greater opportunity for people to move in and out of focussed conversations that made it less demanding and more natural than with a mobile video phone. Consequently, for many of the participants in the current study, an audio call from their mobile was often the preferable choice.

A much stronger reason for people choosing to use mobile video telephony had to do with social and emotional factors and the ability of the mobile and video to enhance some of these factors (cf. Short et al., 1976). As with other kinds of mobile calls, mobile video telephony was used for what has become known as "small talk" – such talk about "keeping in touch" – sharing what is going on in each other's lives, expressing care and affection and through this help nurture personal relationships between friends and family (cf. Dunbar, 1996; Vincent and Harper, 2003; Fox, 2001; Taylor and Harper, 2003). Indeed it accounted for approximately half the video calls logged in the study. Some parallels can be drawn here with early media space motivations and demonstrated values. The ongoing awareness and connectivity of the early media spaces was important in creating social capital. Simply knowing some of the small things promoted through awareness was an important foundation for relationship building in these spaces. While not always connected, the mobility of the video phones and mobile phones in general has allowed people to weave this "small talk" opportunistically into the other threads of their everyday lives. It is the ubiquitous potential for connectivity provided by mobile video telephony that confers some of the properties of a persistent always on connectivity of media spaces despite being a call-based structure.

Yet mobile video telephony cannot be regarded as a simple replacement of normal mobile audio calls for this kind of talk. Rather video calling was perceived to take more effort than audio both in making and participating in a call. This meant that the participants thought of video telephony as more appropriate for special circumstances and special relationships. Indeed, when a video call was made, the extra effort involved helped denote the importance of the call and relationship.

> The video thing becomes a bit more of a special occasion thing because it sort of takes a bit more to achieve it... It's not an everyday use of the phone. SF

Some parallels can be drawn with early media space work where important observations of the system concerned the social meaning that was created through the different models of possible connectivity even in circumstances where underlying technical implementations were the same. What we see here with the mobile video telephony is the ability to demonstrate social meaning through the choice of call type.

Video telephony was then part of the suite of possibilities for keeping in touch with small talk and maintaining ongoing awareness. It tended to be used primarily within "special" relationships or for special circumstances where the visual element would add something extra. Couples were a key example of such a special relationship; in particular, those who are away from each other for an extended period such as travelling for work. For these people, one of the reasons for explicitly choosing to use mobile video calls was because it was seen to add a level of emotional depth to certain communications when they were geographically separated. Of interest here is how mobility plays an important role in allowing particular kinds of these calls to be made in circumstances where fixed media space technologies and setups would be difficult because of the nature of the spaces involved and because of their contingent qualities. A good example here was the "good night" call of a particular couple when one of them was away.

> I like the idea of being able to see my husband when he's away before I go to sleep. HM

The bedroom as a place obviously has certain sensitivities associated with it that would present difficulties for introducing a fixed and persistent media space node. The mobile video phone afforded a certain level of control over when such capabilities could be introduced within such as space. In addition, one end of the connection in these circumstances is unpredictable in terms of its location since different hotels were inhabited accordingly depending on the particular geographic location of the travelling partner. Consequently, until we get to a point of greater ubiquity of media space nodes in different locations such as hotel rooms (as we do with fixed line phones and internet connectivity for example), the mobile video phone was able to provide a capability for easily introducing visual connectivity from a diverse set of locations.

In another episode, we also see how the visual aspect of the video call facilitated the expression of moral support when the one partner was lonely or down. The participant in question had been working away from home and was waiting on the platform at Rugby station at night to get a train home. She was upset at the announcement of all trains being cancelled.

> Dave and I are a couple. So I go away on business and he is stuck at home or he goes away on business and I am stuck at home. It's actually really nice to be able to see your partner. It's nice to see the object of your affections on the other end of the phone.... It gets to be stupid things – here I am on Rugby Station. I'm just about to go and find a taxi to Coventry because they have cancelled all the trains.... If you are particularly miserable a little bit of support would be nice and yeah I can ring him on the audio and he will say things to me but if I'm particularly miserable its quite nice to sort of say here I am Look I'm really miserable do something – he just says 'Hello Bunny it's alright, I Love you [laughs].' SF

Another type of relationship for which the video element of telephony was important was between family members and children: sons, daughters, nieces, and nephews.

> I made a call home the other night to see the children when I was away from home it was just good to see their faces. SB

These parent–child relationships have a special quality that lends itself to video telephony. For other types of family relationships and friendships, people suggested that familiarity made it easy to visualize the people they were talking to. In these cases the video element added little to everyday audio calls. With children, however, there was a sense of a continuous process of getting to know them. Because they undergo rapid change when they are young, the visual element becomes more important.

> With Raj I will happily just call him on audio call but if I think the kids might be home I would prefer to video call. I reckon because there is that whole familiarity – you want to get to know your nephews and kids etc. ... I don't want to waste money on calling someone I am familiar with ... If my brother [Raj] was living in this town I wouldn't phone him up on video call just for the sake of seeing him. I'd just audio call him because he is close to me. Once you have that familiarity with someone you don't need that unless you want to show them something. SM

The visual element of the call was particularly rewarding with children because they did things which were visibly cute or visibly funny and which are missed in audio calls.

> One of the nephews had spaghetti dangling from his mouth which was a funny thing to see. SM.

Indeed the visual was one of the primary ways in which children were able to communicate so:

> They're not really for communicating. It doesn't matter with the kids because all they want to do is jump around in front of the screen. That really ought to be the selling point. HM

For one participant, the mobile video phone allowed him to experience important routines in the children's lives, (e.g., bath time) which he would otherwise miss by virtue of being at work or on the way home from work when this activity took place. The mobility of the video phone is important in this case in part because it could be taken to the bathroom to provide access to the service in that place. But another factor is the flexibility of timing over when the service can be accessed. The argument here concerns the ability to flexibly coordinate different activity schedules of the connecting parties. The father's location was contingent on his particular work schedule and activities for that day and not something that was always fixed and predictable. With the traditional fixed media spaces, connectivity between people is not simply about the physical connection between these spaces but also dependent on an ability to map the activity rhythms of these spaces. An obvious example here can be seen in the time zone differences between PARC and EuroPARC which meant that for large part of each working day there were only small windows of overlapping connectivity between the spaces. Of course mobility does not necessarily overcome differences in time zones, but the point is that it does provide a much greater flexibility for matching activity rhythms between spaces (cf. Churchill and Wakeford, 2001).

A further example of using the mobile video to talk to children and family illustrates another important difference between these mobile video calls and traditional fixed media spaces. In this example participant SM, the uncle of the children concerned, called up the family at home during meal time in order to be able to speak with the children. The father, who received the call, passed it around the children as they sat at the table eating and they *"got very excited by the video phone and Uncle Sanj phoning up."* The issue here is not that fixed media space technologies could not accommodate such family gatherings in the way they are set up. The issue rather is that there are times when traditional media space set-ups require people to configure themselves around. With the mobile device, the ability to pass the phone around the different family members meant that the video call could be fitted within the existing configuration of the family activity which in turn limited disruption of routine family life. This contributes to the ability to accept and manage the call successfully.

### Show and Talk

One of the key motivations behind the traditional media space developments was the ability to show things in support of a conversation. Indeed, the relative benefits of shared object views versus "talking heads" within media space collaborations has been a consistent theme of research in the area over the past 20 years and one of the persistent benefits of video telephony (e.g., Whittaker, 2003). Unsurprisingly then, the desire to show or see something of the caller or recipient context was an important motivation underlying a significant number of video calls reported in the study (28%). What is noteworthy to discuss though is again what is afforded by the mobile properties of the video calls seen in the study both at the macro and micro levels (Luff and Heath, 1998). This is illustrated by an example from one of the participants who made a video call from a shop to discuss with her friends a dress she wanted for an upcoming wedding.

> I tended to use it when opportunities presented themselves. Usually if there was a visual thing that needed to be seen.... Last week I was getting a dress on my own for a wedding and I thought I'll use the video ... I could put a dress on and call Amie and show her it to get her opinion. It was nice doing this because I like to have a second opinion and it was like she was there. FB

Three key features are important from this perspective. First, the mobility of the phone allowed the participant to make the video call in a shop and more specifically in the changing room with a full length mirror. Second was the opportunistic nature of this event. Only because the phone is carried around all the time was such opportunistic use of video telephony possible. The third feature concerns the "framing" of the object to show. Achieving the correct framing is dependent on the "micro-mobility" of the mobile video phone to get it into the correct position and orientation, something that is more difficult with fixed video telephony and media space counterparts. In this instance, successful framing was dependent also on having a full length mirror in the changing room allowing the user to position the phone far enough away from her reflection to show enough of the dress (this would have been difficult to do simply by holding the camera away from her own body, suggesting the need either for a wider angle lens or mechanism for supporting the video phone on a surface). Some of these properties were available to an extent within the early media space experiments with people picking up cameras and moving them in order to facilitate showing episodes. Likewise camera lens zooming could help with framing. But the tethered nature of the cameras did not offer the same level of flexibility that was possible with the mobile video phones.

The act of showing things is also a dynamic process that involves continuous repositioning of the camera during a call. Note though, that video performance would often suffer under movement, becoming broken and pixelated under image-processing algorithms optimized for relatively constant scene components. Mobility, then, both created opportunities as well as sometimes detracting from the experience.

It is important to examine this "showing" behavior within the broader context of the conversation. Talk was used to introduce and narrate over images being shown, requiring a delicately timed choreography between face-to-face and object views displayed on the phone screen. This broader conversational context surrounding opportunities for showing helps understand why some participants reported missed opportunities for showing things with video telephony. These opportunities for showing would come up in the course of audio phone calls, but without an easy way to switch to a video call from audio call, the participants let the opportunity pass in order to avoid the social disruption of ending the audio call and starting a video call.

## Social Barriers to Video Calling

The management of public–private boundaries was something that has been a fundamental concern for media space technology since its introduction 20 years ago (e.g., Bellotti and Sellen, 1993). The introduction of networked cameras into spaces changes a number of the dynamics of privacy management that are seen when people share normal physical space. For example, properties of reciprocity where you can see someone who can see you are no longer available with the media space environment. Lots of the research with these technologies was about understanding these shifting dynamics introduced by the technology, what people did to work within these new parameters and design interventions to provide ways to help support the management of public and private boundaries (e.g., introducing audio announcements for camera glances or social rules for "office share" features).

One important feature of the traditional media space environment was the fact that these technologies were fixed to a place. This provided predictable and knowable parameters within which to make judgments about how to interact with people in the space. Such fixity of space is not something that can be known in the mobile environment. The mobility of the phone has taken personal telecommunications into all sorts of public spaces, giving people the ability to contact others and be contacted. This brings its own unique challenges to the ways people manage their public–private boundaries and what they reveal about us in these contexts (Palen and Dourish, 2003). In this section we discuss the impact of video phones on people's ability to manage various public–private boundaries between self and copresent others, between caller and recipient and the boundaries of the copresent others.

## Managing Boundaries Between Self and Copresent Others

When we consider how people make mobile audio calls in public settings, a range of strategies are available for managing boundaries between themselves and others. These strategies include talking quietly; crafting verbal responses to be meaningful within the context of the "hidden" half of the conversation; physically withdrawing to a less public place (e.g., Fox, 2001; Grinter and Eldridge, 2001; Taylor and Harper, 2003); or simply not making and taking calls when there are other people present. With mobile video telephony a number of new factors are introduced that impact people's ability to adopt these strategies. So while, in theory, having a mobile video phone should provide the capability for making these video calls anytime anywhere, the difficulties with the management of the public–private boundary in these spaces created social barriers to its use.

The problems here stemmed from the need to hold a mobile video phone at arms length or positioned on a surface at a distance from the face (see Fig. 19.1).

**Fig. 19.1** Positioning of mobile video phone for calling

This necessitated use of the phone loudspeaker making the normally "hidden" side of the call audible for those within earshot. This is illustrated by participant FB:

> Yes it does constrain you to some extent as it always tends to be a little loud and everyone can hear what your conversation is about so if the conversation is a little banal everyone can hear both sides of the conversation … you can keep it more discreet with a voice call. FB

Not only was the "normally hidden" side of a call broadcast on loudspeaker, participants also noted how they talked louder on a video call than they would with an audio call. Again this restricted the normal strategies of talking quietly to manage public–private boundaries during mobile calls in public settings. As MW commented:

> When I'm at work or he is at work you don't [make video calls] because it's more obvious that you are making a personal call. Its very obvious because you are stood there like this [holds out arm simulating video call pose] and you tend to talk a bit louder because the mic is over here [reaches out in front of him where the mic would be]…you don't want to be seen to make too many personal calls at work. MW

The concern here is not about keeping secrets. Rather it is about how they present themselves to other people in the public setting through the details of their conversation and how people perceive them as a result (see Chapter 14 for a discussion of the different types of disclosure that people imply when talking about privacy). Consequently, they became self-conscious because the salience of the conversation made them socially accountable to those copresent (cf. Murtagh, 2002). This accountability further related to whether the talk was appropriate within the tacit social rules of their particular context (cf. Palen et al., 2000). For participant FB, her embarrassment was about the "banality" of the conversation in front of strangers. For MW, the concern was how he was being perceived at work and that he was seen to work rather than make personal calls. Personal audio calls at work are easier for him to disguise and so more readily made and received during a normal work day.

Some of these difficulties could be overcome using the earpieces that came with the mobile video phones. While participants considered the concept good for maintaining privacy, the reality was that they are not always available to use.

> You just can't carry them about, you lose them. It's as simple as that. PW

They were therefore never readily available in the situations where calls were being made and received.

### Video Display Available to Copresent Others

The video channel also became a public feature of the communication when making a video call with other people around. Again if we consider the typical position of the phone during a video call (see Fig. 19.1), this made the display available for others around to see. For SF, this created a source of embarrassment:

> It was quite embarrassing. He called me when I was on the train and I was like err I'm talking to my phone – it's embarrassing. "HELLO, I'M ON THE TRAIN" pales into insignificance compared to this – Some poor soul sat next to you. And of course the person next to you becomes quite fascinated and they start staring into the phone. And you are like "do you mind I'm trying to have a conversation here" – it's very public. SF

Of course sharing the display with the copresent others can be valuable creating a more collaborative phone experience for small groups of friends (see Fig. 19.1 for an example of shared use of the display). But the point here is about how the shared visibility of the screen makes it difficult to control the boundaries and when to reveal the display versus when to hide the display from copresent others. This was exacerbated by the fact that people near to the video phone had a tendency to dive in, waving or pulling funny faces. This resulted in somewhat chaotic and unfocussed call as is well highlighted by SM:

> The phone call has a chaotic feel to it that is not so much the case with audio calls – everyone is trying to take part and get in the picture – it is less focussed. The chaos is enjoyable but it makes other things difficult to achieve in the conversation. SM

The consequences of these various difficulties are numerous. Mobile video calls in public situations become an awkward experience and in some cases end abruptly:

> Also there's a slight embarrassment factor as well, when you're out making a call… Shaun called me once from Victoria Station and he said he had to stop the call because he was being stared at… FB

People also became reluctant to make video calls in certain places, as participant DW suggests:

> I haven't been using much because she is at work and a video call – she has only just got her own office and it wasn't very private to have a video chat because the offices were open before. DW

Receiving video calls in public situations was particularly problematic for participants because of the unanticipated nature of the call and the recipient's lack of control over where the video call was made and who was around. As participant LC described it, *"receiving them is inconvenient."* Under such "inconvenient" circumstances, participants either: didn't answer the call at all, answered it only to defer the call until a later time, or ended the video call and made an audio call instead. When asked about his reactions to receiving a video call, participant MW commented:

> It obviously depends on where I am. If it's at work I might say "I'll call you back". I would answer it. There is no point in ignoring it … I might call them back on an audio call or wait until lunchtime. MW

This highlights the difficulties managing the public–private boundaries between self and copresent others and results in missed or deferred opportunities for mobile video calls to take place. What can be seen here is the way mobility creates an unpredictability of place and context that not only makes receiving calls difficult but also makes it difficult for callers to make judgments about when would be an appropriate time to call. With the fixed media space experiments the purpose was to exploit the understandable context of a place to help make judgments about communication. In addition, one of the goals of media spaces was to visually provide awareness to potential communicators that gave further context for the judgments about how to communicate with colleagues.

## Managing the Boundaries Between Caller and Recipient

The way a caller and recipient could present themselves and their circumstances to each other also determined people's acceptance of mobile video telephony.

### Video Reveals Too Much Information

It is well established that video telephony can reveal too much visual information, making people self-conscious about how they come across to the other person. In longer term media space experiments these factors were less of an issue but it was certainly apparent in some of the participants' attitudes towards mobile video calling. The reasons for this again stem from some of the key underlying factors of the ergonomics of phone positioning and unpredictability of context that arises from the mobile capabilities. The ergonomics of positioning the video phone to talk and view creates an odd *"camera angle [that] looks straight up your nose and [makes] you look awful" (PW)*. The main cause, though, was the mobility of the phone which afforded spontaneous use at unpredictable times, places, and behavioral contexts outside the recipient's control. In some of these contexts video calling was regarded as "*invasive*" because it revealed too much information which participants wanted to control, e.g., their appearance, as PW describes:

> I used it in conversation with this French girl. When she used it for the first time, she'd just got out of bed, she was in her pyjamas, her hair was a mess and she's never used it since.... it's too invasive. If I got a video call, half the time I wouldn't use it. It's like having someone walking in your house and saying 'what are you doing?' I don't want that. PW

At other times, there were aspects of the place and behavioral context that would have been too much to reveal. In one such episode, SM had an opportunity to make a video call to his parents but explicitly chose to make an audio call instead since he was at his flat in bed with his girlfriend, both of them only half dressed. He knew his parents tacitly disapproved of him "*living in sin*". *"It's not that they don't know that it is going on but if it is not mentioned, things are fine and there is no conflict."* (SM). So in this situation he chose not to make a video call because it would reveal too much about his current context and make explicit the issue of his living arrangements. This would have led to conflict with his parents which he was able to avoid through the use of audio alone.

### Visual Channel Makes it Difficult to Lie

Video did not just reveal too much information but also made it difficult to "distort the truth" due to the fact that you were looking someone "in the eye."

> You can't really lie can you? You don't want to lie do you but you know...You can't call someone and say look I'm in so and so can you? Say if I call Shaun and say "I'm at so and so and I'll be there in 10 minutes" and really you're somewhere else and you're going to be 20 minutes. You can't do that with a video call. FB

The management of social relationships through "white lies" in this way is complex and subtle. People use ambiguity in how they project their identity and circumstances for all sorts of social reasons, both good and bad. Mobile phones have allowed people to manage these kinds of interactions by exploiting particular ambiguities associated with their use (Plant, 2002). Place, in particular, is difficult to assess during a mobile phone call as is indicated by the standard "where are you?" question that accompanies most opening sections of a mobile phone conversation. Fixed telephony does not have this issue to some extent and neither does a traditional media space. Binding camera to a place means that there is little room for ambiguity of location information for the person on the other end of the connection. Mobile video calls lie some where in between mobile audio calls and media spaces in this regard. While there is uncertainty regarding where someone is when they make or receive a video call, the video channel actually makes it a bit more difficult to convincingly distort the truth about where you are. In part this is the inherent difficulty of lying on someone's face but it also has to do with the fact that the video potentially reveals further information about one's surroundings. These difficulties in managing ambiguities, then, compromise the very social flexibility that has made the mobile audio phone a significant technology in people's lives. Interestingly, in response to the prevalent use of white lies on mobile phones, one participant, who was late for a meeting used a video call to explicitly show she was approaching the entrance to the office building, demonstrating the veracity of her circumstances.

## Managing the Boundaries of Copresent Others

The boundaries being managed during mobile video calls in public places were not just those of the callers themselves. Video calls also had an impact on those in the vicinity. The annoyance caused to people in the vicinity by mobile audio calls in public places has been documented (Plant, 2002).

### Aural Intrusiveness

Study participants felt that mobile video call in public places were even more disruptive due to the increased volume of talk with mobile video calls (see earlier discussion around phone positioning and the consequent perceived need to talk louder) the other conversation half on loudspeaker. Those who considered the needs of others around them were conscious of social pressure to avoid using video telephony in these places. In one episode with PW in a ski cabin on holiday with friends, the complaints from his friends in the vicinity resulted in a lost opportunity for a "show and talk" video call:

> I used the phone in the ski tele-cabin and the other guys complained. PW

It is interesting to think about these issues in light of the early media space experiments. Much of the early work at PARC and EuroPARC with media spaces was located in a workplace organized around individual closed offices. This represents a different challenge from some of the more public locations that mobile video telephony was taking place. In closed offices, there are much less concerns about aural intrusiveness (and indeed some of the privacy concerns that accompany this). It is worth reflecting on whether different types of more open workplace environments would change people's orientation to a media space installation.

### Intrusiveness of Camera

The prime concern in relation to managing others' public–private boundaries, though, came not from aural intrusiveness, but from the intrusiveness of introducing a camera into other people's space.

> I have one friend, basically just didn't want to be seen on the call. When I used it on the train my friend just disliked the idea of being involved in my phone call. PW

What is significant here is how the video call compromised the ability of the copresent other to choose whether or not they got involved in a call. As participant MD said:

> Someone else has the choice of joining in a voice call but on video they are forced to join the call because [of the camera]. MD

With standard audio calls, copresent others can choose not to get involved in a call simply by not speaking. With video calls, copresent people are passively involved which removes their control. This introduces the same issues of managing the presentation of identity and behavioral context discussed in the previous section but this time for the copresent others. In this context though, the copresent other created an additional social pressure against the video call being taken in that place. In the following example, we see this cause recipient of the video call to leave the room.

> The call came through while I was sat on the sofa with my girlfriend. So I got up from the sofa and went to the bedroom to take the call. She was on the sofa in her pyjamas so that is why I went to the bedroom but also with the video calls you are on speaker phone so it picks up a lot of ambient noise more – the TV was on and this gets picked up – it would have been really difficult for the person at the other end. MW

In this instance, the participant exploited the mobility of the video phone to remove himself from the situation where he was compromising his partner's privacy.

There are some related issues with the early media space work. People visiting a media space for the first time would often demonstrate a certain amount of uncomfortableness about inadvertently being on camera, even when the camera was not intended for them. But with a fixed installation, people have some control over whether they enter into a place where there were cameras. By contrast, mobile video phones can be taken into places and in ways that are beyond the control of other people around, making it potentially more difficult to manage.

## *Practical Barriers to Video Calling*

The literature on mobile phone usage reveals that a key value of mobile phone technology is the ability to make use of "dead time" – time spent in places where activities are restricted and which would otherwise be wasted, e.g., while travelling (Perry et al., 2001). The phone's mobility means it can be carried at all times, providing access to telephony when and where people choose. As such, it is always available to exploit "dead time" when it arises. The same argument should of course apply to mobile video telephony and indeed provide some of the spontaneity missing from traditional fixed video telephony. However, some important practical factors prevented frequent, spontaneous video calling in dead time in particular spaces. These included: high ambient noise, poor lighting, and problems of dual tasking while video calling.

### Ambient Noise

As we discussed earlier, the mobile phone during a video call was either held at arms length or positioned on a surface at arms length in order to get a full face view in the camera frame. A consequence of this was that the microphone was left open to surrounding ambient noise which proved to be distracting to the person at the other end of the video call. The position of the phone also necessitated listening to the conversation on loudspeaker and again this had to compete with the ambient noise in public spaces making it difficult to hear. So, for example, several participants experienced difficulties trying to have a video call in a bar. Likewise traffic noise on the street made it difficult to conduct video calls in urban spaces.

> I was in the street and that was a little difficult to hear because of the traffic. IP

In the following quote we see how this had an impact on a participant's ability to use the phone in "dead time" in the pub while waiting for someone else to arrive – a typical and important behavior with a standard mobile phone.

> "After the trial ends I don't think I'd use it … There are just too many problems making the call … if you use it in the street you can't hear it. We often make calls in the pub and you can't hear it… but it is there that you want to do things with your phone while you are waiting for someone. PW

Again, some participants, when possible, worked around these constraints by exploiting the very mobility of the phone from which the original difficulties stemmed; withdrawing to quieter places that met the audio requirements of making a video call. As MW commented:

> If I'm in the pub I'll do like with a normal audio call – I'll go to the loos or find a nice quiet spot or out in the corridor. It's primarily for the audio – you need to be heard. MW

Movement away from places with ambient noise was not always possible causing missed video calling opportunities.

### Lighting

Noise, though, was not the only environmental constraint. Low light levels also hindered people's ability to use mobile video telephony effectively. Several participants had tried video calling while walking on the street at night. Participant KB for example, wanted to video call her partner on the way home from work (again it is typical mobile phone behavior to get in touch with a partner at the end of a work day). However, being dark outside she was unable to. SM reported similar frustrations:

> You can't use it at night either because you just see a little coloured blob on the screen so you think why am I using a video call. SM

Lighting difficulties were not restricted to outdoors at night. People also experienced difficulties in some indoor environments with artificial light. In part this was due to the dimness of the lighting conditions but also because of the position of the overhead lighting with respect to the video phone. Again the positioning of the device during a video call compounds the problems here. The natural position of the phone so that the display seen was lower than the head. This meant the camera pointed upwards towards the head and also the light sources in the ceiling resulting in a silhouetting of the person making it impossible to see them. As participant AB noted:

> You do have to get the position right because of the light and also if you put the camera in the wrong place they can see literally up your nose … there's a certain amount of angling. AB

It is not the case that such environmental constraints could not be overcome with careful positioning or by waiting for more suitable lighting. Rather, these factors added effort to the process of making a call and eroded much of the flexibility a mobile device is meant to create. This reduction of flexibility made it difficult for mobile video telephony to enter all aspects of people's lives in the same way that mobile audio calling has done.

These issues are a significant source of contrast with fixed media space installation. One of the significant things that characterizes fixed installations is precisely the ability to control for the ambient conditions that make up the space in terms of lighting and sound. There is an inherent predictability of fixed space that allows certain assumptions to be made in optimizing the components and settings within a fixed media space. What is clear from the early experiments with media spaces and indeed more recently with HP's Halo collaboration studios (http://www.hp.com/halo/introducing.html), is that attention to detail in terms of audio and video setup and environmental control, such as lighting and ambient noise, can contribute significantly to a successful experience of video-mediated collaboration and presence.

### Problems of Dual Tasking

A particular concern for people was the ability to use time efficiently by dual tasking. Making and receiving telephone calls was often something people would do while simultaneously carrying out other tasks, such as reading email, doing household chores, driving, or even just walking. Unlike audio calls, video calls interfered with the ability to do other tasks. For example:

> When I call on a hands-free [audio] phone I can put the phone down during a call and get on with other things. With a video call you can't do that. It would be a bit rude or there would just be no point in using the video at all. MD

These extracts indicate a concern both to *see* and *be seen* by the person at the other end during a video call. While theoretically possible for these participants to revert to hands-free loudspeaker, they were reluctant to do so. The issue here was not just physical but rather social: it was considered rude to create an asymmetry in the video channel where only one participant was in view.

Of course the mobility of the video phone allowed more flexibility than a traditional fixed video phone. There were some examples when people would move around the house during a video call, but this was more to *get to* another room rather than for ongoing movement while doing other tasks. As participant MW commented, video calls are *"difficult to do while walking"* not only because of the demands of maintaining visual contact but also because holding the phone in front of you is uncomfortable for all but short time periods and ties up your hands. Unlike mobile audio phones, cradling the phone on your shoulder while video calling was not a practical option.

Participants' frustrations about the constraints on dual tasking imposed by video telephony were not simply about time efficiency and convenience but also about safety. Trying to have a video call while walking in the street created concern by not wanting to *"be a prat and walk to a lamp post" (MW)*. Similarly, with driving: the demands on visual attention that video calling makes were simply too dangerous for people to make or receive calls while driving. Yet for many people, the car, to and from work, was a key place for communicating with people during otherwise dead time. The inappropriateness of mobile video telephony for the car context created a barrier to it being used as an everyday tool. So while the mobility of the device enabled ubiquitous access to video telephony, the video element essentially hindered the ability to exploit this ubiquity.

## Discussion and Conclusions

Looking at the everyday practices of mobile video in this way allows us to reflect on the relationship of mobile video telephony with its technical predecessors in the early media space and video telephony work. On a purely technical level, one might argue that mobile video telephony provides the flexibility to create on-the-fly media spaces whenever and wherever people happen to be. But as we have seen with the early media space work, the technology was not simply about making connections between physical spaces and creating new kinds of spaces. Rather, what was important was the ways that these technologies allowed people to act in new or different ways to develop a sense of place and to operate within the social context of the place. With mobile video telephony, what we have seen in the study is how the mobile nature of the device offers new opportunities for how we can act in particular places but also introduces a new set of constraints by virtue of the range of places it potentially inhabits.

The point here is not that mobile is better than fixed or that fixed is better than mobile. Rather, the fixed and the mobile together offer a range of possibilities for action as a result of their particular design characteristics, sometimes similar and sometimes distinct. What is important for us to understand is the ways that the physical and contextual properties of these different communication and awareness devices shape the choices that people are making in terms of how they communicate or maintain awareness of remote others.

Mobile video telephony, then, provided a certain flexibility for calls to be interleaved with the ongoing activities of everyday life in terms of when and where they could be made and received. This applied to large-scale mobility where people were "out and about," as well as to smaller scale mobility (e.g., at home) where they could move the video telephony capabilities from room to room as activities demanded. Such flexibility applied too to the showing of things during a video call both in terms of large- and small-scale mobility. But it is this very flexibility that brings with it some of the difficulties of use that are particular to mobile video telephony relative to its fixed counterparts. What was important about fixed media space setups were that they were more understandable, predictable, and knowable because they were not changing. This made it easier for all parties, local and remote to make judgments about appropriate ways to act within those places. It made it easier also to manage the boundaries between public and private actions. Even though new behaviors had to be learned in this regard, it was in some ways the fixity and persistence of these installed media spaces that facilitated the development of new social conventions. Similarly, with a fixed environment it was much easier to design things to overcome some of the practical constraints such as ambient lighting and noise issues associated with the mobile environment. With mobile video telephony, the flexibility that was otherwise valuable, in some ways made it more difficult to be able to or know how to act appropriately. This is because there is an inherent uncertainty over when and where people can make or receive mobile video calls. When this uncertainty is combined with the rather visually and aurally open nature of video calls, it can lead to certain difficulties in managing the public and private boundaries and in overcoming some of the practical constraints to usage.

It is also worth reflecting on the potentially shifting attitudes towards mobile video telephony. We have identified a number of areas where the mobile nature of video calls creates certain social difficulties. There are undoubtedly inherent properties of the device that create these difficulties but we might expect that work-around behaviors and attitude shifts occur that reduce some of the barriers they create. One of the lessons from the longer-term media space experiments is that attitudes towards them and the ways that they get used change over time as they are assimilated into people's everyday lives and as people learn to shift their behaviors in response to the presence of the technology to create more positive outcomes. We have seen such shifts too with regards to mobile phone use as people's attitudes have changed dramatically over when and where these devices get used. We would imagine that as people learn about some of the properties of mobile video devices as outlined in the study, they will be able to develop some appropriate workarounds to allow a more successful assimilation into their social interactions.

However, we cannot expect such assimilation to be entirely based on workarounds. As with the early media space research, careful design interventions can help users manage the social and practical barriers to mobile video calls to create more opportunities for its use. A key design implication here would be to support a more fluid switching between audio and video modalities such that people can more fluidly exploit the properties of each modality according to particular practical and social circumstances. An interesting solution to consider here would be a "push-to-video" model in which the video channel can be introduced to the conversation from a standard audio call simply by pressing a button. This model would allow callers to default to audio calls (for easier management of privacy and ambient noise in public places). Then, through negotiation over the audio, callers can agree to introduce video if circumstances are appropriate. This "push-to-video" model also helps capture lost opportunities for show and talk by allowing users to respond more opportunistically to the evolving content of a conversation. If an opportunity to show something arises during an audio call, users can push the button to start the video channel. Likewise ways of providing better understanding of recipient context would allow better movement from awareness to dialogue (a key benefit of the early media space work). Interesting ideas to this would revolve around ways of making the receiver's contextual information available to potential video callers without compromising on privacy concerns (e.g., Milewshi and Smith, 2000; Pedersen, 2001). As Tang (Chapter 26, this volume) mentions new sensing and communication technologies are creating new opportunities for how this might be achieved.

In this chapter, we have drawn a number of comparisons and points of contrast with respect to media spaces and mobile video telephony that allow us to understand the possibilities for action and constraints on action. What is important to acknowledge is not simply that fixed media space work has helped inspire some of the technological developments that have brought us to an age of mobile video telephony. Rather, it is the theoretical and conceptual legacy of the early media space work that is more important and long lasting. Take for example the notions of privacy, notions of awareness, models of connectivity (call-based versus always-on-office share) and notions of space and place. It is these foundations that have provided a framework within it has been possible to understand some of the everyday practices of mobile video telephony and the points of comparison and contrast with earlier media spaces. And it is these foundations that will continue to allow us to interpret and understand everyday practices with future instantiations of this genre of technology.

## References

Bellotti, V. and Sellen, A. (1993) Designing for Privacy in Ubiquitous Computing Environments. In *Proceedings of ECSCW'93*, Milano, Italy.

Bly, S., Harrison, S. and Irwin, S. (1993) Media spaces: Bringing people together in a video audio and computing environment. *Communications of the ACM* special issue, 36(1): 29–47, January, 1993.

Brown, B and O'Hara, K. (2003) Place as a practical concern of mobile workers. *Environment and Planning A*, 35, 1565–1587.

Buxton, W. and Moran, T. (1990): "EuroPARC's Integrated Interactive Intermedia Facility (IIIF): Early Experiences", in *Proc. IFIP Conference on Multi-User Interfaces and Applications*, Herakleion, Crete, September 1990.

Churchill, E. and Wakeford, N. (2001) Framing Mobile Collaborations and Mobile Technologies. In B. Brown, N. Green, R. Harper (Eds.) *Wireless World: Social and Interactional Aspects of the Mobile Age*. London: Springer-Verlag.

Dourish, P., Adler, A., Bellotti, V. and Henderson, A. (1996) Your Place or Mine? Learning from Long-Term Use of Audio-Video Communication. *Computer-Supported Cooperative Work*, 5(1), pp. 33–62.

Dourish, P. and Bly, S. (1992). Portholes: Supporting awareness in a distributed work group. In *Proceedings of Human Factors in Computing Systems, CHI'92* (Monterey, CA), pp. 541–547. New York: ACM Press.

Dunbar, R. (1996) *Grooming, Gossip and the Evolution of Language*. London: Faber and Faber.

Finn, K., Sellen, A. and Wilbur, S. (1997.) *Video-mediated Communication*. Hillsdale, NJ: Lawrence Erlbaum.

Fox, K. (2001) Evolution, alienation and gossip: The role of mobile telecommunications in 21st century. *Social Issues Research Centre Report*, Oxford.

Gaver, W., Sellen, A., Heath, C., and Luff, P. (1993) One is not enough: Multiple views in a media space. In *Proceedings of INTERCHI'93*, Amsterdam, The Netherlands, pp. 335–341.

Gaver, W., Moran, T., MacLean, A., Lovstrand, L., Dourish, P., Carter, K., and Buxton, W. (1992), Realizing a video environment: EuroPARC's RAVE system. In Proceedings of Human Factors in Computing Systems, *CHI'92* (Monterey, CA), ACM Press, New York, pp. 27–35.

Gaver, W.W. (1992) The affordances of media spaces for collaboration. In *Proceedings CSCW'92*, Toronto, ON, ACM Press, New York.

Grinter, R. and Eldridge, M. (2001) y do tngrs luv 2 txt msg. In *Proceedings of ECSCW'01*, Bonn Germany, pp. 219–238.

Harrison, S. and Dourish, P., (1996) "Re-Place-ing Space: The Roles of Place and Space in Collaborative Systems", *Proceedings of the 1996 Conference on Computer Supported Cooperative Work*, Boston.

Licoppe, C. and Heurtin, J.P. (2001) Managing one's availability to telephone communication through mobile phones: A French case study of the development dynamics of mobile phone use. In *Personal and Ubiquitous Computing*, 5, pp. 99–108.

Luff, P. and Heath, C. (1998) Mobility in collaboration. In *Proceedings of CSCW'98*, Seattle, WA, USA.

Mackay, W.E. (1999) Media spaces: Environments for multimedia interaction. In M. Beaudouin-Lafon (Ed.), *Computer-Supported Cooperative Work*, Trends in Software Series. Chichester: Wiley, pp. 55–82.

Mantei, M., Baecker, R., Sellen, A., Buxton, W., Milligan, T. and Wellman, B. (1991) Experiences in the use of a media space. In *Proceedings of Human Factors in Computing Systems, CHI'91*(New Orleans, LA), pp. 203–208. ACM Press, New York.

Milewshi, A.E. and Smith, T.M. (2000) Providing presence cues to telephone users. In *Proceedings of CSCW 2000*, Philadelphia, PA, pp. 89–96.

Murtagh, G. (2002) Seeing the "Rules": Preliminary observations of action, interaction and mobile phone use. In Brown, Green and Harper (Eds.) *Wireless World: Social and Interactional Aspects of the Mobile Age*. London: Springer-Verlag.

O'Hara, K., Black, A., and Lipson, M. (2006) Everyday Practices with Mobile Video Telephony. In *Proceedings of CHI 06*, Montreal, Canada.

Palen, L. and Dourish, P. (2003) Unpacking "Privacy" for a Networked World. In *Proceedings of CHI'03*, Fort Lauderdale, FL, pp. 129–136.

Palen, L., Salzman, M., and Youngs, E. (2000) Going wireless: behavior & practice of new mobile phone users. In *Proceedings of CSCW'00*, Philadelphia, PA, USA.

Pedersen, E.R. (2001) Calls.calm: Enabling Caller and Callee to Collaborate. In *Extended Abstracts of CHI 2001*, Seattle, WA.

Perry, M, O'Hara, K, Sellen, A, Brown, B and Harper, R. (2001) Dealing with mobility: Understanding access anytime, anywhere. In *ACM Transactions on Human–Computer Interaction*, 8 (4), 323–347.

Plant, S. (2002) On the Mobile: the effects of mobile telephones on social and individual life. Motorola Report http://www.motorola.com/mot/doc/0/234_MotDoc.pdf

Sellen, A.J. (1995). Remote conversations: The effects of mediating talk with technology. *Human–Computer Interaction*, 10 (4), 401–444.

Sellen, A.J. and Harper, R.H.R (1997) Video in support of organisational talk. In Finn, K., Sellen, A., and Wilbur, S. (Eds.), *Video-Mediated Communication*. Hillsdale, NJ: Lawrence Erlbaum, pp. 225–243.

Short, J., Williams, E., and Christie, B. (1976) *The Social Psychology of Telecommunications*. London: Wiley.

Tang, J. and Isaacs, E. (1993) Why do users like video? Studies of multimedia-supported collaboration. In *Computer-Supported Cooperative Work*, 1(3), 163–196.

Taylor, A. and Harper, R. (2003) The gift of the Gab: A design oriented sociology of young people's use of mobile's. In *Computer Supported Cooperative Work*, 12(3), 267–296.

Vincent, J. and Harper, R. (2003) Social Shaping of UMTS: Preparing the 3G Customer. University of Surrey, Digital World Research Centre.

Whittaker, S. (2003) Things to talk about when talking about things. *Human–Computer Interaction*, 18, 149–170.

# Chapter 20
# Media Spaces, Emergency Response and Palpable Technologies

**Margit Kristensen and Morten Kyng**

**Abstract** In this chapter we present and discuss a case on the development and use of technologies for emergency response, which shares important aspects with Media Spaces. We first describe the characteristics of emergency response, based on field and literature studies. We then present visions for technological support of emergency responders and outline important design issues and principles regarding the design. We finally reflect upon our findings in relation to Media Spaces, and describe a number of possibilities and related challenges, by the use of examples. We suggest that moving from symmetry to asymmetry and from static to non-static spaces and more generally from closed to open-ended use situations and technological setups can bring Media Space research to bear on a large spectrum of future technology, which is outside traditional Media Spaces.

## Introduction

In this chapter we present and discuss a case of the development and use of Media Space-*like* technologies for emergency response. We take emergency response as our starting point and begin with a description of how emergency response in major incidents is carried out typically in terms of organization, division of work, and collaboration. Then we move beyond this to describe our initial observations regarding action and interaction of emergency responders and their use of tools and artifacts. Against this background we present our vision and the important challenges and principles on which we build our technology development. This is followed by a description of the Information Systems (IS) prototypes we are developing, to support those who act in emergency response – prototypes that support *entity information* and *overview*. As part of the prototype descriptions we describe their

M. Kristensen
The Alexandra Institute
e-mail: margit.kristensen@alexandra.dk

M. Kyng
Department of Computer Science, University of Aarhus
e-mail: mkyng@daimi.au.dk

S. Harrison (ed.), *Media Space 20+ Years of Mediated Life*,
Computer Supported Cooperative Work,

purpose, how they are meant to be used in future emergency response situations, and how they have been used in a "real world" event.

The use of these prototypes forms what can be considered media spaces that are dynamically changing and interdependent. It supplements – or challenges – the traditional understanding of the media space concept in several ways:

- The emergency response media spaces have to be dynamic and mobile in the sense that they have to be established in ever-changing physical settings – depending on *where* and *what* the incident is,
- The settings can *also* be outdoor
- It allows the use of a range of (not necessarily predefined) media – in fact the different media applied can be *whatever* the participants want to use
- The people who join the media space(s) are *not* a pre-defined, static, or limited group of users – in fact people come and go, can be unknown to each other, regarding name, appearance, and role.

In media space terms, the prototypes in use create spaces where users of – or participants in – the media spaces obtain and maintain possibilities for orienting themselves in a common space and being oriented about other persons and things. These possibilities of knowing/seeing bodily position (subjects and objects) in the space by itself afford cooperation. We show how this can be practiced in "our" dynamic media space(s) that emerges when and – especially – *where* needed, and we consider the differences and similarities with respect to more traditional Media Spaces. We conclude with a discussion of the advantages and challenges to be explored in the future.

Our discussions of where to take the original Media Space concept are grounded in newly finished work in a large European Union project investigating "palpable computing" (PalCom, http://www.ist-palcom.org). This project researched a future where ubiquitous and palpable computing is a natural part of everyday life.

Ubiquitous computing (Ubicom) refers to a vision of unobtrusive, "natural" computing exploiting the fact that computers are increasingly embedded in small and large devices (e.g., mobile telephones, personal digital assistants, cars, or buildings). Ubicom depends on different digital services embedded in our environment (e.g., networks, storage, geographical information services (GIS), or positioning). Ubicom has an enormous potential for supporting future work and daily life, but currently the vision is far from realized. It was originally characterized as *Invisible* (Weiser, 1991), where invisible could mean literally invisible by being embedded. However, invisibility was also referring to invisible-in-use, where people "just" make use of a technology without paying attention to the technology itself. Making computers invisible has prompted many designers to make computers literally invisible by embedding them, by automating processes, and by transferring control, for example, of network establishment to machines. This in many ways makes our lives easier. However, it also makes it hard for people to know what the technologies are doing, to use them effectively and to trust them.

So, in PalCom our main aim was to provide infrastructural support for making ubiquitous computing "palpable," that is, "noticeable, manifest, obvious, clear"

(Oxford English Dictionary, http://dictionary.oed.com/). In other words, we sought to support people in understanding what computers do, and, to support interaction with them, by letting the computers being noticeable and apprehendable.

So, palpable computing will go beyond state-of-the-art ubiquitous computing by complementing the ubiquitous computing visions with palpable computing visions. Especially we want to complement invisibility with visibility, scalability with understandability, construction with de- and re-construction heterogeneity with coherence, change with stability and automation with user control. However, "complementing" should not be understood as "either" – "or." On the contrary it should be seen as creating the possibilities to continually choose the most appropriate level between (e.g.) total invisibility and total visibility, depending on the actual technology and setting in which it is (to be) used.

Thus palpable computing complements the unobtrusive effectiveness of ambient computing with a focus on making the means of empowering people intelligible.

## Emergency Response: State-of-the-Art

Some of the main characteristics of emergencies are their unforeseen occurrence and the need for immediate response from several types of professionals. The response to an emergency is in almost all cases initiated by someone's call to an alarm center. When activated, emergency response resources are allocated to the incident and directed towards the incident site itself and to assisting sites (e.g., hospitals). This is done by use of a country and/or region-specific code of practice. Each incident and emergency response situation is assessed regarding needs for and availability of resources. In Denmark this is initially done by the receiver of the call at the alarm center, and later on by the incident commander(s) on site and dedicated officers in the involved coordination centers. The larger an incident is (regarding physical spread, severity and/or number of casualties), the more resources (personnel, equipment and hospital capacity) are needed, and the more complex and difficult it becomes for the involved emergency responders to create and maintain an overview of the situation and thus to organize the activities. Many different types of emergency response professionals are involved (especially police officers, fire fighters, medics and paramedics), and they are expected to follow a preplanned and in most cases a well-known set of procedures called the Incident Command System (ICS), see e.g., (LESLP, http://www.leslp.gov.uk/frames.htm; DICS, http://www.brs.dk/uk/danish_preparedness_act.htm). In the ICS the roles of the different professionals, the structure for collaboration and their mutual routes of communication are specified, together with directions for physical configuration of the incident site. A typical spatial organization of the incident site is illustrated in Fig. 20.1.

The actions taken – and the communication – are supposed to happen within a structured hierarchy, both within each profession and across the different professions. Working and communicating within a certain hierarchy is

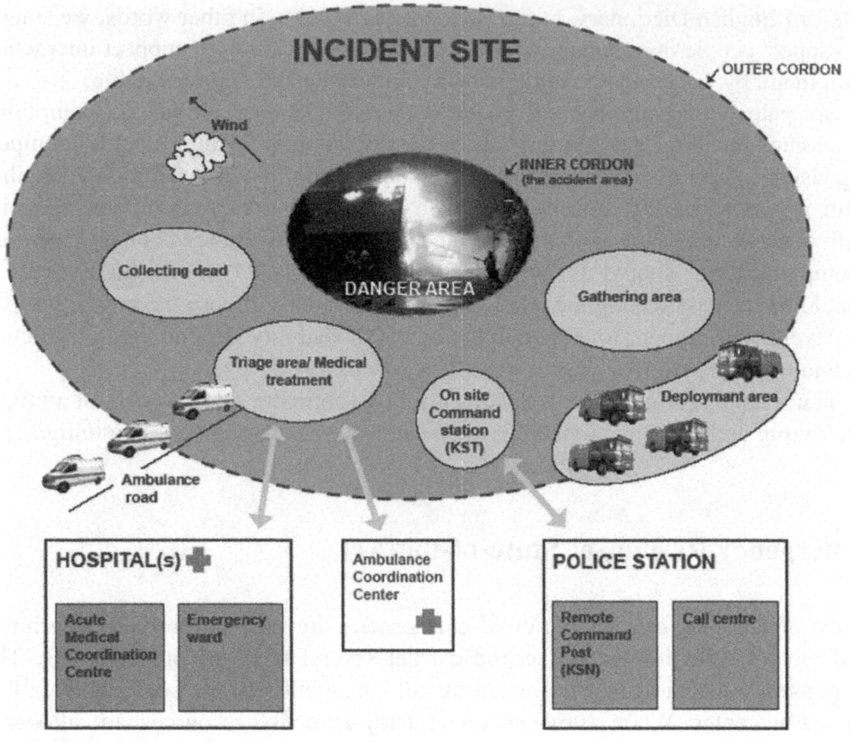


**Fig. 20.1** Spatial organization of the incident site

intended to support each professional in recognizing what to do, who to refer to, and who to collaborate with. This means that each person should be able to concentrate on exactly his/her task in close cooperation with other professionals involved.

Briefly explained the overall division of work between professionals is as follows:

1. The fire fighters are the primary rescuers – they are responsible for securing and getting people out of the primary *danger area*.
2. The police are the overall responsible professional group. They do the cordoning off around the *incident site* and are responsible for deciding on and securing routes for transportation of equipment and people. They are also responsible for registration of all involved people – both injured and noninjured. Moreover, they have to take care of the public, the media and the relatives.
3. The paramedics are responsible for providing ambulances for transportation of injured people to hospital(s) and for the transportation itself. A major part of this is to maintain a flow of ambulances that are as close as possible to the capacity needed.

4. The medics[1] are responsible for handling the injured people – the initial assessment, treatment, and transfer to hospital. This is carried out in close collaboration with the paramedics.
5. The fire fighters, police officers, medics, and paramedics, respectively are managed by their respective managers: the fire brigade incident commander, the police incident commander, the medical incident officer, and the paramedical manager. The fire brigade incident commander and the police incident commander man the on-site command center (KST). These two incident commanders together are responsible for the overall response – the fire brigade manager for the direct, primary rescuing effort and the police manager for the overall effort. Therefore, they need to act in close collaboration with each other and also with the medical incident officer and the ambulance service manager who are responsible for the medical treatment and transportation of injured persons.
6. At the hospital the medical coordinator in the acute medical coordination center (AMK) is responsible for the coordination of medical resources at the hospitals and for coordinating to which hospital the individual casualties are transported. At the hospitals the different medical professionals, most often collaborating in teams, are responsible for the medical examination and treatment of the injured people.
7. The remote command center (KSN) (often physically situated at a police station) is manned with resource persons relevant for the concrete emergency response. The resource persons in KSN are not directly responsible, but they give advises and respond to specific or overall issues regarding the emergency response and carry out concrete tasks of more investigational or nonemergency site organizational nature (e.g., knowledge about overall amount of available ambulances or fire trucks in their own district and request for help from the neighboring districts).
8. The receiver of the alarm call in the alarm center at the police station has a well-defined responsibility; she/he is responsible for the initial judgment of the incident – a judgment resulting in the first allocation of the emergency response resources.

The involved emergency responders are taught to take responsibility for – and carry out as best they can – each of their specific parts of the response work. What they do and how they act depend on the kind and size of the actual incident in combination with the person's role, training, and skills. In everyday emergency response it is comparatively easy for the rescuers to follow the emergency response procedures, described in their ICS described just above. They know what to do; it is simply a deep-rooted way of working. However, the bigger an incident is the more complex,

[1] During recent years it has become more and more a permanent routine in most of Europe that medics (physicians or nurses) work as part of the pre-hospital emergency response team (Lockey et al., 2005, Schønemann et al., 2007; Welling et al., 2005). Additionally special teams of medics are sent out in major incidents, e.g. in response to the London Bombings in 2006 and the Volendam Café Fire in 2000 (Lockey et al., 2005; Welling et al., 2005).

unusual, and rare the situation becomes for most of the responders (most of them have never participated in a real-life major incident's emergency response before) – and this does of course affect the responders: they become more stressed and have to carry out their work within more complex settings. Often, procedures they are supposed to apply are no longer well-known, and – even if they are well-known – in many cases it is not possible to do as prescribed, e.g., due to non-functional communication lines. In addition to this, major incidents emergency response often involves rescuers from "foreign" regions, i.e., the rescuers do not know each other.

With this in mind – (a) that the responders theoretically *know* what to do *also* in a major incidents situation, but they have not necessarily *practiced* it before, and (b) that the bigger an incident is the more complex the whole situation becomes (e.g., physical spread and character of damage, number of casualties and responders) we describe in more depth the relevant observations from our research and its relation to media spaces in the next sections.

## Moving Beyond State-of-the-Art

### *Some Initial Observations*

Emergency service is carried out by responders through direct interaction with a huge amount of different physical entities – both people and things. To illustrate:

A fire fighter interacts with other fire fighters, a fire engine, fire pumps, his helmet, his radio, debris, police officers, medics, and victims (injured and/or not injured).

A medic interacts with injured people, medical monitoring equipment, medical equipment for treatment (e.g., medicine, drips, neck collars, stretchers, bandages, and drainage tubes), paramedics, fire fighters, medical staff at hospitals, radios, mobile phones, ambulances, and documentation forms.

Through interaction with other rescuers, their tools, and artifacts the responders carry out their tasks, but at the same time they *signal* to each other and to people in the surroundings as well – through their specific location, body-language, and use of tools/artifacts. Some examples: (a) The way a police vehicle is parked and the way a police officer positions himself indicates "do not go through here" (Fig. 20.2), (b) a certain hand gesture by a fire fighter manager walking around a crashed train wagon may signal "possible danger near the wagon," that is, others should not come closer, and the change of direction of an approaching police officer talking on his radio signals his awareness of this (Büscher and Mogensen, 2007), and, (c) a large number of rescuers helping with transportation of an injured person from the scene to the ambulance signals that the person on the stretcher is severely injured (Fig. 20.3).

Information from the incident site to hospitals, remote command centers, rescue vehicles, etc. are communicated via incident-site radios and cell phones. In addition, some text-based Information and Communication Technology (ICT) systems are used to communicate between some of the remote command centers, hospitals, and rescue vehicles. Paper documentation is formally required, especially regarding

**Fig. 20.2** Positioning of the police car and the police officer signal "do not go through here"

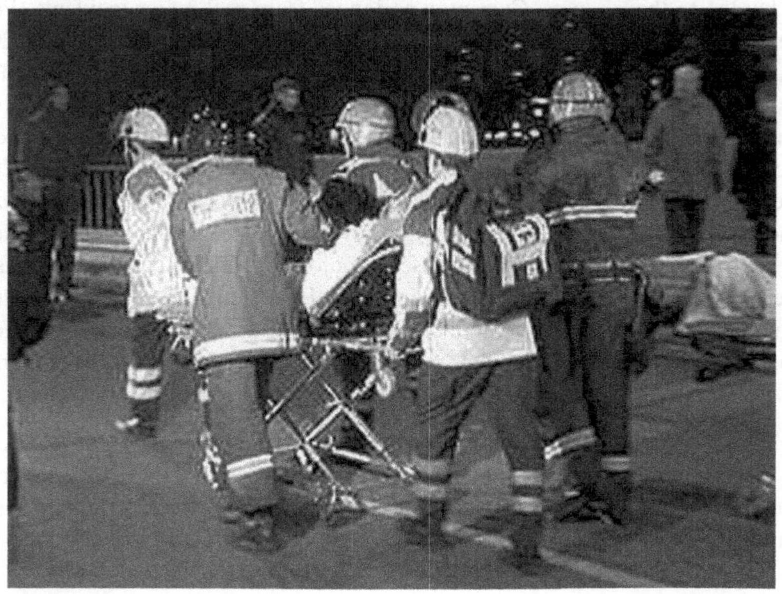

**Fig. 20.3** A large number of rescuers around a stretcher indicate that the person on the stretcher is severely injured

the medical work. It is also used as a means to communicate and collaborate between medical professionals pre- and in-hospital. However, documenting is seldom done on site. Normally the ambulance patient record is partially filled out during ambulance transport and when the emergency response is over, the paper documentation is finally produced, especially by the physicians.

However, most of the information produced and used during the execution of a rescue operation is acquired through interactions in the setting, for example, with (other) rescue workers and injured people at the incident site. Thus *the setting itself* is the primary source of information and for this reason we conceptualize the incident site and the people (casualties and rescuers) and equipment (vehicles, buildings, etc.) as *boundary objects* (Bowker and Star, 1999; Kristensen et al., 2006; Lutters and Ackerman, 2002; Star and Griesemer, 1989). Through these different boundary objects complex and often imperfect work of coordination is done; the victims themselves serve to coordinate the work and work trajectories of emergency response personnel – and so do the rescuers together with the different tools and artifacts used during the emergency response. In this perspective we also refer to the incident site as the "physical information space."

What *matters* to the emergency responders on site is to improve the state of the emergency through direct *action* in the physical world, for to move injured people to safety and to treat them to save lives, to fight a fire or to get control of a chemical spill. ICT is – and can only be – considered as secondary and should support focus on improvement of the direct actions in the physical world without being an extra burden to the rescuers. Current experiences from real major incidents (Peral-Gutierrez de Ceballos et al., 2005; Roccaforte, 2001; Romundstad et al., 2004; Teague, 2004), for example, show that use of ICT systems is usually sparse and that many systems are difficult to use due to, e.g., malfunction, lack of interoperability and integration, and lack of usability and usefulness in the context of the incident. These experiences are supported by findings in our own research (Kramp et al., 2006; Kristensen et al., 2005, 2006; Kyng et al., 2006): The responders are *expected to* use technologies that (a) they do not use in their everyday work and thus are unfamiliar with, or (b) that are *not* developed for use in major incidents situations and thus fits the needs poorly when many people are injured. (Expected) Use of non-proper/non-familiar technologies adds even more complexity and stressfulness to the emergency response. The bottom line is that these technologies most often are not used in major incidents situations, as illustrated by the following two examples:

- In major incidents the medical responders are expected to use (a) colored cards to mark injured people regarding which triage category[2] they belong to, (b) an Incident Site Card per injured person, to document injuries and treatment carried out, and, (c) an Incident Site Log in which all injured people are registered with

[2]During triage casualties are categorized by a physician according to the severity of their injuries and treated according to e.g. the following categories: (1) Needs treatment immediately, (2) needs treatment as soon as possible, (3) treatment can wait or is not feasible, (4) deceased. Every victim is supposed to be marked with a colored (red, yellow, green, or white), numbered card (1, 2, 3, or 0).

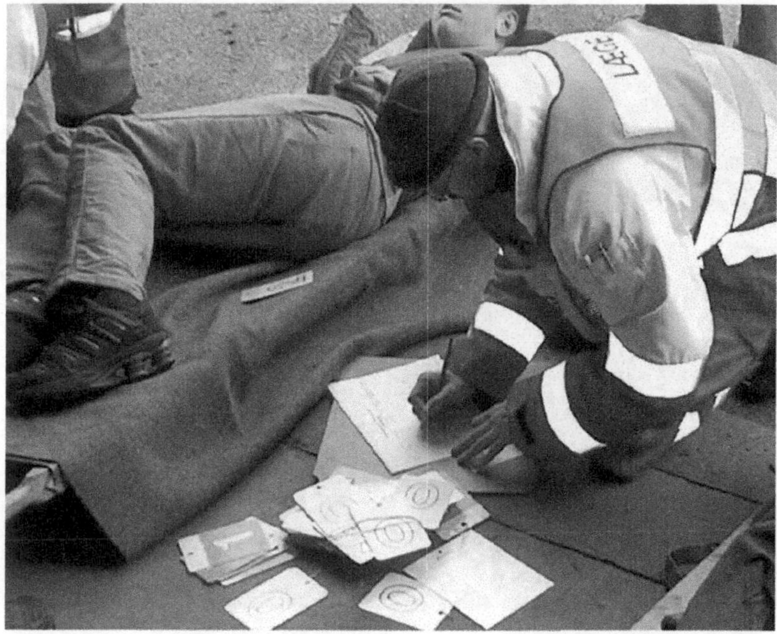


**Fig. 20.4** Triage cards, incident card and incident log – three different documents meant to support documentation, collaboration and coordination during major incidents emergency response

basic data and which hospital they are brought to, to ensure they do not "disappear" (illustrated in Fig. 20.4). None of these three tools are well known from everyday work. Experiences from real major incidents show that the Log is used – the other's are not.

- The audio communication systems are often not used – radios may be left unused in pockets because both hands are needed, cell phone systems get overloaded, the conditions on site may be too noisy, etc. This is well known and has contributed to developing the unofficial but common procedure that the commanders who are responsible for the overall coordination of the emergency response and – because of this – *must* collaborate, try to stay together physically during a response (Fig. 20.5).

In a media space perspective we note that a lot of information is a *visual "by-product"* of doing the real job and that this opens up some unique design possibilities:

- The responders on site carry out their work through interaction with physical entities. Through this direct interaction with each other and/or tools and artifacts they *signal* what they are doing. Moreover, they also signal their evaluation of the situation (e.g., if something might be dangerous or life-threatening). They signal this both to the surroundings (those "outside" the incident area) and to each other.

**Fig. 20.5** Incident commanders physically stay together to ensure mutual communication

- Virtually no information is produced on site specifically *for later use*. This is due to pressing, time critical work, and lack of resources. However, a lot of the information required for documentation, communication and collaboration support, is available through inspection of the rescuer's (mutual) interaction and/or inspection of physical entities, primarily the injured people, for example, when looking at the injured person it is immediately visible if a neck collar has been mounted or intravenous infusion is given.

Thus video seems to have the potential to *provide* information through visual-inspection-at-a-distance of the primary boundary objects in the physical information space, and to do so at virtually no extra cost in terms of time.

At the same time we note that different kinds of videos have the potential of *adding* important qualities to the available information on site. To illustrate: Fire chief Joseph Pfeifer, New Your Fire Department, who was involved in the 9/11 response once said in an interview:

> I have looked and examined the whole response to the Trade Centre. I wish we would have seen while we heard what everyone saw on TV. We didn't get any messages that the top 15 floors were glowing red or the building looked like it was going to collapse. (sent on Danish channel TV2, September 12, 2006)

Thus it seems that Media Space-like technology could play a prominent role in future systems for emergency response. We would like to create spaces where users of – or participants in – the media spaces obtain and maintain possibilities for orienting themselves in a common space and be oriented about other people and things.

## *Vision, Challenges, and Principles*

As mentioned in the Introduction we have in the EU-financed PalCom project (PalCom, http://www.ist-palcom.org) designed for a near future where information and communication technologies, including sensors and actuators are attached to people and artifacts and integrated in many parts of our environments. In some cases we might want these technologies to "disappear" into our environments, but in many cases and situations it will be appropriate – and maybe even necessary – that the users can control their interactions with the technologies: assemble technologies in meaningful constellations, make them work differently from what they were originally programmed to, or inspect them to see if they are working as expected, or to handle break-downs. Viewed in this light our vision is to provide the means for emergency responders to cocreate the organization of the physical incident site. This includes use of the physical incident site's role as physical information space, where the site and people, tools and artifacts act as boundary objects. Moreover, it includes use of a number of partially shared digital information and media spaces. The overall goal is to support and enhance the response work. The crucial thing is to support action in the physical world. So, we have chosen *to align the digital support with the physical world.* One key element in this principle is to augment the physical entities with ICT. Another key element is to align on-site media spaces with 3D models of the incident site.

The emergency response, unfolding at the incident site itself, is however, in many challenging ways very different from settings where traditional media spaces are applied. In addition emergency response has some characteristics, which poses major challenges to ICT support in general. In the following we first discuss the challenges in relation to media spaces and then we go on to consider those in relation to ICT support in general.

Emergency response is what one may describe as "emergent": it starts out as chaos and through their actions the emergency responders appropriate the site and transform it into something they can understand and operate effectively in. Thus the incident site is usually unknown to the responders, the responders may, for a large part, be unknown to one another, and the technologies are not deployed on beforehand. They, so to speak, build up their site and the response, depending on the character of the emergency, the settings it is in and the resources available. In these settings the rescuers cannot spend time on deploying technologies they do not urgently need in their direct rescue tasks. Turning to the command centers and the rescue vehicles the conditions are much different; they are in known territories, and may be equipped with the necessary technology from the outset. This has led to the formulation of the following principle:

*Anchor the media space part of the emergency response in more well-known and stable parts of the response organization, i.e. the command centers and the vehicles, cf. Fig. 20.6.*

In the lower left corner of the dimensions depicted on Fig. 20.7 are the emergency rooms at the hospitals and the command centers. These may be equipped with rather traditional media space hardware. At the upper right corner is the

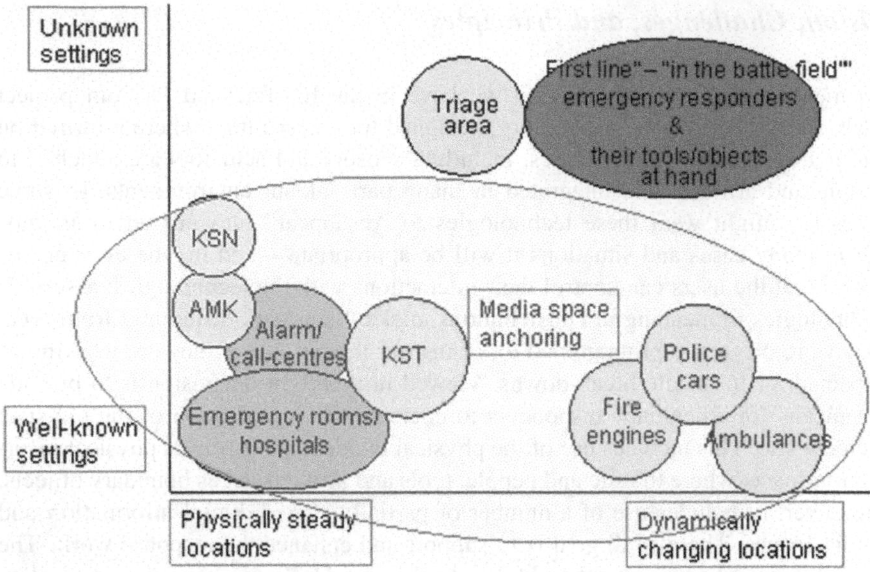


**Fig. 20.6** Characterization of emergency response situations according to "knownness" and stability

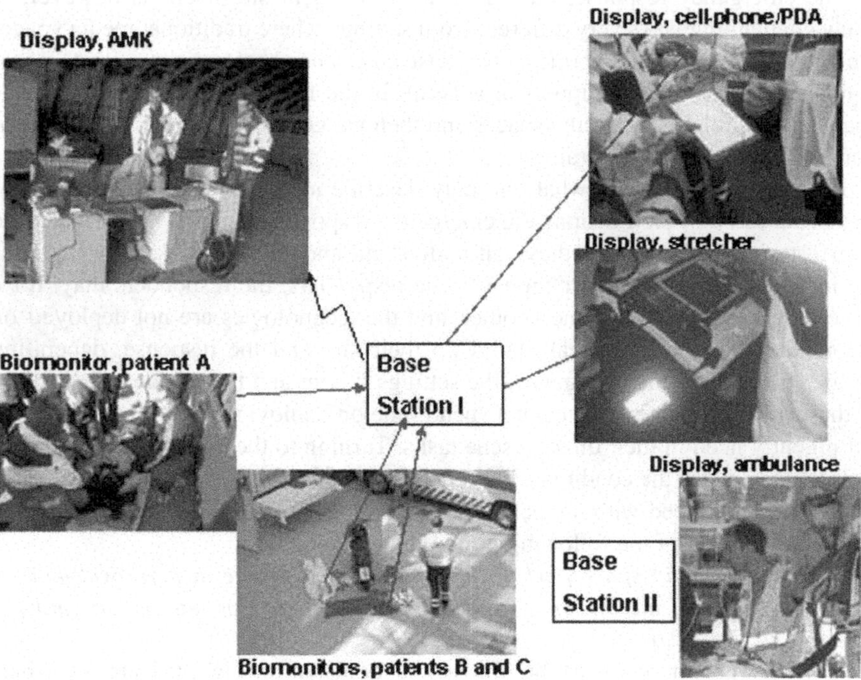


**Fig. 20.7** The BlueBio monitoring system

incident site, which is unknown and where people and equipment come and go. In general such sites are unsuited for traditional two-way media space technology, however, with careful design they may function as "media space information sources," and – to some degree – Media Space inter-actors, cf. also the section "Emergency response and Media Space – Summary and Discussion."

When we then move on to consider other aspects of the ICT support we note that – because of the incident site with its people, tools and artifacts are conceptualized and serve as boundary objects – the ICT should provide effective means of getting and providing information both in the physical and digital world. To avoid adding an extra "information access method," we have formulated the following principles:

- *Physical entities, people, vehicles etc., should act as "access points" also for the digital information.*
- *Representations of physical entities in the digital space should also act as access points for digital information.*

Furthermore to reduce the number of shifts between different spaces we have formulated the following principle:

- *Representations of physical entities in the digital space should also act as points of manipulation of the physical entity.*

In addition, to make systems more efficient and thus uptake more likely, information available through inspection of the physical entities should primarily be accessed physically and not be required to be entered digitally on site. This has led us to formulate the following principle:

- *When asking for digital information focus should initially be on information that is not immediately available through direct or video-mediated inspection of the physical world.*

We also have to consider some characteristics of emergency response that pose major challenges to ICT support in general. Based on findings like those described in the previous section we have, in Kristensen et al. (2006) and Kyng et al. (2006) argued that when developing ICT support to be used in emergency response:

- Focus should be on issues that are immediately relevant to the saving of lives and/or keep damage to materials to a minimum, and
- Systems and devices have to be effective and efficient – in reality this means that they should preferably be understood, well-known, and practiced by the users beforehand,

and as a corollary:

- ICT support for major incidents should preferably also be useful in the daily work with minor incidents – to support "well-known and practiced"

## *Support for Future Emergency Response: Design and Prototypes*

To provide effective and efficient support and to avoid information overload as well as the creation of unused systems, we have chosen a use-driven and experimental-development approach where future users are included in the design team (Bødker et al., 1993; Greenbaum and Kyng, 1991; Kramp et al., 2006; Kristensen et al., 2005, 2006; Kyng, 1994, 1998; Kyng et al., 2006). Our work follows two strands: one on *entity information* and one on *overview*. We begin by briefly describing the support for entity information, since entity information is a major part of the overview.

### Entity Information

The support for entity information, took as its point of departure the need for information about injured people, and the main element of our design is still the 'BlueBio' biomonitoring system providing biosensor information from the victims. The Bluebio system also contains infrastructure for the wireless distribution of the information generated "at" each injured person using ad hoc network infrastructure deployed as part of the emergency response. The system is illustrated in Fig. 20.7 and discussed in more detail in (Kramp et al., 2006; Kristensen et al., 2006).

In addition to biosensor information we also began to work with other types of information pertaining to each injured person, like photos, position, and identity information. Thus we aim at handling the following types of information about injured people:

- Condition, e.g., biosensor data
- Position, e.g., GPS data
- ID, e.g., unique system ID, picture(s), description (e.g., age, gender, hair colour), social security number and name
- Photos
- Video

In addition to the initial focus on injured people we are now considering information on several types of entities:

1. People
   (a) Victims
      (i) Injured
      (ii) Noninjured
   (b) Emergency responders
2. Equipment
   (c) Primary emergency equipment
      (i) Emergency vehicles
      (ii) Medical equipment and other emergency equipment, e.g., for smoke divers

(d) ICT
  (i) RFID tags and scanner
  (ii) GPS equipment
  (iii) Radios and cell phones
  (vi) Video cameras and digital cameras
  (v) Computers and displays

Thus in addition to information pertaining to injured victims (1.a.i) we are also working with the production and distribution of entity information of noninjured victims (1.a.ii), of emergency responders (1.b), and the different kinds of equipment "involved" in the incident (2.a and 2.b). This is no big surprise and was on our agenda from the beginning: one wants to be able to judge the health condition and safety of emergency responders, the position of vehicles, the battery of ECG equipment, etc.

However, we have chosen to represent not only the entities of primary interest and the information available about them, but also the devices involved in providing and handling the information about the entities of primary interest. There are two reasons for this:

First of all, if something indicates a problem, e.g., missing GPS signal from a fire fighter, one wants to inspect the GPS device in question. And in this case it is important that the device itself is also part of the digital information space.

Secondly, when these devices are part of the digital information space we may also support interacting with them through this space. To illustrate: if a motor-controlled video camera is represented in the digital information space we may use that representation to tilt and zoom the camera in the real world.

Finally, it is important to note that the provided ICT support is not static, that is, it does not consist of a certain defined amount of technologies. In contrast it is *dynamic*. To illustrate: in a recent real life test of the system in a harbor it was decided 2 days earlier the test that we should try to include tracking of ships using the Automatic Identification System (AIS). The next day we acquired the hardware and guessed the proprietary protocol and the following day the software developers in the project had managed to add the AIS as a new service, enabling the positions of different ships to be included in our digital space.

## Overview

The second strand took as its point of departure the need for overview of an incident, to support coordination, and collaboration on-site as well as with the remote responders. The key idea is to provide a 3D model, representing the incident site and share this model among all involved parties. The model is accessed via software tools running on a number of devices with different types of displays: some large, interactive displays and several smaller ones, e.g., tablet PCs, PDAs, and smart phones. Thus, those, who use the tools (right now in the form of prototypes) may share views and interact from different locations.

The prototype holds different so-called *workspaces* each containing different kinds of information and interaction possibilities, much of it as a presentation of the *entity information*, sketched in the subsection just above; one workspace contains different drapes regarding the terrain; e.g., a layer with aerial photos, a layer with terrain-data and maps with technical data, indicated by colors. Another workspace provides sketching functionalities, to sketch ideas during a discussion, and save the visuals and other data on approved plans. Yet another workspace contains 3D models of buildings. The overall idea is that as many workspaces as needed can be created (e.g., workspaces containing information about power supply and gas stations).

Sketching and planning will usually be carried out by the different incident commanders and officers, situated on site or remotely (see Fig. 20.8), and be aimed at the professionals carrying out the direct response work "in the field" as well as the involved incident commanders. Thus plans and other information created and or made visible via one display is available at any other display-device, including equipment carried by the personnel "in the field" (e.g., fire fighters inside a crashed train, police officers at barriers, or paramedics in ambulances).

The prototype uses the 43D Topos software product as a starting point (43D, http://www.43d.com/index.php). Development of Topos was initiated in another EU-financed project, called "WorkSPACE" (WorkSPACE, http://www daimi.au.dk/workspace/index.htm).

As mentioned earlier it is argued in (Kristensen et al., 2006; Kyng et al., 2006) that when developing ICT support to be used in emergency response it is important

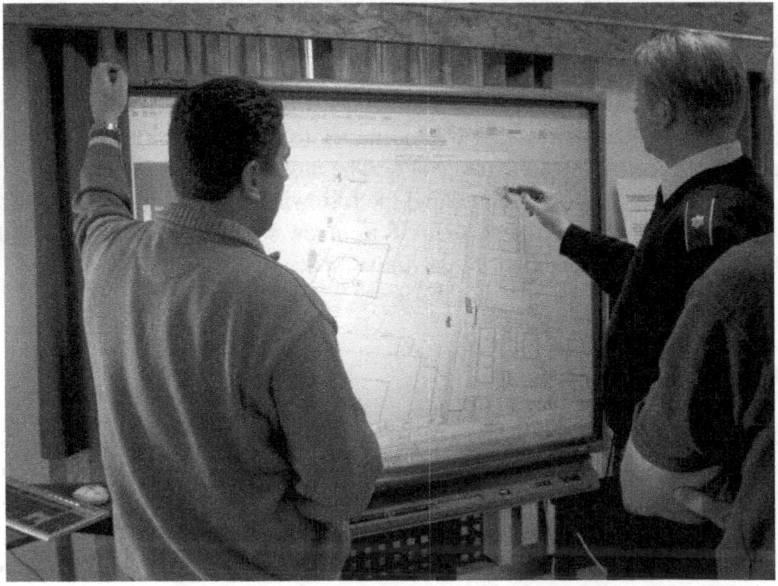

**Fig. 20.8** From an early workshop: Police officer (*left*) and fire brigade incident commander sketch organization of incident site

to develop it so that it is used (and useful) not only in major incident situations but also in the everyday emergency response – to support it being "well-known and practiced." For some time it was a bit difficult for the research group (researchers and users) to see how the overview prototype could be useful also in everyday work. However, though in the winter 2006–2007 the users suggested that we should make a prototype setup in a Command Centre, established during the major event "The Tall Ships Races 2007" in Aarhus, July 5–8 (TSR, 2007). So, we put a great deal of effort into configuration of the prototype - a 3D model, covering the main-area for the Tall Ships Races Event; a 6 × 3 km area of the harbor – and kept it running during the whole 4-day-long event. This testing of the prototype in real life, but not an emergency response situation, gave us a lot of valuable input, which has been described in (Büscher et al., 2008). Below we will describe some of the setups relevant in a Media Space perspective.

A first example on an important workspace is an online Geo-tagged video-stream. In the picture below (Fig. 20.9) a police officer in KST uses a large interactive display with the 3D model and online video streaming to see how status is in one of the pretty crowded places at the harbor. In total we had mounted six video cameras in strategically important places; one of the video cameras could be tilted when interacting with it on the large display. Since each video camera was Geo-tagged, "opening" a camera means opening its stream in the correct position on the 3D map.

A second example on an important workspace is a space showing (GPS) tracked persons and moving objects (e.g., GPS tracked vehicles and AIS tracked boats)

**Fig. 20.9** From Tall Ships Race 2007: Police officer gets an overview of a section of the harbour area by opening one of the online video cameras in the Overview Prototype

**Fig. 20.10** White arrows point to three GPS tracked persons and the GPS tracked rescue boat

In Fig. 20.10 the long white arrows point to three GPS tracked persons and the GPS tracked rescue boat. The GPS is build into a cell phone with a camera and pictures taken by the phone will appear in the workspace in the exact location it is taken. Figure 20.11 shows a picture taken by a police officer patrolling at the harbor. The car is parked in a non-parking area – actually a fire access road, which is not legal.

As demonstrated with the examples above the 3D model gradually has become populated with many different entities of interest and information about an entity may be accessed via its representation in the 3D model.

Finally we note that – as mentioned in the Introduction and in the description of our vision – an important aspect of the PalCom project (PalCom, http://www.ist-palcom.org) is to support inspection of the different devices, tools and services – e.g., what they represent and how they work in our 3D model. Inspection is carried out through interaction with the entity in the digital space.

However, at the same time we have developed information access methods that support the inspection of information pertaining to an entity via direct interaction with the entity in the physical space. An example: A medic, working with the victims in the triage area may want to inspect the biosensor data of a specific victim. He does this by RFID scanning; an action which selects the data of the victim for presentation on the primary display associated with the person doing the scanning, typically a PDA, carried around by the medic.

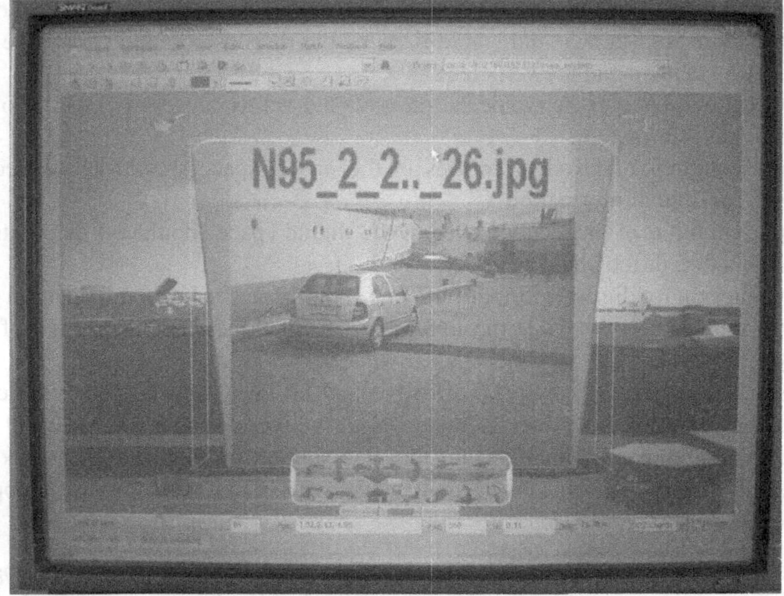


**Fig. 20.11** Picture of illegally parked car, taken by police officer in the field and immediately visible in the Overview Prototype

## Emergency Response and Media Space – Summary and Discussion

In summary our research regarding use of technologies to support emergency responders have pointed to the following *important issues*:

- Most of the information that is created at the incident site during an emergency response situation is a *visual "by-product"* of the real job, carried out at the incident site – it is not *as such* created with the main purpose of being information.
- The incident site with its people, tools, and artifacts serve as boundary objects.
- The primary focus during emergency response is on the rescue efforts. Thus use of ICT is considered as "secondary" in the emergency response action and should therefore support and improve the direct actions in the physical world without being an extra burden to the rescuers.

These issues have contributed to the development of the following *design principles*:

- The digital services and devices should be aligned with the physical world.
- Focus should be on issues that are immediately relevant to the saving of lives and/or keep damage to materials to a minimum.

- The ICT used in the emergency response should as far as possible be anchored in the more well-known and stable parts of the response organization (like the command centers and the vehicles).
- Physical entities (people, vehicles, etc.) should act as "access points" also for the digital information.
- Representations of physical entities in the digital space should act as access points for digital information.
- Representations of physical entities in the digital space should act as points of manipulation of the physical entity.
- When asking for digital information focus should initially be on information that is not immediately available through direct or video-mediated inspection of the physical world.
- Systems and devices has to be effective and efficient – in reality this means that they should preferably be understood, well-known and practiced by the users on beforehand. This indicates that ICT support for major incidents should preferably also be useful in the daily work with minor incidents – to support "well-known and practiced."

We have enhanced the spectrum of traditional emergency response technologies with the possibility of producing and using still-pictures, video-streaming (including audio), and other types of entity information. Thus our prototypes support:

- Overview including 3D area models that can be presented at different kinds of displays, with different interaction possibilities,
- Supplemented with information regarding different kinds (but not a certain predefined amount) of entities, including video- and still cameras, and
- All of it can be shared across different locations, to support – also – remote collaboration.

The technological setup in our prototypes is with these additions in some ways a Media Space-*like* setup. However, it differs from a traditional Media Space in several ways.

Figure 20.12 shows an example on a "traditional" Media Space setup: Video-cameras are mounted in different offices and are connected, so that people in the respective offices can see, speak with, and be aware of people in the other office and in this way are aware of what is going on there. This can be described as a

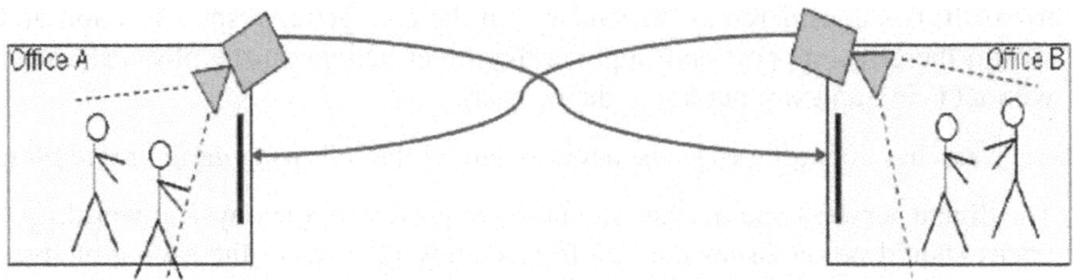


**Fig. 20.12** A (traditional) symmetric Media Space

*symmetric* Media Space. It means that the equipment on the two locations is used by the involved people in similar ways. Moreover, the setup is to a large degree *static*: first it is static in the sense that it is mounted and used in fixed settings – it is mounted to create a media space between two or more offices in stationary buildings. Secondly, when installed it is the same equipment that is used from day to day. Over a longer period of time it might be supplemented with new technologies or parts of it might be upgraded to new units, but basically it is the same day in and day out.

Considering the prototypes for emergency response as a Media Space, and taking into account the *important issues* and *design principles* outlined above we conclude that responders working at the Incident Site do not want to see the people in the remote response centers (AMK, KST, KSN, and different alarm- and call centers). But it makes a lot of sense that the people in the different remote centers can see and follow the responders in the field. So, first of all the emergency response Media Space can be described as *asymmetric*.[3]

Additionally the emergency response media space can be considered as *always changing*; emergency settings are never the same and are often in open space, and thus the conditions (e.g., weather and light) can be very different from response situation to response situation. This poses specific challenges to the technologies in use – to the different media, contributing to create emergency response media spaces. This is what we have focused on in our research and which have let us to design an open-ended, dynamic type of media space.

A media space setup like the one sketched in Fig. 20.13 – including the incident site itself as a part of it – pose several possibilities, but also several challenges:

*First of all* the alignment of the digital information space with all the different types of physical information (or one could say; enhancement of the physical information with production of digital information), including the digital augmentation of physical entities, supports the user in transferring experiences with material qualities, and characteristics to the digital space. To illustrate: Information about an entity may be acquired through direct physical interaction with and inspection of that entity, e.g., examining a person with a broken leg. Here the entity itself (i.e., the person) acts as a boundary object. In addition digital information about the physical entity (the person) may be accessed through physical interaction with a digital information source aligned with the entity, e.g., a biomonitor mounted on the injured person; one possible solution to get access to the collected data is to scan the (RFID-)tagged biomonitor. This causes data to be shown on a display, belonging to the person who did the scanning. Finally, digital information may be accessed through different kinds of representation of the entity on the 3D map (positioning, ID, description, biosensor data, pictures, and/or video).

Secondly the digital representation may support users in dealing with complexity in the physical world, especially when things scale up, i.e., when dealing with a

[3] Parts of it might be symmetric – a setup of video cameras in KST, KSN, AMK and maybe also in the alarm/call-centers (not illustrated).

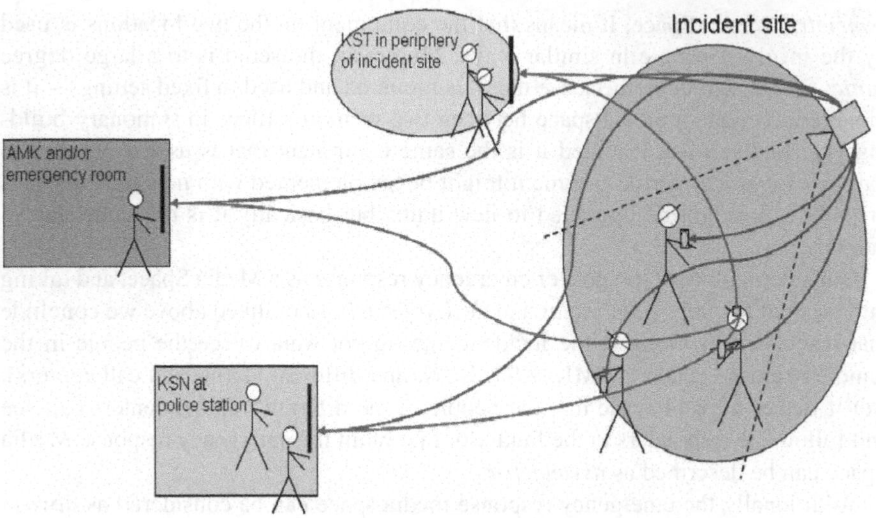


**Fig. 20.13** The emergency response Media Space is asymmetric

major incident, with many injured people, spread over a large area and involving a huge amount of rescuers and vehicles and other equipment. In this case moving around in the digital world – the 3D map – may be used as a way of quickly focusing attention on the entities of interest – instead of physically moving around a huge, chaotic incident site, where specific people and things can be impossible to see or discover. Searching for what/who one wants to find in the digital space can be easier – in the digital space you can use the different workspaces to choose, delimit, and select for specific purposes.

Information access by use of still pictures and online video streaming was in our test during The Tall Ships Races 2007 assessed as being very valuable and useful. In many situations still pictures was very informative (e.g., like the picture of the illegally parked car in Fig. 20.11). However, in many situations the possibility to *see action* adds important information. An example: if the picture in Fig. 20.3 had been a video-stream the way the responders walk (pace and target-ness) would really tell more about the severity.

Different possible solutions are still subject to further research and discussion: Until now we have only experimented with video cameras mounted at a distance from the area of interest, surveying pretty huge areas, supplying the digital space with – among other things – information about how the responders *act*. We have to explore where these should be mounted in a very mobile emergency response world. They *could* be mounted on top of, e.g., fire trucks and/or ambulances, but we need to investigate that in more detail. Moreover, we don't know if the current video-streaming-information could usefully be supplemented with information from video cameras mounted in the responder's helmets, supplying the digital space with video of what the specific responder(s) *see*.

*Thirdly*, the alignment of the on-site media spaces with the 3D model (which is often used away from the incident site) supports transfer from the digital to the physical world by exploiting the "well-known-ness" of maps. To illustrate: discussing, creating – and communicating – digital entities in the 3D map, such as inner and outer cordon (Figs. 20.1 and 20.8), can simplify the work of transferring the position of cordons to the physical world tremendously compared to a verbal description communicated over a radio. Thus, in the 3D digital world you can make drawings of how and where you want something to be (e.g., where the inner cordon or access point should be) and once a drawing is made and is accepted those who are in the field are able to access it on a display they carry – and will in most cases – know how to interpret it. However, how things are decided to be does not necessarily reflect how they are actually executed in the physical world – this calls for *feedback* from the physical implementation, e.g., by tags, GPSs, photo, and/or video.

*Fourthly*, digital representations of the different devices support interaction with and inspection of the devices. Regarding inspectability, the digital representation of, for example, a camera can be used to inspect that device, both regarding its physical and digital state: where it is, if it is working as expected, how the power level is, if failures have occurred, the type of failure, etc.

The digital representations of the devices also support interaction with the devices: the representations, for example, allow for tilting the video camera or sending a message to a cell phone with information about microphone malfunction.

However, several challenges are to be further investigated. To mention a few: If the emergency response Media Space setup is as sketched in Fig. 20.13 – there are on-site commanders in one location (KST) and other commanders in other locations (e.g., AMK and KSN). These commanders are potentially all in control of video cameras that can be manipulated remotely. But how do these commanders decide how to control the camera? How should that be "negotiated"?

Inspectability and interaction refers to all levels of the prototype, from end-user level to programming level. This demands different solutions for inspection and interaction in at least two dimensions: First, it should be possible to inspect and interact both directly and remotely with the devices, tools, and services. Secondly, the inspection and interaction interfaces have to be designed so that they are aimed at different types of users, from software architects and – designers to different types of end-users, including fire fighters, physicians, and police officers. We have the initial designs, but they definitely have to go through several further iterations. It is *not* trivial to develop a viable design for inspectability and interaction, having in mind that additional interaction with technologies during an emergency response should contribute directly to improving the state of the emergency.

*Finally* the mobile setup concept, containing use of different media in an open and not delimited space, seems to have proved its value; it gave a lot of positive and useful feedback during use of it in The Tall Ships Races 2007, where it worked and was used many, many times during the event for many different purposes (Büscher et al., 2008). However, turning it into something *really* mobile, in the sense of being able to bring it as an integrated part of the emergency responder's response setup, demand more well-examined solutions also regarding issues such as bandwidth and wireless network technologies.

To conclude:

In our research we have been able to identify principles for design of technologies to be used in emergency response. The design principles build on (a) extensive field studies of and with end-users and (b) several iterative evaluation sessions where end-users have tested more and more mature prototypes.

Together with the design principles we have outlined several important issues that have to be taken into account when designing the technology. And we have also used these in our design of the prototypes for emergency response.

We see our work as a contribution to think on, work with and research media spaces in new ways. Especially we think that the challenges associated with moving from symmetry to asymmetry and from static environments and technology setups to non-static are important issues to consider if we want to enlarge the perspectives of *Media Spaces*.

**Acknowledgments** The work, this chapter builds on, has been an integral part of research in the PalCom project (PalCom). This project ran from 2004 until end of 2007. The research was funded in part by the European Union, IST, project 002057 "PalCom: Palpable Computing – A new perspective on Ambient Computing"; and in part by the ISIS Katrinebjerg project 118 "Understandable Computing." We thank the emergency responders in Aarhus and our colleagues in the PalCom project for their enthusiastic cooperation.

## References

Bowker, G., Star, S. L. (1999) Sorting Things Out, Cambridge, MA: MIT Press.

Büscher, M., Mogensen, P. H. (2007) Designing for material practices of coordination emergency teamwork. *Proc. of ISCRAM 2007, 4th International Conf on Information Systems for Crisis Response and Management*, Delft, Netherlands, May 13–16, 2007, pp 419–429.

Büscher, M., Kristensen, M., Mogensen, P. H. (2008) When and how (not) to trust IT? Supporting virtual emergency teamwork. Proc. of ISCRAM 2008, 5th *International Conf. on Information Systems for Crisis Response and Management*, Washington DC, USA, May 4–7, 2008, pp 167–176.

Bødker, S., Grønbæk, K., Kyng, M. (1993) Cooperative Design: "Techniques and experiences from the Scandinavian Scene". A. Namioka, D. Schuler (Eds.), *Participatory Design*, Hillsdale, NJ: Lawrence Erlbaum, pp 157–175.

43D homepage: http://www.43d.com/index.php

Greenbaum, J. Kyng, M. (1991) Situated Design. J. Greenbaum, M. Kyng (Eds.), *Design at Work: Cooperative Design of Computer Systems*, Hillsdale, NJ: Lawrence Erlbaum, pp 1–24.

Kramp, G, Kristensen, M, Pedersen JF. (2006) Physical and digital design of the BlueBio biomonitoring system prototype, to be used in emergency medical response. *In Proc. of 1st International Conference on Pervasive Computing for Healthcare*, Innsbruck, Austria, Nov–Dec 2006.

Kristensen, M., Kyng, M., Nielsen, E. T. (2005) IT support for healthcare professionals acting in major incidents. *SHI2005, Proc. 3rd Scandinavian Conf. on health informatics*; August 25–26, Aalborg, Denmark, pp 37–41.

Kristensen, M., Kyng, M., Palen, L. (2006) Participatory design in emergency medical service: designing for future practice. *Proc. of the SIGCHI conference on Human Factors in computing systems CHI '06*. Montreal, April 2006, pp 161–170.

Kyng, M. (1994) Scandinavian Design: "Users in Product Development," *Proc. CHI*, pp 3–9.

Kyng, M. (1998) Users and computers: A contextual approach to the design of computer artifacts, *SJIS* 10(1–2), 7–44.

Kyng, M., Nielsen, E. T., Kristensen, M. (2006) Challenges in designing interactive systems for emergency response. *Proc. of the 6th ACM Conf. on Designing Interactive systems DIS '06*, Penn State University, June 2006, pp 301–310.

Lockey, D. J., MacKenzie, R., Redhead, J., Wise, D., Harris, T., Weaver, A., Hines, K., Davies, G. E. (2005). London Bombings July 2005: The immediate pre-hospital medical response. *Resuscitation 66*, 2005, pp ix–xii.

London Emergency Services Liaison Panel: LESLP Major Incident Procedure Manual, available at: http://www.leslp.gov.uk/frames.htm

Lutters, W. G., Ackerman, M. S. (2002). Achieving safety: a field study of boundary objects in aircraft technical support, *Proc. of CSCW*, pp 266–275.

Oxford English Dictionary, http://dictionary.oed.com/

PalCom project homepage: http://www.ist-palcom.org

Peral-Gutierrez de Ceballos, J., Turégano-Fuentes, F., Pérez-Diaz, D., Sanz-Sánchez, M., Martin-Llorente, C., Guerrero-Sanz, J. E. (2005). "11 March 2004: The terrorist bomb explosions in Madrid, Spain – an analysis of the logistics, injuries sustained and clinical management of casualties treated at the closest hospital," *Critical Care* 9(1), Feb 2005, 104–111.

Roccaforte, J. D. (2001). "The World Trade Center Attack. Observations from New York's Bellevue Hospital," *Critical Care* 5(6), Dec.

Romundstad, L., Sundnes, K. O., Pillgram-Larsen J., Røste, G. K., Gilbert, M. (2004). "Challenges of major incident management when excess resources are allocated: Experiences from a mass Casualty incident after roof collapse of a military command center," *Prehospital and Disaster Medicine* 19(2), April–June 2004, 179–184.

Schønemann, N.K. et al. "Survivors After Catastrophic Prehospital Illness: Long-Term Outcome After Prehospital Life-Saving Treatment", at: http://www.laegeambulancen.dk/survivors_after.htm (22/6/2007)

Star, S. L., Griesemer, J. (1989). Institutional ecology, "Translations," and boundary objects, *Social Studies of Science* 19(3), 387–420.

Teague, D. C. (2004). "Mass casualties in the Oklahoma City bombing," *Clinical Orthopaedics and Related Research*, 422, 2004, 77–81.

The Danish National Level Incident Command System (DICS). Description available at: http://www.brs.dk/uk/danish_preparedness_act.htm

The Tall Ships Races 2007 web-page: http://www.tsr07.dk/?topID=14

Weiser, M. (1991). The computer for the 21st century. *Scientific American* 13(2), 94–10, Sept. 1991.

Welling, L., Perez, R.S.G.M, van Harten, S.M., Patka, P., Mackie, D.P., Kreis, R., Bierens, J.L.M. (2005). Analysis of the pre-hospital education and subsequent performance of emergency medical responders to the Volendam café fire. *European Journal of Emergency Medicine* 12(6), 265–269.

WorkSPACE homepage: http://www.daimi.au.dk/workspace/index.htm

# Chapter 21
# Videoconferencing and Connected Rooms

**Austin Henderson and Lynne Henderson**

**Abstract** This chapter contrasts two practices: videoconferencing and connected rooms, for using video to support distributed meetings. The differences in these practices are based on differing models of social interaction in distributed meetings. Basically, the users' conceptual model of videoconferencing (VC) is that a distributed meeting is composed of two local meetings that are interacting with each other; the users' conceptual model of connected rooms is that a distributed meeting is a single meeting taking place in a virtual space spanning two sites.

## Introduction

This chapter presents some thoughts about how Media Space is different from videoconferencing (VC). These thoughts arose out of consulting work done for the Workplace Effectiveness Group at Sun Microsystems focusing on how to help people work together from a distance. These ideas are not new, but they were to us at the time, and they may surprise you as much as they did us.

## Context

Around 2000, Sun was spilling out of Silicon Valley and the Worksplace Effectiveness Group (a research group within Facilities) was concerned with how Sun employees would work together from a distance. We were asked to look at Sun's experience with various ways of working from a distance and propose some best practices.

One practice we considered centered on video: gathering in special conference rooms equipped with "videoconferencing equipment" – cameras, monitors, and document cameras, with the ability to make connection with other sites using

A. Henderson and L. Henderson
Rivendel Consulting and Design
e-mail: austin.henderson@pb.com
e-mail: lynne@psych.stanford.edu

S. Harrison (ed.), *Media Space 20+ Years of Mediated Life*,
Computer Supported Cooperative Work,

medium-bandwidth, dial-up video codecs. This configuration had detectable but acceptable delay, and was available throughout Sun.

It was a common belief at Sun that videoconferencing was horrible, and to be avoided at all costs. Therefore VC was used very little. However, we discovered a few groups that were using it with singular success and loving it. These groups were using the standard VC equipment, but in a novel configuration with novel practices. They had created what we came to see as dial-up Media Space. To make the point to Sun, we contrasted this Media Space-like practice with that of normal videoconferencing (VC) by calling it "Coupled Rooms" (CR).

In VC, in rooms on both sites, the chairs face the videoconferencing equipment. There are often special-purpose tables and chairs, special lighting, and special microphones in front of the chairs. In CR, on the other hand, the videoconferencing equipment is set up at one end of the table in a small conference room, with the presentation area (screen, whiteboard, document camera) at the other end of the table. In effect, the videoconferencing equipment couples the two rooms together end-to-end, making one long virtual table, surrounded by chairs, and with presentation areas at both ("outboard") ends.

## Practices and Models of Interaction

Most generally, we believe that these two contrasting practices (VC and CR) are two different ways of achieving the same purpose: having a distributed meeting. However, we also believe that the two practices can be seen as reflecting two quite different ideas of what "having a distributed meeting" means. We understand these as differences in the models of the social interaction that takes place in a distributed meeting. These models provide different answers to a number of questions about social interaction in meetings in general, and in distributed meetings in particular. The answers to these questions then drive the physical (including spatial and technical) and social arrangements of the two practices. Different models of social interaction lead quite directly to different behaviors.

In the following sections, we give some examples of these questions about social interaction in meetings, the models and answers provide by VC and CR, and the resulting differences in the practical details of physical and social arrangements.

### *Why Are You Having This Meeting?*

While VC answers, "So that we can meet with those folk who are remote," CR answers, "So that everyone, some of whom are remote, can meet with everyone." With CR, there is just as much interest in people at each site talking with each other as there is in talking between the sites. This means that things should be arranged so that local people can interact easily. In VC, because the focus is on talking to the folks at the other end, the chairs are arranged facing the video equipment. In CR, people are arranged around a single virtual table, leveling the playing field of interaction, inviting mutual participation and discussion.

## What Happens at Meetings?

CR is all about having a discussion between everyone. On the other hand, if you look at the advertising for video equipment, VC is usually about a presenter speaking to a remote audience. VC practice is based on the belief that all the talks in a presentation happen between audience and presenter. However, even in presentation meetings, if you want the folks in the audience to talk to each other (e.g., as part of Q&A), or if you have audiences at both ends, or speakers at both ends (as in an all-hands meeting), the idea of a meeting as a discussion among all parties may be the better model.

## Who Talks? Who Listens? Where Are They? What Are They Doing?

These questions are related to the previous question: Is the presenter the only speaker, or is everyone a speaker? Are they standing/sitting still or are they moving around? VC tends to have an unequal and stationary view of interaction. CR seeks a level playing field. VC says provide microphones for the presenter; CR demands that you arrange microphones to capture the whole room.

## Whom Do You Watch?

One answer is that you watch the speaker. A better answer is that you watch whomever you want, often the person whose reaction to the speaker is of interest to you. That is, let everyone choose who to watch for themselves. VC's model of interaction is so based on watching the speaker that immense effort has been put into the technology to enable the camera to automatically follow the speaker. This technology also works only when switching between speakers is slow, as the camera has to be swung around to each speaker in turn. In contrast, with CR – as at all discussion meetings – the choice of whom to watch is personal. CR encourages people not to move the camera, so that the image of the far end remains stationary, and so that people's ability to find people at the remote end is as good as it is at the local end. VC calls for zoom lenses; CR calls for wide-angle lenses.

## What Do You Watch?

A VC tends to focus on watching presenters; CR focus on watching the whole room. A VC meeting room is considered to be filled with people; a CR meeting room includes not only the people, but also all the furniture, the coffee machine, the whiteboards, the documents, the windows, walls, and doors. People carry things in, share them, write on boards. A VC meeting tends to focus on communicating (one way) or sharing (two-way) information; a CR meeting is focused on working together.

## *Where Do You Present?*

A VC presenter is standing at one end of the room, presenting either to the other end or to both ends. A CR presenter is inside the room, often sitting at the table, or, for more "formal" presentations, standing at the presentation end of the room. In a VC meeting, the video equipment needs to be moved so that the speaker is on-camera. In a CR meeting, the document camera must be put on a long cable so that it reaches the presentation end, but the camera never has to move.

## *Why Use Video Rather than Telephone? Why Videoconferencing Rather than Teleconferencing?*

Both VC and CR answer this one similarly: to provide participants with a sense of presence, a sense of being there and participating. However, VC participation is focused on conveying information, on being there to hear the presentation; CR participation is about engagement, discussion, negotiation, and decision (see other paper). VC often argues for zooming in on faces and document cameras to provide more information; CR focuses on supporting the distributed remote social construction of meaning (e.g., understandings, agreements). With CR you can tell who is in the room, and you can tell from body language the nature of their engagement. You can use the visual channel as a back-channel without interrupting the speaker (e.g., signaling the desire to talk, giving a thumbs-up to the speaker, or a colleague). You can show disagreement, form coalitions, and give support using the visual concurrently with speaking (e.g., waving hands, jumping up and walking around, leaning back in disapproval, or forward in engagement). If agreement is reached, you can know that all have agreed, and that they know that you know. If agreement is not reached, that too is "publicly available." CR supports the undeniable understanding that "you" were there and that you were part of the "we" that were responsible for whatever happened.

Information transfer works pretty well with phones, particularly when supported by machine-to-machine presentations. For this reason, we believe, VC has not been seen as providing significant value beyond teleconferences and webinars. In contrast, telephones and slide presentations are no match for CR in supporting the sense of being there that is necessary for group work.

## Conclusion

The underlying models of social interaction (Heath and Luff, 1991) in distributed meetings are different for VC and CR. To achieve understanding, these examples are based on idealized accounts of VC and CR practices; the real practices are much richer, and are not always as sharply contrasting as we have made them here. Further, we understand that what we learned from these contrasts apply equally to meetings taking place in one room. At heart, the VC users' conceptual model is that a distributed meeting is composed of two local meetings that are interacting with each other; the CR users' conceptual model is that a distributed meeting is a single meeting taking place in a virtual space spanning two sites.

## Reference

Heath, C and Luff, P (1991) Collaborative activity and technological design: task coordination in London underground control rooms. Proceedings of the Second European Conference on Computer-Supported Cooperative Work. Kluwer, Dordrecht.

# Chapter 22
# The Halo B2B Studio

**Mark Gorzynski, Mike Derocher, and April Slayden Mitchell**

**Abstract** Research underway at Hewlett-Packard on remote communication resulted in the identification of three important components typically missing in existing systems. These missing components are: group nonverbal communication capabilities, high-resolution interactive data capabilities, and global services. Here we discuss some of the design elements in these three areas as part of the Halo program at HP, a remote communication system shown to be effective to end-users.

## Overview

If you look around you, on your desk or perhaps in your pockets, you are likely to find examples of technology that have been successfully applied to improve many types of global communication. Telephone services are easily accessible. Data-oriented tools like email, file sharing, text messaging, and a variety of streaming media are located right at your fingertips. Many of us find that these applications and services have become essential business tools that are partly responsible for the growth of our business by giving access to global markets and workforces.

An essential characteristic of communication tools is that they extend capabilities traditionally available locally, so that they work over distance. Many communications processes have become globalized. There are some critical business processes that have not yet been globalized by technology tools. We will describe three key missing processes here.

The first missing process is the ability to extend face-to-face meetings over distance. Voice-only conversations and text sharing are not a problem over distance. However, it is still much more common for businesses to depend on travel for face-to-face social meetings than it is for them to use interactive video conferencing, even though a wide variety of video conferencing and web camera technologies are available. The importance of face-to-face meetings to global business is shown by how much companies

M. Gorzynski, M. Derocher, and A.S. Mitchell
Hewlett-Packard Company
e-mail: mark.gorzynski@hp.com; mike.derocher@hp.com; april.slayden@hp.com

S. Harrison (ed.), *Media Space 20+ Years of Mediated Life*,
Computer Supported Cooperative Work,

still depend on scheduling travel for critical processes. The speed and quality of global business is largely gated by the ability of key personnel to travel, causing significant productivity problems.

The second missing global process involves applications requiring high resolution, smoothly moving images for interactive (two-way) work such as editing of films and CAD, or presentations with interactive animation. A bottleneck with these applications is the human interface. It is difficult to send the high-resolution visual data needed by humans rapidly across the globe. Streaming media solutions like television have solved this problem partially by delaying the streams with buffering and prestoring content; however, this is not satisfactory for interactive work that must run in real time.

The third problem for companies is how solutions for face-to-face communication and data collaboration are provided. Generally, technologies for communication are provided to companies as subsystems that need to be integrated into their IT systems. As these technologies increase in scope and complexity, companies are forced to take on increasing integration and service loads. With communication becoming global and intercompany, it is increasingly unproductive for companies to separately integrate complete global solutions on their own. Companies are missing a solution where communication and collaboration systems are integrated into complete globally oriented solutions. Companies should expect global communication solutions to be provided like power and road systems, largely integrated and ready to use, yet flexible enough to integrate into their local systems. Most video- and data-collaboration systems today are not integrated on this global scale.

The goal of the Halo program at HP is to develop solutions that address these missing processes; face-to-face communication, high-resolution data collaboration, and end-to-end service. The Halo program is designed to build on the large amount of excellent existing work and available subsystems by focusing on the missing pieces, as well as integration and user testing. By concentrating on integrating full solutions, the Halo program has been forced to deal with many small details that together add up to possible sources of failure. Requiring high levels of acceptance by end-users requires us to extend the typical technical team to include significant expertise in design, cinematography, and media reproduction.

## The Halo Experience Framework

Our research on creating a workable global solution for face-to-face collaboration resulted in a wide range of issues. We have categorized these issues based on their impact to user experience in four areas we call the *Halo Experience Framework*. The four areas are:

- The Work Experience,
- The Communications Experience,
- The Interaction Experience
- The Service Experience

## The Work Experience

The primary goal of providing communication and collaboration tools is to enable widely distributed groups to meet, interact, and work together effectively in real time. The creation of environments and tools needs to be optimized for the type of work to be performed. When a space is designed for one type of work, it can promote optimal productivity and human performance for that work. If an environment is designed to be used for multiple work purposes with opposing requirements, it may be more difficult to promote optimal productivity for any one task. For example, a space designed to support large meetings may be less optimal for discussions between a few people.

Optimizing an environment for work also means supplying the technical tools needed for work. When a space needs to support distributed work where some participants are remotely located, technical systems like video and audio are used. These systems are not work tools however, and should not be treated as such. The goal of the work space is to enable all remote and local participants to work together efficiently as if they were all local. Technology must be transparent to that end. Technology used to bring remote participants is part of the communication experience. Communication technologies must be blended into a space in a way that does not degrade the work experience.

## The Communication Experience

Many studies over the years have shown that during work, people communicate in a variety of ways including verbally and nonverbally. For reviews, see books such as Richmond et al. (2007) or Mehrabian (2007). While the specifics of this work, such as Mehrabian's "55% nonverbal" rule, have been widely quoted out of context, the importance of nonverbal communication is clear. Work sessions among groups of people include dynamic verbal and nonverbal signals. These signals are naturally communicated during local work, and face-to-face meetings over distance must satisfy this same basic need. Work environments are specifically tuned to properly enable such communication. When some participants are at remote locations, technology systems must be put in place to encode and preserve these nonverbal signals. The perception of participants is a feeling of transparency through a connection to the remote space. The result of systems with a transparent communication experience is an accurate transmission of nonverbal group signals across remote sites.

The technology required for enabling transparent communication can be extensive including subsystems for camera and audio acquisition, encoding and signal processing, and audio–video reproduction. These systems have limited abilities to acquire, encode, transmit, and reproduce verbal and nonverbal communication. They take up critical work space and increase cost of installation and maintenance. Using them during meetings can require interaction making work more complicated. A principle challenge of creating work experiences with proper communication capabilities is the integration of audio–video subsystems.

In an ideal installation, full nonverbal communication would be enabled as if remote participants were actually local. In real systems, it is often necessary to make tradeoffs. For example, systems vary in the physical sizes of their audio–video reproduction spaces. A cell phone designed to enable communication while traveling has a very small space. A desktop computer or laptop may be larger while a room system can be very large. A goal of enabling work is to preserve needed communication signals in the available spaces. However, we must be clear when a system simply cannot preserve a type of communication. To assist in this task, we have created a simple hierarchy of communication types with dependencies on physical capabilities such as size and spatial resolution.

- Voice, language, and tone
- Visual presence and identity
- Individual facial signals
- Individual body language
- Group nonverbal dynamics
- Proximity

In our work, we have concentrated on the last few items of this list where communication of nonverbal signals of face and body language between members of a group is important. We have found a distinct difference between systems designed to preserve signals from individuals versus those that preserve signals between individuals in a group across multiple remote sites (multipoint). We have found attributes required for preserving group nonverbal dynamics during a multipoint meeting. These attributes are largely those that create a valid perceptual frame of reference for the work space. In other words, group dynamics are preserved if participants are properly seen in the context of a work space. When a first person glances at a second person, it is vital that a third person see this exchange properly in context for group dynamics to be preserved.

Multipoint conferencing requires a local site to receive video and audio signals from multiple other sites. These signals must then be combined in the local reproduction system in a way that allows group nonverbal signals to be properly communicated. We have concentrated on combining signals from remote sites into a panoramic multipoint image following certain rules:

- Magnification constancy. Images from multiple sites must show participants in a size consistent for them being at one location.
- Eye height. Participants should be shown at a position correct for their relative seating.
- Foreground and table height. Objects common to the work should be maintained across all sites.
- Background consistency. Backgrounds should be consistent across all sites.
- Distortion reduction. Efforts should be made to eliminate reproduction distortions such as tilted tables and wall seams.

- Eye contact and gesture awareness. Audio and video acquisition must be aligned with reproduction promoting consistent eye contact across the panorama and spatial alignment between audio and video signals.
- Spatial audio. Knowing not just what is said, but also who is saying it and the relative position of the speaker helps participants direct their gaze appropriately.

## The Interaction Experience

Work typically requires interaction between people and with artifacts of work such as documents. Sometimes, interaction is required to prepare an environment or tools for work. Chairs may be brought in, tables arranged, software set up. There are then two objectives for interaction: first, optimize setup activities in order to prevent them from interfering with the main work and second, provide the tools needed for work.

## The Service Experience

People participating in work benefit from the right work, communication and interaction systems being in place where and when they need them. Trusting that systems will be available and will operate consistently is vital to making collaboration tools useful for business. Insuring that this is true has two service aspects: maintenance and optimization.

Maintenance services cover all bases of installation and maintenance. Components that break need to be fixed. New systems need to be installed. Multiple components across a global system need to be arranged to work correctly together without inconsistencies. Proper maintenance service is the backbone of simple interaction and transparent communications. Many interaction problems are caused by poor maintenance services. Interaction systems are forced to take on maintenance tasks such as aligning cameras or assigning network addresses. If done correctly, proper maintenance services are invisible, working diligently in the background. A concierge service is the public face to maintenance, providing a place to express concerns and ask questions.

Optimization services provide the types of choice needed by workers and provide essential coordination between remote locations. For example, a scheduling service allows people to choose times for meetings. A service for setting up a work environment allows choice of meeting size and seating arrangements. Optimization services allow interaction to be simplified by providing a platform for coordinating event setup and management. They enable transparent communication by helping endpoints coordinate media streams and reproduction.

During our work to establish a system for face-to-face collaboration, we required user testing with full systems. Creating a full system required us to service that system. We soon learned that this service was as important as the design of the work, communication, and interaction systems. In fact, we found that principle causes of failure in communication and interaction can be traced back to service. Insufficient network service design is echoed in audio–video communication systems designed for limited performance. Event setup limitations cause complicated interaction and an inability to create multipoint connections that preserve nonverbal communication. Inconsistent maintenance can result in random failures and a general sense of mistrust in users. Our research with users of previous systems emphasizes these problems. Early on in our work, we became convinced that producing an end-to-end global service was essential to solving problems of face-to-face communications.

## The Halo B2B Studio

### *The B2B Work Experience*

For our research, we worked with DreamWorks studios and user experience researchers to select one type of work scenario important to companies for our first endpoint. The type of work selected for Halo's first endpoint is the B2B (business to business) meeting (Fig. 22.1).

The B2B model for 6 people per table (B2B6) is a relatively small meeting optimized for up to 12 people sitting around a table having a critical business discussion. The focus of the meeting is the conversation among the participants. This is a social group where sharing group nonverbal communication is an essential reason for holding the meeting in person rather than over a voice-only phone call.

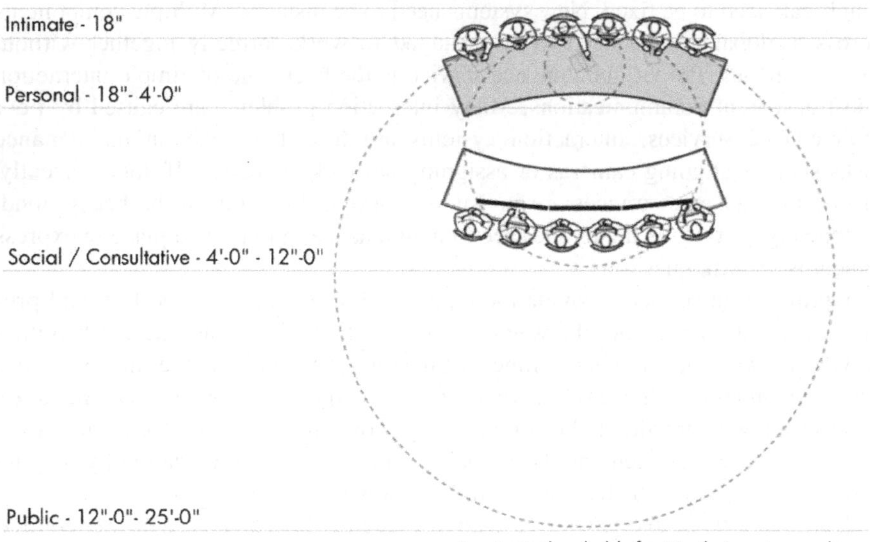


**Fig 22.1** The B2B6 work model

This type of meeting may call for the ability to share supporting materials including digital slides, movies, data or physical objects, and papers. However, the primary focus of the meeting is social communication. Participants' reactions to shared materials should be preserved. Materials should not focus participants' attention away from each other or limit social communication.

We selected the B2B meeting model in favor of other interesting and needed models for several reasons. Smaller, more data-centric work was already represented to some degree with data tools and telephone. Larger meeting venues would require more investment compared to the B2B. Based on interviews with potential customers, we found the B2B meeting type represented a common-sized meeting requiring travel.

Our first step was to outline the work experience required for a high-quality B2B meeting and the implications this placed on space design. We then moved on to a *choreography* phase where the space was modified to incorporate remote communication technologies. A goal of the choreography phase was to enable communication between remote participants that is as close as possible to local communication without sacrificing the work experience. Obviously this required tradeoffs. The result of this phase was a space optimized for work and natural communication rather than a space that emphasized technology. Technology was largely hidden unless it was a tool required for work.

- Room shape:
  - People seated 6–12 ft apart gathered around a two-sided curved table with equal seating positions
  - Room for up to 12 participants at the main tables
- Sharing materials:
  - Ability to share paper and objects placed on the table
  - Ability to bring in a laptop computer for sharing programs such as slides
  - Positioning shared data images centrally at the table rather than individual screens or projections at the end of the room
- Environment:
  - Natural materials and muted color schemes to contrast against highly technical environments
  - No visible technology elements on table surface
  - Quiet, low noise to minimize stress and distraction
  - Lighting providing good visibility and comfort

## *The B2B Communication Experience*

Choreography of communications technology into the B2B work model required careful attention to many details. A model was developed that established viewpoints of participants within the workspace. These viewpoints were then mapped onto audio and video acquisition and reproduction systems. An overview of the model is shown in Fig. 22.2.

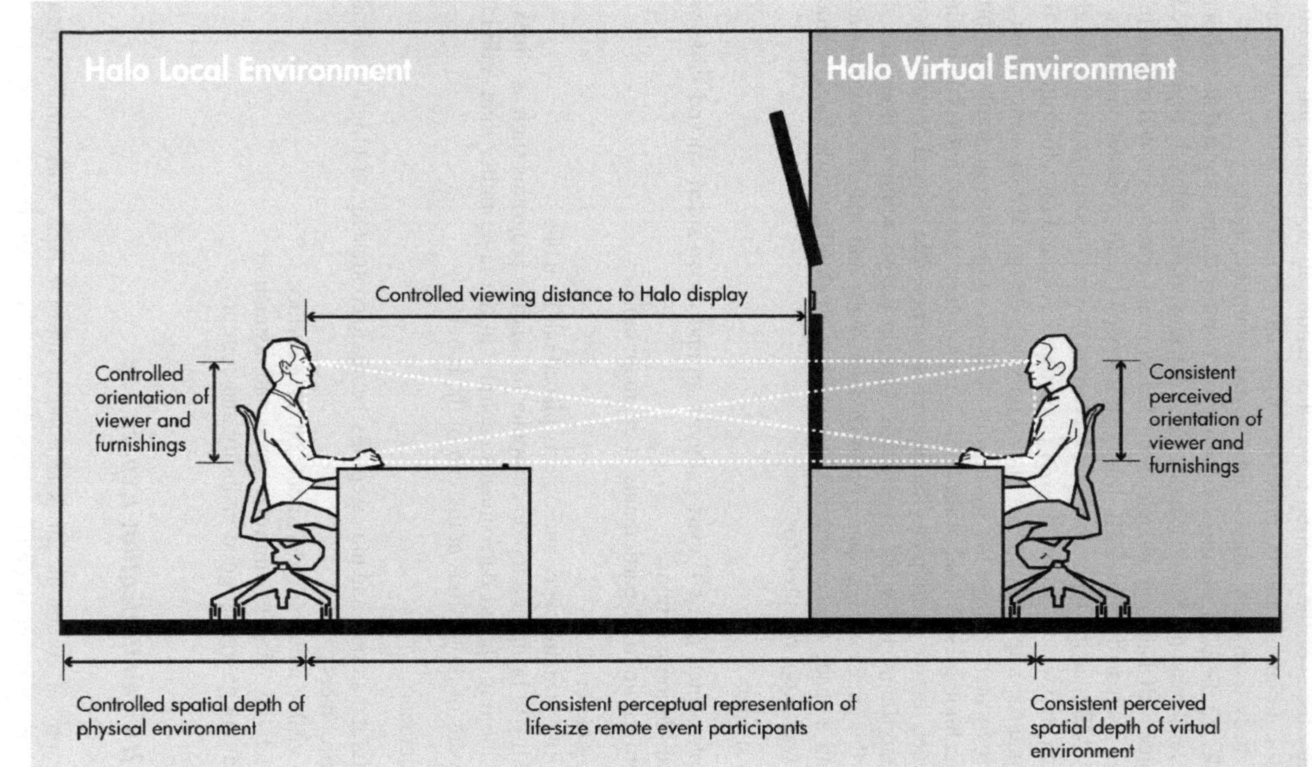


**Fig. 22.2** The Halo B2B communications model

**Fig. 22.3** Front view of the Halo B2B communications model

The model in Fig. 22.2 shows participants seated at opposing tables. The remote participant on the right is mapped into a virtual space defined at a display defining the view into that space. Essential parameters like eye height and magnification are defined at the display surface. This allows construction of a theoretical set of images needed to be generated by the video acquisition system as shown in Fig. 22.3.

Figure 22.3 shows 3 image modules combined into a panoramic multipoint image. In this case, the panorama is made from three tiled displays. Each image forms a standardized module with predefined attributes such as eye height, magnification, and table height. Formation of standardized modules during capture allows flexible arrangement during construction of multipoint panoramas.

Figure 22.3 also shows the position of information display selected for the B2B communication model. Unlike many information arrangements, a position above the participants was selected. This position allows for information visibility closing close proximity to remote participants. Therefore, it is easier to see information and participant reactions at the same time. Focus is maintained on the conversation and nonverbal communication. Information is above, not between participants maintaining social distances. Many systems place information displays either at the sides of the room or below the participants, sometimes directly embedded into the tables. Our testing showed that placing information at the sides refocused attention away from people to the information display. This is appropriate for some meetings but not the work model selected here. Testing with displays below or embedded in the table showed that participant heads were caused to be increasingly directed down with eyes and faces no longer visible. Positioning information at the table places significant technology between participants increasing social distance and reducing nonverbal communication seen with intimate arrangements. The model of Fig. 22.3 was selected for our B2B work model. Other work models can be expected to require different arrangements.

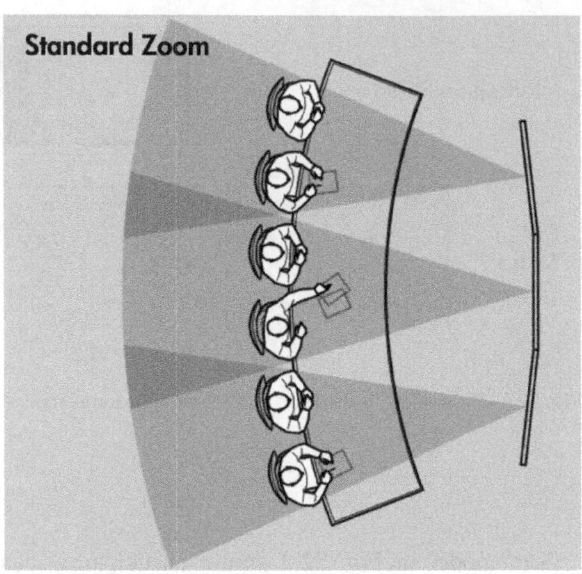


**Fig. 22.4** Halo B2B camera views for a two-point meeting

Figure 22.4 shows camera positions adjusted for a two-point meeting. Camera fields are adjustable being readjusted for different types of multipoint meetings.

A side view of the Halo B2B space is shown in Fig. 22.5 giving a high-level look at planning for lighting, audio, and video geometries. Each was optimized in detail for the communication experience. Lighting was selected to provide even- field illumination and constant color temperature. This was important because it allowed us to optimize tone reproduction for a fixed gain and white balance capture system. This provided very good image clarity and detail, and consistency between sights in a meeting. Audio and video components were carefully arranged. Camera and display height were selected to optimize reproduced eye height and optimize eye contact error. At viewing distances created, vertical eye contact error was insignificant making use of devices like mirrors or camera arms placing lenses in front of the display unnecessary. Background elements were carefully controlled removing objects that could be distorted on camera such as wall seams.

Details such as those shown in Fig. 22.5 contribute to both the work and communication experience. The goal for communication is to preserve nonverbal signals between participants. This means that once the endpoint systems acquired images properly, a network service needed to be provided that maintained the signals accurately and transmit them across the globe to remote locations. The speed of the transmission needed to be fast enough to not be noticeable to participants.

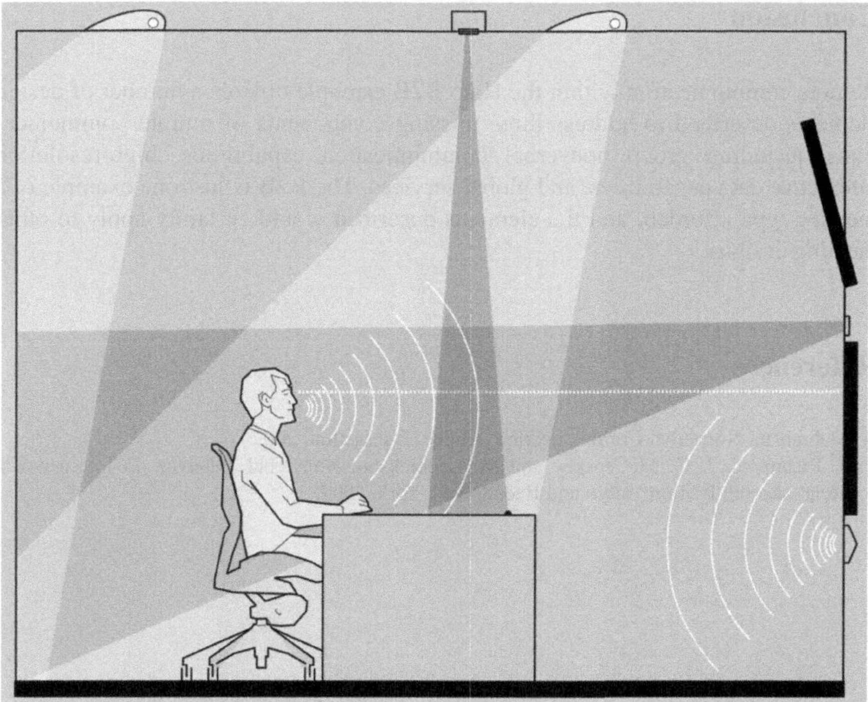

**Fig. 22.5** Lighting, audio, and video in the Halo B2B space

A document camera is shown in the ceiling above the table in Fig. 22.5. This system, in conjunction with a cable for sharing VGA laptop output, gives participants the ability to share objects on the desk or computer output.

## *The B2B Service Experience*

Tests showed that using data-optimized multipurpose networks were not sufficient for connecting Halo endpoints. Problems such as high-transmission latencies, packet loss, and inconsistent service contributed to audio and video quality inconsistency. To solve this, HP constructed a private global backbone using large OC class fiber resulting in the Halo Video Exchange Network (HVEN). HVEN is the network service used by Halo to interconnect endpoints. The HVEN network has quality of service and bandwidth needed to transmit video conference and data collaboration signals at the speeds required. It is maintained as part of a global service interconnecting companies and so has the consistency and availability needed. HVEN has become the foundation of Halo's service experience.

## Conclusion

Remote communication within the Halo B2B example utilizes a number of design elements described to address three missing components of remote communications, including group nonverbal communication capabilities, high-resolution interactive data capabilities, and global services. The B2B is just one example of a meeting type afforded, and the elements described would certainly apply to other meeting designs.

## References

A. Mehrabian, Nonverbal Communication, Aldine Transaction, 2007.

V. P. Richmond, J. C. McCroskey and M. L. Hickson, Nonverbal Behavior in Interpersonal Relations, 6th Edition, Allyn and Bacon, New York, 2007.

# Chapter 23
# Presence in Video-Mediated Interactions: Case Studies at CSIRO

**Leila Alem**

**Abstract** Although telepresence and a sense of connectedness with others are frequently mentioned in media space studies, as far as we know, none of these studies report attempts at assessing this critical aspect of user experience. While some attempts have been made to measure presence in virtual reality or augmented reality, (a comprehensive review of existing measures is available in Baren and Ijsselsteijn [2004]), very little work has been reported in measuring presence in video-mediated collaboration systems. Traditional studies of video-mediated collaboration have mostly focused their evaluation on measures of task performance and user satisfaction. Videoconferencing systems can be seen as a type of media space; they rely on technologies of audio, video, and computing put together to create an environment extending the embodied mind. This chapter reports on a set of video-mediated collaboration studies conducted at CSIRO in which different aspects of presence are being investigated. The first study reports the sense of physical presence a specialist doctor experiences when engaged in a remote consultation of a patient using the virtual critical care unit (Alem et al., 2006). The Viccu system is an "always-on" system connecting two hospitals (Li et al., 2006). The presence measure focuses on the extent to which users of videoconferencing systems feel physically present in the remote location. The second study reports the sense of social presence users experience when playing a game of charades with remote partners using a video conference link (Kougianous et al., 2006). In this study the presence measure focuses on the extent to which users feel connected with their remote partners. The third study reports the sense of copresence users experience when building collaboratively a piece of Lego toy (Melo and Alem, 2007). The sense of copresence is the extent to which users feel present with their remote partner. In this final study the sense of copresence is investigated by looking at the word used by users when referring to the physical objects they are manipulating during their interaction as well as when referring to locations in the collaborative workspace. We believe that such efforts provide a solid stepping stone for evaluating and analyzing future media spaces.

---

L. Alem
CSIRO
e-mail: Leila.alem@csiro.au

S. Harrison (ed.), *Media Space 20+ Years of Mediated Life*,
Computer Supported Cooperative Work,

## Physical Presence of the Remote Specialist Doctor in the Virtual Critical Care Unit

The Virtual Critical Care Unit (ViCCU®) is a telemedicine system that allows a specialist at a major referral hospital to direct a team in a rural hospital. ViCCU® allows remote consultation to take place based on the transmission of multiple channels of real-time video/audio information of the patient, the clinical team, x-ray/paper documents, and patient vital signs from the remote site to the specialist. ViCCU® was installed in the Katoomba Hospital and Nepean Hospital in December 2003 for a 2-year clinical trial. A usability and technical evaluation was conducted by CSIRO after ViCCU® had been used for 21 months.

This study explores clinicians' experience of presence in this telemedicine application using a modified version of the Slater-Usoh-Steed (SUS) presence questionnaire (Slater et al., 1994) to measure clinicians' sense of presence when using ViCCU®. We explore the relationship between presence felt when using ViCCU® and personal, usability, and media factors. Initial results indicate that in this context, personal factors influenced clinicians' experience of presence and that there was a positive relationship between presence and both usability and media factors. Reflections on some of the challenges in conducting this study in an emergency department and the appropriateness of the SUS presence measure in this real setting are also included.

The Virtual Critical Care Unit system is described in Section 1.2, Section 1.3 contains a review of the existing presence measures and the justification for selecting the SUS measure as a foundation for this study, Section 1.4 describes the design of the study, Section 1.5 contains the results, and Section 1.6 presents our conclusion and suggestions for future directions.

## *The Virtual Critical Care Unit*

ViCCU® is composed of two main stations: a specialist station located at Nepean Hospital and a remote station located at Katoomba Hospital. The system transmits digital video (DV) over an 'ultra-broadband' Gigabit optical fiber link between the two hospitals.

### The Remote Station – Katoomba

The system has four cameras that capture and transmit multiple views to the Nepean specialist. These include a camera for general treatment overview, a document camera for transmitting X-rays, ECG reports, and other patient records; a camera on the ceiling for viewing the patient; and an auxiliary video channel for plugging in a mobile camera for close-up examination or other sources such as an ultrasonic scanner and an overhead view camera.

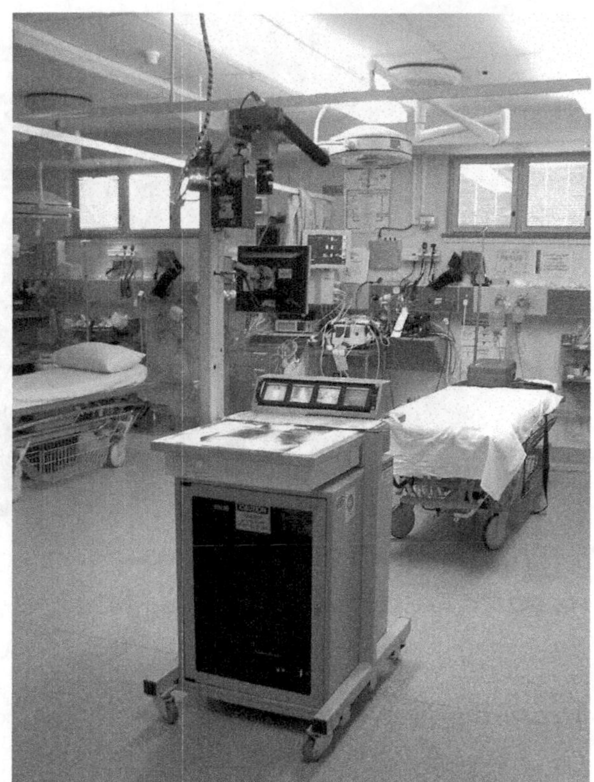

**Fig. 23.1** The remote station at Katoomba hospital

In order to minimize the clutter created by the equipment necessary for ViCCU®, the majority of the equipment for the remote unit was designed as a mobile trolley (Fig. 23.1). The mobile trolley setup allows ViCCU® to be easily wheeled in to the end of the patients' bed when needed – where a specialist would usually stand when physically present.

## The Specialist Station – Nepean

At Nepean, a room was dedicated to house the specialist unit of ViCCU® as shown in Fig. 23.2. It consists of three monitors that are able to continuously display the patient's vital signs as well as different patient views, X-rays, and patient notes to a specialist in the room.

The patient's vital signs are continuously displayed on the top right monitor. On that same screen the specialist may select the patient or document view desired, by selecting the corresponding thumbnail.

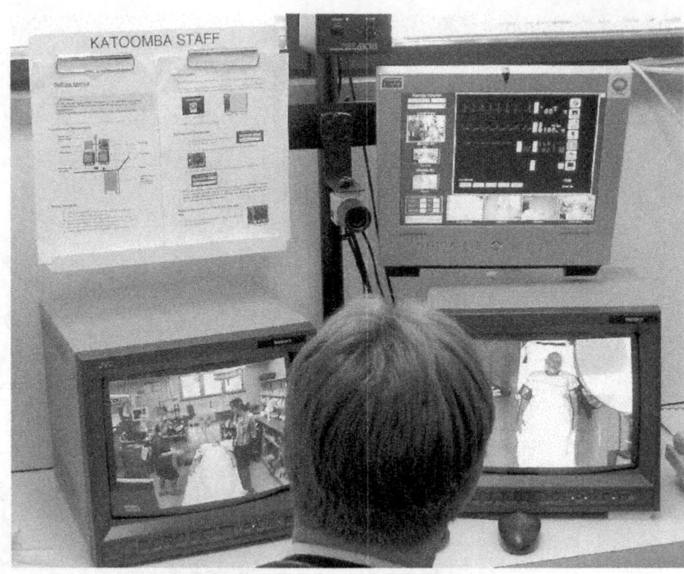


**Fig. 23.2** The specialists' station at Nepean hospital

## *Measuring Presence*

Heeter (1992) defines three aspects/dimensions of presence:

- Physical presence: the sense of being in one place or environment
- Social presence: the feeling of being connected to other people in the place or environment
- Environmental presence: the extend to which the environment itself appears to know that you are there and reacts to you

As one of the aims of ViCCU® was to create a system that gave clinicians located in a rural hospital the feeling that the specialist located in a major hospital was physically "there" at the end of the bed, we decided to focus our initial study on the physical aspect of presence.

Due to the constraints presented by the emergency department environment – which is a highly complex and dynamic environment with continuous interruptions – and ethical constraints, the measure of presence chosen had to be as nonobtrusive as possible. In this environment any external intervention was unfeasible making presence questionnaire the most practical and feasible to consider. Questionnaires are easy to administer, can be completed relatively quickly, and do not require interfering with users during their presence experience. After careful consideration and review of presence questionnaires such as the ITC-Sense of Presence Inventory ITC-SOPI (Lessiter et al., 2000), the Witmer and Singer's Presence Questionnaire PQ (1998), (an extended comparison of subjective measures is proposed by Insko (2003) the Slater-Usoh-Steed SUS questionnaire (Slater et al., 1994) was selected as the most appropriate measure and adapted to suit the conditions of our study. The SUS questionnaire assesses the experience of presence by asking users their sense of being in the virtual environment (VE), the extent to which the environment becomes the dominant reality, and the extent to which the virtual environment is remembered as a place. Even though the SUS instrument was originally designed for measuring presence in artificial environments such as VEs created to somehow simulate real environments, the instrument has since been used to measure presence in real-world settings (Usoh et al., 2000) such as media space environments.

## *Method*

### Design

The aim of this study was to explore clinicians' experience of presence using ViCCU® and the relationship between the sense of presence and the three factors commonly mentioned in the literature as influencing presence. They include:

- Personal factors
  - Employment category, i.e., doctors vs. nurses
  - Gender
  - Prior experience with videoconferencing
- Usability factors
  - Ease of use
  - Ability to focus on patient
  - Satisfaction with overall design
- Media factors
  - Overall satisfaction with Video
  - Overall satisfaction with Audio

Presence in this study is operationalized as the cumulative value of the presence scores from the adapted version of the SUS questionnaire. It was measured using two adapted versions of the SUS questionnaire, one for Katoomba and one for Nepean, as described bellow.

Katoomba clinicians were asked the following questions (based on questions 1, 2, 3, and 6 of the original SUS questionnaire):

- Please rate your sense of the specialist "being" in Katoomba on the following scale: Not at All (1) – Very Much So (7)
- To what extent were there times while using ViCCU® did you feel that the specialist was in Katoomba in reality? None of the Time (1) – Almost All of the Time(7)
- When you think back to your experience interacting with a specialist in Nepean using ViCCU, do you look back on it as an interaction over a video, or more as a face-to-face interaction? Video interaction (1) – Face-to-Face Interaction (7)

- While you were remotely interacting with the Nepean specialist using ViCCU, did you think to yourself that they were actually in Katoomba? Not at All (1) – Very Much So (7)

Nepean clinicians were asked the following questions (based on questions 1, 2, 3, 5, and 6 of the original SUS questionnaire):

- Please rate your sense of being in Katoomba hospital on the following scale. Not at All (1) – Very Much So (7)
- To what extent were there times while using ViCCU did you feel you were at Katoomba hospital in reality? None of the Time (1) – Almost All of the Time (7)
- When you think back of your use of ViCCU, do you think of Katoomba hospital more as something you saw over a video, or more as a place that you visited? Images I Saw (1) – Somewhere I Visited (7)
- Consider your memory of your remote interaction with Katoomba staff using ViCCU. How similar is your memory of Katoomba hospital to other places you have been to? Consider issues such as: Do you have a visual memory of Katoomba hospital? Is your memory in colour? The extent to which your memory of Katoomba hospital seems vivid, panoramic? Not at All (1) – Very Much So (7)
- While you were remotely interacting with Katoomba staff using ViCCU, did you think to yourself that you were actually in Katoomba hospital? Not at All (1) – Very Much So (7)

### Participants

Fifty clinicians in total took part in this study. These participants were identified as staff who had used ViCCU® by the telehealth nurse consultant in charge of ViCCU® and were recruited through a series of informal information sessions. Thirty-six hospital staff (21 nurses, 14 doctors, and 1 person who did not report their employment category) from Katoomba Hospital completed the Katoomba questionnaire. This sample comprised all of the current Katoomba staff who had used ViCCU® during the data collection period. Fourteen staff specialists from Nepean Hospital completed the Nepean questionnaire. This sample comprised all of the staff specialists (13 emergency specialists and 1 neurologist) who had used ViCCU® during the data collection period.

## *Results and Discussion*

This study measured clinicians' sense of presence using the SUS presence measure and explored how the presence score relates to factors known to affect presence. Relationships were observed between presence and personal factors, usability factors, media factors, and how they compared using ViCCU® to the specialist physically being there. These are explored in more detail below.

### Personal Factors

Whilst there was no significant difference between the mean presence scores of Katoomba and Nepean clinicians, the relationship between presence and personal factors was different across the two interfaces. Katoomba Nurses reported a higher level of presence (m = 18.38, s = 5.608) than doctors (m = 13.64, s = 5.329). Katoomba females had significantly higher mean presence scores than males (m = 18.5, m = 13.93, p = 0.018), whereas in Nepean, males had higher mean presence scores (m = 22) than females (m = 14.67). A possible explanation for the difference in mean presence scores for males and females across the two sites could be provided by looking at the presence scores across employment category in the Katoomba data. Nurses had a higher mean presence than doctors in Katoomba, and the majority of nurses in Katoomba were female. As the results were in the opposite direction for the Nepean data, this suggests that the nature of the job may influence presence more than the gender. For example, in Katoomba whilst the nurses' role when using ViCCU was similar to what it would be if a doctor were leading them, the doctors experienced a change in responsibility and power with the specialist present over ViCCU than in their previous work situation.

However, the different direction of presence scores across gender in the two hospitals may not necessarily be due to or solely due to the nature of the job, but the nature of the interface, which may affect the genders differently. Further study and exploration of this is needed in order to clarify the reason for this finding and to see if this finding is consistent.

### Usability Factors

Consistent with the findings of Nosper et al. (2005), the mean presence score of those who found ViCCU® easy to use was higher than those who were neutral across both hospitals. The mean Katoomba presence score of those who found ViCCU® easy to use (m = 17.31) was higher than the mean presence score of those who reported ViCCU® was neutral to use (m = 14.11). Similar to Katoomba, the mean Nepean presence scores of those who found ViCCU® easy to use (m = 21.83) was higher than the mean presence score of those who reported ViCCU® was neutral to use (m = 12.00). There was also a significant moderate positive correlation between Nepean presence scores and ease of use ($r = 0.553$, $p < 0.05$).

However, although there were indications of relationships between the other usability factors, that is, the ability to focus on patient and satisfaction with overall design, there were no other statistically significant relationships.

This could be because with the exception of ease of use, there was no relationship between presence and usability/control factors, the way we operationalized usability, or the way the sample was distributed. That is, most people reported positively on the usability factors with very few or no people expressing dissatisfaction in any of the three categories. The small number, or complete lack of people in these negative categories, although positive for ViCCU®, made it difficult to assess the relationship between presence and these factors.

## Media Factors

There was some evidence of a relationship between presence and media factors in this study. There was a significant positive moderate correlation between the Nepean presence scores and overall satisfaction with video quality ($r = 0.549$, $p < 0.05$). In Nepean, those who reported satisfaction with the overall quality of ViCCU® displayed a higher mean presence score ($m = 22.40$) than those who were neutral ($m = 15.50$). As hypothesized, a positive relationship was found between presence and overall satisfaction with video. No significant relationship was found between overall satisfaction with audio for Nepean specialists. There was no significant relationship between presence and media factors for Katoomba clinicians.

The lack of relationship found in this study between presence felt by Katoomba clinicians and media factors may be due to a lack of relationship or could be due to the fact that very few or no clinicians reported dissatisfaction with the media quality in each category.

This meant that there were either very few or no people to represent dissatisfaction giving a disproportionate weighting to individuals who did express dissatisfaction when comparing mean presence scores across the categories. As the majority of Katoomba and Nepean staff reported high levels of satisfaction with the media factors, similar to the usability factors it was difficult to explore whether these experiences affected presence.

## Comparison of Using ViCCU® to Specialist being in the Room

As face to face is widely considered the gold standard, at best we thought that some clinicians may report that ViCCU® was the same as the specialist being there. Whilst there was no significant difference in the presence experience by Katoomba and Nepean clinicians, a surprising finding was that the majority of Katoomba staff actually felt that using ViCCU® was the same as the specialist actually being there (53%) and almost 20% of the staff felt that it was better. However, the majority of the Nepean clinicians felt that using ViCCU® was worse (62%) than actually being there and about a third (31%) thought it was the same. This could be due to several reasons. From the interviews conducted with nurses, doctors, and specialists it is proposed that this is most likely to do with the nature of their jobs. Although the visual information provided by the vital signs monitor, documentary camera and various patient views give the specialist more information to form a diagnosis than they would have available through more basic communication mediums such as a telephone. In some cases it is important for the specialist to be able to touch and feel the patient, which is not possible through ViCCU®. The nurses and doctors on the remote end only need to hear the specialist's advice, and any additional information is supplementary.

### The SUS Questionnaire

Whilst the SUS questionnaire may not be as comprehensive as the ICT-SOPI, it has shown itself to be a context flexible and adaptable measure of presence. The major advantage of the SUS questionnaire, particularly in this time-critical telemedicine context, is the length of the questionnaire which lends itself to be easily integrated into a larger questionnaire and is quick to fill in. However, the length of the questionnaire could also be its major disadvantage as it may not necessarily be able to capture as wide a range of the elements that contribute to presence and lead to a more accurate measure. If possible, it would be interesting to assess an adapted SUS questionnaire to a more comprehensive measure such as the ICT-SOPI in a real-world telemedicine context and compare the results.

## *Limitations of the Study*

Whilst usability and media factors were found to influence presence in the directions expected, it was difficult to establish statistical significance and explore this comprehensively for two main reasons including the sample size and the nature of the responses.

Although the full sample of Nepean staff specialists using ViCCU® at the time of data collection was captured, this sample size of 14 lacked power and was therefore not sufficiently large to detect some of the potential significant differences. Even in the Katoomba data with the larger but still relatively small sample size of 36, in cases where there were few clinicians represented in a category interpretations of the data needed to be made in a more qualitative manner, that is, from graphical representations of the mean presence scores across each category.

In addition to this, whilst it was great that majority of clinicians were satisfied with the usability and media factors, the ability to assess how these perceptions were related to presence was limited as there were either very few or no clinicians who reported feeling negatively in these areas.

## *Conclusion*

Clinicians reported high levels of presence when using ViCCU®. The study revealed that the presence experienced by the clinicians was influenced by personal factors including employment category, gender, and previous experience with videoconferencing. There was some evidence to support the positive relationship between satisfaction with usability and media factors and presence.

There was also evidence from the study to suggest that the high levels of satisfaction with ViCCU® expressed by the clinicians could be influenced by the high levels of presence experienced when using ViCCU®, making it comparable to actually "being there." The majority of Katoomba staff felt that using ViCCU® was the same or better than the specialist physically being there, although the majority of Nepean staff felt that using ViCCU® was worse.

This study indicates that the SUS is an appropriate presence measure in this context and is sensitive enough to allow the investigation of the influence of different factors such as personal, usability, and media factors on presence. Whilst acknowledging the limitations, this study also represents a positive step in measuring the sense of physical presence in telemedicine applications in a real-world context.

## Social Presence in Playing a Game of Charades Using Videoconferencing

In this study we used the social presence theory as a lens for formalizing and analyzing users experience with videoconferencing systems. While telepresence is the sense of "being there," social presence is the sense of "being together with another." The social presence theory asked the question: how well did one person feel socially and psychologically connected to another person when engaged in a mediated interaction. According to Biocca (Biocca et al., 2001) the assessment of satisfaction with videoconferencing systems is based largely on the quality of social presence they afford. Various measures of social presence have been proposed in the literature. While Short and Christie (Short et al., 1967) define social presence as a constant property of the media, Biocca looks at social presence as the moment by moment awareness of the copresence of another accompanied by a sense of engagement with the other. Biocca identified three theoretical dimensions of social presence: copresence, psychological involvement, and behavioral engagement. Each of these dimensions has empirically determined factors. A recent version of Networked Mind measure (Harms et al., 2004) consists of five factors: copresence, attention allocation, perceived message understanding, perceived affective understanding, perceived affective interdependence, and perceived behavioral interdependence. The Networked Mind measure of social presence consists of multiple questions for each factor scale and has been used to compare face to face and purely mediated conditions. (Biocca et al., 2001; Harms et al., 2004) and to compare 3D videoconferencing with 2D videoconferencing (Hauber et al., 2005).

This study investigates the effect of zooming on user's sense of social presence using a videoconferencing system. In this study participants are engaged in a game of charades, in pairs, in three different conditions; face-to-face, videoconferencing with a fixed view and videoconferencing using a manually adjustable zoom. After the game of charades was completed participants were administered the Networked

Minds social presence scale. In conducting this pilot study we hypothesized that the participants with a control over the zoom will experience a greater sense of presence then the ones who did not, we also hypothesized that the F2F condition will have a greater sense of presence than the mediated one. This section presents what we have learned in exploring social presence using nonverbal communication activity such as charades.

## *Introduction*

Recent studies have shown video to be beneficial in specific tasks, e.g., negotiation tasks with nonnative English speakers (Veinott et al., 1999). Work by Hauber (Hauber et al., 2005) measures the difference in social presence in F2F, 2D videoconferencing, and 3D videoconferencing, with participants engaged in a negotiation task. As far as we know this is the first attempt at exploring social presence in a videoconference domain. In their experiment social presence was measured using Networked Mind measure proposed by Biocca.

Drawing on Hauber's work, this study investigates the effect of zooming on social presence in a situation where users are engaged in an informal and semi-structured game of charades, a highly nonverbal game, via videoconferencing. We have selected the game of charades, as in our view it relies more on social aspects of interpersonal communication than do other specific tasks such as negotiation or design. Although playing a game of charades is not a specific task that would be performed in real-life in the work place its value lies in its isolation of nonverbal communication that occurs in everyday life.

In a game of charades one person attempts to communicate through the use of gestures. As stated by Gaver (1992), the views provided by one or more stationary cameras do not capture enough information to be useful in all tasks. Our approach to this problem has been to use a single stationary camera with a zooming capability. We assume that the zooming function will provide more satisfying user experience. The types of views that can be achieved in our experiment vary from face and headshots to a wide shot, in which viewers can see more of the physical environment of the remote other.

## *Method*

### Experimental Design

Participants were required to play a game of charades, in pairs, in three different conditions; face-to-face, videoconferencing with a fixed view, and videoconferencing using a manually adjustable zoom. After the game of charades was completed participants were asked to fill in Harms', Levine's, and Biocca's (Harms et al., 2004) Networked Minds Social Presence Scale. A confederate was used as the charade actor, in this case the experimenter.

In conducting this pilot study we explore the following questions:

- What is the effect of zooming on social presence?
- Using the game of charades, can we replicate Hauber and Biocca differences between F2F and mediated interaction?

Our findings from this pilot study take preliminary the form of reflections on the task we have used, and the potential effect of the manipulation we did, e.g., zooming.

**Apparatus**

Our videoconferencing system connects two rooms using DV over IP for the video transmission (approximately 30 mbps per interleaved video/audio stream), using PAL video 720 × 576, Mono audio (12bit 48 khz). Echo canceller is ASPI Digital EchoFree1210.

Cameras

ROOM1 – Canon VC-C50i (1/4" single CCD, PAL)
ROOM2 – Panasonic NV-GS120 (1/6" 3 CCD, PAL)

Screens

ROOM1 – Fujitsu (50" Plasma Display, 1,366 × 768)
ROOM2 – Fujitsu (50" Plasma Display, 1,366 × 768)

**Participants**

Eight subjects (5 female and 3 male) participated in the experiment, each playing one round of charades. The age of the participants ranged from 23 to 64 years, and their countries of birth being Hong Kong, China, Australia, Indonesia, Bangladesh, England, and Germany. Out of the eight participants only three reported to have had any videoconferencing experience. The participants were recruited by posting flyers around the university campus and by internal email. Participants were assigned to time slots and dates of participation depending on their availability and preferences. Compensation was provided by way of a movie voucher for our staff and of $50 for external participants.

## *Task*

The game of charades was chosen to be the task for the experiment. The game of charades is a game where one person has to act out a phrase without speaking and other members of the team have to guess what the phrase is as fast as they can. Typically played face to face, two teams of equal size write down phrases on separate bits of paper and place it into a container. These phrases may either be quotations or titles of books, movies, plays, television shows, and songs. So phrases aren't too difficult to guess some basic rules include: no phrases should be longer than seven words, no phrase should consist solely of a proper name, no foreign phrases. For this experiment a list of nine charades were provided for the confederate actor, titles of which included books, movies, songs, and TV show titles. The titles were taken from top 100 lists of these categories on the Internet, as they were thought to be the most likely to be recognized. The list of charades included the following titles:

- Movie: Brokeback Mountain
- Song: YMCA
- Song: Walk like an Egyptian
- Movie: One flew over the cuckoos nest
- TV: Lost
- Book: Hitchhikers Guide to the Galaxy
- Movie: Lord of the rings
- Book: Little women
- TV: The X-files

The experimenter acted out each charade in face-to-face conditions, and over the two videoconferencing conditions.

## Data Collection Tools

The Networked Minds Questionnaire was filled by the participants at the end of the nine charades. We used all 36 questions covering all six factors of social presence: copresence, attention allocation, perceived message understanding, perceived affective understanding, perceived affective interdependence, and perceived behavioral interdependence.

Our demographics questionnaire established gender, age, employment and student status, use of visual aids, country of birth, amount of time in Australia, the participants experience with videoconferencing, knowledge of charades, and familiarity with the charades actor. This questionnaire was administered at the end of the experiment.

Actor and guesser were recorded on video tapes for future analysis.

Informal interviews took place at the end of the session, where participants were asked their views about the videoconferencing systems they just used, their feeling about playing a game of charades, and how they felt after meeting the remote actor F2F.

## Results

Our hypothesis is that Social presence will be higher amongst all six factors in the face-to-face group than those in the video-mediated conditions with adjustable

**Table 23.1** Alpha score (Reliability) of network minds questionnaire

| Social presence factor | Number of items | Alpha |
|---|---|---|
| Copresence | 6 | 0.92 |
| Attention Allocation | 6 | 0.68 |
| Perceived Message Understanding | 6 | 0.95 |
| Perceived Affective Understanding | 6 | 0.65 |
| Perceived Affective Interdependence | 6 | 0.81 |
| Perceived Behavioral Interdependence | 6 | 0.90 |

views, which will be higher than those in video-mediated conditions with fixed wide-shot views.

We performed a reliability analysis of all the items in the questionnaire, and a Cronbach's alpha was calculated for each social presence factor (Table 23.1).

Using cumulative scores for copresence, perceived message understanding, perceived affective interdependence, perceived behavioral interdependence, we report the differences that our data seem to indicate between the three conditions.

## Copresence

The mean copresence score was similar across the face-to-face (m = 42.0) and zoom condition (m = 41.5), both of which looked to be greater than the mean copresence score in the wide-shot condition (m = 34.0).

## Perceived Message Understanding

The mean perceived message understanding score was higher for the zoom condition (m = 39.5) than the wide-shot (m = 30.0) and face-to-face (m = 31.7) conditions.

## Perceived Affective Interdependence

The mean perceived affective interdependence score was similar across the wide-shot (m = 33.3), zoom (m = 33.0) and face-to-face (m = 30.3) conditions.

## Perceived Behavioral Interdependence

The mean perceived behavioral interdependence scores looked to be substantially higher in the zoom condition (m = 40.5) than the other two conditions. The mean perceived behavioral interdependence score was slightly higher in the face-to-face condition (m = 34.3) than the wide-shot condition (m = 29.7).

## *Reflections*

### Low Alpha Score for Intentional Allocation

Playing a game of charade may not afford a good measurement of attention allocation. The guesser is paying solid attention to the actor and the actor is concentrating on acting out charade or thinking of next clue. What we take from this observation is that we may need to reverse the roles during the interaction event, so that each participant plays both the guesser and the actor role. Perhaps by doing this we will obtain a higher alpha score for an attention allocation.

### Reflection on Effect of Zooming on Social Presence

Why the zoom condition indicates a higher level of social presence in factors of perceived message understanding and perceived behavioral interdependence? Could it be there was more detail to the visual information than either the face-to-face or wide shot. Perhaps the actor was standing too far away from the face-to-face actor. Is it possible that the wide-shot participants and the face-to-face participants had a similar feeling of distance between the actor and them? Were the participants who used the zooming capability, able to go beyond that barrier and "get closer." Perhaps participants' perception of the actor proximity affected their responses (Figs. 23.3–23.5).

**Fig. 23.3** View of charade actor in zoomed shot

**Fig. 23.4** View of charade actor in wide shot

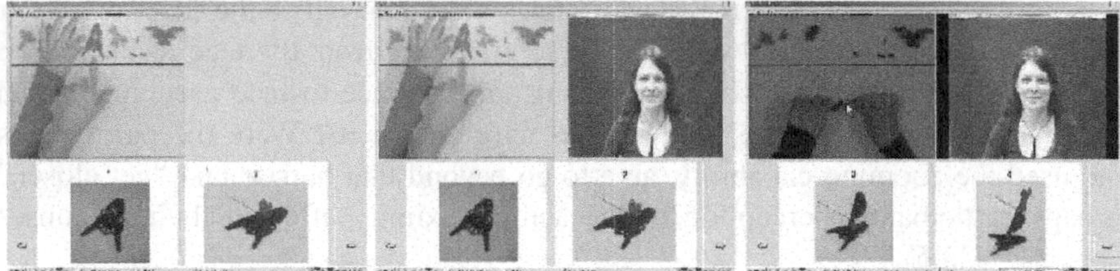

**Fig. 23.5** Screen viewed by each participant during each condition

## *Future Work*

This study presents our initial attempt at exploring social presence using nonverbal communication activity such as playing a game of charades. We have to find the Networked Mind measure and underlying social presence theory useful in formalizing and analyzing users' experience with a videoconferencing system. In a follow-up study we hope to establish that the zooming condition has a higher score in social presence then the fixed-shot condition, and this across the six factors of social presence.

# Copresence in Video-Mediated Collaboration on Physical Tasks

This study reports on a video-mediated collaboration study in which a worker and a helper are assembling jointly a Lego toy. In this study the helper's sense of copresence (i.e., the extent to which they feel in the same room as their remote partner)

was assessed. Kramer's study (Kramer et al., 2006) reports an experiment with a similar design where researchers have found that local deixis and remote deixis were positively correlated to presence. In their study, the sense of presence was measured by a set of questions developed by the authors. As an attempt to further the promising findings of this earlier study, we were interested in investigating if copresence score measure using an existing and established measure of copresence such as Shroeder measure (Shroeder et al., 2001) were correlated to linguistic features such as local and remote deixis. While Kramer reports a positive correlation between both local and remote deixis and presence score, we hypothesized that local deixis will be positively correlated to copresence score and remote deictics will be negatively correlated to presence score.

## *Experimental Set Up*

### Design

Our study was conducted in the context of a more comprehensive experiment which investigated the effects of two different representations of gesture (hand/pointer) in a remote collaboration on physical task. In our experiment we were interested in comparing different representations of gesture (hand/ pointer) the remote collaboration on physical task environment. For that aim we designed four different media conditions during which the participants should accomplish a physical task. The conditions were:

- Condition 1: The pair could see the pieces of Lego toy and the hands of the two participants all in one single view (workspace)
- Condition 2: The pair could see the workspace as well as a view of their remote partner available
- Condition 3: The pair could see the pieces of Lego toy, the worker's hands and a cursor controlled by the helper, all in the workspace view. In addition, each participant was provided with a view of their remote partner
- Condition 4: the participants were asked to perform the task using only verbal communication (i.e., no use of hand gesture on the part of the helper). Therefore, only the workspace view was available. The interface used during condition 1 was used in this condition as well.

Thirty-four participants were grouped into randomly assigned 17 pairs of one worker and one helper. The experiment included the three conditions and a final step: (1) the pair could see the pieces of Lego toy and the hands of the two participants all in one single view (workspace); (2) same as condition one, plus each partner had an additional view of their remote partner (other's view); (3) the pair could see the pieces of Lego toy, the worker's hands and a cursor controlled by the helper, all in the workspace view, and other's view; and (4) a final step: the participants assembled the parts built in the previous conditions, using only verbal communication and without the other's view.

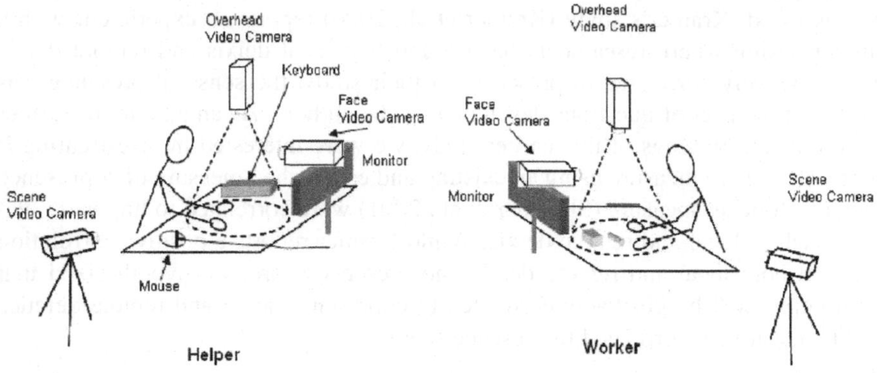


**Fig. 23.6** The technical setup used in the experiment

Much of the technical setup was based on the work by Kirk (Kirk et al., 2005). The physical environment in terms of hardware and setup was similar on both ends (see Fig. 23.6). Each participant faced a standard desktop monitor and had a mat (30.5 × 41.0 cm) on their desk which acted as the shared workspace. A camera was positioned directly above the mat with a field of view encompassing the entire mat. A video feed was distributed via a local network to the helper's computer, broadcasting a shared workspace onto both the helper's and worker's screens. The VIRTUAL TEA ROOM technology functioned as the technical platform for this experimentation. This application uses digital video over IP to provide an extensible and flexible telecollaboration environment for simultaneous multisite conferencing. It was adapted to the technical needs of each condition.

## Participants and Procedure

Forty-two participants were recruited in a university close to the place where the experiment took place. The participants were grouped into randomly assigned pairs with one worker and one helper. In separate rooms, each participant was given an overview of the study, signed voluntary consent and filled in the QCM questionnaire. Pairs then performed their tasks by building two objects in each condition via videoconference. At the end of each task, they completed a post-task questionnaire, reporting assessments of the condition (i.e., Satisfaction) and their perception of the interaction. After all tasks, they completed the final questionnaire, consisting of the demographic information, final motivation, and preference questions. Following this, the participants were debriefed and compensated with AU$ 40. Sessions took approximately 70–90 min.

Reference to an instruction manual by the helper in a training exercise prior to the trial ensured that the helper had familiarity that would enable them to adequately assist the worker in completing the tasks. The manual, which provided step-by-step instruction on the helper's screen, contained pictures of each piece, the orientation needed for assembly, and arrows indicating direction of assembly.

**Fig. 23.7** The bionicle toy

In effect, the manual contained all information needed to successfully build the LEGO toy, except for the physical pieces.

Assembly of a LEGO kit task is common in the literature (Kramer et al., 2006; Kirk et al., 2005). According to Kirk, this task incorporates generic elements such as selection, pattern matching, rotating, inserting, and attaching: allowing investigation of the demands placed on real-world applications.

Assembly was completed on a Bionic LEGO toy (LEGO Bionicle PIRAKA AVAK, (see Fig. 23.7). Three tasks were balanced in a number of steps needed to complete, and the likelihood of equivalent difficulty. As a result, in each condition, participants were asked to build collaboratively two different body parts of the LEGO toy (i.e., leg and body) by assembling 12 pieces of LEGO toys in 11 instructions steps. As we are interested in helper's sense of presence, the findings in this paper are based on data from helpers.

### Measures

In this study we used a combination of methods assessed different constructs such as sense of copresence, user satisfaction, and quality of interaction.

Sense of copresence: was measured using three questions developed by Schroeder (Schroeder et al., 2001) to assess issues related to participants' experience during the trial and perception of technology used during the experiment. The three questions were:

- How much did you have a sense of being together with your partner in the same room while solving the task?
- Were there moments while solving the task that the technology (i.e., interface) became "invisible"?

**Table 23.2** Categories of words used for linguistic analysis

| Word category | Examples |
|---|---|
| I | I, my, me |
| We | We, our, us |
| You | You, your |
| Cognitive Processes | Cause, know, ought |
| Remote Deixis | That, those, there |
| Local Deixis | This, these, here |

- Think back of previous interactions when building or manipulating a real object together with another person. How similar was this former experience to today's experience?

In this study we have used two methods: a set of subjective measures of copresence and a linguistic analysis based on full transcription of the trials. The sense of copresence was measured using Shroeder's questionaire (Shroeder et al., 2001). The transcriptions were fed to a text analysis software (Pennebaker et al., 2001). The software determined the rate at which the speakers used 70 dimensions of language. In this study, we used the categories in Table 23.2 below.

Satisfaction: Satisfaction is an index used to qualify the user's feeling of adequacy with a given situation. Typically if the technology or tool is adequate, the user will be "satisfied." The overall satisfaction was captured after each condition for each participant by self-assessment on a 5-point scale (range 0–4).

Quality of interaction: The quality of interaction is measured by questions we have developed to measure

- The participant's perception of how well the pair is at coordinating their effort
- The participant's perception of their remote partner

Participant's perception of how well they coordinated their effort was operationalized by the following three questions:

- I always realized when my assistance was needed by my partner
- My partner always realized when I needed his or her assistance
- We worked very well together on the task

Participant's perception of their remote partner was operationalized by the following three questions:

- My partner acted very cooperatively
- My partner acted very competently
- My partner acted in a very friendly way

## *Research Hypothesis*

We hypothesized that we would find a positive correlation between the frequency of local deixis and copresence score (as established by Kramer in (Kramer et al., 2006);

and a negative correlation between local deixis and remote deixis as opposed to the findings reported by Kramer in (Kramer et al., 2006).

## *Results*

In this study we have used an average measure of copresence of the whole trial. This average copresence score and general measure of the linguistic features were used for investigating potential correlation between copresence score and linguistic features such as local and remote deixis. An initial analysis indicates a high positive correlation between the copresence score and the frequency of local deixis, and a negative correlation between presence score and the frequency of remote deixis, and finally, a high negative correlation between local and remote deixis (see Table 23.3).

A regression analysis was performed in order to check the linguistic features ability to predict copresence score. The regression analysis used the frequency of local deixis and the frequency of We category (words as we, our, and us). Results indicate that those linguistic variables may predict about 38% of the whole the copresence score (R Square = .381; F [12,680] = 4.31).

Investigation of the relationship between copresence score and satisfaction and quality of interaction is of interest to us and will be reported in future publications.

## *Discussion*

In this study we replicated some aspects of Kramer study (Kramer et al., 2006) using Shroeder's copresence measure (Shroeder et al., 2001) developed and used by the presence research community. The use of Shroder's measure as opposed to a measure developed by the authors for the purpose of the study, increases our level of confidence in the interpretation of our findings. Aligned with previous results, we have found a high positive correlation between the copresence score and the frequency of local deixis. In opposition with the result reported by Kramer, we have found a negative correlation between the copresence score and remote deixis and a negative correlation between the frequency of local deixis and remote deixis. Our results validate what we have intuitively hypothesized. It seems reasonable to assume that users during their remote interaction with their partner will either

**Table 23.3** Correlations between local and remote deixis and presence score (N = 17)

| | Remote deixis | Local deixis | Copresence |
|---|---|---|---|
| **Remote deixis** | 1 | −.667(**) | −.379 |
| **Local deixis** | −.667(**) | 1 | .581(*) |
| **Copresence** | −.379 | .581(*) | 1 |

** $p < 0.01$; * $p < 0.05$ level (2-tailed)

mostly use local deixis (e.g., their linguistic behavior is as if they were copresent with their partner), or mostly use remote deixis (e.g., their linguistic behavior is indicative that they are not in the same place as their partner). Users' linguistic behavior is hence one indicative of aspects of their experience while engaged in remote collaboration, more specifically their sense of copresence. From a methodological point of view, analysis of targeted linguistic features such as remote and local deixis while requiring a lot of effort (full transcription of the trials) is a good candidate method for developing an objective measure of copresence.

It is proposed to target future work in developing a more cost-effective way of deploying linguistic features analysis methods and in exploring relevance of the linguistic approach for measuring/evaluating other aspects of users' experience such as their sense of social presence.

## Conclusion and Discussion

We have reported, in this chapter on a set of video-mediated collaboration studies conducted at CSIRO in which different aspects of presence are being investigated.

A first study reports on the sense of physical presence a specialist doctor experiences when engaged in a remote consultation of a patient using the virtual critical care unit (Alem et al., 2006). The study revealed that the presence experienced by the clinicians was influenced by personal factors such as employment category and gender. There was some evidence to support the positive relationship between satisfaction with usability and media factors and presence. There was also evidence from the study to suggest that the high levels of satisfaction with ViCCU® expressed by the clinicians could be influenced by the high levels of presence experienced when using ViCCU®, making it comparable to actually "being there."

A second study reports on the sense of social presence users' experience when playing a game of charade with remote partners using a videoconference link (Kougianous et al., 2006). In this study the presence measure focuses on the extent to which users feel connected with their remote partners. The zooming condition indicates a higher level of social presence in factors of perceived message understanding and perceived behavioral interdependence.

A third study reports on the sense of copresence users' experience when building collaboratively a piece of lego toy (Melo and Alem, 2007). The sense of copresence is the extent to which users felt presence with their remote partner. In this final study the sense of copresence is investigated by looking at the word used by users when referring to the physical objects they are manipulating during their interaction as well as when referring to locations in the collaborative workspace. Aligned with previous results (Kramer et al., 2006) we have found a high positive correlation between the copresence score and the frequency of local deixis. In opposition with the study, we have found a negative correlation between the copresence score and remote deixis and a negative correlation between the frequency of local deixis and remote deixis. Hence, users' linguistic behavior is indicative of aspects of their experience while engaged in remote collaboration, more specifically their sense of copresence.

One important observation from these three studies is our effort to evaluate video-mediated collaboration systems beyond traditional measures of time on task and task accuracy by attempting to qualify users' experience and at the same time explore the relationship between presence and other factors at pay such as usability, media, and behavioral factors such as linguistic features. The three studies reported in this chapter differ from the type of presence being investigated (physical, social, and copresence), the type of activity users/participants engage in (medial consultation, playing a game of charade, and building a lego toy), and finally the nature of the study (field study and laboratory study). We believe that such effort provide a solid stepping stone for evaluating and analyzing future media spaces.

**Acknowledgments** I would like to thank my colleagues from CSIRO, Susan Hansen and Jane Li who conducted the ViCCU study with me, Lizz Kougianous and Paulo Melo who conducted respectively the charade study and the linguistic analysis study, during their internship at CSIRO with me. My thanks to Cara Stitzlein, Laurie Wilson, Anja Wessels, and Alex Krum-Heller for their technical support and the CSIRO Networking Research Laboratory for funding and supporting this research.

## References

Alem, L., Hansen, S., and Li, J. (2006) Evaluating Clinician Experience in a Telemedicine Application: A Presence Perspective. In Proceedings of OZCHI'06. Sydney, Australia.

Baren and Ijsselsteijn (2004). http://www.presence-research.org/Overview.html

Biocca, F., Harms, C., and Gregg, J. (2001) The networked minds measure of social presence: Pilot test of the factor structure and concurrent validity. 2001 May 21.

Gaver, W. (1992) The affordances of media spaces for collaboration. In Proceedings of CSCW'92, 1–4 Nov, Toronto.

Harms, C., Levine, T., and Biocca, F. (2004) The effects of media type and personal relationship on perceptions of social presence, in Unpublished dissertation.

Hauber, J., Regenbrecht, H., Hills, A., Cockburn, A., and Billinghurst, M. (2005) Social Presence in Two- and Three-dimensional Videoconferencing. In Proceedings of ISPR Presence 2005.

Heeter, C. (1992) Being there: the subjective experience of presence. Presence: Teleoperators and Virtual environments, 1(2), 262–271.

Insko, B.E. (2003) Measuring presence: subjective, behavioral and physiological methods. In G. Riva, F. Davide, and W.A. Ijesslsteon (Eds) Being there: concepts, effects and measurement of user presence in synthetic environments. Ios Ptress, Amsterdam, The Netherlands.

Kirk, D.S., Fraser, D.S., and Rodden, T. (2005) The effects of Remote Gesturing on Distance Instruction. In Proceeding of the International Conference on Computer Supported Collaborative Learning, Taipei, Taiwan, pp. 301–310.

Kougianous, L., Alem, L., and Adrieenson, T. (2006) Supporting the Non verbal Aspect of Tele Collaboration: An Interface Perspective. In Proceedings of International Workshop at CHI2006, 11 Sept, London.

Kramer, A., Oh, L., and Fussell, S. (2006) Using Linguistic Features to Measure Presence in Computer Mediated Communication. CHI 2006 Notes. ACM Press, New York, pp. 913–916.

Lessiter, J., Freeman, J., Keogh, E., and Davidoff, J. (2000) Development of a new cross media presence questionnaire: The ITC-sense of presence inventory. Presence: Teleoperators and Virtual Environment (special issue).

Li, J., Wilson, L.S., Hansen, S., Qiao, R., Krumm-Heller, A., Stapleton, S., Cregan, P., and Murphy, M. (2006) Meeting user needs for quality – design and technical evaluation of a telehealth system for critical care. Proceedings of Second IASTED International Conference on Telehealth 2006, Banff, Canada.

Melo, P. and Alem, L. (2007) Selective Analysis of Linguistic Features Used in Video Mediated Collaboration: An Indicator of User's Sense of Co-presence. In Proceedings of INTERACT'07, Sept 7, Rio de Janeiro, Brazil.

Nosper, A., Behr, K.M., Hartmann, T., and Vorderer, P. (2005) Exploring the relationships between the usability of a medium and the sense of spatial presence perceived by the user. Presence, 261–266.

Pennebaker, J.W., Francis, M.E., and Booth, R.J. (2001) Linguistic Inquiry and Word Count (LIWC): A Computerized Text Analysis Program. Erlbaum, Mahwah, NJ.

Schroeder, R., Steed, A., Axelsson, A.-S., Heldal, I., Abelin, A., Wideström, et al. (2001). Collaborating in networked immersive spaces: as good as being there together? Computer & Graphics, 25, 781–788.

Short, J., William, E., and Chritie, B. (1967) The social psychology of telecommunication. Wiley, London.

Slater, M. (1999) Measuring presence: a response to the Witmer and Singer questionnaire. Presence, 8(5), 560–566.

Slater, M., Usoh, M., and Steed, A. (1994) Depth of presence in virtual environments. Presence: Teleoperators and Virtual Environments, 3, 130–144.

Usoh, M., Catena, E., Arman, S., and Slater, M. (2000) Presence questionnaires in reality, Presence, 9(5), 497–503.

Veinott, E., Olson, J.S., Olson, G.M., and Fu, X. (1999) Video helps remote work: Speakers who need to negotiate common ground benefit from seeing each other. in CHI '99, ACM, Pittsburg, PA.

Witmer, B.G. and Singer, M.J. (1998) Measuring presence in Virtual environments: A presence questionnaire, Presence, 7(3), 225–240.

# Chapter 24
# Build It: Will They Come?

## Media Spaces in the support of Computational Science

**Brian Corrie and Todd Zimmerman**

## Introduction

Scientific research is fundamentally collaborative in nature, and many of today's complex scientific problems require domain expertise in a wide range of disciplines. In order to create research groups that can effectively explore such problems, research collaborations are often formed that involve colleagues at many institutions, sometimes spanning a country and often spanning the world. An increasingly common manifestation of such a collaboration is the *collaboratory* (Bos et al., 2007), a "... center without walls in which the nation's researchers can perform research without regard to geographical location – interacting with colleagues, accessing instrumentation, sharing data and computational resources, and accessing information from digital libraries." In order to bring groups together on such a scale, a wide range of components need to be available to researchers, including distributed computer systems, remote instrumentation, data storage, collaboration tools, and the financial and human resources to operate and run such a system (National Research Council, 1993). Media Spaces, as both a technology and a social facilitator, have the potential to meet many of these needs. In this chapter, we focus on the use of scientific media spaces (SMS) as a tool for supporting collaboration in scientific research. In particular, we discuss the design, deployment, and use of a set of SMS environments deployed by WestGrid and one of its collaborating organizations, the Centre for Interdisciplinary Research in the Mathematical and Computational Sciences (IRMACS) over a 5-year period.

B. Corrie
Simon Fraser University
e-mail: bcorrie@sfu.ca

T. Zimmerman
University of British Columbia - Okanagan
e-mail: todd.zimmerman@ubc.ca

S. Harrison (ed.), *Media Space 20+ Years of Mediated Life*,
Computer Supported Cooperative Work,

## Computational Science and Scientific Media Spaces

Computational science is the domain of scientific research in which the computer is one of the key scientific research tools. Computational science complements, supports, and extends the traditional experimental and theoretical approaches to scientific investigation. The dramatic increase in the amount of data that is available to scientific researchers, using high-resolution instruments and/or increasingly complex computational simulations, is transforming the way scientists perform research.

Scientific research, and in particular computational science research, is fundamentally collaborative in nature. Many of today's complex scientific problems require domain expertise in a wide range of disciplines. This need is exacerbated by the size and complexity of the computational simulations and experimental apparatus that are used in research today. In order to explore such problems, research collaborations are often formed that involve colleagues at many institutions, often spanning several universities and sometimes spanning the world.

### *Scientific Collaboratories*

Over the last 20 years, large-scale distributed research groups, or collaboratories (as originally coined in 1989 by Wulf [Bos et al., 2007]), have become common in many areas of science. The US National Research Council's report on collaboratories (National Research Council, 1993) defines a collaboratory at the abstract level, using Wulf's terminology, as a "*…center without walls in which the nation's researchers can perform research without regard to geographical location, interacting with colleagues, accessing instrumentation, sharing data and computational resources, and accessing information from digital libraries.*"

Collaboratories and the related scientific research infrastructure have been explored in some detail in the recent research literature. The Science of Collaboratories project has conducted a broad review of a wide range of collaboratory projects, creating a taxonomy of collaboratory types (Bos et al., 2007). Other researchers have explored individual collaboratory projects, including research that attempts to understand how collaboratories use data (Birnholtz and Beitz, 2003), identify factors that can help to predict success and failure in collaboratories (Finholt and Olson, 1997), and evaluate specific aspects of a collaboratory (Sonnenwald et al., 2003).

### *Media Spaces*

Media Spaces facilitate the creation of place from space. Space is the reality that surrounds us, be it physical or digital (a room, the chairs in a room, a display, and an image on that display). Such a space becomes a place through the utilization of the environment to facilitate social interactions among individuals. For example, a meeting room is a space that contains chairs, a table, a computer, and a computer display. At times, such a meeting room is transformed into a place for holding a meeting, next, a place for holding a birthday party for a colleague, and then a place for a casual conversation among colleagues. It is the appropriation of space for a social endeavor that gives place meaning to the participants.

Media Spaces are designed to support a wide range of person-to-person interactions, with a Media Space transformed into a Media Place based on the social context of those interactions. Bellotti and Dourish describe a media space as "… providing a wider set of services based around people's different reasons for wanting to be in contact with each other" and state that the "… integration between these components is as much a matter of use as of construction" (Bellotti and Dourish, 1997). Media spaces provide an environment in which users can construct a meaningful place for collaboration through use of the technological tools that exist within them. The aim of Media Space is to provide the infrastructure to support creating an effective Media Place while attempting to avoid dictating the form of the communication that occurs.

From a technology standpoint, media spaces are a set of technology-based components that support distributed communication, providing technologies that extend physical space to include distant people, events, and other spaces. The aim of a media space is not to replicate face-to-face communication, but instead to provide the ability to create a set of tailored communication places that encompass the social communication needs of the collaborators. One of the key defining concepts of the media space environment is the notion that it is always active, allowing users to walk into a local physical space and feel that they are immediately a part of the larger virtual space. Participating in a media space environment typically has little or no overhead from the user perspective. Many media space environments require no direct action from the user to begin interaction (Harrison et al., 1997). In some cases, a minimal interaction is required to instantiate a set of media space services that tailor the environment for a communication task (Bellotti and Dourish, 1997).

## *Scientific Media Spaces*

Communication is a fundamental component of supporting distributed collaborative science. If the goal is to create a large, distributed laboratory, a question follows naturally; can media space technologies be leveraged to provide an environment that meets the collaboration needs of a distributed scientific community. In many ways, early media space research environments were Scientific Media Spaces (SMS). The PARC (Harrison et al., 1997) and EuroPARC (Bellotti and Dourish, 1997) media space systems were created to support scientific research in computer science. They brought together distributed communities of researchers working on a common project. This community was distinct in that the research area being studied was in fact the media space environment itself. The question we explore in the remainder of this chapter is in what ways a media space environment might support the general scientific community.

## *AccessGrid*

The AccessGrid (AG) is a technology platform for the support of distributed, scientific collaboration (Childers et al., 2000). Originally developed by Argonne National Lab in the USA, the original vision of AccessGrid was in many ways as a modern scientific media space. Designed to support group-to-group collaboration in a room-based environment, AccessGrid directly supports multiple, high resolution, large-screen displays, multiple cameras, high-quality acoustically echo-cancelled full duplex audio, and a range of interaction technologies. The drive for the creation of the AccessGrid environment stemmed from the Argonne group's frustration in using currently available tools to support their distant collaboration needs (Childers et al., 2000). In particular, they found the following:

1. A wide-area group-to-group collaboration tool was needed.
2. Although formal meetings were important, much of their productivity came from unstructured discussion around brainstorming, problem solving, casual conversation, and idea generation. Thus, a range of interactions was required, from formal meetings to casual unstructured discussion.
3. Users brought artifacts to meetings on their laptops to share with their collaborators. Thus, it was necessary to bring these devices into the environment as first class devices.
4. The perceived need to support a wide range of hardware and software platforms plagued existing efforts to provide a successful environment. Thus, a consistent set of technologies across all participants would be beneficial.

The ideal collaborative environment envisioned by the AccessGrid developers consisted of "an intentionally designed space, one that would be rewarding to be in, one that provides a sense of copresence with other groups using similar spaces. We envision a space with ambient video and audio, large-scale displays and with software to enable the relatively transparent sharing of ideas, thoughts, experiments, applications, and conversation. We envision a space where we can 'hangout' comfortably with colleagues at other places, and then use the same space to attend and participate in structured meetings such as site visits, remote conferences, tutorials, lectures, etc." (Childers et al., 2000). This description is very similar to how one would describe many media spaces. Two examples of AccessGrid collaboration rooms are shown in Fig. 24.1.

AccessGrid is designed to manage complex collaboration spaces. A single physical AccessGrid Node (a physical room like those shown in Fig. 24.1) typically consists of multiple computers, with each computer providing one or more collaboration capabilities to the Node. Collaboration capabilities are instantiated by NodeServices, where a typical node service might be responsible for handling video capture for one or more cameras, audio processing for the room, or display on one or more of the projection surfaces used in the room. The NodeService infrastructure is extensible, and the AG community has created a wide range of complex node services. The multiple computers within a single physical AG Node (and the

**Fig. 24.1** A theatre (*left*) and meeting room (*right*) Scientific Media Space

NodeServices that run on those computers) are coordinated by a ServiceManager, which are in turn coordinated by the user front end to the system, the VenueClient. It is possible to add and remove NodeServices to an AG Node as required and different Node configurations can be loaded at the press of a button. Thus, it is possible to tailor an AG Node with different NodeServices for different purposes.

The AccessGrid uses a spatial metaphor to scope collaboration, utilizing "Virtual Venues" as virtual meeting spaces. Virtual venues are connected to each other through "doors" and one navigates from virtual venue to another by traveling through these virtual doors. Physical AG rooms (such as the one pictured in Fig. 24.1) connect to other physical rooms by both rooms navigating to a single virtual venue. The system coordinates the node services (audio, video, visualization, shared documents) of the rooms that are connected to a virtual venue such that they create a single, distributed collaboration space.

Since its inception in 2000, AccessGrid usage within the scientific community has grown extensively. There are a number of regional efforts that support AccessGrid around the world, including efforts in the USA, the UK, Europe, Canada, and the Asia Pacific region. In the UK region alone, there are over 70 AccessGrid AG Nodes in operation and it is estimated that there are hundreds of such nodes in active deployment around the world.

## *AccessGrid as a Modern Scientific Media Space*

Many of the concepts encapsulated in Media Spaces are reflected in the AccessGrid. An AccessGrid Node (a physical room) is a flexible and extensible media space environment. AccessGrid can provide a range of collaboration services to SMS users across a number of computers within a physical room. It supports advanced display, video, and audio collaboration services. These services can be composed into a media space that meets a wide range of purposes. Like the EuroPARC media spaces, an AccessGrid node "... is comprised of a constellation of more or less independent parts. Integration between these components is as much a matter of use as of construction; such technology can be appropriated by its users for an unlimited variety of collaborative and social activities" (Bellotti and Dourish, 1997).

In addition to providing connectivity on a room-to-room basis, AccessGrid also facilitates collaboration from users at their desktop, at home, and while traveling. Although designed to support multi-computer, multi-camera, and multi-display rooms, it is straightforward to have an office- or laptop-based AccessGrid node. Such an environment is a first class "Node" in the AccessGrid world, and participates in the SMS at the same level as any other participant. Single-computer AccessGrid use is common (at the office, at home, and on the road), and complex configurations (multi-computer, multi-camera, and/or multi-display) in people's offices are often used.

Moving from media space to media place is facilitated through the AccessGrid's ability to flexibly compose resources and tools in different configurations for specific purposes (formal meetings, casual discussion, or providing presence). This is possible at two levels. It is possible (at the click of a button) to configure a local physical node to provide a set of specific services to the rest of the participants connected to a venue. For example, during a scientific research meeting, multiple video services, a high-quality audio service, and a shared visualization service might be instantiated as part of the SMS. Alternately, if I am in my office connected to the SMS, I may only want to provide a very low frame rate video feed and a reception-only audio service as a means for providing presence information. Note that switching from this configuration to a configuration that is usable for an informal conversation or a formal meeting can be made at the click of a button.

The second mechanism for customizing behavior for a specific purpose in AccessGrid is through the use of venue customization. In AccessGrid, it is possible to create virtual venues that are tailored for a specific purpose. Using this approach, it is possible to create a virtual venue where collaborators can share specific documents or connect to specific visualizations (the documents and visualization are relative to the venue, not a specific node). It is also possible to have shared applications attached to a virtual venue that control and/or modify the node services that are being used by participants when they are in that venue. For example, it is possible to create a virtual venue that is tailored to provide "presence information" only (low frame rate video and receive-only audio). This control is based on the venue and not the physical node, and therefore it is the process of navigating to a virtual space that changes the behavior of the environment.

The AccessGrid, like many Media Space environments, is designed to be an always-on environment. There are a range of national and international AccessGrid VenueServers available for use by the scientific community, including servers in the USA, Canada, the UK, and the Asia Pacific region. Many physical AccessGrid rooms are "always on" and "always connected." For example, at any given time there are typically from 10 to 20 AG nodes connected to the Argonne AccessGrid VenueServer. The community served is primarily the developers and users of AccessGrid technology. This parallels the use of media spaces as described in Bellotti and Dourish (1997) and Harrison et al. (1997) in that some of the main users of the media space environment are the key developers and users of the technology itself. Thus, the group lives and breathes the technology that it is developing.

## Scientific Media Spaces in Action

In the remainder of this Chapter, we describe our experiences in planning, building, and operating an extensive SMS infrastructure in support of the computational sciences in Western Canada. WestGrid (www.westgrid.ca) is a computational science consortium in Western Canada, spanning the four westernmost Canadian provinces or roughly half the country geographically. It provides computational science resources (high-performance computers, data storage, networking, collaboration, and visualization technologies) to over 1,000 researchers. Originally funded in 2001, designed in 2002, and implemented in 2003, this infrastructure currently spans 14 universities and 4 provinces.

An important aspect of the computational science infrastructure that WestGrid has created is a set of SMS environments. These media spaces are designed to provide distant collaborating researchers with the ability to communicate effectively with colleagues across campus, across the country, and around the world. Our analysis of the use of this infrastructure pays particular attention to the development and use of SMS environments in the Centre for Interdisciplinary Research in the Mathematical and Computational Sciences (IRMACS) at Simon Fraser University (SFU). IRMACS is located at one of the WestGrid consortium institutions and collaborates extensively with WestGrid in this area.

We targeted the SMS infrastructure across WestGrid and IRMACS at meeting the collaboration needs of a wide range of scientific users. From an SMS perspective, this presents an interesting design problem. Most media space environments are targeted at a single community need, and therefore can be customized to support a community of practice. The WestGrid and IRMACS infrastructure must address user needs across a wide range of scientific communities and across a wide range of collaboration scenarios. Although one of the defining properties of a media space is its ability to support a range of needs, the WestGrid diversity of use amplifies this requirement. The WestGrid and IRMACS SMS infrastructure needs to be highly configurable and at the same time maintain simplicity of use.

In the remainder of this section, we explore the community of users that have taken advantage of the WestGrid and IRMACS SMS infrastructure over the past several years. We focus on the usage of the IRMACS infrastructure in particular, as relevant user statistics are available for the SMS rooms in that center. This is by no means a rigorous study of SMS, but instead is an anecdotal exploration of our experiences building and operating such an infrastructure over the past 5 years. In particular, we discuss how the usage of the IRMACS Scientific Media Spaces have changed during this time and explore some of our successes, some of our failures, and some of the opportunities we see for the future. For a more detailed study of scientific collaboration in this context, please refer to Corrie and Storey (2007).

## WestGrid Scientific Media Space Design

The design goal of the WestGrid collaboration infrastructure was to support a wide range of distributed scientific research. In the early design for this infrastructure (2001), there was a recognition that having collaboratory or media-space-like technologies available for the scientific user community would be highly beneficial. At this time, the WestGrid collaboration designers did not think in terms of media spaces, but a number of the principal collaborators had built and were performing research in iRoom (Fox et al., 2000) or collaboratory style rooms (Borwein et al., 2006; Berry et al., 2005) and a number of researchers had experience with AccessGrid technologies (Patrick et al., 2004). Thus, it was towards these environments that the WestGrid collaboration infrastructure was targeted.

One of the key early design decisions for this infrastructure was that each WestGrid institution should have access to an advanced, technology-rich collaboration room. Termed GridRooms in the WestGrid literature, but referred to as Scientific Media Spaces in this document, these environments were envisioned as collaboration rooms that would support most, if not all, collaboration needs for WestGrid users. We chose AccessGrid as a collaboration tool for WestGrid because of its widespread use in the computational science community, the fact that it was an open source software project, and because it was designed to be extensible. Extensibility in particular was thought to be of high importance, given the diversity of the collaborations that WestGrid needed to support. The choice of AccessGrid drove the technology infrastructure in the SMS environments, resulting in all rooms having high-quality full duplex echo-cancelling audio systems, two or more display surfaces (projectors, plasma displays, and sometimes table-top displays), and multiple cameras. All rooms were connected to each other using advanced networking (typically at gigabit connection speeds).

## IRMACS Scientific Media Space Design

At approximately the same time as WestGrid was deploying its SMS, another related research center was in the implementation stages. The Center for Interdisciplinary Research in the Mathematical and Computational Sciences (IRMACS – www.irmacs.sfu.ca) at Simon Fraser University (SFU) has taken a somewhat novel approach to supporting interdisciplinary research. Most interdisciplinary research centers exist as one of two types: a center that has a focus on a specific interdisciplinary research problem or a virtual center that attempts to bring interdisciplinary researchers together through online communication about research activities, the support and facilitation of meetings, and sometimes direct funding of research projects.

IRMACS took a somewhat different approach. IRMACS supports research across a wide range of disciplines by creating a physical “meeting place” for its research community (25,000 $ft^2$ of open office, lab, and meeting space) and

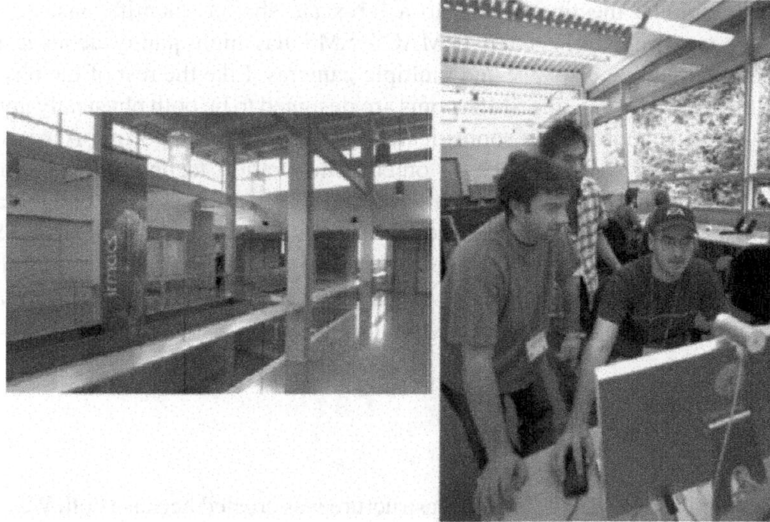

**Fig. 24.2** The IRMACS Atrium (*left*) and an IRMACS lab (*right*)

providing the technological infrastructure to perform that research in as effective a manner as possible. IRMACS is designed as an attractive environment, both architecturally and socially, with an open plan, many windows in the lab space, and easy access to meeting rooms for break-out sessions (see Fig. 24.2). IRMACS extends its physical space to remote interdisciplinary collaborators using SMS environments. From the perspective of media space research, the goal of IRMACS is not to create a **space** for interdisciplinary research, but instead to create a **place** that draws interdisciplinary researchers together academically and socially, both locally and at a distance. As of April 2008, IRMACS hosts 60 research projects and 288 researchers, with research projects spanning 16 disciplines/departments.

Distance collaboration was always a fundamental part of the IRMACS vision. Leveraging the fact that IRMACS was one year behind WestGrid in its funding and implementation of its SMS infrastructure, IRMACS was able to provide one of the most advanced SMS environments of the WestGrid institutes. The IRMACS SMS rooms are designed meeting room spaces (i.e., they are not retrofitted meeting rooms), with the ability to be used as both traditional colocated or distributed collaboration spaces. It was recognized early on in the IRMACS design that we did not want to build spaces for distance collaboration, but instead spaces that were designed for colocated collaboration that could be utilized for collaborating at a distance at the "touch of a button." That is, we wanted to have the ability to transform a designed collaboration space (e.g., a meeting room) to a distributed media space on demand.

IRMACS has created six SMS rooms, with rooms designed to fill specific roles in terms of the type of collaboration that they support. Rooms range from a 75-seat lecture theatre (with a high-resolution stereoscopic 3D visualization capability), through traditional meeting rooms, to a lab-scale shared scientific visualization laboratory (see Fig. 24.1). Each IRMACS SMS has high-quality acoustic echo cancellation, multiple displays, and multiple cameras. Like the rest of the physical environment at IRMACS, the SMS rooms are designed to be both physically appealing as well as technologically sophisticated. In addition to supporting AccessGrid, the rooms support a wide range of other collaboration technologies, including traditional teleconferencing, video conferencing (H323), and desktop collaboration technologies such as iChat, Skype, and VNC. In addition, all of the IRMACS SMS environments make use of touch-sensitive screen overlays (SmartBoards), allowing users to interact with applications by directly touching the screen or annotating documents by writing on the screen with a digital pen.

## *We Built It – Did They Come?*

The WestGrid and IRMACS SMS infrastructure was created because both WestGrid and IRMACS recognized that scientific researchers had a need to collaborate with remote colleagues and that this was an important aspect of the emerging computational science research community. This need was not as well-defined as perhaps it could have been, and the infrastructure was in some sense created with a "build it and they will come" approach. We recognized a need, but did not understand the usage pattern of this community well.

### How Often Do They Come?

The vision of an SMS infrastructure that supports a wide range of scientific uses is ambitious in its scope, but over the 5-year period of its planning, deployment, and use we view our infrastructure deployment as fundamentally successful. There are many aspects of the SMS infrastructure that could be more effective, but the increased frequency of use of our users, the increasing number of users using the facilities, and the level of sophistication demonstrated by our users all indicate that the SMS infrastructure is increasingly meeting the needs of our users.

In order to understand the change in the research community's level of use of the SMS infrastructure, it is necessary to understand what was available to this community before the WestGrid and IRMACS SMS were available. We focus on SFU for this analysis. Starting in 1995, distance collaboration was supported at SFU through an administrative unit that supported learning and instructional development. Initially, this unit provided a single room that supported ISDN (phone line based) H323 video conferencing on the SFU main campus (SFU has three distributed campuses). Over time, this infrastructure was upgraded to include IP-based H323 video conferencing and the addition of a mobile H323 unit that could be wheeled into a classroom or meeting room. The primary use for these facilities was to support teaching, although the units were also used for administrative meetings, thesis defences, and research meetings.

The WestGrid and IRMACS infrastructure significantly changed the collaboration landscape at SFU. One key dimension of this change was the target audience of the SMS infrastructure. Rather than supporting remote teaching, the IRMACS and WestGrid infrastructure was almost exclusively focused on supporting distributed scientific research. A second equally important dimension of change was the number and capability of the SMS spaces that were built by WestGrid and IRMACS. The main SFU campus went from having one room and one mobile videoconferencing space to having an additional seven technologically sophisticated SMS rooms. Although we do not gather detailed statistics on facility usage at all WestGrid sites, the IRMACS SMS facilities at SFU have tracked usage since January of 2005. We utilize these statistics to explore how the culture of collaboration has changed over the 4 years that this infrastructure has been in use at SFU.

The first SMS facility at SFU was built by WestGrid to service the collaboration needs of the high energy physics (HEP) research community. The need to collaborate within the HEP community has existed for many years. HEP research involves the carrying out of experiments using large-scale, unique devices (such as the ATLAS detector of the Large Hadron Collider at CERN in Switzerland). The ATLAS experiment involves over 1,900 physicists from more than 164 universities in 35 countries. The experiments involve the design of the ATLAS detector, experimental planning, and in 2008 when the experiment comes on line, intensive data analysis. These collaborations require meetings among researchers from around the world, with meetings often occurring on a weekly basis.

Since its completion in 2004, the Physics SMS room (located in the Physics Department at SFU) has been used extensively for both local meetings as well as remote collaborations. The room was designed so that its normal role as a meeting room could be extended to include the functionality of an SMS. Although we don't have detailed statistics for this room over an extended period of time, current SMS usage levels are quite high. During the first quarter of 2008 the room is on average used five times a week for approximately 9 h of SMS activity. These SMS sessions range from collaborations with colleagues at other Canadian universities to international collaborations with colleagues around the world. The room is used for traditional colocated meetings about the same number of times per week, resulting in approximately 50% of the room's usage and 20% of the working hours in the week for SMS activities. This alone is a significant increase over the level of collaboration that was available before this SMS facility existed at SFU.

The IRMACS SMS infrastructure adds six SMS environments to the SFU collaboration capability. Detailed statistics about usage of these SMS spaces have been kept since January of 2005. Since January 2005 the use of the IRMACS SMS environments for distant collaboration has steadily increased (see Figs. 24.3 and 24.4). At the end of its first year of operation (the end of 2005) it supported 20 research projects and 74 researchers. During the 2005 calendar year 73 SMS meetings occurred with a steady growth in the number of SMS meetings as the IRMACS community grew in size and as the researchers became familiar with the IRMACS SMS capabilities. By the end of the 2007 calendar year the IRMACS research community grew to 60 projects and 288 researchers. The IRMACS SMS

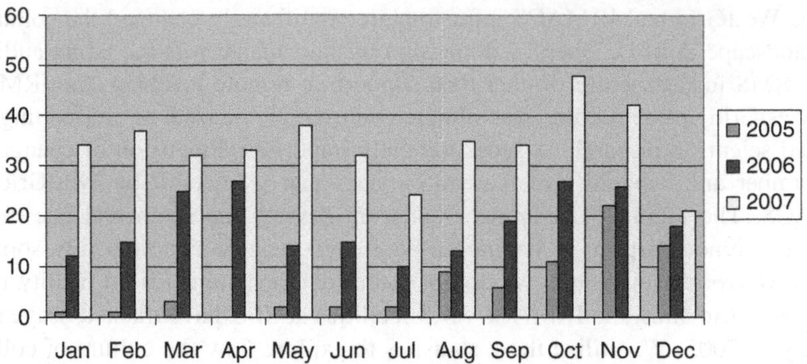


**Fig. 24.3** Number of monthly IRMACS SMS meetings

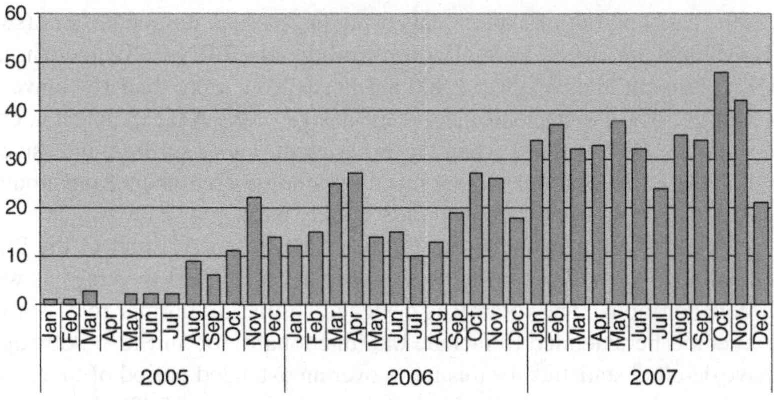


**Fig. 24.4** IRMACS SMS meetings, 2005–2007

spaces were used for distant collaboration 397 times during 2007 for approximately 720 h of SMS collaboration time (on average seven meetings and 13.5 h of SMS time per week). During the same calendar year, the IRMACS meeting rooms were used for a total of 1,450 meetings (both traditional and remote SMS sessions) and a total of over 2,950 hours of meeting time. This implies that approximately 27% of the meetings (and 24% of the number of meeting hours) in the IRMACS facility had remote collaborators participating through use of the IRMACS SMS infrastructure. We believe that the SFU SMS infrastructure, and in particular the IRMACS approach to deploying that infrastructure, has resulted in a fundamental shift in the way SFU researchers collaborate.

Today, many of our users use the SMS technologies seamlessly. There has been a cultural change in terms of our user's ability and desire to use the SMS infrastructure for distant collaboration. In many cases this use occurs with no need for technical support. In fact the technical support staff for the IRMACS facility sometimes only discovers a meeting is SMS based if something goes wrong. The users of the IRMACS Centre expect to be able to collaborate with remote colleagues wherever and whenever they have such a need.

## What Do They Come For?

The usage pattern of the WestGrid and IRMACS SMS infrastructure is a complex one. The SMS infrastructure is used for a wide range of purposes, by a wide range of users, each with a wide range of experiences with using the technologies. Some of our research groups use the SMS rooms for distant collaborations several times a week, while other researchers use the rooms once (for a Ph.D. defence for example) and never use them again. Some uses are for formal presentations to a large and widely distributed audience (left image in Fig. 24.1) while others are informal, exploratory, and often intense research group meetings with only one or two distant collaborators. We can break down our major SMS usage into four broad categories:

- *Research meetings*: One of the primary uses of scientific media spaces is of course to support scientific research. Our SMS environments are used to support a range of research groups that span WestGrid, Canada, and the world. In many cases, these collaborations involve the joining of two or more physical SMS environments while at other times the meeting may only involve one or two remote researchers joining a larger group of collaborators in a single SMS environment. These collaborations are usually interactive in nature and many of them revolve around the sharing of digital artifacts.
- *Research dissemination*: In addition to supporting research meetings among individual research groups, SMS are also used to disseminate research results to a wider audience. For example, IRMACS leads the Coast-to-Coast (C2C) Seminar Series (Borwein et al., 2006) a biweekly seminar series that brings together researchers from across Canada to present and discuss their research. These sessions are interactive presentations that involve up to ten sites across the country, with upwards of 60 attendees at some sessions. This activity has been occurring since 2005.
- *Training meetings*: WestGrid technical support staff use SMS for providing advanced training courses to the scientific community. Courses are given on using, programming, and optimizing computational algorithms for high-performance computing systems, using scientific visualization, and using collaboration technologies. These sessions typically involve many of the 14 WestGrid institutes and can have anywhere from 2 to 20 participants at a given site. The sessions are always interactive in nature, with the training sessions often involving live interactive demonstrations that are shared between all sites. Such training sessions have been delivered since 2004.
- *Operational meetings*: WestGrid, as a distributed consortium, uses the SMS infrastructure for operational purposes including financial, technical, and strategic meetings. These meetings involve all WestGrid institutes with 1–4 people at each site. They have been occurring on a regular basis since 2004.

## *What Worked?*

We often think of IRMACS and its SMS infrastructure as a social experiment. We designed the IRMACS Center to bring people together both socially and intellectually, and the IRMACS SMS infrastructure has played an important role in accomplishing this. The statistics on SMS usage indicate that distance collaboration is an important part of our computational science research communities work practice. We believe that the IRMACS SMS infrastructure has had a significant impact on both the intellectual and social dimensions of this research community. We explore some of these impacts below.

### Meeting Researcher Need

During the 2007 calendar year, the IRMACS SMS infrastructure was used to support remote collaboration approximately 13.5 h per week. Although we cannot state this definitively, we believe that many of these remote collaborative meetings would not have taken place had IRMACS not existed. That is, rather than synchronous distributed work, researchers would have either collaborated using asynchronous tools (email), collaborated at a much lower frequency, or possibly not collaborated with their remote colleagues at all.

The addition of the IRMACS SMS infrastructure has literally changed the way researchers work at SFU. Although it is difficult to document quantitatively the value to the researchers and the success of their projects, the level of demand that we see from our user community clearly indicates a need for SMS technologies. Some users of this infrastructure state the value of the SMS infrastructure quite clearly, with statements like "…we would not function effectively without it", "… can't live without these things [SMS rooms]", and "… if WestGrid had not provided such a facility we would have had to look for some funding to do it ourselves". Spreading such a need across the 60 projects and 288 IRMACS researchers makes the value to the research community clear.

### Location, Location, Location

We believe, as do many researchers (Olson and Olson, 2000), that "Distance Matters" and that it is important to have our SMS facilities close to the user community. The fundamental precept behind IRMACS was to bring people together in a single, interdisciplinary research space. Having an SMS infrastructure as a core technology in a physical space that supports 288 researchers is an effective mechanism for bringing this technology to the user community. Researchers come to IRMACS on a daily basis to meet with colleagues, have research group meetings, and attend talks. Making use of the IRMACS SMS technologies is a simple and natural extension to a researcher's typical day at IRMACS. This "on at the touch of a button" capability of the SMS rooms within IRMACS brings a new level of capability to our research community. One regular user of the WestGrid SMS room in Physics states that "…The closer it is and the easier the access the more often it will be used" and "The AG [SMS] room in physics is almost [as] close [as my office] but much higher quality…." We have found that proximity to the user community is fundamentally important to achieving the levels of use that we see in our SMS facilities.

## Everything but the Kitchen Sink…

One of the key successes of the IRMACS SMS infrastructure stems from its support of a comprehensive range of technologies within the physical SMS rooms. Originally, we had planned on using AccessGrid as our primary collaboration tool. We rapidly realized that although AccessGrid provided the most capability in terms of creating an advanced SMS environment, our user community was going to ultimately determine the set of software and hardware tools that met their needs the most effectively. Rather than dictate the technology that one uses for collaboration, the IRMACS SMSs provide the ability for researchers to create new and dynamic collaboration spaces as required. The ability to tailor a room to the purpose in which the room is going to be used is a fundamental and important dimension of the Media Space concept.

It is our belief that had we dictated the technology available to our users, the SMS usage in our facility would be significantly less than current levels. It is important to note that this does not mean that we allow the collaboration technologies used to be dictated by the remote site. Instead, we consult with our researchers, try to determine what their collaboration needs are, and then try to map that on to a set of technologies that will meet those collaboration needs. Fortunately, our SMS environments have been designed such that most collaboration tools can be used seamlessly in our SMS rooms.

## User Expertise in SMS Usage

One of the key changes that we have noticed in our user community is the ability of our more frequent SMS users to function with a high level of expertise in our SMS rooms. These rooms, although designed to be as seamless as possible, are complex technical environments and often require a learning period. Note that this period involves technological as well as social learning and adaptation. Our users need to adapt to the technology, but perhaps more importantly they also need to adapt to different social processes. Like any group that starts to work together, it takes time for the group to "learn" how to work together. It is possible to mitigate the technological learning process through careful technical design, but the social process is malleable and can only be learnt over time. It is our experience the pervasive SMS infrastructure at IRMACS has accelerated this adaptation. Our users are exposed to distance collaboration technologies on a regular basis, leading to an understanding and even an expectation that remote collaboration is a standard tool that they can use in their research.

Some of our users have become very sophisticated in their use of our SMS environments. Some groups make regular use of SmartBoard touch-screen technologies for interacting with and annotating documents and sharing a range of those documents (including digital whiteboards) with remote users. Although usage at this level of sophistication is not the norm for our user community, it is not uncommon. We have seen a number of research groups go from new users to extremely sophisticated users (both technically and socially) over a relatively short period of time (several months) (see Corrie and Storey [2007] for details).

### What Do You Mean, I Can't have an SMS Meeting?

Having access to the IRMACS SMS capabilities has significantly changed our users' expectations about being able to work with the wider research community. Even though not all of our community uses the IRMACS SMS infrastructure directly for their research, almost everyone within IRMACS has experienced SMS environments in some form or another, through either our Coast-to-Coast seminar series or other distributed events that IRMACS has hosted. Today, our users expect to be able to collaborate remotely with distant colleagues whenever and wherever they are. Unfortunately, it is not always possible to meet these expectations. Not all institutions have the same level of collaboration capability as that available to IRMACS researchers and it is therefore sometimes difficult to provide the level of quality interaction that we try to attain within our SMS rooms. Fortunately, the way our SMS environments are designed allows us to install collaborative software and seamlessly use it with the audio, visual, and interaction technologies in our rooms. Thus, it is possible for our SMS rooms to accommodate some sort of collaboration with most remote sites.

## *What Didn't Work?*

In the previous section, we painted a very rosy picture of the way the research community uses our SMS infrastructure. Over the last 3 years, we have seen a dramatic growth in usage. We also have a user community that is rapidly becoming familiar with the capabilities of our SMS technologies. Of course, getting to our current state has not been without its problems and issues and we would be remiss if we did not discuss these in as much detail. In fact, we have learned at least as much from our failures as we have from our successes. In the following sections, we look at the struggles we have gone through in creating and operating this infrastructure over the past 3 years. We concentrate on the operational aspects of supporting this infrastructure as the research community began to use the IRMACS SMS environments.

## Can You Ever Get It Right?

Building an easy-to-use SMS environment is an extremely difficult task, especially when the SMS environment needs to support a wide range of collaboration tasks. While our SMS environments were designed to be flexible, we could not have guessed all of the current uses of these systems, nor understood the limitations of some of the originally selected equipment. In order to adapt to both the ever-changing ways our rooms are utilized and the constantly changing software tools and collaboration protocols required by those uses, it has been necessary to constantly update and adapt our systems. While in some cases, these changes amounted to something as simple as installing a new piece of software, other cases required a complete redesign and reimplementation of certain equipment and technologies. Given the constantly shifting requirements of our users, and the rapidly changing collaboration landscape, this need is not likely to decrease in the future.

Within this ever-changing environment, maintaining an easy-to-use interface to the technology environment of our SMS rooms is also problematic. It is interesting to note that although our SMS rooms are "production rooms" (as opposed to research spaces) the technologies we use are similar to those discussed in the early Media Space (Harrison et al., 1997; Heath and Luff, 1992) and advanced interaction research (e.g. ClearBoard; Ishii and Kobayashi, 1992). In essence, we have attempted to commoditize the Media Space concept. Our SMS rooms have multiple cameras (typically three), multiple displays (at least two), touch-screen interaction (SmartBoards), sophisticated acoustic processing, and multiple computer platforms (computers and H323 units). Although many of these technologies are commodity technologies, the overall environment is still very complex and results in many possible points of failure. We try to limit the number of controls that a user has to deal with, we document our rooms extensively, and provide "dummy's guide" style step-by-step instructions for common usage scenarios. Despite these efforts we continually struggle with maintaining ease of use.

We have learned an enormous amount about both our user community and how we can use SMS technologies to support their collaboration needs, and we believe that we have made significant progress in this regard. This is at least partially reflected in the steady growth in SMS usage (see Figs. 24.3 and 24.4). Unfortunately, this is a never-ending process as collaboration software, technology platforms (e.g., high-definition videoconferencing), and our user's needs continually evolve. As a result, we are in a continuous cycle of improving the usability of our SMS environments to meet those needs.

## You Can't Win Them All...

Even if we were able to create an SMS environment that was flexible, powerful, and easy-to-use, a remote collaboration can break down in many ways. In many cases, much of the technology an SMS session depends on is outside of our control. This can include the quality of the technology at the remote site (acoustic quality, video quality, etc.), the networking infrastructure that joins the sites, security infrastructure at the remote sites (e.g., firewalls), and even the familiarity of the remote participants with collaboration technologies. Further, even the definition and terms of success are dependant on the expectations of the users and can vary widely based on past experience and the users' understanding about technical capabilities. We are often fortunate that the remote sites we are connecting with are at universities, and therefore the network is high bandwidth, low latency, and relatively free of congestion. However, at the other extreme, we also facilitate important research meetings between one of our SMS rooms and a collaborator in a hotel room, dialing in on a cell phone from the other side of the world and sharing complex documents using a hotel Internet connection. Unfortunately, the quality of an SMS session typically degrades to the quality level of the site with the poorest quality. When something goes wrong, there is little that one can do other than be flexible and creative in trying to find a way to make the collaboration work. Interestingly, in some instances our researchers have become so accustomed to having successful advanced collaborations over high bandwidth connections that they don't understand why this doesn't work in other, less desirable environments such as over hotel and/or wireless connections. Managing the users' expectations based on the realities of their collaboration and making sure they understand why the collaboration is failing is a very important aspect in making sure they are satisfied.

Our approach to mitigating these problems has been to be as proactive as possible in establishing a quality initial collaboration for our researchers. By investing time and effort in determining appropriate technologies to use, the quality of network between the collaborating sites, and the familiarity of the users with collaboration technologies, we attempt to avoid problems during the SMS session itself. Further, by defining the needs of the collaboration up front, many times the researcher themselves will have a better understanding of the role of technology within the overall goals of the collaboration. While it is not possible to remove such problems completely, our experience indicates that understanding the context of the collaboration is the most effective way of building an ongoing collaboration. Having a strong negative experience in an initial SMS collaboration can stop an emerging collaboration as quickly as any other problem that might arise.

## Well, It Worked Yesterday!

Even when you have everything planned and working today, there is no guarantee it will work tomorrow. No matter how much preparation is carried out, computers can fail, networks can go down, firewalls can change, and software can crash. One of the most surprising issues that we have in our SMS rooms is the seemingly unending desire of our users to disconnect and reconnect (often incorrectly) the devices in our rooms. Despite the fact that we try and make it as simple as possible to use the rooms and as difficult as possible to get access to devices that we do not want the user to touch, it is surprising how often we go into an SMS room after a meeting (or more often, at the beginning of the next SMS meeting when it isn't working) and find cabling unplugged, cabling connected incorrectly, or equipment turned off. This clearly indicates that despite our efforts, we still have a long way to go in making our SMS environments simple to use. When users encounter problems it leaves them with the option of asking for help (which they seem reluctant to do) or trying to make the SMS environment work for them selves. They clearly prefer doing it themselves, with the expected results – SMS rooms that no longer function correctly.

## Dealing with Success

One of the main problems we have at IRMACS today is dealing with our success. Our SMS usage has increased from 73 SMS meetings in 2005 to 397 meetings in 2007, with approximately 27% of the meetings held in IRMACS involving interaction with a remote collaborator. IRMACS is fortunate in that it has personnel who are dedicated to supporting this distant collaboration, but our personnel resources are currently oversubscribed. The vision of the IRMACS Center is to push the boundaries of how technology can be used in support of computational science. Given our current resources, the daily usage of our SMS environments makes it difficult to support our researchers at a level that fits with our mission of pushing technological boundaries. Although this is a result of our success, we also view it as a major failing of our effort to help our researchers bring these collaborations to a new level.

## To Adapt or Not to Adapt…

One of the key obstacles to having a successful collaboration is the change to social interaction that is required in these spaces. Although our SMS environments are technologically sophisticated, they do not reproduce a face-to-face environment. An SMS both presents barriers to the collaboration and at the same time provides new opportunities. The user primarily drives use of the SMS environment and we believe that we are only at the beginning of users developing new and innovative applications of these technologies.

It is clear that it is necessary for our users to adapt socially to the environment in which they are working. We have found that the level of adaptation is something that is naturally learned, but is learned differently across different users and for different tasks. Some users become adept at using advanced SMS technologies quickly, while others adapt slowly.

The level to which users adapt to these environments can be quite striking, to the point where we have seen collaborating research groups use components of our SMS environments in ways that were never intended. For example, one of our collaborating research groups uses Microsoft Excel as a modelling and visualization tool. They share Excel documents with remote collaborators and mark up and manipulate those documents with touch-sensitive digital SmartBoards. This group has gone so far as to develop a multiuser interaction technique that allows two users to simultaneously control a single user application (Excel). This group has been observed (see Corrie and Storey, 2007 for details) manipulating Excel documents with one user utilizing the keyboard to manipulate which cell is being discussed and the other using either the mouse and/or the SmartBoard to scroll around the document. This interaction is facilitated by the fact that the two users are remote, and therefore are not affected by some of the typical affordances of a single user application. We have seen this behavior develop over time as the group interacts with and manipulates Excel documents in complex ways as part of their collaboration.

## What About the Future?

The IRMACS and WestGrid SMS infrastructure has been in operation since 2004. We have learned an enormous amount in the 4 years that we have planned, deployed, and operated this infrastructure. The dramatic increase in the use of our facilities indicates that SMS is an important tool to the computational science community. It has also been an excellent opportunity to learn and understand how to support the collaboration needs of this community.

Despite the fact that we have been carrying out the social experiment we call IRMACS for 4 years, practically speaking we are only half way through this experiment. WestGrid has recently received a second round of funding that will extend the WestGrid SMS collaboration effort to 2013. In addition, WestGrid is one of seven collaborating computational consortia that make up Compute Canada, a national computational science initiative in Canada. This will result in similar SMS environments being installed across Canada. IRMACS is also only partially through its current round of funding, and we expect to continue developing our SMS infrastructure as new display, video streaming, and interaction technologies are developed and commoditized.

We believe that there are two fundamental reasons why the IRMACS/WestGrid SMS infrastructure has been successful, in particular in the context of the IRMACS Centre. First, through the funding provided by WestGrid and IRMACS we were able to build an advanced, distributed SMS infrastructure that allowed us to collaborate in ways that were difficult, if not impossible, before. Second, the technical support staff across WestGrid, and in particular at IRMACS, have allowed us to support the technical infrastructure in a way that empowered our researchers to use the facilities with little investment in time and effort. We believe that it is the combination of these two factors that have resulted in the dramatic increase in SMS usage at IRMACS and Simon Fraser University. We believe that without the dedicated IRMACS support personnel this level of collaboration would not have occurred. Through the continuation of the WestGrid and IRMACS efforts, we believe that the computational science community's use of SMS technologies is only beginning to evolve. We look forward to the opportunity to observe and analyze the continuing usage of Scientific Media Spaces in the future.

## References

Bellotti V, Dourish P (1997) Rant and RAVE: experimental and experiential accounts of a media space. In: Finn K, Sellen, A, Wilbur S (eds) Video Mediated Communication, Lawrence Erlbaum, Hillsdale, NJ.

Berry L, Bartram L, Booth K (2005) Role-based control of shared application views, Proc. UIST 2005, Oct 23–26, 2005, Seattle, USA. ACM.

Birnholtz JP, Beitz MJ (2003) Data at work: supporting sharing in science and engineering. Proc. GROUP 2003, Sanibel Island, USA, Nov 9–12, 2003, ACM.

Borwein J, Jungic V, Langstroth D et al. (2006) Coast-to-Coast Seminar and Remote Mathematical Collaboration. Proc. HPCS 2007, Saskatoon, Canada.

Bos N, Zimmerman A, Olson J, et al. (2007) From shared databases to communities of practice: A taxonomy of collaboratories. J. Comput.-Mediat. Commun., 12(2), 16. Available at http://jcmc.indiana.edu/vol12/issue2/bos.html. Accessed June 1, 2008.

Childers L, Disz T, Olson R, et al. (2000) Access Grid: Immersive Group-to-Group Collaborative Visualization, Proc. of Immersive Projection Technology Workshop, Ames, USA, June 19–20.

Corrie B, Storey M. (2007) Towards understanding the importance of gesture in distributed scientific collaboration, Int. J. Knowl. Inf. Syst., 13(2), Springer, London.

Finholt T, Olson G (1997) From laboratories to collaboratories: A new organizational form for scientific collaboration. Psychol. Sci., 8(1), Blackwell.

Fox A, Johanson B, Hanrahan P, et al. (2000) Integrating information appliances into an interactive workspace, IEEE CG & A 20(3), May/June 2000.

Harrison S, Bly S, Anderson S, et al. (1997) The Media Space In: Finn K, Sellen A, Wilbur S (eds) Video Mediated Communication, Lawrence Erlbaum, Mahwah.

Heath C, Luff P (1992) Media Space and Communicative Asymmetries: Preliminary Observations of Video-Mediated Interaction, J Human–Computer Interact., 7(3).

Ishii H, Kobayashi M (1992) ClearBoard: a seamless medium for shared drawing and conversation with eye contact. Proc. CHI 1992, Monterey, US, May 3–7.

National Research Council (U.S.) (1993) National Collaboratories: Applying Information Technology for Scientific Research, National Academy Press, Washington, DC.

Olson G, Olson J (2000) Distance Matters, J. Human–Computer Interact., 15(2/3), Lawrence Erlbaum, Mahwah.

Olson J, Teasley S, Covi L, et al. (2002) The (currently) unique advantages of collocated work. In: Hinds P, Keisler S (eds) Distributed Work, MIT Press, Cambridge.

Patrick A, Singer J, Corrie B, et al. (2004) A QoE sensitive architecture for advanced collaborative environments, Int. Conf. on Quality of Service in Heterogeneous Wired/Wireless Networks, Oct. 18–20, Dallas, TX.

Sonnenwald D, Whitton M, Maglaughlin K. (2003) Evaluating a scientific collaboratory: Results of a controlled experiment. ACM Trans. J Computer–Human Interact. 10(2) Jun. 2003.

# Chapter 25
# Section 4: Where Are We?

## Reflections on Media Space

**Steve Harrison**

The concluding chapters in this volume are reflections on media space research. There are two kinds of reflections: one about research that often leads to further questions and directions for further investigation, and the other about design that are often discussions on refinement of products and evaluations of processes. In an enterprise like media space, we see both.

We have three reflections: John Tang reflects on the utility of lessons from 20+ years of media space research; Saul Greenberg, his students, and colleagues reflect on some of the metaphors used in the design of media spaces and media space interfaces; and Austin Henderson reminds us of the dreams that drove early media spaces and how we can, by staying awake to our everyday world, see new ones.

While there is no need to further introduce those chapters, the reader should approach them understanding the general context of what media space research got right and what it missed.

## Got Some Things Right

Media space research was predicated on the basis of some predictions of technological enablers. Therefore, we set the context for the reflections by revisiting those technological assumptions:

*Video and audio part of networked computing*. YouTube, Skype, iChat, iTunes, built-in microphones, and cameras – we accept and expect it in commercial computing.

*Cheap high bandwidth to fixed locations*. DSL and broadband service are considered standard communications fare in offices, homes, and hotels. Whether directly or wirelessly connected, the optical and wired services form the backbone of this ubiquitous and relatively inexpensive communications sea. The answer to the question raised over 30 years ago, "Who needs all these bandwidths?" now seems obvious – pretty much everybody.

S. Harrison
Virginia Polytechnic Institute and State University
e-mail: sHarrison@vt.edu

S. Harrison (ed.), *Media Space 20+ Years of Mediated Life*,
Computer Supported Cooperative Work,

*Ubiquitous webcams*. Probably the element of early media spaces that at the time seemed the most wild and improbable was the idea that cameras would be cheap enough and found useful enough to be everywhere. But today, they are.

*Environmentally embedded technology*. While computers are still archetypically boxes with keyboards, mouses, and displays, more CPUs are put in automobiles than traditional computers. DVD players, cable and satellite decoders, and DVRs are practically indistinguishable from computers and often interoperate with them.

## Got Some Things Wrong

*Webcams address anxieties and fears rather than connect people and places*. Webcams are used for security, to monitor children at rest or play, to record mundane transactions and possible theft, to hunt for terrorists, and make sure that employees do not pilfer office supplies. In addressing anxieties, their presence communicates the idea that the location of the camera is in some way special and potentially dangerous, that the sense of being private is more difficult and less under individual's control, and that the someone who put up the camera (and is presumably watching) does not trust those who are being watched. This is rather the opposite from the trusting relations or engendering a feeling of connectedness.

*Displays did not get cheap (or flat) as fast as bandwidth and computing did*. The ubiquity of cameras was not matched by the ubiquity of display. Although many promising technologies are promoted as just about to make ubiquitous wall size or at least full-body size visual display possible, it has not yet happened in a way that would make the integration of digitally generated visual illusion and remote connection part of the everyday built environment. In fact, Time Square in New York is still enough of an anomaly that it remains an icon of mediated places and a tourist destination.

*Missed near-ubiquity of wireless, particularly (relatively) high bandwidth*. One crucial idea in the early media space work was that bandwidth necessary to create useful visual and acoustic simulations of remote locations would require a wire or optical cable. WiFi is rapidly becoming the network connection of choice for computing. Where the early media spaces were deeply identified with particular physical locations that in turn were associated particular social settings, wireless connectivity breaks the technological imperative for specific locations.

*Missed cell phones and the camera phone*. At the outset of media space research, the cell phone was not anticipated as a significant technology, and particularly not one that would act as a dislocator/relocator of space and social setting. As it became ubiquitous and added multimedia capabilities coupled to social conventions ("I'm in the supermarket; they don't have fresh salmon, so should I get the Ahi tuna? I'm sending you a picture so you can decide."), cell phones started to provide many of the coordinative and sociality envisioned for media spaces. And they have altered the meanings associated with space and place such as what constitutes "private" and "public," how deixis is resolved at distance, and so forth.

We invite readers to reflect on how visions shape realities since:

*Nothing ages faster than our visions of the future*.

# Chapter 26
# Fast Forward: Applying Media Space Experiences to Current Technologies

**John C. Tang**

**Abstract** It has been over 20 years since the initial media space research, and we are still not experiencing routine audio-video connections in everyday worklife. Yet, the popularity of instant messaging, photo and video sharing web sites, blogs, and other Web 2.0 tools can be largely explained by the lessons learned from that early media space research. These tools are reviewed in light of insights learned from the early media space research with some reflections on future directions.

In this chapter, I explore how to apply what we learned from studies of the social phenomena around media spaces to explain some of the popularity of recent services such as instant messaging (IM), photo and video sharing, blogging, and virtual worlds. Furthermore, what we learned from media space research can be used to guide the design and development of new Internet services, now that a networking infrastructure for delivering audio, video, and other media has been pervasively deployed. Thus, by updating the range of technologies under consideration and focusing on the social affordances of media spaces, we can leverage what we learned from media spaces some 20 years ago to guide innovation in the Web 2.0 space today.

I reflect on the recent popularity of IM, photo and video sharing, blogging, and virtual worlds, to illustrate how our experiences with media spaces help explain their popularity. In each case, I describe similarities with and differences from media spaces, to explain how we can or cannot apply insights gained from our media space studies to these current user experiences. Without worrying too much about whether all these services actually fit within the definition of a media space, using our media space experiences to explain their popularity can guide future exploration in these areas.

J.C. Tang
Microsoft Research
e-mail: johntang@microsoft.com

S. Harrison (ed.), *Media Space 20+ Years of Mediated Life*,
Computer Supported Cooperative Work,

## IM: Using Text and Icons to Share Awareness

Clearly, IM has become a popular Internet-based service around the world. A Pew report (Horrigan, 2007) notes that 37% of American Internet users use IM. Furthermore, IM use has been growing in both number of users and frequency of use. And IM, which was initially popularized in the home market for on-line socializing, has become increasingly popular in the workplace, where workers discovered that they also need to maintain an awareness of their distant colleagues to ease finding times to communicate (Nardi et al., 2000).

Like media spaces, IM as a system is always on, although individual users can log off or set blocked states for intervals of time. This always-on, shared awareness updated in real-time enables people to coordinate good times to initiate communication, much as media spaces do. Just as peeks at a video window would help suggest good times to try to contact a remote colleague, the dynamically updated awareness cues in IM (log-in status, availability states, keyboard idle times, etc.) help users coordinate good times to start a text chat. Research experiences in studying commercial IM (Nardi et al., 2000) and other IM prototypes in the workplace (Tang et al., 2001; Isaacs et al., 2002) document the ways in which IM can help colleagues (especially those remote from each other) find good times to start conversations in the workplace.

On the other hand, unlike media spaces, IM has very low fidelity, relying on text and icons to share awareness and communicate. Yet, by requiring an infrastructure that only needs to exchange text, it lowers the barrier to entry so that IM has enjoyed pervasive deployment, perhaps outnumbering by over a million-fold those who have actually experienced a media space. Despite these technical differences, the usage of IM closely resembles the way media spaces were used to help coordinate the starting of conversations. While IM may have developed wholly independent of the media space research (indeed its development may have been nearly contemporaneous), the social phenomena around IM usage is accurately predicted by how media spaces were used to set up conversations.

Even though the awareness cues shared by IM have much lower fidelity than those transmitted in the video of media spaces, it appears to be enough to help people coordinate their interactions. Furthermore, sharing the log-in status and availability states in IM raise less privacy concerns than sharing the full-motion video of media spaces. And while IM interruptions may be imperfectly timed, due to the lower fidelity awareness cues available, responding through text chat messages appears to be lightweight enough that people are willing to entertain and manage these IM interruptions. Indeed, the minimal distraction afforded by text-based IM enables some interaction in situations that would be off-limits to audio–video connections, such as doing IM while at the same time attending a meeting.

One likely direction for future development is to enable lightweight services such as IM to share higher fidelity cues, such as pictures and video. An infrastructure for sharing video in real-time is emerging, and commercial developments, such as Apple's iChat A/V, are demonstrating the feasibility of lightweight, reliable video connections over the internet. In fact, we are beginning to see IM as a mechanism for integrating together several other communication channels, such as IM, Voice over IP (VoIP) telephony, and desktop video conferencing.

## Photo and Video Sharing: Asynchronously Uploading and Sharing High-Fidelity Context

Web-based services that enable sharing photos (e.g., flickr) and video (e.g., YouTube) are a prominent part of the recent wave of Web 2.0 social networking technologies. These services depend on users to generate and share content (photos and videos) and also help manage the organization of this material (through tagging, rating, or even passively monitoring the amount of viewing each resource experiences).

A Pew report estimates that 19% of American Internet users have shared online something that they created (artwork, photos, stories, videos) (Horrigan, 2007). Furthermore, 16% of American Internet users have viewed a web cam (Rainie, 2005). These statistics indicate both a maturing network infrastructure that enables sharing photo and video data, and broader user uptake of working with pictorial and video data. The popularity of these photo and video sharing services is a product of the ease of both inexpensively capturing these materials (through digital cameras, camcorders, camera phones, etc.) and sharing them, via well-designed, easy-to-use web-based sites for photo and video sharing.

Like media spaces, photo and video-sharing services enable sharing high-fidelity data in the form of pictures or video clips. And while the systems are always accessible to view and upload data, the data is only periodically updated. In this sense, they are somewhat like Portholes, which only periodically updated still images from video cameras (Dourish and Bly, 1992). Casually browsing through photo-sharing sites shows that one practice for which they are used is to publicly share "stream of consciousness" pictures for all to see. While this might initially seem like amateur exhibitionism, our experiences with media spaces would indicate that there is enough value and interest in sharing high-fidelity cues of my context that others will pay attention to it and discover some shared interests or experiences, or even coordinate activities around that context.

While the awareness that these photo and video sharing services offer does enable shared context, this is not usually used to coordinate starting an interaction. Instead, it tends to be used to share context and experiences with selected social contacts over distance. For example, while it may seem initially puzzling to find photos of what I ate at meals or other seemingly everyday activities on photo-sharing web sites, our experiences with media spaces would predict that sharing rich contextual cues with other interested parties enabled collaborators to have a stronger, more interesting connection through their shared awareness of each others' context. A rather common special case of this kind of high-fidelity sharing occurs around sharing photos and videos while traveling, typically with close social contacts who are left behind.

## Blogging: Intentionally Sharing What Is on My Mind

Blogging, the practice of periodically updating a web-accessible journal, has also been gaining popularity, although perhaps mostly from reading blogs than actually creating them. The Pew Institute reports that 8% of American Internet users have created or worked on an online journal or blog, whereas 39% indicate that they have read a blog (Lenhart and Fox, 2006). Of those who created a blog, the most popular primary topic (37%) is cited as "my life and experiences."

Blogs are asynchronously updated and read, although publishing them on the web makes them always accessible. And since blogs are mainly text (although some also rather sparingly include pictures), their low fidelity and asynchronous exchanges seem most unlike the always-on, real-time video shared in media spaces. Aggregators and feed readers enable users to configure a dynamically updated stream of information on topics of selected interests.

Yet, blogging fundamentally relies on a premise that information about me is of interest to others. More specifically, everyday information about me, my thoughts, opinions, and life experiences that are not otherwise newsworthy can attract an audience if it is easy enough to access and monitor. In one sense, media spaces demonstrated the potential of that premise. Before media spaces, it was not clear that always-on, live video feeds of everyday offices would attract any persistent attention. Yet, our early experiences with media spaces showed that the video feeds transformed from initial curiosity to a useful mechanism for coordinating interaction. People found enough interest in the shared context, which media spaces offered that they used that shared context to coordinate interaction or strengthen their connections with other media space inhabitants.

The asymmetry of blog producers contrasted with consumers is where blogging perhaps differs most from the media space experience. The Pew statistics above indicate that almost five times as many Internet users have read a blog than have created one. By contrast, in most media space installations, those who viewed output from a media space also contributed a video input to it. I think this asymmetry reflects the increased effort needed to contribute intentional content to a blog, contrasted with the more passive sharing of context more typical in a media space arrangement (and to some extent, exhibited in use practices around some photo-sharing services).

## Virtual Worlds: Fad or Future?

More recently, virtual worlds have enjoyed a resurgence of public interest. Second Life and Active Worlds have attracted recent interest among both consumer and business audiences (Hof, 2007). Multi-player games such as World of Warcraft and Star Wars Galaxies set challenging games in a virtual world that often require players to work together to advance to higher levels (Ducheneaut et al., 2007; Nardi and Harris, 2006). Yet, this is at least the second wave of interest in virtual worlds, as the work on Habitat back in the 1980s (Morningstar and Farmer, 1991) launched a range of virtual worlds, such as Worlds Away and Microcosm (Isaacs, 1998), that enjoyed periods of success.

A recent study of interactions in virtual worlds observed the role of enhanced awareness information in them that reflects the coordinating nature of media spaces: "We see then that the ability to see what activities teammates are currently engaged in enables players to achieve tighter coordination in interaction than they can without such awareness information" (Moore et al., 2007). Unfortunately, in current virtual worlds, the awareness comes at the expense of considerable effort from the user to manually pose and move their character in the virtual world. The question remains whether the interface for interacting in virtual worlds can be made as easy to use as the way video passively records interactions in the media space. Virtual worlds present an intriguing platform for adding richer context to online interactions if the interface issues for naturally interacting in those environments can be addressed.

## Reflecting on Future Directions

Twenty years ago, a dozen or so researchers began experimenting with always-on, audio–video connections among locations within research laboratories. Today, hundreds of millions of people share awareness information through IM, photos, and videos through web sites, information through blogs, and experiences in virtual worlds. While today's services do not look like the network of video connections of the early media spaces, they offer similar affordances of coordinating communication and activities, socially negotiating starting an interaction, and sharing experiences and context. So while they do not fit the *spatial* definition of a media space, people have used them to construct a system that shares some *social* characteristics of a media space. Conversely, our experiences learned from using media spaces help explain the popularity of these services.

Looking forward to future developments, the next opportunities for deploying media space affordances are in mobile and asynchronous environments. We are already seeing this with IM clients appearing on mobile devices and using camera phones to capture and transmit photos. More recently, the Twitter system enables users to enter text from a number of locations and mobile devices to publish your current status to share with others. In the future, a more elastic version of "always on" may translate to easily accessible and easily updateable. So, while mobile devices especially may not support always-on video connections, we may still get similar benefits from occasionally updated photos posted on a web site accessible from mobile devices (i.e., a mobile version of Portholes).

It is not only the technical limitations of mobile devices that dissuade mobile media spaces to be always on, but also the privacy implications of deploying in a mobile environment. Privacy concerns about capturing scenes in the mobile world may suggest that initial versions be of lower fidelity (i.e., lower quality photos rather than video) and more asynchronous (i.e., occasionally uploaded snapshots rather than always-on video).

Rather than sharing video, which literally conveys the sensory information that people can use to maintain awareness of others' activities, mobile media spaces may convey other sensed information that people can use to accurately infer their awareness status. Whittaker (2003) reviewed computer-mediated communication systems according to whether they focused on sharing the following:

- The raw sensory information
- The cognitive cues that a person uses to interpret that sensory information into behaviors
- The social cues that people collectively use to provide a context for interpreting the behaviors and information

For example, seeing that a colleague is not currently in the office is an observation based on *raw sensory information*. Noticing that there is also no coat or briefcase in the office leads to a *cognitive inference* that the colleague has not yet arrived in the morning. Finding the colleague's office empty at around 12 noon would likely be *socially interpreted* as being away at lunch, according to the social norms of people eating lunch around that time.

While video affords literally sharing raw sensory information, Whittaker called for further exploring the effects of cognitive and social cues in supporting shared awareness. Supporting the cognitive and social cues that people use to mediate their communication does not require literally re-creating the sensory inputs that provide those cues. Thus, we are beginning to see systems that piece together various kinds of sensor information (i.e., location data, samples of audio to determine the quietness of a user's setting, rhythmic patterns based on historical usage) that would enable people to cognitively or socially infer whether it is a good time to start an interaction.

In reflecting on what we learned from the usage of media spaces, perhaps it is easier to generalize the lessons learned from the social perspective on media spaces to apply to the design of current and future technologies in this space. As noted earlier in the book, the social perspective allows more elastic variations in how media spaces of today are constructed and deployed. Thus, I find it striking how the media space research from over 20 years ago is still very relevant to explaining the popularity of current social phenomena as well as guiding the development of future technologies to support group interaction.

**Acknowledgments** I have worked with many people over the past 20 years that have helped me learn about media spaces that I want to thank. I am indebted to the Media Space group at Xerox PARC who first introduced me to media space research: Steve Harrison, Scott Minneman, Sara Bly, and Bob Stults. I also thank the Collaborative Computing group at Sun Microsystems, Inc. who explored digital version of media spaces: Rick Levenson, Monica Rua, Ellen Isaacs, Trevor Morris, Tom Rodriguez, and Alan Ruberg. I also thank the Network Communities group at Sun who explored IM and awareness prototypes: Bo Begole and Nicole Yankelovich. And, I thank the many anonymous users who gave us feedback on our research prototypes. By persisting through the trials of using prototype technology, they gave us valuable input to guide future designs.

## References

Dourish P, Bly S (1992) Portholes: supporting awareness in a Distributed Work Group, *Proceedings of Conference on Computer-Human Interaction (CHI)'92*, pp. 541–547.

Ducheneaut N, Yee N, Nickell E, Moore RJ (2007) The life and death of online gaming communities: a look at guilds in World of Warcraft, *Proceedings of Conference on Computer-Human Interaction (CHI 2007)*, pp. 839–848.

Hof, RD (2006) My virtual life, *BusinessWeek*, May 1, 2006, pp. 72–82.

Horrigan JB (2007) A typology of information and communication technology users, *Pew Internet: Pew Internet ICT Typology*, May 7, 2007, Pew Internet & American Life Project, http://www.pewinternet.org/PPF/r/213/report_display.asp (Verified May 25, 2007).

Isaacs E, Walendowski A, Ranganathan D (2002) Hubbub: a sound-enhanced mobile instant messenger that supports awareness and opportunistic interactions, *Proceedings of the Conference Computer-Human Interaction (CHI) 2002*, pp. 179–186.

Isaacs EA (1998) Microcosm: support for virtual communities via an on-line graphical environment, *Proceedings of the Conference Computer-Human Interaction (CHI) 1998*, pp. 5–6.

Ito M, Okabe D (2005) Technosocial situations: emergent structuring of mobile e-mail use. In: Ito M, Okabe D, Matsuda M (eds) *Personal, portable, pedestrian: mobile phones in Japanese life*. MIT Press, Cambridge, MA, pp. 257–273.

Lenhart A, Fox S (2006) Bloggers: a portrait of the internet's new storytellers, Pew Internet: Pew Internet – Bloggers, July 19, 2006, Pew Internet & American Life Project, http://www.pewinternet.org/PPF/r/186/report_display.asp (Verified May 25, 2007).

Moore RJ, Gathman ECH, Ducheneaut N, Nickell E (2007) Coordinating joint activity in avatar-mediated interaction, *Proceedings of the Conference on Computer-Human Interaction (CHI) 2007*, pp. 21–30.

Morningstar C, Farmer FR (1991) The lessons of Lucasfilm's Habitat, In: Benedikt M (ed) *Cyberspace: first steps*. MIT Press, Cambridge, MA, pp. 273-302.

Nardi B, Harris J (2006) Strangers and friends: collaborative play in world of warcraft, *Proceedings of the Conference on Computer-Supported Cooperative Work (CSCW) 2006*, pp. 149–158.

Nardi B, Whittaker S, Bradner E (2000) Interaction and outeraction: a study of instant messaging in the workplace, *Proceedings of the Conference on Computer-Supported Cooperative Work (CSCW) 2000*, pp. 79–88.

Rainie L (2005) Use of webcams, *Pew Internet: web cams*, June 2005, Pew Internet & American Life Project, http://www.pewinternet.org/PPF/r/159/report_display.asp (Verified May 25, 2007).

Tang JC., Yankelovich N, Begole JB, Van Kleek M, Li F, Bhalodia J (2001) ConNexus to Awarenex: extending awareness to mobile users, *Proceedings of the Conference on Computer Human Interaction (CHI) 2001*, pp. 221–228.

Whittaker S (2003) Theories and methods in mediated communication. In: Graesser AC, Gernsbacher MA, Goldman SR (eds) *The handbook of discourse processes*. Lawrence Erlbaum, Mahwah, NJ, pp. 243–286.

# Chapter 27
# Reflecting on Several Metaphors of MUD-Based Media Spaces

**Saul Greenberg, Gregor McEwan, and Michael Rounding**

**Abstract** Over the last decade, we designed and used three media spaces: Teamrooms, Notification Collage, and Community Bar. All were oriented towards creating a shared environment supporting a small community of people: about 2 to 20 members were expected to inhabit the media space. All provided others with a sense of presence through portrait images and/or snapshot-based video of its members, and all emphasized creation and sharing of real-time groupware artifacts. They differed in that each was designed around a different metaphor: multiple rooms for Teamrooms, a shared live bulletin board for the Notification Collage, and an expandable sidebar that contained multiple places for Community Bar. This chapter briefly reflects on how the systems and their metaphors served as a communal place. We saw that many factors – both large and small – profoundly affected how these media spaces were adopted by the community. We also saw that there was a tension between the explicit structures offered by media space design (rooms, places, bulletin boards, and so on) versus the very lightweight and often implicit ways that people form and reform into groups and how they attend to information in the real world.

## Introduction

Media spaces come in many forms and flavors, but all try to encourage awareness leading to informal interaction between people (typically coworkers or collaborators) who benefit from casual interactions with one another. In the classic media space experiments – the late 1980s and early 1990s – such systems typically comprised always-on or easily available video/audio connections between interested

S. Greenberg
University of Calgary
e-mail: saul.greenberg@ucalgary.ca

G. McEwan
National ICT Australia – NICTA

M. Rounding
SMART Technologies, Inc.

S. Harrison (ed.), *Media Space 20+ Years of Mediated Life*,
Computer Supported Cooperative Work,

parties (see Bly et al., 1993 for examples). Over time, these were augmented by computational tools that allowed people to move from conversation to actual work over computer artifacts. Around the same time, another popular class of social space was evolving: Multi-User Dungeons (MUDs and MOOs). Born of adventure games, traditional MUDs were text-based systems: game controllers created a space by using a server that hosted a variety of different rooms, each with a unique description and set of objects. A person could enter any number of different rooms, chat with other people in those rooms, and type commands to create and modify objects in the rooms. Multi-user virtual environments (MUVEs) visualized MUDs as graphical worlds where people could present themselves as avatars that could navigate the world and encounter others (e.g., DIVE, Carlsson and Hagsand, 1993). Text or audio connections to others were typically triggered by being collocated within a room or by proximity. MOOs combined MUDs and MUVEs within a richer graphical user interface, and sometimes augmented their communication so that people could converse over richer channels. For example, the Jupiter project (Curtis and Nichols, 1993) added MBONE audio and video conferencing, as well as graphics capabilities through shared whiteboards. More recently, MUDs have been transformed yet again into the very popular MMORPG: massive multiplayer online role-playing games, with examples being World of Warcraft and Second Life.

Technically, there is not much difference between a video-based media space augmented with computation tools and a MOO augmented with video; both serve the same purpose of providing a social world to its members by giving them awareness of who is around, and using that awareness to move into conversation and interaction. However, there are two key differences.

1. ***Real vs Virtual Worlds***. Video-based media spaces are centered on the real-world environment. The video connects two or more physical spaces so people appear somewhat co-located; add-on computational tools provide additional "virtual" resources to the group. In contrast, MOOs are centered on a "virtual" environment. People inhabit the virtual world, and add-on video/audio capabilities provide additional "real-world" connectivity.
2. ***Intimate Collaborators vs Loosely Knit Communities***. Video-based media spaces tend to focus on very small groups of intimate collaborators: members are often goal-oriented and have a real need and desire to stay connected. In contrast, MOOs support large, loosely knit virtual communities, where anyone can enter the space (sometimes anonymously or with pseudonyms).

Our own interest was to merge the two approaches, where we wanted to refashion MOO-like virtual environments so they would better fit the real-world needs of modest-sized groups of intimate collaborators. The primarily problem was not technical, for the capabilities of both video-based media spaces and MOOs began to overlap as they evolved. Instead, the challenge was how to redesign MOOs so they fit this different audience. Between about 1995 and 2007, I and my students developed, designed, and used three MOO-based media spaces that offered both video snapshots and groupware artifacts. While each has superficially similar capabilities, they are designed around quite different metaphors.

- **Teamrooms**, commercialized as Teamwave Workplace, is based on the notion of multiple rooms (Greenberg and Roseman, 2003; Roseman and Greenberg, 1997);
- **Notification Collage** is a shared live bulletin board viewable on a large public display and from people's workstations (Greenberg and Rounding, 2001)
- **Community Bar** is an expandable sidebar that holds multiple places (McEwan and Greenberg, 2005; Romero et al., 2006).

This chapter briefly reflects on each system – and each metaphor – as a communal place.

## Teamrooms

Similar to MOOs, Teamrooms was designed around a rooms metaphor. However, our goal was to provide multiple virtual rooms that exploit features inherent in physical rooms used for team purposes (e.g., team rooms, war rooms, etc.). Its interface, features, and use are fully described in (Greenberg and Roseman, 2003; Roseman and Greenberg, 1997). Figure 27.1 shows a screen snapshot of the commercial version of Teamrooms, called TeamWave Workplace. Some of Teamrooms' key ideas included:

- *A bounded space* that affords *partitioning* into a collection of rooms
- *Containment* through individual rooms, where they collect people and groupware objects
- *Permeability* of rooms allowing people and things to enter and leave them
- *Persistence* of objects within the room over time
- *Socially mediated ownership* that controls who should enter and use that room and how privacy is managed;
- *Customization* of that room by how its occupants create and manipulate objects within it
- *Spatial location* where objects and people within a room are spatially positioned in a way that maintains common reference and orientation, and where proximity influences action and reciprocity
- *Habitation* where people can be aware of others across and within rooms, and where they can inhabit particular rooms

Figure 27.1 illustrates the main components of its user interface. Figure 27.1a displays the "Rooms on this Server" window that lists all rooms currently available to the community, who is in it, and even a degree of privacy as suggested by the door icon. Figure 27.1b shows similar information, but in this case as a list of logged-on people identified by name, photo, and what room they are in. Clicking a person's name reveals their business card (1c). A person enters a room by selecting that room from the list. The large window on the lower half of Figure 27.1 shows one of the many rooms created by this community. In this case, user Carl has entered a room called "TeamWave Demo"; Saul and Mark are also present in this room as shown by their icons (Fig. 27.1h).

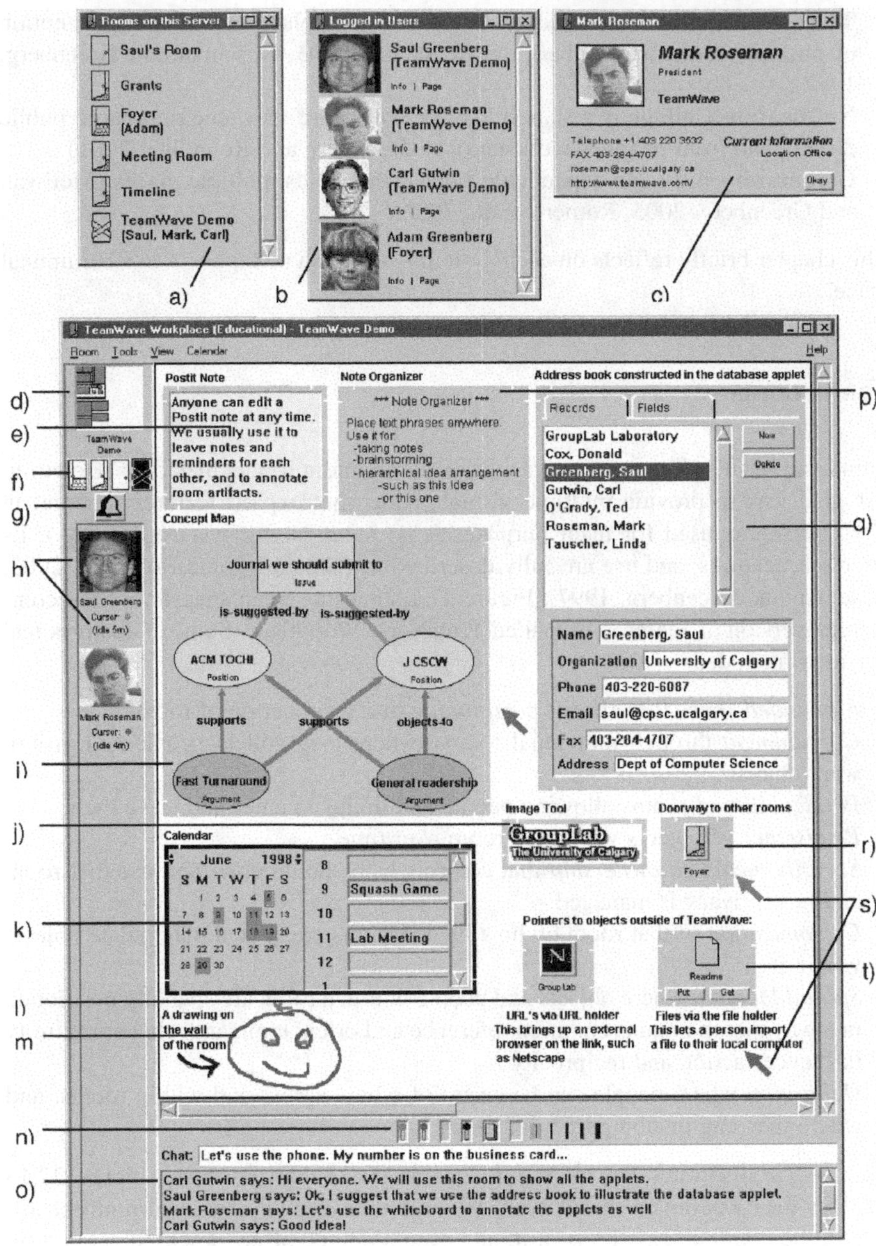

**Fig. 27.1** TeamRooms/TeamWave Workplace user interface, showing a room and peripheral windows as seen by user Carl

Rooms have many resources. The side bar includes a radar overview (1d), the ability to set privacy via the door state (1f), the ability to attract attention by dinging others (1g), and a list of people in the room, their cursor shape and idle time (1h). Depending on the system version, the images in 1h are static photos or video images updated every few moments in real time. The bottom bar includes a text-based chat dialog (1o) and a set of drawing implements (colored pens, eraser, and line thickness).

The center area is a groupware space: all see each other's cursors in this space, all can work simultaneously, and all actions and artifact changes are seen by others in real time. The back wall is a sketchpad, and people can draw, erase, and type on it (e.g., 1m). People can add a variety of special purpose applets to the room, such as a Postit™ note that serves as a multiuser text editor (1e), a groupware concept map editor (1i), a groupware calendar (1k), a note/list editor (1p), and/or a groupware database (1q). Within this space, they can also place and retrieve files (1t), URLs (1l), images (1j), and even doorways to other rooms (1r). Other tools (not shown) include a groupware web browser, a groupware file viewer, and even collaborative games. What is important is that the act of entering the room automatically connects these people together, where they can immediately see each other and all the things in the room, and where they can immediately chat and simultaneously interact over the groupware artifacts. Rooms and their artifacts persist, so people can come and go as they please.

We thought that groups would construct social places within these rooms, as the system no longer had many of the "seams" found in conventional groupware. Rooms could serve as a place for both individual and group work; the distinction between the two was simply a matter of who occupied the room and the purposes the room was used for. Rooms also encouraged modeless interaction: real-time interaction was just a consequence of people inhabiting the same room at the same time, while asynchronous interaction was a consequence of how people left artifacts (i.e., groupware objects showing content) within the room for others to see. Rooms would also let the social place develop over time; because things persisted (including writing that people could put on its back wall), people could craft the social meaning of the room by how they included objects within it, and how they decorated it. The collection of rooms would also form a community: while access control dictated who was allowed into a particular collection of rooms, any community member, once in Teamrooms, could create a room, could enter other rooms, and could see who was around. That is, access within a community was mediated through social versus technical protocol.

In spite of the rich intellectual premises behind its design, Teamrooms did not live up to its promise as a social environment. While people did create their own rooms, we saw little actual interaction over time. Eventually, the commercial version of this product – Teamwave Workplace – was pitched as a place to hold planned classroom meetings rather than as a media space supporting casual social interactions and ongoing work.

We believe that Teamroom's shortcomings were not with the room metaphor, but with the ways rooms were realized within it. With hindsight, we identified two major problems. The first was that Teamrooms did not effectively support awareness leading to casual interaction. A person could see who was around and thus available for interaction only ***after*** they actually logged into the system. Because logging in was relatively heavyweight, people would rarely do it just to see if someone was there. In addition, people would not leave the system up and running just for awareness purposes, as it consumed considerable screen real estate. This defeated the "always on" premise behind most media space designs. Thus there was little opportunity for casual interactions simply because no one was in a room long enough for others to notice. Another way to think of this is that Teamrooms was too MOO-like; people had to enter and inhabit the virtual world before they could see and interact with others. Unlike video-based media spaces, Teamrooms did not connect people's real-world activities.

The second problem was that Teamrooms did not really support actual work. It only had "toy" applications within it. While people could do simple tasks, they could not really share their real work done with commercial applications such as Microsoft Word, Excel, and so on. In addition, voice was not supported, meaning that people would have to use an awkward chat system to mediate their real-time interactions over these applications.

## Notification Collage

To partially solve these two problems, we determined that our next system should somehow stress real-world (vs. virtual world) social interaction, and information sharing relevant to the group (vs. "toy" groupware applications). First, we decided to base our design around the metaphor of a public bulletin board that would always be visible on a person's screen or on a public display; the idea was that this always-on visible bulletin board would exist within the person's real-world environment and context. Second, the bulletin board would contain a collage of interactive information fragments, called *media items*, which are interactive groupware applications that let individuals post information they thought relevant to the group, where others could view and manipulate the media item's content. The result was a new groupware system called Notification Collage (Greenberg and Rounding, 2001).

Notification Collage (NC) is illustrated in Fig. 27.2 and works as follows. Distributed and colocated colleagues comprising a small community create a central server (a fairly trivial process). Each person in that community then connects to this server via an NC Client, which appears as a large window – a real-time collaborative surface – on their screen (Fig. 27.2). Because of its size, we recommended people place NC on a second monitor located at their periphery. At this point, individuals can post media items (selected from the Posting Menu, Fig. 27.2), and all members see these immediately. Akin to collages of information found on public bulletin boards, NC randomly places incoming elements onto

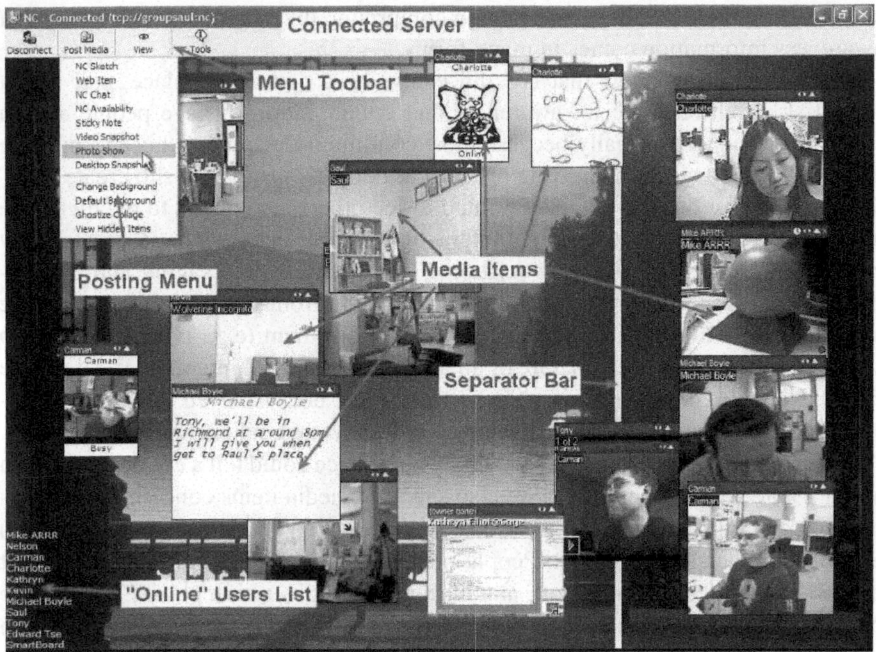


**Fig. 27.2** Notification Collage

this surface. While all see the same items, people can rearrange them as desired on their individual displays, for example, in order to increase their visual prominence or hide less interesting ones from view. In particular, items placed on the right of a separator bar are never covered by new items. As illustrated in the figure, people can post assorted media: live video from desktop cameras; editable sticky notes; activity indicators; slide shows displaying a series of digital photos, snapshots of a person's digital desktop, and web page thumbnails. Some items allow people to move into direct interaction: people can move into an audio/video conference by selecting a person's video, and they can share a person's desktop by selecting a particular desktop image.

Unlike Teamrooms with its many virtual rooms as social places, this metaphor gives a group a single public place that holds meaning to them. First, it serves as a combined media-rich bulletin board, chat room, and video-based media space. We hoped that their focus on this single place would encourage sufficient postings and interactions to make it worth keeping always on, always visible on their display, and thus always present. Second, because it is a single bulletin board, we could post it in a large public display situated in a meaningful location, as well as on people's individual workstations, for example, in a room or hallways populated by coworkers who are part of the NC community. Thus people could see its content as they walked by, or engage with others over it. Third, the overlap of items inherent in a large collage acknowledges that there may be a large number of information fragments, too many to tile neatly on the display. Finally, collages are customarily used to present unstructured information comprising diverse media, conceding that awareness information comes in many forms.

User experiences show that NC did evolve as a communal place, and that it served as a rich resource for awareness and collaboration. It gave people a keen sense of presence, especially because most community members chose to indicate their presence to others by posting live video. People's instinct was to create a visible presence for themselves: they wanted to see others, and others to see them. We also saw that media items triggered interaction. People acted on its information by engaging in text and video conversations. Unlike instant messaging and conventional media spaces, conversations sometimes began from people seeing interesting artifacts within the space and wanting to talk about them (e.g., photos or desktop snapshots). Next, the public nature of all actions encouraged interaction. All people could overhear conversations and see all postings; because even directed conversations and postings were visible to the group, anyone could monitor and join in. Furthermore, those cohabiting a public physical space could tell a collocated person about a note addressed to them. We also saw that media items concerning communication and information sharing (vs. the work-oriented groupware of Teamrooms) encouraged social engagement. People posted items they believed would interest others, such as desktop snapshots, announcements and vacation photos. Finally, the public display acted as a way for telecommuters to reach people (including room visitors) visible from its attached camera, and for those people to respond.

While successful as a place supporting a single small community, the Notification Collage had several limitations that restricted how it could be used by less well defined groups. As a single public place, it was all or nothing. People were either "in" or "out" of this community. This meant that people on the periphery of this group were sometimes reluctant to join in. The group was also very conscious of the appearance of "strangers" (usually a friend of only one group member), where conversations would cease until that person was somehow introduced by an "in" group member. Similarly, Notification Collage did not really support ad hoc groups. People were either a member of the community, or they were not. Its interface also proved somewhat heavy-weight in terms of how awareness was supported. People had to constantly review its contents to see what (if anything) had changed since they looked, although appearances of new items of changes to an item's content typically stimulated a glance. Notification Collage was also more space-intensive than we would have liked. People without second monitors were severely disadvantaged, as the large size of the main window competed with other foreground applications.

## Community Bar

The Community Bar (CB) (McEwan and Greenberg, 2005; Romero et al., 2006) extends our earlier work by trying to overcome the limitations of the Notification Collage while still building on the successes of media items. In particular its design is theory driven, where it is built around the Locales social science framework (Fitzpatrick, 2003) and the Focus and Nimbus model of awareness (Rodden, 1996). Generally, CB supports ad hoc groups by letting people create and enter *locales* (called *Places* in CB jargon). CB also balances providing rich awareness information versus space requirements through its use of a *sidebar metaphor* that leverages the query in depth properties of the Microsoft Sideshow awareness display (Cadiz et al., 2002). Both these design considerations are described below.

The Locales Framework (Fitzpatrick, 2003) suggests that people inhabit multiple social worlds, where each "world" contains not only people, but offers a site and a means for their interactions. CB supports multiple locales through rapid creation of "Places." For example, the particular individual's CB client in Fig. 27.3 displays two Places (i.e., two sites) called "mike test" (top) and "CSCW class" (bottom). Each comprises different sets of media items representing the various people who inhabit each place (e.g., the Presence media item in Fig. 27.3 shows each person's live video or image) and various means (e.g., people communicate through the Chat item; they share web pages through the Web item, they can post personal photos through the Photo item; they can even share their screens through the Screen sharing item). People can inhabit as many places as they wish. For example, Gregor, MB, and Mike R are in the "mike test" place, while Kim, MB, and KT are in the "CSCW Class" place; MB cohabits both places. Long-standing and ad hoc groups can create, maintain, and destroy these places as needed. Through the media items, people within a place can present themselves to others, engage in conversation, and interact with group artifacts as desired. Each person can act in distinct ways in each of the Places they inhabit. Within a Place (and similar to MUDs), all information and interactions are public to all other people currently in that Place. Place members are able to share awareness information, to send broadcast queries (e.g., "Is there anyone who knows about X?"), and to overhear conversations and join those of interest to them. Unlike Notification Collage, CB supports multiple places rather than a single place. Unlike a room in Teamrooms, people can be in multiple places at the same time, and interact within any Place at leisure.

The Sidebar metaphor is important for lightweight transitions from peripheral awareness to foreground interaction. It recognizes the tension between a person's desire for a *minimal* amount of unobtrusive yet dynamic awareness information of their intimate collaborators, against the need to act upon that information, e.g., to explore that information in depth, or to engage in rich communication as desired. Community Bar relieves this tension by offering people a progressive view of information. Rich yet not overwhelming awareness information is located at the periphery of the screen in a space conservative sidebar (shown in Fig. 27.3, right). Moving the mouse pointer over items causes a "tooltip grande" to appear (Fig. 27.3, left) that displays more information and provides interaction opportunities. Clicking on the tooltip grande title raises a "full view" permanent window (not shown in Fig. 27.3) providing full information and interaction opportunities. To show this in more detail, Fig. 27.4 shows this progression for the screen-sharing media item, which allows people to post part or all of their desktop to the group (Tee et al., 2006a, b). The tile view (left) shows a small image of Kim's desktop, updated every

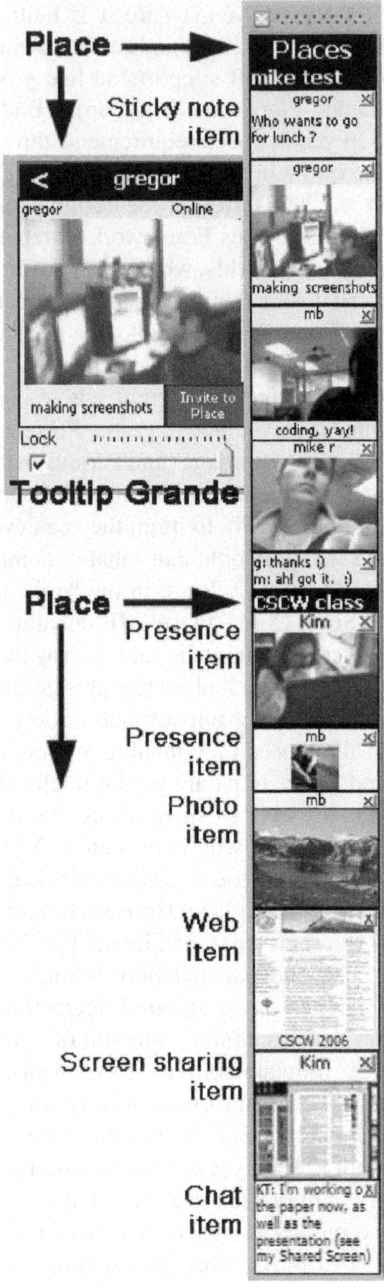


Fig. 27.3 Community Bar. Visible are two labeled places ("mike test" and "CSCW class"), five types of items, and the Presence Tooltip Grande

several seconds. The size and resolution suffice to give others a broad sense of what she is doing. The Tooltip Grande (middle) offers a somewhat higher fidelity view of the same information at a faster update rate. The Full view (right) is at full fidelity; people can zoom into information and even request remote pointing to move into

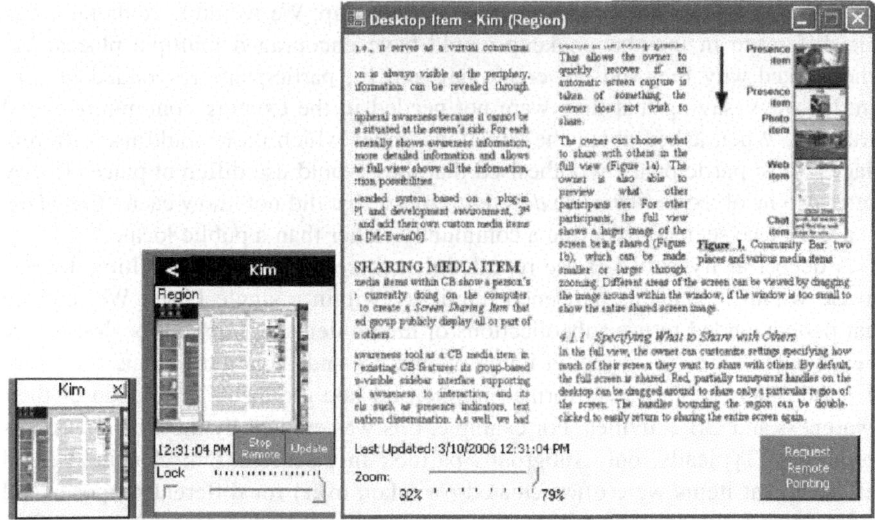


Fig. 27.4 The Tile, Tooltip Grande, and Full View of the screen-sharing item (Tee et al., 2006a, b)

interactive screen sharing. Collectively, this progression of views allows the user to quickly stay aware of peripheral information, and to easily move into foreground interaction with information and people.

Finally, Community Bar uses the focus/nimbus model (Rodden, 1996) to represent center and periphery relationships. People express their involvement within a Place by using sliders to adjust both their nimbus (what others can see of them) and focus (how much they see of others). In this way, views and memberships become somewhat more fluid. Unlike Teamrooms, where people are either in or out of a room, people can now adjust their focus/nimbus to control how much they are "inside" a place.

We performed a field study of CB in use (Romero et al., 2006). Many things worked as predicted by the Locales theory, in particular, how people were able to maintain awareness and how they could move into interaction with others. However, the multiple Place functionality was not used heavily by this user community. We initially thought this was because the group was fairly cohesive, where they enjoyed working within one large Place (i.e., as in the Notification Collage). We thought this group did not see a strong need to splinter themselves into long-term subgroups. Yet on closer inspection, we found that our study participants were easily divided into two groups: a "core" group who often worked together closely and interacted with each, and a peripheral group comprising everyone else who had less work ties to the first group. This led to a divide in how CB was considered. Core group members consistently talked about the sense of belonging to the community that CB gave them. In contrast, peripheral members often reported that they felt like outsiders, and that most of the explicit communication on CB did not involve them directly. This was not necessarily a bad thing, as all people, whether core or peripheral, expressed sentiments on how useful CB was for maintaining an idea of what was going on with the rest of the group. We would have thought that this difference in member makeup would have encouraged multiple places. Yet when asked why they did not create new places, participants responded in very similar ways, saying that they were not needed in the existing community social structure. When asked about the situations under which they would use different places, most participants hypothesised that they would use different places if they were also involved in *distinctly different groups* that did not know each other. That is, a CB Place seemed to define a community rather than a public locale.

A deeper analysis of CB use revealed that there actually were multiple locales in use within it, but this happened implicitly within a single Place. We realized that people tended to use subcollections of media items as implicit locales, where they would "tune in" to media items of interest and "tune-out" items that were of lesser interest. They also formed implicit ad hoc groups as a function of their awareness and CB activities. For example, this was evident by the way chat items were used. Typically, only subgroups partook in discussions in chat items, and different chat items were often created (or taken over) for different purposes and people. Similarly, different sub-groups were interested in different things at different times: this likely led to some of the differences in how people interpreted some media item awareness information as useful versus as clutter and distracting. Yet people seemed comfortable – even those who were "on the periphery" – of doing all this ad hoc group formation within the context of the larger CB community versus within the explicit structure of CB Places. On reflection, actual CB use is somewhat akin to how people inhabiting a common physical area selectively attend only some activities within it, and how they rapidly form and quickly reform ad-hoc subgroup clusters.

## Discussion

All three systems were built around the notion of a collection of public media items that portray people (usually as live video snapshots), their interactions (usually as text chats), and their things (usually as information containers or mini-groupware applications). They differ considerably in the metaphors they followed, which in turn affected how each system structured and presented these items. What we saw is that many factors – both large and small – profoundly affect how these media spaces are adopted by the community. In spite of its rich-room metaphor, Teamrooms was not adopted as we had expected, simply because it lacked the light-weight awareness critical to casual interaction and because the "walls" comprising its room were too hard – they isolated community members rather than brought them together. This left it more suitable as a meeting tool rather than an always-on media space. Notification Collage did work as it offered a rich multimedia space for casual interaction. However, it was limited as being an "all or none" system; people were either in the group defined by the single media space, or out of it. Community Bar achieved the same effect as the Notification Collage while doing a better job at balancing awareness and distraction. Yet its key property – that of Places – was not used in the way we expected, i.e., Places defined the entire community versus ad hoc groups. Still, we did see subgroups evolve within a single Place through how people used its items and how they attended them.

## *Implicit versus Explicit Structures*

It seems there is a tension between the explicit structures offered by media space design (rooms, places, bulletin boards, and so on) versus the very lightweight and often implicit ways that people form and reform into groups. In real life, we do this through a variety of social mechanisms – by physically moving closer together, by sharing things in particular ways, by cohabiting a space, by moving between multiple spaces, and by selectively attending and responding to the world around us. In the computer world, these everyday physics don't apply. Instead, we substitute explicit structure through our metaphors as a mitigating surrogate that anticipates how groups form and reform, and that controls the social mechanisms of groups. In practice, we see that these explicit structures are often ignored or become hurdles. In contrast, systems with little structure do seem to work better because people use their own attentive and social resources to define their group in a subtle, highly flexible, and tacit way. Yet we expect an unstructured approach will have problems, as they likely will not scale beyond small reasonably cohesive groups. A challenge is how we can provide explicit structure as a flexible backbone to peoples' social activities, where it suggests rather than forces people to interact in a way that works well for them.

## *Transitions Between Real versus Virtual Worlds*

Let us now reconsider the main difference between media spaces and MUDs. As mentioned, media spaces connect intimate collaborators and are centered around the real world; the idea is that because people live in the real world, technology can create a virtual portal connecting geographically separated real-world locations. In contrast, MUDs collect loosely knit communities centered around a virtual world; the idea being that this virtual place transcends the physical boundaries and physics that could otherwise limit community formation and interaction.

While both views appear reasonable, they are incomplete in themselves, as they assume that people primarily "live" in either the physical world (which favors the media space approach) or the virtual world (which favors the MUD approach). Yet the reality today is that most people live in both places. What has happened since the late 1980s (when media spaces and MUDS were first introduced) is that the desktop computer has become an integral part of people's physical world. Many people are now heavy computer users, spending at least a few hours a day at their screens, or referring to them repeatedly over the course of a day. Yet these same people inhabit a physical world, where they also attend to life off the screen. Thus computer use is interwoven with physical activity.

On reflection, we realize now that the evolution of our three systems moved their design towards a space that somewhat blends the distinctions between media spaces and MUDs, as they were progressively centered around having a real-world component that transitioned into the virtual world. This was a good thing. For example, CB and Notification Collage were successful as awareness systems as their always-on state meant they "lived" in the real world. Its information was always available, where people habitually monitored their display while pursuing some other real-world activity or while working at their computer. The lightweight manner that people could attend this information within the Notification Collage and CB place better reflected their real-world engagement with information and with the other people inhabiting the place. CB's sidebar also did a better job of managing people's real-world awareness needs, where they could move from information easily available in the real world (i.e., via a quick glance), to more in-depth information held by the virtual world (e.g., by navigating to tool-tip grandes and full interaction views).

The failures we noted previously show where transitions between the real and virtual world were not well supported. First, the state of activity in a Teamrooms room was visible only if one was in the place; in practice, this meant that critical information was rarely accessible "at a glance" from the real world. Out of sight became out of mind. Second, both the Notification Collage and Teamrooms demanded a large amount of real estate. People mediated this by either devoting a large part of a second display to it (which was expensive in terms of cost and desk space), or by covering up the window with other windows or shrinking it down to the toolbar if the screen was used for other things (which fundamentally changed the ease of accessing its information). When the window was in full display, it was visually dominant, that is, it demanded attention in a way that could have been out of proportion to how people wanted to use it. If people expended excessive time-monitoring activity in the virtual world that did not match its real-world importance, then it would become a distraction. The result is that people would likely turn off the system, or shrink it out of view, or simply not use it. Third, the explicit structure of a virtual group suggested by both a Teamrooms' room or a CB place was largely ignored, as it often did not reflect how people perceived, managed, and attended their real-world groups.

## *Embodied Interaction*

Dourish's (2001) theory of *embodied interaction* can help us reconsider the phenomena noted above. Embodied interaction is the way that physical and social phenomena unfold in real time and real space as a part of the world in which people are situated, right alongside and around us, and how people create meaning about the world through their own actions and those of others.

Under this theory, we should now understand that people are including their virtual systems as part of these physical and social phenomena. We suspect that the specific successes as seen in NC and CB have more to do with having some portion of these system – usually the attentional devices that promote awareness – embedded in the real world where people were doing all of their other activities. People's world as a whole thus incorporated a complex mixture of social, physical, and virtual components. Each system provided an extension from the physical to the virtual world in which people were currently acting, with smooth transitions in and out of this new space. In contrast, MUDs and Teamrooms created a separate world to inhabit, where the transitions are heavyweight. Thus people had to choose to be embodied in one world or the other. While appropriate for dedicated activities (such as meetings), this split embodiment does not work well for casual interaction. Again we come back to and stress the need for transitioning from informal awareness to casual and formal interaction if the system is to become a social place. It is not a matter of connecting our physical worlds (as done in media spaces) *or* connecting our social worlds (as done in MUDs), but rather of blending those worlds together in a way that eases the transitions between them.

While our three systems all worked to varying extents, none are optimal. The design challenge is how to strike a balance between the offerings of the virtual world and how they manifest themselves in the embodied interaction of the moment-by-moment real world. Perhaps ubiquitous computing approaches may help this process, where we may see virtual information and people situated in our real world in a way that preserves our natural social ways of interacting with the world around us (Dourish, 2001; see Greenberg and Kuzuoka 2000, for an example).

**Acknowledgments** Research was partially funded over the years by the NSERC Discovery Grant, the NSERC NECTAR Research Network, by Microsoft Research, and by the NSERC/iCORE/Smart Technologies Chair in Interactive Technologies.

**Software Availability** Community Bar and the Notification Collage are available for download at http://www.cpsc.ucalgary.ca/grouplab/cookbook/. Both were designed around earlier versions of Microsoft Windows.

## References

Bly S, Harrison S, and Irwin S (1993) Media spaces: bringing people together in a video, audio, and computing environment. *Communications of the ACM*, 36(1), January

Cadiz JJ, Venolia GD, Jancke G, and Gupta A (2002) Designing and deploying an information awareness interface. *Proc ACM CSCW*, , 314–323

Carlsson C and Hagsand O (1993) DIVE – A platform for multi-user virtual environments. *Computers and Graphics*, 17(6), 663–669.

Curtis P and Nichols D (1993) MUDs grow up: Social virtual reality in the real world. In *Proceedings of the Third International Conference on Cyberspace*, Austin, TX

Dourish P (2001) *Where the Action is: The Foundations of Embodied Interaction.* MIT Press, Cambridge, October

Fitzpatrick G (2003) *The Locales Framework: Understanding and Designing for Wicked Problems.* Kluwer, Dordrecht

Greenberg S and Kuzuoka H (2000) Using Digital but Physical Surrogates to Mediate Awareness, Communication and Privacy in Media Spaces. *Personal Technologies*, 4(1), January, Elsevier

Greenberg S and Roseman M (2003) Using a Room Metaphor to Ease Transitions in Groupware. In M. Ackerman, V. Pipek, V. Wulf (Eds) *Sharing Expertise: Beyond Knowledge Management*, 203–256. MIT Press, Cambridge, MA, January

Greenberg S and Rounding M (2001) The Notification Collage: Posting Information to Public and Personal Displays. *Proc ACM CHI*, 515–521, ACM Press

McEwan G and Greenberg S (2005) Supporting Social Worlds with the Community Bar. *Proc ACM Group* 2005, ACM Press, Sanibel Island, FL

Rodden T (1996) Populating the Application: A Model of Awareness for Cooperative Applications. *Proc. ACM CHI*, 88–96

Romero N, McEwan G and Greenberg S (2006) A Field Study of Community Bar: (Mis)-matches between Theory and Practice. Report 2006-826-19, Department Computer Science, University of Calgary, Calgary, Alberta, Canada, T2N 1N4, March 17

Roseman M and Greenberg S (1997) A Tour of TeamRooms. Video *Proc ACM CHI*, ACM Press. Videotape

Tee K, Greenberg S, and Gutwin C (2006a) Providing Artifact Awareness to a Distributed Group through Screen Sharing. *Proceeding of the ACM CSCW'06 Conference on Computer Supported Cooperative Work*, ACM Press, November

Tee K, Greenberg S, Gutwin C, and McEwan G (2006b) Shared Desktop Media Item: The Video. Video *Proceedings of ACM CSCW'06 Conference on Computer Supported Cooperative Work*, November, ACM Press. Video and two-page summary. Duration 4:00

# Chapter 28
# Making Contact

**Austin Henderson**

**Abstract** Starting an interaction is a significant barrier to interaction in many current Media Spaces. This critical activity needs to be understood and supported in future Media Spaces.

I am working along, and it occurs to me that I want to talk to Lynne about the chapter. I have three things to do: decide how I can reach her, decide if this is a good time to talk, and go through the negotiation of starting the conversation. This is the activity of "making contact," a key part of all communications.

If Lynne and I are in the same space (same room, within earshot), I have all the information I need to support making contact: the space can provide me with an on-going awareness of Lynne's presence, the appropriateness of interrupting her, and the means for starting the talk. In contrast, if we are not in the same space, I will have to make an effort on all three fronts, finding a media for communication, addressing her within it, and staging an unanticipated "blind" interrupt at the risk of intruding.

One of the nicest things about Media Space is that, at its best, it extends the feeling of being in the same space to situations in which people are separated. My experience when Annette Adler and I had coupled rooms (in OfficeShare) was that I was aware of her absence or presence, and whether she was likely to be OK with an interruption, and could start a conversation with "Lunch?," unheralded by "Hello," or even "Annette?" Steven Pemberton remarked at CHI2008 that he has noticed that when on an extended trip and coupled to home through video Skype, his children simply come up to him (via their computer, of course), engage and depart, just as they do when he is working at home.

Of course not all Media Spaces have the luxury of being "always on." Indeed, the technology is such that getting them going is often a considerable effort. How many distributed meetings are started with ten minutes of fighting the technology?

A. Henderson
Rivendel Consulting and Design
e-mail: austin.henderson@pb.com

S. Harrison (ed.), *Media Space 20+ Years of Mediated Life*,
Computer Supported Cooperative Work,

These difficulties not only take effort, but more importantly, they tend to make the technology the subject matter; as such, they are usually a serious intrusion into the social interaction of the meeting. As a result, many people with good cause avoid distance collaboration using video.

My hope is that Media Spaces of the future will address these difficulties in making contact. I imagine making it easy to identify the space that you want to couple your space to, easy to set up the coupling, and therefore easy for people to negotiate the interruption with the full resources of coupled spaces. Many distance collaboration technologies allow you to explicitly make public your availability for interruption. The problem is that the work to make your availability explicit is itself a distraction. Some technologies attempt to supply that automatically (state of presence in IM), but these work best when an immediate response is not required. From the initiator's side, peeking and probing have been tried, without good solutions for the problems of privacy and intrusion. In physical space, secretaries are the making-contact experts; houses have front porches where access is negotiated; glass windows in closed doors provide for negotiating interruptions, often one-sidedly. Social systems permit ignoring intrusions that are not convenient, provided there is a way of "plausibly denying" that people were ignored ("I must not have been home," or "My cell phone must have been turned off.").

I think the problems can be solved only by considering the whole technical-social design of the human activity of making contact. I think new developments in making contact in Media Spaces are essential to making space as central to our communicating as sound is.

# Chapter 29
# About the Authors

**Leila Alem**
CSIRO ICT
*Leila.alem@csiro.au*

Dr. Leila Alem is a senior research scientist at CSIRO ICT Centre http://www.ict.csiro.au/. Her group is conducting research in Human Factors in tele collaborative settings. She is interested in formalizing and measuring users' experience when engaged in synchronous computer-mediated collaboration, more specifically, users' sense of presence. In recent years, she has conducted several laboratory and field experiments to investigate the various factors affecting users' sense of presence. She has also investigated novel approaches for developing objective measures of presence using gaze tacking and analysis methods, as well as linguistic analysis approaches.

**Paul Aoki**
Intel Research Berkeley
2150 Shattuck Ave., Ste. 1300
Berkeley, CA 94704-1347, USA
*aoki@acm.org*

Paul M. Aoki is a research scientist at the Intel Research laboratory in Berkeley, California. He holds a B.S. in Electrical Engineering and a Ph.D. in Computer Science from the University of California, Berkeley. His research interests include mobile computing and communication systems, human–computer interaction, and computer-supported cooperative work. His current work focuses on mobile sensor devices for community action and on the design of technologies for emerging regions.

**Alison Black**
Alison Black Consulting
56 Alexandra Road
Reading RG1 5PP, UK
*alison@alisonblack.co.uk*

Alison Black works with organizations to develop user-focused products and services. After completing a degree in cognitive psychology at Sussex University and a Ph.D. at Cambridge, she held a postdoctoral research fellowship in the Department of Typography and Graphic Communication, University of Reading; from there she went on to set up and lead the London-based human factors team of international design consultancy, IDEO. She has worked independently since 2000, focusing particularly on telecoms and new media applications.

**Sara Bly**
24511 NW Moreland Rd.,
North Plains, OR 97133, USA
*sara@bly.net*

Sara Bly provides consulting services, while designing and conducting user studies. The studies encompass a wide range of methodologies to inform the design of systems, organizations, and technologies throughout the early conceptual stages, iterative design stages, evaluation stages, and deployment stages. Methodologies include fieldwork, observations, in-depth interviews, usability studies, laboratory-designed experiences, Web questionnaires, and diary studies (e.g., day-in-the-life, camera studies). Sara Bly Consulting also provides research expertise in computer-mediated communication and collaborative work. Sara Bly Consulting works closely with clients to ensure a shared understanding of goals and results. The work is iterative, learning from each phase, and using that learning as grounding to inform the next steps.

**Michael Boyle**
SMART Technologies ULC

Michael Boyle is a Distinguished Developer in the software development group at SMART Technologies. He came to SMART in 2005 after he earned his Ph.D. in Computer Science from the University of Calgary. At SMART, Michael is focused on developing classroom-centered collaboration software for teachers and students. Usability and social workability of software inside and outside the classroom are his key areas of interest.

**Jamika Burge**
The Pennsylvania State University
University Park, Pennsylvania, USA
*jburge@ist.psu.edu*

Jamika D. Burge is currently a Postdoctoral Research Scholar in the College of Information Sciences and Technology at The Pennsylvania State University, University Park. She is managing a wireless network research project under the guidance of John M. Carroll at Penn State University. Burge completed her Ph.D. in Computer Science from Virginia Polytechnic Institute and State University (Virginia Tech) in Blacksburg, VA. She has received several awards, including IBM Ph.D. Research Fellow (2005–2006), and she has served in several leadership positions, including president of the Computer Science Graduate Student Council while at Virginia Tech.

**William (Bill) Buxton**
Principal Researcher
Microsoft Research Building 99/4134
One Microsoft Way
Redmond, WA 98052, USA
*www.billbuxton.com*

Bill Buxton is the author of *Sketching User Experiences: Getting the Design Right and the Right Design*, published jointly by Morgan Kaufmann and Focal Press. He is the Principal Researcher at Microsoft Research and has a 30-year involvement in research, design, and commentary around human aspects of technology, and digital tools for creative endeavor, including music, film, and industrial design, in particular. Prior to joining Microsoft, he was a researcher at Xerox PARC, professor at the University of Toronto, and Chief Scientist of Alias Research and SGI Inc. In 2007, he was named Doctor of Design, *Honoris Causa*, by the Ontario College of Art and Design, and in 2008 became the 10th recipient of the ACM/SIGCHI Lifetime Achievement Award for fundamental contributions to the field of human–computer interaction.

**Elizabeth Churchill**
Yahoo! Research
2821 Mission College Blvd.
Santa Clara, CA 95054, USA
*Elizabeth@elizabethchurchill.com*

Elizabeth Churchill is a researcher, designer, and observer of communication technologies. Originally a psychologist by training, for the past several years she has drawn on diverse areas to consider how to design effective communication situations – both face to face and technologically mediated. At the center of her work is a fascination with people's passions, proclivities, and practices. She has studied and written about mobility and mobile work, distributed collaboration, interaction in graphical and textual virtual spaces, and the augmentation of public spaces with digital artifacts. Applications designed and/or evaluated include cell phone interfaces, textual and 3d graphical environments, interactive digital posterboards, and animated interface personas. She currently works at *Yahoo! Research*, and is based in Santa Clara, California. Formerly, she worked at *PARC*, the Palo Alto Research Center in Palo Alto, California in the Computing Science Lab (CSL). Prior to that she was the project lead of the Social Computing Group at *FX Palo Laboratory*, Fuji Xerox's research lab in Palo Alto.

**Brian Corrie**
Technical Director for the Centre for Interdisciplinary Research in the Mathematical and Computational Sciences
Simon Fraser University
8888 University Drive
Vancouver, BC, Canada
*bcorrie@sfu.ca*

Brian Corrie is the Technical Director for the Center for Interdisciplinary Research in the Mathematical and Computational Sciences (IRMACS), a multidisciplinarian research center located at Simon Fraser University (SFU). He is also the Collaboration and Visualization Coordinator for WestGrid, a large multi-institutional grid computing project in Western Canada. He leads a small research group in collaboration and visualization at SFU, focusing on the integration of visualization technologies with collaborative environment. He is also a Ph.D. student at the University of Victoria. His research interests are in advanced collaborative environments, computer graphics, scientific visualization, and coupling computational simulation to visualization. Over the last 10 years, Brian has held a number of applied research positions. These include positions as the Project Leader for the Collaborative VE project at the Australian National University, the Technical Leader at the Virtual Environment Technology Centre at the National Research Council of Canada, and the Focus Area Leader for the Immersive and Collaborative Environments research program at the New Media Innovation Centre in Vancouver. He is currently combining these experiences with his research to explore advanced collaborative environments.

**Mike Derocher**
Experience Design Manager
Hewlett-Packard Halo Project Team
Corvalis, Oregon
*mike.derocher@hp.com*

Mike Derocher manages experience design for HP Halo, which is a unique expression of video teleconferencing designed to enable an evocative social connection between meeting participants. Mike's expertise and background are in industrial and interaction designs. Since joining HP in 1987, he has worked in numerous businesses and roles including designing palmtop pc's, directing mobile computing design, setting design strategy for personal printers, and leading efforts to create the Halo multipoint interface and experience. He holds a Bachelor of Fine Arts degree from the University of Michigan.

**Batya Friedman**
Professor
The Information School
370E Mary Gates Hall
Seattle, WA 98195-2840, USA
*batya@u.washington.edu*

Batya Friedman is a Professor in the Information School and an Adjunct Professor in the Department of Computer Science and Engineering at the University of Washington where she Co-directs the *Value Sensitive Design* Research Laboratory. She received both her B.A. (1979) and Ph.D. (1988) from the University of California, Berkeley. Her research interests include human–computer interaction, especially human values in design, social, and cultural aspects of information systems, and design methodology. Her 1997 edited volume (Cambridge University Press) is titled *Human Values and the Design of Computer Technology*. Her work on Value Sensitive Design has focused on the values of informed consent, privacy in public, trust, freedom from bias, moral agency, and human dignity, and engaged such technologies as web browsers, large-screen displays, urban simulation, robotics, open-source code bases, and location-enhanced computing. She is also a Co-director for The Mina Institute (Covelo, CA).

**Bill Gaver**
Goldsmiths, University of London
New Cross, London, SE14 6NW, UK
*w.gaver@gold.ac.uk*

Bill Gaver is a Professor of Design and leads the Interaction Research Studio at Goldsmiths, University of London. He has pursued research on innovative technologies for over 20 years, following a trajectory that led from experimental science to design. Currently, his research focuses on design-led methodologies and innovative technologies for everyday life. With his group, he has developed approaches to design ranging from Cultural Probes to the use of documentary film to help assess peoples' experience with designs, pursued conceptual work on topics such as ambiguity and interpretation, and produced highly fashioned prototypes that have been deployed for long-term field trials and exhibited in major international exhibitions. Much of this work has been pursued with and for companies such as Intel, France Telecom, Hewlett Packard, IBM, and Xerox, as well as with UK and European Council funding.

**Brian Gill**

Brian Gill is a statistician with an interest in applications of statistics in social and health sciences; he is an Associate Professor in the Department of Mathematics at Seattle Pacific University.

**Mark Gorzynski**
Hewlett-Packard Halo Project Team
Corvalis, Oregon
*mark.gorzynski@hp.com*

**Saul Greenberg**
Professor and iCore Chair
Human–Computer Interaction & Computer-Supported Cooperative Work
Department of Computer Science
University of Calgary
Calgary, Alberta, Canada T2N 1N4
*saul.greenberg@ucalgary.ca*

Saul Greenberg is a Full Professor in the Department of Computer Science at the University of Calgary. While he is a computer scientist by training, the work by Saul and his talented students typifies the cross-discipline aspects of Human–Computer Interaction, Computer-Supported Cooperative Work, and Ubiquitous Computing. He and his crew are well known for their development of toolkits enabling rapid prototyping of groupware and ubiquitous appliances, innovative and seminal system designs based on observations of social phenomenon, articulation of design-oriented social science theories, and refinement of evaluation methods. His research is well recognized. He holds the iCORE/NSERC/Smart Technologies Industrial Chair in Interactive Technologies. He also holds a University Professorship, which is a distinguished University of Calgary Award recognizing research excellence. He received the CHCCS Achievement Award in May 2007 and was also elected to the ACM CHI Academy in April 2005 for his overall contributions to the field of Human–Computer Interaction. Saul is a prolific author who has authored and edited several books and published many refereed articles, as listed at http://grouplab.cpsc.ucalgary.ca. He is also known for his strong commitment in making his tools, systems, and educational material readily available to other researchers and educators.

## Jennifer Hagman

Jennifer Hagman is an information scientist with an interest in the role of informed consent in human–computer interactions; she was a Research Analyst in the Information School at the University of Washington at the time of this research.

## Steve Harrison

Department of Computer Science and Art and Art History (by courtesy)
121 VTKW II, 2202 Kraft Drive
Virginia Polytechnic Institute and State University
Blacksburg, VA 24061, USA
*sHarrison@vt.edu*

Steve Harrison's research has been to use video to break time and distance. It is informed by studies carried out of creative people working together. His research focuses on the life outside the computer box as much as within it; getting an understanding of the settings of use shapes the design of a system. He has done field and laboratory studies of collaboration, looking at the communications between people. And he has brought innovative ideas from the lab out to real work situations for evaluation. This unique approach produced the seminal CSCW system known as the Media Space and contributed to the development of a number of shared drawing tools, culminating in the DrawStreamStation, all of which employ video in novel ways. Being a student of design, as well as media, he has led most recently in developing exhibits and the overall program for "XFR: experiments in the Future of Reading." These have been reported in numerous technical publications and conference proceedings, the popular press and cited with two prestigious design awards. This interwoven design and research approach continues with a study of the practices of design review in many disciplines. He is an architect, licensed in California.

**Christian Heath**
King's College London
Strand
London WC2R 2LS, England, UK
*Christian.Heath@kcl.ac.uk*

Christian Heath is a Professor of Work and Organisation and leads the Work, Interaction and Technology Research Centre. He specializes in video-based studies of social interaction, drawing on ethnomethodology and conversation analysis, with a particular interest in the interplay of talk, bodily conduct, and the use of tools and technologies. He is currently undertaking projects on auctions and markets, medical consultations and operating theaters, and museums and galleries. These projects are funded by the UK research councils and the IST Programmes of the European Union. A number of these projects also involve the design and development of advanced technologies including, for example, media spaces, trust systems, and tools to interweave paper and digital documents. These projects involve close collaboration with academic, private, and public sector organizations in the UK and abroad. He has published five books and more than 100 academic articles in journals and books and is co-editor of the book series *Learning and Doing* (Cambridge University Press). He has held positions at the Universities of Manchester, Surrey, and Nottingham and visiting positions at various Universities and industrial research laboratories in the UK and abroad. He currently serves on various schools, colleges, and external committees including the ESRC Information and Communications Committee.

**Austin Henderson**
Director, Knowledge Management
Advanced Concepts & Technology
Pitney Bowes
35 Waterview Dr., MS 26–31
Shelton, CT 06484, USA
*austin.henderson@pb.com*

Austin Henderson has been in the field of Human–Computer Interaction since 1964. He has a B.Sc. in Mathematics from Queen's University, Canada, an M.S. in Computer Science from the University of Illinois, and a Ph.D. in Computer Science from MIT. He has built applications in areas including manufacturing, air traffic control, electronic mail (Hermes), user interface design tools (Trillium), and workspace management (Rooms, Buttons). He has done research and user interface architecture with Xerox at both PARC and EuroPARC, Apple Computer, and Pitney Bowes and industrial design with Fitch, and research consulting with his own firm, Rivendel Consulting. Currently, he is the Director of Knowledge Management in the Advanced Concepts & Technology group of Pitney Bowes in Shelton, CT, USA. Professionally, Austin has been active in ACM/SIGCHI since 1983, including as conference chair (1985), and organization chair (1989–1993). His research interests are in the areas of the design of systems that can be collaboratively evolved by users, and in the management of the integration of research and development in corporations.

**Lynne Henderson**
Faculty, Continuing Studies
Stanford University
Stanford, CA 94305, USA
Shyness Institute
2000 Williams St.
Palo Alto, CA 94306, USA
*lynne@psych.stanford.edu*

Lynne Henderson is a Principal at Rivendel Consulting and Design. She is the founder of the Social Fitness Center, and founder and Co-director, with Philip Zimbardo, of the Shyness Institute. Dr. Henderson has been a visiting scholar in the Psychology Department at Stanford, and is a faculty member in Continuing Studies. She is an adjunct research faculty at the Institute for Transpersonal Psychology. Her research interests include the influence of personality variables and cultural influences on interpersonal perception, cultural influences on self-conceptualizations, interpersonal motivation, leadership styles, and distance collaboration.

**Peter Kahn**
Associate Professor
Department of Psychology
Box 351525
University of Washington
Seattle, WA 98195-1525, USA
*pkahn@u.washington.edu*

Peter H. Kahn Jr. is a developmental psychologist with interests that lie at the intersection of technology, nature, and social and moral development; he is an Associate Professor in the Department of Psychology and an Adjunct Associate Professor in the Information School at the University of Washington.

**Karrie Karahalios**
Assistant Professor
Siebel Center for Computer Science
201 N. Goodwin Ave.
3110Urbana, IL 61801, USA
*kkarahal@cs.uiuc.edu*

Karrie Karahalios is an Assistant Professor in Computer Science at the University of Illinois where she heads the Social Spaces Group. Her work focuses on the interaction between people and the social cues they perceive in networked electronic spaces. Of particular interest are the interfaces for pubic online and physical gathering spaces such as chatrooms, cafes, parks, and Facebook. The goal is to create interfaces that enable users to perceive conversational patterns that are present, but not obvious, in traditional communication interfaces. She completed an S.B. in electrical engineering, an M.Eng. in electrical engineering and computer science, and an S.M. and Ph.D. in media arts and science at MIT.

**Margit Kristensen**
Innovation Manager (Pervasive healthcare)
Alexandra Institute A/S
Aabogade 34 B
DK-8200
Aarhus N, Denmark
*margit.kristensen@alexandra.dk*

Margit Kristensen is an innovation manager and the vice-director of the Centre for Pervasive Healthcare at the Alexandra Institute, situated at Katrinebjerg in Aarhus. Margit has a professional background from the health care sector and moreover has a master's degree in Health Informatics. She has for the last several years worked with R&D within ICT, especially for health care, and she was a member of the PalCom project research group (www.ist-palcom.org). One of her main foci has been on use of participatory design in the R&D processes. Currently, Margit – together with Morten Kyng – is developing a new research and innovation program in health care and ICT based on national as well as EU funding.

**Hideaki Kuzuoka**
Professor
Graduate School of Systems and Information Engineering
Department of Intelligent Interaction Technologies
University of Tsukuba
1-1-1 Tennoudai, Tsukuba, Ibaraki 305-8573, Japan
*kuzuoka@iit.tsukuba.ac.jp*

Hideaki Kuzuoka is a Professor in the Graduate School of Systems and Information Engineering at University of Tsukuba. His main research field is CSCW and groupware. He received his bachelor's degree in Mechanical Engineering and has experience in developing hardware and systems of many different kinds. While he has been one of the proponents of using robots and other electromechanical systems for CSCW research, he has also been working with ethnomethodologists for more than 10 years. This research collaboration has enabled the iterative refinement of a number of systems and methods for assessing those systems. Professor Kuzouka has published widely, principally in the fields of CSCW and HCI at international conferences like CHI, CSCW, and ECSCW.

**Morten Kyng**
Professor
Department of Computer Science and Director
Centre For Pervasive Computing
University Of Aarhus
Aabogade 34 B, DK, 8200 Aarhus N
*mkyng@daimi.au.dk*

Morten Kyng is a Professor of Pervasive Computing and Director of the Centre for Pervasive Computing, www.pervasive.dk, a national research center with headquarters at Katrinebjerg in Aarhus. He also directs the Centre for Pervasive Healthcare, www.pervasivehealthcare.dk. He has a long-standing track record of research in participatory design, computer-supported cooperative work, and human–computer interaction. Together with the late Kristen Nygaard from Norway and Pelle Ehn from Swedenm, Morten has led the development of the Scandinavian school of participatory design, which has set the agenda for vast body of international research. In recognition of his work Morten was, in 2001, appointed to the ACM CHI Academy for leadership in the field of computer–human interaction. He has created and managed a dozen national and international research projects including the ground-braking Scandinavian project Utopia on participatory design and the Palcom project: Palpable computing – a new perspective on ambient computing. Palcom ended in 2007 and was part of the European Union's 6th Framework Programme. He has published several articles and books, organized international conferences, and served on university committees and governing bodies. Currently, Morten – together with Margit Kristensen – is developing a new research and innovation program in health care and ICT based on national as well as EU funding.

**Matthew Lipson**
Orange
The Point
37 North Wharf Rd
London, UK
*matthewlipson@yahoo.co.uk*

Matthew Lipson is on sabbatical from Orange where he is an insight manager leading efforts to represent user needs in the design of new and emerging products. Previously, he worked for the Appliance Studio in Bristol, UK as a user researcher. He has a degree in Psychology from Sheffield University and a Ph.D. from Oxford University. During his sabbatical he is studying for a Masters in Environmental Technology at Imperial College.

**Paul Luff**
Centre for Work, Interaction and Technology
Department of Management
King's College
The Franklin-Wilkins
Building150 Stamford Street
London SE1 9NN, UK
*Paul.Luff@kcl.ac.uk*

Paul Luff is a Professor of Organizations and Technology at the Department of Management, King's College, London. His research involves the detailed analysis of work and interaction and drawing upon video recordings of everyday human conduct. With his colleagues in the Work, Interaction and Technology Research Centre, he has undertaken studies in a diverse variety of settings including control rooms, news and broadcasting, health care, museums, galleries, and science centers, and within design, architecture, and construction. Over the past few years, Paul Luff has been particularly concerned with the use of apparently mundane objects, specifically paper documents, and how these support what are often very complex work practices. He has drawn from this research in a number of projects concerned with the design of novel systems, including advanced media spaces that allow for the manipulation of paper documents and technologies that can interleave the use of paper and electronic materials. This research, and related studies, has been reported in numerous articles in the fields of CSCW, HCI, Requirements Engineering, Studies of work practices, and ubiquitous and mobile systems. Paul Luff is co-author with Christian Heath of *Technology in Action*, published by Cambridge University Press.

**Gregor McEwan**
National ICT Australia, NICTA

Gregor McEwan is currently a Research Engineer at National ICT Australia (NICTA), with a full-time commitment to the (braccetto) project. Before starting with NICTA in September 2006, he was completing his M.Sc. at the University of Calgary in Canada. Gregor's expertise is in Computer-Supported Cooperative Work with a special emphasis on creating groupware environments for small communities. His recent graduate work applies social theories of interaction to groupware design. Previous to his graduate work he was involved in designing and implementing a complex groupware environment, and also research into social communities formed around sharing of web resources. At that time, he was also involved in research about combining Participatory Design and eXtreme Programming development methodologies. Gregor has previously worked as a Research Scientist at the Distributed Systems Technology Centre (DSTC) and was involved in the Information Ecology, Ambience, Elvin and Orbit projects.

**April Mitchell**
Researcher Engineer
Multimedia Communications & Networking Lab
Hewlett Packard Labs
1501 Page Mill Road
MS 1181/3U – H37
Palo Alto, CA 94304, USA
*april.slayden@hp.com*

April Slayden Mitchell is a member of the Multimedia Communication and Networking Laboratory at Hewlett-Packard. April's expertise lies in the area of user experience research and design. Since joining HP Labs in 2002, she has worked on multiple projects including BiReality telepresence, the DJammer music manipulation device, and Halo video collaboration where she led the design for the original user interface. April holds a Bachelor of Science degree from Millsaps College in Jackson, Mississippi, and a Master of Science in Computer Science from the University of Rochester in Rochester, New York.

**Les Nelson**
Palo Alto Research Center, Inc.
3333 Coyote Hill Road
Palo Alto, CA 94304, USA
*lesnelson@acm.org*

Les Nelson is a researcher at the Palo Alto Research Center working on web-based support for collaboration. His work considers how existing technologies get adapted to meet changing social practices. Les joined PARC in 2004, studying information sharing and collaboration support tools used in system engineering practices. His latest work is on the study of the measurable impacts of social annotation software and in usable access control for selective information sharing in close collaborations. His involvement with Xerox goes back to 1995, where he was the first researcher hired into the FX Palo Alto Laboratory. His work on human–computer interaction leads to two products and a variety of patents and publications in social computing, mobile technology, and tangible user interfaces. Before FXPAL, Les worked for Lockheed Research and Development in the systems and software engineering for very large systems, software reengineering, and software reuse. Les started out in corporate life with the IBM Federal Systems Division as a software engineer on large scale, mission-critical, real-time systems. He received an undergraduate degree in Mathematics and Computing from Trinity College, Hartford, Connecticut, and an M.S. in Computer Science from the University of Wisconsin in Madison specializing in mathematical programming and systems science.

**Carman Neustaedter**
Kodak Research Labs
1999 Lake Avenue
Rochester, NY 14580, USA
carman.neustaedter@kodak.com

Carman Neustaedter is a Research Scientist in the Computational Science & Technology Research group at Kodak Research Labs and an Adjunct Professor in the Department of Computer Science at the University of Rochester. Carman's research is in the areas of Human-Computer Interaction, Computer-Supported Cooperative Work, and Ubiquitous Computing, where he studies social culture to inform the design of technologies to support human activities. This research has involved studying, designing, and evaluating a wide range of computer technologies including email systems, instant messaging, video conferencing, digital photo software, calendars, online games, and pervasive location-based games. Carman holds a PhD in Computer Science from the University of Calgary, Canada.

**Kenton O'Hara**
CSIRO ICT Centre
Pembroke Road
Marsfield 2122
NSW, Australia
*kenton@gwork.org*

Kenton O'Hara is a Principal Scientist at the Commonwealth and Scientific Industrial Research Organisation, in Sydney Australia, where he is the Director of the HxI initiative. His research explores the social and behavioral factors that shape the design and use of emerging technologies. Over the years he has looked at a wide variety of topics including social and collaborative aspects of mobile video consumption, collaborative music consumption, location-based computing, public and situated displays, pervasive media, local and remote collaboration, context aware computing, and mobile communication. He has worked at key research labs such as HP Labs and Rank Xerox EuroPARC. He has published many articles on these areas of interest as well as the books, *Social and Collaborative Aspects of New Music Technology* and *Public and Situated Displays*. He has a degree in Psychology and a Ph.D. in human–computer interaction.

**Michael Rounding**
SMART Technologies, Inc.

Michael Rounding is currently a User Experience Specialist with SMART Technologies where he researches, designs and evaluates interactive technologies used globally in classrooms and corporate boardrooms. He is an active field researcher, and teaches courses internal to SMART regularly. He received his MSc in 2004 at the University of Calgary in Computer Science, specializing in Human Computer Interaction, working with Dr. Saul Greenberg on groupware interfaces and architectures used to promote communication and collaboration in groups of partially co-located and distance-separated collaborators. In addition to his current work with SMART, he has also applied his training to the Medical Imaging industry, designing imaging products to help doctors improve patient care.

**Nicolas Roussel**
LRI, bat 490
Université Paris-Sud, 91405 Orsay Cedex, France
*Nicolas.Roussel@lri.fr*

Nicolas Roussel is an Associate Professor at the Computer Science Department of Paris-Sud University where he teaches human–computer interaction and computer graphics. He is also a member of In Situ, a joint research project between LRI (Paris-Sud University – CNRS) and INRIA Saclay – Île-de-France. His research mainly concerns the design of environments to support coordination, communication, and collaboration between distant people. He also works on the design of novel software architectures and tools adapted to a new generation of interactive systems.

**Rachel Severson**
Department of Psychology
Box 351525
University of Washington
Seattle, WA 98195-1525, USA

Rachel L. Severson is a developmental psychologist with an interest in subject–other relations; she is a Ph.D. student in the Department of Psychology at the University of Washington.

**Robert Stults**
P.O. Box 620
Woodstock, NY 12498, USA
*calmbob@gmail.com*

Robert Stults worked from 1975 to 1990 as a researcher in design processes and in media space, first at Evans & Sutherland Computer Corporation and then at Xerox Palo Alto Research Center; since then, he has worked as an architect for large, distributed enterprises in integrating their edge operations and systems with their centralized structures. He is currently working on an extended essay, From Architecture to Architecture, that addresses the translation of traditional architecture of buildings to emergent architecture of nonphysical systems.

**Peggy Szymanski**
Workscapes & Organization Area
Computer Science Laboratory
Palo Alto Research Center
3333 Coyote Hill Road
Palo Alto, CA 94304-1314, USA

Margaret "Peggy" Szymanski is a senior researcher in the Computer Science Laboratory at Palo Alto Research Center (PARC). Before joining PARC, Szymanski was a bilingual, elementary school teacher in Los Angeles studying how native Spanish-speaking children transition to English literacy. Szymanski earned her Ph.D. from the University of California, Santa Barbara specializing in the study of Language, Interaction and Social Organization (LISO). Her research interests include collaborative learning activity, copresent and remote states of incipient talk, and cultural practices around food.

**John C. Tang**
Microsoft Research
1310 villa street
Mountain View, CA 94041
*johntang@microsoft.com*

John Tang works in the VIBE group at Microsoft Research. His research interests are focused on understanding the needs of users to shape the design of technology to support collaboration. He applies a mix of qualitative (video-based observation, interviews, surveys to collect user perceptions) and quantitative (usage logs) methods to understand how people currently use technology and to design new technology to improve their work. He has a special interest in interfaces for distributed groups to enable sharing awareness information and social networking to encourage coordinating contact.

**Deborah Tatar**
Associate Professor of Computer Science and, by courtesy, Psychology
2202 Kraft Dr.
Room 123
Virginia Polytechnic Institute and Sate University
Blacksburg, VA 24060, USA
*dtatar@cs.vt.edu*

Deborah Tatar (Ph.D., Psychology, Stanford) is an Associate Professor of Computer Science and, by courtesy, Psychology at Virginia Tech. Starting with the seminal Co-lab project at Xerox PARC, her work has been concerned with the effects of technology on interpersonal interaction. She edited the first two proceedings of the Conference on Computer-Supported Collaborative Work. Her doctoral work was concerned with social and personal effects of inattentive listeners.

**Allison Woodruff**
Intel Research
2150 Shattuck Avenue #1300
Berkeley, CA 94704, USA
*Allison.Woodruff@Intel.Com*

Allison Woodruff is a researcher at Intel Research Berkeley. Her primary research interests include environmentally sustainable technologies, technology for domestic environments, mobile and communication technologies, and ubiquitous computing. Prior to joining Intel, Woodruff worked as a researcher at PARC from 1998 to 2004. She holds a Ph.D. in Computer Science from the University of California, Berkeley, an M.S. in Computer Science and an M.A. in Linguistics from the University of California, Davis, and a B.A. in English from California State University, Chico.

**Jun Yamashita**
Lecturer
University of Tsukuba
1-1-1 Tennoudai, Tsukuba City
1-1-2 Ibaraki Pref.
305-8573 JAPAN
jun@iit.tsukuba.ac.jp

Jun Yamashita is lecturer in the Department of Intelligent Interaction Technologies at the University of Tsukuba. For his PhD at the University of Tsukuba he developed two enhanced video communication systems: AgoraG and AgoraPro. In 2004 he was technical director of a special exhibition held at the National Museum in Tokyo. For this, he was responsible for developing a ubiquitous mobile guide that was used by over 20,000 visitors in six months. Jun's research interests include human-computer interaction, both with the design of technologies that support remote collaboration and mobile ubiquitous applications, and with the analysis of users' behaviour using these technologies.

**Keichi Yamazaki**
*BYI06561@nifty.com*

**Todd Zimmerman**
University of British Columbia, Okanagan
FIP326 – 3333 University Way
Kelowna, BC V1V 1V7, Canada
*todd.zimmerman@ubc.ca*

Todd is the Collaboration and Visualization Specialist for WestGrid, a large multi-institutional grid-computing project in Western Canada, and the University of British Columbia – Okanagan. He has co-designed, technically set up, and managed numerous advanced collaborative facilities including those at the IRMACS Centre, the CECM Colab, and the Physics Collaboration room at Simon Fraser University. For WestGrid, his role also includes the technical management of the collaboration infrastructure and AccessGrid servers, and the coordination of many large-scale AccessGrid seminars and events.

# Index